Army Techniques Publication
ATP 3-39.12

LAW ENFORCEMENT INVESTIGATIONS

August 2013

United States Government
US Army

Army Techniques Publication (ATP)
No. 3-39.12 (FM 3-19.13/FM 19-25)

Headquarters
Department of the Army
Washington, DC, 19 August 2013

Law Enforcement Investigations

Contents

Distribution Restriction: Approved for public release; distribution is unlimited.

*This publication supersedes FM 3-19.13, 10 January 2005 and FM 19-25, 30 September 1977.

Figures

Tables

Preface

Army Techniques Publication (ATP) 3-39.12 is aligned with Field Manual (FM) 3-39, the Military Police Corps Regiment's operational doctrine, and Army Tactics, Techniques, and Procedures (ATTP) 3-39.10. It is intended as a guide and toolkit for military police investigators, USACIDC special agents (SAs), and military police Soldiers conducting law enforcement (LE) and LE investigations. It also serves to educate military police commanders and staff on LE investigations capabilities, enabling a more thorough understanding of those capabilities. This increased understanding facilitates staff planning, resource allocation, and the ability to articulate LE investigative capabilities and requirements to supported commanders and organizations.

The principal audience for ATP 3-39.12 is Army military police personnel, which include Department of the Army (DA) civilian police, conducting LE investigation activities while assigned to military police brigades, battalions, companies, detachments, United States (U.S.) Army Criminal Investigation Command (USACIDC) elements, military police platoons supporting brigade combat teams, and Provost Marshal (PM) staffs. The manual also provides military police commanders and staffs with a framework and understanding of LE investigations and investigative capabilities that support decisive action.

Commanders, staffs, and subordinates ensure their decisions and actions comply with applicable U.S., international, and, in some cases, host-nation (HN) laws and regulations. Commanders at all levels ensure their Soldiers operate in accordance with the law of war and the rules of engagement (see FM 27-10).

ATP 3-39.12 uses joint terms where applicable. Selected joint and Army terms and definitions appear in both the glossary and the text. Terms for which ATP 3-39.12 is the proponent manual (the authority) are marked with an asterisk (*) in the glossary. Definitions for which ATP 3-39.12 is the proponent publication are boldfaced in the text. For other definitions shown in the text, the term is italicized and the number of the proponent publication follows the definition.

ATP 3-39.12 applies to the Active Army, Army National Guard (ARNG)/Army National Guard of the United States (ARNGUS), and United States Army Reserve (USAR) unless otherwise stated.

The proponent of ATP 3-39.12 is the U.S. Army Military Police School (USAMPS). The preparing agency is the USAMPS. Send comments and recommendations on DA Form 2028 (*Recommended Changes to Publications and Blank Forms*) to Commandant, USAMPS, ATTN: ATZT-CDC (ATP 3-39.12), 14000 MSCoE Loop, Suite 270, Fort Leonard Wood, Missouri 65473-8929; by e-mail to <usarmy.leonardwood.mscoe.mbx.cdidcodddmpdoc@mail.mil>; or submit an electronic DA Form 2028.

A listing of preferred metric units for general use is contained in Federal Standard 376B at <http://www.usaid.gov/policy/ads/300/fstd376b.pdf>.

Unless this publication states otherwise, masculine nouns and pronouns do not refer exclusively to men.

Introduction

Whether supporting LE activities in support of bases and base camps; maintaining and restoring order in an effort to stabilize an area of operations (AO); providing training and support to HN police; or supporting humanitarian relief operations, Army LE investigators and other military police Soldiers provide capabilities that are invaluable to the supported commander. Recent history and experience have expanded the Army's understanding that LE investigative skills are relevant and arguably critical to success in the operational theater, especially during the conduct of stability tasks. Military LE investigations are correctly focused on activities conducted to solve criminal cases, investigate incidents or accidents, and provide evidence sufficient to achieve a successful administrative recourse or conviction within the military justice system. However, the Army has identified the need for investigative skills, especially in the areas of evidence collection and forensic analysis, as a critical requirement in combating the criminal and hybrid threats that operate on the modern battlefield. USACIDC SAs have always investigated incidents of war crimes as well as deaths or other serious or sensitive incidents occurring in a deployed operational environment. Investigative activities, training, and doctrine for all other Army LE elements were largely confined to the installation or base at home station.

The requirement for investigative skill sets to support decisive action has led to a requirement for revised doctrine and associated training for military police investigators (MPIs) and other military police personnel that addresses the investigative capabilities and application of LE investigative skills to support decisive action. Investigation of criminal activity requires deliberate, methodical, and disciplined actions and analysis on the part of LE investigators and supporting personnel. These skills and the associated knowledge and experience can be applied in all environments. They are critical to successful LE activities directly associated with a criminal investigation and can also be critical to the support of military operations—to include site exploitation, HN police training, and collection and analysis of evidence to attack criminal and other threat networks.

ATP 3-39.12 is a full revision from the superseded FM 3-19.13 and FM 19-25. The revision has been driven by changes in the operational environment, available and emerging technologies, and Army and joint doctrine. This manual builds on the previous version and applies collective knowledge and lessons learned through recent operations and shifts in doctrinal focus and operational requirements. It is rooted in time-tested fundamentals and technology, while accommodating new technologies and emerging mission sets.

ATP 3-39.12 is written primarily to be a toolkit for military LE investigators; however, it acknowledges current and likely operational environments and the requirement for the skill sets and capabilities of Army LE investigators and the technologies they employ. USACIDC SAs, MPIs, TMCIs, and military police Soldiers must be knowledgeable and proficient in accepted investigative techniques, practices, and technologies while understanding how those capabilities apply to criminal and traffic investigations and applications supporting decisive action that fall outside the scope of direct criminal investigations in the traditional sense. They must be prepared to operate in any operational environment and apply their craft in support of the commander while dealing with a wide range of threats and other influences.ATP 3-39.12 provides specific techniques required for Army military police personnel and USACIDC SAs to conduct successful LE investigations. It also provides a descriptive framework of LE investigative organizations, personnel, and capabilities. This manual also provides military police commanders and their staffs with a thorough understanding of Army LE investigative capabilities and their application, enabling informed planning and succinct articulation of general LE investigative capabilities to supported commanders and their staffs. This doctrine will assist Army leaders and trainers at branch schools to plan, integrate, and teach LE investigative capabilities and applications in support of Army, joint, and interagency operations.

Where appropriate, the manual describes nationally recognized methods of investigation and evidence examination adopted from the Department of Justice (DOJ); the Federal Bureau of Investigation (FBI); the Bureau of Alcohol, Tobacco, and Firearms; the National Association of Fire Investigators (NAFI); the National Institute of Justice (NIJ); and the United States Army Criminal Investigation Laboratory (USACIL) and other LE agencies. In addition to the techniques described in this manual, Army LE personnel are encouraged to seek guidance on police and investigative matters from other approved official LE sources. Additionally, this manual—

- Incorporates terminology changes consistent with Army Doctrinal Publication (ADP) 3-0, Army Doctrine Reference Publication (ADRP) 3-0, and other recent doctrinal changes.
- Expands LE investigations doctrine to include collision (traffic accident) investigations.
- Incorporates the latest task analysis and synchronizes LE investigations doctrine and task alignment to the Army Universal Task List (AUTL) in FM 7-15.
- Describes Army LE investigation capabilities and integration in support of Army operations including techniques for properly handling evidence and the establishment of evidence response teams, forensics laboratory support, and building HN police investigative capabilities.
- Applies lessons learned through the conduct of recent operational experiences.
- Expands on the investigations, evidence collection, and forensics analysis framework established in ATTP 3-39.10 and FM 3-39.
- Incorporates emerging technology updates to material from other relevant publications and sources.

This manual is organized into thirteen chapters with eleven appendixes to provide additional details on selected topics. Chapter 1 describes the doctrinal framework for LE investigations including organizations relevant to criminal and collision investigations. Chapters 2 through 6 are focused on collection of evidence pertinent to investigative efforts. Chapters 7 through 12 address investigative considerations for specific types of criminal investigations. Chapter 13 covers collision investigations. A brief description of each chapter and appendix is provided below:

- Chapter 1 describes LE investigations capabilities and support. It provides a framework for understanding the application of LE investigative capabilities and describes the various LE investigative organizations, personnel, and specific capabilities. It introduces revised nomenclature for deployable forensic organizational elements consistent with recent organizational changes.
- Chapter 2 describes the collection of physical evidence. It provides detailed techniques and considerations for collecting and preserving various types of physical evidence under various environments and conditions. It includes information on specific forensic analysis capabilities and requirements for successful evidence processing.
- Chapter 3 describes methods, strategies, and considerations for conducting interviews and LE interrogations. It introduces the forensic experiential trauma interview (FETI) and associated physiological evidence.
- Chapter 4 discusses crime scene processing and documentation. It also addresses analysis and reconstruction of crime scenes.
- Chapter 5 focuses on LE investigation surveillance activities. It describes the varying types of surveillance, methods, and considerations for planning and conducting LE-related surveillance.
- Chapter 6 discusses undercover activities supporting LE investigations. It addresses planning, preliminary investigations, personnel selection, suspect contacts, and other considerations.
- Chapter 7 provides investigative techniques specific to death investigations.
- Chapter 8 provides investigative information regarding assault and robbery investigations.
- Chapter 9 discusses investigation of sex crimes.
- Chapter 10 focuses on investigating crimes against property. It also includes a discussion of arson and explosion investigations.
- Chapter 11 provides information regarding fraud investigations and associated economic crimes.
- Chapter 12 discusses investigation of drug offenses.
- Chapter 13 addresses techniques for collision investigations (also called traffic accident investigations). It discusses requirements for collision investigations, collision photography, and traffic accident reports. The other portions of FM 19-25 were previously incorporated into ATTP 3-39.10, including discussion of traffic planning, traffic control and enforcement, and traffic assessments. FM 19-25 will be rescinded upon publication of this manual.

- Appendix A provides information on investigations support in an operational environment.
- Appendix B describes electronic devices that may provide evidence.
- Appendix C provides a description of the FETI introduced in chapter 3.
- Appendix D provides examples of investigative forms used by Army LE investigators.
- Appendix E describes considerations for managing investigative sources.
- Appendix F provides example checklists for use in the conduct or support of LE investigations.
- Appendix G describes common drugs of abuse encountered by Army LE investigators.
- Appendix H provides guidelines for use when investigating environmental crimes.
- Appendix I provides techniques for investigators preparing for and conducting courtroom testimony.
- Appendix J describes requirements and techniques for diagramming traffic-related collisions.
- Appendix K provides instructions and examples of calculations required for traffic-related collision investigations.

Chapter 1

Law Enforcement Investigation Capabilities and Support

Within the military LE context, LE investigations are official inquiries into alleged crimes or incidents (of known or undetermined cause) involving the military community. Properly conducted LE investigations can result in the collection of evidence that supports allegations of criminal conduct or negligence. They can also provide evidence exonerating persons suspected of such activity. LE investigations are conducted within strict procedural guidelines to ensure integrity and preservation of evidence. They require trained investigators with knowledge and skills that enable observation and critical reasoning. LE investigations require investigators to identify and collect evidence and apply forensic analysis capabilities to fulfill forensic requirements. Advances in technology have greatly increased the capabilities of LE investigators in the application of their craft. The rapid increase in terrorist, criminal, and hybrid threats has significantly increased the need for the capabilities and skills associated with LE investigations in environments outside traditional LE investigative missions. LE investigators must be able to apply their specific knowledge, skills, and capabilities to environments across the entire range of military operations.

FRAMEWORK FOR LAW ENFORCEMENT INVESTIGATIONS

1-1.   Investigation of criminal activity and traffic-related matters may be required in any environment in which military operations occur, from home station to austere operational environments. Regardless of the operational environment, criminal activity committed against U.S. forces and property degrades military discipline, morale, and operational capabilities. Army LE works in coordination with federal, state, local, and foreign LE agencies to investigate crimes and incidents in support of the commander's effort to protect personnel, resources, and critical assets.

1-2.   Army LE activities, including LE investigations, are typically conducted within the framework of the military police law and order (L&O) function. L&O activities are the primary function of military police. They shape the actions and perspective of military police Soldiers and leaders in the conduct and execution of all other functions.

1-3.   LE investigations are primarily conducted as a supporting LE task within the military police L&O function. See ATTP 3-39.10 for a detailed discussion of the L&O function and the L&O framework. LE investigations typically fall into two primary categories—criminal investigations and collision (traffic accident) investigations.

1-4.   Criminal investigations supporting Army operations are conducted primarily by USACIDC SAs and MPIs; see Army Regulation (AR) 195-2 for information on investigative purview. TMCIs are a specialized investigative asset focused on investigation of traffic collisions and other traffic-related concerns. All military police Soldiers must be knowledgeable in basic investigative techniques and are required to identify and secure crime scenes, document initial observations and identify and preserve evidence, conduct preliminary investigations, and assist dedicated investigative assets as directed by their supervisor or the lead investigator.

CRIMINAL INVESTIGATIONS

1-5.   A criminal investigation is the process of identification, collection, preservation, documentation, analysis, preparation, and presentation of both physical and testimonial evidence to prove the truth or falsity of a criminal allegation. Criminal investigations are typically conducted by trained criminal investigators (USACIDC SAs and MPIs) supported by military police patrol elements. They cover a broad spectrum from nonviolent incidents of larceny or fraud to physical attacks such as homicide or rape. The sheer magnitude and range of possible crimes that may be investigated requires a large body of knowledge and skills for criminal investigators to master, as well as a significant pool of technical experts supporting the investigator within their areas of expertise.

1-6. Criminal investigation is both an art and a science. In science, the absolute truth is often achieved. Experience has shown that in criminal investigations a less decisive hypothesis may sometimes be all that is possible to achieve. Objectives of criminal investigations include—

- Determining if a crime was committed.
- Collecting information and evidence legally to identify the perpetrator or responsible party, victims, and witnesses.
- Apprehending the person(s) responsible or reporting the individual (or group) to the appropriate civilian police agency.
- Recovering stolen property.
- Presenting the best possible case to the prosecutor.
- Providing clear, concise testimony.

1-7. While criminal investigators conduct deliberate criminal investigations, all military police must be knowledgeable in basic investigative techniques. Military police patrols are typically the first on the scene and must always secure the scene, observe, and document their initial observations (including personal behavior of witnesses and potential subjects). They are also in the best position to identify and preserve potential evidence and conduct initial interviews of witnesses and potential subjects. The majority of this publication is focused on criminal investigations.

COLLISION INVESTIGATIONS

1-8. A collision investigation is the process of observation, collection and documentation of evidence (including physical measurements of objects, markings, and vehicles), analysis, preparation, and presentation of both physical and testimonial evidence to determine the cause or causes of a collision or mishap involving a vehicle. Collision investigations are typically conducted by a trained TMCI; however, any military police patrol may be required to conduct investigations of minor traffic incidents or assist TMCIs in major incidents or complex collision investigations.

1-9. MPIs or USACIDC SAs may assume investigative responsibility over criminal offenses discovered as a result of the collision. If evidence of criminal activity is identified by responding military police patrols or TMCIs, MPIs, or USACIDC SAs should be notified as soon as possible. Military police will notify the supporting USACIDC element whenever a traffic accident involves a fatality or an offense within USACIDC investigative responsibility as described in AR 195-2. In all cases, TMCIs or military police patrols will complete the investigation of the actual collision and provide a copy of the report to the USACIDC element or MPI as appropriate. Collision investigations are covered in chapter 13.

SUPPORT TO DECISIVE ACTION

1-10. Military police L&O support to decisive action includes a wide range of missions and tasks. See ATTP 3-39.10 for more information. Military police L&O capabilities are relevant within all four tasks associated with decisive action by supporting command efforts to maintain good order, enable freedom of action, protect the force, and shape conditions for mission success. See ADP 3-0 and ADRP 3-0 for a detailed discussion of unified land operations. L&O is conducted throughout all tasks associated with decisive action; LE (including LE investigations) is heavily associated with stability operations. Military police conduct LE (and associated LE investigations) as critical tasks within the L&O function, in support of decisive action within three contexts or conditions, including support of—

- A commander's internal efforts to maintain good order and discipline. This includes support for bases and base camps within the United States and its territories. It also includes support to base camps and other operational sites within operational theaters outside the United States and its territories. This effort is aimed at policing our own Soldiers and civilians and deterring, mitigating, and preventing criminal and terrorist threats. Deliberate LE activities and LE investigations are significantly reduced during operations in immature theaters and during operations external to a base of operations. Minor infractions are typically handled by the chain of command without direct military police support. Major crimes (including those involving death, serious bodily injury, and war crimes) will be investigated by USACIDC SAs, regardless of the environment or relative maturity of the theater of operations. See appendix A for discussion of war crimes investigations.

- A commander's efforts to establish and maintain civil security and civil control within a HN to enable self-governance under the rule of law. This effort is aimed at maintaining order within the local population where HN police and security capability is either nonexistent or inadequate. This is a temporary effort until sufficient HN capability and capacity exists to allow transition of all LE activities to HN control. Support to a HN can range from U.S forces providing all LE support (including LE investigations) to the HN population in cases where the security and LE infrastructure has been either decimated or is otherwise nonexistent, to providing support and training to existing HN police forces to increase their capability and capacity, enabling self-sufficiency.

- Local LE agencies within the United States or its territories in times of crisis during defense support of civil authorities. In emergency conditions, local LE agencies within the United States or its territories may require additional resources, capability, and capacity. Defense support of civil authorities that involves LE support is extremely restricted by U.S. law (the Posse Comitatus Act). USAR and active duty military police elements, including federalized National Guard Soldiers, are generally prohibited from direct participation in civilian LE activities. National Guard military police and Criminal Investigation Division (CID) elements may support their respective state governors in this function while operating as state assets under Title 32, U.S. Code (32 USC); upon federalization of National Guard assets all legal restrictions apply. National Guard CID elements become USACIDC elements upon federalization and transition to Title 10 status. While acting as state assets, National Guard military police and CID elements do not have federal authority and may not use federally issued badges or credentials while conducting their state duties. See FM 3-28 and FM 3-39 for details regarding Posse Comitatus and other restrictions.

1-11. The security environment during high intensity major combat operations (MCO) is typically not conducive to successful LE activities, although limited LE activities are conducted. This is also true in the immediate areas where offensive and defensive tasks are being executed, even when the primary task within the AO is stability, and in extremely immature theaters even when MCO is absent, such as humanitarian or peacekeeping activities. The effective enforcement of laws on a population requires a level of security and stability not typically present during offensive and defensive tasks; likewise the deliberate nature of LE investigative activities requires a relatively secure environment for LE personnel to operate. LE investigations associated with LE activities are typically reduced when offensive and defensive tasks are dominant (as during MCO) but can approach levels consistent with normal operations in support of bases and base camps during long duration stability activities. The level of military, civilian, and HN LE and LE investigative activities is directly tied to the level of security and stability in the area.

1-12. Internally focused LE and supporting LE investigative activities are normally limited to major crimes falling within the investigative purview of USACIDC. USACIDC SAs conduct required criminal investigations of serious crimes regarding U.S. personnel, war crimes, detainee abuse, Department of Defense (DOD) civilian employees, contractor personnel, and other persons accompanying the force regardless of environment or which element of decisive action is dominant. As a theater and its base camp infrastructure mature, dedicated LE activities are required by military police in support of U.S. commanders. Over time, these LE activities may closely resemble those associated with L&O support provided by military police in support of bases and base camps at home.

1-13. Experience in recent conflicts, specifically in combating networked hybrid threats, has highlighted the requirement for capabilities to collect evidence at criminal and other incident sites, conduct forensic and deductive analysis of gathered evidence (physical and testimonial), investigate individuals and organizations threatening U.S. forces, and provide appropriate products required for targeting these threat networks. These requirements are reinforced by increased pressure to prosecute threat personnel captured by military forces for the crimes they commit, significantly increasing the relevance for LE investigative capabilities throughout all elements of decisive action. Focused externally, LE and associated investigative and associated support capabilities of military police and the USACIDC provide significant technical capabilities to support the operational commander and staff. These technical capabilities include—evidence collection, preservation, and documentation; forensic and pattern analysis activities; production of police intelligence products; and dissemination of information to operational elements. Military police elements may provide these capabilities in support of site exploitation activities, investigation of alleged war crimes, or in support of HN police requirements. Information from evidence gathered feeds the operations process and can be analyzed by investigators, police intelligence analysts within PM sections, or by LE personnel attached to maneuver units, to provide commanders with enhanced situational understanding of the criminal and threat environment. See ATTP 3-90.15 for more information on site exploitation operations.

> *Note.* Dissemination of information and records subject to privacy restrictions are discussed within Department of Defense Directive (DODD) 5400.11, DODD 5400.11-R, and internal organizational regulations and policies. All LE organizations must comply with the privacy guidelines and restrictions within these documents; other legal restrictions to dissemination may also apply. The servicing office of the Staff Judge Advocate (SJA) should be consulted for clarification when required.

1-14. Investigative efforts to determine the existence and capability of criminal and terrorist networks within the AO can be focused through coordinated police engagement activities and integrated police intelligence activities that enable identification of criminal networks, individual elements and cells, their level of organization, and specific capabilities. These activities can be critical shaping mechanisms enabling the targeting and attack on criminal, terrorist, and hybrid threat networks and ultimately restoration of order and establishment of a secure environment. Investigative efforts can also contribute to weapons technical intelligence efforts focused on identification and targeting of explosive devices; their components and capabilities; organizations, cells, and networks; individuals involved in design, manufacturing, and distribution of devices; and logistics and finance processes supporting the organizations, cells, and networks.

LAW ENFORCEMENT INVESTIGATORS

1-15. LE investigators conduct systematic and impartial investigations to uncover the truth. They must remain impartial to ensure that investigations and subsequent conclusions are objective and based on the evidence. Investigators must avoid the trap of developing a bias favoring a particular suspect or theory of the investigation; early biases can lead to exclusion of evidence during the collection process or subconscious exclusion of evidence in formation of the investigator's conclusions. Investigators' efforts are focused on finding, protecting, collecting, and preserving evidence discovered at the crime scene or elsewhere. Beyond initial training, investigative skills are honed through experience and mentorship from more seasoned investigators. Less experienced investigators gain valuable experience by reviewing cases, consulting with peers, and working with experienced investigators. Likewise military police patrol personnel gain experience through performance of their duties alongside more experienced military police personnel. All military police and USACIDC personnel expand their knowledge through formal military and civilian LE courses designed to teach nationally recognized policing and investigative techniques.

1-16. Their professional knowledge and skills include crime scene processing, identification of critical evidence, evidence collection and preservation, an understanding of forensic analysis capabilities and requirements, and knowledge of the techniques and methods used to interview witnesses and conduct interrogations of suspects. They ensure that evidence is accounted for by maintaining a complete chain of custody to ensure its admissibility in court. They must be skilled in providing professional testimony during judicial and administrative proceedings. An investigator's charter is to find, examine, and make available unbiased evidence that will clear the innocent and allow prosecution of the guilty. As professional fact finders, investigators maintain unquestionable integrity—whether during a criminal investigation or a collision investigation. USACIDC SAs, MPIs, and TMCIs are specifically trained and charged with conducting LE investigations. They are trained through separate courses tailored to the scope of their regulatory and investigative responsibilities.

Special Agents

1-17. SAs are the most highly trained of all Army LE investigators and are recognized as federal LE officers. Their training begins with the USAMPS Criminal Investigation Division Special Agent Course and includes further training in Advanced Fraud Investigations, Child Abuse Prevention and Investigative Techniques, Crisis and Hostage Negotiations, Combating Terrorism on Military Installations, Protective Service Training, and other specialized training. As their careers progress SAs attend additional advanced training and may specialize in forensic science, economic crimes, or other investigative areas.

1-18. Beyond criminal investigations in support of U.S. bases and base camps, their extensive training and experience may be leveraged in support of operational requirements of U.S. forces. Criminal investigation capabilities are particularly relevant in site exploitation and other evidence collection requirements on the battlefield, training and assistance to HN LE organizations, and collection of police information and analysis and production of police and specific criminal intelligence critical in identifying, understanding, and attacking criminal networks operating against U.S. interests. USACIDC SAs also provide administrative, analytical, and investigative support to multiple U.S. criminal investigative and terrorism task forces.

Military Police Investigators

1-19. Minor crimes, such as relatively low-value thefts (under $5,000 in value) or simple assaults, are normally investigated and processed by MPIs and DA civilian investigators assigned to L&O detachments or tactical units. MPIs receive training at the USAMPS Military Police Investigators Course. Their training includes evidence collection and crime scene processing, basic interviews and LE interrogations, investigating crimes against property and persons, drug identification, and court room testimony. They also routinely conduct—

- Juvenile crime investigations.
- Gang-related investigations.
- Crime prevention activities.

1-20. MPIs provide the operational commander with significant expertise in evidence collection and preservation; these skills can be instrumental during site exploitation activities in support of military operations overseas. They can also provide training and assistance to HN police, specifically in basic criminal investigation activities and techniques.

Traffic Management and Collision Investigators

1-21. TMCIs are trained at the Traffic Management and Collision Investigation Course at Lackland Air Force Base, Texas. TMCIs receive specific training to conduct traffic management and enforcement which includes specialized technical capabilities in traffic investigations. Traffic management and enforcement activities are L&O tasks that directly support the maintenance of good order and discipline as part of a broader L&O mission set conducted by military police.

1-22. L&O tasks related to traffic management and enforcement include those tasks associated with mobility and collision investigations. Traffic management and enforcement activities (less collision investigations) are discussed in ATTP 3-39.10. The investigative activity of traffic management and enforcement is discussed in this manual at chapter 13. TMCIs possess specific capabilities in collision investigations and enforcement of traffic-related laws, including suppression of driving under the influence violations. They are skilled at postincident reconstruction of traffic-related incidents to determine cause and effect. TMCIs also play a critical role in HN police support. They provide expertise in the training and implementation of HN police traffic enforcement capabilities and can be instrumental in the identification of other crimes discovered during collision investigations.

MILITARY POLICE SOLDIERS AND DEPARTMENT OF THE ARMY CIVILIAN POLICE

1-23. All military police Soldiers and DA civilian police, are trained to conduct initial investigations and support LE investigators during the conduct of deliberate criminal investigations. While SAs, MPI, and TMCI personnel conduct dedicated, complex criminal and collision investigations, all military police personnel must have a basic foundation and understanding of investigative techniques and capabilities including evidence collection and preservation, forensic analysis capabilities and requirements, conducting interviews, and establishing and maintaining the chain of custody. They must be proficient at conducting preliminary investigations and limited follow-on investigations. These skills must be trained and certified as part of initial training and certification and should be reinforced through cyclical training of all military police.

1-24. Military police, as first responders to many (if not most) crime scenes are regularly required to conduct preliminary investigations and canvas interviews of witnesses, victims, and potential subjects. Preliminary or initial investigations begin when the first patrol arrives at the scene of an incident. The preliminary investigation should include—

- Observing and documenting—
    - The general condition of the scene.
    - Activities occurring upon approach and after arrival.
    - Any spontaneous statement or comments by victims, witnesses, or potential subjects.
- Maintaining and protecting the crime or incident scene by—
    - Establishing a protective perimeter around the crime scene.
    - Establishing an access point and briefing area to control and document entry into the controlled area.
- Conducting evidence collection as required.
- Locating and identifying victims, witnesses, or potential subjects.
- Conducting initial interviews with victims, witnesses, or potential subjects, as required, and ensuring that witness statements are properly documented.
- Apprehending subjects as required.
- Completing all required—
    - Patrol reports.
    - Witness statements.
    - Chain-of-custody and evidence documentation.
    - Briefing of MPIs, TMCIs and USACIDC SAs on all aspects of the preliminary investigation and providing copies of all reports, statements, and evidence documentation.

1-25. Follow-up investigations by LE patrols may be directed by the desk sergeant, the patrol supervisor, or the operations section when required to fill information gaps or complete LE administrative requirements. Most follow-up investigations are conducted at the request of LE investigators to fill identified information requirements on open investigations. They can also be initiated by the original responding patrol when gaps in required information are identified. Follow-up investigations can include additional searches or interviews, the apprehension of subjects, and victim or witness assistance.

> *Note.* If an MPI or USACIDC SA has taken over the lead in an investigation, military police desk and patrol personnel must coordinate with the lead investigator before conducting any follow-up activities to ensure investigative efforts are synchronized.

TRAINING CONSIDERATIONS

1-26. Military police and investigators must stay current with new investigative techniques and capabilities. Even experienced investigators must learn new investigative methods and understand the evolving nature of threat and LE capabilities. Ongoing education and training for USACIDC SAs, MPIs, TMCIs, and military police patrol personnel can be obtained through several sources including—

- LE training embedded within professional military education courses.
- Functional courses through USAMPS.
- Civilian LE training opportunities.
- In-service certification and refresher training.
- Unit mentorship programs.

Evolving Technology

1-27. LE investigators must stay current with emerging technology and understand the capabilities and limitations of the technology as it applies to LE investigations. More advanced analytical software and databases continue to be developed, providing additional tools and faster analytical capability to LE personnel. Advances in electronic media capability have made protecting and retrieving electronic evidence a challenge for the LE community. The development of new technologies for analyzing biological and other trace evidence, including deoxyribonucleic acid (DNA) testing, has expanded the range and credibility of forensic analysis and increased the number of tools available to investigators and legal professionals. These new technologies have become established and accepted elements of LE and criminal justice procedures. LE investigators must understand these new capabilities and how they can impact an investigation.

Safety

1-28. Personal safety is a priority for investigators. Beyond the obvious physical threat posed by a subject, responding to a crime scene often places the investigator in danger of exposure to environmental hazards or other unsafe conditions. The collection of some types of evidence can increase the risk of exposure to dangerous substances. Personal protection against chemical, biological, radiological and nuclear (CBRN) threats and hazards and physical hazards often requires special training and equipment. LE managers should ensure that all police personnel receive hazardous material training and critical incident management training, and that appropriate safety equipment is available in investigative kits. Numerous federal, state, and local agencies provide such training. Emergency management agencies at the federal, state, and local levels often provide hazardous material and critical incident training at no cost to police, fire, and emergency medical personnel.

ORGANIZATIONS AND CAPABILITIES

1-29. Both USACIDC and military police organizations provide investigative capabilities supporting L&O activities in all environments. These organizations have a wide range of subordinate organizations, elements, and individuals that either act as the investigative lead or provide critical support to the LE investigator.

UNITED STATES ARMY CRIMINAL INVESTIGATION COMMAND

1-30. The mission of the USACIDC is to conduct and control all Army investigations of serious crimes, as defined in AR 195-2, and less serious crimes upon request or as needed to enforce Army law or regulations. USACIDC is a direct reporting unit headquartered at Quantico Marine Corps Base, Virginia. It is commanded by a general officer and staffed with officers, warrant officers, enlisted Soldiers, and DA civilian employees. USACIDC provides overarching management and supervision of all Army criminal investigation functions and is the approving authority and manager of all agent accreditation functions. LE investigative personnel within the organization are referred to as SAs. When performing LE investigative responsibilities, they operate within the USACIDC command structure to enable independent, unbiased investigations, free from fear of improper command influence by the supported commander.

1-31. Regardless of the environment, USACIDC has the responsibility to investigate serious crimes involving Army personnel, DA civilians and agencies, and companies working for the Army. USACIDC investigates war crimes and crimes involving personal and government property affecting the Army's mission and logistics security. USACIDC SAs may also conduct investigations based on international treaties, status-of-forces agreements (SOFAs), and joint investigations with the HN, if requested by the supported commander in support of the overall Army mission. Outside of the United States, USACIDC's investigative authority and investigative responsibility are determined by international treaty or agreement, including SOFAs, the policies of the HN government, the U.S. ambassador, and AR 195-2.

> ***Note.*** Foreign countries are sovereign entities; this prohibits direct contact and information exchange between LE personnel unless a Mutual Legal Assistance Treaty or other official legal document between the countries is in place. Investigators should consult with their servicing legal advisor to ensure that any coordination with foreign officials is covered by an appropriate legal agreement.

1-32. USACIDC is structured with a headquarters, two geographic CID groups, and a "special services" CID group. These CID groups are further broken down into CID battalions and CID elements with specific geographic areas of responsibility. The 701st CID Group provides specialized investigative capabilities (and exclusive investigative authority for certain offenses) in general support across the Army; investigative elements of this group are discussed in detail in paragraph 1-40. See figure 1-1 for a diagram of USACIDC investigative and investigative support assets.

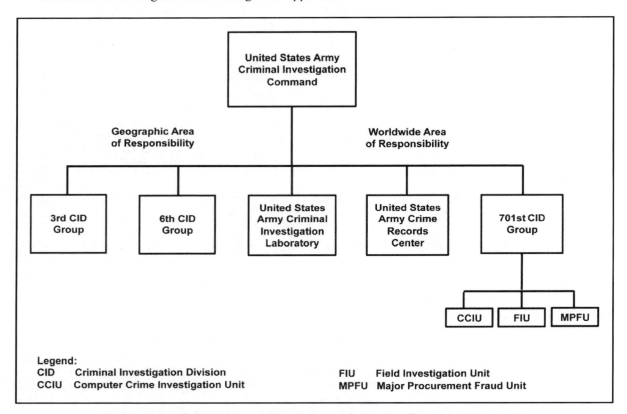

Figure 1-1. USACIDC investigative and investigative support assets

1-33. The two geographic CID groups and their subordinate CID elements have the organic capability to conduct a wide range of criminal investigations. The commander of each CID group, battalion, or element is responsible for the conduct of criminal investigative activity within their assigned geographic area of responsibility (AOR). When investigative requirements exceed their capabilities, technical experts from other elements within USACIDC can be employed to assist. Investigations typically fall into the following six primary categories:

- **Serious crimes against persons.** These investigations consist of the most serious offenses. SAs conduct a complete investigation into all deaths that occur on an Army installation or that the Army may have an interest in. Other examples of this type of investigation would include robbery, assault, and child abuse.

- **Drug suppression activities.** CID elements conduct installation-level drug suppression activities both on and off the installation. These activities frequently require—
  - Undercover (covert) activities in unit and social environments.
  - Coordination between CID drug suppression teams and local, state, federal, and HN LE agencies.
  - Overt activities that assist unit commanders in unit drug suppression activities through training, education, and the conduct of health and welfare inspections.
- **Economic crimes investigations.** USACIDC units conduct investigations of fraud, waste, and abuse at the installation, unit, and individual levels. These include the full range of investigations from the theft of an individual Soldier's checkbook or debit card up to and including installation-level contract fraud.
- **Sex crimes investigations.** SAs complete investigations of rape, sexual assault, or unwanted sexual contact involving active duty Soldiers at any location and civilians on government property. These investigations require—
  - Extensive specialized training.
  - Close coordination with, trial counsel, the sexual assault response coordinator (SARC), social work services, victim advocacy, and medical treatment facility personnel.
  - Coordination with off-installation professional services (this coordination is accomplished in concert with Army victim advocacy personnel).
- **Crime prevention.** SAs evaluate installation activities and units to determine areas susceptible to theft or diversion of military assets or other crime-conducive conditions. Recommendations are then made to the supported commander for improvements that may limit risks.
- **Criminal intelligence.** *Criminal intelligence* is a category of police intelligence derived from the collection, analysis, and interpretation of all available information concerning known and potential criminal threats and vulnerabilities of supported organizations (ATTP 3-39.20). SAs collect, analyze, and process criminal intelligence from both the installation and external sources. CID elements—
  - Evaluate, collate, and forward this information to their higher CID headquarters.
  - Receive information from external sources including criminal information and intelligence from military, civilian, and foreign intelligence services.
  - Report, when required based on threat and investigative impacts, specific criminal intelligence—such as methods of operation, distinct patterns, crime techniques, investigative leads, gang violence, and terrorism—to commanders and supported installation activities, and share with various intelligence and LE agencies.

United States Army Criminal Investigations Laboratory

1-34. The successful investigation and prosecution of crimes can require the collection, preservation, and forensic analysis of evidence, which can be critical to determine the guilt or innocence of an individual. The USACIL provides forensic analysis and other technical services to LE investigators and other military and nonmilitary investigative entities. The USACIL is a nationally accredited criminal investigative laboratory located at the Gillem Enclave, Forest Park, Georgia. It is accredited by the Forensic Quality Services' Forensic Accreditation Program.

1-35. USACIL personnel conduct examination and analysis of all evidence submitted, whether from USACIDC elements, military police units, other DOD investigative agencies, or other federal LE agencies, when required. It is primarily staffed with a civilian staff, providing stability and continuity of the mission. The USACIL provides state-of-the-art forensic analysis in several areas and disciplines including drug chemistry, biological evidence (serology/DNA), latent impression examination (including fingerprints, tire tracks, and other impressions), questioned documents examination, digital evidence evaluation, and firearms and tool marks examinations. The USACIL can also provide technical support to SAs for processing crimes scenes in any operational environment. USACIL examiners provide expert witness testimony in court cases regarding the results of forensic examinations.

1-36. In addition to many innovative forensic techniques, the USACIL contributes to the Combined DNA Index System (CODIS). The CODIS is an FBI program used to store DNA profiles. It allows federal, state, and local crime labs to compare DNA profiles and to generate investigative leads. All military criminal investigators should become thoroughly familiar with CODIS. USACIL analysts also provide data and use the Integrated Automated Fingerprint Identification System and the National Integrated Ballistics Information Network. These important databases can be useful to LE investigators and crime lab analysts for comparative analysis of fingerprint data and firearms evidence (such as cartridge casings) recovered in an investigation.

Expeditionary Forensic Division

1-37. The USACIL Expeditionary Forensic Division provides global forensics support. It provides forensic expertise, infrastructure, and reachback capability to the Combatant Commands enabling actionable information for targeting, criminal prosecution, protection activities, and other emerging requirements. The Expeditionary Forensic Division consists of three Expeditionary Forensic Laboratories (EFLs) and a Reachback Operation Center that provides a deployable, trained, and equipped forensic capability supporting decisive action.

Expeditionary Forensic Laboratory

1-38. The EFL is a deployable, adaptive forensic capability that enhances the exploitation of captured enemy materiel and evidence gathered supporting criminal investigations. The EFL provides a standardized exploitation process by integrating weapons technical exploitation capabilities, including explosive exploitation and electronic reengineering, with their inherent forensic disciplines of serology, DNA, chemistry, latent prints, and firearms/tool marks. EFLs provide support to combatant commanders based on operational priorities. EFLs have on-site capabilities and the ability to obtain institutional support from the USACIL through reachback. This combination of on-site and reachback capability allows the lab to prioritize in-theater capabilities while ensuring full forensic analysis support.

United States Army Crime Records Center

1-39. The United States Army Crime Records Center (USACRC) receives, maintains, accounts for, disseminates information from, and disposes of Army crime records. It coordinates automation of crime records data and information and serves as the functional proponent for the electronic imaging of crime records. The USARC retrieves and correlates data and statistics from the stored records and provides crime data to authorized recipients. It also administers the USACIDC Polygraph Program and the Freedom of Information Act Program. Army LE investigators routinely access data from USACRC databases to determine if suspects have a past record or if victims have ever been victims of another crime. Archived case files from previous investigations can sometimes be helpful when criminal or victim histories are determined.

Specialized Investigative Capability

1-40. The 701st CID Group is a special services group which has a worldwide area of responsibility and provides mission command over units and activities with specific technical or administrative capabilities and missions. USACIDC investigative and investigative support assets are shown in figure 1-1, page 1-8. Elements within the 701st CID Group include the Computer Crime Investigative Unit (CCIU), the Field Investigative Unit (FIU), and the Major Procurement Fraud Unit (MPFU). This group retains jurisdiction over activities within its purview worldwide. The unique missions of these elements, as well as other specialized activities and capabilities, are discussed below.

Computer Crimes Investigative Unit

1-41. The CCIU is the Army's sole organization for conducting worldwide criminal investigations of intrusions and related malicious activities involving Army computers, networks, personnel, and data. As needed, the CCIU also provides expert investigative support to USACIDC field elements conducting criminal investigations involving computers and digital media evidence. The CCIU maintains liaison and works with other LE agencies; the CCIU coordinates with U.S. federal and foreign government intelligence agencies.

1-42. Most USACIDC SAs do not possess the required technical skills to conduct advanced computer forensic analysis and complex computer crime investigations. Due to the highly technical nature of investigating computer crimes and computer forensic analysis, CCIU personnel receive advanced computer training from the Defense Cyber Investigations Training Academy, Federal Law Enforcement Training Center and other sources of technical expertise.

1-43. USACIDC SAs and attorneys assigned to the CCIU provide guidance and subject matter expertise to other USACIDC SAs in the field who are conducting investigations involving computers and associated networks. The CCIU has sole investigative responsibility and authority to investigate offenses related to Army networks. The CCIU maintains personnel with advanced training in processing and analyzing digital evidence capabilities. These CCIU SAs can provide assistance to USACIDC SAs in the field as well as the USACIL and other LE agencies requiring computer forensic analysis capability.

Field Investigative Unit

1-44. The FIU is a unique investigative organization and conducts the most sensitive criminal investigations in the Army. The FIU has a specific mission to investigate criminal allegations involving highly classified Army programs and other sensitive situations of interest to the Secretary of the Army and the Army Chief of Staff.

1-45. Much of the activity of the field investigative unit is classified. The unit investigations frequently support both the intelligence and acquisition communities. In addition, it conducts investigations of classified programs and senior Army personnel where discretion is required during the investigative process. The FIU also provides investigative support to other USACIDC elements and Army organizations when the security requirements exceed available investigative resource capability.

Major Procurement Fraud Unit

1-46. The MPFU is compromised of highly skilled SAs who conduct investigations into allegations of fraud involving major Army contracting activities and acquisition programs. These units may be collocated at an Army installation or they may be standalone elements located near a major Army contracting epicenter. MPFU SAs conduct complex multifaceted investigations that frequently take years to complete. They are typically staffed with civilian USACIDC SAs to ensure longevity based on the complexity and duration of MPFU investigations.

1-47. The MPFU conducts all investigations into allegations of fraud, defective pricing, corruption, kickbacks, antitrust violations, and other miscellaneous incidents involving major procurement actions. The MPFU Fraud Field Office is the basic operating unit and conducts procurement fraud investigations within an assigned geographical area of responsibility, designated by the MPFU. Each MPFU Fraud Field Office is assigned six or more SAs, depending on the area of responsibility, and is resourced for full operational capability but has limited administrative and clerical capacity and may require support from its higher headquarters.

1-48. MPFU elements are further broken down into MPFU resident agencies. An MPFU resident agency operates in a limited geographical area within its parent MPFU Fraud Field Office's area of responsibility. The MPFU resident agency is typically assigned one to four special agents and has no organic administrative capability. It is completely dependent upon its parent MPFU Fraud Field Office for all clerical, administrative, and logistical support.

Forensic Science Officers

1-49. The forensic science officer (FSO) is a specially trained USACIDC SA—limited to warrant officers only—with the knowledge, skills, and abilities to conduct complex forensic investigations. FSOs receive graduate-level education in forensic science at civilian universities, the USACIL, and through the Armed Forces Medical Examiner System (AFMES); upon completion of their specialized training, they are typically assigned to CID group or battalion-level CID elements. These technical specialists have advanced training in identification, preservation, collection, and analysis of evidence. They provide subject matter expertise regarding evidence collection and preservation at crime scenes and coordinates with the USACIL on behalf of field agents when technical aspects of the evidence require advanced discussion beyond the capability of agents not specifically trained as FSOs. FSOs also can perform crime scene reconstruction in areas such as bloodstain spatter analysis and bullet-path or trajectory analysis.

Polygraph Examiners

1-50. AR 195-6 is the governing regulation for polygraph requirements and support. Polygraph examiners are experienced LE investigators that meet extensive screening, training, and certification requirements in order to perform polygraph examinations. The basic polygraph examiners training course is taught at the Department of Defense Polygraph Institute. Polygraph examiners are normally geographically located within the CID battalion; however, they operate independently from the CID battalion headquarters to which they may be assigned. Polygraph examiners are typically limited to the conduct of polygraph examinations as assigned by the USACRC; emergency authorization for polygraph examinations is delegated to specific CID commands only under specific circumstances as outlined in AR 195-6.

MILITARY POLICE ORGANIZATIONS

1-51. Military police LE investigative capabilities exist across many military police elements. Authorizations for trained MPIs and TMCIs exist on military police brigade and battalion staffs and military police companies. Because duty as an MPI or a TMCI is not a permanent career track assignment, it is not uncommon for military police units to have Soldiers with MPI and TMCI training and experience within their force structure in numbers well beyond authorizations in the modified table of organization and equipment documents.

1-52. Military police Soldiers are also trained to observe and report information about persons, activities, and their environment based on published information requirements and intuitive understanding of unidentified critical information requirements. This information can be critical to LE investigators and provide critical police information for analysis and production of police intelligence relevant to criminals, criminal activity, and crime conducive conditions. In an operational environment this information not only fulfils LE investigative information requirements and police information requirements, it also feeds the operations process enabling fusion with traditional intelligence elements. See ATTP 3-39.20 for more information.

Note. Commanders should query USAR and ARNG units during operational deployments to identify those personnel with careers in civilian LE. During operational deployments, military police Soldiers from USAR and ARNG elements may possess significant LE investigative capabilities and skills based on experience in their civilian LE careers.

1-53. Military police brigade, battalion, and PM staffs conduct police intelligence activities which directly support LE investigations and collection of police information. Each operations section within these organizations should be staffed with trained police intelligence analysts to help conduct analysis of incoming information and produce police intelligence products to support LE investigators and commanders in fulfilling information requirements.

1-54. All military police organizations have a basic level of investigative capability within their force structure based on training and experience in basic LE patrol activities and the presence of personnel trained as MPIs or TMCIs. However, the highest density of dedicated MPI and TMCI capability is structured within the L&O detachments through the MPI and traffic management and enforcement teams. For additional information regarding the PM and other military police organizations see FM 3-39.

Law and Order Detachments

1-55. Within military police formations, most capabilities required to conduct dedicated LE activities, including LE investigations, are associated with the L&O detachment and associated teams. L&O detachments are built as teams with specific capabilities; these teams are designed to be deployed to support specific LE requirements in an AO. L&O teams are found across active, reserve, and National Guard force structures. At home stations, the teams that comprise the L&O detachment are assigned LE duties within the Provost Marshal Office, making up the core of dedicated technical policing expertise supporting U.S. Army bases and base camps. When deployed to provide LE support for U.S. forces, L&O detachments are normally assigned to a military police brigade and placed under the operational control of the base camp commander for L&O support to the base camp. When deployed to provide HN support, they are typically assigned to a military police brigade or battalion to provide appropriate mission command and task organization, ensuring optimum use of the limited assets of the L&O detachment.

1-56. Specialized teams within the L&O detachment provide skills and capabilities required for military police to conduct police station activities supporting either U.S. forces or HN LE requirements, including criminal and collision investigations. The L&O detachment has teams to fill the full range of capabilities required for police station activities including military police headquarters and station activities that provide administration, military police operations, and military police desk capabilities. L&O detachment teams also provide expertise to support required force protection programs and associated requirements, provide military working dog (MWD) capabilities, conduct criminal investigations, and conduct traffic management and enforcement investigations. The two teams dedicated to LE investigations are the MPI team and the traffic management and collision investigation team; these teams are discussed below. See ATTP 3-39.10 and FM 3-39 for detailed descriptions of the full capability of the L&O detachment.

Military Police Investigation Team

1-57. The military police investigation team provides technical capabilities for investigating criminal incidents and associated activities. MPIs that make up the team are specially trained to analyze police information, collect and properly store evidence, document criminal investigations, and prepare evidence for appropriate adjudication through the military justice system. When required, they coordinate with USACIDC SAs, sister service military criminal investigative service SAs, or other military and civilian LE agencies operating within the AO to synchronize and deconflict ongoing investigations and share LE information. They also directly support USACIDC drug suppression efforts. MPIs assigned overseas work with HN military and civilian police agencies when conducting joint and multinational investigations.

1-58. MPIs support HN police development and transition teams by working with HN criminal investigators to build baseline investigative capability and capacity, supporting the operational commander's efforts to establish civil control. MPIs experience and technical expertise in evidence collection and preservation enable successful site exploitation and follow-on forensic evaluation in support of military police and multifunctional commanders. They are trained to conduct interviews and LE interrogations. These skills are honed for use in criminal investigations, but can be extremely valuable when conducting tactical questioning of personnel detained in an AO during military operations or at an incident site during follow-on response and exploitation. These same capabilities are also valuable in conducting interviews of HN citizens, local officials, and other personnel to gain valuable information and increase situational understanding of the criminal and general threat environment.

Traffic Management and Enforcement Team

1-59. The traffic management and enforcement team provides technical capabilities required for investigating traffic-related collisions and subject matter expertise beneficial to military police traffic enforcement and education activities. TMCIs assigned to the team are trained in collision investigation and reconstruction to assess the causes of collisions, including operator error, environmental conditions, and equipment failures. TMCI capabilities are critical when conducting collision investigations involving fatalities or extensive property damage and collisions involving injuries or damage to government property. Collision investigations are covered in depth at chapter 13. Other duties and responsibilities of TMCIs include—

- Conducting traffic control and safety tasks.
- Conducting traffic enforcement.
- Conducting drunk driver suppression activities.
- Identifying and processing abandoned vehicles.

- Preparing traffic studies.
- Preparing and tracking traffic reports, including citations.
- Conducting special traffic enforcement during special events, emergency operations, or other incidents and events.

1-60. The knowledge of traffic control and flow, protection measures associated with vehicle movement, and traffic study capabilities of TMCIs can be a valuable asset to military police and multifunctional commanders in their efforts to protect U.S. personnel and assets, ensure freedom of movement, and establish and maintain civil order and control. These aspects of traffic management and enforcement are covered in depth in ATTP 3-39.10 and linked in the discussion of mobility operations in ATTP 3-90.4.

Military Working Dog Teams

1-61. MWD teams provide a valuable asset to military police, combined arms, the DOD, and other governmental agencies. The dog's sight, smell, and hearing ability enhance detection capabilities and provide commanders with a physical and psychological deterrent to criminal activity. MWD teams are key resources for use in Army LE. There are three types of MWDs in the Military Police Corps Regiment—the patrol explosive detector dog, the patrol narcotics detector dog, and the specialized search dog. Specialized search dogs are not typically used to support L&O missions, because they are trained to work off leash and are not trained to perform patrol dog functions required for LE applications. Patrol explosive detector dogs and patrol narcotics detector dogs are also trained as patrol dogs. Patrol dogs are used in routine military police LE patrol activities supporting decisive action in all environments. Their explosive and narcotics detection capabilities can provide significant support to Army LE investigators for detection of contraband and protection of personnel. See ATTP 3-39.10 and ATTP 3-39.34 for more information.

Evidence Response Teams

1-62. Evidence response teams can be a valuable asset to both LE investigators and operational commanders. An evidence response team is an ad hoc team of technical experts, expediently formed and mobilized to respond to a crime scene, incident site, or other significant event requiring the collection and preservation of evidence. These teams will typically be manned by military police Soldiers and led by MPIs or USACIDC SAs. The mission of an evidence response team is to—

- Identify and mark the crime scene or incident site boundaries. Military police should receive guidance from the senior MPI or USACIDC SA to determine the boundary limits to ensure that an adequate area is marked and protected.
- Protect the scene.
- Collect and preserve physical evidence.
- Document evidence and establish the chain of custody.

JUDGE ADVOCATES

1-63. Throughout an investigation, LE personnel coordinate with appropriate judge advocate (JA) personnel within the office of the SJA concerning their investigation. Along with obtaining a legal opinion as to whether an investigation is complete and legally sufficient, LE personnel should involve JAs throughout the investigation to ensure that all appropriate criminal offenses have been considered, and to assist in the goal of obtaining legally competent evidence. Additionally, some JAs, such as trial counsel and defense counsel, may contact LE personnel directly to discuss ongoing or closed investigations. Office of the SJA legal personnel who may interact with LE personnel include the—

- **SJA.** The SJA is the primary legal advisor to the commander exercising general court-martial convening authority. Among other things, the SJA provides military justice advice to the commander.
- **Military Justice Division.** This may include the—
  - Chief, Military Justice Division. The Chief of Military Justice advises the SJA on all military justice matters. The Chief also leads and supervises all JAs within the division.

- **Trial counsel**. JAs who work under the supervision of the Chief of Military Justice are trial counsel. Trial counsel (many of whom are assigned at the brigade level) prosecute courts-martial arising within their jurisdiction. The trial counsel reviews all military justice actions that arise within their jurisdiction.

Special Victims Prosecutor

1-64. Army special victims prosecutors (SVPs) are assigned to the U.S. Army Legal Services Agency but are stationed throughout the world and serve area jurisdictions. These JAs primarily prosecute sexually related and domestic violence offenses. SVPs are accessible to all LE offices and personnel, regardless of the SVPs duty location. The SVPs serve regionally and review all military justice actions involving sexual or domestic violence offenses within their jurisdictions.

United States Army Trial Defense Services

1-65. All JAs who serve as defense counsel are assigned to the United States Army Trial Defense Services (USATDS). They generally defend Soldiers within their geographical area. However, USATDS attorneys may be detailed to cases anywhere in the Army. Defense counsel, whether assigned to a specific installation or remotely located, may contact LE personnel for office calls to review evidence or case files or to schedule interviews with investigators or USACIDC SAs. Requests from trial defense attorneys should be accommodated to the extent possible in order to ensure the timely processing of cases. If LE personnel have questions or concerns regarding communications with USATDS personnel, they should contact their servicing military justice JA.

Chapter 2

Physical Evidence

Successful criminal prosecution is dependent on the ability of LE investigators and military police organizations to properly secure, collect, and preserve physical evidence for subsequent analysis in support of LE activities and other mission requirements. Beyond traditional LE activities, increased pressure to prosecute terrorist and other threat elements captured within the context of decisive action have increased both awareness and operational requirements for evidence collection and forensic analysis capabilities during military operations. Advances in technology have enhanced forensic analytical capabilities and increased the sensitivity of forensic testing. This chapter provides an understanding of the key activities involved in evidence collection and forensic analysis. It focuses on techniques for use in evidence collection by Army LE investigators and military police. The processing and analysis of collected evidence is also covered briefly in other publications to include ATTP 3-39.10 and ATTP 3-39.20.

TYPES OF EVIDENCE

2-1. Evidence is anything that helps to ascertain the truth of a matter, or gives proof of a fact in an investigation; evidence may be physical or testimonial. Physical evidence includes any object, material, or data gathered to establish facts relevant to a specific crime or incident. Testimonial evidence includes documented written or verbal statements typically collected during interviews or LE interrogations conducted during a LE investigation. This chapter will focus on physical evidence; testimonial evidence will be discussed in chapter 3.

2-2. Physical evidence is exchanged anytime two objects or persons make contact with each other; this is known as Locard's principle of exchange. The principle is based on the assumption that anytime two objects touch physical evidence is exchanged, or cross transferred, between the two objects. These exchanges may leave obvious visible material or marks, or the physical exchanges may not be visible to the investigator. The challenge for investigators is to identify and collect this deposited evidence. Evidence properly collected and analyzed can provide elements of fact or lead to associations or patterns that establish proof (or a high probability of proof) that a conclusion or judgment is true. Collection of physical evidence can be broken down into three primary tasks: identification or recognition of potential evidence, protection of evidence, and collection and preservation of evidence.

2-3. The collection of physical evidence and follow-on forensic analysis enables LE investigators to identify persons in relation to space and time, thus enabling the identification of individuals specific to crimes or other incidents; linkages between persons, material, and equipment (including weapons); and trends, patterns, and associations pertinent to crimes and criminal activity. It can also enable operating forces to identify enemies and add depth and scope to the intelligence picture. Evidence such as fingerprints or DNA can enable U.S. forces to specifically identify who handled an item, such as an improvised explosive device (IED), and to connect a particular person with a certain place or event. The resulting information can support—

- **Criminal investigation and prosecution.** Evidence collected, analyzed, and exploited by Army LE investigators can link individuals to particular locations, events, or devices and establish trends, patterns and associations. These results can be used to further criminal investigations of crimes and individuals suspected of involvement in criminal acts against U.S. forces, family members, and resources.

- **Protection efforts.** Collected evidence and subsequent analysis can enable protection efforts by identifying threats and enabling commanders to implement measures to mitigate hostile actions against U.S. personnel, resources, facilities, and critical information.
- **Targeting actions.** Timely collection and analysis of evidence results in targeting of criminal elements in conjunction with ongoing LE investigations or targeting, using lethal and nonlethal means, against threat elements in contingency operations.
- **Sourcing actions.** Collection of evidence and subsequent forensic analysis can be fused with other information obtained through LE or intelligence channels to increase the situational understanding of criminal networks. This enables further investigation and targeting to disrupt, interdict, apprehend, or eliminate criminal elements.
- **Medical processes.** Medical examiners (MEs) conduct autopsies to identify individuals and determine the cause and manner of death. The recovery of forensic materials can enable research and analysis by Armed Forces MEs to increase knowledge regarding Army deaths and identify trends and preventive risk factors.

2-4. Military police and LE investigators should have a basic understanding of the analytical process and requirements of forensic scientists and technicians. This must be accompanied by a broad understanding of collection, preservation, and packaging techniques that reduce the chance that evidence will be destroyed or contaminated. Improper handling of evidence can render it useless. This understanding will enable the collector to identify potential evidence, understand what potential information can be obtained through analysis of the evidence, and ensure proper handling of the evidence to mitigate the chance of destruction or contamination. Proper identification, collection, and packaging of evidence during crime scene processing or site exploitation are critical to the success of subsequent forensic examination. ATTP 3-39.10 contains information on basic evidence collection techniques.

RULES OF EVIDENCE

2-5. Army LE personnel, especially investigators, must develop skills and techniques to recognize, collect, evaluate, process, and preserve evidence. Evidence is the source from which a court-martial or jury must form its conclusions regarding the guilt or innocence of an accused. Evidence is the means by which any alleged matter of fact is proven or disproved. Evidence includes all matters, except comment or argument, legally submitted to a court.

2-6. Army LE investigators conduct inquiries to find evidence and make it available for presentation in court. Something more than a mere collection of evidence is required of a successful investigation; the evidence obtained must be admissible in court or lead to admissible evidence. A basic knowledge of the rules governing admission and rejection of evidence is fundamental to an investigation. This knowledge is needed to conduct inquiries and prepare cases that will present enough admissible and reliable information to the court for a proper decision to be rendered. Only evidence that satisfies the rules of admissibility is admitted.

2-7. Admissibility of evidence in court is generally dependent on whether the evidence is relevant, whether it was obtained legally, and whether positive control (chain of custody) over the evidence has been maintained to ensure that the evidence has been protected and unaltered. To be admissible, evidence must be relevant. Relevancy requires that the specific evidence in question has some direct bearing on the alleged crime. "Relevant evidence" means evidence having any tendency to make the existence of any fact that is of consequence to the determination of the action more probable or less probable than it would be without the evidence. Military Rules of Evidence (MRE) rule 401 describes relevant evidence. The MRE are included as part III within the Manual for Courts Martial (MCM). All relevant evidence is admissible at trial unless some rule of law forbids its consideration by the court. Part III, section IV of the MCM discusses relevancy of evidence including its limits and exceptions.

2-8. Army LE is most directly impacted by rules concerning search and seizure of evidence and rules affecting the admissibility of information, including confessions, obtained during interviews and LE interrogations. Evidence from a search or a seizure will not be admissible if it was obtained as a result of an unlawful search or interview. The Fourth Amendment to the U.S. Constitution establishes the right to be free from unreasonable searches and seizures. The MRE, included as part III of the MCM, is the primary reference for rules concerning search and seizure of evidence. Additional information can be found in ATTP 3-39.10. Though not all inclusive, the following text provides an overview of the basic rules of evidence that are most commonly faced by Army LE personnel.

THE EXCLUSIONARY RULE

2-9. The Fourth Amendment to the U.S. Constitution establishes the right to be free from unreasonable searches and seizures. Army LE personnel must know and understand the law surrounding the Fourth Amendment and lawful searches and seizures; failure to understand and act according to the Fourth Amendment, and subsequent judicial rulings, can result in the exclusion of evidence. This is known as the *exclusionary rule*. The exclusionary rule applies to—

- Evidence obtained as a result of an unlawful search or seizure which violated the Fourth Amendment rights of the accused.
- Any derivative evidence obtained as a result of an unlawful search. This includes any evidence obtained as a result of the original Fourth Amendment violation, as a product of the violation, or as evidence which flowed from the violation, often referred to as *fruit of the poisonous tree.*

2-10. The following key criteria need to be considered to determine if there is a violation of the Fourth Amendment:

- Whether there is an intrusion into an area where a person has a reasonable expectation of privacy. Areas where a reasonable expectation of privacy is typically understood to exist include within an individual's home, personal belongings, automobile, desk, lockers, personal computers, personal cell phones, items on the individuals body (including clothing), and other areas. Exceptions are discussed later in this section.
- Whether the intrusion was effected by a U.S. Government official or agent. The Fourth Amendment does not apply unless there is U.S. Government intrusion. Private searches and foreign searches are not covered by the Fourth Amendment as long as the private individual or foreign officials are not acting as agents of the U.S. Government.

SEARCHES AND SEIZURES

2-11. A search is an examination, authorized by law, of a specific person, property, or area for specified evidence or property or of a specific person for the purpose of seizing such property, evidence, or person. A seizure is the taking of property from the possessor by an authorized person or the restriction of freedom of movement of an individual against their will by an agent of the government. Army LE personnel must have probable cause, search authorization, or a search warrant for a search and seizure of evidence to be lawful, unless a valid exception exists.

2-12. A search is not considered unreasonable when conducted pursuant to a search warrant or authorization that was issued upon a showing of probable cause. Probable cause to conduct a search or seizure exists when there is a reasonable belief that a crime has been committed and that the person, property, or evidence sought in connection with the crime is located in the place (a room, barracks, privately owned vehicle, quarters) or on the person to be searched. The existence of probable cause is required for search or apprehension of a suspect. MRE 315(f)(2) covers the rules for these searches.

2-13. A competent military or civilian authority must make a probable cause determination that there is a reasonable belief that the person, property, or evidence sought is located in the place or on the person to be searched and approve the search authorization. This probable cause determination is based on the totality of the circumstances at the search time. A competent civilian authority is required when USACIDC SAs conduct criminal investigations off the installation and the Uniform Code of Military Justice (UCMJ) is not applicable or in cases dealing with civilians on a military installation who are not subject to the UCMJ. A competent military authority includes a military judge, a military magistrate, or a commander "who has control over the place where the property or person to be searched is situated or found." MRE 315(d) outlines who has the power to authorize a search.

2-14. Although a search authorization is generally required, there are instances when a search authorization is not required. The following searches are exceptions to the search authorization requirements:

- Consent search.
- Search incident to lawful apprehension.
- Operable vehicle search.
- Exigent circumstances.
- Medical emergencies.
- Plain view.
- Investigative stops, also known as "Terry stops."

Consent Searches

2-15. A consent search may be conducted of any person or property as long as lawful consent is given. MRE 314(e) discusses consent searches. A person can consent to search their own person or property, unless that person no longer has control of the property. Likewise, a person who is in control of property but who does not own it, can usually give consent to search that property. Consent can be withdrawn anytime; Army LE personnel must then stop the search and get proper authorization if the search is to continue. Ideally, the consent to search should be obtained in writing.

Lawful Apprehension

2-16. When a person is lawfully apprehended, that person and the surrounding area can be searched. MRE 314(g) discusses searches incident to a lawful apprehension. The search may be conducted for weapons or destructible evidence. The surrounding area of the person consists of the area within immediate control and the area in which the person being apprehended could reasonably reach with a sudden movement to obtain a weapon or evidence. This immediate control area may include a vehicle; this search **does not** include the trunk or the engine compartment. In 2009 the Supreme Court of the United States limited the authority to search a vehicle subsequent to apprehension (*Arizona versus Gant*). LE personnel may only search a vehicle subsequent to an apprehension with a valid search authorization (legal search authorization or consent to search), or if—

- It is reasonable to believe that the apprehended individual might access the vehicle at the time of the search.
- It is reasonable to believe that the apprehended individual's vehicle contains evidence of the offense that led to the arrest.
- The officer has probable cause to believe that there is evidence of a crime concealed within the vehicle, assuming the vehicle is readily mobile.

Note. It is impermissible for the arresting officer to "manufacture" a situation where the arrested individual could still have access.

2-17. These restrictions on vehicle searches do not affect the legitimate conduct of an inventory of a vehicle. LE personnel may still inventory a vehicle subsequent to an apprehension, a vehicle being towed due to a legitimate violation, or if the vehicle is towed for safety reasons; for example, if it represents a danger to other motorists or persons in the area. The inventory must be conducted strictly in accordance with approved agency procedures. During the inventory, the contents of the entire vehicle may be inventoried, with the exception of secured/locked areas that are not subject to open view and access. All accessible areas of the vehicle may be inventoried in order to protect the LE organization from allegations of theft or loss and to protect the driver of the vehicle from having his belongings pilfered while the car is impounded.

Exigent Circumstances

2-18. An exigent circumstance is one where there is a compelling reason to search immediately rather than wait for authorization. Exigent circumstance exceptions apply for a search based on probable cause when there is a reasonable belief that the delay in obtaining a search warrant or search authorization would result in removal, destruction, or concealment of evidence or when there is a reasonable military operational necessity that prohibits or prevents communication with a person empowered to grant a search warrant or search authorization. There must also be a reasonable belief that the delay necessary to obtain a search warrant or search authorization would result in the removal, destruction, or concealment of evidence.

2-19. Both probable cause and the specific exigent circumstance must exist. Under exigent circumstances, Army LE personnel may enter an area normally requiring a search authorization (such as a residence, a barracks room, an office, or a vehicle) to detain or apprehend a subject without written search authorization. Examples of exigent circumstance exceptions include the following:

- A subject committing a crime, or located by Army LE personnel in a public area, that is wanted for a previous offense can be pursued into a private area if he flees to avoid detention or apprehension. MRE 315(g)(1) discusses exigencies related to insufficient time. In this case, the fact that the subject is running to evade Army LE personnel subsequent to a crime makes a delay in the pursuit to obtain a written search authorization impractical. The perpetrator knows they are under suspicion and will likely attempt to destroy evidence prior to intervention by Army LE personnel.

- An operable vehicle may be searched if there is probable cause that the vehicle contains evidence of a crime. MRE 315(g)(3) discusses exigencies related to operable vehicles. The elements of probable cause and exigent circumstances that make obtaining a search authorization impractical must be present, and the vehicle cannot be in a condition that obviously renders it inoperable. The search in this case is not limited to the interior of the vehicle, but may include the entire vehicle. For example, a military police patrol conducts a lawful traffic stop for a traffic violation. Upon approaching the vehicle the LE official detects the sound of someone in distress emanating from the trunk of the vehicle. The trunk is beyond the immediate control of the operator; therefore any routine search incident to the traffic stop does not include the trunk. The sound of the person in distress or the smell of marijuana coming from the vehicle provides probable cause that a crime may be in progress; the fact that the vehicle is in operating condition and can be driven away provides the exigent circumstance for Army LE personnel to immediately search the trunk of the vehicle.

- Observations of a crime in progress warrant immediate action. Under this circumstance, Army LE personnel may enter a home or vehicle without a formal search authorization. For example, an Army LE patrol moving through a neighborhood hears screams for help emanating from a residence. Taking time to obtain a search authorization to enter the home could result in serious injury or death to the victim as well as loss or destruction of evidence; no formal search authorization is required. LE personnel with probable cause may take immediate action during these incidents to secure evidence in the immediate area that is in danger of being destroyed. MRE 315(g)(2) discusses exigencies related to lack of communications.

- When there is a valid medical emergency, Army LE personnel may take necessary actions to preserve the health of personnel. MRE 314(i) discusses exigencies related to emergency searches to save life or for related purposes. For example, if an LE patrol finds an unconscious person, that person may be searched in an attempt to find some identification and determine the cause of his condition.

2-20. The presence of an exigent circumstance does not provide a permanent authority to search. Once the exigency is eliminated, LE personnel must follow search and seizure rules as if no exigency ever existed. For example, if LE respond to a report of gunfire at a residence and respond to find an injured person inside, they along with other emergency medical personnel may enter to render aid. While legally inside the residence (due to the exigent medical emergency) any evidence in plain view may be seized as evidence. Once the person has been stabilized and taken by medical personnel the exigent circumstance has been removed; LE personnel may not search the residence for evidence without legal search authorization or a search warrant issued by competent authority.

Plain View

2-21. At any point in which Army LE personnel make contact with the public, items that are in open view can be seized if identified as contraband. This is known as *plain-view doctrine*. Plain-view doctrine has several key elements. Army LE personnel may seize an item of evidence in plain view if the following elements are met:

- The LE officer is lawfully in the place from which he observes the item—the officer did not violate the Fourth Amendment in arriving at the place from which the evidence can be plainly viewed.
- The item is immediately recognizable as contraband (meaning no manipulation of that item occurred to determine its contraband nature).
- The item may lawfully be reached from the LE officer's location.

Investigative Stops

2-22. An investigative stop is a brief detention of a person when Army LE personnel have reasonable suspicion of criminal activity; these are also known as Terry stops (*Terry versus Ohio*, 1968). Reasonable suspicion is a lesser belief than probable cause; but, like probable cause, it is based on the totality of the circumstances. Investigative stops may be conducted based on many factors including—

- The experience of Army LE personnel.
- Crime conditions (such as a high crime area).
- Mannerisms, dress, and activities of the individual.
- The time of day.

2-23. A frisk may be conducted during an investigative stop for the safety of Army LE personnel. The frisk should only be performed when there is a reasonable belief that the person is armed and presently dangerous. MRE 314 (f)(2) discusses frisks during lawful stops. A frisk consists of a pat down of the outer clothing only unless a weapon is detected. If a weapon is detected a search of the pockets, belt area, or other areas of the outer clothing to locate and seize any found weapons is authorized. Within the context of LE officer safety and frisks, weapons are defined very broadly and can include any object that can be used as a potential weapon such as a screwdriver; scissors; or any other sharp, heavy, or dense objects.

2-24. Any other contraband discovered during the conduct of a lawful frisk may be seized. An investigative stop can transition from a detention to an apprehension if probable cause develops that a crime has been committed by the detained person. If Army LE personnel feel an object with a contour and mass making its identity immediately apparent as contraband, the officer may seize the object. The contraband may be seized without a formal search authorization and "would be justified by the same practical considerations that inhere in the plain-view context" (see *Minnesota versus Dickerson*, 1993). This action is also known as *plain-feel doctrine*.

2-25. If an LE officer conducts a traffic stop (based upon a reasonable and articulable suspicion that criminal activity is occurring) and develops the reasonable belief that the persons in the vehicle are presently armed and dangerous (not limited to only firearms), the officer may order the occupants of the vehicle out of the vehicle and conduct a "Terry frisk" for officer safety. This "frisk" may extend to all unlocked containers in the vehicle (backpacks, purses, and such) and to the passenger compartment of the vehicle itself to look for weapons that could be used to harm the officer. Any contraband found during the "frisk" of the car would be admissible in court, assuming that the frisk was supported by the LE officer's reasonable belief that the suspects were armed and dangerous.

Note. LE personnel must understand the limitations of their authority to search persons and property. The authority to search and process a crime scene is subject to fourth amendment protections. LE personnel may not continue searches beyond the exigent circumstances that justified the initial entry to an area or a search of a person or property without proper search authorization. For example, LE personnel may enter a residence to render aid or intervene in a crime-in-progress situation; however, once the immediate threat or exigency is mitigated, any search of the area must cease and search authorization is required. Any searches and seizures of evidence after the exigency is over may render the evidence inadmissible. Plain view doctrine still applies to items clearly in open view while LE personnel are authorized to be in the area, but any overt action to search the area is prohibited until legal search authorization is obtained.

COLLECTION OF EVIDENCE

2-26. Evidence collection and subsequent forensic analysis are conducted across all operational environments and are employed with great success in both traditional LE applications and in efforts to target, apprehend, and prosecute criminals, terrorists, or enemy combatants. These activities occur in support of LE activities within both stable and unstable environments associated with contingency operations. Military police and USACIDC SAs conduct evidence collection directly supporting U.S. military LE efforts, in support of multinational LE efforts, or as part of general military activities supporting site exploitation. Forensic laboratories deployed to the theater of operations provide significant expansion, timeliness, and relevance for evidence collection and forensic analytical capabilities.

2-27. Evidence collection is conducted by Army LE investigators as well as by military police patrols. In support of LE activities in relatively stable environments, the bulk of crime scene processing and evidence collection at most crime scenes and complex sites is typically conducted by, or under the direct supervision of, Army LE investigators. Military police patrols typically conduct collection of evidence as a result of a search incident to apprehension; a seizure of objects and weapons that may present a danger to LE personnel, other responding personnel, and bystanders; or a seizing of contraband or other evidence that is easily destroyed or concealed. These items include weapons, drugs, or other items found either on a subject's person or within immediate control of a subject or bystanders. In minor cases when Army LE investigators are either not employed or readily available, military police patrol personnel collect any items deemed to have evidentiary value; less experienced military police patrols can obtain guidance regarding evidence collection from patrol supervisors, military police desk personnel, or on-duty MPIs when required. Chapter 3 discusses crime scene processing in-depth.

2-28. Evidence collection is sometimes conducted in operational environments in support of military contingency operations. Evidence collection in support of HN police activities is conducted consistent with normal LE activities, though the threat may be significantly increased depending on the relative stability of the operational environment.

2-29. Evidence collection may be required in support of hasty or deliberate site exploitation activities. The information obtained during these activities can be critical in identifying perpetrators of violence against U.S. or other friendly forces; developing an understanding of threat networks operating in the area; enabling U.S. forces to attack these networks to disrupt, interdict, or destroy the network; and enabling the capture and potential criminal prosecution of the perpetrators. Hasty site exploitation is typically time constrained. This is especially true when the threat is too high to risk extended presence on the incident site or crime scene. Hasty site exploitation can result in immediate and timely evidence (including statements from personnel in the area) that enable exploitation of the threat information collected. Hasty site exploitation is warranted in many instances, to include—

- Immediate response to an incident such as the explosion of an IED or other attack.
- Following discovery of a weapons cache, an IED construction site, or a suspect material storage area.
- As a planned phase of a raid or an assault where information, personnel, or material require collection.
- Following a tip from an informant regarding threat activity, personnel, or material or during deliberate site exploitation when evidence of a previously unknown site is discovered.

2-30. Deliberate site exploitation is conducted when there is sufficient time and conditions are conducive to secure the site, conduct deliberate planning and rehearsals, and move dedicated site exploitation assets to the site. Deliberate site exploitation is typically a combined arms operation employing technical specialties from numerous branches, including USACIDC SAs and military police. Hasty site exploitations can evolve into deliberate site exploitation if the commander's critical information requirements or other critical information is identified. Deliberate site exploitation teams should include technical and functional experts; the specific technical capabilities required should be based on the type of site being exploited and the material expected at the site. HN police support is addressed in ATTP 3-39.10; site exploitation activities are addressed in ATTP 3-90.15.

GENERAL COLLECTION CONSIDERATIONS

2-31. Evidence at any crime scene or incident site is as varied as the incidents or crimes associated with those locations. One of the first tasks when conducting evidence collection is to establish a priority of effort. The collection of material must be prioritized and conducted based on the type of incident, any threat or hazards associated with the site, the state and relative fragility of the evidence, and other environmental conditions. Site hazards include both hazards to personnel and environmental conditions that may threaten specific types of evidence.

2-32. Many items of evidentiary value are obvious, such as stolen vehicles, weapons, or drug paraphernalia; these items can be collected and transported for further processing with relative ease. This is not the case with many types of evidence. Some evidence is not readily obvious or visible to the collector and may not be as easily identified by untrained personnel. Also, evidence may not be easily collected by simply picking the item up because of its physical state or size. For many types of latent and trace evidence, additional techniques must be employed to identify, collect, and preserve the evidence for further evaluation by a forensic laboratory. If conducting evidence collection in an operational environment, evidence may be used to support criminal prosecution or future operations.

> *Note.* All evidence should be photographed before it is seized or moved. The entire crime scene should be photographed including all interior and exterior areas associated with the crime scene. This includes every room or area in which the victim or accused may have had access. Crime scene photographs help investigators, and eventually a court, determine relevant facts. Photographs of the scene are important even when significant time has passed between the crime and the processing of the scene. All photographic evidence must be preserved to maintain evidentiary value. See chapter 4 for detailed information on crime scene photography and preservation of photographic evidence.

HANDLING AND PACKAGING TO PREVENT CONTAMINATION

2-33. Contaminated evidence can be rendered useless to forensic analysts and risks being eliminated as admissible evidence during criminal procedures. Evidence can be contaminated through contact with people or animals (fingerprints, hairs, saliva, or other contaminants), from cross contamination between items of evidence, or from environmental factors. Individuals exposed to the incident site must exercise care to avoid contamination of evidence. While it may be difficult to mitigate all possibilities of evidence contamination, there are measures and techniques that limit the risk of contamination that would hinder future forensic analysis.

2-34. When conducting evidence collection, all personnel should use personal protective equipment (PPE) to reduce the risk of evidence contamination. See paragraph 2-39 for additional information regarding PPE. Items of evidence should be handled with gloved hands at all times. Evidence items should be handled with care to avoid destruction or alteration of the evidence. Evidence containing known or potential latent prints should be handled on corners, edges, or other areas least likely to contain prints.

2-35. Extreme care should be used when using instruments such as tweezers, knives, or other tools to collect evidence to prevent possible destruction or alteration of the physical characteristics of the evidence. When tagging or marking evidence, avoid writing directly on the item; any writing should be attached using an evidence tag or on the exterior packaging.

2-36. Cross contamination between evidence items can easily occur; efforts must be taken to mitigate this risk. Items of evidence should be packaged separately. Never place multiple samples or items of evidence in the same container. Any evidence processing areas should be cleaned thoroughly with a 10 percent bleach solution between processing different types of evidence or evidence from different locations or persons. Never transport victims and subjects in the same vehicle.

2-37. Exercise care to maintain the integrity of evidence from the crime scene or incident site to the laboratory or analysis facility. Evidence must be protected from physical alteration or destruction, contamination, and hazardous conditions. Investigators must package evidence to protect it from physical breakage, contamination, bacterial growth, or other environmental conditions. Appropriate containers should be used to store evidence. Packaging that is in direct contact with evidence (the inner most packaging) should be free of contaminants. Packaging in direct contact with evidence must be new and clean. When standard collection containers are not available, improvised packaging may be required, especially in contingency operations where logistical support is limited. Ensure that improvised packaging is as sterile as possible to avoid introduction of contaminants such as transfer of residue from ammunition or other items from ammo cans.

2-38. A druggist or pharmacy fold of clean paper is a good method for protecting small or trace items of evidence. There are multiple techniques for creating a druggist fold. See figure 2-1 for a description of how to make a druggist fold. A simple method for creating a druggist fold includes the following steps:

- Obtain a sheet of clean white bond paper and fold it into thirds.
- Place evidence in the center section of the paper between the folds.
- Fold the two outer folds down to cover the evidence.
- Take the folded paper with the evidence and fold it again into thirds.
- Tuck one fold inside the other to secure it.

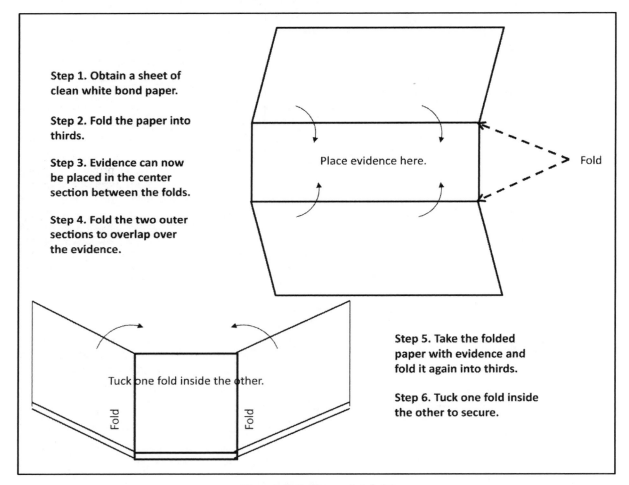

Figure 2-1. Druggist fold

Note. Handle latent print items with care because the collector's fingerprints can still be transferred to the item with gloves on. Double or thick gloves are recommended.

UNIVERSAL SAFETY PRECAUTIONS

2-39. Personnel conducting evidence collection must always wear gloves when gathering evidentiary material, both for their safety and the protection of evidence. In many cases, full PPE including suits, gloves, eye protection, and foot covering may be necessary. The use of PPE can greatly reduce the chance of evidence contamination as well as provide protection for the collector from environmental hazards. For most crime scenes and incident sites, collectors should have the following PPE available for use to ensure protection of personnel and the evidence being collected:

- **Latex, nitrile, or other nonporous polymer gloves**. Gloves should be changed often to avoid cross contamination, specifically when moving from one type of evidence to another and/or to another area or room. Leather, cotton, or other natural or synthetic work gloves should not be used as a substitute for latex gloves, especially when handling fluids. Double-gloving can offer an additional layer of protection.

Note. It is important to remember that when an unprotected piece of investigative equipment, (such as a camera, fingerprint brush, or even a pen) is picked up or touched with a gloved hand, that glove may now be contaminated. Disposable items should be discarded with other PPE equipment while durable equipment must be thoroughly cleaned after each use.

- **Surgical face masks**. Surgical face masks aid in the protection of the collector and evidence from airborne biological materials or particulates. Surgical masks are not effective at protecting against the effects of chemical hazards.
- **Disposable shoe coverings**. Disposable shoe coverings can limit cross contamination of the crime scene or incident site. They lessen the potential of tracking materials to clean areas and help to prevent the introduction of contaminants into the site. They can also prevent unintended exposure of the collector to hazardous material.
- **Full-body overgarments with hoods**. These garments can be used to provide complete protection over the entire body. They should be used in conjunction with shoe coverings, a surgical-type mask, and gloves.

2-40. Many crime scenes and incident sites may present exceptional hazards due to the presence of chemicals or explosives including clandestine drug labs, major chemical spills, terrorist incidents, and many other scenarios where explosive material or chemical hazards may be present. When explosive material or chemical hazards are encountered, the area should not be processed until rendered safe by trained personnel. When these materials are encountered, immediately contact explosive ordnance disposal (EOD), CBRN, or other specialized units that assist with hazard mitigation requirements.

BIOLOGICAL EVIDENCE

2-41. Biological evidence that is found during an LE investigation needs to be evaluated, collected, and preserved to ensure that the evidence is not degraded or contaminated. LE and laboratory personnel are responsible to provide an account and possibly court testimony of their involvement with the evidence. Biological evidence includes any item containing blood, semen, hair, saliva, skin tissue, fingernail scrapings, bone, bodily fluids, or any other identifiable biological material collected as part of a criminal investigation. Biological evidence can be similar to trace evidence in that it can easily be overlooked or destroyed. Biological evidence can be microscopic particles that are not obvious at a crime scene. They can be easily overlooked, destroyed, and/or taken away from the crime scene or incident site.

2-42. Suspects, victims, and witnesses may leave blood, hair, and fibers at a crime scene; likewise, these persons may carry biological evidence away from the scene. Biological evidence that is found on an individual or crime scene can be processed by multiple forensic analysts and laboratory examiners (to include DNA examiners).

2-43. Biological evidence is collected directly from individuals for use in comparative DNA analysis or for toxicological tests to determine drug, alcohol, or other chemical content in the blood. Effective use of biological evidence in a LE investigation begins the moment that Army LE personnel arrive at a scene. It includes the processes used to evaluate, collect, and preserve biological evidence. It also includes the preparation and delivery of court testimony provided by LE personnel and laboratory examiners.

DEOXYRIBONUCLEIC ACID

2-44. DNA is the basic component of an individual's entire genetic structure and is the hereditary material in humans and almost all other organisms. Nearly every cell of the body has the same DNA. DNA sequences do not change throughout a person's life; they remain the same from the day you are born (with the exception of recipients of a bone marrow transplant). DNA analysis is a technical process performed in a laboratory setting that allows forensic scientists to identify individuals by comparing and contrasting genetic profiles from known samples to genetic profiles from evidence collected at the scene.

2-45. DNA is a powerful investigative tool because, with the exception of identical twins, no two people have the exact same DNA sequence. The uniqueness of an individual's DNA can positively identify a suspect or exonerate an innocent suspect. DNA collected from a crime scene can link a suspect to the evidence, establish a person's presence at a particular location, or eliminate a subject from suspicion. DNA from relatives can assist in identifying a victim even when remains are not present. In cases when a direct DNA profile from a witness, suspect, or victim is not available, DNA from close family members can be helpful. The individuality of DNA can enable the linking of a suspect from one crime scene to another when evidence from separate crime scenes is compared.

2-46. Even though DNA analysis can aid in an investigation, there are limitations that should be understood. These limitations include the following:

- Casual contact may not transfer enough DNA for laboratory analysis (although touch DNA is becoming more viable).
- Washing can remove or destroy DNA, but does not always do so.
- Environmental factors such as mold, heat, humidity, bacteria and sunlight can quickly degrade DNA.
- The time that the evidence was deposited cannot be determined through DNA analysis.
- A DNA profile cannot determine the biological material that yields DNA evidence.

2-47. Biological evidence may not be obvious or even visible; however, there still may be enough biological material present for DNA analysis. Biological evidence can be collected from virtually anywhere. Only a few cells are required to obtain useful DNA information relevant to an investigation. When anyone comes into contact with another person or object, there is a possibility that the transfer of biological material has taken place. The transfer does not always have to be as obvious as blood. Beyond obvious deposits of biological evidence, table 2-1 shows a wide range of items that may contain biological evidence, locations on the identified item where the biological evidence can be obtained, and the source material that may provide DNA. This table is not all inclusive.

Table 2-1. Biological evidence

Item Containing Evidence	Possible Location of Evidence	Possible Source of Evidence	Collection and Packaging
Baseball bat or similar weapon	Handle and striking surface	Skin, blood, tissue	Place in a clean paper bag after allowing it to air dry.
Hat, bandana, or mask	Inside	Hair, dandruff (skin cells), perspiration	Place in a clean paper bag.
Eyeglasses	Nosepiece, earpieces, and lenses	Skin	Place in a clean paper bag.
Facial tissue or cotton swab	Surface area	Mucous, blood, semen, earwax	Place in a clean paper bag after allowing it to air dry.

Table 2-1. Biological evidence (continued)

Item Containing Evidence	Possible Location of Evidence	Possible Source of Evidence	Collection and Packaging
Laundry (dirty or washed)	Surface area	Blood, semen	Place in a clean paper bag.
Used cigarette	Cigarette butt	Saliva	Allow it to air dry, place in clean bond paper (druggist fold).
Stamp or envelope	Licked area	Saliva	Allow it to air dry, place in clean bond paper (druggist fold).
Tape, ligature, or binding material	Inside and outside surface	Skin, blood	Place in a clean paper bag.
Bottle, can, or drinking glass	Sides or mouthpiece	Saliva	Place in a clean paper bag.
Used condom	Interior and surface area of the condom	Semen, vaginal cells, rectal cells	Allow it to air dry, place in clean bond paper (druggist fold).
Blanket, pillow, sheet	Surface area	Hair, blood, semen, saliva, urine	Place in a clean paper bag after allowing to air dry.
Bite mark	Skin, clothing, or other material bitten	Saliva	Swab saliva with a clean cotton swab and place in a clean paper bag.
Fingernail or fingernail pieces	Scrapings	Blood, tissue	Place in clean bond paper (druggist fold).

GENERAL COLLECTION AND PRESERVATION GUIDELINES FOR BIOLOGICAL EVIDENCE

2-48. Identification, collection, preservation, and protection of biological evidence from contamination are key to successful DNA testing. Successful DNA results are dependent on the amount and condition of the material collected. Environmental factors such as mold, heat, humidity, bacteria, and sunlight can degrade DNA. All these factors should be considered when collecting and submitting evidence for processing. Investigators and laboratory examiners must work together to determine the most probative pieces of evidence and establish priorities for collection and submission of biological evidence.

Personal Protection and Contamination Prevention

2-49. Efforts to prevent contamination are necessary when identifying, collecting, and preserving biological evidence; the same methods used to prevent contamination of evidence also protect personnel from possible exposure to pathogens that may be present in biological material. Biological evidence can become easily contaminated when biological material from another source gets mixed with the evidence relevant to an investigation. Initial responders, investigators, and laboratory personnel sent to the scene of a crime or incident site must all take appropriate precautions to reduce the risk of exposure and to protect the evidence from contamination. Army LE personnel should—

- Wear gloves and change them before each new item of evidence is handled.
- Wear a surgical mask.
- Use disposable instruments or clean them thoroughly according to the standard operating procedures (SOPs) before and after handling each sample.
- Avoid touching an area where biological evidence may exist.
- Thoroughly clean evidence processing areas with bleach after each type of evidence or evidence from different areas or persons is processed.
- Never package different items of evidence together.
- Never transport victims and suspects together.

- Avoid talking, sneezing, and coughing over evidence.
- Avoid touching the face, nose, head, and mouth when collecting and packaging evidence.
- Air-dry the evidence thoroughly before packaging. Avoid contact between items.
- Properly package and store biological evidence using the following techniques:
  - Store evidence in a clean, dry paper bag, envelope, cardboard box, or other paper-based storage container. Biological evidence should never be placed in a plastic bag or plastic storage container; this can produce moisture that can damage the evidence.
  - Protect evidence from extreme heat or direct sunlight; these conditions can degrade the evidence.
  - Seal, label, and maintain a proper chain of custody. Proper identification of the evidence and the location from where it was obtained are crucial to the chain of custody.

Note. It is important that personnel handling biological evidence be aware of the potential for the presence of hazardous pathogens, such as the human immunodeficiency virus (HIV) and hepatitis B and hepatitis C viruses. Dried material can be disturbed and become airborne creating inhalation hazards for the collector; the minimum PPE required for handling biological evidence should be a face mask and latex, nitrile, or other nonporous polymer gloves. Additional PPE such as eye protection, head and hair covering, foot coverings, and a protective suit with hood may be required, depending on the specific situation, for individual safety and to avoid contamination of the evidence.

Collection of Bodily Fluid Evidence

2-50. When collecting body fluids, extreme care must be taken to avoid contamination of the evidence and exposure of the individual collecting the evidence to biohazards. Always wear PPE when handling biological evidence of any kind.

2-51. Bodily fluids may be located on virtually any surface. Biological evidence may be on a surface in solid or liquid form. The method of collection will depend on the location and the physical state of the evidence. Regardless of the method used for collection, never store or submit wet or moist material. Collected biological evidence should be air dried on a piece of clean paper in a ventilated area. The following methods may be used to collect evidence of bodily fluids:

- **Collect the entire object.** Whenever possible the entire object containing the biological evidence should be collected. This can be done for most small items such as clothing, bed linens, knives, tools, and other items small enough to be placed in a bag or box. This method is not typically feasible for large items of furniture, structures, or other extremely large items. If it is not possible to seize the entire object, a decision must be made to either collect a sample of the item or to swab a sample of the biological evidence off of the object.
- **Collect a sample of the item.** If the item on which the biological evidence is deposited is too large or otherwise impossible to collect, a sample or piece of the item may be cut from the object as a whole. This method is typically used for stained fabric on upholstered furniture, carpeting, walls, flooring, or other large cumbersome items, especially those objects that are made of a porous material (for example, cloth, leather, or wood).
- **Collect a swab of the biological evidence.** In some cases collection of an entire item, or portion of an item, is impossible. In these cases collection of a swabbed sample of the biological material may be conducted. This method is preferred when the object is nonporous (for example, glass, metal, or plastic). Techniques for collecting swab samples are as follows:
  - Collect a sample of the stain with a sterile cotton swab.
  - Slightly moisten the swab with sterile water if the material is dried.
  - Swab the material gently but firmly to ensure that adequate cellular material is collected; the sample should be well concentrated on the tip of the swab. Two well-coated swabs are typically sufficient. Swab the area again with a sterile dry swab.
  - Allow the swabs to air dry and place them in clean paper packaging.

2-52. Dry collected evidence completely before packaging, then place it in a clean paper container (such as a bag, an envelope, or a box). Dried bloodstains can be scraped into a druggist fold using a clean razor blade. The razor blade should then be placed in the envelope with the scrapings. Although not the preferred method, a small gel lifter or fingerprint tape can also be used to lift dried blood from shoe prints or fingerprints in blood when other collection methods are not feasible. Ensure that the items are properly labeled and sealed.

2-53. All biological evidence should be placed in paper packaging. Avoid using plastic bags or plastic storage containers; they can cause moisture and produce bacterial growth that can damage the evidence. Ensure that all items of evidence are packaged separately. Never package evidence from a victim and a suspect in the same containers. Collect a comparison standard from each individual involved in the incident. Use clean bags and boxes to hold collected evidence; used bags and boxes may contain contaminating DNA.

COLLECTING COMPARISON STANDARDS

2-54. The effective exploitation of biological evidence and derivative DNA may require the collection and analysis of comparison standards. Comparison standards are necessary to determine whether the evidence came from the suspect or from another source. If a crime occurred in the specific location where biological evidence is being collected, Army LE personnel responding to a scene must think ahead and attempt to determine who would normally be present at that location and who may have left biological material. When DNA profiles are developed for comparison, it is imperative that comparison standards are collected from all persons known to have been associated with the crime scene. This includes any identified suspects, victims, witnesses, and any persons known to have been present at the location including friends, neighbors, boyfriends, girlfriends, spouses, housekeepers, baby-sitters, LE personnel or other persons. Collection of comparison standards enables laboratory personnel to develop comparison standards for each sample submitted. These comparison standards can then be used to positively identify DNA extracted from submitted evidence, identify unknown DNA profiles, or eliminate some persons from the sample pool that do not match evidentiary DNA collected at the scene. These comparisons can either tie a person to a crime scene or clear an individual from wrongful implication.

2-55. Buccal (oral) swabs are typically used to collect required comparison standards. A buccal swab is designed to collect epithelial (skin) tissue from the interior of the cheek by rubbing a sterile swab vigorously on the interior of the cheek surface. The swab should be vigorously rubbed along the interior cheek; usually 30 seconds to a minute will ensure enough cells are collected. Typically two swabs are taken (one on each cheek) to ensure that an adequate amount of cells are recovered for analysis. The swab should be allowed to air dry and then placed into an envelope, sealed, and marked as evidence. The sample can then be sent to a forensic laboratory for processing.

2-56. Sometimes liquid blood samples may be required. A medical officer or a trained medical technician must draw blood samples. The samples should be taken at a medical treatment facility where proper precautions can be taken to prevent contamination of the samples. The amount of liquid blood required for a laboratory DNA examination is about 5 milliliters or one tube. Medical treatment facilities have sterile containers available for sending samples to the laboratory. The tube of blood should be sent with an anticoagulant in a purple-topped tube. Tubes for drawing blood samples are standardized with different colored tops. The tube color designates different materials within the tube that maintain the sample in a desired state for further analysis. For LE purposes, the two types of tubes typically used are—

- **Purple-topped tubes.** These tubes contain K2EDTA, usually referred to as simply EDTA. EDTA is an anticoagulant and is generally used when whole blood is needed for analysis. This tube is required for DNA analysis.
- **Gray-topped tubes.** These tubes contain sodium fluoride and potassium oxalate. Sodium fluoride is an antibacterial and prevents enzymes in the blood from working. Potassium oxalate is an anticoagulant. This tube is required for toxicology examinations to determine the content of substances in the blood such as alcohol, drugs, or other chemicals.

2-57. If there is a delay in sending drawn blood to the laboratory, the sample must be refrigerated but not frozen. Medical personnel may take samples of body fluids like blood and urine from Soldiers without their consent when authorized to do so by a search authorization. Samples for comparative analysis (specifically from blood samples) of a deceased victim of a crime are collected by the ME and provided to the investigator.

2-58. Collecting comparison standards may be very sensitive, especially in sexual assault cases. It may be necessary to collect DNA samples of a victim's recent consensual partners, if any, to eliminate them as potential contributors of DNA believed to be from the suspect. If this is necessary, the help of a qualified victim advocate should be enlisted. Extreme sensitivity and a full explanation of why the request is being made should be given to the victim and consensual partners.

SPECIFIC TYPES OF BIOLOGICAL EVIDENCE

2-59. Biological evidence, including body fluid stains can be valuable evidence. It can be used to associate a victim or suspect with a specific crime or location; it can also eliminate an individual as a suspect. Laboratory testing of collected biological evidence is conducted to identify what the biological evidence is, such as blood, semen, saliva, or other substance; whether the material is human or not and; if confirmed to be human biological material, to attempt to establish a DNA profile for the material.

2-60. There are many types and sources of biological evidence. The biological evidence most commonly encountered is bodily fluids (blood, seminal fluid, and other secretions), hairs, and tissue (skin cells), though other types of biological evidence may be found. Proper collection and storage of biological evidence can result in useable evidence for many years after the sample was collected.

Blood

2-61. In crimes of violence, blood evidence is very valuable if properly identified, collected, and processed. It can indicate (through bloodstain spatter analysis) whether a victim's body was or was not moved, positions of the victim and subject during the crime, the relative level of violence, and a variety of other information that could be useful in an investigation. These deductions can be indicated by the presence (or absence) of blood pooling, smears, spatters, or other evidence of blood transfer. See chapter 3 for more information. The DNA evidence extracted from blood can physically place a suspect at a crime scene or in contact with a victim; it can also eliminate an individual from the list of potential suspects.

2-62. Examiners perform a preliminary laboratory examination of an alleged bloodstain (serology testing) to determine if the stain is a bloodstain. These preliminary chemical tests may not be conclusive. Other substances, common chemical compounds, and certain body discharges may also give positive results. The inability of the laboratory to provide definitive results about bloodstain evidence is due to inadequate quantity, improper storage, and/or contamination of a sample. If testing shows that the stain is a bloodstain, it must then be determined if the blood is human. The evidence value of a bloodstain may be seriously impaired unless the stain is shown conclusively to be human blood.

Seminal Fluid

2-63. Seminal fluid (or semen) is a colorless, sticky fluid produced in the male reproductive organs. In its dried state, semen appears as a grayish white, sometimes yellowish, stain. It gives a starchy stiffness to the part of the fabric that has been stained. The presence of seminal fluid can positively place a suspect at the scene of a crime or eliminate an individual as a suspect. In the case of a rape or sexual assault, it may be alleged that the suspect had an emission. If so, the identification of seminal fluid is of paramount importance.

2-64. Semen contains thousands of minute organisms, known as spermatozoa, which die as the seminal fluid dries. Spermatozoa keep their shape indefinitely if they are not destroyed through handling. Epithelial (skin) cells are present in semen, which makes it possible to identify an individual donor through DNA without the assistance of live sperm. Suspected fluid or stains may be identified as seminal fluid by the laboratory even if the attacker has had a vasectomy. Inspection of an area or item of evidence under ultraviolet (UV) light or a blue 450nm forensic lamp sometimes helps find the location of seminal fluid stains. Seminal fluid stains have fluorescent qualities. Even though laundering or dry cleaning may remove traces of seminal stains, laundered materials should be collected for laboratory testing to determine if seminal fluid residue remains. Typical objects and materials holding seminal fluid evidence are clothing, bedding, condoms, carpeting, upholstery, vehicles, and other objects. Seminal fluid evidence can also be obtained from swabs taken from victims or suspects from sexual assault kits. Collection of evidence from victims and subjects (sexual assault kits) is only performed by properly trained medical personnel. See chapter 9 for specific information and considerations for sexual assault cases.

Other Bodily Secretions

2-65. Body fluids also include other bodily secretions that can be collected and processed to establish DNA profiles and comparative analysis. Though not all inclusive, these secretions include saliva, perspiration, and vaginal fluids.

2-66. Saliva is secreted from the salivary glands in the mouth. Saliva can be deposited on anything that is placed in the mouth or that comes in contact with the mouth during a bite. Saliva can be extracted from cigarette butts, gum, clothing, and even bite marks that have not been cleaned. It can also be collected in the form of spit that has been purposefully projected by an individual onto another person or object. DNA evidence can be extracted from saliva collected by LE personnel and matched to known samples from individuals.

2-67. Perspiration is the fluid secreted through the skin by the sweat gland. It is composed primarily of water, salts, and metabolic waste products. Perspiration itself does not contain cells, therefore contains no DNA. However, the friction between clothing, caps, or other items that touch the skin can cause skin cells to be deposited (along with the perspiration) on materials in contact with the skin. These skin cells may be recoverable within the perspiration samples. Typical items that can be collected with productive perspiration samples include hats, jackets, ski masks, bandannas, gloves, handled objects, weapons, eyeglasses, and such.

2-68. Vaginal fluids are useful in sexual assault cases as they may contain traces of seminal fluid deposited by the perpetrator of the assault. Clothing (especially underpants worn immediately following the assault), bedding, condoms, and other objects may contain such evidence. Vaginal fluid evidence can also be obtained from swabs taken from victims or suspects during sexual assault examination (sexual assault examination kits). Collection of evidence from victims and subjects (sexual assault examination kits) is only performed by properly trained medical personnel. See chapter 9 for specific information and considerations for sexual assault investigations.

Hairs

2-69. Hair, being a biological specimen of the body, can sometimes be associated to an individual through DNA analysis; however, DNA is not always successfully extracted from hair. Hairs may not provide conclusive evidence but, in conjunction with other evidence, they have proven to be important and essential evidence. The origin and texture of hairs found at a crime scene or on the body, clothing, or headgear of a suspect or a victim may be important as evidence. This is especially true in homicides and sex crimes. Properly handled, even when DNA evidence is not retrievable, hair and fibers may yield investigative leads and add to the evidence facts being assembled. Comparative examinations of hair are conducted by trained laboratory examiners.

Note. Even though hair is a biological material, many agencies and resources characterize hair as trace evidence rather than biological evidence.

Characteristics

2-70. Structurally, a hair is composed of the tip end, the cuticle, the cortex, the medulla, and the bulb or root. The best source of DNA from a hair is at the root or bulb of the hair; there tends to be more skin cells attached to the root of the hair as opposed to a part of the hair further away from the scalp. Each of these parts provides the laboratory examiner with definite information. Examination of hair evidence can yield several findings to include—

- Whether the hairs are animal or human.

- The species of animal (if determined to be animal hair).
- The hair's origin on the body (such as the head, face, chest, armpit, limb, or pubic area).
- Whether the hair was removed naturally or forcibly.
- If the hair was bleached, dyed, or otherwise altered.
- If the hair was cut with a dull or a sharp instrument (if a cutting was recent).
- Whether the hair had been crushed or burned.
- The blood grouping and sex of the donor in rare occasions.
- DNA profile.

2-71. When extraction of DNA evidence from a hair sample is not possible, definitive comparative linkage to a specific individual is impossible. Laboratory comparisons of hair in these instances will generally result in one of the three following conclusions—

- The hairs are dissimilar and did not come from the same individual.
- The hairs match in terms of microscopic characteristics and blood groupings and came from a person or persons whose hair has the same microscopic characteristics.
- The comparisons show that no conclusion could be reached concerning the origin of the hair.

Collection of Hair Evidence

2-72. Hair evidence can be collected either as material deposited on an object or surface (bed, counter, comb, clothing, or other object or surface), deposited on an individual following contact with another person, or as a known sample taken directly from an individual's body. Locating hairs deposited at a crime scene can be accomplished through multiple methods including—

- A visual search.
- An alternate light source.
- An additional magnification search aid.
- Taping.

2-73. Evidence gathered from a suspect and a victim must never be intermingled. It must be individually collected, marked, and kept separated during packing for shipment. Several methods can be employed to collect hair evidence including—

- **Collecting individual hairs (picking).** This is typically conducted when a minimal number of hairs are located on an object or surface. Gloved fingers or tweezers are normally used to collect the hairs. Place hairs in a druggist fold, then seal them within a paper envelope that can be completely sealed around all edges.
- **Using adhesive tape.** This technique is conducted by patting over the item or surface to recover the identified evidence using fingerprint tape, cellophane tape, or other clear adhesive tape. When transparent adhesive tape is used to collect the hairs, the tape should be placed with the adhesive side down on a clear plastic transparency, the inside of a clean document protector, the inside of a clean plastic bag, or other similar plastic material; under no circumstances should the tape be affixed to an index card or other paper material. The plastic material, with the tape and hair affixed, should be sealed in another container. Place the collected hair samples that have been affixed to the plastic, inside a paper envelope that can be completely sealed around all edges.
- **Combing and representative samples.** This technique is used to collect evidence and obtain hair samples for comparison directly from the body of a suspect. Medical personnel will collect sample hairs from the body of a victim or a suspect. A witness should be present, preferably of the same sex as the individual the samples are collected from. Never allow an individual of the opposite sex to collect samples from a victim or subject. This technique is conducted by running a comb thoroughly through an individual's hair over the area of the body being sampled to recover transferred hair evidence. These samples should be obtained from any of the parts of the body that could be involved in the crime. If multiple body areas are sampled, the evidence collected from each area should be kept separate and a different comb should be used for each area. Once a comb is used in an area, it should be placed in the container or envelope with the

collected samples. Clean cotton can be placed in the teeth of the comb to maximize the chance of recovery. A clean sheet of white paper should be placed under the area being combed (this may include having the individual stand on a large sheet of clean white paper) to collect any falling hair or debris. Any hair collected should be placed on a clean piece of paper; the paper should be folded into a packet and put into a clean paper envelope or other paper container. Any required representative samples are then extracted, sealed, and packaged separately. Twenty-five hair strands, taken from different parts of the head and/or pubic region, are considered a minimum sample.

- **Vacuuming.** This technique employs a portable vacuum equipped with removable traps to lightly vacuum the target area suspected of having hair (and other trace evidence). The traps should be covered with a cap to seal the collected evidence. The entire trap should then be placed in a separate clean paper bag or cardboard box for storage and shipment.

Tissue (Skin Cells)

2-74. Tissue evidence includes skin cells deposited on an object and can be processed to develop a DNA profile of the donor. It may be latent or visible to the naked eye. Tissue evidence includes fingernail fragments and scrapings. This type of evidence can be found in many places including on a vehicle, tape or ligatures, eyeglasses, earrings, and guns or knives. Skin cells can be collected by swabbing both live and dead bodies to collect skin cells that may have been transferred from a suspect to a victim, especially in violent assaults.

2-75. Most types of tissue evidence should be collected with the item on which they are discovered or suspected when possible. Photograph the evidence in place to document the evidence. Small items of evidence can be placed in a druggist fold and placed within a larger clean paper envelope. Larger items may be wrapped in clean paper and placed in a larger clean wooden or sturdy cardboard box. For items that cannot be removed, the evidence may require collection using a swab or tweezers (depending on the size and state of the evidence). The material should then be air dried, placed in a clean paper container, and packaged in a clean paper envelope or box.

2-76. Some of the most productive types of tissue evidence are fingernails and fingernail scrapings. Broken fingernail fragments can provide DNA evidence that can link a suspect to a crime scene or victim. They should be collected and processed in the same manner as other physical evidence. Fingernail scrapings should be exploited to the fullest advantage. The cause of abrasions and scratches found on many parts of the body due to resistance from both the victim and the suspect during an assault are often from fingernails. The face, neck, arms, thighs, and genitals are the places commonly attacked. Evidence of scratch marks or gouges in these places on a suspect or victim can indicate a high probability that evidence may be found on the counterpart to the altercation. The residue under the fingernails of a victim or suspect may have traces of substances from the crime scene or from the corresponding suspect or victim's body or clothing. For cases not involving physical assault, residue under the fingernails of a suspect may have traces of substances from the crime scene that can link the suspect to the scene or materials used in the commission of a crime. Particles recovered from fingernail scrapings can include—

- Minute particles of fibers, skin, blood, hair, and cosmetics found under the fingernails that may help link the suspect and the victim.
- Evidence of narcotics, marijuana, or poison.
- Evidence of explosives or other chemicals.

2-77. Scrapings from each hand should be taken from all of the suspect's fingers, preferably before the suspect can bathe or clean his nails. Scrapings should be kept separate and placed in appropriate containers. In taking fingernail scrapings from a suspect or a victim, a knife, a file, or any other hard, sharp instrument should not be used. It may cause bleeding and contaminate the nail scrapings. The best item to use is the blunt end of a flat, wooden toothpick. A different toothpick should be used for each hand. As the scrapings from each finger are taken, the toothpick and the scrapings should be placed on a clean piece of paper. The paper should be folded and placed in a clean paper envelope or container. Each container should be marked to show the finger from which the scraping was collected. The packed scrapings are then sent to the laboratory for examination.

2-78. For deceased persons, fingernails should be clipped close after scraping to ensure that all available evidence is obtained. Clippings from each hand should be collected separately. Clipping the fingernails close on rape victims should be considered as well. This is especially important when the victim's nail or nails are damaged, as there may be skin cells in the damaged nail that cannot be retrieved by scraping.

COMBINED DEOXYRIBONUCLEIC ACID INDEX SYSTEM

2-79. The CODIS is an FBI program that consists of a database containing DNA profiles. This program allows federal, state, and local crime laboratories to compare DNA profiles with existing profiles in the database. The CODIS consists of separate indexes or parts of the database. Each index contains a different type of DNA profile. Searching the indexes against themselves and each other to find matches can generate investigative leads. These indexes include the—

- **Forensic index.** This index is a database of DNA profiles developed from biological material, believed to belong to a suspect, that was collected at a crime scene or material that was carried away from a crime scene and subsequently collected during a criminal investigation. Some common sources for the forensic file can include—
  - Semen from vaginal swabs, panties, bedding, and such taken from rape investigations.
  - Cigarette butts or beverage containers left at burglary scenes.
  - Blood from suspects left at crime scenes, such as a burglary, an assault, or a murder.
- **Convicted offender index.** This index is a database of DNA profiles developed from samples of individuals convicted of qualifying offenses. The federal government, all states, and the military have laws requiring sample collections from convicted and suspected individuals. Under the Military Convicted Offender Program, samples from individuals convicted by a general court-martial or special court-martial of qualifying military offenses are collected and sent to the USACIL CODIS laboratory for processing. Department of Defense Instruction (DODI) 5505.14 further directs that DNA samples be taken from individuals fingerprinted due to apprehension and investigation of criminal activity in accordance with DODI 5505.11.
- **Unidentified human remains index.** This index contains profiles developed from bodies or body parts found and deduced victim profiles. A deduced victim profile is one developed from DNA thought to belong to the missing victim. Examples include the victim's toothbrush and blood found at a scene, believed to belong to a victim, even though a body has not been recovered.
- **Arrestee index.** This index contains profiles of arrested persons (if state law permits the collection of arrestee samples).
- **Missing persons index.** This index contains DNA reference profiles from missing persons.
- **Biological relatives of missing persons index.** This index contains profiles voluntarily contributed by the relatives of missing persons for comparison to unidentified human remains. Search restrictions apply to this index.

2-80. To gain access to CODIS, the investigator must submit a request to USACIL. The USACIL reviews the case to ensure compliance with FBI CODIS requirements and then submits the DNA profile to the CODIS laboratory. Both known and unknown subject profiles can be submitted for DNA analysis and subsequent input and comparison in CODIS. An unknown subject case is the type of case in which CODIS can be most helpful.

2-81. The CODIS laboratory enters the profile into the forensic file and initiates a comparison search through the database. If a match is detected in the CODIS software, it must go through a confirmation process. If a match is confirmed, the investigator is notified and provided a formal report. Regardless of whether there is a match to a suspect in CODIS, the submitted profile will remain in the forensic index. The profile continues to be searched routinely.

TOXICOLOGY

2-82. Some investigations require collection and submission of controlled samples of blood and urine for testing to determine the presence of alcohol or drugs. Generally samples should be collected within 24 hours for alcohol tests and 72 hours for drug testing. The Division of Forensic Toxicology, AFMES provides support to Army LE for toxicological analysis required for criminal investigations, including driving under the influence (DUI) or driving while intoxicated (DWI) cases. Toxicology testing should be considered in all cases in which an individual is incapacitated or alcohol or drugs are involved.

2-83. Analysis routinely performed by the Division of Forensic Toxicology includes tests for volatiles (including ethanol, methanol, and other substances) and drugs of abuse. Complete drug screens can be conducted upon request; if known, the suspected drug should be disclosed. Specimens submitted should include—

- Blood. 14 to 21 milliliters in gray-topped specimen tubes.
- Urine. 50 to 70 milliliters in a standard sealed specimen cup.

2-84. Collected specimens should be forwarded to the Division of Forensic Toxicology, AFMES for processing. Specific procedures and requirements can be found in the Division of Forensic Toxicology, AFMES publication *Guidelines for the Collection of and Shipment of Specimens for Toxicological Analysis.* This document and the AFMES Form 1323, *Toxicological Request Form,* which acts as laboratory request and chain of custody document for Division of Forensic Toxicology submissions, can be found on the AFMES Web site at <www.afmes.mil>.

ELECTRONIC DEVICES AND DIGITAL EVIDENCE

2-85. Digital evidence is binary information that is stored or transmitted by means of a digital device (including computers, mobile phones, scanners, flash drives, and other devices) that can be collected for its investigative value. Properly retrieved and documented digital evidence can be extremely useful to LE investigations. Digital evidence can provide direct proof of criminal activity such as credit card fraud, transmission and storage of child pornography, and many other forms of economic crimes. It can also provide important information regarding perpetrators intent or motives. Digital evidence can be used to prove a suspect's whereabouts or activity at a specific time and establish connections to other persons and organizations. Appendix B describes a wide variety of the types of electronic devices commonly encountered in crime scenes. It provides a general description of each type of device, describes its common uses, and presents the potential evidence that may be found in each type of equipment.

2-86. The capability of electronic devices is rapidly expanding, and crimes committed using these tools are among the fastest growing crimes in our society today. Electronic devices can be used to commit a crime, contain the evidence of a crime, and even be the targets of crime. Understanding the role and nature of electronic devices and digital evidence, including how to process the crime scene containing potential digital evidence, are crucial issues facing all LE personnel. Due to a rapid increase and the serious nature of these crimes, several federal agencies have organized special units that investigate computer crimes. The DOJ through the NIJ provides training and information on digital evidence collection. The USACIL is the primary supporting agency for Army LE investigators with regard to electronic evidence. The CCIU provides backup expertise in networks and digital evidence forensics. Ideally, trained subject matter experts (SMEs) from these organizations should conduct examination and data retrieval from digital devices to ensure that the evidence is properly secured for criminal investigators. However, Army first responders and LE investigators must have a basic understanding of identifying digital evidence and techniques to protect data on collected digital devices.

2-87. Digital evidence is fragile; it can be just as fragile as DNA and fingerprints. Digital evidence can also be hidden from access by untrained personnel. Equipment and software may be required to retrieve the evidence. Expert testimony may be required to explain the examination process and any process limitations. Digital evidence can be altered, damaged, or destroyed by improper handling, storage, and examination. For this reason, special precautions must be taken to document, collect, preserve, and examine this type of evidence. Failure to do so may render it unusable or lead to an inaccurate conclusion. Investigators should ensure that—

- Actions taken to secure and collect digital evidence do not change the evidence.
- Persons conducting the examination of digital evidence are trained for that purpose.

- Activity relating to the seizure, examination, storage, or transfer of digital evidence is fully documented, preserved, and available for review.

2-88. Digital evidence is acquired when data or physical items are collected and stored for examination purposes. Precautions must be taken when digital evidence is collected to ensure that the evidence is preserved for analysis by trained examiners. Collection and preservation of evidence requires an understanding of the characteristics of electronic evidence. Electronic evidence—

- Is often hidden, encrypted, or otherwise not readily accessible.
- May not be confined to the physical device at the crime scene or incident site. Networking and internet capabilities provide almost unlimited ability to access, transmit, and store digital information in locations that transcend borders with ease and speed.
- Can be easily altered, damaged, or destroyed.
- Can sometimes be time sensitive.

COLLECTION OF EVIDENCE

2-89. Computer evidence, like all other evidence, must be handled carefully and in a manner that preserves its evidentiary value. This relates not just to the physical integrity of an item or device, but also to the digital data it contains. The nature of digital evidence requires some additional considerations for collection, packaging, and transportation. These include actions to protect data that may be susceptible to damage or alteration from electromagnetic fields, such as those generated by static electricity, magnets, radio transmitters, and other devices. Appropriate information technology, USACIL, or CCIU personnel may be consulted for guidance on collecting, transporting, and storing electronic technology and digital evidence.

2-90. Special tools and equipment may be required to collect electronic devices containing digital evidence. As technology advances, the tools and knowledge required to collect and retrieve the evidence may change. Ongoing training will likely be required to maintain currency with rapidly emerging technology, to include tools and equipment beyond normal evidence collection and processing equipment and supplies such as cameras, notepads, sketch pads, evidence forms, crime scene tape, and markers. Each aspect of the process (documentation, collection, packaging, and transportation) dictates the specific type of tools and equipment required. The following are additional items that may be useful to have in a tool kit at an electronic crime scene:

- Documentation tools such as—
  - Cable tags.
  - Indelible felt-tip markers.
  - Stick-on labels.
- Disassembly and removal tools in a variety of nonmagnetic sizes and types that include—
  - Flat-blade and cross-tip screwdrivers.
  - Hex-nut and secure-bit drivers.
  - Star-type nut drivers.
  - Needle-nose and standard pliers.
  - Small tweezers.
  - Specialized screwdrivers (manufacturer specific).
  - Wire cutters.
- Packaging and transporting supplies such as—
  - Antistatic bags and bubble wrap.
  - Isolation bags.
  - Cable ties.
  - Evidence bags.
  - Evidence and packing tape.
  - Packing materials (avoid materials such as foam peanuts that can produce static electricity).

- Sturdy boxes of various sizes.

2-91. Recovery of nondigital physical evidence at the crime scene or incident site can be crucial in the investigation and should not be overlooked. These items are frequently in close proximity to the computer or related hardware items and should be secured and preserved for future analysis. Take proper care to ensure that such evidence is recovered and preserved. Items relevant to subsequent examination of digital evidence may exist in many forms including—

- Written passwords and other handwritten notes.
- Blank pads of paper with indented writing. These can sometimes reveal relevant data when processed by qualified examiners.
- Hardware and software manuals.
- Calendars or planners.
- Literature, text or graphical computer printouts, and photographs.

Secure and Identify Evidence

2-92. The crime scene or incident site should be secured to ensure the integrity of evidence at the location. Chapter 4 discusses securing and processing crime scenes. This includes ensuring that all persons are removed from the immediate area where the evidence is located; no one should be allowed to touch any electronic devices or peripherals. This ensures that subjects, victims, or witnesses do not intentionally or unintentionally destroy or alter digital evidence. Personnel processing the crime scene should make every effort to—

- Protect perishable data (physical and electronic). Perishable data may be found on computers, pagers, answering machine or caller identification (ID) boxes, electronic organizers, mobile phones, and other similar devices. Any device containing perishable data should be immediately secured, documented, and/or photographed. Once a digital device is located, do not change its current operating condition. If the device is on, it should be left on; if the device is off, it should be left off.
- Identify external connection lines and cables. This includes telephone lines attached to devices; telephone lines can be attached directly to computers, modems, caller ID boxes, or other digital devices. Document, disconnect, and label each telephone line to record the wall connection and what device(s) was connected. Identify cables for local area network (LAN), wide area network (WAN), or other network technologies.
- Protect and preserve any peripheral components. This includes computer mouse, keyboard, diskettes, compact disks (CDs), digital video disks (DVDs), printers, external hard drives, or other components that may have other latent physical or digital evidence. Chemicals used in processing latent fingerprints can damage equipment and data. Therefore, latent prints should be collected after the completion of digital evidence recovery.

Conduct Preliminary Interviews

2-93. Army LE personnel should conduct preliminary interviews to gain background information. These preliminary interviews can be conducted by responding military police patrols, MPIs, or USACIDC SAs. Preliminary interviews should begin by separating and identifying all individuals (witnesses, subjects, or others) at the scene and recording their location upon initial arrival by first responders. The following information should be obtained:

- Passwords and user names of owners and/or users of electronic devices found at the crime scene and the Internet service provider. Obtain any passwords required to access the system, software, or data if the person provides them voluntarily. An individual may have multiple passwords, such as basic input-output system, system login, network Internet service provider, application files, encryption pass phrase, e-mail, access token, scheduler, or contact list.
- The purpose of the system.
- Unique security systems or destructive devices.
- Any off-site data storage.

- Any social media sites, Web logs, or other interactive internet media used.
- Documentation explaining the hardware or software installed on the system.

Documentation of Evidence

2-94. Documentation of the evidence, within the context of the entire crime scene, creates a permanent historical record of the placement and configuration of the evidence. Crime scene documentation includes inventories of evidence, sketches, and photography of the scene to document the physical configuration of the scene. It is important to accurately record the location and condition of computers, storage media, other electronic devices, and conventional evidence. Moving of a computer system while the system is running may cause changes to system data. A computer system should not be moved until it has been safely powered down. Information technology, USACIL, or CCIU personnel may need to be consulted for guidance on how to power down while maintaining and protecting digital evidence. The initial documentation of the physical crime scene should include—

- Observing and documenting the physical location and layout of electronic equipment at the crime scene or incident site. This documentation should include the—
  - Position of the mouse.
  - Location of components relative to one other (a mouse on the left side of the computer may indicate a left-handed user).
  - Information displayed on screens. This may require photographing the front of the computer, monitor screen, and other components as well as written notes on what appears on the monitor screen. Active programs may require video recording or more extensive documentation of monitor screen activity.
  - Connections between components.
  - Cable and phone line connections.
- Documenting the operating condition of the computer system. This documentation may include—
  - The power status of the computer (on, off, or in sleep mode). Most computers have status lights to indicate that the computer is on. Likewise, if fan noise is heard, the system is probably on. Furthermore, if the computer system is warm, it may also indicate that it is on or was recently turned off.
  - Any damage to the system, especially if there is evidence of recent efforts to destroy equipment or data.
- Identifying and documenting related electronic components that will not be collected.
- Photographing the entire scene to create a visual record as noted by the first responder. The complete room should be recorded with 360-degree coverage, when possible.

Standalone Computers

2-95. A standalone personal computer (PC) is a computer that is not connected to a network or another computer. Standalone computers may be desktop machines or laptops. Desktops typically have a keyboard, a monitor, and a computer case or tower along with a mouse and other peripheral devices (although some desktop computers may have integrated monitors, keyboards, and computer cases); desktop computers typically require an electrical an external power source to power the computer. Laptops and notebooks incorporate a computer, monitor, keyboard, and mouse into a single portable unit. They differ from desktop computers in that they can be powered by an external source or an internal battery source. Therefore, they require the removal of the battery in addition to standalone, power-down procedures.

Note. Wireless networks are becoming more prevalent; the lack of network cabling does not necessarily ensure a standalone computer.

2-96. If the computer is on, document existing conditions and consult the appropriate information technology, USACIL, or CCIU SME for assistance. This is especially important if there are indications of obvious criminal activity, open text documents, financial data, open chat rooms or messaging programs, data encryption, or remote storage. If a computer expert is not available, document all actions taken and any changes observed in the monitor, computer, printer, or other peripherals resulting from those actions taken. Observe the monitor and determine if it is on, off, or in sleep mode. Once the monitor status is determined, the following steps can be taken based on the situation that applies:

- **Situation 1:** The monitor is on and the work product, Web site, and/or desktop are visible.
    - *Step 1.* Photograph the screen and record the information displayed.
    - *Step 2.* Proceed to situation 3, step 3.
- **Situation 2:** The monitor is on and the screen is blank (sleep mode) or the screensaver (picture) is visible.
    - *Step 1.* Move the mouse slightly without pushing buttons. The screen should change and show the work product or request a password.
    - *Step 2.* Do not perform any other keystrokes or mouse operations if mouse movement does not cause a change in the screen.
    - *Step 3.* Photograph the screen and record the information displayed.
    - *Step 4.* Proceed to situation 3, step 3.
- **Situation 3:** The monitor is off.
    - *Step 1.* Make a note of the "off" status.
    - *Step 2.* Turn the monitor on, then determine if the monitor status is as described in either situation 1 or 2 above and follow those steps.
    - *Step 3.* Regardless of the power state of the computer (on, off, or sleep mode), remove the power source cable from the computer, not from the wall outlet. If dealing with a laptop, in addition to removing the power cord, remove the battery pack. The battery is removed to prevent any power to the system. Some laptops have a second battery in the multipurpose bay instead of a floppy drive or CD drive. Check for this possibility and remove that battery as well.
    - *Step 4.* Check for evidence of outside connectivity such as a telephone modem, a cable, a satellite dish, an integrated services digital network (ISDN), and a digital subscriber line (DSL). If a telephone connection is present, attempt to identify the telephone number.
    - *Step 5.* Avoid damage to potential evidence by removing any floppy disks that are present, packaging the disk separately, and labeling the package. If available, insert either a seizure disk or a blank floppy disk. Do not remove CDs or touch the CD drive.
    - *Step 6.* Place tape over all the drive slots and over the power connector.
    - *Step 7.* Record the make, model, and serial numbers of all components.
    - *Step 8.* Photograph and diagram the connections of the computer and the corresponding cables.
    - *Step 9.* Label all connectors and cable ends (including connections to peripheral devices) to allow for exact reassembly at a later time. Label unused connection ports as "unused." Identify laptop computer docking stations in an effort to identify other storage media.
    - *Step 10.* Record or log evidence on an evidence custody document.
    - *Step 11.* Package any components as fragile, if transport is required.

Networked Systems

2-97. Multiple computers may indicate a computer network. Work environments frequently have multiple computers connected to one other, to a central server, or both. In these situations, specialized knowledge about the system is required to effectively recover evidence and reduce your potential for civil liability. Securing and processing a crime scene where the computer systems are networked poses special problems. Improper shut down of a networked computer may destroy data. The possibility of various operating systems and complex hardware configurations requiring different shutdown procedures make the processing of a network crime scene extremely complex, requiring significant expertise (beyond the scope of this manual). When investigating criminal activity in a work environment, the presence of a computer network should be planned for in advance, to include coordination for appropriate SME support. Computer networks can also be found in a home environment and the same concerns exist. Indications that a computer network may be present include—

- Multiple computer systems.
- Cables and connectors running between computers or central devices, such as hubs.
- Information provided by informants or individuals at the scene.
- Network components.

2-98. Computers and other electronic devices can be fragile and sensitive to temperature, humidity, physical shock, static electricity, and magnetic sources. Special precautions should be taken when packaging, transporting, and storing electronic evidence. To maintain the chain of custody of electronic evidence, document its packaging, transporting, and storing. If multiple computer systems are collected, label each system so that it can be reassembled as found; for example, system A: mouse, keyboard, monitor, and main base unit; system B: mouse, keyboard, monitor, and main base unit. When packaging collected evidence, ensure that—

- All collected digital evidence is properly documented, labeled, and inventoried before packing.
- The presence of latent or trace evidence on the devices being collected is considered and action taken to preserve it.
- Magnetic storage media is packed in antistatic packaging (paper or antistatic plastic bags). Avoid materials that can produce static electricity, such as standard plastic bags.
- Care is taken to avoid folding, bending, or scratching computer media, such as a diskette, compact disk-read only memory (CD-ROM), or tape. Ensure that all containers used to hold evidence are properly labeled.

2-99. Ensure that computers and other components that are not packaged in containers are secured in the vehicle to avoid shock and excessive vibrations. For example, computers may be placed on the vehicle floor and monitors placed on the seat with the screen down and secured by a seat belt. Extra padding such as blankets or foam may be required to provide additional protection. When transporting evidence—

- Keep all digital evidence away from magnetic sources. Radio transmitters, speaker magnets, and heated seats are examples of items that can damage electronic evidence.
- Avoid storing digital evidence in vehicles for prolonged periods of time. Conditions of excessive heat, cold, or humidity can damage electronic evidence.
- Maintain the chain of custody on all evidence transported.

ON-SITE SEARCHES WITHOUT SEIZURE AUTHORIZATION

2-100. In most cases Army LE personnel should not conduct a search of a computer or open electronic files on a suspect device. In some circumstances, a consent or authorization to search a computer is granted, but seizure is not authorized. Typically, this occurs in one of two situations. The first is when consent to search a computer is authorized by a suspect, but he does not agree to allow the computer to be collected and shipped to the laboratory for examination. The second situation results when a commander or supervisor suspects that criminal activity has been committed using a government computer but has no means to verify it. Further, authorization to take the computer is not granted because the commander or supervisor does not wish to deprive the organization of the use of the computer. In these cases when it is impossible to seize the device for laboratory examination, a limited search may be required.

2-101. If a consent type search of a computer is required based on a scenario indicated above, it is essential that the search is terminated immediately upon discovery of a file containing evidence of a crime. At this point probable cause has been met, and a formal search authorization should be obtained from an authorized authority. The computer should be sequestered but not removed from the site pending authorization. All activities pertinent to the consent search (including every keystroke and mouse click that led to the discovery of the criminal material) should be documented. It is important that additional files not be accessed, because the date-time group of the accessed file is modified and can result in the suppression of the file as evidence in subsequent judicial proceedings. Upon receipt of the search authorization, the computer can be seized and sent to the laboratory for processing. The subsequent seizure of the computer is now based on the evidence identified during the consented search and subsequent authority of the formal search authorization, rather than the consent to search.

FINGERPRINTS

2-102.   Fingerprint evidence remains one of the oldest, most reliable, and most accepted means of personal identification. A good reference for information on fingerprints and associated processes and technology is *The Fingerprint Sourcebook* published by the Scientific Working Group on Friction Ridge Analysis, Study and Technology; the publication can be found at the NIJ Web site.

2-103.   Fingerprints, or simply prints, are friction ridge impressions left by an individual on a surface. These impressions are primarily left through contact with an object by the palmer surfaces (fingers and hands) or plantar surfaces (toes and feet) of the individual's skin. They can be caused by pressure or from residual oils from the skin which leaves an impression on the object touched by the individual. They are typically associated with impressions from the fingertips and palms but can be obtained from the feet and toes. Individual prints can be identified and isolated by examination of the loops, whirls, arches, and other characteristics of the print. These characteristics appear in differing combinations and patterns on each individual and are unique to each individual. Generally prints are categorized as latent prints or record prints.

LATENT PRINTS

2-104.   The word "latent" means hidden, but within the LE context normally the term latent prints refers to those prints left at crime scenes and/or on items of evidence—whether visible or not. They are typically deposited unintentionally by an individual through routine or accidental contact with surfaces. In many cases latent prints deposited on a surface are partial prints (not a complete impression of any one digit) or they may be smudged, overprinted with another print, or otherwise distorted making analysis, comparison, and positive identification difficult or impossible. Prints that are not visible or faint may require development by physical, chemical, or electronic techniques.

2-105.   Another category of latent prints is patent prints. Patent prints are impressions visible due to transfer or displacement of material or contaminant when the body touches a surface. The material or contaminant is usually a fine particulate such as dust, powder, or flour. Mediums such as wet clay or other fine soils can also cause patent prints. Patent prints are typically visible to the naked eye and do not require enhancement techniques. Patent prints must be photographed before any attempt to lift the print from the surface. Plastic prints are those impressions left in materials such as wax, window putty, or other pliable materials that retains the impression after contact. Plastic prints are also typically visible to the naked eye.

Locating and Preserving Latent Prints

2-106.   Prints can be deposited on any surface contacted by an individual. For this reason it would be impossible to process every latent in most crime scenes. Investigators processing latent prints should examine the area to determine what objects or surfaces would likely be touched by persons pertinent to the investigation. They should consider which of these surfaces or objects are likely to provide recoverable prints. Finally, they should consider what objects with recoverable prints are relevant to the investigation. Considering these questions can help focus the investigator's efforts.

2-107.   Army LE personnel must understand the varying characteristics of different surfaces. Knowledge of these characteristics enables Army LE personnel to identify and properly process prints deposited on various surfaces. Prints deposited on items of evidence are generally divided into two categories—porous and nonporous.

2-108.   Care must be exercised when handling prints. Wearing gloves does not protect the latent prints from being destroyed if they are touched, rubbed, or smeared; gloves only prevent additional prints from being deposited. Photography, cyanoacrylate fuming, and fingerprint powder processing are techniques used to preserve latent prints.

Porous Surfaces

2-109. Porous surfaces absorb fingerprint residue into its surface; evidence with a porous surface can be best described as a sponge that absorbs residue; for example, paper, checks, currency, unfinished wood, cardboard, and other similar material. These items do not require treatment by personnel processing the crime scene. LE personnel should not attempt to process fingerprints on porous items because laboratory processing techniques are best for this type of evidence. Prints deposited on porous surfaces are relatively stable. While the danger of destroying latent prints on porous surfaces is low, the risk is high that personnel handling the evidence can accidentally deposit additional latent prints. Clean gloves should be worn at all times when handling porous evidence.

2-110. All porous evidence containing prints should be placed in a paper envelope, bag, or box or wrapped in paper and sealed. The USACIL cautions against the field use of chemical agents commercially marketed for the development of latent prints on porous materials. Some of these products are of poor quality and can damage or destroy latent prints. Latent prints developed in the field can fade or disappear before laboratory examination. An example is latent prints that are developed using iodine and ninhydrin, which produce "fugitive" prints or prints that fade within a short period of time after initial development. If investigators processing a scene believe that the scene or evidence could best be processed using such chemicals on-site, he should consult with USACIL for advice and guidance.

Nonporous Surfaces

2-111. Nonporous surfaces do not readily absorb water or other liquids into its surface; for example, plastic bags, painted or sealed woods, metal, glass, some glossy magazine covers, knives, guns, computer equipment, and like materials. Latent prints on nonporous evidence are often deposited on the surface of an item and are extremely unstable and vulnerable. When it cannot be determined from appearance whether a drop of water would be absorbed into a surface, the evidence should be handled and processed as nonporous (such as a leather wallet, cigarette cartons, and shiny cardboard boxes).

2-112. Due to the extremely fragile nature of prints deposited on nonporous surfaces, all nonporous evidence selected for latent-print examination should be processed as soon as possible. If ridge detail is visible, photographs should be taken of the print before further processing. All nonporous evidence should then be processed by cyanoacrylate fuming to enhance the print. See the section below on cyanoacrylate fuming.

Photography

2-113. The first step in latent print preservation is photography. Visible latent prints must always be photographed to prevent the loss of evidence. Latent prints deposited in grease, blood, paint, and other visible substances will often not require additional processing before photography.

2-114. Always use a scale in evidence photography and steady the camera using a tripod. Both general crime scene photographs and examination quality photographs should be taken. See chapter 4 for a detailed discussion of crime scene photography. General crime scene photographs (mid-range) should be taken to document the evidence as it relates to a specific area of the scene and other pieces of evidence. Examination quality (close-up) photographs should be taken to provide detail of the print suitable for examination.

Cyanoacrylate Fuming

2-115. Cyanoacrylate fuming (also known as "superglue" fuming), remains the most effective way to develop, protect, and preserve latent prints on nonporous evidence. All nonporous evidence should be processed using cyanoacrylate fuming to enhance the print. Studies conducted by the USACIL have shown that latent prints on evidence that was fumed in the field are preserved better and have a significantly greater chance of being identified than latent prints not fumed, but forwarded to the laboratory as found. Cyanoacrylate fuming preserves latent print evidence making it stable for shipment to the laboratory without any further processing. It can simply be placed in an envelope, bagged, or wrapped in paper without special packaging materials and shipped to the laboratory. The cyanoacrylate fuming process includes the following steps:

- **Step 1.** Place evidence in a suitably sized, sealed container and in an area that is well-ventilated.
- **Step 2.** Prepare a test print. The test print should be placed on the same type of material as the questioned evidence. A test print can be made by wiping an ungloved finger on the face or neck to collect skin oils; the finger is then applied to the test surface to deposit a latent fingerprint.
- **Step 3.** Place the object with the test print applied into the chamber at a height consistent with the evidence to allow for consistent results between test print and evidence. The object with the test print must be placed where it is observable.
- **Step 4.** Place a few drops of liquid cyanoacrylate on a piece of foil or laboratory tin and placed on a coffee cup warmer, or a similar heat source, inside the container. The cyanoacrylate fuming process can be accelerated using heat or chemicals. USACIL suggests heat to accelerate the fuming process.
- **Step 5.** Observe the test print and evidence—this is critical. When the test print has developed, any latent prints on the evidence will also develop.
- **Step 6.** Remove the evidence from the container for further processing or preparation for shipment.

Note. Caution must always be used to ensure the safety of investigators who are using this fuming process. Cyanoacrylate fumes must not be inhaled and exposure to the eyes should be avoided, especially if contact lenses are worn. Masks and eye protection must be worn while in the area where cyanoacrylate fuming is being conducted.

2-116. In some cases following the fuming process, latent prints exposed to cyanoacrylate fumes can be photographed, powdered, and lifted. Do not submit evidence to the laboratory if the investigator has powdered the latent prints and they are capable of being lifted. Send only the photographs taken before lifting and the actual lifts. Some evidence does not reveal prints sufficient for photography and lift after the fuming process. This evidence should be appropriately packaged and shipped to the laboratory for additional processing as soon as possible. Evidence should be placed in a paper envelope, bag, or box or wrapped in paper to be transported to the laboratory.

2-117. Large items of evidence can be fumed in much the same way as smaller items. The investigator may have to build a makeshift tent to enclose the evidence. Latent prints developed with cyanoacrylate fuming on large or immovable items of evidence should be dusted with fingerprint powder, photographed, and lifted. Only the photographs and lifted prints should be sent to the laboratory. This effort saves shipping and handling costs of large or bulky items.

Note. Some evidence may require processing beyond print identification and lifting. This may include processing for other trace material or physical examination. Evidence requiring examination by other divisions of the USACIL must never be processed with fingerprint powder because contamination can hinder other examination processes. Cyanoacrylate fuming must not be used on any evidence being submitted for trace evidence examinations.

Powder Processing

2-118. The traditional fingerprint powder processing technique is still an important and widely used method for processing fingerprint evidence. The preferred method of recovering latent fingerprints from a crime scene (especially those that are located on large, bulky, or immovable items) is to apply cyanoacrylate fume first and then powder and lift the latent prints.

2-119. Many latent prints can be developed and preserved using a fingerprint brush and powder. All latent prints developed with a brush and powder must be photographed (with a scale) before lifting. Latent prints found in dust, grease, blood, or other contaminants should not be processed using fingerprint powders. Fingerprint powders are supplied in crime scene kits in several colors. In most instances, the best powders to use are the black or gray general purpose powders. Always choose a powder that contrasts best with the background of the evidence and the color of the lift medium used.

2-120.   Fluorescent powders can be used to develop latent prints on multicolored surfaces. These powders require the use of an alternate light source or UV light to be able to photograph. Effective use of these light sources requires training and experience. They are very costly and can cause health issues. Only long-wave, UV light should be used; short-wave, UV light is harmful to the eyes and skin. Anytime UV light is used to develop latent prints, investigators and anyone else in the room exposed to the light must wear protective goggles and clothing. Fluorescent powders with UV light should only be used when absolutely necessary.

2-121.   Magnetic powders are available for use on plastics such as water bottles, plastic bags, or other plastic storage containers. Magnetic powders also work well on shiny or glossy paper such as magazine or pamphlet covers. A magnetic applicator is required when using magnetic powders.

2-122.   Many types of fingerprint brushes are used to apply fingerprint powder. Examples of these brushes are fiberglass, animal hair, and feather brushes. For overhead work or in situations where it is critical that the brush elements do not come in contact with the surface, magnetic wands and magnetic powders are used. The requirements for using fingerprint powders are—

- **Step 1.** Check the surface first using a test print. Lightly brush an area away from the subject surface and determine if any latent prints are present. If none are present, wipe the surface and apply and process a test print to determine how acceptable the surface is to the fingerprint powder processing. The test print can be made using the same method described in the cyanoacrylate fuming section above.
- **Step 2.** Pour a very small amount of powder out into a cupped sheet of paper. The brush must never be dipped into the container; this contaminates the powder and can spoil the working properties of the powder.
- **Step 3.** Apply powder to the brush by touching the powder only with the tip of the brush. Lightly shake off any excess powder and brush the surface using only the very tips of the powdered brush. The key to proper print development is to use a small amount of powder and a light touch.
- **Step 4.** Brush the area being processed, following the contour of the ridges and using a twirling method to ensure that the sides of the bristles are not coming into contact with the surface and destroying latent prints.
- **Step 5.** Watch for the latent print to become visible to ensure that it is not overbrushed. Brushing should continue only until there is enough detail to see the ridge flow on the print. Overbrushing can destroy the print. Stop brushing when the ridge detail is developed or immediately if the ridge contrast begins to diminish.
- **Step 6.** Remove excess powder. This can be done with light strokes from a clean powder-free brush, by lightly tapping the edge of the evidence being processed, or by lightly blowing excess powder from the print.

Note. If too much powder adheres to the surface around the print and it cannot be brushed away, an initial lift can sometimes remove the excess powder. A second lift will usually obtain an acceptable print. Powder can be lightly reapplied following the first lift if too much powder is removed.

- **Step 7.** Photograph the print as soon as the ridge flow is observable. All developed prints should be photographed and then lifted.
- **Step 8.** Discard any unused powder; never return contaminated powder to the container.

2-123.   All lifts and photographs should be submitted to the USACIL for evaluation, examination, and comparison. All latent print photographs should include a scale. Cyanoacrylate fumed prints can be powdered and lifted many times without destroying the print; however, latent prints that have not been fixed using the fuming process can diminish or be destroyed while attempting multiple lifts.

Lifting Latent Prints

2-124.   The most common means to lift latent prints is to physically lift the print using commercially produced lifting devices, such as hinge lifters, lifting tapes, rubber or gelatin lifters, and various types of liquid lifting mediums. Chemical processing using applications including iodine fuming, silver nitrate, and ninhydrin to lift prints can also be conducted. Most chemical processing of latent print evidence should only be conducted by trained laboratory personnel in an approved facility; however, there are some instances where chemical processing can and should be conducted in the field by trained investigators. The USACIL should be consulted when there is doubt about using chemical processing.

Lifting Devices

2-125.   There are numerous devices on the market for lifting latent prints. They range in size from single fingerprint to lifting shoe prints. There are also choices in the lifting medium; the choice is largely driven by the surface on which the desired print is deposited. A lift background that contrasts the color of the powder should be used. Hinge and rubber lifters as well as lifting tape store well; gel lifters may require refrigeration. A description of these common lifting mediums follows:

- **Hinge lifters.** Hinge lifters (as well as transparent lifting tape) have the advantage of presenting the lifted latent print in its correct perspective. They come in a variety of sizes and can be obtained in clear, white, or black to ensure appropriate contrast with the powder used. They are best used on smooth surfaces. Textured surfaces can result in voids in the lifted print; rubber or gelatin lifters are best for textured or rough surfaces.

- **Rubber or gelatin lifters.** Rubber or gelatin lifters are used when the surface area being processed is rough or has texture. The material in these lifters is more flexible and will fill irregularities, thus reducing the chance of voids in the lift. They are preferred for fragile surfaces that are prone to tearing if tape or conventional hinge lifters are applied such as paper, cardboard, or wallpaper. They work better on rough or irregular surfaces. They are not as tacky as tape or hinge lifters. This makes them preferable for use on surfaces that are more fragile, such as where paint or other material might be pulled away with a powdered print and are excellent for lifting dust prints. Like the standard hinge lifter, they come in a variety of sizes and can be obtained in clear, white, or black to ensure appropriate contrast with the powder used. The downside to rubber and gelatin lifters is that the print, when lifted, is in a reversed or mirror image perspective. The print must be reversed again using photographic or other electronic techniques to properly visualize and compare the latent print.

- **Transparent lifting tape.** Transparent lifting tape is similar to the material in the standard hinge lifter but is dispensed in a roll. Lifting tape works better for taking prints from curved or uneven surfaces. Transparent tapes used in office work, such as cellophane tape, are not suitable for lifting fingerprints except in dire circumstances.

- **Silicone, putty, or other liquid casting materials.** Silicone, putty, and other liquid casting materials can be useful in filling voids to lift prints from semisolid and uneven surfaces. This technique is rarely used for fingerprints and is more common for larger casting requirements such as footprints, tire impressions, or toolmarks. Most types work by pouring them over the powdered latent print and removing them after they dry.

2-126.   Hinge and rubber or gelatin lifters are all used in basically the same manner. A lifter large enough to cover the entire print should be used. The plastic cover should be removed from the lifter with care in one steady movement. A pause can result in a crease being left on the lifter surface and obliterating a ridge upon lifting. The adhesive side of the lifter should be placed to the developed, powdered print. It should be pressed down evenly and smoothed out over the surface. If an air pocket is sealed under the surface of the lifter, an attempt should be made to force it out. Use pressure or a pin to puncture the lifter and release the air by applying pressure to the bubbled area. The lifter should be peeled from the surface in one smooth, even motion.

2-127.   Transparent lifting tape is applied in much the same way as commercial lifters. Bending one corner of the tape before application will provide a "tab" for the collector to use when removing the tape from the applied surface. One end of the tape should be placed on one side of the latent print and smoothed out across the surface of the print. Air bubbles should be worked out using a rubberized roller or a pin, if necessary, to expel air trapped under the surface of the tape. The tape should be pulled free with one continuous motion and then mounted on clean materials that contrast the fingerprint powder used. A black background should be used for gray or white powders. A white background should be used for black or dark powders. Commercial mounting cards usually offer the best types of mounting surfaces and have contrasting surfaces on each side of the card. Lifting tapes can be used to lift large areas of latent prints (such as shoe prints) by applying in overlapping strips. All of the strips should be pulled free from the surface in one continuous motion with all of the strips connected together. They should be mounted as one connected piece.

2-128. Silicone, putty, and other liquid casting materials are typically applied by pouring the compound onto the surface being processed or applying it with a spatula. The material is then allowed to set before being removed from the target area. The material fills the voids and creases without disturbing the surface area and can result in a successful lift. Like rubber or gel lifters, the image is reversed and must be processed using photographic or other electronic techniques to properly visualize and compare the latent print.

Chemical Processing

2-129. Typically chemical processing of latent prints is not conducted in the field and is reserved for personnel at the USACIL. The main exception is cyanoacrylate fuming which is regularly conducted in the field by investigators. The premature or improper use of chemical processes in the field can result in the loss and/or damage of latent print evidence. Most chemical processes are "fugitive" in nature and are not enduring, meaning that once the latent prints are developed with chemical processes, they will fade and often disappear before the occurrence of proper photography and comparison of the evidence. One type of processing that may be used is small particle reagent (SPR). SPR may be more of a physical process than a chemical process in that the resulting action is physical in nature.

2-130. SPR can be applied to lift prints from wet nonporous evidence, items that have been lightly washed or rinsed, items that may be covered in dirt or mud making them impossible to process by normal means, or items that have been submerged or covered in moisture. The target evidence is sprayed with the SPR. Metallic particles suspended in the solution adhere to the oily and waxy residue of the latent print after the moisture has washed everything else away. SPR is then simply rinsed away with water. It can then be photographed and lifted as with powdered prints, after drying. SPR also works on metal and masonry type surfaces. SPR comes in contrasting colors and UV formulas so that the latent print appears in a contrast to the item of evidence being processed.

RECORD PRINTS

2-131. Record prints, also referred to as exemplar prints, are the controlled recordings of fingerprints deliberately collected from an individual. Record prints will typically at minimum include rolled prints from each finger taken individually, plain flat prints from all fingers taken simultaneously from each hand, and a flat print of each thumb. Record prints are normally recorded on a standardized fingerprint card. Record prints can be obtained using an ink pad and fingerprint cards or electronically through automated fingerprint scanning devices. These electronic scanning devices can produce high quality prints without the use of ink. Though there are many variations on how to obtain record prints, the principles are the same. Record prints can also be taken from feet, which also bear friction ridge skin.

2-132. Record prints may be collected subsequent to apprehension of a criminal subject. Army LE is required to submit offender criminal history data to the Criminal Justice Information Services Division of the FBI for crimes listed within DODI 5505.11. They can also be used for enrollment in a print database for security or background checks. During a criminal investigation, record prints should also be taken from the victim, witnesses, suspects, medical and law enforcement personnel, and anyone known or suspected of handling evidence or entering a crime scene. Once legible and complete elimination prints for investigators are on file at USACIL, there is no requirement to resubmit record prints for each investigation conducted. In some cases, it may be necessary to record ear and lip prints for comparison. The laboratory should be contacted for guidance in these cases.

2-133. To classify, analyze, and compare record fingerprints, they must be complete and clear. It takes practice to obtain suitable record fingerprints and could take several attempts to obtain suitable prints from a particular individual. All administrative data including signatures and dates should be completed on the fingerprint card before the printing process. This reduces the chance of smearing wet ink. The subject being printed should wash and dry their hands thoroughly to remove dirt, sweat, or grime. The subject's hands should be examined to ensure that they are absent of intentional disguises, such as coatings and any disfiguring. Ensure that ink formulated for use in fingerprinting is used to obtain the best results; standard printer's ink or ink for ink pads dries too slowly and is more susceptible to smudging. The following equipment is normally required for printing:

- A fingerprint card.
- Plain bond paper.
- A fingerprint card holder.
- Fingerprint ink.
- An ink roller.
- An ink plate.

COLLECTING RECORD PRINTS

2-134. Record prints are taken to show the entire friction ridge skin surface of the digit or body part being printed. Record fingerprints for submission to the USACIL consist of at least two completed fingerprint cards. To prepare for recording the prints, the fingerprint card should be secured in the holding device. A small dab of ink should be placed on the inking plate and rolled until a thin, even film covers the surface. The ink should appear opaque black on the inking plate but not wet. If the ink plate appears wet, then too much ink has been applied; if the color appears gray rather than black, more ink is required. Ensure that the fingers of the individual being printed are clean and dry. Contaminants on the hands will result in poor prints.

Individual Fingerprints

2-135. The individual collecting the prints uses the same motions for inking the finger and recording the finger on the fingerprint card. The fingers are rolled from nail edge to nail edge and from approximately 1/8 inch below the crease of the first joint to as far up as possible. This area will allow for the recording of all ridge characteristics required for correct classification of each finger. The finger is rolled through the ink and then rolled in the corresponding block of the fingerprint card. The individual taking record fingerprints should grasp the top of the subject's hand to ensure that the finger to be printed is extended. The investigator uses his other hand to hold the subjects finger at the base where it meets the palm. The subject should be instructed to look away, relax, and allow the person collecting the print to guide all movements.

2-136. Each finger should be rolled in one continuous and smooth motion. The fingers and thumbs are rolled from awkward to comfortable (fingers rolled away from the individual's body and thumbs rolled toward the body). A roll should be processed to capture the entire surface area of the skin from nail edge to nail edge. This allows the collector to work with the anatomic features of the hands without fighting the natural resistance of the hands. The finger should not be rolled back and forth on the ink or the card since this will cause over inking, distortion, and ink lines to appear on the recordings. The pressure should be firm and even. Pressing too hard causes the furrows (grooves between the ridges) to fill in with ink. It is important that the individual collecting the prints ensures that the correct finger is rolled in the designated block.

Plain or Simultaneous Prints

2-137. After all fingerprint blocks have been completed, the plain or simultaneous prints at the bottom of the card should be completed. They verify the order of the rolled record fingerprints and show characteristics that are sometimes distorted in rolled prints. Simultaneous prints are made on the card by pressing (not rolling) the four inked fingers onto the card in the appropriate blocks at a slight angle so that they fit the space. The subject should hold his fingers straight and stiff. The subjects hand should be level with his wrist. His wrists should be grasped with one hand and the fingers should be pressed onto the cards with the other hand. Plain thumb prints are recorded by inking each thumb and pressing it on the appropriate thumb impression block.

FULL RECORD PRINTS

2-138.   Full record prints, sometimes referred to as major case prints, are typically required for criminal cases and generally require more extensive printing than the standard rolled and plain prints required for standard identification purposes. Full record prints will typically require collection of all the friction ridge detail on the entire hand. This includes rolled and plain fingerprints discussed previously, and also includes palm prints that include the entire flat palm, the thenar edge (thumb edge of the hand), the hypothenar edge (knife edge of the hand), a roll of the entire tip of the fingers, and prints of the entire friction ridge surface area of each thumb and finger. Prints of the subject's feet may also be required in some cases. See figure 2-2 for an example and instructions for taking a full record print of a subject's hand.

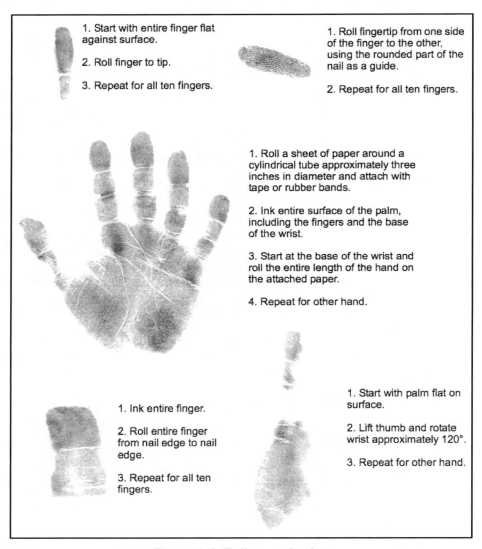

Figure 2-2. Full record print

Palm Prints

2-139.   Palm prints may be required from a person when their record fingerprints are obtained for a major criminal investigation, especially if the prints are being submitted to the laboratory for comparison. Ink should be applied directly to the subject's palms using the ink roller, covering completely from the base of the hand at the wrist crease to the end of the fingertips. Using the inking plate to apply ink will cause ink lines created by the edge of the plate to appear in the record palm print. The palm print card or a piece of bond paper should be wrapped around a cylindrical object that is uniform in diameter; typically, a three- to four-inch tube or cylinder, such as an aerosol spray can, works best. Wrap the cylinder with a print card or heavy bond paper and secure at the edges with tape or rubber bands.

2-140. Place the subject's heel or the base of his palm at the wrist crease on the covered cylinder and roll the palm using a pulling motion from the heel of his hand to his fingertips. Ensure that the thumbs are extended to the side; thumbs are printed separately. Ensure that the entire center areas of the subject's palms are recorded; this requires direct pressure to be applied to the back of the hand. After rolling the palm and an acceptable print is obtained, remove the card or paper from the cylinder and carefully lay it out on a flat table or other surface. Several recordings of each palm may be required to ensure that all areas are recorded properly.

2-141. The edge of the palm on the thumb side (thenar edge) and the side of the palm opposite the thumb side (hypothenar edge, knife edge or writer's palm) should also be recorded. The thenar edge of the hand, with thumb fully extended, should have ink applied with the roller and pressed firmly to the fingerprint card. The thenar print of the right hand should be placed on the left side of the rolled palm print of the same hand; the thenar print of the left hand should be placed to the right of the rolled palm print of the same hand. The knife edge or writer's palm is recorded in the same manner with the little finger fully extended. The knife edge print of the right hand should be placed to the right of the rolled palm print of the same hand; the knife edge print of the left hand should be placed on the left side of the rolled palm print of the same hand. If there is no room on the print card with the rolled palm print to place the thenar and knife edge prints, a separate card can be used and clearly marked to identify the prints applied.

Complete Friction Ridge Print of the Fingers

2-142. When complete recordings of the entire surface of the fingers and thumbs (all friction ridge detail) are required, use the following steps:

- **Step 1.** Use the ink roller to apply ink to the entire friction ridge surface of the thumb from the nail to the base of the thumb including the sides).
- **Step 2.** Record the thumb by pressing the left side of the thumb, from the base to the tip, firmly onto the print card or paper and removing.
- **Step 3.** Press the center or underside of thumb and remove it, followed by the right side of the thumb.
- **Step 4.** Apply the left side thumb print to the lower left side of the paper, the center thumb print in the center of the paper, and the right side thumb print on the right side of the paper.
- **Step 5.** Above the three prints roll the thumb tip from one extreme side of the tip to the other.
- **Step 6.** Clearly label the print for identification; for example, right thumb.
- **Step 7.** Repeat the process for the remaining thumb and fingers.

Footprints

2-143. The techniques for collecting footprints are similar to that of collecting the palm print. When collecting a footprint the paper used to record the print should be legal sized (8.5 inches by 14 inches) to ensure enough surface area to accommodate the entire foot. A larger cylinder or tube should be used as well—typically a cylinder of at least 5 to 6 inches in diameter. The paper should be attached to the cylinder in the same manner as described for obtaining palm prints.

2-144. Apply ink with the ink roller over the entire bottom surface of the foot from the heel to the tips of the toes. Roll the prepared cylinder from the extreme edge of the heel toward the toes, ensuring that the entire toe passes over the cylinder. If this method is not feasible, a print may be obtained by placing the subject in a sitting position and supporting the outstretched leg and foot. Paper mounted on a flat board can then be pressed against the subject's inked foot to obtain the footprint.

Problem Prints

2-145.   Excessive perspiration, dirty hands, and dirty equipment may cause problems when recording prints. The collector must always start with clean equipment and clean fingers. When a subject's fingers are wet from perspiration, each finger should be wiped with alcohol, quickly inked, and rolled onto the fingerprint card. Some people have dry and/or rough hands that can make collecting adequate prints a problem. Rubbing them with lanolin, lotions, or creams can often make them soft enough to obtain clear, unsmudged prints. When all efforts have failed to obtain adequate prints, USACIL can be consulted for guidance.

2-146.   If the hands and fingers are deformed, normal printing steps cannot be followed. The ink should be applied directly to the fingers with a spatula or small roller, then a square piece of paper should be rotated around the finger. When an acceptable print has been made, the square should be taped to the proper box of the fingerprint card.

2-147.   If there is an extra finger (usually a little finger or a thumb), the innermost five are printed as usual on the card. The extra digit is then printed on the reverse of the card. Webbed fingers should be printed as best as possible in the rolled and plain impressions blocks of the fingerprint card. If a finger or a fingertip has been amputated, it should be noted in the proper box; for example, AMP, 1st joint, FEB 1993 or TIP AMP.

COLLECTING POSTMORTEM RECORD PRINTS

2-148.   LE investigators must always attempt to obtain full record finger and palm prints from deceased individuals related to LE investigations. These record prints are used to identify the deceased and/or eliminate them as the source of the latent print evidence. The process of taking postmortem record finger and palm prints is cumbersome and difficult, but can be critically important to the investigation. Prints are often obtained from recently deceased persons using methods similar to collecting from living subjects. Many factors can inhibit postmortem printing including decomposition, desiccation (drying), or maceration (separation and/or softening of skin from prolonged exposure to liquid) of the friction ridges. The technique used to obtain postmortem prints is driven by the condition of the friction ridges on the area being printed.

2-149.   In many cases there is limited opportunity to obtain postmortem prints before the body is interred. This process must be completed with accuracy and diligence. Proper preparation is critical to ensuring successful collection of postmortem prints. The following items should be available for use when processing fingerprints and palm prints of deceased individuals:
- Fingerprint ink.
- An ink roller.
- Fingerprint powder.
- A fingerprint brush (soft-hair type).
- Transparencies made from fingerprint cards without a textured surface.
- White paper or fingerprint cards, precut to an appropriate size.
- Fingerprint tape.
- Blank transparencies or document protectors.
- A permanent marker.
- Extra large sealable zip-type plastic bags.
- An inking spoon.
- A spatula.
- PPE (latex gloves, masks, and goggles).

Note. For safety, the person collecting the prints must wear latex gloves, a mask, and eye protection to protect from biohazards. When finished and before removing PPE, place the postmortem prints into a sealable zip-type plastic bag and discard the magic marker used to label the prints.

2-150. Collecting prints from recently deceased individuals follows the same basic process as for live subjects. The process of inking the fingers directly, using inking spoons, and square paper tabs on the fingers might be used. When rigor mortis is present, it may be necessary to break rigor in the hands and fingers by massaging and straightening the fingers; this technique of massaging the fingers and hands takes time (about 10 minutes per hand). Rigor may be broken by bending the fingers backward and pressing down on the middle joint of the finger. In some cases pressing the hand toward the inner forearm and/or pressing the fingers just above the knuckle toward the palm can flatten the palm and straighten the fingers, enabling acquisition of prints.

2-151. It is recommended that deceased individuals are at room temperature when taking prints to lessen problems of condensation during recording. The easiest position from which to take the record prints is to place the deceased in a prone position (face down) with the arms stretched out in front of the body. It may be necessary to massage the fingers and palms to make them more pliable and receptive to the print-taking process. This massaging will open up the palm area for better record taking. A small worktable should be used for supplies and equipment.

2-152. During the printing process, ink is applied to the right thumb of the deceased, covering the area to be printed. The ink can be applied directly to the surface being recorded with an ink roller. Ink can also be applied using a spatula that has a thin coat of ink applied. The hands of the deceased should be clean and dry; alcohol swabs may be used on the deceased's hands and fingers to ensure that the skin is clean and dry enough for printing. Start with the right hand in the following order: thumb, index finger, middle finger, ring finger, little finger, and then the left hand in the same finger order; this will help the collector stay organized and prevent mistakes with labeling. Fingerprint cards can be cut into strips so that each row on the card equals one strip or individual finger, and plain print sections can be cut out ahead of time. Place precut card material being used to record the print on the tip of the finger and gently roll or press as appropriate to obtain the print. Inking spoons may be extremely helpful when performing this procedure. As the prints are taken, they are affixed to the fingerprint card in the appropriate space. The process is repeated until the complete fingerprint card is full. Simultaneous plain prints are taken in the same manner using paper cut to the appropriate size. Multiple attempts may be necessary on each finger or other area being printed to obtain acceptable prints.

2-153. Fingerprint powder may be used to collect prints from deceased persons when the ink method is unsuccessful. During the printing process, the fingerprint powder should be brushed on the area to be printed. The hands of the deceased should be clean and dry; alcohol swabs may be used on the deceased's hands and fingers to ensure that the skin is dry enough to receive a light dusting of powder. As with the ink process, start with the right hand in the following order: thumb, index finger, middle finger, ring finger, little finger, and then the left hand in the same finger order. After applying powder to the target area, fingerprint tape can be applied tacky side down and gently smoothed around the finger or area being printed. The tape can then be lifted and applied to the fingerprint card. Prints taken in this manner will be displayed in a reverse orientation and must be manipulated in the same manner as latent prints collected in the same manner. One way to eliminate the problem of reverse orientation of the print is to use white-backed tape to lift the print and then apply the tape with the lifted print to clear transparency material. The result when the print is viewed transparency side up is a correctly oriented print.

2-154. In many cases deceased persons are in a condition that makes standard field processes ineffective. There are numerous processes that can be conducted by MEs or laboratory personnel. Consult the USACIL for guidance when standard printing methods are unsuccessful or impossible due to degradation of the body.

FIREARMS AND AMMUNITION

2-155. Solving a crime involving firearms and ammunition often depends on the scientific examination of evidence by a qualified examiner at USACIL. Testing by laboratory examiners can provide information that cannot be determined by field examination; Army LE personnel do not perform firearms identification tests in the field.

2-156. Firearms examiners perform the required forensic examinations at the crime laboratory and provide the test results to the requesting investigator. Firearms examiners can also provide expert testimony in court, when needed. The ability of USACIL personnel to provide relevant identification, comparisons, and associated expert testimony is dependent on proper collection of evidence by Army LE personnel in the field. The weapon may contain evidence such as prints, gunshot residue (GSR), blood, hair, fibers, or other material that can be recovered for analysis. If other evidentiary material is identified on the weapon, ensure that it is noted for USACIL examiners to process. In addition to other evidence deposited on the firearm or projectile, collected firearms, projectiles, and expended cartridge casings and wadding material can enable firearms examiners to determine many facts to include—

- The class characteristics of the weapon including the make, caliber, manufacturer, and type of firearm (automatic pistol, revolver, rifle, and such) that was discharged as well as the type of propellant used to fire the projectile. If two or more projectiles are collected, laboratory examiners may be able to determine if they were fired from the same weapon. The number and width of lands and grooves in the rifling and the direction of twist may also be determined.

- A confirmation or elimination of a firearm as the weapon that fired a bullet when the bullet or cartridge casing (or both) and the firearm are both collected and available for comparison. Weapons alone can be matched to bullets collected from previous crime scenes or incident sites when the bullets are available for comparison or bullet data is available for comparison through databases such as the National Integrated Ballistics Identification Network.

- The determination of shot size from collected shot pellets (from shotguns).

- The gauge of the shotgun used from recovered wadding.

- The proper function of the weapon which can show that an accidental discharge was possible. All firearms uncovered during the investigation of homicides, suicides, assaults, and robberies should be submitted for function testing. The value of learning if a firearm will function and if it functions safely is often overlooked. It may be determined that a firearm is malfunctioning and could have discharged accidentally as stated by a suspect or that a particular firearm could not be fired at all.

- The presence or absence of gunpowder residues in the barrel of a firearm.

- Serial numbers, die stamps, or other distinctive markings that may have been removed or made unreadable through wear or deliberate action. Firearms examiners may be able to restore these numbers or markings to a readable state through laboratory processes.

RECOVERY AND PRESERVATION OF FIREARM EVIDENCE

2-157. Items of evidence associated with firearms must be collected and maintained in the state in which they were found upon arrival of LE personnel on the scene to avoid altering or damaging the evidence. After properly photographing the evidence, firearms identified and collected at a crime scene or incident site should immediately be rendered safe by the LE personnel collecting the evidence. Handle collected evidence with care to ensure that it is not altered or damaged. Wrap firearms and firearm-related evidence (including projectiles, shell casings, cartridges, and wadding) in paper and place it in a wooden or sturdy cardboard box. Zip ties may be used to secure the weapon in place; for field expediency, wrap in paper and protect with cardboard. All items of evidence must be wrapped separately.

2-158. Never place anything inside the barrel or cylinder of a weapon (pencils, pens, flex cuffs, plastic ties, or other material); foreign objects placed in the barrel or cylinder can mark the barrel or cylinder and alter the identifying characteristics of the weapon. The location of the weapon and expended and live cartridge casings; positions of safeties, hammers, indicators, and control features; and other pertinent details should be recorded by responding Army LE patrols and investigators. When possible to safely do so, leave the items in place until photographs and measurements can be made by crime scene personnel. Never clean projectiles recovered; this can destroy potential evidence. If the projectile is wet from blood or other liquid, air dry it before packaging.

2-159. Under normal conditions, firearms and associated ammunition and spent shell casings must never be packaged in plastic bag or wrapping. If a firearm is found submerged in water, collect the weapon with the original water. In this case, lower a watertight container into the water to capture the weapon and the surrounding water. This allows any trace evidence within the water to be collected and prevents the weapon from being exposed to other contaminants.

2-160.   Recovering projectiles at a crime scene can be difficult. Many times projectiles will be found lodged in walls, ceilings, paneling, wood framing, furniture, or other material. Projectiles should not be touched with bare fingers. Used gloved hands to collect projectiles found loose on the floor, street, or other area. Loose projectiles may also be recovered expediently by carefully sliding a clean sheet of paper under the projectile, then folding the paper over to protect the evidence before packaging.

2-161.   When a projectile is found lodged within a structure, objects, or materials at a crime scene or incident site, remove a section of the area around the lodged projectile without disturbing the projectile itself. The entire section can then be packaged and forwarded intact to the laboratory. This limits the chance of damage to the projectile. If removal of a section of the impacted area is not possible, the projectile may require recovery by extraction from the impacted material. Always use rubber-tipped or heavily padded tools to extract a projectile; never probe for a projectile or attempt to extract it with metal or other hard-surfaced objects.

2-162.   Examination of entry holes created by projectiles can be critical in determining the shooting distance and direction. This can be determined by trace evidence of GSR around the entry hole in close range incidents involving single projectile weapons. Material that has been penetrated by projectiles may require collection for processing by laboratory examiners; projectile holes can be collected in the same manner as collecting lodged projectiles by removing the entire area around the hole. This includes clothing worn by victims. LE investigators should monitor medical personnel and ensure that if clothing is removed from a victim that the area around the hole created by the projectile is protected. Garments should be cut a good distance away from bullet holes to leave the holes and area surrounding them intact. The clothing should be gathered and protected as evidence as soon as possible to prevent contamination. If the bullet passed through the clothing into the body, obtain a photograph of the entry wound that clearly shows the location of the wound. Use a ruler to demonstrate scale.

> *Note.* FSOs can conduct bullet trajectory analysis at the crime scene to determine many aspects of bullet path including distances, angles, and positions of individuals involved in the shooting incident.

2-163.   Only laboratory examiners are qualified to provide expert opinions on powder residue on clothing or other materials. By firing a suspect firearm and using ammunition of the type that left the residue, a laboratory examiner can conduct tests to learn the approximate distance from the muzzle to the target. These range of fire tests are based on the dispersion of gunpowder residues. They are, of course, subject to limitations. A scaled photograph of the wound may be helpful to a firearms examiner who is examining the clothing worn by the victim. Normally no discernible gunpowder residue pattern will be present if the muzzle-to-target distance is in excess of 2 1/2 feet. Only pathologists or other qualified medical individuals can give expert opinions on gunshot wounds to the flesh and their powder patterns.

2-164.   The firing distance for weapons firing shot shell ammunition can be determined at much further ranges by analyzing the spread of the shot pattern on the impacted objects. In many cases the pattern covers an area too large to collect. Photograph and measure the shot pattern to determine the spread or overall size of the pattern. Include the firearm and ammunition with the scaled photograph and measurements to enable laboratory determination of firing distance.

2-165.   All ammunition found in the possession of a suspect or at the scene of a crime must be seized and processed as evidence. USACIL may require the seized ammunition to conduct analysis. The laboratory firearms division should be contacted to determine if the seized ammunition is required for laboratory analysis. If required, the ammunition collected as evidence should be packaged and sent to the USACIL for analysis with the firearm.

2-166.   Latent print processing can be very difficult on the parts of firearms that have a slight oily film; however, it is possible to get usable impressions. Latent print fuming techniques typically conducted in the field will not normally hinder analysis by the firearms examiner and does not have an impact on GSR in the barrel or chamber. Other types of processing such as application of fingerprint powder to lift prints should not be conducted; these techniques can affect required analysis. USACIL fingerprint and firearms examiners will coordinate their efforts at the laboratory to ensure that analytical processes are prioritized for optimum results.

Marking Firearm Evidence

2-167.   Firearms evidence should be physically marked so that it can be readily and positively identified later. Firearms may be sealed without being marked, especially if they require examinations for trace evidence, biological evidence, or latent prints; marking the weapon may destroy evidence. Firearms seized or impounded before determination of evidentiary value should not be marked, scratched, or defaced in anyway; these items are marked only after it is determined that the firearm has value as evidence. Common sense should be used in marking antique and/or highly engraved firearms; since the purpose for physically marking is positive identification, it is likely that they can be identified without physically marking the firearm. Physical marking should not be done in areas where latent prints could be found during laboratory processing.

2-168.   The weapon should be marked by placing the investigator's initials and the time and date of recovery on each item of evidence so he can positively identify the evidence at a later date. When several similar items are found, an identifying number should be added on each item. No two items of evidence in the same case should bear the same identifying numbers. The investigator should put a description of each item and all identifying marks involved in the same case in his notes. The identifying number has no bearing on the numbers of the exhibits in the Report of Investigation (ROI).

2-169.   Marking tools may be used for inscribing identifying markings on firearms evidence. Diamond point pencils or scribers are ideal. Dental picks make excellent marking devices when the curved tip is cut off and the point made needle sharp. Firearms are usually marked on the side of the frame. All parts of the firearm that leave imprints on either the bullet or cartridge case should be removed and marked; all parts of a firearm should be marked the same. Place marks where they can be seen but do not interfere with or alter existing markings or stampings on the firearm. Mark magazines on the floor plate (bottom) or on the exterior portion of the magazine body and then submit them with the suspect firearm; rounds in the magazine should be left in place (do not unload the magazine).

2-170.   Mark a conventional 9-millimeter caliber semiautomatic pistol in three places: the barrel that marks the bullet; the slide that contains the extractor, the breech face, and the firing pin; and the receiver that includes the ejector that marks the cartridge case. See figure 2-3, page 2-40, for an example of a marked 9-millimeter pistol. Mark revolvers, especially those with interchangeable cylinders, on both the cylinder and barrel. If the revolver has a removable side plate, mark it on the side of the frame that cannot be removed. See figure 2-4, page 2-40, for an example of a marked revolver. When revolvers having loaded cartridges or fired cases are obtained, make a diagram of the rear face of each cylinder reflecting the exact position in which it was found. Show the position of the loaded cartridges or the fired cases with respect to one another and the firing pin. Scratch an arrow on each side or the rear face of the cylinder (under the firing pin) to show the position that the chamber was in when the revolver was found. This should be done on the revolver and also on the diagram. The diagram, complete with legend, lets the laboratory examiner relate the fired cartridges to the chamber of the cylinder in which they were fired. See figure 2-5, page 2-41, depicts notation of the position of the cartridges in a recovered revolver. Army LE personnel should never disassemble a weapon; the weapon should be rendered safe and remain intact.

2-171.   Firearms with removable bolts, such as a semiautomatic, an automatic, or a bolt-action, should be marked on the bolt, barrel, and frame. If the barrel of a firearm cannot be removed without tools, it does not need to be marked. But marking the barrel, even under these circumstances, adds certainty. A projectile submitted as an exhibit may be jacketed or lead. No markings should be placed on the projectile. Identification marks may cause the loss of trace evidence or evidence marks. Containers, such as pillboxes and plastic vials with cotton packing material can be used for sealing fired bullets. The containers must be sealed with evidence tape. The containers must be marked with the date, time, and initials of the individual packing the evidence so that the markings cross over the sealed tape. If the package is opened before it arrives at USACIL, it will be apparent. Deformed projectiles and jacket fragments must also be placed in a container and marked as described above. Cartridge cases are not marked. They are treated the same as projectiles and then placed in containers. Shotgun shell cases, wads, or shot columns are not marked. Shot pellets, such as bird shot and buckshot, known to be from one source can be placed together in a container. Containers must be marked for identification.

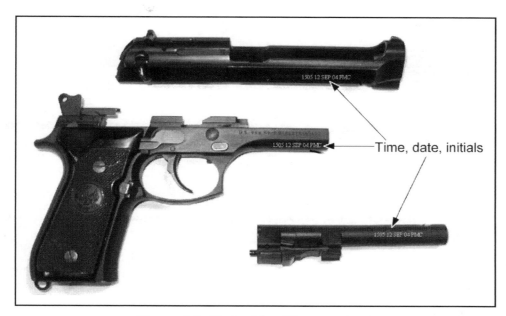

Figure 2-3. Marked 9-millimeter pistol

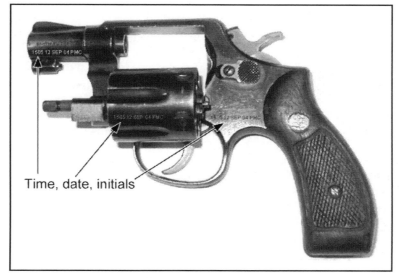

Figure 2-4. Marked revolver

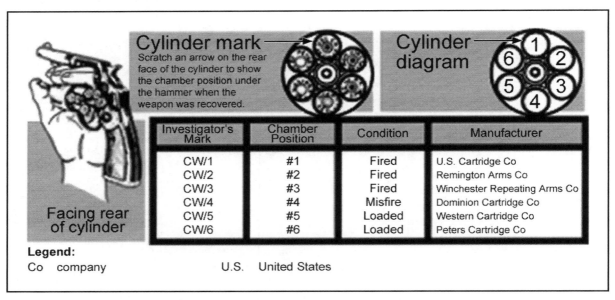

Figure 2-5. Notation of the position of the cartridges in a recovered revolver

TOOLMARKS

2-172. A toolmark is an impression, cut, scratch, gouge, or abrasion made by a tool in contact with an object. Close examination of a toolmark can determine the type, size, and contour of a tool as well as the presence of trace evidence. A tool can make a negative impression, an abrasion or friction mark, or a combination of the two.

2-173. A negative impression is made when a tool is pressed against or into a receptive surface. The mark made by a crowbar used to pry open a door or a window is a negative impression. An abrasion or friction mark is made when a tool cuts into or slides across a surface leaving striations in the object marked by the tool. A pair of pliers, a bolt cutter, a knife, an ax, a saw, a drill, a plane, or a die used in manufacturing can make this type of mark. A combination mark is made, for example, when a crowbar is forced into the space between a door and its facing and pressure is then applied to the handle of the tool to force the door open. The forced insertion of the crowbar makes an abrasion or friction mark. The levering action produces a negative impression. The visible result is a combination of both the friction and a negative impression mark.

2-174. No two tools are alike in every detail; thus, they will not leave identical impressions. Tools may have obvious differences in size, width, thickness, or shape. They also have minute differences that are only seen when the tools are examined under a microscope. These minute differences can be caused by manufacturing, grinding and finishing, and uneven wear from normal use of the tool. They may also be caused by accidents, sharpening, and alterations or modifications made by the users of the tools. From these minute differences, it may be possible to identify the tool that made a given impression. Laboratory examination of toolmarks is based on the same principles and techniques used for fingerprint and firearm identification. Tools leave unique characteristic traces that cannot be exactly reproduced by any other tool. In the laboratory, test marks are made with suspect tools on materials like those on which the toolmarks are present. The test marks are then compared with the suspect toolmarks under a comparison microscope.

COLLECTING TOOLMARK EVIDENCE

2-175. Original evidence (the actual tool and marked object) is always more credible in court than reproductions and should be obtained when possible. Often, photographs and casts do not show the evidence well enough for identification purposes at the laboratory. Casting or other means of taking impressions of a toolmark should only be used as a last resort; a casting is never as good as an original impression. This is especially true of toolmarks made in soft materials like wood, putty, and paint. Many of the casting media suited to these materials will not reproduce the fine details needed for identification. An impression or a cast cannot reproduce scratches in paint from minute irregularities in the edge of a tool.

> *Note.* While original evidence bearing the toolmark is always better than casts, pictures, and other means of documentation, the decision to seize and remove an area bearing a toolmark should be made based on the relative importance of the case and potential value of the evidence compared with other evidence available. Wholesale removal of property or parts of valuable structures is not desired or needed in many cases.

2-176.   When a toolmark is discovered, photograph it with a measuring device in the picture for scale before moving, disturbing, or altering it in any way. Photographs provide a permanent record of the evidence in its original state and location. They are used to match and corroborate original evidence with casts or molds made from the toolmark. They also satisfy the legal requirements for records of original evidence.

2-177.   If a toolmark can be removed for examination in the laboratory, collect a piece of the object holding the toolmark. The piece should be large enough to ensure that the toolmark does not splinter, bend, twist, or receive friction, causing damage to the original toolmark during shipment. This also provides a large enough piece to allow proper marking. If the marked part of a door, window sash, windowsill, or other area is removed for examination, inspect and collect adjacent portions of the area if necessary. Obtain any window latch, door latch, bolt, hasp, or lock that has been cut, broken, or forced for entry. Suspect tools found at the crime scene should be sent to the laboratory with the toolmarks. When submitting toolmark evidence, provide as much information as possible regarding the tool(s) used and the location of the toolmarks to include the—

- Method and angle at which the tool was used when it made the mark, if known.
- Measurements of the toolmark from the floor.
- Location of any door, window, or other object containing the toolmark such as basement, first floor, or second floor.

> *Note.* The ownership of an object removed for analysis should be determined so that the owner can be contacted to arrange for the return, replacement, or payment for the items removed. Ensure that witnesses are present and documented during the removal of the evidence, preferably other Army LE personnel. This prevents later claims against the U.S. Government and provides personnel who can corroborate the original condition of the evidence.

2-178.   Mark each item of evidence to show the inside, outside, top, and bottom surfaces and the area bearing the toolmark, taking care to mark well away from the toolmark. If the surface bearing the toolmark is painted, samples of the paint should be sent to the laboratory. Even though paint could not be seen on the tool, enough particles may be present for analysis and comparison at the laboratory. Since some tools are also painted, there may be paint from the tool on the toolmark surface. This can also be compared for possible common origin.

2-179.   A toolmark may not be removable due to its location or the material in which the toolmark is made. If this is the case, take samples of the area and send them to the laboratory for analysis. Particles of material holding the toolmark may adhere to the tool (such as metal, paint, resins, or other material). The samples can be analyzed and identified by the laboratory examiner. If the toolmark cannot be moved, a cast can be made of the toolmark. These casts are typically made from a silicone or rubber-based product applied to the toolmark. Rubber- and silicone-based products are best for the fine striations and indentions in the toolmark required for matching. Rubber- and silicone-based products designed for casting toolmarks are available in a variety of formulations. They typically require mixing with a hardening agent before application; some manufacturers also market products with accompanying application devices that mix the materials automatically as the product is applied. The silicone is normally pressed into the toolmark with a spatula or wooden tongue depressor. Most silicone-based casting compounds dry in 15 to 20 minutes after application.

2-180. If cut pieces of wire are collected for analysis, clearly mark the suspect end of the wire. Never cut the wire with the suspect tool. The laboratory can sometimes match the cut ends of wire to help identify related items; for example, wire used in a crime matched to a collected spool of like wire or matching a radio wire to the wire attached to a car to show it to be originally from a specific vehicle.

2-181. Wrap and package toolmark evidence so that the toolmark and any suspect tool will not be damaged and trace particles will not be lost. Each piece of evidence sent to the laboratory must be marked for identification and wrapped separately. Evidence samples should not share the same package unless each individual piece is wrapped separately within a larger container to eliminate risk of contact between objects. Cover the cutting blades or tips of the tool to prevent damage. If the item to be examined has to be collected by cutting, always mark the end that is cut by the collector and the questioned end to be examined to ensure there is no confusion.

IDENTIFYING SUSPECT TOOLS

2-182. If a suspect tool is not readily identifiable, a search may be required. To help identify the type of tool to look for, the toolmark should be visually examined to note its gross appearance. This can tell you what type of tool or shape of tool to look for as a suspect tool for comparison analysis. The gross appearance of a tool impression may not be complete or well-defined. For example, a hammer impression on a steel safe may not include the edges of the hammerhead. Thus, the shape of the head cannot be shown. When this occurs, all suspect tools that could have made the mark should be collected and sent to the laboratory to be examined. USACIL can be contacted for assessment and comparison of toolmark images to assist in identifying items that would likely produce the markings discovered.

2-183. The surface that bears the impression of a toolmark may have been painted. If so, a careful check may show that flakes or chips of paint were removed. The paint flakes may be sticking to the tool that made the impression and can be compared to the paint from the impression surface to determine possible common origin. If a tool is found with paint similar to that of the painted surface and the flake patterns look comparable to the paint pattern formation, the tool should be photographed in the event some of the paint flakes become dislodged during transmittal to USACIL. Additionally, flakes of paint could have been removed and transferred from a painted tool to the surface bearing the impression. A trace-evidence examiner can examine paint flakes to determine their origin.

2-184. A suspect tool should never be placed into a toolmark to see if it fits or if it could have made the impression. This could alter the toolmark and prevent any evidence on the tool, the associated mark, or transfer evidence on the tool and the object bearing the toolmark from being admitted as evidence in court.

2-185. If a suspect tool cannot be located, an examination of toolmarks without a suspect tool can still be of value. In such cases, the examination may yield other valuable characteristic information about the tool used and possible trace evidence deposited that can be used as a lead for further investigation. Comparing the toolmarks found at each scene may link a series of burglaries. A match of the lengthwise markings on two pieces of wire may show that both were manufactured at the same time, having been drawn through the same die during production. A suspect's possession of a piece of wire matching a piece found at a crime scene would show the possession was more than accidental.

SERIAL NUMBERS AND OTHER MARKINGS

2-186. Serial numbers or private marks may be stamped, molded, etched, or engraved. Serial numbers are placed on many manufactured objects to distinguish one item or model from another. Owners of items lacking manufacturer's serial numbers often place their own marks or serial numbers on the items. This helps identify the item if it is stolen.

2-187. Serial numbers may consist of numerals, letters, symbols, or a combination of the three. Serial numbers are often the only way to show ownership. Items with serial numbers can often be traced from the manufacturer to the wholesaler and on to the retailer and, potentially the purchaser. Some items, such as automobiles, firearms, and watches, bear serial numbers on several parts. If an object is found and the serial numbers seem to have been removed, the object should be searched for other numbers. Such numbers are often found in hard-to-find places. Restoration of removed or obliterated serial numbers requires processing by laboratory personnel. Neither the material from which an item is made nor the method used to affix the serial number can automatically preclude restoration. Serial numbers have been restored under the most adverse conditions. Conversely, restoration attempts have failed when conditions seemed most favorable.

2-188. Military services buy tools in large quantities and often do not initially record individual serial numbers. Lot numbers and shipping and receiving documents account for the shipments. Sometimes, other means are used to speed the movement of supplies. Often, the manufacturer of a serially numbered item can give the lot number. The manufacturer may also have data of other recorded items bought by military services. As the bulk shipment is broken down for issue to units, the serial numbers are often used for records and identification. Lot numbers or shipping document numbers often narrow the search to the unit of ownership.

2-189. A jeweler's mark is a distinctive mark or symbol, typically placed on a piece of jewelry, watch, or other small item by an individual jeweler who has worked on or created the specific item in question. While jewelers' marks are not serial numbers, their use in tracing stolen property can be of value. When an item is created by a jeweler or given to a jeweler for repair, it is common practice for the jeweler to place a small, identifying mark in a hard-to-see place on the item. This mark is often inscribed with a very fine engraving tool. The mark is engraved under magnification. Therefore, the mark is often visible only when viewed under equal magnification. Jewelers in the same location often know one another's markings. When a mark is found, an attempt should be made to locate the jeweler who inscribed it. The jeweler may be able to identify the person who brought the item to the jewelry shop.

IMPRESSIONS AND CASTS

2-190. Impression evidence is created when a pattern or indentation is retained on the surface of an object or area, typically through transfer of material or pressure. The pattern or indentation left behind retains the characteristics of the object that formed the pattern and can be used to identify the object forming the impression. The most common impressions are from tires, footwear, and toolmarks. Toolmarks were discussed in the previous section.

2-191. Footwear and tires are highly complex and precisely engineered. Features that are incorporated into the manufacture of footwear and tires can become very useful in impression examination. Logos, lettering, numbers, or other markings may be clues to the brand, style, or manufacturer. Expert examiners take advantage of these unique aspects of footwear and tires to place or eliminate individuals at crime scenes. It is what occurs to the footwear and tires after they are put into use that makes them individual and highly identifiable. The individual wear and damage to the friction surfaces makes every item of footwear and every tire unique. Locating and recovering impression evidence requires patience, attention to detail, and some basic techniques.

FOOTWEAR AND TIRE TRACK IMPRESSIONS

2-192. Footwear and tire track impressions can be one of the most overlooked types of evidence at the scene of a crime; largely due to a lack of awareness and training for Army LE personnel regarding the collection and preservation of impression evidence. Crime scenes may contain numerous footwear and tire track impressions from witnesses, police, fire, and medical responders. Army LE personnel should limit foot and vehicle traffic to the absolute minimum level required by response personnel to avoid contaminating a scene with additional impressions and to reduce the chance of destroying evidence left by potential suspects. Impression evidence is typically very fragile and can be destroyed by weather, placement of objects on the impression, or foot or vehicle traffic over the impression, but if protected, impressions can be preserved for a significant period of time. All footwear and/or tire impressions should be documented and collected even if police, fire, and medical responders may have interacted with the scene.

2-193. Impressions can reveal many facts about the footwear or tire that deposited the impression. Recovered impressions can be analyzed to—

- Help determine the type, make or manufacturer, and size of the shoe or tire that left the impression. Do not confuse shoe size with the size of the shoe and tread left behind. Some shoes have larger bases or treads and do not necessarily correspond with a shoe size.
- Identify unique imperfections caused from wear on the surface of the shoe or tire. These unique imperfections can aid in matching the impression to a specific shoe or tire, thus placing the item at the scene; this can help in identification of potential subjects.
- Differentiate separate impressions deposited at a scene. This can help LE personnel determine if a single or multiple subjects are involved and can help in determining paths of entry and exit to the crime scene or incident site.
- Assist in the formation of an accurate reconstruction of the events that took place.
- Corroborate or refute subject and witness accounts of a specific event.

2-194.   There are two different types of impressions—two-dimensional impressions and three-dimensional impressions. Two-dimensional impressions are imprints or patterns left from tires, shoes, or other means deposited on hard surfaces such as concrete, tile, and wood. They leave impressions of width and length but no measurable depth and are typically lifted using techniques similar to those for lifting fingerprints. Three-dimensional impressions are deposited in soft material such as dirt, mud, or other material leaving impressions with measurable width, length, and depth. These impressions are pressed into the material and are typically collecting by casting the impression with a compound that will harden and retain the impression upon removal.

2-195.   Full impressions are not always required to place a perpetrator at the scene; successful identification is often made from partial impressions. Many times footwear impressions are not visible in existing ambient light conditions. Proper lighting and search techniques can assist in locating valuable impression evidence. Most surfaces are conducive to footwear impressions. Surfaces such as rough, uneven carpeting or even masonry should never be discounted without proper examination. Although poor weather conditions can destroy some impressions, this should not be accepted as fact in all cases. Excellent footwear impressions can still be found in mud puddles, under fallen snow, below the overhang of a house, under shrubs, and other places.

IMPRESSION SEARCHES

2-196.   Impression evidence is often overlooked at crime scenes. A systematic and logical approach to locating impression evidence can increase the likelihood of detection and successful collection of impression evidence. A knowledge of the direction of travel, the number of suspects involved, and the mode of transportation (foot or vehicle) can greatly assist the search for impression evidence. In some cases this information may not be known, especially in relatively cold crime scenes or incident sites or outdoor areas where ingress and egress routes may not be known or obvious. In these cases, it is imperative that the entire area be searched, especially likely entry and exit routes around the actual crime scene.

2-197.   Once the scene is secured, the area should be searched systematically using a grid, circle, or other search technique; these techniques are discussed in chapter 4. This ensures that the entire target area is covered. There are specific areas that should be focused on during the search due to the increased probability of deposited impressions. Areas to search for footwear and tire track impressions include—

- The point(s) of entry, both interior and exterior.
- The path or route traveled from the point of entry to the area where the crime occurred.
- The immediate area where the crime took place.
- The path or route traveled from the area where the crime occurred to the point of exit.
- Other identified areas where the perpetrator may have walked, driven, or parked to include beyond the scene.
- The point(s) of exit, both interior and exterior.

Note. Searches beyond the scene can sometimes reveal areas where a vehicle has paused waiting for an accomplice or where a vehicle has been hidden until it was needed.

2-198. Locating impression evidence sometimes requires the Army LE personnel to view the target area from various vantage points with different lighting angles until the best viewing angle and lighting is achieved. Large areas may be searched from the vantage point of a helicopter, if available; this is especially applicable when looking for vehicle tracks or entry and/or exit routes that may not be obvious due to dense vegetation. Latent impressions may be located by using oblique lighting. UV lighting and electrostatic methods can also be used to locate latent impressions.

LIGHTING TECHNIQUES

2-199. Existing lighting conditions should be used first to detect obvious footwear impressions; especially those made in some form of material such as blood, grease, mud, and other visible residues. As each impression is located, it should be marked using a system of placards, signs, or labels with some form of alphanumeric designator that is easily seen and identifiable in a photograph.

2-200. As a general rule, the deeper the impression, the higher the angle required for best visualization. A portable floodlight is most effective; however, a bright flashlight will also work well. A search using oblique lighting is an excellent technique for detecting impressions on smooth surfaces such as flooring and furniture. The area should be darkened, if possible, and searched using a bright, intense light at an oblique, side-lit angle. The light source should be held just above and aimed diagonally (almost parallel) to the surface being searched. Shining the light source diagonally over the target area rather than straight down (vertically) creates shadows caused by the light aimed across the ridges of the impression. Raising and lowering the light will cause the shadows to fall differently in the impression and allow for adjustments for the best possible visualization of the impression. Impressions on carpeting or other rough or porous surfaces may still be invisible even with the oblique light; UV light sources may be effective in locating latent impressions.

CHEMICAL SEARCHES

2-201. Chemical searches are often necessary to detect and develop latent footwear impressions such as faint blood impressions. The techniques used for latent footwear impressions are similar to those used in identifying and lifting fingerprint evidence and should be performed by trained laboratory personnel. When an impression is suspected, the floor, substrate, or other surface should be removed and sent to the laboratory for processing. In some instances, on-scene assistance from laboratory personnel may be necessary.

COLLECTION AND PRESERVATION

2-202. Both footwear and tire track impressions are collected and preserved using the same methods and techniques. Footwear and tire track impressions are extremely fragile in nature. Environmental elements, improper safeguarding of the scene, time, and improper processing and collection techniques can often destroy this type of evidence.

2-203. Impressions must be collected and preserved as close to their original state as possible to be useful. The evidence should be protected from destruction by natural elements or accidental damage; this can be done by covering it with a clean trash can lid, cardboard box, or another suitable object. Large areas may have to be cordoned off, and guards may need to be posted. A suspect's footwear must never be placed in or near a crime scene impression because it could contaminate the impression and jeopardize its integrity, making future findings invalid.

Photographs

2-204. Impressions must be photographed before any attempts to cast or lift the impression. Photography establishes the integrity of the evidence and is one of the best techniques for capturing and preserving impressions. A measurement scale or ruler must always appear in the evidence photograph. Photographs should be taken at a 90-degree angle to the impression. Fill the field with the measuring device visible in the screen. Ensure lighting is oblique (not directly on top of the impression) and does not wash out the details but enhances and illuminates them. Both general crime scene photographs and examination quality photographs should be taken. See chapter 4 for a detailed discussion of evidence and crime scene photography. These photographs—

- Document the evidence and establish the location and orientation of the impression in relation to its surroundings.
- Provide a photograph with enough quality and clarity to enable evaluation, comparison, identification, and verification by evidence examiners.

Lifting Two-Dimensional Impressions

2-205.   The optimum method for collecting a two-dimensional impression is to collect and properly protect the object (or portion of the object) containing the impression. When the item bearing the impression cannot be readily removed from the crime scene, or removal and shipment is not cost effective, the impression should be lifted. Coordination should be made with the USACIL before the collection and shipment of this type of evidence. Examples of situations requiring an impression to be lifted include—

- Footwear impressions on doors of vehicles.
- Footwear impressions on immovable or heavy objects.
- Dusty tire track or footwear impressions on a garage or warehouse floor.
- Impressions on a heavy, bulky, valuable, or sensitive surface or item.

2-206.   There are multiple methods available for lifting two-dimensional impression evidence. These methods are similar to those used for lifting fingerprints, but typically require larger lifting mediums to accommodate the size of the impression. Methods for lifting impressions include standard lifters, rubber or gelatin lifters, electrostatic lifters, and chemical processes. Most standard lifters are not useful in lifting footwear impressions. They are normally too small to work effectively and are too tacky. Even though some products are specifically cut to footwear size, many have backing that are too flimsy causing air bubbles and distorting the impression.

2-207.   Rubber and gelatin lifters (also called gel lifters) differ from standard fingerprint lifters and are excellent for footwear impressions. They are made with reduced adhesive properties and can be used successfully on fragile surfaces. They are soft and pliable and can lift good detail from rough surfaces. Rubber and gel lifters can provide excellent results in lifting footwear impressions and come in a variety of colors and sizes. Contrast must be considered when using rubber or gel lifters. If the footwear impression is in dust, the black gel lifters are typically the best choice; if the impression is in a darker substance, white gel typically works best. The collected image is always in the reversed position after using rubber or gel lifters to lift it and must be reversed at the laboratory using photographic techniques. Electrostatic lifting should be considered before attempting to lift an impression with a rubber or gelatin lifter.

2-208.   An electrostatic dust print lifter is a device used to make lifts of dry surfaces and substances, such as dust, powder, and other lightweight dry residues and debris deposited in impression evidence. It works by applying a static electrical charge to a thin piece of Mylar® film; typically by using a portable power source. The statically charged Mylar® film attracts the dust particles to the film, collecting the impression. It is a highly effective method of collection and renders excellent detail suitable for identification. Considerations for using electrostatic lifting include the following:

- An electrostatic dust print lifter can be used on porous or nonporous evidence.
- The technique is considered to be nondestructive and may be used for searching as well as for collecting. Blind searches can be made by laying out the film over an area suspected to contain latent dust impressions, charging the film, and examining the lift. This works well on carpeted entrance and exit ways.
- Lifts can be made of vertical surfaces. Lifts can be made on doors and walls, by taping the film to the surface and lifting as normal.
- Electrostatic lifts are very fragile. The film may continue to holds much of its charge even after the collection process and continues to attract dust and particles, which can obscure the impression. Over time the charge can dissipate and the collected dust forming the impression could move or fall from the film. Impressions lifted by electrostatic means should be photographed as soon as possible, in the manner discussed previously, to ensure that the

impression is recorded. The film should be placed in a suitable box and sealed as soon as possible to prevent damage. A flat, sturdy box (such as a photographic paper box, shirt box, or clean unused pizza box) is recommended for collection of this type of impression. Wipe out the box before use to clean away dust or paper residue. Place the film in the bottom of the box with the impression side (dark side) up. Secure the film to the bottom of the box by taping down its four corners. Close the box and tape shut all the edges of the boxes, making it nearly airtight.

2-209.   The static or cling vinyl lifter is another option for lifting prints from dry surfaces and substances, such as dust, powder, and other lightweight dry residues and debris deposited in impression evidence. Cling vinyl works similar to an electrostatic dust print lifter to capture dust impressions; however, its advantage is that no equipment beyond the vinyl sheet is required. The sheets can be carried in a folder or duty bag, are sized to capture most shoe prints, and require minimal training. Like other lifters, these vinyl lifters can be purchased commercially in a variety of sizes and colors.

2-210.   There is a wide range of chemical processing techniques available to develop and lift impressions. However, trained laboratory personnel must perform all chemical processing of impressions in an approved laboratory facility. Laboratory examiners and technicians are trained to use many types of chemical processes in a safe and efficient manner. The premature or improper use of chemical processes in the field can result in the loss and/or damage of impressions. Most chemical processes will fade and often disappear before proper photography and comparison of the evidence.

Casting Three-Dimensional Impressions

2-211.   When casting a three-dimensional impression, there are several steps to consider. Each step is important to ensure that the impression is protected from destruction and contamination and it is properly preserved and documented. The steps for casting an impression are as follows:
- **Step 1.** Prepare the impression.
- **Step 2.** Prepare the casting material.
- **Step 3.** Cast the impression.

Preparing the Impression

2-212.   To obtain a good cast, it is sometimes necessary to prepare the impression. The impression must always be photographed first. When the impression is located outdoors, it should be determined whether any debris might have blown into it. Carefully remove debris using a pocketknife or tweezers. Do not attempt to remove debris that is part of the impression or was present when the impression was made. Impressions that are made over rocks, sticks, or other debris can reveal excellent reproduction or detail in the immediate area of the foreign matter; attempting to remove the material can destroy the detail. If loose material such as leaves, twigs, or blown trash has managed to fall into the impression after it was made, it can be carefully removed.

2-213.   A practice cast of an impression created by LE personnel in the same material as the suspect impression may be cast to determine the strength of the ground and its ability to withstand casting. It may be necessary to strengthen the soil in which the impression is found by spraying it with a plastic spray or lacquer. Hair spray and spray paint may also be used. Spraying directly on the print may damage individual characteristics used to effect identification. Instead, direct the spray against cardboard or other material so that a fine mist settles gently into the print. Allow it to dry and then resprayed. The number of coats required can be determined by conducting the same procedure on a test impression. Three to ten coats are not unusual in sandy soil. Thin coats are better than heavy coats, which can damage the impression.

Preparing the Casting Material

2-214.   In most cases dental stone or die stone is the best casting material for footwear and tire impressions. Plaster materials are not recommended; they do not dry quickly, mix uniformly, and are not as strong as dental or die stone and are more prone to breakage after casting. Dental stone is much more durable and stronger than other casting materials; it dries faster, captures greater detail, does not require reinforcement materials, and does not require frames. Dental stone is readily available from local dental supply companies or military dental facilities in emergency situations.

2-215.   Dental stone comes in a powder form and can be premeasured and stored in large plastic, sealable bags. Normally about 6 ounces of water to every 1 pound of dental stone provides the appropriate consistency. A typical footwear impression requires about 2 to 3 pounds of dental stone and 12 to 15 ounces of water. A clean beverage can (which typically holds 12 ounces) makes a good field expedient measuring device for the proper amounts of water. Large batches of dental stone are required in casting tire tracks; the exact amount is dependent on the size of the track being cast. Dental stone is very forgiving. If the mixture is too dry, more water can be added; if the mixture is too wet, more dental stone is added. The water is simply poured into the bag of premeasured dental stone powder. The materials (powder and water) are mixed inside the plastic bag by kneading the mixture until it is thoroughly mixed and uniform in consistency. A good mixture is typically about the consistency of pancake batter; it is better to have a mixture a little too thin rather than too thick. This technique should be practiced before actual impressions are collected.

Casting the Impression

2-216.   When using dental stone, forms are seldom required as long as the surface is somewhat level. On surfaces with extreme slopes, forms can be purchased or built and placed around the impression to hold the casting material. A partial form can be used for slight slopes to control the flow of castings on the lower side of the impression. A good technique is to cut off the bottom corner of the plastic bag used to mix the stone and allow the mixture to flow out of the hole; the mixture should not be poured directly into the impression. The mixture should be poured by holding the opening at ground level next to the edge of the impression (on the high side if there is a slope) and allowing the mixture to flow onto the ground and into the impression. If the impression is deeper in one area, pouring the mixture into the deep end first can also slow the flow through the rest of the impression.

2-217.   If the material is flowing too rapidly, use pieces of cardboard or other stiff materials to deflect and slow the flow of liquid to prevent damage to the impression when pouring the cast. Once the entire surface of the impression is covered, gently overfill it with any excess material to build the thickness of the cast for strength. If necessary, a second batch can be poured directly over the first. When casting a tire impression, an entire rotation of each available tire impression should be cast in removable segments. Cast the track in 12- to 18-inch segments. Reinforce the cast with tongue depressors or screen material if the cast is over 12 inches long. Dams to establish the edges of each segment must be emplaced. These can be formed with stiff cardboard and tape, or commercially produced adjustable dams can be purchased and used.

2-218.   After pouring the casting material, but before it dries, the cast should be marked for identification. The data can be written into the surface of the cast using a paper clip, toothpick, or similar item to make a permanent marking. The minimum data should be the investigator's initials and the time and date. If known, the case number should also be inscribed. An arrow indicating north may be inscribed in the cast to help determine the relationship of the cast to other evidence and help to prove the direction of travel. If the impression has been marked for photography, the identifying number or letter used should also be annotated on the cast.

2-219.   Typical footwear casts will be sufficiently dry to enable collection after approximately 30 to 45 minutes; extreme heat or cold may alter the drying time. After collection, the cast should be allowed to dry another 72 hours before packaging and shipping to the laboratory. The cast should not be cleaned; laboratory personnel will perform any required cleaning before processing. Cleaning techniques and equipment can damage and scratch the surface of the cast, rendering it useless and destroying its individual characteristics.

Special Casting Considerations

2-220.   Impressions are not always found on dry surfaces. Sometimes impressions can be found in water or snow. It is possible to retrieve castings of impressions left in water or snow if the proper technique is applied.

Snow Casting

2-221.   Impressions in snow can be cast by stabilizing the impression and the area immediately around it with a spray wax. A spray wax made specifically for impression recovery should be used. After stabilizing the impression with the spray wax, photographs should be taken. The spray wax will provide better contrast in the photograph. A single can of spray wax is normally enough for about three impressions.

2-222.   The spray wax should be cured for approximately 15 minutes before the dental stone mixture is poured into the impression. Use water that is as cold as possible to mix with the dental stone for the best results. This reduces the risk of melting the snow before the cast can be formed. One technique is to set a bucket of water in the snow while working and add snow to the water until the snow stops melting. This is a good indication that the water is cold enough not to melt the snow in the impression. Pour the dental stone slowly into the impression, not off to the side as in other impressions. If it is poured off to the side, especially if the snow is deep, the impression could cave in. Allow the cast to dry, then removed it from the snow. The snow should not be removed from the cast; it should be allowed to melt away and then air-dried indoors for 72 hours before packaging for shipment to the laboratory. If spray wax is not available, a contrasting spray paint can be used as a substitute. While not as strong as spray wax, spray paint can highlight the print for photography and can provide a strong enough coating to seal and stabilize the impression for casting.

Water Casting

2-223.   It is possible to cast an impression that is submerged beneath the water, especially in puddles of water and at the edges or banks of a lake or stream. Sometimes it is possible to dam around the impression and siphon off most of the water; experience has shown that it is not a good idea to siphon away all of the water because the water sometimes acts as a stabilizer for the impression. If possible, a form should be placed around the impression extending above the waterline; the form should not be placed so close to the impression that it will disturb or destroy the impression.

2-224.   After removing as much water as possible, slowly sprinkle dry dental stone over the impression, allowing it to precipitate down through the water and into the impression. A flour sifter or large saltshaker can help evenly disperse the dental stone. Continue this process until the cast begins to build up. Allow about one inch of dental stone to settle into the impression. While the dry dental stone settles and builds within the impression, prepare a mixture of dental stone and water (enough to completely fill the framed area). Pour the mixture into the framed area of the impression, displacing the water from the impression. If framing the impression was not possible, pour enough mixture to slightly overfill the impression. Allow at least two hours of drying time before removing the cast from the impression. The cast should be fully air dried (minimum of 72 hours) before shipping to the laboratory for examination. The cast should not be cleaned.

2-225.   Casts must be carefully packaged since they are fragile evidence. One of the most important considerations in sending a cast to the laboratory is ensuring that the cast is completely dry. Casts that are not dry may develop fungus and subsequently deteriorate. Casts should not be packaged in plastic wrappings, only dry paper. Plastic promotes moisture and moisture promotes decay. Other packaging considerations are the same as for preparing evidence to be sent to the laboratory. However, the outer packaging should state "Do Not Refrigerate" as refrigeration damages the cast. Submit all shoes, tires, and casts using a chain of custody document.

QUESTIONED DOCUMENTS

2-226.   For many investigations, a document or a document-related item becomes evidence of the crime or about a suspect who committed a crime. Often, a document is the instrument of the crime. A questioned document is any document collected as evidence in an investigation in which the authenticity or reliability may be challenged in a criminal, civil, or administrative proceeding. The Questioned Document Division, USACIL, conducts forensic examinations of document evidence. Examinations commonly conducted include handwriting and handprinting comparison, alteration and obliteration examinations, typewriting examinations, photocopy examinations, and other nonchemical examinations relating to document evidence.

HANDWRITING AND HANDWRITING COMPARISONS

2-227.   A forensic document examiner conducts handwriting examinations by comparing the writing on the questioned document to the collected writings and standards (known writings) submitted. Handwriting and handprinting identification is based on the many individual characteristics that distinguish each individual's writing from that of others. In natural writing, these characteristics are made by habit, and the writer is not usually consciously aware of them. In handwriting and handprinting examinations, these characteristics are compared to determine if there are enough matching characteristics or different characteristics to support the identification or elimination of a writer. These characteristics can include the—

- Size.
- Slant.
- Letterforms.
- Proportions.
- Height relationships.
- Beginning and ending strokes.
- Connecting strokes.
- Characteristics of 'i" dots" and "t" crossings.
- Spacing.
- Baseline habit.

Line Quality

2-228.   Line quality is perhaps the single most important characteristic evaluated in the comparison of handwriting for identification. The success of a handwriting comparison is largely dependent on the naturalness of the writings involved (both the questioned and the known). Anything other than natural writing is, to some degree, artwork. The authorship of artwork is not identifiable because it does not contain the habitual, unconscious writing habits that make handwriting identifiable. Line quality is the tool the document examiner uses to gauge the naturalness of the writing submitted for comparison. An awareness of the difference between good and poor line quality in writing can help investigators identify possible forgeries when screening records during an investigation and enable recognition of efforts to disguise dictated exemplars created by a suspect.

2-229.   The natural writing of a skilled writer flows smoothly. The beginning and ending strokes are tapered because the pen is moving when it touches the paper and when it is removed from the paper. Long curving strokes are smooth in their curving movements and free of tremor or signs of hesitation. Vertical up and down strokes display natural variation in pen pressure by changes in the width and darkness of the ink line. Connecting strokes between small internal letters are regular direction changes, short smooth curves, and small well-formed loops. There is an absence of false starts and retouching. They appear to have been rapidly and reflexively written, without conscious thought about the writing process. Handwriting with poor line quality lacks one or more of these features.

2-230.   Poor line quality sometimes appears in genuine writing. Illness or injury may affect the quality of the written product. Fear or stress may influence the skill displayed by the writer. Handwriting ability may be affected by the ingestion of drugs and alcohol. The conditions under which a person writes may also detract from the quality of the written line. It is very difficult to write fluently while riding in the back seat of a moving vehicle or when the paper is resting on the rough surface of a well-used field table.

2-231.   Poor line quality may also be the result of a writer forging, tracing, or simulating the handwriting habits of someone else. Signs of tracings or simulations include blunt beginning and ending strokes; a tremulous writing line indicative of slow, careful drawing; curved lines which lack smoothness; corrected mistakes; and misinterpretations of letterforms. Unskilled forgers are also prone to patch, touch up, or try to improve a completed forgery. Poor line quality can also be indicative of disguised writing and efforts by an individual to consciously control their writing. Indicators of disguised writing are inconsistent letterforms, bizarre letterforms, unnaturally large or small writing, extreme angularity, and excessively elaborate writing. In an effort to hamper handwriting identification, the suspect may disguise both questioned and exemplars.

Copies as Evidence

2-232.   Original documents, rather than copies, must be obtained as evidence when they are available. Originals are the best evidence to present in court and are the best for the purpose of forensic examinations. Some forensic examinations can only be performed on an original document. Handwriting comparisons using copies typically yield poorer results than could have been obtained with an original.

2-233.   An original document may not be available because it cannot be located or has been destroyed. In other cases, a copying process has been used to fabricate a document that did not exist as an original. In these cases, a copy is obtained as evidence. It is important to get the best copy available. If a copy has been used as the instrument of a crime, the specific copy used should be obtained. If a copy is obtained as a substitute for a missing original, every attempt should be made to locate and obtain a copy that was made directly from the original. Avoid getting copies of copies.

2-234.   If an original document exists, but is not available, then a copy of the original must be obtained to use as evidence. A copy should be obtained even if there is an expectation that the original can be obtained later. The copy the investigator submits to the USACIL for examination must be the evidence copy, not a case file copy or a copy made especially for laboratory submission. If expert testimony or a laboratory report will be used in court, the same copy examined by the laboratory examiner must also be introduced as evidence in court. Whether the evidence is an original or a copy, it must be accounted for according to AR 195-5.

Court Authentication

2-235.   For expert testimony or a laboratory report to be admitted as evidence in a trial, the evidence examined must have been admitted as evidence. To be admitted, the evidence must be authenticated, that is, shown to be what its proponent claims. The presiding judge decides authentication and admissibility. It is important to be aware of this requirement with regard to exemplars. Dictated exemplars may be authenticated by the testimony of the investigator who obtained them. Standards may be authenticated by one of several means. The investigator should review section IX of the MRE (specifically rules 901, 902, and 903) or Federal Rules of Evidence (as appropriate) and consult the servicing JA.

COLLECTION OF QUESTIONED DOCUMENTS

2-236.   Any collected questioned documents must be protected from damage, and the facts surrounding the collection should be documented. The investigator should take detailed notes describing the circumstances of the collection of the questioned document. All of this information may be of value later in the investigation or in any criminal, civil, or administrative proceedings. These notes should include the—

- Place, time, and date the document was collected.
- Name of the person providing the document, if applicable.
- Exact location where the document was found or retrieved.
- Condition of the document.
- Identifying markings placed on the document.
- Information about the history and contents of the document.
- Handling and disposition of the document.

2-237.   Care should be taken to protect question documents from damage or contamination. Questioned documents may hold trace evidence or latent prints retrievable by laboratory examiners. Any tears, indentions, or stains added to the document can destroy evidence and degrade the ability of examiners to make definitive findings. The following measures should be applied to protect collected documents:

- Handle the questioned documents with tweezers or cloth gloves whenever possible. The document may need to be examined for fingerprints or other trace evidence; this limits the chance of adding fingerprints or other material to the document. For safety purposes always use nitrile gloves when handling question documents that may be contaminated with chemicals or biological fluids.

- Never fold, crumple, staple, or carry a questioned document unprotected in a pocket or container with other material or evidence that may damage the document. Never clip two or more questioned documents together. Collected documents should be placed within a protective cover. A paper envelope large enough to easily accommodate the document is the best method to protect the evidence; the document should never be folded to fit the envelope or container.
- Never write on the envelope with the document inside; this can leave indentations on the document that can affect the examiners findings. Documents should be handled so that any indented markings are not destroyed or added.
- Do not subject the document to strong light for prolonged periods. The document may be viewed with a UV light for a short time to compare or contrast its fluorescence or reflectance with other similar documents or possible paper sources.
- Place torn documents in a protective covering with the pieces placed in the most obvious and logical positions. Do not attempt to make repairs on a document that is torn or otherwise damaged. Do not attempt to straighten crumpled paper; package it in a container large enough for the crumpled paper to rest unaltered.

2-238. The questioned document should be marked for identification to distinguish it from other documentary evidence and to enable positive identification by Army LE personnel at a later date. Use a pencil for the markings and place the markings in a location less likely to have been handled by the suspect. Examine the document carefully to find an inconspicuous location to mark the document with their initials, date, and time of collection. The location of the mark should not interfere with any writings or impressions on the document; a corner on the back of a document is most commonly used. The location and how the document was marked should be documented in the investigators notes. Copies of the questioned document should be made for use during the investigation. The original must then be placed in the evidence depository until the laboratory requires it for examination. Photocopying and photographing are acceptable methods for making copies. Avoid feeding the document through any kind of sheet-feeding mechanism; this could result in damage to the document.

2-239. An evidence tag should be attached to the outside of the envelope or other container holding the document. When shipping to the laboratory for examination, wrap the protected document with enough heavy wrapping material to prevent it from being bent, torn, or folded in transit; placing the document (within its protective envelope) between two stiff pieces of cardboard works well. Transparent plastic document protectors are generally not suitable for use in packaging document materials. If plastic document protectors are used they should be of acid free material designed for protecting fragile documents. Print applied by typewriters, printers, and photocopiers may stick to the plastic and be lifted off the paper.

2-240. Questioned documents often document valuable transactions between a victim and another party. Evidence of these transactions can be important to both criminal and civil proceedings. The victim may need the document returned for use as evidence in a civil proceeding to recover losses suffered from a fraudulent transaction. A property receipt should be provided to the person providing the document to enable the return of the document upon conclusion of the investigation and any criminal trial. The receipt should describe the document in enough detail to permit future identification. The description should be limited to the physical aspects of the document.

Interviews Related to Questioned Documents

2-241. All persons that were affected by or handled the document should be interviewed. For example, in a case concerning a forged check, the investigator should question the cashier or the teller who accepted the check, the person whose signature had been allegedly forged, and a representative of the bank on which the check was drawn. Any bank, business, or other organization that will be affected by the questioned document should be contacted. Information about past dealings with the person whose signature was allegedly forged may give helpful clues. Other incidents in which the same forms or method of operation were used may be discovered.

2-242. If the document was prepared or signed in the presence of a witness, the witness should be questioned about the person preparing the document and the method of preparation. This information can be used to eliminate suspects or to confirm suspects from which exemplars should be obtained. Witnesses should be interviewed to determine facts including—

- The number of suspects and other individuals present.
- A description of the suspect's appearance.
- The suspect's actions leading up to, during, and immediately following any document preparation or transaction.
- Conversations by the suspect.
- Any identification or names used.
- The writer's physical state at the time the document was written including whether the writer was nervous, intoxicated, or physically impaired as a result of injury or illness.
- Specifics pertaining to document preparation including whether the document was written—
  - With the right or left hand.
  - Quickly or slowly.
  - On top of other papers or on an irregular, soft or hard surface.
- The method or reason the document was identified as false or questionable.

2-243. All victims and witnesses should be asked to name any possible suspects and the reasons for their suspicions. This list, along with persons of interest identified by investigators, should be used to check on victims and suspects to determine potential motive and opportunity. These victim and suspect checks can include examining their—

- Financial status.
- Interrelationships.
- Business practices.
- Emotional stability.
- Major life events such as death of family or close associates, ongoing or recently diagnosed major illnesses, recent marriage or divorce, financial windfalls or losses, or legal troubles (either civil or criminal).

2-244. In some cases, a questioned document must be shown to a victim or suspect. If a signature on a questioned document is that of a known person, that person should be interviewed to verify that he or she denies writing or signing the document. If possible, avoid showing a questioned document to a victim or potential subject until after dictated exemplars are obtained. If the document must be shown to a victim or potential subject before obtaining an exemplar sample, there should be a significant time lag between the two actions so that the format of the questioned document is not fresh in the individual's mind.

2-245. The document should not be handled by the victim or potential subject as it may negate a latent fingerprint examination. Always obtain and submit exemplars of the victim for laboratory examination. Exemplars of the victim can assist the document examiner in determining whether a questioned writing is a simulation of the victim's writing style; it may also confirm that the victim of a case may have actually made the questioned writing.

Known Writings

2-246. Handwriting and handprinting examinations are done by comparison. The known writings, also referred to as standards or exemplars, must be comparable in kind to the questioned writing. Handwriting (cursive writing) generally must be compared to handwriting; handprinting generally must be compared to handprinting. Capital letters must be compared to capital letters. Lowercase letters must be compared to lowercase letters. The exemplars must be representative, meaning it must contain the same words or, at least, the same letters and letter combinations as the questioned writings. Both standards and exemplars have advantages and disadvantages; when possible both types of documents should be collected.

Collected Known Writings (Standards)

2-247.   Collected writings are obtained from various sources that the writer prepared for purposes usually unrelated to the investigation. For example, they may include military records, other government documents, employment documents, financial records, personal correspondence, or negotiated personal checks. The advantage of these types of standards is that they were usually written naturally with no intent to disguise the appearance. Multiple samples can also show the individual's writing over a period of time. The disadvantages are that they may not be fully comparable to the questioned writing and the number available may be limited.

Dictated Known Writings (Exemplars)

2-248.   Dictated writings are prepared under the supervision of the investigator. The advantage of this type of writing is that the form used, the content of the writing, the type of writing, the number of samples prepared, and the manner in which the writings are prepared can be controlled. The main disadvantages are that the writer may attempt to disguise the writing and the writings only show the individual's writing as it appears on a single occasion. Dictated exemplars are obtained as follows:

*   Obtain the questioned document and standards first.
*   Be familiar with the appearance of the individual's natural writing.
*   Obtain paper or forms similar to the questioned document.
*   Use a writing instrument similar to that used for the questioned document. If the writing instrument is not an ordinary ballpoint pen, obtain some writing samples with a black ballpoint pen.
*   Provide a material for the subject to write on that is similar in paper size, quality, and arrangement to that on which the questioned document was written—similar quality bond paper, pad paper, or blank forms (such as government forms or checks). When using copies of forms or checks, ensure that they are clean copies with white backgrounds (not gray, dark, or patterned) so that the writing is readable.
*   Use a copy of the questioned document to dictate the questioned text and ensure comparability of the exemplars.
*   Do not allow the subject to see the questioned document.
*   Have the writer positioned in a natural position during the dictated writing (sitting or standing).
*   Dictate the questioned writing to the writer at a comfortable writing speed.
*   Provide no assistance to the writer for spelling or format of text on the paper or form.
*   Include all entries that the person may have written on forms, checks, or other formatted documents. Obtain several examples without giving the writer any instructions; as each sample is completed, remove it from the writer's sight. If instructions are necessary to ensure comparability (such as cursive versus printing or capital versus lowercase letters), document the instructions given on the back of the first sample to which it applies. Each sample should be numbered sequentially and marked with the investigator's initials and the time and date. If the writer is suspected of trying to disguise their writing, additional samples should be obtained.
*   Do not collect multiple samples, such as signatures, on the same sheet of paper. Obtain writings on one side of the paper, only. If the questioned document has writing on both sides, the back should be duplicated separately.
*   Collect multiple exemplars of each writing sample from the individual using their strong hand. The strong hand is the right-hand for a right handed person and the left hand for a left-handed person. If there is evidence that the individual is ambidextrous, obtain samples from both hands as if they are both strong hands. There is no set standard for the number of samples to be taken; however, as a general rule obtain—
    *   About 25 repetitions for questioned signatures, personal checks, and similar brief writings.
    *   About 10-15 samples for questioned documents about the length of a short note.
    *   One complete repetition of the text plus additional repetitions of important parts, such as admissions or text that establishes a motive or supports the elements of the crime, for

questioned text that is one or more full pages in length. If there is no one part of a questioned document that is deemed significant, consider getting additional repetitions of the first and last paragraphs.

- One to three samples written with the individual's weak hand (the hand that he does not normally use for writing). If the person shows real ability with this hand, or if the writing bears strong similarity to the questioned document, more samples should be obtained.

2-249. For documents that contain classified words or phrases, dictated exemplars may be made without the classified information if the subject you are obtaining the exemplars from does not possess the appropriate level of clearance to be made aware of the classified material. In this case, the use of this language must present a national security risk to justify excluding it from the exemplar.

2-250. If omitting the classified portion and substituting similar words can produce an acceptable dictated sample, this technique should be used. In these cases, words with the same letters and letter combinations as the classified words should be substituted. Ensure that the dictated words chosen include the beginning and ending letters of the eliminated words or phrases. The substitute words should be in the same position in the sentence. The Questioned Document Division at the USACIL can provide guidance in these cases. Close coordination with the servicing JA is recommended before making any decisions on how to proceed with the collection and/or alteration of this type of exemplar as evidence.

Tracings and Simulations

2-251. A tracing is a duplicate of another individual's writing, typically a signature, made using the writing line of a genuine writing as a model or guide. Several methods may be used to duplicate another person's writing. The most common methods involve viewing the model through the paper onto which the tracing will be placed, with or without the aid of backlighting, or transferring a guideline from the model signature to another piece of paper using carbon paper or other means. A simulation is a freehand imitation of another individual's writing, typically a signature. It commonly involves the use of a genuine writing as a model. Both tracings and simulations may show signs of having been slowly drawn.

2-252. The author of a tracing or simulation usually cannot be identified by handwriting comparison because these writings are not the author's natural handwriting. However, tracings and simulations may retain enough identifying characteristics to enable a successful comparison with the specific genuine writing used as a model to produce it. Investigators must attempt to identify and seize the genuine writing that was used as a model when a tracing or simulation is suspected. Tracings are usually identified by pen lifts, stops and starts, and hesitation in writing where ink pools or is darker in places along the signature.

Writings on Walls or Similar Surfaces

2-253. Some questioned writings are written on walls, doors, and similar surfaces. Questioned writing on walls and similar surfaces must be photographed. Ideally, photographs should be taken using a normal focal length lens from a position directly in front of the writing using available light. The photograph should include all of the writing, along with a scale indicating size. Lack of space or size of the questioned writing sample may make it necessary to use overlapping photographs (photographs taken from a variety of angles or a wide-angle lens). It may also be necessary to use a flash or other artificial light. A flash pointed directly at a flat surface usually produces a glare in the center of the photograph that obliterates the writing. Consider using a bounced, diffused, or low-angle flash; a variety of approaches may be tried to ensure usable results.

2-254. If possible, remove the surface area with the writing to secure the writing as evidence. If possible, dictated known writing should be obtained in a manner that duplicates the original writing to compare with such questioned writings. Large sheets of paper taped to a wall or a large tablet on an easel may be used to simulate the vertical surface and the large writing size of the questioned writing.

Writing Indentations and Alterations

2-255. Writing indentations are produced when the pressure of writing on a sheet of paper is transmitted to the sheet or sheets of paper beneath it. This often occurs with writing on tablets or pads of paper. It can also occur on loose sheets and any other paper underneath the sheet being written on. Writing indentations can be important in many types of investigations, but they can be especially helpful in cases involving anonymous notes. The note may bear indentations of earlier writing that can identify the writer.

2-256. It may be possible to read writing indentations in the field with the help of a light held at a low angle to the page. Do not attempt any other method, such as a pencil or fingerprint powder, to enhance these indentations. The Questioned Document Division at the USACIL is equipped to develop and preserve writing indentations, even those too faint to see. When handling possible indentation evidence, ensure that no new indentations are added to documents collected for examination. Protect the document with cardboard or place it in a rigid container. Ensure that it is not placed beneath other documents or in an envelope that will be written on.

2-257. An alteration occurs when someone tries to change a document or obliterate part of the text on a document. A superimposed signature block on a second document is also a form of alteration. Varying font sizes and types, misaligned margins, and tell-tale lines along the center of the page are indicative of a document where the signature has been cut and copied onto a second document. Documents with either known or suspected alteration can be submitted to the Questioned Document Division at the USACIL. The USACIL can attempt to determine if an alteration has occurred or decipher the original entry that was altered or obliterated.

Typewritten Documents

2-258. Typewritten questioned document can sometimes be linked to the typewriter used to type the document. For a positive comparison to be possible, the typewriter or the typing element (if present) must have developed individual characteristics, usually in the form of damage or other mechanical defects, which appear on documents typed on the machine in question. Typewritten text from a typewriter with no individual characteristics may not be distinguishable from that of another typewriter of the same make and model in good condition. The individual characteristics may include damaged letters, alignment problems, or other things. On typewriters of the older, type bar design, the individual characteristics belong to the typewriter. On newer, single-element (such as daisy wheel or ball element) typewriters, the individual characteristics are likely to be on a removable typing element. It is important to locate the typing element used to type the questioned document.

2-259. It may be possible to reduce the number of suspect typewriters or typing elements by doing a field comparison of the type style on the questioned document with the type style of the typewriters or typing elements available. General steps for a field comparison include the following:

- **Step 1.** Identify any obvious differences in type size, style, and spacing. A very different type size or type style may indicate that a different typing element (in the case of removable element machines) or typewriter (in the case of type bar machines) is involved. On older machines, different letter spacing such as 10 characters per inch versus 12 characters per inch can narrow the search to a specific machine; on newer typewriters, this setting can be changed.
- **Step 2.** Examine the typed characters, specifically—
  - Check the upper and lowercase letters of the "M" and "W" first, as they are often the most distinctive in style. Their differences may be easily recognized. The bottom of the staffs of the lowercase letters may or may not have serifs (cross strokes) at the bottom. The two outside staffs may have serifs, and the center staffs none. The center V-like formation of the capital M may descend to the baseline or stop varying distances above it. If it descends to the baseline, it may or may not have a serif. The inverted V of the center formation of the W may or may not extend to the top of the line formed by the outer portions of the letter and may or may not have a serif at the top.
  - Check other characters. Characters other than the "M" and "W" that typically are prone to designs that help distinguish between typestyles are the letters g, t, a, r, y, i, f, and the numerals. Again, look for positioning of the letters in relation to each other and the baseline and any obviously unique flaws in the letter or number. If the letters and numerals are not distinguishable with ease, submit typewriter exemplars standards to the laboratory.

Typewriter Ribbons and Correction Tapes

2-260.   Before obtaining typewriter exemplars, check the ribbon of the suspect typewriter. If the ribbon is a carbon film ribbon that passes through the typewriter only once and bears transparent images of the letters typed, remove the ribbon cartridge; do not take exemplars on this ribbon. Seize the ribbon as evidence and preserve it for a possible typewriter ribbon examination. Another ribbon known to be unconnected with the investigation should be used to obtain the exemplars.

2-261.   The Questioned Document Division at the USACIL can read these ribbons and attempt to locate a questioned text or to determine what was typed on the typewriter from which the ribbons were taken. Fabric ribbons or multistrike carbon film ribbons cannot be read. Sometimes it is possible to link a carbon film ribbon to a document by comparison of irregularities in the carbon transfer, the paper fiber impressions on the ribbon, or other characteristics. If a typewriter has a correction tape that is used to strike over or lift off typographical errors, the tape should be seized. It may be possible to match characters on the tape to corrected errors on a questioned document.

Typewriter Exemplars

2-262.   When obtaining typewriter exemplars, the content and formatting of the questioned document should be duplicated. It is desirable, but not essential, for the document examiner to be able to overlay the questioned document and exemplars. The investigator should pay particular attention to the letter case (upper or lower), margins, tabs, spacing between letters and words, and line spacing. If the questioned document consists of about one-half page or less, it should be reproduced in its entirety. If the document is lengthy, the first 20 to 30 lines should be reproduced. The remainder of the questioned document should then be examined. Any words, numerals, or symbols not appearing in the first 20 to 30 lines should be added to the sample. The words preceding and following the material to be added should be included and typed as they appear in the questioned document.

2-263.   The make, model, and serial number of the typewriter should be documented on the exemplars. If possible, find out when the ribbon on the machine was last changed and the nature and date of the latest repair work done on the typewriter. Samples of known typewriting produced on the suspect typewriter should be collected from office files or wherever they might be found. Typewriter characteristics can change with use, maintenance, or repair, and it may be important to locate documents typed on about the same date as the questioned document. Sometimes changes in the condition of a typewriter, combined with dated typewriter standards collected, can be used to determine the approximate date a questioned document was typed. It may be possible to complete the examination using only the typewriter exemplars; however, the suspect typewriter may need to be seized as evidence. Coordinate with the USACIL before shipping a typewriter for examination.

Photocopied Documents

2-264.   A copy produced on a photocopier or similar device can sometimes be linked to the copier that produced the document. This is done by matching individual markings placed on the photocopy by the copier with those on known photocopies from the suspect photocopier. Such markings may result from trash particles or marks on the glass platen of the machine, damage to the copying drum, images of parts of the machine included in the copy, or other sources. It is also possible to eliminate a particular photocopier or similar device from having produced a questioned copy; this is usually done by comparing class characteristics of a questioned copy with those of known copies made by the suspect machine.

2-265.   It is important to locate and seize the specific copy that was used as an instrument of the crime to be seized as evidence. The copy seized is evidence and must be accounted for according to AR 195-5. Additional copies of seized documents are commonly made after the offense for administrative purposes, and these subsequent copies are much less useful, both as evidence and for the purpose of forensic examinations.

2-266.   Analysis of a photocopied questioned document requires production of exemplar copies from the photocopier used to make the questioned document. A clean, blank sheet of paper the same size as the questioned copy should be collected for submission to the USACIL. This sample should be without paper impurities or other marks that can be copied by the copier. This sheet of paper should be saved as evidence as an item separate from the exemplars subsequently created and submitted to USACIL. Use the following steps to make copier exemplars:

- **Step 1.** Place the sheet of paper on the glass platen of the copier and make 10 copies on paper the same size as the questioned copy.
- **Step 2.** Remove the sheet of paper, close the copier lid, and make 10 additional copies.
- **Step 3.** Open the copier lid and, with no paper on the platen, make 10 copies.
- **Step 4.** Feed the blank sheet through the feeder, if the copier uses a sheet feeder, and make 10 copies.
- **Step 5.** Keep the blank sheet and each group of copies separate and note how they were obtained.

2-267. Individual characteristics of photocopiers can be changed or eliminated by cleaning and maintenance. To help account for these changes, attempt to collect existing photocopies known to have been made on the suspect machine. Ideally, these existing photocopies should have been made around the same time that the questioned document was produced. Similarly, collected standards can sometimes be used to determine the approximate date that a questioned copy was produced.

Printed Documents

2-268. Documents produced by one of the various types of printing processes, such as offset, letterpress, or flexography, may become evidence in a criminal investigation. There are several forensic examinations that may be requested for these documents, depending on the circumstances. These include examinations to determine—

- The method used to print the document.
- Whether the document is genuine or counterfeit.
- Which printing job the document was printed on.
- The approximate date on which the document was printed.

2-269. Other examinations may be possible. The information and standards needed by the USACIL will vary depending on the circumstances. The Questioned Document Division at the USACIL should be contacted for guidance.

Mechanical Impressions

2-270. Documents with mechanical impressions made by a device, such as a check protector or an embossed seal, may be encountered. A forensic examination may be needed to determine whether the impression is genuine or whether it can be associated with a seized device alleged to have produced a fraudulent impression. In these cases, obtain the suspect device and submit it to the USACIL for comparison with the questioned document.

2-271. If seizing the device is not possible, prepare about 20 exemplars with the device for submission to the USACIL for examination. If the device has data that can be changed, such as on a check protector, the device should be changed to duplicate the information on the questioned document. Every attempt should be made to collect standards prepared with the device at about the same time and date as the questioned document. Specimens of genuine impressions should be collected and submitted for comparison with the suspected fraudulent impressions. Coordination with the USACIL is recommended.

Rubber Stamps

2-272. Questioned rubber stamp images on documents can be compared to suspect rubber stamps or to documents bearing rubber stamp images from a known source. Although rubber stamps can be mass produced, they may acquire individual features, such as manufacturing defects or damage and wear resulting from use.

2-273. It is best to seize suspect rubber stamps and submit them to USACIL for comparison with the questioned stamp impression. If the stamp cannot be seized, prepare rubber stamp exemplars. They should be prepared using varying amounts of ink, with different amounts of pressure, and at different angles to replicate as many possible impressions from the stamp. Ensure that the entire surface of the stamp is reproduced.

2-274. It is important to locate and obtain existing documents that were created with the stamp. Because the individual characteristics of rubber stamps may change with use and cleaning, it may be necessary to have existing documents on which the suspect rubber stamp was used, preferably around the same time as the questioned stamp image. With such documents, it may be possible to establish the approximate date the questioned rubber stamp image was made.

OTHER LABORATORY EXAMINATION CAPABILITIES AND SUPPORT

2-275. The USACIL has a wide range of capabilities that can be employed by examiners to extract information from collected document evidence and provide LE investigators with useful information. While the areas discussed previously are the most common types of comparative analysis conducted by the USACIL to support Army LE, there are other capabilities that investigators should understand and consider when requesting laboratory support.

Charred Document Examinations

2-276. Text on charred documents can often be recovered to a readable state. A charred document is different from ashes. A charred document has been blackened and made brittle from exposure to high heat without enough oxygen to burn. To be examined, the pieces must be large enough to have legible text. Charred documents are very fragile. Pick them up by sliding a sheet of paper beneath them and use this sheet as a support. Transfer the charred documents to a shallow, cotton-lined box (such as a pie box). Sheet cotton stapled to the top and bottom inner surfaces of the box will prevent movement of the charred document.

2-277. Charred documents that are relatively flat may be placed between two panes of glass that are then taped together. Charred documents should be sent to the laboratory by courier. This will reduce unneeded handling and mitigate the risk of destruction. In some cases, the laboratory examiner may be asked to come to the location of the document. If both of these two preferred methods are impractical, careful packaging is required to reduce the risk that the evidence is destroyed. Coordination with the USACIL is recommended to obtain specific packaging guidance.

Computer Printer Document Examinations

2-278. Most types of modern computer printers are simple and reliable devices that are less likely than typewriters to place individual characteristics on the documents they produce. However, individual characteristics may be present, so consider obtaining known documents from suspect printers and submitting them for examination. High-quality printers and copiers used in business applications are more likely to embed data on printed pages. Some high-quality color printers and copiers steganographically embed their identification code into the printed pages. This is may appear as a series of fine and almost invisible patterns of yellow dots. Coordinate with the Questioned Document Division of the USACIL before submitting the printer for examination.

Ink Examinations

2-279. The Questioned Document Division of the USACIL is equipped to do nondestructive examinations of inks including infrared, infrared luminescence, UV, and other nonchemical examinations. These examinations are usually performed for the purpose of detecting alterations, deciphering obliterations, or determining that entries were made in different inks.

2-280. Nondestructive ink examinations are conducted to detect a difference between inks. Nondestructive examinations are limited to findings that the inks are different or that no difference was detected between the two inks. A finding that no difference was detected does not conclusively mean that the inks are the same; it simply means that examiners could not detect any differences. Destructive ink examinations are currently conducted by the U. S. Secret Service. The optimum potential finding by destructive examination is that no differences exist between two inks.

Latent Print Examinations

2-281. A latent print examination on questioned document evidence should be considered when documents are submitted for other examinations. Latent prints on paper are relatively permanent. Using gloves or forceps while handling these documents and placing them into an envelope is typically sufficient to protect latent prints on questioned documents.

2-282. When both questioned document and latent print examinations are to be done, the questioned document examination is done first, and the document is protected for the latent print examination. Latent print examinations on paper normally degrade the document in a manner that would hamper a subsequent questioned document examination.

Paper Examinations

2-283. Paper can be examined to determine its physical characteristics. Pieces of paper can be compared to determine whether they are different or whether no difference can be found. Some characteristics found in some papers, such as watermarks, may help determine the source of the paper or even when it was produced.

2-284. A paper examination, along with other evidence, may be useful if you suspect that the paper used for a document is the wrong kind or a page has been added or substituted in a multipage document. It may also show that the paper of a questioned document is of a type available to a particular suspect or from a particular source.

Torn, Cut, and Shredded Document Examinations

2-285. Examining torn, cut, or shredded documents may serve one of two purposes. One is to match a paper fragment to another piece of paper from which it was separated. This is typically done for the purpose of associating the fragment with a source document or paper sample. The second purpose is to reconstruct torn, cut, or shredded pieces of a document so that the document may be seen whole. In these cases, it is important to recover all fragments and protect them from further damage.

2-286. Sometimes document fragments can be reconstructed in the field without USACIL involvement. In such cases, the investigator should not use tape, glue, or other permanent adhesive. When a high-security or other high quality shredder has been used to shred a document, it may be impossible to reconstruct the document.

Submission of Evidence

2-287. All evidence should be submitted to the USACIL at one time. A case cannot be examined until all evidence is received. If evidence or documents are requested from another office, the added material should be obtained before forwarding the referrals to the laboratory. This precludes the laboratory having to hold referrals that cannot be examined pending receipt of other evidence.

2-288. If the examination requires an original document on file at the Defense Finance and Accounting Service (DFAS) and DFAS will not release it to the investigator, request that the DFAS send the document directly to USACIL. The investigator should retain any other document evidence (that is to be submitted to the laboratory for examination) until notified by DFAS or USACIL that such documents have been sent or received.

On-Site Assistance

2-289. Some investigations justify on-site assistance by USACIL forensic document examiners. When large numbers of questioned documents are involved, document examiners can assist investigators in screening the documents for those most likely to be productive for handwriting and other examinations. When large numbers of suspect writers, copy machines, typewriters, and other sources of documents are involved, document examiners can screen the sources (such as personnel records or post locator cards) to identify the source of questioned documents. On-site assistance trips by USACIL document examiners have been extremely successful and can result in more rapid and efficient examination of questioned document evidence.

TRACE EVIDENCE

2-290.　Trace evidence can be described as small amounts of material that are easily transferred from one individual or item to another through contact or other means. Trace evidence is easily overlooked, mishandled, and discarded as useless. Trace evidence is often referred to as contact evidence, contact transfer evidence, or transfer evidence. The utility of trace evidence is based on the premise that every contact leaves a trace; therefore, finding these traces can help establish associations or links. Trace evidence may be left by an individual and found at a crime scene or incident site; it may also be carried away by an individual and found at another location.

2-291.　Virtually any type of material can play a potential role as trace evidence. Trace evidence at a crime scene may be as obvious as soil or as inconspicuous as dust particles or microscopic particles. Army LE personnel must be aware of the potential presence of trace evidence to avoid destruction of valuable evidence. They must be aware that poor handling techniques and failure to maintain positive control of the crime scene or incident site can negate the value of evidence that would otherwise be admissible in court.

2-292.　Destruction or contamination of trace evidence can easily occur by many means. For example, if a scene is not properly secured and a suspect is allowed to return to the scene of a crime before it is completely processed, the suspect can plausibly claim that trace materials found there were left during the time of his return visit and that he was not present during the crime. Improper safety and collection techniques can result in cross contamination between trace evidence found at different locations of the crime scene, resulting in the value of the evidence being diminished or destroyed. Failure to protect identified evidence before collection can result in destruction by animals or environmental conditions such as wind or rain. Army LE and other personnel handling evidence must always be aware of these risks and practice sound evidence protection and collection techniques to avoid contamination.

GUNSHOT RESIDUE

2-293.　GSR may be defined as material (other than the actual projectile) that exits a firearm during its discharge. GSR projected from a fired weapon can be detected to show that the weapon was indeed fired and that surfaces (including persons) with deposited GSR were present when the weapon was fired. It can also be analyzed to determine the distance from the weapon to an impacted surface. All GSR testing is completed by laboratory examiners. The following two types of GSR tests are conducted at the laboratory:

- **Range of fire test.** The range of fire test is performed to search for and identify unburned powder particles and to measure muzzle-to-target distances using the residue patterns left on a target.
- **Gunshot residue test.** The GSR test is performed to detect primer residue in determining if an individual has handled or fired a weapon. Gunshot residue may be found on the individual's hands; it may also be found on their clothing and the weapon fired.

2-294.　GSR residues originate primarily from the primer mixture, the propellant, the bullet, the bullet jacket, and the cartridge case. Primer particles are formed when components of the primer mixture are vaporized and subsequently cool and condense upon discharge of a firearm. Primer particles are usually microscopically small, spherical particles (1 to 5 micrometers in diameter) containing lead, barium, and antimony. Spherical particles in this size range (containing all three of these elements) are considered highly specific for GSR. Using scanning electron microscope with electron dispersive spectroscopy analysis, the particles are imaged and the elements present in each individual particle are determined.

2-295.　GSR can be collected from many surfaces including the hands of a suspected shooter, the clothing worn by the shooter, the weapon fired, and surfaces in the immediate vicinity of the fired weapon. GSR is extremely fragile. It must be collected as soon as possible, especially on a live subject. As time passes between an incident and the collection of GSR, the levels of detectable GSR remaining on the subject's hands will likely diminish. On live individuals, GSR will rarely last much beyond three hours. On deceased victims, the hands should be bagged; bagging the hands helps to extend the time GSR remains collectible, but it should still be collected as soon as possible.

2-296. Items suspected of having GSR should be collected whenever possible and forwarded to the USACIL for processing. Typical items collected are weapons suspected of being fired, clothing worn by a suspected shooter, and clothing worn by victims (especially if the shooting was at close range). Items that cannot be collected such as a person's hands or surfaces in the immediate vicinity of a fired weapon (such as walls, counters, or car doors), should be processed using commercially available GSR kits to collect suspected GSR. GSR kits containing cotton swabs and dilute nitric acid, designed for bulk analysis, should not be used. Evidence collected with bulk collection kits cannot be analyzed at USACIL.

2-297. When collecting GSR, gloves should be worn to prevent contamination; the collector must not have fired or cleaned a weapon within the past day. The collection kits contain everything necessary for proper collection of potential primer particle evidence. The kits consist of aluminum stubs covered with an adhesive material similar to double-sided tape. A container and a lid protect the stubs. The lid doubles as a holder for the stub when it is removed from the container. The stub is used to remove potential primer particles by repeatedly pressing the stub against a surface suspected of holding GSR particles (such as an individual's hand) using a blotting motion, much like using a piece of tape to remove lint from clothing.

2-298. When collecting powder pattern evidence and items of evidence suspected of having GSR for laboratory examination, take care not to disturb any GSR that may be present. Wrap items in clean paper and place them in a clean cardboard box for transport. Additional guidelines for packaging GSR and shot pattern evidence include—

- Handling cloth and clothing items as follows:
  - Send any clothing that contains bullet or shot penetration to the USACIL for examination.
  - Mark each article of clothing suspected of having GSR by attaching a tag indicating its source and relation to the fired weapon. Mark linings with ink or an indelible pencil in an area away from the suspected residue.
  - Send to the USACIL laboratory a written description of the garment containing the suspected shot or powder residue, including the location of the suspected shot or powder. The person recovering the evidence must maintain a copy of this description.
  - Wrap clothing in clean paper after it has been dried and forward it to the USACIL laboratory.
- Marking and documenting firearms as described earlier in this chapter.
- Photographing and measuring surfaces such as skin, walls, doors, or similar surfaces to document any shot or GSR pattern. See chapter 4 for more information. The USACIL should be consulted for further processing guidance.

FIBERS

2-299. Fiber evidence can help provide corroborative evidence that places a suspect at a crime scene or incident site. This can be accomplished when fibers are collected from the victim's clothing or the crime scene and matched to fibers collected from a suspect's clothing. Textile fibers can be exchanged between two individuals, between an individual and an object, and between two objects. Whether a fiber is transferred and detected is dependent on the nature and duration of the contact between the suspect and the victim or objects contacted. It also depends on the persistence of the fibers after the transfer and the types of fabric involved in the contact.

2-300. Fiber evidence can be recovered from many surfaces such as clothing, fingernails, hair combings, weapons, tools, bedding, furniture, structures, and vehicles. When fibers are shed, they can adhere to clothing, furniture, or other surfaces for a short period of time; if located and properly collected they can be used to establish a possible link between a suspect, a victim, and the crime scene. Fiber evidence can rarely produce a positive match between two pieces of fabric, carpet, or other material; determinations made during a fiber examination can include the—

- Type of fiber.

- Possible product uses such as carpeting, clothing, or upholstery.
- Similarity between evidence fibers and standards.
- Physical match (fracture or jigsaw match) to a potential source material.

2-301.   When fibers are matched with a specific source (such as fabric from the victim, the suspect, and/or the scene), a relative value or significance is placed on that association. This value is dependent on many factors including the type of fiber found, the color or variation of color in the fiber, the relative uniqueness of dyes or fibers, the number of fibers found, the location of fibers at the crime scene or on the victim, and the number of different fibers at the crime scene or on the victim that match the clothing of the suspect.

Assigning Value or Significance

2-302.   The large volume of fabrics produced reduces the significance of any fiber association and can make it difficult to definitively match two fibers. It can never be stated with certainty that a fiber originated from a particular garment because other garments were likely produced using the same fiber type and color. The inability to positively associate a fiber with a particular garment to the exclusion of all other garments, however, does not mean that the fiber association is without value. Single fibers, by themselves, do not individualize; however, finding multiple fibers on a subject that correspond closely to fibers that come from a victim's clothing can be significant evidence of similar class characteristics that can approach the level of individualization.

2-303.   When a fiber examiner matches a questioned fiber to a known item of clothing, there are only two possible explanations: either the fiber actually originated from the item of clothing or the fiber did not originate from the item of clothing. In order to say that the fiber originated from the item of clothing, the clothing either had to be the only fabric of its type ever produced or still remaining on earth, or the transfer of fibers from the clothing had to be directly observed. Conversely, the only way to say that a fiber did not originate from a particular item of clothing is to know the actual history of the garment or to have actually observed the fiber transfer from another garment. Since neither of these situations is likely to occur or be known, when fibers are matched fiber examiners will conclude that the fibers could have originated from the clothing or that the fibers are consistent with originating from the clothing.

2-304.   Even though positive matches are impossible without direct observation of a transfer, some fabrics and fibers may have unique characteristics that, while not enabling a positive match, can increase the significance of the association. Matching dyed synthetic fibers or dyed natural fibers with complex dyes and color variations can be very meaningful and assigned a high level of significance. Matching common fibers, such as white cotton or blue denim cotton, in most areas of the United States would be less significant. The discovery of cross transfers and multiple fiber transfers common between a suspect's clothing and the victim's clothing can dramatically increase the value of the association and provide significant circumstantial evidence that the two individuals had physical contact. Multiple fiber types found on different items of clothing or fabric from the suspect, the victim, and the crime scene greatly increase the likelihood that contact occurred between these individuals and the scene. Each associated fiber type is considered to be an independent event, and multiple associations undermine a coincidence defense.

Natural Fibers

2-305.   Many different natural fibers originating from plants and animals are used in the production of fabric. Cotton fibers are the plant fibers most commonly used in textile material with the cotton type, the fiber length, and the degree of twist contributing to the diversity of these fibers. Processing techniques and color applications also influence the value of cotton fiber identification. Other plant fibers used in the production of textile materials include flax (linen), ramie, sisal, jute, hemp, kapok, and coir. The identification of less common plant fibers at a crime scene or on the clothing of a suspect or victim would have increased significance.

2-306.   Wool is the animal fiber most frequently used in the production of textile materials, and the most common wool fibers originate from sheep. The end use of sheep's wool often dictates the fineness or coarseness of woolen fibers. Finer woolen fibers are used in the production of clothing, whereas coarser fibers are found in carpet.

2-307. The diameter of fibers and the degree of scale protrusion of fibers are other important characteristics. Although sheep's wool is most common, woolen fibers from other animals may also be found. These include camel, alpaca, cashmere, mohair, and others. The identification of less common animal fibers at a crime scene or on the clothing of a suspect or victim would have increased significance.

Manmade Fibers

2-308. More than half of all fibers used in the production of textile materials are manmade. Some manmade fibers originate from natural materials, such as cotton or wood; others originate from synthetic materials. Polyester and nylon fibers are the most commonly encountered manmade fibers followed by acrylics, rayons, and acetates. There are also many less common manmade fibers. The amount of production of a particular manmade fiber and its end use influence the degree of rarity of a given fiber.

2-309. The shape of a manmade fiber can determine the value placed on that fiber. The cross section of a manmade fiber can be manufacturer-specific. Some cross sections are more common than others, and some shapes may only be produced for a short period of time. Unusual cross sections encountered during examination can add increased significance to a fiber association.

Color Characteristics

2-310. Color influences the value given to fiber identification. Several dyes are often used to give a fiber a desired color. Individual fibers can be colored before being spun into yarns. Yarns can be dyed, and fabrics made from them can be dyed. Color can also be applied to the surface of fabric, as found in printed fabrics. How color is applied and absorbed along the length of the fiber is an important comparison characteristic. Color fading and discoloration can also lend increased value to a fiber association.

Number and Location of Fibers

2-311. The number of fibers on the clothing of a victim identified as matching the clothing of a suspect is important in determining actual contact. The greater the number of fibers, the higher the likelihood that contact actually occurred between these individuals. Where the fibers are found also affects the value placed on a particular fiber association. The location of fibers on different areas of the body or on specific items at the crime scene influences the significance of the fiber association.

Fiber Transfer and Persistence

2-312. Textile fibers are transferred to the surface of a fabric either by direct transfer or indirect transfer. Direct transfer occurs when a fiber is deposited from one material to another through direct physical contact. Indirect transfer occurs when a fiber is deposited onto a surface from one material, then is picked up by another material after contact with the same surface at a later time. The likelihood of transfer depends on the types of fabric involved in the contact and the nature and duration of the contact. The type of physical contact between a suspect and a victim can also determine the number of fibers transferred and the value placed on their discovery. Violent physical contact of an extended duration will often result in numerous fiber transfers.

2-313. Studies have shown that transferred fibers are lost rather quickly, depending on the types of fabrics involved and the movement of the clothing after contact. The greater the amount of movement the higher the probability that transferred fibers will be lost. Emergency personnel, MEs, and LE personnel must handle a victim's clothing carefully to minimize fiber loss. Fibers transferred onto an assault victim's or suspect's clothing will be lost if the garments are aggressively moved, brushed, shaken, or washed. It is important for investigators to retrieve and preserve the clothing of victims and suspects to protect and preserve any fiber evidence that may be present.

Locating and Collecting Fibers

2-314. The processing considerations given to fibers are similar to those for hair evidence. Locating fibers can be difficult due to their size; they may also blend in on materials of similar color. The following are methods used to locate fiber evidence:

- A visual search.
- An alternate light source.
- An additional magnification search aid.
- Taping.

2-315. When obtaining samples of fabrics as possible fiber donors, the samples should be representative of all the types and colors in the fabric of the item. All items should be sealed and labeled for identification. Since fiber evidence is generally small in nature, care should be taken to prevent loss or contamination. Evidence gathered from separate sources should not be intermingled. It must be individually collected, marked, and kept separated during packing for shipment. Recovery of evidence should be the most direct but least intrusive technique practical. Techniques for recovering fiber evidence include—

- Collecting individual fibers (picking).
- Using adhesive tape.
- Scraping.
- Vacuuming.

SOIL

2-316. Soil can easily transfer from the ground to other objects as they make contact with the surface. Comparative analysis of soil composition between questioned samples collected from a suspect's shoes and comparison standards taken at the crime scene can produce an associative link. LE personnel should understand that soil comparison results can be limited. Soil sample quantity and levels of soil contamination can affect the success or failure of soil comparisons. Soil evidence may be collected in sufficient quantities from a suspect's shoes or vehicle, but contamination collected from surfaces after leaving the crime scene can limit the effectiveness of soil comparison.

2-317. Soils and rock may vary throughout a localized area. The differences between two visibly different soils, such as sand or clay, are easily recognized. However, minor differences between similar appearing soils may only be revealed by a thorough examination of their mineral compositions. Therefore, comparison standard samples should be collected of the soil at the crime scene for comparison with the soil recovered from a suspect; for example, from his clothing, shoes, or vehicle.

Collection of Evidence

2-318. Soil evidence is extremely prone to contamination. Movement of the suspect, whether by foot or by vehicle, after departing the crime scene or incident site will inevitably add material to the soil collected at the crime scene. Because of this likelihood for contamination, thin layers of soil are less likely to provide desired results than thicker samples; when collecting questioned soil samples, thicker samples are preferred. Adequate soil evidence is typically found on a suspect's footwear and in or on a suspect's vehicle. Areas of focus when collecting questioned soil samples include the—

- **Shoes of the suspect.** Shoes worn by a suspect may be located with caked mud or dirt. If soil evidence is located on a suspect's shoes, collect the shoes (with soil intact) and forward them to the laboratory for analysis. Do not attempt to remove the dirt from the shoes.
- **Floor mats and the brake, clutch, and gas pedals of the vehicle.** In situations where a suspect has walked through wet or muddy areas, it is likely that soil from the scene will be deposited on the floor mats and pedals of the vehicle. Examine these areas for the presence of soil similar to that at the scene. If similar soils are found, remove the mats and/or pedals from the vehicle and submit them to the laboratory for examination. Collect distinct clumps of soil that may be present and package them separately. General debris that is present on most automotive floor mats or floorboards consists of material that has accumulated over a period of time and is generally of little or no value for comparison.
- **Tires, fenders, or wheel wells of the vehicle.** Collect questioned soil as discrete clumps from the tires, fenders, or wheel wells of the vehicle. Package each of these samples individually to ensure that each one represents a single source. Soil from vehicles, especially in the wheel wells,

may have been deposited in layers. The soil should be collected in a manner that preserves the full thickness and layers of the soil.

2-319. Suspects should be questioned regarding the origin of any soil that may be present, such as on their shoes or in or on a vehicle. Collect soil samples from the locations indicated by the suspect along with comparison standards from the crime scene. These are the suspect's alibi standards. If the soil on a suspect's shoes matches that from the crime scene, but not that from the location where the suspect claimed, this provides doubt for the suspect's alibi. If it matches the standards from where the suspect claimed it originated, it provides corroboration of the suspect's statement.

Collection of Soil Comparison Standards

2-320. Soil samples should be collected throughout the crime scene or incident site to ensure that a representative sample of the entire crime scene is obtained. When distinct footwear, tire track impressions, or areas of disturbed earth are present, soil samples should be collected in the immediate vicinity of each impression or disturbed area. Exercise care to ensure that actual impressions are not disturbed. These comparison standards should be collected to a depth equal to that of the corresponding impression. Deep impressions may require collection of several samples from varying depths, especially if there are obvious differences in soil composition or color at different levels throughout the depth of the impression.

2-321. Many scenes may have no distinct impressions or disturbed areas of soil. For crime scene where no distinct footwear, tire track impressions, or areas of disturbed earth and the soil are present, samples should be collected from throughout the scene in an attempt to obtain samples that are representative of any variety that may be present in the area. If there are obvious variations in soil color and texture, samples of each visually distinct soil should be obtained. If the scene appears to have soils of similar composition, representative samples from throughout the scene should be obtained. Focus on areas with exposed soil such as flower beds, beaten pathways, and other areas with limited ground cover vegetation; these areas are more likely to transfer soil from the ground to a subject or vehicle. Collect comparison standards from the upper-most layer, not more than 1/4 to 1/2 inch, since the materials at that depth are most representative of what may have been transferred. At a minimum, collect six soil samples. A garden trowel is a common tool that can be used to collect soil standards; thoroughly clean the trowel between each sample.

2-322. Plastic screw-top, urine specimen containers capable of holding at least 120 milliliters may be used for packaging comparison standard soil samples. Each container should be filled completely. If urine specimen containers are not available, collect approximately 1/2 to 1 cup from each area and secure it in a sealable glass or metal container.

Laboratory Testing

2-323. Given a sufficient number of comparison standards and adequate quality questioned samples for comparison, laboratory testing can show if a questioned soil removed from a suspect's clothes, shoes, or vehicle could have come from the crime scene. In rare instances, sufficient unique and inclusive materials such as vegetable matter (including seeds or other plant material) and nonorganic materials (such as paint chips or glass), are present in both the standard and questioned soils to achieve a direct association. Laboratory comparisons of comparison standard and questioned soils may demonstrate that the questioned soil could not have originated from the same source as the standard samples.

BUILDING MATERIALS

2-324. When a structure is broken into, the suspects may damage or break through a variety of building materials such as glass, paint, plaster, fiberglass, insulating materials, sheetrock, cinder block, mortar, brick, and caulking and sealing materials. It is possible that these materials may have been transferred to the clothing of the suspect or to the tools used during the break-in. Samples should be obtained from any of these materials that exhibit signs of damage or tampering. Preserve any identified toolmarks or other impressions. These impressions should be processed and submitted to the laboratory for examination (see the section on toolmarks in this chapter). Collect samples of—

- Each type of building material that appears to be involved in the crime. The composition of a specific material may vary. If a specific material (such as a door facing or window) shows damage in multiple locations, collect samples from each area of damage.
- All fragments of any broken glass at the scene. Ensure glass from different locations is collected and packaged separately. Collect glass from both sides of a window break, packaging and documenting the inside and outside evidence separately. Analysis of the glass can determine the direction of force causing the breakage. See the section on glass fractures and fragments below.
- Materials that may be present in areas, including dust and fine shavings, where access to cabinets, safes, or other security storage containers is evident. Penetration of the walls of a safe or other security cabinet may cause its insulation to be broken and deposited in the area along with other shavings and dust particles unique to the container. Pieces of insulation, metal shavings, and dust may be scattered about the scene and become deposited in or on the suspect's clothing and on any tools used to commit the crime. Collect known standards of the safe insulation as comparison standards.

2-325. Suspects in the investigation may carry particles on their clothing and bodies that is consistent with the evidence collected at the scene. All clothing worn at the time of the crime should be collected for examination. Suspects may have evidence on their bodies, especially if identified quickly and they have not bathed or cleaned themselves. Fragments of building material, especially glass, may be found in cuts on the suspect's skin or hair. If the suspect left the scene in a vehicle, the entire passenger compartment and trunk should be examined for potential evidence, including any tools that may have been used.

GLASS FRACTURES AND FRAGMENTS

2-326. Even though glass is usually considered to be class characteristic evidence, variations in its composition and properties make it a potentially valuable type of physical evidence. When a piece of glass that has been broken is reconstructed (such as from a headlight in a hit and run collision), it may assume an individuality when the fractured pieces fit together. It is for these reasons that care must be exercised when collecting glass.

2-327. When a window or other glass pane is broken, glass particles rebound up to ten feet or more toward the direction from which the force is applied. This creates a shower of glass that will shower any individual that is breaking the glass from close proximity. This effect is known as backward fragmentation. Glass fragments can easily be embedded in the shoes and clothing of any individual who is within range of the breakage. Additionally, glass fragments can get into hair and wounds and on or in the skin of the suspect or individuals who are near the scene. The object or projectile used to break a window may also have glass fragments in it. Biological or trace evidence from suspects or victims may be deposited on glass fragments. Investigators should take care to identify these fragments and appropriately process those pieces with biological or trace material to preserve valuable evidence.

Collecting Glass

2-328. When glass from a window or doorframe is broken, pieces of glass often remain in the frame. The original inside or outside surface and the orientation (such as top or bottom) of each remaining piece of window glass should be marked before removal. The entire frame may be removed if toolmarks or other evidence is relevant. Standards of wood, putty, paint, or other materials should be collected at this time. Techniques for collection of glass and glass fragments include the following:

- Wear gloves while collecting glass.
- Photograph all glass fragments exactly as they are found and document their location on the crime scene sketch before collecting them.
- Consider activities at the crime scene from the time of the incident to the time of evidence collection. Consider whether the suspect caused the characteristics in the broken glass or whether other individuals, such as medical personnel or witnesses, introduced them. Be aware that moving glass pieces and extracting the remaining glass pieces in the window or doorframe may extend fractures; this can affect findings by the laboratory technician.
- Remove all larger pieces of glass. Be sure to—

- Handle the glass carefully to preserve any latent prints on the glass.
- Pick up larger pieces of glass by their edges avoiding the flat surfaces as much as possible.
- Wrap each piece of glass separately in soft paper, cotton, or other similar material.
- Secure the pieces to avoid shifting and breakage during movement. Friction, shifting, or contact with other items can destroy or contaminate the evidence.
- Never package glass fragments in glass containers.
- Mark all wrappings and containers as "Fragile."
  - Collect small glass fragments. Be sure to—
    - Take care to protect the edges of glass fragments as they are collected. The edges can help laboratory technicians determine the manner in which the glass was broken.
    - Use rubber-tipped tweezers or similar type tools to handle smaller fragments. This will help prevent further damage to the fragments.
    - Wrap smaller fragments in bond paper using the druggist fold.
    - Place fragments in containers and stabilize them so that the glass will not shift during movement. Friction, shifting, or contact with other items can destroy or contaminate the evidence.
    - Mark all wrappings and containers as "Fragile."
  - Collect samples of known glass from each broken window or source.
  - Submit all pieces of glass collected from the scene for laboratory examination. Package questioned pieces of glass separately from known pieces of glass.
  - Collect and submit the victim's and the suspect's clothing to the laboratory for examination. Package each clothing item separately in a paper bag. The laboratory may be able to determine if glass fragments from the scene are on the suspect's clothing, establishing a link between the suspect and the scene.

Marking the Fragments

2-329. Glass fragments should be marked with an indelible marker, a scriber, or a diamond point pencil. A piece of properly marked adhesive tape may also be used. Initial, date, and annotate the time on each piece of glass. Place marks where latent prints or where material of evidentiary value are not likely. Place marks on the side of the glass that was facing up when it was found; place marks on the inside if the glass was taken from a window frame or door. This helps in the reassembly of fragments and in the reconstruction of the incident. Fragments that are too small for marking should be placed in containers. Mark both the container and the lid.

Field Examination of Fractures

2-330. In the field, investigators must be able to distinguish between fractures caused by heat and those caused by blunt force. They must also be able to distinguish these kinds of fractures from those created by a high-speed impact like that of a bullet. A basic knowledge of the characteristics of safety glass is also helpful. There are two types of safety glass—laminated and tempered. Laminated glass will generally remain intact when fractured; tempered glass is made to produce many small fragments and will not remain intact when fractured.

2-331. Army LE personnel should understand the manners in which glass reacts to force. This knowledge is often critical in determining whether a crime has been committed in the manner presented by the parties at the scene. Broken glass can exhibit several fracture patterns that can provide clues to the direction of force applied to the glass. Glass fracture patterns can include—

- **Radial fractures.** Radial fractures appear like the spokes of a wheel as they radiate away from the point of pressure, such as the point in which a rock is thrown or a projectile is shot through a window. Radial fractures start on the opposite side of the force applied. Figure 2-6, page 2-70, provides an example of a radial fracture.

- **Concentric fractures.** Concentric fractures form a series of broken circles or arcs around the point of impact and between the radial lines. Concentric fractures start on the same side of the glass as the original force applied. Figure 2-6 provides an example of a concentric fracture.
- **Cones or craters.** A cone is the result of a high velocity impact such as a bullet or pellet. The cone will form on the opposite side of the original impact. The entry hole will be smaller than the exit hole.
- **Wallner lines**. Wallner lines are rib-shaped marks visible on the edges of an impacted glass. They will appear in a wave-like pattern and will appear concaved, curved in the direction of impact. Figure 2-7 provides an example of Wallner lines.

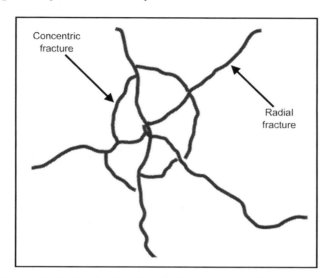

Figure 2-6. Example of radial and concentric fracture

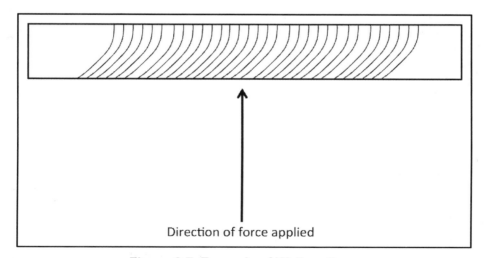

Figure 2-7. Example of Wallner lines

Bullet Hole Fractures

2-332.   Checking glass for bullet holes may provide useful information. Many times the direction from which a bullet enters a piece of glass is easily discernible. A bullet makes a somewhat clean-cut hole in the side of entrance. As it penetrates, it pushes glass fragments ahead of it. This causes a saucer-shaped or coning depression on the exit side with a greater diameter than the entrance hole. Determining the direction becomes more difficult when several bullets enter safety glass closely together. When the last bullets enter the glass surface there are already a number of cracks. As a result, small pieces are knocked out around the holes on both sides.

2-333.   At times it is important to know which of two or more bullet holes in a pane of glass was made first. This may be determined from the fractures. When a fracture traveling across glass meets a fracture that is already present, the newer fracture will be stopped. If fractures from one bullet hole are stopped by those of another, it may be concluded that the blocking fracture was made first.

2-334.   A general angle from which a bullet enters a piece of glass may be found by the amount of chipping at the exit crater. If a bullet strikes glass straight on, chipping around the exit hole will be fairly even. If a bullet enters from an angle, chipping will be greater in the direction of travel. For instance (always orienting from the same side of the glass) if a bullet enters at an angle from right to left, the amount of chipping found on the right side of the exit hole will be less than that on the left side of the exit hole. The entrance hole will show straight and short radial fractures on the right, while one or two longer radial fractures should appear on the left. If a bullet enters from the left of the glass, these fractures will be reversed.

Blunt-Object Fractures

2-335.   Glass fractures caused by a blunt object will show a pattern of fractures like, but not as regular as, those from a bullet. This difference is mainly due to the impacting force being dispersed over a greater area. It may be more difficult to tell which side the impact came from, but it can still be determined by the ridgelines on the edges of the radial fractures. Anomalous fracture patterns can occur if the impact is close to a frame that is rigidly holding the glass pane. It is not recommended that the investigator attempt to partly reconstruct the object to find the radial and concentric fractures. Radial fractures will always originate on the side opposite the impact. The *4R rule* (*ridges* on *radial* fractures are at *right* angles to the *rear*) applies most of the time; however, anomalous patterns do occur under some conditions. The 4R rule is unreliable for laminated glass, tempered glass, and small windows tightly held in a frame. This rule is valid only from the point of impact to the first concentric fracture and valid only to the first bend in the glass. You must find the point of impact to be able to find the direction of force.

Heat Fractures

2-336.   Recognizing heat fractures in glass can help you eliminate areas of concern in your investigation. Fractures due to heat are wave-shaped. They do not show a regular pattern of radial and concentric lines like fractures caused by impact. Heat fractures also show little, if any, curve patterns (stress lines) along the edges. If the stress lines are smooth, or almost smooth, and no point of impact is found, the fracture may have been caused from excessive heat. Expansion of the glass (stretching action) occurs first on the side exposed to the heat. Glass splinters will often fall toward that side. Reconstruction of a glass object fractured by heat will show the wave-shaped fracture pattern.

Laboratory Examination of Fragments and Fractures

2-337.   Glass fragments and fractures may yield important leads when examined by trained technicians. Examiners can analyze glass fragments and fractures to determine a variety of facts. Laboratory examiners can—

- Reconstruct shattered glass, including fracture matching.
- Determine the cause and direction of force.
- Conduct chemical analysis.

Reconstruction and Fracture Matching

2-338.   LE personnel on a crime scene should not attempt to reconstruct glass fragments; attempts to reconstruct the fragments can further damage the glass. Laboratory examiners will conduct reconstruction of fractured glass. How the reconstruction is done depends on the size and shape of the object. The fragments should not be sent to the laboratory in a reconstructed form as damage may result during shipping and handling.

2-339. It is more difficult to reconstruct a curved or irregular-shaped piece of glass, such as a bottle or a jar; both the size and the shape of the object must be determined. However, a partial reconstruction of curved glass that originated from a bottle, lenses, or a similar curved item may be possible. This may allow an approximation of the size and curvature of the original object. Lenses are made in round, oval, and other shapes with their spherical surfaces not always being completely regular in contour; these irregularities can make lens reconstruction difficult unless all pieces are retrieved. Some pieces (such as automobile headlight lenses) may have patterns cast or cut into them. These can be compared and matched more easily than smooth glass surfaces. In many cases, the pattern may be matched independent of the fractured edges. But the exact matching of edges is still the most conclusive evidence of common source.

2-340. Fracture matching can sometimes be useful to physically match larger fragments of questioned glass to glass from the broken item. In this case, it is possible to conclude that the questioned and the suspected source were, at one time, a single unit. Examination of fractured glass may yield information as to the type of glass from which it originated. The manufacturer's name or logo may be imprinted or molded in the glass and could provide additional information.

Determination of Direction of Force

2-341. Examination of reconstructed glass items, such as windowpanes, may enable examiners to identify the direction of a blow and the angle of impact. It may also show the sequence of breaks and, in the case of multiple bullet holes, the sequence of the holes and the side from which they originated. These determinations are conducted through analysis of fracture patterns in the glass and reconstructed glass fragments.

2-342. Laboratory examiners can determine a more precise angle of travel for the bullet than field evaluators. This requires examiners to compare the bullet hole with test shots fired from varied known angles. The test shots should be fired through the same type of glass and under the same conditions with the same type of weapon and ammunition as the original bullet hole. The laboratory is equipped to conduct test fires of weapons and ammunition.

2-343. The type of ammunition can sometimes be learned from the size and features of the bullet hole. Bullet holes in safety glass offer more evidence than those in window glass because safety glass fragments do not fall. When a bullet goes through a pane of glass in a sideways fashion, it is often harder to determine the caliber of the bullet. Coordinate with the laboratory to learn the best way to submit evidence for this type of examination.

Chemical Analysis

2-344. Scientific examination of the physical and chemical properties of the glass may establish that the questioned glass could have originated from a specific window glass or it could eliminate that possibility altogether. A known sample of glass from the frame must be obtained for comparison. Results of chemical analysis can also be used to establish commonality of chemical composition and associate fragments collected from a suspect or victim.

PAINT

2-345. Paint evidence commonly results from breaking and entering incidents, automobile collisions, and other crimes in which forcible contact has been made with painted surfaces. The resulting paint evidence is usually in the form of chips and smears. When a suspect attempts to break into a safe, vault, window, or door, paint can be transferred to and from the tools that are being used to commit the offense. Paint evidence should be carefully collected for examination by the USACIL. General guidelines for collecting paint evidence include the following:

- Collect tools contain paint evidence and forwarding them to the laboratory intact; do not attempt to remove the paint from the tool. If the tools are suspected of having left impression marks, such as on a windowsill, send sample impressions with the tools.
- Collect paint samples from a surface, such as around the windowsill, by chipping the paint from the surface to the foundation to obtain a sample of the full thickness or depth of the paint; do not

scrape samples from the surface. Chipping the paint allows its layered structure to remain intact. Each layer can then be a point of comparison.

- Conduct a field examination for paint fragments on clothing collected as evidence. Field examination risks the loss of paint chips, especially those too small to be seen with the naked eye. These items should be marked for identification, packaged, and sent to the USACIL for examination.

2-346. Paint chips are frequently produced in automobile collisions between two vehicles. These situations can also produce paint smear evidence, such as when two vehicles sideswipe each other. When the collection process is a result of an automobile collision, the investigator should—

- Search the collision scene for paint fragments and pieces of vehicle body parts.
- Pick up paint chips using tweezers or by placing a piece of clean paper under them and lifting them up. Place paint chips in a box with a soft lining to prevent altering the chips.
- Pack multiple paint evidence separately.
- Be aware that smears may require removal and submission of vehicle components. Submit entire vehicle components, such as a fender or bumper, when paint transfer is minimal and the severity of the crime warrants.
- Collect samples of questioned paint transfers from each vehicle area. In addition, collect control samples of paint from undamaged areas on the same body panel and directly adjacent to each area where a questioned transfer has been collected.
- Mark the evidence container with the exact location from where the paint evidence was collected, the date, and the investigator's initials.

EVIDENCE MANAGEMENT AND CONTROL

2-347. The proper management and control of evidence is critical to any criminal investigation and subsequent legal proceeding. Lawfully collected evidence loses its evidentiary value if the chain of custody is not properly documented. All personnel engaged in Army LE activities, including patrol and security personnel, desk sergeants, investigators, and evidence custodians, must be familiar with the procedures for properly receiving, handling, accounting for, storing, and disposing of evidence. To admit lawfully seized items into evidence at a trial, they must be authenticated. Critical to authentication of evidence is a well-documented chain of custody. All persons from the initial collector to the evidence custodian share this responsibility. Regulatory guidance and detailed instructions for evidence collection, management, storage, and security are outlined in AR 195-5. In addition to the guidance provided by AR 195-5, LE managers are encouraged to develop local SOPs that serve as quick references for evidence management and control.

Chapter 3

Interviews and Law Enforcement Interrogations

Conducting interviews and LE interrogations is an investigator's means of obtaining testimonial evidence from persons connected with an incident. Proper and effective interviewing skills are among the most basic and essential tools an investigator can possess. These skills are a significant facet of obtaining some of the most critical aspects of the criminal acts committed by an individual. The importance of the testimonial accounts obtained from the victim of a crime, and the witnesses who were present or have personal knowledge of what happened, cannot be overemphasized. In most cases the most critical testimonial account of the criminal acts committed by an individual is obtained from the person who committed the offense. Doctrinally, LE interrogations are differentiated from intelligence interrogations conducted by human intelligence collectors trained and certified to conduct interrogations in support of military operations. LE interrogations are different from intelligence interrogations. Intelligence interrogations are described in FM 2-22.3 and governed by DODD 3115.09. LE interrogations are covered by AR 190-30 and AR 195-2. For the purpose of brevity, references to LE interrogations within this chapter will be referred to as simply interrogations.

TESTIMONIAL AND PHYSIOLOGICAL EVIDENCE

3-1.   Testimonial evidence includes documented written, verbal, and/or recorded statements typically collected during interviews or interrogations conducted during a LE investigation. Testimonial evidence is a statement based on personal knowledge, experience, or belief that can be used as evidence or proof concerning a crime or incident under investigation. To obtain testimonial evidence, Army LE personnel gather information by asking questions designed to extract essential information. Physiological evidence is information obtained which tends to prove or disprove the matter under investigation based on documented psychological and physical reactions to a crime experienced or witnessed by an individual. These reactions can include nausea, flashbacks, muscle rigidity, trembling, terror, memory gaps, or other psychological or physical responses to the incident in question. Physiological evidence is typically documented during the interview process.

3-2.   Effective interviews and interrogations require an understanding of human nature, good interpersonal communications abilities, and good observation skills. Army LE personnel must continuously strive to be objective while conducting interviews. They must build a picture or view of the incident at hand from all physical, physiological, and testimonial evidence collected; this will help investigators determine if the information provided should be considered questionable or if critical information is missing or altered. Testimonial evidence can rarely stand alone. It must be compared and assessed in context with all other aspects of the investigation, including physical, physiological, and other testimonial evidence.

3-3.   Although testimonial evidence can be the most beneficial evidence in many investigations, it is also the least reliable form of evidence. The assessment of testimonial credibility requires a greater level of objectivity and interpersonal skill than other forms of evidence identification, collection, and preservation. Human nature, education level, personality, psychological sophistication, trauma, and a number of other influences can greatly affect a witness's ability or willingness to provide reliable information. Understanding the factors that affect a witness's ability or willingness to provide accurate and reliable information can enable investigators to mitigate the effects of these factors and assist in discovering the truth. This understanding can also be extremely helpful in identifying less-credible testimonial information. Army LE personnel must be aware of these factors and take steps to mitigate the possibility of receiving tainted information. There are several factors that can contribute to reduced credibility of testimonial evidence, including—

- The limits of human memory.
- Trauma.
- Fear.
- Personal experiences and biases.
- Poor vantage points from which a particular event is witnessed.
- Impairment due to mental illness, extreme emotions, or the influence of drugs or alcohol.
- Personal motivations.
- The period of witness exposure to other witnesses.

3-4. Most people want to be as helpful as possible and will attempt to help Army LE personnel when asked; they do not want to be considered unhelpful and unobservant. Their unconscious efforts to prove their value as witnesses can result in unreliable eyewitness testimony. In some instances, with the passage of time, memory can fade and some details may be lost, resulting in the loss of valuable information. Postevent influences can alter perception and recollection. If witnesses are allowed to discuss their observations with one another before being interviewed, they tend to incorporate statements and observations (provided by other witnesses) into their account of the incident. Typically, this is not an intentional effort to derail the investigative process; however, erroneous information provided to a witness after an incident is frequently incorporated into future witness accounts.

3-5. Over a lifetime, all individuals have been influenced by their surroundings experiences, culture, education, religious beliefs, or other environmental factors. All these experiences affect the way in which individuals perceive their surroundings and events that they witness. Although an individual's observations are factually accurate, they may be skewed by perception. Army LE personnel must be aware of potential biases that individuals may have that influence their perceptions of an incident. Army LE personnel are likewise affected by these same influential factors and, therefore, must be careful not to allow their own personal biases to affect their perceptions of an incident or the persons they are interviewing or interrogating.

3-6. Investigators should understand that different vantage points, especially when coupled with biases discussed previously, can result in multiple witnesses to the same event "seeing" the event differently. This can result in multiple witnesses providing seemingly contradictory information. When possible, the scene should be viewed from the same viewpoint as the witness and at the same time as the incident. This can help the investigator understand what obstructions, distances, and other factors may have affected the witnesses' perception of the incident.

3-7. In some cases an individual may have been present during an event but may not be able provide reliable information due to mental or emotional issues. These issues can be due to chronic mental illness or short-term emotional distress, or possibly due to emotional distress and physiological trauma caused by witnessing or being a victim in the event. Persons may also be impaired due to consumption of drugs or alcohol. Finally, some witnesses may intentionally and/or unintentionally lie or withhold information due to personal motivations. These motivations can include fear of police, peer pressure, fear of retribution by criminal elements, embarrassment, self-blame, or even pressure from family members. In some cases these factors can be overcome if investigators can determine the factor influencing a witness's behavior, although in many cases the personal motivations may be so ingrained in the individual that cooperation is not attainable.

FACTORS INFLUENCING INFORMATION SHARING

3-8. Rapport is widely regarded as an essential foundation for most successful interviews and LE interrogations. It is the gateway upon which an investigator begins to understand an individual's personal motivations and obstacles to gaining information. Building rapport is merely an initial step toward motivating a subject to cooperate and share information. The establishment of rapport enables the investigator to influence the subject through other means. It allows exert techniques of persuasion to increase the suspect's motivation to share information. Techniques and considerations for building rapport are discussed in detail below.

FACTORS AFFECTING MOTIVATION

3-9. Successful investigators are adept at influencing others to provide information. They must develop skills to overcome any reluctance an individual may have to provide information and to encourage continued cooperation beyond the initial information provided. Investigators should be aware of factors affecting interpersonal influence. They must also understand when and how they can influence these factors. Factors that can greatly affect an individual's motivation to share information include—

- **Likeability.** One significant factor is how much an individual likes the other person. The factors that determine whether a person is likeable or not can be affected by the area of the world where the individual was raised and the associated dominant culture. While some factors are consistent across all cultures, others may be unique to a specific culture. Investigators must be aware of these differences when operating in areas where "Western" culture is not dominant. Some factors that affect a person's "likeability" are within an individual's control while others are not. Within Western cultures we tend to like others who—
  - Are physically attractive. This is a relative factor and may be stronger in the negative where a person is uncomfortable with an individual with unattractive features.
  - Appear to like us (directly and indirectly communicated).
  - Behave in a friendly and positive manner.
  - Are similar to us.
  - Are familiar to us.
  - Cooperate with us or generally behave consistently with our own interests.
  - Appear to possess positive traits such as intelligence, competence, kindness, and honesty.
- **Reciprocity.** This is a mutual or cooperative interchange of favors or privileges or "give and take." People are more likely to give to those from whom they have already received or expect to receive something. This applies not only to material goods, but also to social commodities such as favors and information. People are more likely to respond positively to suggestions or requests for compliance from someone who has first provided a benefit to them than from someone who has not. This may be a benefit to investigators. Suspects may be more willing to "give" to an investigator if they have first provided something; this could be intangible, such as fair treatment or sincere concern for their predicament, or something tangible such as reading material or something to eat.
- **Commitment and consistency.** People want to see themselves, and be seen by others, as fulfilling their promises and commitments, possessing a coherent set of beliefs and values, and always acting consistently with those beliefs. Investigators may be able to leverage an individual's sense of duty and commitment to influence cooperation. If an individual holds extreme loyalty to a group that operates on the fringes of or outside the law, their sense of commitment to that group can be a major obstacle to an investigator's efforts to gain information.
- **Authority.** An investigator's perceived authority is another major relationship-based determinant of influence. Individuals are more likely to be influenced by the argument of a person whom they perceive as an authority or an expert, especially if their expertise is directly relevant to the current issue. Similarly, they are more likely to comply with instructions, requests, or directives made by someone who has status, authority, or relevant expertise. Some individuals may be likely to defer to the authority of LE personnel. In other cases authority can work against the investigator; an individual's deference to authority may be stronger to specific members of their family than to LE personnel. Individuals who are members of criminal organizations are likely to maintain loyalties to their organizational leadership over LE personnel.
- **Social validation.** People want to fit in and be accepted. One force that inclines people to action is the belief that others have already performed the action before—especially if the belief is that

many have already acted. For example, an individual might be more likely to provide information if he believes that other individuals have already done so. Strong family or peer values associated with justice and a sense of right and wrong can influence an individual to cooperate with authorities. The desire for social validation can also work against the investigator. Strong family or peer pressure, including association with criminal elements, can be exerted on an individual to remain uncooperative with LE personnel. In some social groups revenge can be a strong motivator; individuals may lie in an effort to gain revenge on a personal foe or rival group.

- **Scarcity.** Something that is abundant or easily attainable is not nearly as desirable as something scarce or rare. Within the context of obtaining information, an investigator might offer an incentive for information that is only available to the individual if he provides the information immediately or within a short, specified time frame. If the individual does not comply within the set parameters, the offer is no longer valid. The diminishing availability of the incentive will increase value of the incentive and may result in the individual's cooperation in exchange for the promised reward.

- **Fear.** Fear can be a strong motivator for individuals. Fear on its own will generally work against the investigator. The individual may be fearful of retaliation by other persons or elements. These fears may be justified or irrational. Emotional distress or physiological trauma can place an individual in a fearful state that inhibits his ability to cooperate or communicate at all. Investigators must learn techniques to alleviate these fears and gain the confidence of the individual. Creating or increasing fear to gain information can be risky. For the use of fear to be effective, the individual must consider the threat credible and must believe that the investigator will withdraw it if the individual complies. For example, threatening an individual with harm is not particularly effective because they may believe that an investigator who is willing to harm them might be willing, or even likely, to harm them whether they comply or not. The individual's motivation to comply, therefore, diminishes. People who believe they are being coerced are likely to feel disrespected and become less likely to comply or cooperate. The use of fear to gain information is generally discouraged; the recommended technique is to reduce the individual's fear by building rapport and gaining his confidence.

Note. Using techniques to create or increase fear in an individual to gain information is not recommended. Fear can be a strong motivator but the results that an individual provides from a position of fear can be questionable. Some traditional notions of interrogation suggest that fear can be a powerful motivator and that the fear of a specific threat or consequence often affects behavior even more than the threat or consequence itself. Reality is that fear may motivate an individual to talk, but not necessarily to provide accurate information.

BUILDING RAPPORT

3-10. Establishing a good rapport with those involved in an investigation will aid the investigator immensely in conducting a thorough and timely investigation. Developing a good rapport does not mean that the investigator must become friendly or "buddies" with the individual. It means that a sense of mutual respect and understanding is established.

3-11. Rapport building begins immediately upon first contact with a victim, witness, suspect, commander, or other LE agencies and continues throughout the course of the investigation. Investigators must always be cognizant of their behavior and conduct when in the presence of these persons. Rapport usually begins to develop during normal conversation, maybe even "small talk," and serves at least two functions. It helps to or facilitates compliance with subsequent requests and gets the suspect talking. It also allows the investigator to identify and assess potential motivations, interests, and vulnerabilities. The way the suspect perceives the investigator and their relationship becomes especially critical under conditions in which the suspect is unmotivated or unable to devote mental energy to thinking about, and analyzing the investigator's arguments.

3-12. Victims, witnesses, and suspects will immediately begin sizing up the investigator. An investigator who is perceived as unprofessional, rude, lazy, unprepared, or uncaring will not gain the trust and confidence of the victim or witness and is more likely to be challenged by a suspect. An investigator who presents a professional appearance and attitude and conveys a genuine concern for the individual being interviewed will obtain a much higher level of cooperation. Each person must be treated with dignity and respect, regardless of the investigator's personal views or opinions. Investigators displaying these positive attributes will see a greater level of cooperation from commanders and other LE agencies as well. Rapport is the cornerstone of testimonial evidence and must be maintained throughout the investigative process.

3-13. Establishing and maintaining effective rapport with suspects during an interrogation is instrumental in obtaining their cooperation and getting them to expose facts they would not otherwise feel comfortable disclosing. The key to establishing rapport lies almost entirely within the mind of the interviewer. If the investigator cannot relate to the suspect as an innocent person, he will not be able to effectively develop rapport or display sincerity. The investigator must look for characteristics or commonalities between himself and the suspect in order to see the suspect as an individual. It is important for the investigator to remember that no one is inherently evil and that good people sometimes do bad things. If an investigator is able to separate the crime from the person being interrogated, he is more likely to get the suspect to like, trust, and respect him. Guilty persons are substantially more likely to confess to an investigator they like, trust, and respect; whereas, innocent suspects are provided the greatest safeguards from false confessions through rapport-based interrogation techniques.

3-14. Sincerity is the most difficult component of rapport building for most investigators. It is the best tool to employ to emotionally move the suspect. The capacity to listen to, and hear about, trauma-related events and criminal activity on a day-in, day-out basis, does not come easily or all at once. The same can be said for learning to conduct correct and productive interviews and interrogations. These processes must be developed. Developing this capacity requires an active, willing, empathic extension of the self into areas of human failure and malevolence; this takes practice. Investigators often believe they can "pretend" to care about the suspect's situation in order to gain their trust; however, sincerity is difficult to fake. Investigators should be truly sincere in their dealings with individuals during an investigation. Separating the crime from the suspect and finding something within the suspect that the investigator can relate to are the most effective means by which investigators can develop genuine concern for the suspect. This is the key to developing and maintaining rapport with the suspect and gaining his confidence.

INTERVIEW TYPES

3-15. *Interviews* are nonstructured discussions, where open-ended questions are asked to determine facts about an incident or crime (ATTP 3-39.10). They are used for fact-finding about personal experiences and are probative in nature; interviews are conducted by all Army LE personnel to gather information and determine facts about a crime, experience, or incident. Interviews conducted during LE activities and investigations are less structured then interrogations.

3-16. There are several types of interviews that may be conducted. The type used depends on the situation and the person being interviewed. Interview types include—
- Canvass interviews.
- Victim interviews.
- Witness interviews.
- Suspect interviews.

3-17. Interrogations are usually a deliberate and structured form of interview. They are conducted by trained LE personnel, typically MPIs or USACIDC SAs. A *law enforcement interrogation* is the systematic effort by law enforcement investigators to prove, disprove, or corroborate information relevant to a criminal investigation using direct questioning in a controlled environment (ATTP 3-39.10). An investigator conducting an interrogation in support of a criminal investigation often uses an understanding of human nature and natural human responses to obtain information from individuals during questioning. LE interrogations are employed when there is reasonable suspicion of the guilt of the subject.

CANVASS INTERVIEWS

3-18. Canvass interviews are useful in developing background information and evidence from personnel who may have direct or indirect knowledge about the reported offense, the behavior of persons involved in the incident, and other key factors that may corroborate information obtained from other key witnesses, victims, and suspects. During a canvass interview, the target for the interview would be anyone who might be likely to have seen, heard, or experienced something significant to the crime. Canvass interviews are designed to cover the entire area surrounding a crime scene, gather information, and identify potential witnesses. In some cases individuals who were not aware that a crime was committed possess material facts that can aid in the investigation. These individuals may not think to report something they had heard or observed based solely on a person, activity, or behavior being suspicious, out of place, or simply unknown within the neighborhood. For example, if someone observed a stranger in their neighborhood, they may mentally take note of their observations but not report it to the authorities unless informed of a crime and asked if they had heard or seen anything out of the ordinary during the time frame in question.

3-19. Canvass interviews are most effective if conducted within 24 hours of the incident being investigated. Some human memory fades with time, and people tend to recall information for long periods of time only if it is significant to them. Merely seeing a person or vehicle in a neighborhood or hearing a loud bang that awakened them from sleep would probably not be a significant event. As time passes, it becomes increasingly difficult for the individual to recall specific details, such as what time an event occurred; the color, make, and model of a vehicle; and the physical descriptions of any suspicious people.

3-20. During a protracted, difficult case it may be beneficial to revisit the area canvass several times. Follow-up contacts may allow the initially reluctant witness to now feel more comfortable about speaking to investigators. It is also possible that the individual may have learned vital new information about the incident. Witnesses may acquire fresh facts; they will rarely divulge that knowledge to investigators unless asked directly. Also, by repeating the canvass, witnesses who were not originally available, or who were previously unknown, may now be located.

3-21. Canvass interviews should be conducted by physically walking through the immediate area where a crime was committed, such as a neighborhood, business district, or public gathering place. Every individual that might have been in a position to see or hear something of evidentiary value should be located and interviewed. In many cases military police patrol personnel can be tasked to assist with canvass interviews. An effective technique for obtaining information in a canvass interview is to ask the potential witness if he "saw or heard anything out of the ordinary or that caused some concern" during the time frame in question. Each person talked to should be fully identified and documented by name, address, and phone number and a brief description of what the witness observed or did not observe. This information not only documents the contact but also enables follow-on investigation when more detailed interviews of persons identified are warranted.

3-22. In some situations retaliation for "snitching" to LE personnel is a real life possibility that must be understood by Army LE personnel. Witnesses who refuse or are reluctant to cooperate with LE personnel may have ample reason for their reluctance to talk. That is why each person approached should be provided with a contact number and assurances that they may remain anonymous.

3-23. In some cases, it may be beneficial to conduct the canvass interviews at the same time of day or night that the crime occurred. Additionally, some instances may require conducting canvass interviews on the same day of the week that the crime occurred. Some witnesses may only be in a particular area on a certain day or at a specific time as part of their routine. This is especially helpful in locating potential witnesses who work shifts or are only in the area during specific times of the day, such as postal workers or people who jog or walk pets past the area.

VICTIM INTERVIEWS

3-24. Victim interviews are conducted to obtain specific information concerning the crime or incident that has occurred and resulted in harm to the individual or his property. If the victim was assaulted or present to witness a crime against his property, the victim may be able to describe items used in the commission of the offense that may not otherwise be identified during a crime scene examination. Although victim interviews and other investigative actions often occur simultaneously, it is important that the scene not be released until after the victim is interviewed.

3-25. When interviewing a victim, always be aware that the victim may be traumatized and emotionally affected. Persons may be more affected by trauma as a result of experiencing certain crimes such as child abuse, attempted murder, sexual assault, aggravated assault, robbery, and such. Victims of larceny, fraud, simple assault, and such may be more or less affected by trauma dependent on the meaning of the crime to that individual.

> *Note.* Investigators should be familiar with the provisions of DODD 1030.01 and DODI 1030.2. These directives implement statutory requirements for victim and witness assistance and provide guidance for assisting victims and witnesses of a crime. Together, the directive and the instruction provide policy guidance and specific procedures to be followed for victim and witness assistance in all sectors of the military.

3-26. For victims of violent crimes (such as sexual assaults, attempted homicide, and robbery) it might be necessary to delay obtaining an in-depth statement for an appropriate period of time to allow the victim to sufficiently recover from the traumatic event. However, a delay in the acquisition of an in-depth statement does not negate the need to conduct an initial oral interview. A brief initial victim interview should be conducted as soon as possible to obtain basic investigative facts, such as the identity of the subject/suspect, the location of the crime scene, and possible witnesses. Establish who, what, where, when, why, and how so that the investigators can preserve the crime scene, including the suspect, and evidence for processing. It is also critical to preserve and document the emotional and/or physical changes the victim is experiencing as a result of the traumatic event.

3-27. Because the victim interview is necessary in order to obtain important information, the viability of the investigation depends on proper handling of the interview. It is important to understand that the victim could potentially be a walking crime scene and eyewitness. Mishandling an interview with a trauma victim can irreparably damage the investigation, as the victim alone can provide much of the necessary evidence in developing the case.

WITNESS INTERVIEWS

3-28. A witness is anyone having knowledge of a crime or incident. Witnesses can include—

- **Eyewitnesses.** An eyewitness is anyone who has direct knowledge about a crime or incident through sight, smell, touch, or hearing activities or aspects of the actual crime or event.
- **Significant parties.** Significant parties are persons who do not possess direct knowledge or observations of the crime, but have information that could help prove or disprove aspects of the crime being investigated. For example, they may provide an alibi for an individual, confirm or refute historical facts about a crime scene or incident site, or may have been witness to, and be able to document statements made by, an individual involved in a crime or incident. This can be true even though they were not present when the crime was committed.

3-29. Witnesses should be interviewed individually to obtain facts about the incident under investigation. In the event that there are multiple witnesses to the same event, they should be separated before the interview and not allowed to discuss the case before being interviewed. If they are traumatized as a result of what they observed, they will often want to be with people that they feel comfortable with, such as family or friends who also may have witnessed the incident. These situations must be evaluated case-by-case to determine the best way to proceed; in some instances it may be appropriate to accommodate such requests. However, the investigator should instruct the witnesses not to discuss the incident and explain why their discussions could affect what each individual remembers about what they observed or heard. If these requests are deemed appropriate, an Army LE or other appropriate person should wait with the witnesses to ensure that discussions do not occur.

3-30. Investigators should take a sympathetic approach, allowing the witness to tell their story for the first time without interruption. While listening to the entire account, investigators should be supportive and understanding of the witnesses' emotional states. Once the story is fully disclosed, it becomes easier for the witness to talk about it. This will provide the investigator the opportunity to seek out details more directly relevant to the investigation.

3-31. A written sworn statement should be obtained from all witnesses. Caution should be taken in providing witnesses with copies of their statements. The release of these documents can create difficulty later in the investigation, especially if a victim or witness becomes a suspect at a later point in the investigation. Additionally, witnesses who are provided with a copy of their statement tend to read them again before subsequent interviews. This makes it difficult for investigators to identify inconsistencies in stories over a period of time. It is normal for a person's memory to fade over a period of time; guilty persons tend to think through their story (or even rehearse), making their story more consistent over long periods. Individuals who read their previous statements before subsequent interviews will tend to provide the same level of details months after the incident. If another investigator is unaware that the witness had access to their previous statement, this can cause unwarranted confusion and suspicion.

> *Note.* Not releasing copies of statements is an accepted practice. It is done to protect the integrity of the investigation. If the person who rendered a statement requests a copy of it, consideration must be given as to whether or not releasing the statement will hamper future investigative efforts. In many of these situations, it may be better to provide copies of these statements only after the completion of the investigation. If a formal Freedom of Information Act request is received that requests the release of investigative products, it should be coordinated with USACIDC or appropriate installation release authority.

3-32. Occasionally, an investigator may encounter an individual who is reluctant or refuses to cooperate with the investigation and provide a statement. This is a common situation in cases where the individual has been traumatized by the event. Other reasons may exist; for example, the victim or witness may be afraid of retribution or may be a friend of the suspect and does not want to see the suspect prosecuted. Attempts should be made to understand why the victim or the witness does not wish to cooperate. With that understanding, the interviewer can attempt to alleviate any fears the witness may have and explain the importance of their cooperation. Some victims or witnesses may believe that they have a "right to remain silent" even though this is not the case. If necessary, military members can be ordered to cooperate with investigators. This should be used as a last resort. In the case of civilians, the prosecutor can issue a subpoena and compel them to testify. In either case, the investigator should consult with the appropriate prosecutor to determine the best course of action when dealing with uncooperative victims and witnesses.

SUSPECT INTERVIEWS

3-33. Before beginning an interview of a suspect, safety is paramount. All suspects should be searched for weapons and or contraband. The first thing that must be addressed in determining whether to interview or interrogate a subject is to recognize the difference between an interview and an interrogation. An interview is generally unstructured and can take place in a variety of locations, such as a residence, a workplace, or a police station. It is conducted in a dialogue format where investigators are seeking answers—typically to open-ended questions—and the guilt or innocence of the person being interviewed is generally unknown.

> *Note.* Any person reasonably suspected of a crime must be advised of his rights before questioning.

3-34. When questioning a suspect for the first time, if there is no reasonably certainty of guilt, an interview is the preferred investigative tool. During this process, the subject will be asked questions about his actions during the time of the incident. Investigators should obtain detailed descriptions of the individual's activities for the periods of time before, during, and after the crime occurred. By obtaining this information, investigators will be able to determine the accuracy of any alibis and whether or not there is evidence that is in conflict with the reported actions of the suspect. Through observation and assessment of the subject's verbal and nonverbal responses, the investigator can determine if any indications of deception are present; this may cause the interview to transition to an interrogation.

3-35. When conducting an interview, the subject is asked questions and is encouraged to speak freely. Note taking should be avoided throughout this process if at all possible. Interviews are not confrontational in nature; do not directly accuse the subject of committing the crime under investigation. However, questions pertaining to the subject's possible involvement, motivation, or other issues that could connect the individual to the crime may be explored. Avoid asking the suspect questions that will likely result in denial; this will make getting to the truth more difficult during the interrogation.

3-36. Even in cases where there is a reasonably certainty that the individual is responsible for the crime under investigation, it is generally recommended that an indirect interview technique be used to initiate discussion with the subject. This may produce enough incriminating information, and possibly an admission or confession, without conducting an interrogation. If the indirect approach does not produce the information being sought, an interrogation may be required. The interaction between the interviewer and the suspect should not be adversarial. It should provide the suspect with dignity and respect. Specific interrogation techniques are discussed later in this chapter.

INTERVIEW AND INTERROGATION STYLES

3-37. Selection of the appropriate interview style depends on many factors including whether the subject being interviewed is a victim, a witness, or a suspect. The level of certainty the investigator has regarding the guilt of a suspect can also affect the interview approach chosen. When reasonable certainty of guilt is not established, the individual should be interviewed using an indirect style; if the individual's guilt is relatively certain, an advanced or direct style is typically the proper choice.

INDIRECT STYLE

3-38. When interviewing witnesses, victims, or potential suspects when the individual's guilt is uncertain or doubtful, indirect questioning is used to gain a detailed account of the individual's activities before, during, and after the time the offense took place. If the individual was previously interviewed, the investigator should review documentation from any previous interviews to determine what the individual stated during these earlier interviews. When selecting an interview style, consideration should be given to using the FETI technique, even in cases where trauma is not an issue. The FETI is nonconfrontational, and different from what an accused expects. This style may disarm defensiveness and lead to disclosure. Regardless of the style chosen by the investigator, the ultimate goal is to gain the cooperation of the subject and to extract required information. See appendix C for more information on the FETI technique.

3-39. The indirect style of questioning is exploratory in nature and is generally initiated by merely asking the person to tell the investigator his story or to explain his actions on the date in question. The investigator listens making observations of both verbal and nonverbal mannerisms and reactions to questions. Questions are generally asked for clarification or to explore apparent inconsistencies. Questions posed in this style are generally open-ended and are not inclined to lead a suspect in any direction with their answer. Facts that definitively show or strongly suggest the individual's guilt are used to formulate questions designed to evaluate the suspect's verbal responses and physical reactions.

3-40. Although neither the indirect style nor the FETI technique is designed to cause perpetrators to confess, it may provide both admissions and confessions. These techniques are designed to arm the investigator with an extremely detailed account of the individual's activities, which can be verified or refuted by facts developed through the investigative process. Once sufficient evidence is established to warrant an interrogation, the investigator may transition to the direct style.

ADVANCED OR DIRECT STYLE (INTERROGATION)

3-41. The advanced or direct style of interviewing is designed to prevent the suspect from becoming psychologically entrenched in a lie. If a suspect is allowed to repeatedly espouse fabrications that are known to be untrue, over time the suspect becomes comfortable with his lies which will make getting to the truth more difficult. In this style, the suspect is not allowed to speak freely; the session is not an open two-way communication. The investigator dominates the conversation, almost to the point of a monologue. The investigator lays out case facts and works on the emotions, logic, and reasoning of the suspect in an attempt to get him to see his situation in a more realistic light, without enabling him to build a wall of lies. This style of interviewing is very structured and should be well planned before initiating the interrogation.

3-42. While occasionally some case facts are provided to the suspect to make him feel that he was identified as the person responsible for the crime, other evidence is withheld from the suspect to identify or corroborate admissions or confessions. Investigators must decide which evidence to reveal and which to withhold. For this style to work effectively, the investigator must present no uncertainty as to the suspect's guilt, but should seem relatively uncertain as to motivation. If the investigator seems uncertain, the suspect will be significantly more likely to hold out hope that his involvement in the crime will go undetected.

VICTIM AND WITNESS INTERVIEWS

3-43. It is important to select a physical setting or environment that is conducive to gaining the trust and confidence of an individual being interviewed and therefore produce the most meaningful information. The setting of any interview or interrogation can be structured as comfortably or as starkly as the investigator deems appropriate for the circumstances of the individual being interviewed.

ROLE OF THE INVESTIGATOR

3-44. Conducting a better interview begins with a realistic understanding of the role of the investigator. The investigator's primary role during witness and victim interviews is to gather information. Once the information is gathered, the investigator must work to confirm or corroborate that information to establish it as fact. If the information cannot be confirmed as fact, the information may be suspect. Investigators must remember that while corroboration of information as fact is important, the inability to directly corroborate a specific item of information does not necessarily mean that the information is false unless other validated information directly contradicts the uncorroborated information.

3-45. Investigators should corroborate as many facts as possible, no matter how insignificant they may seem. This enables the investigator to establish the validity of the individual's story, even when there may be other problems with the investigation. Verifying as many details as possible, even when they are not directly relevant to the elements of the crime, can bolster the individual's credibility. The purpose of conducting a thoughtful, thorough, and accurate interview is to gather and corroborate as much as the individual's story as possible to protect and improve his credibility as a potential prosecution witness.

3-46. While the investigator should seek to give a witness or victim the benefit of the doubt, the investigator must maintain his objectivity. One approach in this process is to focus on developing at least three hypotheses of the reported incident. These may include the following:

- That the incident happened as the individual described.
- That the incident happened but in a different manner than the individual described.
- That the incident did not happen.

3-47. The investigator should attempt to prove or disprove each one of the hypotheses to remain unbiased throughout the interview. An investigator must also have a constant awareness of both societal and his own personal stereotypes in order to overcome biases that can unfairly challenge the individual's credibility. A critical element in applying this concept is to find ways to understand the individual's experience during the interview. Ask questions related to the smells, tastes, sounds, and feelings that are associated with the individual's experience; realize that the truth is in the details, so understanding and documenting the experience is important.

OBSTACLES TO EFFECTIVE INTERVIEWING

3-48. Obstacles encountered during criminal investigations are common occurrences. Most of these obstacles can be overcome by the investigator through experience, creativity, and determination. Many of these same methods that prove successful during many areas of the investigation can be detrimental in an interview. Some approaches and techniques serve as hindrances to an effective and accurate interview, and should be avoided. These approaches and techniques include—

- **Asking for "just the facts."** Many investigators feel that just asking for the "who, what, where, when, why, and how" is sufficient for a thorough interview. It is important to take the time to ask thoughtful questions and become involved in the interview in order to heighten the chances of a productive dialogue. Asking only the basic questions limits an investigator to only the basic facts.

- **Displaying the LE personality.** The LE personality, in very general terms, tends to be a very action-oriented, problem-solving mentality. While this personality type can serve well in some circumstances, it can be counterproductive, especially in cases where an individual is upset or traumatized. Interviews of upset or traumatized persons, conducted correctly, can be drawn-out, detail laden, and emotionally taxing for all persons involved. An investigator may constantly fight to "move on" with the interview, rather than provide the individual the time and delicate touch necessary to achieve the required results.

- **Displaying the "tough-guy" act.** This is especially prevalent in domestic and sexual assault cases, especially when children are involved, because the cases can be so emotionally difficult. These cases are difficult not only for the individual but for the investigator as well. An investigator may have a tendency to adopt a tough act when responding to these cases. This false exterior is an attempt by the investigator to distance himself from the emotion of the case and maintain an unbiased image in front of the individual. While adopting this image may help investigators feel more in control of themselves and their emotions, it can serve as a significant barrier to effectively connecting with the individual and conducting a productive interview.

- **Using poor interview techniques.** Many investigators learn much of their interview techniques under less than optimal interview conditions, where time and technique are considered a luxury. It is critical to consider that time spent early to learn and conduct good interview techniques is time well invested that will potentially save the need for additional man-hours to conduct follow-up interviews and may also prevent possible emotional harm to the individual.

- **Misinterpreting verbal and nonverbal cues.** Investigators should be cautious about placing too much value on the reliability of verbal and nonverbal cues as indicators of deception or truthfulness. The belief that there are reliable cues to deception is frequently incorrect. These indicators can be extremely unreliable, especially when accepted without full understanding of the individual, his specific traits and mannerisms, and other environmental factors. It is essential that nonverbal behaviors and verbal cues are identified and documented as appropriate. They may be useful in determining some general characteristics such as demeanor, affect, and reaction to current physiological pressures, but they are generally limited in determining the truthfulness of an individual or the statements being made. Great care must be taken to correctly understand the meaning of these indicators; nonverbal behaviors and verbal speech patterns may have different meanings to different people.

INTERVIEW PREPARATION

3-49. Crafting a desirable and minimally damaging interview atmosphere is an important aspect to a conducive and productive interview. In addition to establishing a physically and psychologically appropriate location, investigators must manage their demeanor and reactions throughout the interview process. An individual will speak more freely and fully if he believes that the investigator is truly listening. The listener must simultaneously portray a sense of tolerance and convey to the individual that he understands and believes what the individual is saying.

Select the Interview Settings

3-50. Interviews or fact-finding explorations can be conducted in a variety of settings, locations, and environments. An interview can be effectively conducted in environments either supportive to the witness or the victim such as their home or another location of their convenience or choosing, or nonsupportive such as a police station. Interviews may be conducted at a police station, although this setting may intimidate many individuals and produce less than optimum results. It is completely acceptable to conduct an interview at a suspect's work, home, or other location where he may feel more comfortable. Comfort sometimes allows a suspect to talk more openly and freely, which can lead to more and better information.

3-51. Equally important is the task of making the individual feel comfortable and at ease in the interview setting. This can be thought of as setting the stage and consists of several important considerations including—

- Selecting an appropriate location. Investigators should—
  - Ensure that the site is safe and comfortable for the individual, both emotionally and physically.
  - Ensure that the site is private and free from distractions and unnecessary noise.
- Maintaining a physical position that is equal to or inferior to that of the individual. This allows the individual to sense a feeling of regaining a small portion of control over his physical surroundings and help put him at ease despite the discomfort of the interview. For example, sitting on steps, with the individual at a higher point than the investigator or in a hospital setting, sitting in a chair while a victim remains on the hospital examining table, may help accomplish this goal.
- Asking the individual if he would like anyone to be present during the interview.
- Explaining the purpose of the interview and address any immediate concerns. Understand that—
  - The purpose is to gather evidence and obtain the individual's statement, not to find fault or blame.
  - There will be questions the individual may be unable or unwilling to answer.
- Having the appearance of being accepting and compassionate. Investigators should acknowledge the gravity of the ordeal, allow the individual to vent, and demonstrate empathy. Use the following guidelines:
  - Appropriate things to say include, "I'm sorry this happened to you," or "How are you feeling?" or "I can see this is very difficult for you."
  - Inappropriate things to say include, "Everything will be okay," or "It could have been worse," or "You shouldn't feel that way," or "Don't cry."
- Helping the individual regain control. Allowing the individual to make these seemingly insignificant types of decisions accomplishes several goals. It allows the individual to feel a sense of control and builds rapport and trust with the interviewer. It can assist in long-term emotional healing. Finally, it helps facilitate long-term cooperation throughout the investigation. When appropriate, let the individual decide—
  - Where to sit or conduct the interview.
  - Who is present.
  - How you are addressed (first or last name, titles, and such).
  - Whether you can get in touch with someone for them.

Explain the Process

3-52. Creating and maintaining an open interview is important to the success of the interview, especially when interviewing an upset or traumatized individual. Investigators should explain the interview process and why specific things are asked. Explaining questions dealing with sensitive issues helps put the individual's fears at ease. Investigators can use the law to explain why specific information is needed to further the investigation. In some cases, an individual may have participated in high-risk behavior leading up to the incident; investigators should explain that the individual's activities do not cause the investigator to doubt the individual's story.

Be Aware of Physical Gestures and Language

3-53. An investigator's physical actions and gestures can greatly affect the success of an interview. Maintaining eye contact with the individual during the course of the interview is vital to maintaining the flow of communication. While it is important to look the individual in the eye when addressing him, it is more important to make eye contact when he is answering your questions. This lets the individual know the investigator is listening to him and appreciates what he is saying. Be aware that some individuals, especially victims of domestic or sexual assault, feel shame and cannot look the interviewer in the eye;

investigators should not force eye contact in these cases. In some cultures it is offensive behavior for a man who is not a woman's husband to look her in the eye. Additionally, if the individual appears to be upset or embarrassed, it may be helpful to look the other way for the period of time in which he demonstrates distress or discomfort.

3-54. Investigators should be aware of their body language. They should generally use open body language, maintaining a relaxed, although not dismissive, manner with the individual. Positive head nodding can also indicate to the individual that the investigator is listening and is concerned. Gestures, body movement, and tone of voice should all express an air of reassurance and support, and that the individual is being allowed space and as much time as necessary to explain his story. Investigators should avoid touching the individual, especially victims of assault. It is unadvisable to touch a victim of sexual assault because of the extreme personal and violating nature of the crime that has been perpetrated against them. The victim could construe any uninvited physical contact as an additional violation of his personal space.

3-55. Investigators should speak to the individual in plain language. Avoid using LE terminology. Although unintentional, this may be interpreted as intimidating and may be confusing to the individual. Clarify slang terms that the individual may use to ensure complete understanding and to minimize assumptions later during the writing of the investigative report. For example the individual may say, "I saw them get nasty." The investigator should clarify by saying, "What do you mean by get nasty?"

3-56. Ask the clarifying question in an open-ended manner; do not provide a leading question. This forces the individual to provide the clarification and not merely agree with the investigator's statement. Duplicate the terminology the individual uses, without displays of shock or embarrassment. Using the same terminology as the individual will help him feel more comfortable and relaxed in expressing his experience. Conversely, acting shocked, embarrassed, or uncomfortable with certain terminology may cause the individual to withdraw.

VICTIM OR WITNESS NARRATIVE

3-57. Avoid any leading or accusatory questions when obtaining the individual's story. This will help eliminate any concern that the individual was unduly influenced in any way. Victims of violent attacks, especially sexual attacks, are highly susceptible to influences of those around them, especially of people in power. An investigator may unwittingly influence the individual's account of events. Also, by asking leading questions, the investigator may convey the idea that answering a question in a certain way would be the "right" answer.

3-58. During this stage of the interview, the investigators should use open-ended prompts and allow ample time for a thoughtful response. This allows the individual to tell his story completely, giving him control over the process. The individual should be leading the conversation with occasional encouragement from the investigator. By allowing this method of conversation flow, the investigator is likely to get more accurate and uncorrupted information.

3-59. Engage in active listening without interrupting the flow of the individual's narrative. The investigator should occasionally try to interject comments that indicate he has been listening; encouraging the individual to continue talking while acknowledging what he said will show him that the investigator is listening intently. However, excessive interruptions by the investigator should be avoided. Interruptions by the investigator conducting the interview can be a major obstacle to obtaining a thorough and complete interview. Interrupting an individual's narrative, even just to clarify a point, may interrupt the individual's train of thought and potentially cause him to be confused, skip a detail, or forget a detail he was about to convey.

3-60. The investigator should use open-ended questions to both show interest and avoid leading the interview. These questions and responses allow the individual to provide much more detail. They will enable the individual to describe the event in a conversational format. In turn, this will help investigators better understand the situation and overcome most, if not all, challenges to the individual's credibility. Appropriate open-ended questions or responses include—
- What do you remember doing next?

- Help me understand.
- Tell me what you were thinking at that point.
- Tell me what you were feeling (physically/emotionally) when he did that.
- Tell me more about that.

3-61. Avoid leading or accusatory questions. These questions include—
- Did he/she use physical force to restrain you?
- Was he/she bigger than you?
- Did you resist?
- Why didn't you_____?

3-62. Upon completion of the initial narrative, the investigator can clarify specific points. This provides an opportunity to gather additional details about the individual's experience, again using open-ended follow-up questions.

INTERVIEW CONCLUSION

3-63. Ask the individual if they have any additional information that they want to report. Allowing the individual to stop to collect their thoughts, especially after a lengthy or emotionally intense interview, may prompt them to provide additional information that may be useful. Reassure and thank the individual and continue to extend empathy. For victims of assault, reassure the individual that the attack was in no way his fault. The investigator may also thank the individual for his cooperation and for enduring the interview.

3-64. Explain future proceedings. The investigator should explain to the individual what the next steps in the investigation will be, how the investigation should proceed, and that follow-up interviews may be necessary. Because most people have no experience with LE procedures, taking the time to explain to the individual the follow-up process will potentially lead to better cooperation. This is also the time to arrange for future periodic briefings to the individual to keep him informed on the status of the investigation.

INTERROGATIONS

3-65. Interrogations are structured activities and require thought and planning. An interrogation consists of four phases. Each phase serves a distinct purpose and allows the investigator to move in a structured and meaningful manner through the interrogation process. The four phases include—
- Preparation.
- Opening.
- Body.
- Closing.

PREPARATION PHASE

3-66. Probably the most neglected phase of the interrogation process is the preparation phase. By nature, interrogations are structured; however, it is difficult to develop this structure without adequate planning. There are several key components of preparation that provide the greatest advantage to the investigator. These components include—
- Researching the suspect's background.
- Researching case data.
- Planning and mentally preparing for the interrogation including—
  - Developing the theme.
  - Selecting the approach.
- Establishing the most appropriate interrogation environment.

Researching Suspect Background

3-67. Researching the suspect's background involves collecting as much background information on the subject as possible. This will aid the investigator in analyzing the suspect's training, education, financial situation, upbringing, and other factors that may be useful during the interrogation. The more background information an investigator has at his disposal, the better. This information will have a dramatic psychological impact during an interrogation. Presentation of this background information during the interview causes the suspect to realize how thorough the investigation is and will continue to be. This is extremely beneficial in increasing anxiety at key points of the interrogation process. Investigators should consider numerous sources when seeking background information on a suspect including—

- Employment or military records.
- Evaluation reports.
- Service record briefs.
- Medical records.
- National Crime Information Center data.
- Financial Crimes Enforcement Network records.
- Education records.
- Internet sources.

Researching Case Data

3-68. Another key component of the preparation phase is to research case data. A complete understanding of the incident under investigation is paramount to a successful interrogation. This should include physically visiting the crime scene, viewing all crime scene photos and sketches, reading all statements collected during the investigation to date, and discussing the investigation in detail with the case agent and other investigative personnel involved in investigating the offense.

3-69. While conducting this review, the investigator should identify all actual and potential evidence that could link the suspect to the scene, the victim, or the crime. Evidence is the pressure plate used in the interrogation that forces a suspect to face the fact that at the end of the investigation, there will be no doubt who committed the offense. Actual evidence is any evidence that is known to exist, such as physical evidence collected; surveillance tapes seized; testimonial evidence from victims, witnesses, or co-conspirators; or other items that the investigative organization already knows to exist. Potential evidence is evidence that could be identified during the investigation and might link the perpetrator to the crime.

Planning

3-70. Planning and mentally preparing for the interrogation involves a thorough analysis of all known case facts, the suspect's personal background, and what trends indicate why others have committed similar crimes. This enables the investigator to speculate what the suspect's motive was for committing the crime with a relatively high degree of accuracy. Once the investigator understands the likely motive for the crime, he should determine the most effective means of approaching the suspect. Investigators may ask themselves, "If I did this, how would I have to be approached, and what would I have to be confronted with for me to tell the truth about this?" Investigators should also prepare written questions during the planning phase. The investigator should prepare questions he will ask the suspect before initiating the interrogation. The investigator must be flexible during the interrogation as other questions may come to mind when asking a prepared question or the suspect's answers may prompt questions that were not planned.

3-71. By seeking to understand the mental state of the suspect and answering these questions, an investigator can develop the appropriate theme and select an approach that is best for getting the suspect to see his situation in the most realistic light while not making him defensive. If the investigator causes a suspect to take a defensive posture, a psychological barrier may be placed between the suspect and the investigator. This hampers the investigator's ability to maintain rapport. Mapping out the interrogation process in this manner provides the structure required for an interrogation. It will enable the investigator to more effectively control the process, ultimately resulting in full disclosure of the truth by the suspect being interrogated. Themes and approaches are discussed later in this chapter.

Establishing the Interrogation Environment

3-72. Establishing the most effective interrogation environment is a very important component of the interrogation process. An advanced or direct interrogation needs to be strictly planned and controlled. An interrogation should rarely, if ever, be conducted in a suspect-supportive environment. The location selected for an interrogation should be supportive to the investigator, controlled by the investigator, and provide absolute privacy that is free from distraction or disruption.

3-73. With an emphasis on safety and to avoid interruptions, a police station is the most appropriate location for an interrogation. If possible, a room specifically designed for interviews should be used. An ideal interrogation room would be one in which the surroundings of the room promote a relaxed and nonstressful environment in which the subject feels free to give candid and open responses in relating his experience of the incident under investigation. The room should be one which is free of exterior windows; however, including a floor or table lamp, a throw rug, and a plant (artificial would suffice), may serve to lessen the intimidating environment that is associated with being in a LE building.

3-74. Interrogation rooms should not be equipped with phones, outside windows, wall ornamentation, and such. The room should be strategically arranged to ensure the most practical and conducive environment. Where feasible, having a two-way mirror installed in the interview room may prove helpful in allowing other investigative personnel to observe the interrogation and take copious notes instead of being physically located in the interview room and serving as a distraction. If the room is equipped with a two-way mirror, the suspect should not face directly toward it. This serves as a constant reminder that someone may be monitoring the interview from another room and allows the subject to become distracted by his own reflection. Recording the interrogation (preferably video recording) is highly recommended if it is allowed and procedural requirements for this practice are in place. See the section in this chapter on documentation of statements.

3-75. It is generally a good idea to have a small table in the room to complete paperwork, such as interview worksheets and rights warning certificates. A suspect or uncooperative witness that is feeling threatened may attempt to use the table as a physical barrier between himself and the investigator. It is important to position the table and chairs in such a manner that they do not allow the table to become a physical barrier once the interrogation stage begins. Ideally, there should be two different types of chairs in the room. The suspect's chair should be a standard four-legged chair that is comfortable but not mobile. A chair for the suspect that can easily roll around the room can be distracting to the suspect and the investigator. The investigator's chair should be equipped with wheels and a swivel mechanism, allowing the investigator to move around subtly during the interrogation process. This allows the investigator to move back and forth from the table to the suspect as paperwork is being completed.

Establishing Themes

3-76. Themes are essentially the vehicle used by investigators to frame their overall direct, advanced interrogation approach. Themes are used to help the suspects see and appreciate their situation more clearly without making them defensive in the process. Themes can be as simple as the development of a theory of the suspect's motive that influences the suspect to open up about their involvement or as complex as a story that allows the suspect to draw his own conclusion about the right thing to do. Story-type themes are very effective in getting suspects to participate in the interview process in a philosophical manner without actually discussing the crime in question; this helps to keep the suspect from becoming defensive and putting up barriers.

3-77. Other story themes can be used to prevent the initial lie from being told and to humanize the investigator. If an investigator is reasonably certain of a suspect's guilt, it is significantly easier for the investigator to stop the lie before it is told. Once a suspect lies and the more he is allowed to lie, the more difficult it is to get beyond the lie to the truth. If a suspect knows that he is going to be interviewed, he typically goes over in his mind what he believes he will be confronted with and what evidence may exist that can link him to the crime. Then he explores his options to include what he can say to explain the evidence away in an attempt to get away with the crime. Themes can frequently help get beyond the preparation that suspects have done by enabling investigators to distract them from their prepared story and influence them to modify their view of the situation to a more realistic and practical one.

3-78. A theme may be designed to use the suspect's conscience against him and pry at those things most important to the suspect. This is why it is vital during the rapport-building stage for investigators to seek out the things important to the suspect such as values or relationships. This knowledge can be used by the investigator to influence a suspect to be honest. For instance, if a suspect has a strong relationship with his mother, investigators may want to have him reflect on how his mother would feel about the situation. If the suspect is extremely patriotic and loyal to the Army or his unit, this can be used as leverage.

3-79. Other themes may be designed to humanize the investigator and change the suspect's perspective of the investigator. Frequently in interrogation settings, the suspect has a predisposed view of the investigator as the enemy or someone who does not care about him; he sees the investigator as someone who just wants to solve the investigation and put someone in jail. Themes of this nature are designed to show the suspect that the investigator is a human being who cares about doing the right thing for the right reason. These types of themes attempt to show the suspect that the investigator is impartial, understanding, and trying to ensure that the most thorough efforts are undertaken to protect the interests of all involved in an ethical manner. Enabling suspects to recognize these facts helps them to relate to the investigator as an individual, cultivates trust, and builds respect between themselves and the investigator.

Selecting Approaches

3-80. Various approach methods may be used in the direct-interrogation technique. Investigators may use a single approach or they may be required to use multiple approaches, changing their approach during the interrogation based on the individual's personality and reactions. For example, the investigator may choose to initially flatter the suspect and then transition to the cold-shoulder approach to achieve the desired results. The following paragraphs discuss the different types of approaches including—

- Flattery.
- Suspect versus suspect.
- Sympathy.
- Logic and reasoning.
- Cold shoulder.
- Transference of blame.
- Hypothesis.

Flattery

3-81. Flattery is used to build self-esteem within the suspect or feed his ego. It is accomplished by making favorable observations, telling the suspect positive things that his command, friends, or loved ones have said about him. By complimenting his appearance, prior positive conduct, character, patriotism, or other attributes, the investigator can make the suspect feel better about himself. As long as this approach is delivered with sincerity, it will help the investigator build and maintain rapport and a sense of mutual trust and respect. After a suspect makes an admission, he may feel depressed or uncertain that confessing his actions was a good course of action. The use of flattery at this point helps reinforce his decision to be honest and enables him to continue telling the truth. The subject knows he did something wrong; condemning his actions serves no useful purpose. Flattery can help him maintain his self-respect, ease inner turmoil, and maintain a positive interview environment.

Suspect Versus Suspect

3-82. The suspect versus suspect approach is an option when investigating a crime involving more than one suspect. In these situations it is often effective to pit the suspects against each other. Seat the suspects where they can see each other through the door to the interview room, but where they cannot communicate. When a suspect realizes that other possible suspects to the crime have been identified and are also being interviewed, he will likely realize that the evidence against him is mounting and that another suspect may attempt to place himself in the best light by detailing a story that shifts blame or greater responsibility to his accomplices. This approach can have dramatic psychological impacts on a suspect and compel him to relate his story first in order to cast himself in the most credible and understandable situation possible.

Sympathy

3-83. The sympathy approach is designed to let the suspect know that the investigator understands what he did and why he did it. The investigator should be careful not to condone or condemn the offense, merely to understand the suspect's emotional state. To some extent, people want pity and understanding. The investigator should try to truly understand the suspect's motivation and emotional state, which will allow him to show sympathy and sincerity when talking to the suspect. Sincerity is important to this approach. Suspects will quickly identify attempts at sympathy that are void of sincerity as hollow words, resulting in a lack of cooperation and greater obstacles to overcome with the suspect.

Logic and Reasoning

3-84. This approach is generally the favored mechanism in cases with a great deal of evidence or when interviewing someone who is street-smart and has dealt with police on numerous occasions. The logic and reasoning approach is most effective with hardened or career criminals. In delivering this approach, the investigator should be rational, tell the suspect that the facts prove the case, and lay out those facts. The suspect should understand that the facts already show who, what, when, where, and how. At the end of the interview, the only thing left to understand is why the suspect committed the offense.

Cold Shoulder

3-85. The cold-shoulder approach is typically used on an egotistical individual after a lot of flattery. After building up the suspect's self-esteem, the investigator begins the interview process. However, when the suspect offers a denial that is clearly untrue, the investigator does not verbally respond to the statement, but merely realigns himself in his chair, leans back, and looks at the suspect in blank silence. Frequently, the suspect will realize how implausible his statement was and will attempt to clarify his statement or, in some cases, retract it. Investigators may follow up with a request that they be treated with the same respect that they have provided to the suspect. They may further request that their intelligence not be insulted. These tactics can result in an agreement to provide mutual respect and honesty.

Transference of Blame

3-86. In some cases, especially theft, a suspect will feel that the victim's actions justified the crimes. For instance, a suspect may feel that the government owed him compensation for the many long hours he worked and attempt to gain restitution by taking items of value from the Army. Sometimes a suspect may rationalize that the victim really did not want the stolen items or he would have secured them better. Occasionally, it may be effective for investigators to allow and encourage a subject's justifications. However, care must be exercised by investigators. In some cases a suspect may attempt to use transference of blame as a crutch to legally justify his actions, such as self-defense in an assault situation. The investigator must evaluate all case facts to determine if the claims being asserted by the suspect are reasonable and indisputable.

Hypothesis

3-87. This approach is used after a thorough evaluation leads the investigator to know with reasonable certainty how and why a crime was committed. The investigator may be able to propose an overall hypothesis that includes an explanation of the suspect's motivation. This, in turn, may result in a suspect realizing that the investigation has uncovered the facts pertinent to the case, including the suspect's motivations, resulting in the suspect cooperating and providing the details of his involvement. This approach should only be used if the investigator reasonably believes the hypothesis to be accurate based on case facts.

Using Proximal and Haptic Techniques

3-88. It is important to realize that within the structure of rapport-based direct interrogations, the object is to help the suspect become comfortable with the investigator. The proper use of proximal (physical proximity) and haptic (physical contact) techniques reduces psychological barriers and improves rapport building. With the intent to build rapport rather than to increase anxiety or to intimidate, the distance between the investigator and suspect can be adjusted as the interrogation progresses.

3-89. All persons have personal space, an invisible comfort zone around their body, within which they only allow trusted or intimate persons to enter. This space is different for everyone and is determined by a number of factors including personality, culture, previous experiences. Most individuals will exhibit unconscious physical reactions as persons they are not comfortable or intimate with move closer or enter their personal space. Investigators, while observing the individual's reaction, can adjust their position to move closer, enter, or move away from an individual's personal space to achieve a desired result.

3-90. Similarly, touching can be extremely effective; however, extreme caution should be used when employing this technique. Frequently, investigators misunderstand what a touch accomplishes during the interrogation process. A touch should generally be executed at a key point in the interrogation—when the suspect becomes emotional, when he is about to make an admission, or immediately after he has made an admission. The message a touch sends is that the investigator understands and can relate to the suspect and does not judge him. The delivery of a touch is the most critical aspect of this technique. The investigator should not reach out and grab or pat the suspect, as it may be interpreted as condescending and insincere. A touch should be delivered using a couple of fingers on the outer portion of the suspect's leg or arm. The more unintentional a touch appears, the more effective it is in relaying the desired message.

Using Trickery or Deceit

3-91. Historically, the reason LE officers have felt the need to present false evidence during the conduct of interrogations was to apply pressure on the suspect. Convincing a suspect that the evidence clearly links him to a crime may pressure him into telling the truth. Although applying pressure is essential in the interrogation process, investigators do not need to resort to lying to exert pressure and convince a suspect to confess or tell the truth. The presentation of potential evidence is far superior to deceit. Potential evidence not only creates evidentiary pressure for a suspect, but it allows the investigator to do so with absolute integrity and credibility.

3-92. The use of trickery, deceit, ploys, and lying is legally permissible during the course of an interrogation. However, although it is legally permissible to employ deceitful tactics when conducting interrogations, it is not advised or recommended for several reasons including—

- The perpetrator knows more about the crime than the investigator. It can be relatively easy for a perpetrator to catch the investigator in a lie if the investigator uses a deceit tactic. Once caught in a lie by the suspect, the investigator loses all credibility.
- Juries and judges do not like to place their trust and confidence in police officers who appear to manipulate case facts by using deceit. Although lying rarely results in a confession being thrown out, it is frequently a factor used in a deliberation for panel members and judges who are considering evidence from an investigator who has proven that he can be a convincing liar and possibly untrustworthy. This can result in reduced sentences and occasional acquittals. Defense attorneys have become very adept at bringing out lies told during interrogations in courtroom settings and at turning these lies into credibility issues for the panel.

3-93. While the use of deceit in an interrogation may be legal, there are restrictions. No form of trickery or deceit may be used to gain a voluntary waiver of legal rights. Additionally, no lies, ploys, trickery, or deceit can be of a nature to shock the conscience of society or to cause an otherwise innocent person to confess. For instance, threatening a mother with the loss of her children may likely cause her to choose her children over the truth and, consequently, confess even if she is not guilty. Conversely, it would be permissible to tell a suspect that his fingerprints were found on evidence or that a witness observed him at the scene because an innocent person would know that he was not there and refute the statement, whereas a guilty person may feel trapped by the overwhelming evidence and confess.

3-94. Presenting potential evidence to cause a positive reaction from the suspect is generally a better tactic than using deceit in an interrogation. The use of potential evidence works well in many different situations. For example, reminding a suspect that a parking lot or store is equipped with surveillance cameras may cause him to believe he was recorded on tape. If the investigator does not know if the location was equipped with cameras, he can send another investigator to check. He can then tell the suspect that he just sent someone over to obtain any videotapes that may exist. Although the investigator does not know whether or not this evidence exists, he presents the potential for the recovery of evidence that will link the suspect to the crime.

3-95. Rather than telling the suspect that his fingerprints were found on an item of evidence when they have not been found at the scene, the investigator should consider telling the suspect, "We have recovered several latent fingerprint impressions from the crime scene, and I am going to send them to the laboratory with your record fingerprints." Remind the suspect that he may find it very difficult to explain how his fingerprints were discovered at the scene if he continues to insist that he was never there.

3-96. In just about any situation where an investigator can develop a lie to apply evidentiary pressure to a suspect, he can just as easily identify potential evidence to apply the same pressure without lying. If challenged in court, the investigator can explain potential evidence to a panel without losing credibility, but it is difficult to explain deceit and lying as a legitimate interrogation technique without losing credibility.

OPENING PHASE

3-97. The opening of a direct interrogation is essential in establishing the tone. Before beginning the interrogation, attempt to assess the power base and anxiety level of the suspect. This is typically determined through an assessment of the suspect's perception of his status in the community. Power base refers to how much control and power the suspect believes he has as compared to the investigator. For example, if a senior military officer were being interviewed, he would likely feel that he has greater power and control over the interview process than someone of lesser rank. Likewise, the anxiety level of a senior officer would likely be lower. The investigator's introduction is designed to appropriately adjust the power base and anxiety level. When the power base is anticipated to be high and the anxiety low, the investigator should seek to reduce the power base while increasing the anxiety level. Whereas, when the power base is low and the anxiety is high, the investigator should seek to increase the power base while reducing the anxiety.

3-98. In an optimal situation, a suspect's power base as he perceives it should be about equal to that of the investigator. However, in actuality the investigator should control the structure and conduct of the interrogation. If a suspect's anxiety level is too low, there is a lack of concern on the part of the suspect, which reduces the possibility of emotionally affecting him. However, if the anxiety level is too high, the investigator will not be able to accurately assess the suspect's nonverbal communication or get him to focus on key issues.

Persons With a High Power Base

3-99. When investigators introduce themselves to a suspect with a high power base, they should not subordinate himself to the suspect. For example, if the suspect is a senior officer who outranks the investigator, the investigator should use the suspect's rank and last name when he initially introduces himself. He should then refer to himself by using his official title and last name; for example, "Good morning Lieutenant Colonel Johnson. My name is Special Agent Smith. I am glad you could come in today. Could you please follow me?"

> *Note.* Generally, the investigator always walks behind the suspect for safety reasons; however, when interviewing senior personnel, walking in front of them subtly diminishes the suspect's perception that the investigator is subordinate.

3-100. The investigator may then ask the suspect if he would like to take off his coat. If the suspect responds affirmatively, he should be shown where a hanger is and instruct him to hang it up. The investigator may then ask the suspect if he would like some coffee. Again, if he accepts, the investigator should then point out the coffee pot and instruct him to help himself. During this process, the investigator should be polite, courteous, and professional; however, he should not refer to the suspect as "sir" or "ma'am"; he should just use the rank and/or the rank and last name. This approach has proven itself in modifying the power base and anxiety level to the desired levels.

Persons With a Low Power Base

3-101. Suspects who have a lower power base are often uncomfortable and very apprehensive. Consequently, when an investigator first meets the suspect, the suspect should be referred to as "sir" or "ma'am," even if the person is a janitor. The investigator should use the subject's first name if he is a junior enlisted soldier. Investigators should then introduce themselves using only their first and last name in a very friendly and congenial manner. The investigator should then thank the person for coming in and tell the subject that he understands that the subject is very busy, but it is good to see that he wants to take care of the issue. The investigator should cater to the suspect by offering to hang up his coat, pouring him a cup of coffee, putting cream and sugar in his coffee for him, or other minor actions. This makes the suspect feel that he is important in the process and that the investigator sees him as an individual, not by the status that he sees himself or others may see him as having in the community.

3-102. The opening portion of the interrogation is where investigators begin the rapport-building process. In building rapport, the investigator should explore the suspect's interests, looking for common ground that they can relate to on a personal level. When those interests are identified, the investigator should spend a reasonable period of time discussing these topics from a purely personal vantage point. This not only helps the suspect to see the investigator as a person with whom he can relate, but also aids the investigator in a similar fashion and is paramount to successful interrogations. See the earlier section in this chapter on building rapport.

3-103. After establishing the initial tone of the interview and rapport, the investigator should complete a biographical data sheet. While completing the biographical data sheet, the investigator should maintain the previously established environmental tone, continuing to build rapport. Being friendly and polite will reduce anxiety, whereas being more rigid and professional will increase anxiety.

BODY PHASE

3-104. It is during this phase of the interrogation that the investigator strives to get the suspect to tell what happened in a detailed statement, which includes determining the "who, what, where, when, why, and how" of the crime. It would also be extremely beneficial for the investigator to determine what the suspect experienced. As with trauma victim interviews, obtaining physiological evidence can yield substantially more information than the traditional "who, what, where, why, when, and how" method of questioning. This physiological evidence will assist the investigator in corroborating or refuting portions of the suspect's rendition of events. The end result should be a complete description of events, people, places, things, and thoughts (planning and intent), and all elements of proof for each offense should be clearly established.

CLOSING PHASE

3-105. It is important to close an interrogation in a manner that leaves suspects feeling good about themselves and the investigator. After a suspect confesses, don't tell the suspect that he is going to jail or make any judgmental statements about his actions. It is not uncommon to have to interview the same subject again at a later date. Any statements or actions at the end of an interrogation that may break the trust developed between the investigator and the suspect can result in an uncooperative witness or suspect during future interviews. Allowing the suspect to leave the interview with a sense of dignity and the perception that the investigator cared about him as a person, leaves the opportunity for positive future contact with the suspect.

DOCUMENTATION OF STATEMENTS

3-106. Statements from suspects are important documents. They must be recorded and included as a permanent part of the investigation records. There are many methods for recording information obtained through the interview process; however, they all have strengths and weaknesses that make some more appropriate than others based on the situation.

AUDIO AND VIDEO RECORDING

3-107.   Both interviews and interrogations may be recorded. Recording interrogations can provide valuable evidence as well as protection for both LE personnel and suspects. Recording victim or witness interviews should be carefully considered by the investigator.

Recording Interrogations

3-108.   Investigators are encouraged to video record suspect interrogations when practical. Video recording the entire interrogation from start to finish can be an indispensable tool in preserving the integrity of the process. This documentation can also be extremely useful in refuting claims of police misconduct in interrogations. Video-recorded interrogations can show a lack of coercion and can clearly depict whether the suspect provided protected details. It can also provide proof that the investigator did not provide details, invent the details, or otherwise prompt the suspect.

3-109.   Start the recording with an introduction of all parties being recorded and the time and date of the interrogation. Turning on a video camera to record just the confession negates nearly all of the safeguards sought from the recording process. Breaks may be taken during the recording. When a break is taken, the investigator conducting the interview should state that a break is being taken and include the time and date of the break. The recording equipment should not be turned off during the break. Once the interrogation resumes, the investigator should annotate on the tape the parties that are present along with the time and date and a brief description stating what occurred during the break, such as ate lunch or took a rest room break. The tape generated from the interrogation should be maintained with the case file and written transcripts.

Recording Interviews

3-110.   Video recording a victim interview can assist by depicting the demeanor and physical characteristics the victim displayed, as well as recording in his own words the events as he remembered them at the time. Generally, investigators should not video record the initial victim or witness interview. Investigators should consider making any necessary video recording during scheduled follow-up interviews of the victim. Investigators must obtain the necessary approvals before any video recording of a victim interview.

3-111.   If a determination is made to record witness or victim interviews, the individual's permission must be obtained unless there is Army general counsel approval for recording and/or intercepting. Permission can be obtained verbally or in writing. When an interview is recorded, the recording should start with an introduction of the parties being recorded and the time and date, and should include the agreement of each party to the recording. If the individual refuses to permit recording, all recording should cease unless other legal approval has been obtained. Record the entire interview from start to finish; maintain the recorded interview with the case file and written transcripts.

WRITTEN STATEMENTS

3-112.   Written statements are permanent records of the pretrial testimony of accused persons, suspects, victims, complainants, and witnesses. They may be used in court as evidence attesting to what was told to investigators. They also are used to refresh the memory of the persons making the statements.

Typewritten Sworn Statements

3-113.   Typewritten sworn statements are one method for recording and preserving statements from victims and witnesses. Statements are typically recorded on a DA Form 2823, *Sworn Statement*; see appendix D for a detailed example of a completed DA Form 2823. The benefit of a typed statement is that it is generally brief, concise, and well written. It also tends to address the elements of proof in a very clear manner. Typewritten statements can be taken in conjunction with handwritten statements, interview sketches, letters of apology, and/or audio recording or video recording.

3-114. Handwritten statements are many times difficult to read and may cause confusion or doubt about the content. However, when documenting typed confessions from a suspect, defense attorneys have grown very adept at attacking the credibility of these statements. They suggest that the words in the statement are those of the investigator and not the suspect. Defense attorneys will try to establish that the investigator manipulated what the suspect said. This defense tactic is easily defended by following specific techniques for taking statements to include—

- Asking the individual clarifying questions throughout the writing of the statement.
- Providing the individual the opportunity to read the statement as it is being typed.
- Encouraging and allowing the individual to change any aspect of the statement that did not accurately capture what they were trying to say.
- Including as the last question on the statement, "Is there anything you would like to add or delete from this statement at this time?" The suspect's response is recorded and appropriate action to delete and/or add information is taken at that time. If corrections were made as a result of this question, the question should be asked again and the process repeated until no further corrections are made. Adhere to the following guidelines:
  - Never delete corrected or retracted statements. They should be lined through and initialed by the individual providing the statement.
  - Ensure that each body of text provided by the individual is initialed by the individual at the end of the text. For example if the individual provided an initial narrative that was typed, he should initial at the end of the narrative. For each clarifying question asked, the individual should initial the end of each response.
- Ensuring that after the statement is completed (including all corrections by the suspect) the suspect—
  - Reads the statement completely.
  - Signs the transcript.
  - Swears or affirms that the statement is true and accurate.
- Ensuring that at the end of the statement the words "End of Statement" are added and any remaining space is lined through with a diagonal line to prevent addition of text after the statement is closed.

3-115. Generally the investigator will type the statement and facilitate this process. A second option for obtaining typewritten statements from a suspect who has admitted to criminal culpability is to ask the suspect if he can type. If he states that he can, the investigator may ask him to type his own statement. This approach bears the same protections against defense assertions as if the investigator edited the statement. If this technique is employed, the first question asked in the question and answer portion of the statement should be, "Did you type the statement above?" Additional questions should be used to clarify or explore aspects of the suspect's typed narrative.

Handwritten Sworn Statements

3-116. Handwritten sworn statements are tools that can be used by investigators to record statements. This tool is most appropriate for suspect statements but can be used for victim or witness interviews. These types of statements are very effective in recording confessions. They are written by hand, by the witness or the suspect, and in the words of the witness or the suspect, making it very difficult for defense attorneys to suggest manipulation of the facts by investigators. This has become a defense attorney's routine tactic when typewritten sworn statements are presented in court.

3-117. Typically the statements will be recorded on a DA Form 2823 as with the typed statement discussed previously. As with any tool, there are some advantages and disadvantages to using the handwritten statement. One disadvantage is that the person providing the statement may not be able to write the statement in a clear and concise manner based on their educational level. Their handwriting may be so poor that it is difficult to determine exactly what was written. However, after the suspect has written his statement, it is the responsibility of the investigator to carefully read over the statement and ensure that all elements of proof are adequately addressed and all reasonable questions are answered. The question and answer section is no different than in the typewritten sworn statement. The investigator will ensure that the question and answer section clears up any doubt or confusion in the suspect's statement. He ensures that all the elements of proof have been addressed appropriately. This type of statement will frequently require many more clarification questions than would be required of typewritten statements.

3-118. Handwritten statements may lend themselves to a technique known as statement analysis. Statement analysis may be employed to further assess the credibility of a statement or written narrative. Statement analysis should only be conducted by trained personnel. Statement analysis can be used for relatively long statements, letters, or other written narratives. Statements subjected to statement analysis techniques are typically free-flowing narratives or statements of what happened. Analysts trained to perform statement analysis identify linguistic cues and discrepancies to detect concealed or withheld information. Identification of these linguistic cues and discrepancies can lead to a determination of truthfulness or deceit by an individual.

3-119. In some cases, there may be a need to conduct a statement analysis of a victim's statement—not because the victim is suspected of lying or criminal complicity, but to identify aspects of his story that may be embellished or omitted out of embarrassment or other factors. This is especially useful in sexual assault complaints. Even bona fide victims frequently omit information they feel could cause them to be judged or otherwise scrutinized. Statement analysis on a victim's statement should be considered on a case-by-case basis and used only when there is a definite and specific benefit.

INTERVIEW SKETCHES

3-120. An interview sketch is a free-hand drawing of a scene or object relevant to the crime and describes the actions taken during the crime. The sketch should only be obtained after full disclosure is made to the investigator. It is obtained after completing the body of the interview or interrogation of the suspect and before the closure. The sketch should be hand drawn by the suspect and should outline the area of the crime scene. The investigator can ask the suspect questions to document or clarify specifics that answer the "who, what, where, when, and how" of the crime. As the suspect answers he should annotate his response on the sketch. Investigators should not provide information that is pertinent to the crime; however, they can guide the suspect in the completion of the sketch. The suspect must draw the sketch as he remembers it.

3-121. Interview sketches are very effective in capturing routes that the suspect took in committing the crime and fleeing from the scene. They also capture actions taken in the commission of the crime, which include locations along the travelled paths or routes where each action occurred. Relevant facts, such as buildings, structures, and other pertinent features, should be included in the sketch if possible, along with the entrance and exit points, avenues of approach, and evidentiary items. The suspect should use the word "I" when annotating his location in relation to the sketch and when writing directions or routes he used during the commission of the crime. Once the sketch is completed, the investigator should have the suspect sign and date it. The investigator's printed name and signature should also be on the sketch as a witness. See figure 3-1 for an example of an interview sketch.

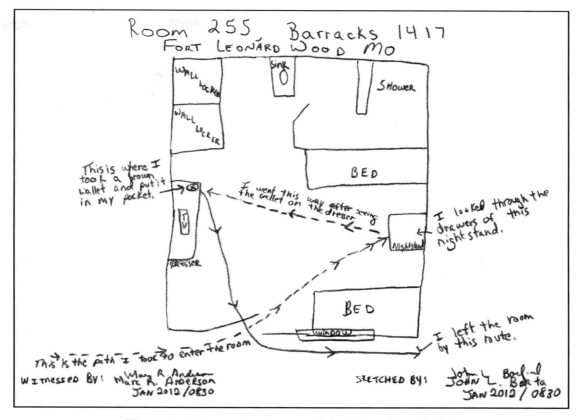

Figure 3-1. Example of a completed interview sketch

ADDITIONAL CONSIDERATIONS

3-122.   When conducting interviews, an investigator may encounter individuals or situations that require special consideration. Specific regulations or guidelines may govern the conduct of certain interviews, but they should not take away from the basic guidelines on conducting interviews. When this occurs, the investigator should maintain his focus of discovering the truth while appropriately following applicable guidelines and regulations.

CONFESSION SUPPRESSION COUNTERMEASURES

3-123.   In recent years, trial defense counsel has adopted numerous standardized tactics designed to suppress confessions. An analysis of this trend indicates that confessions are very difficult obstacles for the defense counsel to overcome with panel members, especially when evidence and investigator testimony implicates the accused, along with a confession. Consequently, panel members tend to be more ready to convict suspects who admit to criminal misconduct.

3-124.   In an attempt to gain acquittals, defense counsel will frequently attack the veracity of confessions so they may more effectively argue away other evidence presented during the trial process. The defense counsel may use a variety of tactics to attempt to get confessions dismissed or degrade their credibility during judicial proceedings. They may counter the confession by claiming that—

- Coercive tactics were employed to gain a confession.
- Suspects were denied their basic human rights.
- Suspects were not allowed to eat, sleep, or take breaks.

- Suspects were not allowed to take medication, or they were on medication and the LE personnel did not know about it.
- Suspects did not actually read the statement.
- Investigators put words into the suspect's statement that were not derived from the suspect.
- Investigators were overbearing and/or abusive.

3-125. Confession suppression countermeasures are designed to thwart future claims made by the defense counsel. Many of these countermeasures have been discussed throughout this chapter. One of the most basic countermeasures is to identify typographical errors within the body of a statement made by the suspect, have the suspect correct those errors, and have the suspect initial the correction. When the suspect corrects the errors, it demonstrates that he read the statement and felt comfortable making changes to it before swearing that it was true and correct.

3-126. If the rapport-based interview style is used appropriately during interrogations, suspects will like, respect, and trust the investigator at the time of the interview. However, after speaking to counsel, the suspect will often claim to have been maltreated. Asking questions within the body of the statement designed to explore the suspect's perception of his treatment at the conclusion of the interview are very effective in refuting or preventing future claims of abuse or coercion. Examples include—

- "How were you treated by CID (and/or MPI) today?"
- "Why did you decide to tell me the truth today?"
- "You were questioned for 10 hours today, were you allowed bathroom, smoking, or meal breaks?"

3-127. Suspects who are treated with dignity and respect will respond in a similar fashion. They will frequently answer with—

- "I was treated well" or "I was treated with respect."
- "You were very professional and nice."
- "You were courteous but persistent."

3-128. Although the defense counsel may try to attack sworn statements typed by the investigator, interview sketches and handwritten statements will diminish future claims that investigators put words in the suspect's mouth or that the suspect did not read his statement. Video recording interviews and interrogations can also be instrumental in disproving claims of coercion, overbearing investigators, and other alleged acts of misconduct on the part of investigators. In the rapport-based interview process, investigators are kind, caring, and compassionate toward suspects, which is in direct contradiction to claims of abuse. However, the defense counsel will use television interview and interrogation tactics common within popular culture to reinforce these claims in the minds of panel members. Recording the interview or interrogation can prevent or mitigate these claims.

CUSTODIAL VERSUS NONCUSTODIAL SETTINGS

3-129. According to federal law and USCIDC regulations, investigators may conduct noncustodial interviews of suspects who are not subject to the UCMJ. According to the decisions and case law stemming from *Arizona versus Miranda*, LE personnel who question suspects who are in custody must issue a "Miranda" warning. Accordingly, suspects not in a custodial status may be interviewed without issuing a "Miranda" warning; however, the standard for whether a person is in custody is measured by the suspect's perception regarding their ability to leave or terminate the interview, not the police officer's perspective.

3-130. The most effective means for investigators to ensure that a suspect knows their custodial status is to advise him by saying, "You are not under arrest or apprehension, you are free to leave at any time, and you do not have to answer any questions." Once the suspect acknowledges his understanding of his status and the interview is conducted, the investigator should document this statement on the first line of the suspect's statement which serves as a written record of the notification of custodial status.

3-131. If a suspect's ability to leave is in any way impeded, he is reasonably in custody and must be issued the "Miranda" warning. If a civilian suspect is interviewed in a custodial setting, he must be advised of his "Miranda" rights. These rights are on the reverse side of DA Form 3881, *Rights Warning*

Procedure/Waiver Certificate. Properly executing DA Form 3881 in such instances is the appropriate mechanism for administering this warning.

3-132.   Article 31(b) of the UCMJ states that anyone subject to the UCMJ may not elicit self-incriminating statements from anyone else subject to the manual until that person has been advised of his rights. Article 31(b) of the UCMJ requires that the suspect be informed of the nature of the accusation, that he does not have to make any statements regarding the offense, and that any statements made by the suspect may be used as evidence against him. This applies whether the suspect is in custody or not. DA Form 3881, which incorporates the warning requirements from both the UCMJ and "Miranda," should be used whenever feasible in conducting suspect interviews of military personnel or civilian personnel in a custodial setting. There is no relief from the requirements of Article 31(b) UCMJ, and failure to comply will result in the suppression of all statements. The UCMJ reads, "No statements obtained from any person in violation of this article, or through the use of coercion, unlawful influence, or unlawful inducement may be received in evidence against him [or her] in trial by court-martial."

FALSE CONFESSIONS

3-133.   Although false confessions are rare, there have been cases where people who confessed to a crime were subsequently convicted, but later proven to be innocent through forensic evidence. Because juries tend to place a great deal of weight on confessions when deliberating a case, it is important that investigators implement safeguards to prevent false confessions.

3-134.   A variety of factors, such as stress, age, fatigue, distraction, and intoxication, can impair the capacity to retrieve and perceive memories accurately. At the extreme, there are rare instances of people confessing to crimes they did not commit. Some false confessions result from some form of coercion, such as being threatened with the death penalty or the loss of their children or being forced into a situation where they felt the need to protect someone close to them. Many false confessions are given by people with cognitive impairment or by juveniles interrogated without an adult present. Investigators must be aware that false confessions can be produced and know how to prevent and/or delineate them from viable confessions.

3-135.   A confession should never stand alone on its own merit; it must be corroborated. Safeguards for preventing and/or identifying false confessions are primarily employed through control of information and specific details of the crime. It is important that investigators not provide the suspect with details from the investigation that only the perpetrator would know. Investigators should not show crime scene photos to a suspect or take him to a crime scene before he provides this protected information. Protected details should also be shielded from the media. The details of the crime scene and investigation can be used to assess whether a confession is true or false. These protected details should be known only by the actual perpetrator, and authorized LE personnel; therefore, a suspect who confesses should be able to provide these details of the crime. In contrast, an individual that did not commit the crime should not know the details, and their confession will lack the required detail to be considered viable.

3-136.   All investigators conducting interrogations should ensure that a suspect who confesses is able to provide information he would not otherwise know unless he was involved in the commission of the crime. Investigators should ensure that investigative personnel did not provide the information in the suspect's confession. Additionally, when an investigator suspects that an interviewee is making admissions merely to stop the interview process, he should consider providing information that is not true to see if the suspect incorporates this information into his statement. If a suspect attempts to incorporate this information into his statement, the investigator should recognize the propensity of the individual to accept responsibility for the things he did not do and should implement strong safeguards to prevent false confessions.

FALSE REPORTS

3-137.   Sometimes false reports are made by individuals who are not victims or witnesses to a crime. The reasons for making a false report are complicated and sometimes indefinable. It is possible that these reports may be initiated to gain attention, inflict revenge on another individual, or conceal other illicit behaviors; however, it is critical for the investigator to not jump to conclusions at the time a report is made. To conduct a complete and thorough investigation, even when a report is suspected to be false, it is best to accept all reports at face value and to thoroughly investigate the report while maintaining an objective and unbiased mindset. If it is determined at the conclusion of the investigation that the complaint was false, the complainant's status may change to that of a suspect. Until evidence is obtained that shows the initial report to be false, always proceed as if the complaint is legitimate. It is important to remember that mere contradiction does not mean that the person is giving a false report. Similarly—

- Inconsistencies do not mean that a report is false.
- Lies about collateral misconduct, such as alcohol or drug use, do not constitute a false report.
- An incomplete report is not necessarily a false report. Traumatized victims or witnesses may confuse chronology or may not remember details.

INTERPRETERS

3-138. Investigators may have to question suspects who do not speak English. In an ideal scenario, the investigator should be able to conduct the interview in the suspect's native language; however, this is not always possible or practical. Investigators should not attempt to conduct interrogations by themselves in a foreign language unless they are fluent in the required language. When using interpreters, there are several considerations that should be planned before the interview. Those considerations include the interpreter's—

- **Affiliation.** It is best if the interpreter is a member of the U.S. armed forces or is a U.S. citizen. If this is not possible, a qualified local national can be used.
- **Trustworthiness and reputation.** It is essential that the interpreter being used is completely trustworthy and understands that he should not edit what the investigator or the suspect says. The interpreter must be honest and free from criminal tendencies or affiliation. If he is native to the area, he should be free from unfavorable notoriety among the local populace. A good reputation and standing in the community prevents an interpreter from being intimidated by persons of higher rank or standing.
- **Ability.** Interpreters should be intelligent and articulate. They should be able to quickly learn the habits, methods, and ways of different investigators. They should be educated in the use of their own language and English. Social and educational levels are often discernible by speech habits or peculiarities. Interpreters must be able to express themselves clearly and intelligibly to all persons whom they are likely to question.
- **Role.** Interpreters must be willing to accept a subordinate or supportive role in the actual questioning of a suspect, which means they must be willing to permit the investigator to ask the questions and to receive and evaluate the answers. Additionally, they should understand that they are not to ask questions on their own accord unless told to do so by the investigator.

3-139. If investigators have an understanding of the language being used in the interrogation, they will be better equipped to check the accuracy, loyalty, and obedience of the interpreter. If they do not have any familiarity with the language used, it is a good practice to have another linguist observe the interview and report his observations to the investigator.

3-140. The investigator asks the suspect the questions, and the interpreter translates the questions as close to verbatim as possible. The interpreter then translates the answer back to the investigator who evaluates it and formulates the next question. Investigators should prepare the questions they intend to ask before initiating the interview. Questions should be clear and concise and designed to invoke brief, factual answers. Direct the interpreter to make his translation of long statements at regular and convenient pauses during the suspect's utterances. The interruptions must come at the end of complete thoughts, but not after extended statements, as the interpreter will naturally abbreviate the response to only include those portions he believes are most relevant. This may be challenging if the subject is allowed to give extensive narrative versions of his account. Therefore, investigators should try to avoid questions that take long explanations and invite diversion from the intended subject.

3-141. Whenever possible, the investigator should give the questions to the interpreter in writing before the interview, so he can adequately prepare and clarify questioning approaches before the interview. Additionally, the interpreter may need to research specialized vocabulary in relation to the specific offense. The investigator should directly face the suspect and look at him while issuing questions and listening to the responses. The interpreter should generally observe the suspect, but try to limit eye contact. This will encourage the suspect to look at the investigator during the interview process.

3-142.   The interpreter should stand or sit to the side and slightly forward of the investigator. This will allow the investigator to converse with the interpreter, but still portray to the suspect that the investigator is conducting the interview. The interpreter should not move around or do anything that will distract the suspect's attention from the investigator. The investigator should address the suspect directly, looking the suspect in the eye to hold his attention. Ask questions slowly and clearly in concise and unambiguous English. Do not use slang words or expressions unique to a region, which could confuse the interpreter. Do not tell the interpreter to ask the suspect a question. For example, do not say to the interpreter, "Ask him if he knows John Doe." Instead, say the question directly to the suspect in English, "Do you know John Doe?" The interpreter translates the question into the language of the suspect. The interpreter should do this promptly in a clear and well-modulated voice. The interpreter should try to reproduce the tone and emphasis used by the investigator. When the suspect answers the question in his native language, the interpreter should repeat the answer in English, translating it as literally as possible. Insist that the interpreter translate the suspect's answer directly. Do not permit the interpreter to reply, "He says he does." Investigators should get the answer through the interpreter as though the suspect answered it in English, such as, "Yes, I know him," using the first person. If the investigator feels an explanation is warranted as to the word selection of the suspect, he should ask the interpreter at a later time. If fact clarification is required, additional questions should be posed directly to the suspect by the investigator.

3-143.   Hold diversions from the intended topic to an absolute minimum. Do not allow the suspect and interpreter to begin an extensive conversation or argument. If the investigator wants to take detailed notes, he should instruct the interpreter to speak slowly and distinctly and to pause while notes are being recorded. Use of a stenographer or a recording device may be warranted and used within appropriate guidelines. If the stenographer speaks both languages, he should record all statements made in both languages. This gives a means of cross-checking the accuracy of the translation.

> *Note.* SOFAs, if in effect, are different in every country and effects how local nationals are interviewed. Appropriate coordination must be made before conducting these interviews.

JUVENILES

3-144.   A juvenile is identified as a person who is less than 18 years of age at the time of the incident being investigated and who is not active duty military. Certain precautions must be observed when questioning juveniles, regardless of whether they are the victim, a witness, a suspect, or a subject.

3-145.   As with most interviews or interrogations, an interview or interrogation of a juvenile by an investigator of the opposite sex should be conducted in the presence of a witness. When possible, the witness should be of the same sex as the juvenile being interviewed. If the juvenile to be interviewed is considered a suspect, the parent or guardian of the juvenile should be present during the rights advisement process. The juvenile should be advised of his rights against self-incrimination with the consent of the parent or guardian. Further, the juvenile should be advised that the interview could be terminated at anytime. In some cases, the presence of the parents may be beneficial to the interview process. However, in many instances, juveniles are reluctant to discuss misconduct in the presence of their parents, and consideration should be given to asking the parents to observe the interview in another room.

3-146.   To get a complete and accurate story, investigators must avoid alienating the juvenile. The use of abusive language, threats, or otherwise abrasive behavior toward juveniles will in almost all cases make it more difficult to relate to them and gain their cooperation. Do not use condemning terms like juvenile delinquent, thief, or liar. An investigator must be in control of his emotions and temper at all times. In some situations, feigning anger momentarily may be appropriate in adjusting a juvenile's power base and anxiety level, especially for extremely street-wise juveniles. In most cases, these behaviors will only create distance between the juvenile and the investigator.

3-147.   Avoid coercive practices or any acts that might push an innocent, but frightened or emotionally troubled juvenile to falsely confess. What most juveniles, especially troubled juveniles, want more than anything is to be respected, listened to, and understood. One of the greatest frustrations in young people is that nobody listens to them, and most authority figures talk down to them. Strong-arm tactics will reinforce this frustration and cause the juvenile to retreat into his feelings of being misunderstood and oppressed.

3-148. Investigators can gain a juvenile's confidence by treating him with respect and dignity and encouraging him to take care of his immediate needs. Juveniles should be encouraged to reciprocate the respect being offered to them. A juvenile will normally be interviewed in a noncustodial setting. Juveniles should not be interviewed in front of their peers because they will feel the need to maintain a hard-line stance with authority figures. Consider questioning a juvenile in his home if the parents are cooperative and willing to work with investigators. If the parents are making excuses for the juvenile or are otherwise obstructing the process, investigators will have to gain the support of the parents before conducting an effective interview. To get the interview started, establish a bond of mutual interest, respect, and experience. Treat a juvenile with consideration and be friendly. When getting personal information, tell him why the information is needed. While obtaining information from a juvenile, investigators may offer information about themselves that will help the juvenile relate to them and keep the interview going.

3-149. Avoid contacting juveniles at school, if possible. If circumstances require that interviews be conducted at a school, the investigator must observe certain precautions. Contact the school principal first and explain the circumstances related to the interview and why it must be conducted at school. Do not contact the student's teacher or the student first. Ask if there is a room in which the student can be interviewed. Never enter the classroom to question or apprehend a student. Do not contact students at school during hours when a number of other students may see investigators with the juvenile.

3-150. Remove a juvenile from school only as a last resort. If a student is to be apprehended, investigators must explain this to the school officials and get permission to take the juvenile from the school, unless specific court instructions mandate otherwise. Ensure that the juvenile's parents have been notified if the student must be removed from school. When an investigator detains or takes a juvenile into custody for an offense, the following actions should be taken:

- Promptly notify his parent or guardian and the local office of the SJA.
- Immediately advise the juvenile of his rights in language that he understands with parents present.

3-151. When juvenile subjects are in custody, they will not be fingerprinted or photographed without the written permission of a federal judge responsible for juvenile cases. This permission is required, regardless of consent by the juvenile, parent, or guardian.

SELF-INCRIMINATION

3-152. Many times during an interview, information is obtained from a victim or a witness indicating that he committed a criminal offense that is not directly related to the crime under investigation (such as drinking under age, drug use, or other criminal activity) in the course of events related to the reported offense. In these cases, the individuals must be advised of their legal rights before being asked any questions about the suspected misconduct. It is generally advisable to complete the victim's interview without addressing the offenses for which he is suspected before executing the rights warning and asking about his criminal conduct. As long as no questions are asked pertaining to the individual's criminal behavior, the interview can proceed to extract information about crimes committed by others. Once the witness or victim interview is complete, the rights warning can be issued pertinent to the incriminating statement and any suspect interview or interrogation activities can proceed according to legal parameters.

3-153. If the interview cannot be completed without addressing a witness or victim's criminal activity, appropriate rights warnings must be rendered. If the individual is in the military, he must be advised of his legal rights. If the individual is a civilian, then a noncustodial warning is appropriate and the witness or victim should be advised that his suspected actions constitute a crime. If the offense is of a nature that is not under the investigative purview of the organization conducting the investigation, those offenses and activities should be referred to the appropriate authority. This could range from other LE agencies to the unit commander.

SENIOR MILITARY OR CIVILIANS

3-154. Whenever an allegation of criminality or impropriety against a senior military officer or civilian person is received, the local provost marshal and USACIDC offices should be notified immediately of the allegation. A determination will be made whether the investigative responsibility is kept locally or sent to the Department of the Army Inspector General (DAIG) to investigate the allegation. Under no circumstances will a senior person be interviewed as a suspect without specific prior authorization from the designated investigative command.

3-155.   When a senior person reports to either the military police or a USACIDC field element that he is a victim of (or witness to) a crime, he should be interviewed to begin the investigative process. Whenever a senior person needs to be interviewed as a victim or witness to an investigation, the USACIDC field element concerned will conduct the interview according to normal investigative procedures. Senior persons are identified as—

- A general or flag-grade officer (includes active and reserve component).
- A general or flag-grade officer designee.
- A DA civilian in the grade of general schedule (GS)-15 or higher.
- Any other person of equivalent rank who occupies a key position as designated by the appropriate commander.

Chapter 4

Crime Scene Processing and Documentation

There is no steadfast rule that can be applied to defining the dimensions of a crime scene. Areas that are well removed from the actual crime scene frequently yield important evidence. The scene of a crime is, in itself, evidence. Valuable physical evidence is normally found at or near the site where the most critical action was taken by the criminal against the victim or property. Just as it is likely to discover and develop critical evidence in the immediate area surrounding the body in a homicide, the site of forcible entry into a building often has the greatest potential for yielding evidence. Technological advances in forensic science, coupled with the ability of crime laboratories to successfully analyze evidence, have greatly increased the investigator's responsibility. Items not previously thought to be of evidentiary value may hold the key to the successful identification or elimination of a suspect or lead to the identification and conviction of the offenders. Army LE personnel, normally investigators, are responsible for conducting a thorough investigation of the crime scene and ensuring the proper collection, preservation, documentation, and transportation of evidence.

LEGAL AND SCIENTIFIC REQUIREMENTS

4-1. For evidence to meet legal requirements and therefore be relevant to a criminal investigation, the crime scene must be controlled and well documented. Loss of control of the scene can result in contamination of the evidence. The legal requirements concerning evidence include—

- Identifying each piece of evidence.
- Recording a description and the exact location of each item.
- Documenting when each item was collected
- Maintaining a proper chain of custody.
- Documenting any changes that occur in the evidence between the time it was collected and its introduction as evidence before the court.

4-2. An investigator's notes, photographs, and sketches become the legal record of his actions. These documents can be critical when introducing and authenticating physical evidence in court. The written and photographic records of the scene also put the presented evidence into perspective. This can help laboratory experts determine what tests are needed; it also helps investigators, counsel, judges, jurors, and other persons involved in the case and/or court proceedings visualize the crime scene after the fact. Finally, investigator's notes, photographs, and sketches are a valuable historical reference of actions taken during crime scene processing.

4-3. Strict procedures concerning evidence collection are in place to ensure the physical integrity of the evidence and that collected evidence meets scientific requirements for forensic analysis. This increases the probability that useful information can be obtained through forensic analysis and reduces the probability of evidence degradation and contamination, or other concerns associated with evidence handling. Scientific requirements for handling and processing evidence include taking precautions to minimize any change or modification to the evidence. Biological evidence will degrade over time; these materials must be packaged and stored to reduce or slow the natural degradation of biological materials. Weather and other unavoidable circumstances may induce change in some types of materials. Some evidence may be fragile and prone to breakage, scratching, or other types of damage that alter the evidence from the state in which it was collected at the crime scene or incident site. Improper packaging can result in cross contamination between two different items of evidence. Army LE personnel collecting evidence must ensure that proper collection, storage, and shipping procedures are followed to mitigate this risk.

4-4. Army LE personnel rely on many techniques and tools to document crimes and crime scenes. These include any available means to legally obtain or capture information that may be relevant to the incident and that can be helpful in understanding the facts of the case. The success of Army LE personnel in processing crime scenes and conducting criminal investigations depends on the training, knowledge, skill, and experience of the military police and investigators working the case. Critical to successful crime scene processing are the observation skills of the military police and investigators and their ability to document those observations to support the investigation.

OBSERVATIONS, DESCRIPTIONS, AND IDENTIFICATIONS

4-5. Army LE personnel rely on their senses to observe, describe, and identify persons, places, events, and objects. While sight and hearing are the most commonly used senses when observing a crime scene, other senses, such as smell and touch, can also provide clues to help Army LE personnel understand the crime scene and environment. The senses of sight, hearing, smell, and touch all together should be honed and employed to observe, describe, and identify threats, evidence, victims, suspects, and other elements of the crime scene and follow-on investigations.

4-6. Observations help Army LE personnel build descriptions of persons, places, events, and objects so that who or what was seen may later be identified. Written or oral descriptions help the observer convey what he saw to others. They may be either written or oral. They include signs, gestures, sketches, and other means to convey information about what was seen by an observer. Accurate observations and descriptions add to credible identifications of persons, places, and objects in an investigation.

FACTORS INFLUENCING OBSERVATIONS

4-7. The ability to observe accurately is developed through training, practice and experience. Most people are not trained in remembering and evaluating what they see, so the observations and descriptions they provide may not be as detailed or as objective as those of a trained observer. Trained observers, such as investigators, know that their observations can be affected by lack of sleep, illness, perceptions, or other outside influences. Army LE personnel must be aware of these influences and their potential impact on their observations as well as those of witnesses. Influences that can affect observations include—

- Environmental factors, such as weather and light.
- The presence of unrelated, distracting events. These events cause an individual to focus his attention in a particular direction; for example, a spectator watching an exciting play on a football field may fail to note the actions of a person sitting next to him.
- The passage of time between when an event is seen and when it is recalled. This time delay can cause the observer to forget or confuse the details of the event, thus influencing his description of what he saw.
- Conversations with other people. Conversations between persons who witnessed the same event can affect the perceptions and recollections of the individuals. People can consciously or unconsciously fill in gaps or alter their recollection due to interaction with other persons. This is why separation of witnesses, victims, and subjects as soon as possible is important.
- The location of an observer at the time he sees an event. It is unlikely that more than one or two people will view an event from exactly the same place; therefore, a difference in location may account for a difference in their observations. Someone observing an event from a great distance may be able to give a good overall description of what took place, but he might not be able to see and give the details that someone at close range could give. Likewise, the closer person may be unsure of the overall picture.
- Psychological, physiological, and experiential factors. These factors influence what people see and how they retain the information. People tend to evaluate and interpret what they observe by their past experiences with like incidents. They are inclined, for instance, to compare the size of an object with the size of another object with which they are familiar. A very short or very tall

person may fail to judge another's height correctly. Someone 6 feet tall may seem "very tall" to an observer only 4 feet 10 inches tall. The same 6-foot person would appear to be "normal height" to a person 5 feet 10 inches tall.

- Unfamiliar sounds, odors, tastes, and other perceptions. A bartender can relate to and accurately describe these factors and his relationship to a fight that occurred in his place of business. However, a young 21-year-old man who made his first visit to the bar on the night of the fight probably could not recall much about any of these factors because they were new and unfamiliar to him. A stimulus, which cannot be easily compared to a past experience, is often mistakenly interpreted in terms of familiar things; a wrong interpretation of a past experience may influence the perception of a present experience.

- Personal interests and training. Specific interests or specialized training and education may increase one's power of observation in those areas, but it may also limit the focus on other details. Specialists often have acute perception within their own field, but fail to be observant in other fields. An artist may take special note of color, form, and proportion, but fail to discern or properly interpret sounds or odors. Conversely, a mechanic may quickly note the sound of a motor or an indication of the state of repair of a car, but fail to clearly discern the appearance and actions of the driver.

- Pain, hunger, fatigue, or an unnatural position of the body. Discomfort may cause an observer to fail to correctly interpret things he would normally comprehend. The senses of taste and smell are often distorted by physical illness and external stimuli. These senses are generally the least reliable basis for interpretation. The presence of a strong taste or odor may completely hide the presence of other tastes or odors.

- Emotions (fear, anger, or worry) and mind sets (prejudice or irrational thinking patterns). For example, a victim of a robbery may have been in great fear of the weapon used by the criminal. He may only be able to recall the size of the bore of the weapon and not be able to describe the offender. Such a person might be expected to exaggerate the size of the bore. Sometimes an observer may have great prejudice against a class or race of people. For example, a person who dislikes police may unwittingly permit this prejudice to affect his view of the actions of a night watchman or a security guard. How he interprets what he sees may be wrong, even if his senses recorded a true report of what occurred.

OBSERVATIONS AND DESCRIPTIONS BY ARMY LAW ENFORCEMENT

4-8.   Army LE personnel should use a systematic approach to observations and descriptions in conjunction with the use of notes, photographs, videos, and sketches. These help the investigator to remember what he observed and also help to improve the accuracy of descriptions. Generally, accuracy is most assured if an established pattern is followed. Use of these observation techniques requires training and practice to gain proficiency. The pattern used most often for observations starts with general features and moves to specific features. For example, when observing a person to develop a description, use the following steps:

- **Step 1.** Look first at general features like sex, height, and race.
- **Step 2.** Check features like color of hair and eyes, unusual scars, and specific body weight.
- **Step 3.** Note changeable characteristics like clothing, eyeglasses, hats, and hairstyles.
- **Step 4.** Note the person's mannerisms and behavior.

4-9.   When a military police patrol or investigator observes a person and attempts to match the individual to a description, it may be useful to change or reverse his pattern of observation. This is most likely done if the person being sought has some very noticeable feature. For example, if a man with a limp or large obvious birthmark were being looked for, the first feature one would look for would be the limp or birthmark, followed by his general features, and then his specific features. Even when reversed, a pattern using a systematic approach is being followed. The exact pattern used is not as important as the fact that a pattern is applied.

4-10. When observing and describing a person, start with the person's general features then progress to specific personal features. General features are very broad descriptions of an individual that, although important, by themselves provide limited detail. General descriptive features of an individual include—

- Gender.
- Ethnic background or race.
- Height.
- Build and posture, such as stout, slim, or stooped.
- Weight.
- Age.

4-11. The observer should then focus on the individual's specific personal features, noting features at the head and progressing downward to the feet. Every individual has personal features or a combination of features that are unique or distinguishing only to that individual. Because these features set him apart from others, they are the most important part of the description of a person. Some of these features are relatively stable; they are generally harder to change and are in some cases permanent. They are physical traits and characteristics that are part of the person. These characteristics may include color of hair and eyes, unusual scars or tattoos, and other distinct facial features.

4-12. Lastly, focus on transient or changeable features and mannerisms. Some features or traits are not a physical part of the person; they are changeable characteristics. These features may be clothing, hairstyle, use of cosmetics, or any other items that are used by the individual. Most persons use these items and materials rather consistently based on personal tastes; they may reflect the individual's personality, occupation, or activity at the time of the observation. These items can also be used by individuals to manipulate their appearance. Army LE personnel should be alert to deceptive ploys while observing changeable characteristics, such as the person having a false limp or wearing a hairpiece or glasses. Table 4-1 provides examples of descriptive features.

Table 4-1. Descriptive features for individuals

Feature	Relative Permanence of the Feature	Descriptions
Face	Relatively permanent	Long, round, square, fat, or thin. Had scars, acne, birthmarks, moles, or other feature.
Forehead		High, low, or wide.
Eyebrows		Thin, bushy, average thickness, painted, or none.
Eyes		Color, wide or narrow.
Nose		Large, small, long, short, pug-nosed, broad, narrow, straight, or crooked. Large or small nostrils, deep-pored, scarred, or hairy.
Ears		Large, small, high or low on head, close to the head or protruding. Were they pierced (how many times)? Were hearing aids worn?
Mouth		Large, small, upturned or drooping.
Lips		Thick or thin.
Teeth		Large, small, bucked, spaced, close set or crowded, crooked, or missing. Were any dental attachments or work present such as gold, retainers, or braces?
Chin		Broad, narrow, short, long, square, pointed, round, or double-chinned.
Neck		Thick, thin, long, or short.
Shoulders		Broad, narrow, squared, drooped, thin, or muscular.
Arms		Length (compared with the rest of the body), thin, heavy, or muscular.
Hands		Slim, thick, well-groomed, dirty, rough, missing or crooked fingers.
Distinguishing marks		Tattoos, birthmarks, scars, moles, or amputations.

Table 4-1. Descriptive features for individuals (continued)

Feature	Relative Permanence of the Feature	Descriptions
Hair	Changeable	Color (to include fad colors), thick, thin, long, short, wavy, curly, or straight. Was the hair groomed or unruly? Specific styles and texture, balding (completely bald, partially bald, or receding), obvious wig or hairpiece.
Mustache	Normally relatively permanent over the short term	Color, long, short, thick, thin, style (handlebar, pointed, and such).
Beard		Color, long, short, thick, thin, bushy, groomed or free-flowing, and style of beard (such as full or goatee).
Clothing		General description (including hat, scarf, or gloves); military or civilian uniform; well-groomed, distressed, or dirty; obvious stains (blood, grease, and such); specific footwear (boots, sneakers, high heels, dress shoes, and such).
Jewelry		Any that was noticed including rings, watches, necklaces, piercings, or toe rings.
Makeup		Type of makeup worn and whether it appeared to disguise or cover the natural face (such as wore lipstick to make lips look larger or heavy dark makeup not consistent with other features).
Wounds		Any obvious wounds or injuries sustained during the crime or incident. These can range from serious gunshot or stab wounds to relatively minor twisted ankles or injured hands.
Personal mannerisms	Normally relatively permanent; some traits can be faked.	Calm, nervous, male with feminine traits or female with masculine traits; obvious habits such as scratching nose; picking at face, fingers, or other body part; running hands through hair or beard; jingling keys; flipping coins, pencils, or other items.
Individualities		Limp, unusual gait, muscle twitches (especially around the eyes, mouth, or other obvious location), tics or major muscle twitches, unusual smile or other feature, stutter.
Voice and speech		Tone (low, medium, or loud), soft, gruff, nasal twang, drawl, foreign or regional accent, or mute condition. Spoke in cultured, highly educated, vulgar, clipped, fluent or broken English.

4-13. Though not characteristics of the individual, many observations related to crimes and crime scenes include vehicles and weapons. It is important that descriptions of vehicles and weapons are recorded when their use by individuals is relevant to the investigation. For weapons, describe the location and the type of weapon including guns, knives, baseball bats, screwdrivers, hammers, or any item used as a weapon. For firearms, describe whether it was a pistol or long gun, revolver, semiautomatic, bolt action, or shotgun. Knives should be identified as having long or short blades, fixed or folding blades, double or single edges, or serrated or smooth edges. Descriptions of how the weapon was carried (such as in the open or concealed, in the right or left hand, in a nervous manner or comfortably) and who had the weapon in their possession are useful.

4-14. Vehicle descriptions should include the color and type of vehicle (sedan, pickup, van, or cargo truck) and where the vehicle was observed as well as a description of any obvious damages or unique paint (including locations of damages on the vehicle). If possible, identify the make, model, year, state of registration, and tag number. Even partial tag identification can be helpful.

Objects

4-15. The pattern of observation used to describe objects is similar to the pattern used to describe people; note observations from the general features of the object to the specific features. This same pattern is used when trying to find objects to match an already built description. Start with the general features that clearly define the broad category of the object. This prevents it from being confused with objects of other classes. When identifying objects—

- Use a noun to describe it, such as a car, a gun, or a club.
- Note its type, size, and color. Avoid using single color descriptors that may have multiple meanings; for example, when describing a ring, say it is gold in color instead of simply gold.
- Look for other general features that are easy to discern and that may help give quick, sure recognition.
- Describe the specific features of the object that differentiate it from all other like items, such as whether or not the car has a sunroof or whether or not the radio or computer is portable.
- Search for any damage or alterations that make the item unique. Distinguishing marks, scratches, alterations, damaged parts, worn areas, signs of repair, faded paint, identifying markings, and missing parts must be noted in detail.
- Look for serial numbers or other identifying marks and labels.

4-16. For example, when observing and describing a computer, begin with the brand name. Then list it as "portable, notebook type model, blue in color, serial number NM97JT02." Include remarks like "No observable damage or markings" or identify any damage or markings that are observed such as "scratched across top, keyboard worn, corner of the case cracked." Follow the same procedure for all other objects.

Places

4-17. During criminal investigations, Army LE personnel must make detailed observations of places and locations where crimes or incidents have occurred. Descriptions should cite the elements that the military police patrol or investigator observes. The goal is to give a concise and easily understood word picture of the scene. Sketches and photographs obtained later in the investigation will support the word description. The pattern of observation will depend on whether the investigator is looking at an outdoor scene or an indoor scene.

Outdoor Scenes

4-18. When observing an outdoor scene, start by noting general characteristics and then fill in specific details. Locate natural or manmade landmarks to use as reference points when available; Global Positioning System (GPS) coordinates may be used if no useable landmarks exist. Sometimes it is necessary to place markers if the area has no obvious landmarks such as in open fields or desert locations. With landmarks or markers identified—

- Note the general scene and its relation to roadways, railways, and/or shore lines. Use these features to pinpoint the general site.
- Pinpoint exact site locations in relation to fixed or semifixed features, such as buildings, bridges, or power line poles.
- View outstanding objects or features within the scene.
- Check the details of the scene and any items of high interest. Some outdoor sites may not have such landmarks, so they will need to be marked for reference.
- Mentally assign boundaries to the area. Use boundaries that are neither too far apart nor too close together.

Indoor Scenes

4-19. Indoor scenes have obvious and definite boundaries like walls, hallways, and basements and are easier to observe and define than outdoor scenes. Because an indoor area often contains many objects, it is very important to use a methodical pattern of observation. Observe indoor scenes by—

- Noting the exact location of the place observed such as—
  - At the front or rear of the building, off a main corridor, or relatively remote or hidden location.
  - Within a large open area or small confined space.

- The floor level (1st floor, basement, and so forth).
- Noting the distances to stairways, entrances and exits, and elevators.
- Identifying the room number or other designation. Observe details near the entries to the area that is the specific point of concern, and note the objects located within the area.
- Determining the exact location as it relates to other objects of interest or areas of concern.

Events

4-20. In most cases, Army LE personnel arrive at the scene of an incident after the crime has occurred. They seldom see an event as it takes place. If a military police patrol or investigator is present when an unlawful event occurs, they must observe and remember it systematically and quickly. They must take in the important factors of time, place, persons, objects, and actions involved and the immediate results of the event. Any description of an event must be later supported with sketches, photographs, and collected evidence. The description of an observed event should be as complete as the circumstances allow and should include the—

- Time.
- Location.
- Order of action or key events.
- Objects and persons involved.
- Cause and effect sequences (what happened as a result of specific actions).
- Specific sounds or odors and combinations of sounds or odors in relation to observed events. For example, hearing a "pop" then an explosion or smelling gasoline shortly before a fire erupts.
- Verbal remarks, emotional states of excitement, gestures, looks of concern, or other observations regarding persons at the scene.
- Direction of movement of crowds or individuals.

OBSERVATIONS AND DESCRIPTIONS BY WITNESSES

4-21. Witness observations and descriptions are important to LE investigations. However, the recollections and observations of untrained observers can be unreliable without aids to spark their memory. A witness is typically not trained to commit details to memory about things they have observed; they may not be able to recall details without being asked specific questions. Asking specific questions such as, "What color eyes did the suspect have?" without suggesting clues or hints can trigger the recall of a witness. A military police patrol or investigator may need to ask a witness specific questions about the general, specific, and changeable features of a person using the same systematic approach outlined for Army LE observations and descriptions. Descriptive features from the items listed in table 4-1, pages 4-4 and 4-5, can be used to trigger witness memories of an individual. Having witnesses recount the incident in reverse chronological order may sometimes yield additional memories or observations that may have otherwise been forgotten.

4-22. A witness must be interviewed as soon as possible after the observed incident. This interview should be conducted before the witnesses have had an opportunity to talk to others or to consciously or unconsciously change their recollection to fit an evolving memory developed from other influences. Imaginative persons often use conjecture to fill in the gaps in their knowledge of an incident. This is particularly true if they later learn that the incident is important in an investigation. Investigators must evaluate the information of a witness and compare it with all related data before using it to investigate further. Investigators must also be aware of, and make allowances for, the many factors that may influence a person's understanding and retention of the details they relate.

4-23. When obtaining a description from a witness, Army LE personnel should learn what background influences might affect the perception of the witness's observation. They must determine if there are influences that might cause a witness to give false answers or to withhold information. To help put the witness at ease, the interviewer can talk to him briefly before questioning him. They should ask the witness to repeat his descriptions to reveal discrepancies made on purpose or by incomplete observation. These flaws should be clarified in an attempt to get a better description. The questions may lead a witness to admit that he distorted the truth. Usually, a witness who lies or hides information makes unconscious slips that can be detected by LE personnel conducting the interview.

4-24. When a witness or victim identifies a person or object involved in a crime or event, it helps the investigator to associate that identification with a specific incident. Before a witness makes an identification, ensure that they have made as complete a description as they can; this will help avoid false identifications and reduce the chance for error. The witness should make the identification of a person or object from among a group of like persons or objects (persons or objects with similar characteristics); showing a witness only one weapon or one person for identification may result in a false result. A witness can identify a person through means of field identification, photographic lineup, or physical lineup.

Field Identification

4-25. Field identification can be used when the person (suspect) is apprehended while committing a crime or is apprehended in the general vicinity of the crime scene. Witnesses and victims are asked to make on-the-scene identification of the suspect as soon as possible after the occurrence of a crime. Field identification is sometimes discouraged by prosecutors; investigators should coordinate with their servicing JA before conducting field identifications.

Lineups

4-26. A lineup is appropriate when a witness may be able to recognize a perpetrator of a crime and the witness does not know the identity of the perpetrator, but the investigator suspects one or more persons of being the perpetrator. Lineups may be either physical or photographic. A physical lineup is preferred to a photographic lineup unless—

- The presentation of a physical lineup would unduly delay the investigation.
- The witness is fearful of confronting a physical lineup and facilities are not available which will preclude a confrontation.

Photographic Lineup

4-27. When conducting a photographic lineup, the suspect does not have the right to a lawyer, does not need to be present, and does not need to be informed that his picture is used in photographic identification. Booking photographs, also known as mug shots, may be used if the suspect has a previous police record with a photograph. Sequential presentation of the photographs—one photograph at a time—is the preferred method, except for cases involving juvenile witnesses; however simultaneous lineups can be used. If photographic lineups are used, the lineups will be attached as exhibits to the final police report.

4-28. In a sequential photographic lineup photographs are presented to witnesses sequentially, in a previously determined order, and removed after it is viewed before the next photograph is presented (the witness sees only one photograph at a time). In a simultaneous photographic lineup all photographs are presented at the same time, enabling the witness to see all persons in the lineup at the same time. Requirements for a photographic lineup include the following:

- The photographs included in the lineup must be identified and documented with an individual number (for example 1 through 6) and their position in the lineup.
- At least six photographs should be included in the lineup; five fillers and the suspect.
- The photograph of the suspect is contemporary and, to the extent practicable, resembles the suspect's appearance at the time of the offense.
- The photograph array is composed so that the fillers (persons other than the suspect) generally resemble the eyewitness description of the suspect, while ensuring that the suspect does not unduly stand out from the fillers. General appearance must be considered when choosing comparable photographs. All subjects (fillers plus the suspect) included in the lineup must resemble the eyewitness description of the perpetrator as much as practicable; they should be of similar height, age, race, weight, and general appearance.
- If the eyewitness has previously viewed a photographic lineup in connection with the identification of another person suspected of involvement in the offense, the fillers in the lineup

in which the current suspect participates must be different from the fillers used in any prior lineups.

- If there are multiple eyewitnesses, the suspect will be placed in a different position in the photographic array for each eyewitness. Each eyewitness must view the lineup independently of other eyewitnesses.
- Only one suspect will be included in a single lineup. Do not present the same suspect to the same witness more than once.
- No writings or information concerning any previous arrest, non-judicial or judicial proceeding involving the suspect will be visible or made known to the eyewitness.
- Nothing may be discussed with the eyewitness regarding the suspect's position in the lineup or regarding anything that might influence the eyewitness in his decision or identification of the suspect.
- No one known to the witness should be included in the lineup. If persons known to witness are included in the lineup, this impermissibly narrows the number of choices the witness has to select from and raises a valid ground for reversible error.
- If possible, the investigator conducting the lineup should not be involved in the case; using an investigator that is not involved with the case reduces any perception of bias. This precaution is relevant to photographic and physical lineups.
- The investigator administering the lineup will document a clear statement from the eyewitness, at the time of any identification and in the eyewitness own words, describing the eyewitness's confidence level that the person identified in the lineup is the offender. This may include a statement of what features of the person were especially persuasive. If the eyewitness identifies a person as the offender, the eyewitness must not be provided any information concerning the person before the investigator obtains the eyewitness's confidence statement about the selection.
- The lineup may be recorded (audio or video) if deemed appropriate by a supervisor. Prior to any recording, all persons present must be notified the lineup is being recorded.

4-29. The location and identity of the individual used in the photographic lineup is documented in the investigators notes and report. A photograph or copy of the images in the lineup should be maintained with the lineup documentation. Document and save all lineups, whether or not the witness is able to identify anyone. When a witness or victim is viewing the lineup, stress the point that he need not identify anyone from the photographs. When having an object identified, such as a gun or knife, the lineup should be conducted in a like manner. The items should be similar. For example, if a particular name-brand revolver is in question, all pictures should be of a revolver of that name brand. If a fixed-blade knife is the suspect weapon, all knives in the lineup should be fixed-blade knives of similar size and construction.

Physical (Live) Lineup

4-30. When a suspect is in custody and there were witnesses to the crime, a physical lineup may be used for identification. A physical lineup must be conducted so that all aspects of the lineup are fair and impartial. There must be no indication that might identify which participant is suspected of being the perpetrator. The requirements are basically the same as those for photographic lineup. In a sequential physical lineup persons are presented to witnesses sequentially, in a previously determined order, and removed from view of the witness prior to the next person entering the view of the witness (the witness sees only one person at a time). In a simultaneous physical lineup all persons are presented at the same time, enabling the witness to see all persons in the lineup at the same time. Requirements for a physical lineup include—

- Participants will be identified by the use of position numbers or letter cards displayed for each participant.
- Before a physical lineup, each subject will be informed of the purpose of the lineup and the general procedures to be followed during the lineup.
- All lineup participants must be out of view of the eyewitness prior to the lineup.
- The lineup will be composed so that the fillers (persons other than the suspect) generally resemble the eyewitness description of the suspect, while ensuring that the suspect does not

unduly stand out from the fillers. General appearance must be considered when choosing comparable photographs. All subjects (fillers plus the suspect) included in the lineup must resemble the eyewitness description of the perpetrator as much as practicable; they should be of similar height, age, race, weight, and general appearance.

- If the eyewitness has previously viewed a photographic lineup in connection with the identification of another person suspected of involvement in the offense, the fillers in the lineup in which the current suspect participates must be different from the fillers used in any prior lineups.

- If there are multiple eyewitnesses, the suspect will be placed in a different position in the lineup for each eyewitness. Each eyewitness must view the lineup independently of other eyewitnesses.

- At least six persons should be used; five fillers and the suspect.

- Only one suspect will be included in a single lineup. Do not present the same suspect to the same witness more than once.

- No writings or information concerning any previous arrest, nonjudicial or judicial proceeding involving the suspect will be visible or made known to the eyewitness.

- Nothing may be discussed with the eyewitness regarding the suspect's position in the lineup or regarding anything that might influence the eyewitness in his decision or identification of the suspect.

- No one known to the witness can be included in the lineup.

- If one person is asked to perform a movement, then all who participate in the lineup must be required to perform the same movement. The same is true with verbal statements. If one person is directed to make a certain statement, then all persons must make the same statement.

- Witnesses and victims must be told that they do not have to identify anyone from the lineup.

- Each eyewitness must view the lineup independently of other eyewitnesses. Only one witness at a time may view the lineup.

- The investigator administering the lineup will document a clear statement from the eyewitness, at the time of any identification and in the eyewitness own words, describing the eyewitness's confidence level that the person identified in the lineup is the offender. If the eyewitness identifies a person as the offender, the eyewitness must not be provided any information concerning the person before the investigator obtains the eyewitness's confidence statement about the selection. Each viewing will be photographed and the photographs will be attached as exhibits to the final police report.

- The lineup may be recorded (audio or video) if deemed appropriate by a supervisor. Before any recording, all persons present must be notified that the lineup is being recorded.

- All lineup participants must be photographed.

4-31. A military subject who was apprehended based on probable cause may not refuse to participate in the lineup. A military subject who was not placed under apprehension and civilians may not be forced to participate in a military lineup. When the lineup is conducted with a subject in a custodial situation, such as pretrial, military police custody or pending pretrial, he will be afforded the right to consult with an attorney. The subject may waive his right to counsel if the waiver is freely, knowingly, and intelligently made. If an attorney is assigned to represent the military suspect, that attorney must be afforded the opportunity to observe the lineup. Attorneys who are assigned to observe physical lineups may not issue guidance, participate, and/or interfere in any way. They are restricted to an observer role. For more information on this topic see MRE 321, MCM.

Note. In some cases a witness may identify a specific location where a crime has or will occur. Care must be taken not to "lead the witness" to describe or identify a specific location. Never offer the witness specific information of a known location. Allow the witness to make the identification based on his own knowledge and memory. When a witness identifies a place, the witness should describe the general location in relation to known landmarks and then describe the location in detail. The witness should then be asked to take the investigator to the scene.

Composite Sketches

4-32. Composite photographs or sketches may be used to help identify persons. If a witness or victim can provide substantial information concerning a suspect's appearance, a composite sketch may be attempted. A composite will never look exactly like the offender. Every detail that is not identical produces material for cross-examination of the witness. For this reason, composites should be used as a last resort. Composites are typically developed when the victim or witness observes and chooses examples from photographs, templates, or sketches of foreheads, eyes, noses, mouths, chins, or other facial features. The witness selects the example that most nearly looks like the particular facial feature of the person to be identified. Do not show a witness a photograph lineup before having him help develop a composite. It may influence his memory of the subject. There are multiple techniques and methods for completing composite sketches including—

- **Commercially manufactured kits.** These kits are packaged with a wide range of photographic or template examples of facial features that can be used to make composite drawings or photographs from verbal descriptions. The drawing from such a kit can resemble a person so closely that it removes others from suspicion. Kit models that use true photographs of facial features, hairstyles, eyeglasses, and hats can produce realistic photograph-like composites.
- **Sketch artists.** A sketch artist can draw a composite likeness based on verbal descriptions by the witness. Sketch artists can sometimes create composite sketches based on descriptions given by multiple witnesses.
- **Computer software.** Another consideration for making composites is the use of computer programs. These composite-generating programs allow the user to make an initial sketch based on information provided by the witness. The sketch is carefully created based on multiple-choice and free-form questions. The witness views the sketch and recommends changes that can be quickly made.

NOTES

4-33. Taking good notes may be one of the most important actions a military police patrol or investigator completes while responding to and processing a crime scene. There are two main reasons why notes are important. They represent the basic source of information, or the raw material that will be used in the written report of the investigation, and they aid in the recall of events for testimony in court.

4-34. The type of notebook an investigator uses may seem to be immaterial, but it can be of significant importance. A notebook with investigator notes may be examined and introduced as evidence in court. If notes from several cases are included in the same book, there is a chance of unauthorized disclosure of information on matters not relevant to the case at hand. Investigators must be aware that evidence of removed pages allows an inference of "shredded" exculpatory information. The preferred method is for investigators to use a separate notebook for each case, preferably hardbound from which no pages are ever removed. This method ensures that there is no question regarding the integrity of the case notes. Additionally, if the notebook becomes evidence, it contains only notes of the case at hand. Use of a separate notebook for each case may be logistically impractical. A hardbound notebook may be used for multiple cases; however, notes from each case must be clearly marked to differentiate them from separate cases, such as "Smith larceny page 1," "Smith larceny page 2," and so forth. This method requires the trial counsel to manage disclosure and protect information from unrelated cases during court proceedings. Trial counsel can move to have the sensitive information from other cases hidden from view. A loose leaf notebook may also be used. If a loose leaf notebook is used, ensure that pages for each case are accounted for using a unique numbering system for each case, similar to the previous example. The inside cover of the notebook should have the military police Soldier's or investigator's name and pertinent business information in case it is misplaced. At no time should the investigator's home addresses, phone numbers, or other personal information be placed in the notebook.

4-35. The objective of any notes taken should be the documentation of meaningful facts to be referenced months after the event. Notes that are unclear shortly after they are written will likely be unintelligible as time passes. Never expect to rely on memory of associated events to provide full meaning to single-word notes. This becomes especially important when the investigator has to write the report or testify in court.

The formal written report may not require the level of detail that is required for a testimony. When notes pertaining to a crime are taken, the writer should anticipate both the requirements and level of detail for the written report and those required for testimony in court.

4-36. In cases involving a lot of physical material and a large crime scene, a portable audio and/or video recording device can be useful. By taping observations and findings, more details can be included in the notes. In all cases, the tapes should be transcribed into a written record. All investigators' notes should—

- Be kept in a safe place within the local office case file. Even after a criminal has been convicted and sent to prison, there is always a chance that an appeal or another civil action will require an investigator's appearance in court again.
- Be printed if the writer's handwriting is not easy to read. Use blue or black ink that will not smudge easily.
- Be numbered on each page. Also ensure that the investigator places their name, title or rank, case number (when known), and current date on each page.
- Document the time when an action is taken, information is received, and an event is observed.
- Not be edited or erased. Line out an entry if a mistake is made, initial it, and then write the correct information.
- Include a detailed description of the scene and any item believed to be pertinent to the case. The description should be as complete as possible.
- Record the exact location (the measurements and triangulation of evidence) of where an item was found.
- Cite the relative distances separating various items.
- State the techniques used to collect evidence, and record identifying marks placed on the item or the package in which the evidence was placed.
- Tell what techniques were used to provide crime scene security and the methods used to search the scene.
- Include any actions taken that may have a bearing on the evidence obtained or that may significantly affect the investigation.

PHOTOGRAPHS AND VIDEO

4-37. One of the most valuable aids to a criminal investigation is quality photographs. When properly taken, photographs and associated documentation can supplement notes and sketches, clarify written reports, provide identification of personnel, and serve as a permanent record of fragile or perishable evidence. USACIDC FSOs have extensive training in forensic photography and may be consulted regarding crime scene photography requirements and techniques.

4-38. Photographs are of great value during every phase of the investigation and any subsequent judicial proceedings. They may be a judge's or jurors' only view of a crime scene. Photography of crimes scenes and other investigative activities is typically used to—

- Create a permanent record of a crime scene, an incident site, or other evidence.
- Supplement investigative reports.
- Aid in testimony.
- Assist in evaluating investigative leads; for example, reexamining photographs of the crime scene to help determine credibility of a suspect, victim, or witness.

4-39. They should accurately document the exact scene as seen by the investigator. For a photograph to have the highest quality as evidence it must depict the scene, person, or object precisely as it was found; photographs must not include people working or extraneous objects in the image. Photograph every part of a crime scene, even if it appears that it was not directly part of the crime. This is the only chance to preserve the appearance of the entire scene. Further investigation may make a different part of the scene important. Photographs must be authentic, properly exposed, and accurately depicted without blur to be useful to the investigative process; the most common errors in crime scene photography are blurry and improperly exposed photographs. Investigators must be able to testify that the photographs accurately depict the area or item observed. Crime scene sketches and investigator's notes can provide substantial corroboration to the accuracy of the photographs.

Note. The Scientific Working Group on Imaging Technology is a source of information to LE organizations and personnel regarding procedures for digital photography, video, and image processing; documenting image enhancement; and several other topics important in today's forensic environment. The Scientific Working Group on Imaging Technology can be accessed at <http://www.theiai.org/guidelines/swgit/>.

PRESERVING AND DOCUMENTING PHOTOGRAPHS

4-40. Preserving and safeguarding images is important to the successful introduction of forensic images in a court of law. The original image should be stored and maintained in an unaltered state. This includes maintaining the original digital images. Do not record photographs from multiple crime scenes on a single storage media (digital disks or memory cards); any photographic media used should be dedicated to a single crime scene. Do not discard or delete digital image files; discarding or deleting files can cause the validity of the photographic evidence as a whole to be questioned. Keep all digital images taken during crime scene processing as part of the photographic record of the scene and record them in the photograph log. Digital cameras record the date and time in the metadata; it is important to ensure that the date and time settings on digital cameras (and on any computers used to process files) are verified. Crime scene photographs should be taken in fine or RAW mode. Original files should be write-protected; duplicates or copies should be used for working images. All files should be archived to a long-term storage media such as archival grade CDs or DVDs.

4-41. Images are initially processed and stored on the digital camera's storage media. Any images taken should be previewed at the scene and retaken if required to ensure that an adequate photograph is captured. When the investigator completes all photography of the crime scene and returns to his or her office, all images are transferred from the digital camera's storage media to a designated folder on an office computer hard drive. The computer folder should be named with a unique title that includes a brief description and the appropriate incident report number such as "Original Crime Scene—Military Police Report (MPR) number," "Original Autopsy—ROI number," or similar naming convention. Once the investigator confirms all images have been properly transferred to the computer's hard drive, he or she will delete the images from the camera's storage device and the device may be used again.

4-42. The investigator must then record or "burn" the computer file containing all transferred images, to a recordable media. The following medias are recommended for the preservation of original images because of their quality, durability, permanence, reliability, and ease with which copies may be generated:

● Write-once compact disk recordable (CDR).
● Digital versatile disk recordable (DVD-R).

4-43. During the "burning process," the investigator must ensure that the CDR or DVD-R writing program closes and finalizes the writing session. The CDR or DVD-R created is considered the "original" and should be protected from loss or damage within the case file. The disc is then labeled with the full case number, with a felt-tip permanent marker or similar non-abrasive writing instrument. A separate CD or DVD will be used for each case.

4-44. The usefulness of photographic evidence depends on two key factors: the quality of the photograph and the admissibility of the photographic evidence. Photographs of poor quality do not accurately reflect the crime scene. They may also be useless to laboratory analysts when conducting forensic examination of the photographs. The quality of the photographs relies on the quality of the camera and storage media (film or digital storage) as well as the knowledge and skill of the photographer. Crime scene photographers should train on the specifics of crime scene photography and become familiar with the use of their equipment. Different methods and types of film and/or digital media produce different results; the photographer must know the best method and equipment for the specific application.

4-45. Admissibility of the photographic evidence depends on the ability to preserve the images in an unaltered state. The use of film technology has long been accepted, and standards for producing, storing, and protecting photographic evidence on film are well established. Digital photography, likewise, has become more prevalent and accepted in criminal courts. Regardless of the method for storing the image, the following techniques must be adhered to for photographic evidence:

- The evidence must be recorded and preserved in an unaltered form.
- The evidence must be documented and a chain of custody maintained.
- Any alteration or manipulation of an image for forensic analysis, such as enhancement or enlargement, must be documented completely.
- The photographer or investigator must be able to testify to the credibility of the images in court.

4-46. All photographs should be documented. A photograph log with camera positions indicated on a sketch must be prepared if the camera does not have the capability to store requisite data on the image file; most digital cameras have this capability. The crime scene photograph log records the photograph and describes the type of photograph. The photograph is precisely identified, and the identifying data is recorded as each shot is taken. The camera positions and distances are also recorded in the crime scene photograph log. This is achieved by measuring from a point on the ground directly below the camera lens to an object used as the focus point for the picture.

EQUIPMENT

4-47. Crime scene photography requires some basic photographic equipment. While additional equipment and technology is available, especially for use by highly trained crime scene photographers, the minimum equipment required includes—

- A single-lens reflex (SLR) camera.
- Film if using a film camera.
- A wide-angle lens. Use 28-millimeter for a 35-millimeter film camera or approximately 18-millimeter for an Advanced Photo System Type C format digital SLR.
- A normal lens. Use 50-millimeter for a 35-millimeter film camera or approximately 30-millimeter for an Advanced Photo System Type C format digital SLR or short zoom lens.
- Filters (red, orange, and yellow).
- A close-up or macro lens.
- A flash with a cable remote.
- A remote shutter release.
- A tripod.
- Scales or rulers.
- A flashlight.

Cameras

4-48. All cameras, whether they are film-based or digital, share common characteristics. They all have a lens to form the image, some ability to focus the image, and a place in a light-tight box to hold film. All cameras work on the same principle; light enters the lens and strikes either the film or the digital chip. In the case of film, the chemicals (silver halide) in the film are "exposed." This makes some areas darker on the negative than other areas. The resulting negative can be printed.

4-49. In the case of a digital camera, the light energy is converted to electrical energy and the information is converted to a usable computer-based file. Most crime scene photography can be conducted using either film or digital cameras. The main components of the typical camera are the lens, the camera body, an exposure meter, and film. Both film cameras and digital cameras can be point and shoot cameras or SLR cameras. Point and shoot provide minimal control over camera settings, thus they have limited capabilities. SLR cameras allow numerous variables to be controlled by the operator including aperture and shutter speed; SLR cameras also allow the operator to change lenses based on specific photographic requirements.

4-50. Typically SLR cameras are used for most crime scene photography; cameras with over 8 megapixels are preferred for general photography; close-up photography requires at least 8 megapixels. Table 4-2 provides a list of basic photography terms that crime scene photographers should understand.

Table 4-2. Photography terms

Term	Description
Aperture	An adjustable opening in the camera which allows the amount of light to be controlled.
Cable release	An attachment that allows you to trip the shutter mechanically while not touching the camera. This allows operation of the camera from a distance and can reduce camera shake.
Depth of field	The amount of the photograph, from foreground to background, that is in focus.
F-stop	Measures the opening of the aperture. In general terms, low f-stop numbers (f2-f6) allow more light, but less depth of field. In general, very small or large apertures should be avoided to eliminate distortion and diffraction.
International Organization for Standardization (ISO) rating	A rating given that measures sensitivity to light. Generally, cameras should be set to 100 to 400 ISO. The lower the number, the more light is needed, but the greater the quality. High ISOs, 800 and above, present a grainy appearance. However, they may be used for night surveillance when use of a flash is contraindicated.
Exposure (light) meter	A device that allows the photographer to determine if appropriate light is present to allow a properly exposed photograph.
Shutter	A mechanical device that opens and closes within a camera to control the amount of light—similar to a shutter on a window.
Shutter speed	The speed at which the shutter opens and closes. Most shutter speeds are measured in fractions of a second—60 is 1/60th of a second, 250 is 1/250th of a second, and so on. Shutter speeds which occur over one second or longer are generally displayed with the second symbol (for example, 2", 3", and so on). The bulb setting allows a shutter to be held open until the photographer closes the shutter. Slower shutter speeds (those less in proportion to the focal length of the lens) will generally result in camera shake if not on a tripod. For example, a camera with a 50-millimeter lens must have at least a 1/50th-second shutter speed to avoid camera shake if not on a tripod. Fast shutter speeds are able to freeze motion.
Shooting mode	Settings that allow the operator to control specific functions of the single-lens reflex cameras. They include aperture priority, auto, manual, program, and shutter priority as described below. Aperture priority mode: The user selects F-stop, the computer selects the rest. Auto mode: The camera computer selects all settings (generally safe, but may not produce the best effect). Manual mode: The user controls all settings. Program mode: The user selects either F-stop or shutter speed; the camera automatically sets the remaining settings. Shutter priority mode: The user selects the shutter speed, computer selects the rest.
Through the lens	A flash setting which can be adjusted on the flash unit that allows the camera to detect automatically when sufficient light has been captured.

Lenses

4-51. Lenses are usually made of glass and metal or plastic components. Lenses are used to form an image on the film or chip. A 50-millimeter lens is considered a normal lens for 35-millimeter photography. This means that the 50-millimeter lens approximates what the eye sees when you look at a scene or object with minimal distortion. Most overall and evidence-establishing crime scene photography can be completed with a 50-millimeter lens.

4-52. There are instances when a wide angle (28-millimeter) or telephoto (200-millimeter) lens may be required. These lenses should only be used when necessary due to the specific requirement on scene because of the inherent distortion that will occur. Wide-angle lenses will elongate the image between the foreground and background; telephoto lenses compress the foreground and background distance. A wide-angle lens may be required when photographing an object in a confined space, such as a vehicle inside a garage. Telephoto lenses may be required when photographing an inaccessible or extremely expansive area; they are also used routinely during surveillance. These lenses produce the following results:

- Telephoto lenses—
  - Magnify the target area or object.
  - Narrow the field of view.
  - Narrow the depth-of-field range.
  - Compress the distance between the foreground and background.
- Wide angle lenses—
  - Widen the field of view.
  - Increase the depth-of-field range.
  - Elongate the foreground-to-background distance.

4-53. A close-up or macro lens is used to magnify a small image to fill the frame of the photograph. Most 50-millimeter lenses cannot properly focus within an 18-inch distance from lens to target. Macro lenses typically provide a 1:1 or 1:2 magnification ratio; a 1:1 magnification ratio is normally recommended for close-up crime scene photographs. Attachments placed on normal 50-millimeter lenses can also provide close-up photography capabilities. Extension tubes or bellows can be used. They attach between the primary lens and the camera body. This moves the optical center of the primary lens resulting in a magnified image. Close-up filters can be used to increase the magnification ratio. While these attachments can produce a magnified result, they are typically not as effective as using a 1:1 macro lens.

4-54. The lens usually has the following two aspects that require input from the photographer: focus and aperture or F-stop. Turning the front ring on the barrel of the lens changes the focus. Point-and-shoot cameras sometimes have a fixed focus, where anything from 8 feet to infinity is in the acceptable focus. Other point-and-shoot cameras may have a variable or automatic focus. SLR cameras have a variable or automatic focus. The ability to precisely control focus is one of the main benefits of the SLR. If the lens has an optical stabilizer, it should be activated. It helps reduce camera shake and thus reduces the likelihood of blurry photographs.

4-55. Most cameras have an aperture range from F-2.8 to F-22. The aperture should be viewed as a fraction of the length of the lens. A good rule of thumb is to make the aperture a fraction. Instead of F-16, view it as 1/16. Instead of F-2.8, view it as 1/2.8. That will assist in understanding why an F-stop setting of F-16 is a smaller aperture than F-2.8. The aperture controls the amount of light entering the lens/camera. A small aperture such as F-16 or F-22 allows less light to enter the camera over a given time than a large aperture such as F-2.8. Another way to understand the F-stop is by describing the aperture size. For a 50-millimeter lens with an aperture setting of F-25, multiply the fraction for the F-stop (as described above) by the lens size (F-25 = 1/25); 50 millimeters x 1/25 = a 2-millimeter opening. Similarly for an F-2 aperture setting (F-2 = 1/2), 50 millimeters x 1/2 = a 25-millimeter opening.

4-56. The aperture also controls the depth of field. The depth of field is the amount of the photograph, from foreground to background, that is in focus. The higher the F-stop the better the depth of field. At F-16, a sharp focus may be obtained over a range from 3 to 100 feet. At F-2.8, sharpness may be obtained only from 3 to 5 feet. Investigators should try to maximize the depth of field.

GENERAL CONSIDERATIONS

4-57. Time is an important consideration when photographing the crime scene. This is especially critical for fragile trace evidence, such as tire tracks in rain or fresh snow, that is vulnerable to damage or destruction. The crime scene should be photographed as soon as possible and before any evidence is disturbed; photography of the crime scene should be done before any other crime scene processing. This ensures that the scene is captured in an undisturbed state. Military police patrols and investigators should avoid touching or disturbing evidence until after photographs have been taken. The Scientific Working Group on Imaging Technology is a good resource for additional information on photographic guidelines.

4-58. One of the most important elements in investigative photography is maintaining perspective. Photographs must reproduce the same view of relative position and size of visible objects as it appears to the photographer. Any significant distortion in perspective may impact the evidentiary value of the photograph. Photographs should be taken from a natural perspective, in most cases. When taking crime scene photographs the photographer should—

- Always wear appropriate PPE for personal safety and to protect evidence.
- Not assume that the confines of the crime scene have been properly identified or that they have been properly secured.
- Photograph the scene and all evidence before recovery. Ensure that—
  - Long range or overall photographs are taken to document the scene. Overall, mid-range or evidence establishing, and close-up photographs are described in detail later in this chapter.
  - All evidence is photographed at least three times.
  - A mid-range photograph is taken to show the evidence and its position in relation to other evidence, and a close-up photograph that fills the frame is taken.
- Always document—
  - Ingress and egress routes to the scene.
  - Interior, exterior, and surrounding areas of structures (houses, office buildings, sheds, garages, and such) that are part of the crime scene.
  - Entry and exit points of suspects or victims; photograph most likely entry and exit points if they are not apparent.
  - Any damaged areas, especially if they were likely access or exit locations.
  - Evidence-establishing photographs of all evidence to document its location and position in relation to other evidence, structures, objects, or bodies.
  - Close-up photographs of all evidence before collection; photograph at a 90-degree angle to the focal point of the picture. Keep the camera back parallel to the item being photographed. If the evidence leaves a mark, stain, outline, or any other change to the surface, photograph the area underneath the evidence after it has been removed.
  - Anything that seems out of place or that may help investigators understand the scene.
- Always consider that evidence is present. Take careful steps to reduce the chance of walking on evidence while concentrating on obtaining photographs.
- Use a scale when photographing evidence. The scale must be placed on the same level and as close as possible to the same plane as the evidence. A scale or ruler used for latent prints or impressions allows for the photograph to be enlarged to the exact scale of the evidence enabling one-to-one comparison. Ink pens, coins, or business cards should not be used. For close-up photography the recommended scale is one prescribed by the American Board of Forensic Odontologists. It is an L-shaped measuring device that measures the length and width; this will produce the most useful results.
- Ensure labels or markers are in place to identify evidence.
- Photograph a room or area from eye level to represent a normal view.

TYPES OF PHOTOGRAPHS

4-59. The purpose of crime scene photography is to document the scene and specific evidence as it was found by responding LE personnel. There are three types of photographs typically required to document a crime scene: overall photographs, medium- or mid-range photographs, and short-range or close-up photographs. Ensure that a progression of long-range, mid-range and close-up photographs of any objects of evidence are collected. Each type of photograph is taken for a different purpose.

Overall

4-60. Overall photographs are taken to capture the entire crime scene; these are also known as outside establishing photographs. They are not intended to document specific evidence, although evidence may appear in the photograph. Overall photographs provide documentation of the overall scene and its relationship to the surrounding area and specific landmarks such as street signs, intersections, and other buildings. They can also document an approximate time of day and general weather conditions at the time the scene was processed. Overall photographs should be taken from multiple directions or vantage points to ensure that the entire scene is captured. They should be taken at eye level unless deliberately duplicating a subject, witness, or victim's viewpoint. Placement of evidence markers will aid the viewer in understanding the spatial relationship of evidence in the scene. The number of overall photographs is based on the specifics of the scene. Considerations for overall photography include the following areas:

- **The exterior.** Use the following guidelines for exterior photography:
  - Take photographs from all sides of the building, structure, or vehicle. Photographs should cover every angle of view (360 degrees around the scene). Photographs should slightly overlap.
  - Maintain enough range to include adjacent landmarks in the photographs such as adjacent houses, roadways, tree lines, ditches, water features, other vehicles, or power lines.
  - Capture any barriers around the scene such as fences or walls.
  - If the structure is named or numbered, capture the address markings or name designation.
  - If the scene has multiple elevations (either from terrain or structure), capture shots from varying levels and vantage points.
  - Consider aerial photography to capture large areas, roads, and other means of approach or departure. Coordinate with the laboratory on proper aerial-photography techniques.
- **Entrances and exits.** Capture all entrances and exits from the structure; including doors, windows, sidewalks, driveways, or other pathways.
- **The interior.** Take overlapping photographs of interior scenes, moving in one direction around the room or area to ensure that all areas are covered. Be sure to cover all of the room from floor to ceiling.

Mid-range (Evidence Establishing)

4-61. Mid-range or evidence-establishing photographs are taken to portray specific evidence in relation to other objects or structures in the immediate vicinity. These are also known as evidence-establishing photographs. They provide more detail than overall photographs but do not typically provide enough detail for positive identification of a specific piece of evidence.

4-62. The purpose of mid-range photographs is to illustrate the particular piece of evidence in relation to a fixed object or so that one can view the orientation of the evidence at the scene. They can be used to show blood spatter on a wall, broken glass at a suspected point of entry, foot or tire impressions on a section of lawn, or a gun or knife left at the scene in relation to a body. They can also document the absence of items such as a dust-free area on an otherwise dusty surface where a television or computer may have been removed. Considerations for mid-range photography include—

- Take photographs from multiple vantage points, overlapping the frames to ensure complete documentation.
- Mark known evidence locations (shell casings, impressions, weapons, and such) with evidence markers to help identify evidence.
- Use a tripod when necessary to stabilize the camera.

Close-up

4-63. Close-up photographs are taken to capture specific items of evidence. Close-up photographs can be used to show position and detail within a narrow frame; for example, close-up photographs can be taken to show a weapon in relation to the hand; a bullet, shot, or pellets lodged in the wall; spent shell casings; ligatures, gags, or bindings; or toolmarks or other damage to door jambs, window sills, or other points of entry. They can be exposed to provide enough detail for positive identification of the evidence and to provide adequate quality and detail for forensic analysis when appropriate. Close-ups of all evidence should be accomplished before collection, measuring, and sketching take place.

4-64. Use a ruler to show scale when taking close-up photographs; always photograph the item without the ruler first. Scales should be placed on the same plane as the evidence. Typically the target item will be photographed in a manner that fills the entire frame of the picture. Always use a tripod for close-up photographs. Close-up photographs should be used for documenting—

- Latent fingerprints, palm prints, or footprints.
- Toolmarks or tire or footwear impressions.
- Evidence that will be collected for processing off-site.
- Serial numbers, vehicle identification numbers (VINs), or other markings.

4-65. Examination quality photographs (sometimes referred to as specific evidence photographs) may be required for critical comparison of evidence to known standards. These are close-up photographs, typically used for impressions, latent prints, and toolmarks. Examination quality photographs are solely focused on the specific item of evidence; spatial comparison to surrounding objects is not a consideration. Examination quality photographs provide sufficient detail for evaluation, comparison, identification, and verification by an evidence examiner. The camera must be equipped with a close-up (macro) lens; always use a tripod and a scale. Oblique lighting is often used to provide greater clarity and detail. A tripod is absolutely necessary for examination-quality photography. Due to the slow shutter speed settings required, the camera cannot be held steady enough for examination-quality photographs. When the image is enlarged, the distortion caused by any slight movement is exaggerated and becomes obvious.

4-66. The camera should be placed on a tripod directly over the print or impression. This sometimes requires inverting the center rail of the tripod so that the camera can be mounted underneath. The back of the camera or the film plane should be parallel to the impression to avoid distortion and allow for the greatest possible resolution when enlarging photographs. The camera should be focused on the impression or print and the target should fill the entire frame. This allows for the greatest possible resolution when enlarging the photograph. When using digital cameras, the operator must be aware of the limitations of their equipment. Table 4-3 provides a list of required camera resolutions for corresponding sized areas to be photographed. Photographing a larger area than what is recommended for the camera's resolution will capture less detail and may limit the success of laboratory comparison efforts.

Table 4-3. Digital photography requirements for latent prints

Digital Camera Resolution	Largest Area That Should Be Photographed
6 megapixels	2 x 3 inches
8 megapixels	3.25 x 2.5 inches
10 megapixels	2.6 x 3.9 inches
12 megapixels	2.85 x 4.25 inches
16 megapixels	3.3 x 5 inches
22 megapixels	4.1 x 5.4 inches
39 megapixels	5.4 x 7.2 inches

4-67. Close-up photographs are typically required for evidence such as latent fingerprints, bite marks, toolmarks, or dust impressions. Photographing these items of evidence close-up requires additional considerations to obtain acceptable evidentiary photographs. General steps for taking close-up photographs of fingerprints, toolmarks, or similar evidence are as follows:

- **Fingerprint and toolmarks.** Use the following techniques:
  - Remove the flash from the camera. Use a flashlight to provide oblique lighting.
  - Set the camera to the aperture priority setting. This setting allows the operator to set the appropriate F-stop and enables the camera to automatically set the appropriate shutter speed (experienced photographers may keep the camera in manual mode and retain control over all settings).

- Never allow International Organization of Standardization (ISO) settings to be higher than 400. ISO settings from 50 to 200 will produce the best quality, so use a lower ISO if lighting allows.
- Set aperture to an F-stop setting of F-8 to F-13.
- Place the camera on a tripod; do not attempt to hold it by hand.
- Ensure that the camera back is parallel with the latent print. If the photograph is taken at an angle, the print will not be completely in focus.
- Focus on the evidence being photographed, filling the viewfinder of the camera. Get as close as possible and focus carefully; due to the extremely shallow depth of field, even being slightly out of focus will cause poor results.
- Use oblique lighting to illuminate the target area. Hold the light source 1 to 2 feet away and at about a 4-degree angle from the evidence being photographed.
- Depress the shutter release; the camera will automatically close the shutter when enough light has been captured to expose the photograph.
- Bracket the target, exposing several frames using different oblique lighting distances and angles.
- Take photographs with and without a scale; ensure that the scale is placed level with the injury and parallel to the target being photographed.
- **Bite marks and other skin injuries.** Before taking close-up photographs take an overall photograph of the person to show the part of the body where the bite mark impression is located and evidence-establishing photographs of the bite mark and the immediate area around the bite mark impression. Bite marks are generally processed in the same manner as fingerprints or toolmarks (except a tripod is generally not required); however, photographing the skin can produce challenges not inherent in fingerprints or toolmark evidence due to the variations in skin tone. If the methods above do not produce adequate results, the following techniques may be used:
  - Place the camera in manual mode.
  - Use of a detachable flash.
  - Set F-stop at F-8, shutter speed 1/125th of a second, and ISO at 200 to 400, and through the lens (TTL).

Notes.

1. When photographing light skin, the aperture may need to be opened up to allow more light. When photographing dark skin, the aperture may need to be closed to allow less light. Bracket in single increments until a proper exposure is achieved.

2. If the flash is producing "hot spots" the flash should be diffused. This can be accomplished by moving the flash further away, placing tissue over the flash, or using commercial diffusers attached to the flash. The light can also be bounced of the ceiling or wall to diffuse the light instead of aiming the light directly at the injury. Bite marks will typically require oblique lighting to gain enough clarity.

  - Consider the depth of the impression and the contour of the area of the bite mark impression. A bite mark impression on a curved portion of the body may require more than one photograph of the mark.
  - Consider taking additional photographs 24, 48, and 72 hours after the initial photographs. They may produce better photographic evidence for comparison; sometimes bruising becomes more pronounced with time.
- **Footwear and tire track impressions**. Use the following techniques:
  - Set the camera to the aperture priority setting. Experienced photographers may keep the camera in manual mode and retain control over all settings.

- Set aperture to a small F-stop setting; F-11 during night or low light areas and F-22 during daylight or brighter areas.
- Remove the flash from the camera to project oblique lighting and create shadows in the impression; this increases contrast and detail. Place the flash in manual mode.
- Place the camera on a tripod, and ensure that the legs of the tripod do not obscure the footwear or tire track impressions.
- Ensure that the back of the camera is parallel with the impression. If the impression is on sloping ground, ensure that the camera back slopes in the same direction and at approximately the same degree.
- Shade the impression in bright sunlight to reduce shadows.
- Focus and fill the frame.
- Hold the flash about 3 feet away at a 45-degree angle to the impression. A flashlight or other light source can also be used. For very deep impressions where details are too dark, set up a bounce card (folded white piece of bond paper) in the opposite direction of the flash to add additional illumination and reduce shadows.
- Take the photograph and view results. Adjust light by decreasing or increasing flash intensity. Decrease intensity by moving the flash further away, or diffuse the light by placing a tissue or diffusing attachment over the flash. To increase light intensity, move the light source closer to the impression.
- Bracket the impression, exposing several frames using different oblique lighting distances and angles to achieve the best contrast.
- Take at least three exposures without scale. Place a scale next to the impression and take three with the scale.
- Repeat the sequence exposing photographs from all four directions—front, back, and two sides of the impression. A complete set of photographs from four directions will produce 24 photographs; 12 with scale and 12 without.
- When photographing in snow, it may be necessary to place the camera in manual mode to allow the operator to adjust F-stop and shutter speed. Bright objects can fool in-camera exposure meters. Take some photographs at the recommended meter setting, such as 1/250 at F-11, and then shoot several photographs at a higher exposure, such as 1/125 or 1/60 at F-11.
- Photograph longer impressions, such as tire tread patterns, in segments of 1 to 2 feet in length. Ensure that the sections overlap. Place the camera on a tripod to assist in keeping the same camera-to-subject distance.
- **Dust impressions.** Use the following techniques:
  - Set the camera to the aperture priority setting.
  - Set aperture to a small F-stop setting of F-11.
  - Place the camera on a tripod; do not attempt to hold it by hand.
  - Ensure that the back of the camera is parallel with the impression.
  - Focus on the impression to fill the frame.
  - Provide oblique lighting with a flashlight; the scene must be dark. Pan the evidence in an even manner, from about 2 to 6 feet away at a very oblique angle to obtain the best contrast.
  - Take the photograph with and without a scale; the shutter may take a few seconds to close due to minimal lighting.
  - Take additional photographs with increased and decrease angles and amounts of light.
- **Dust impressions collected on Mylar.** Use the following techniques:
  - Lift the print as discussed in chapter 2.
  - Tape Mylar Paper to the wall about shoulder height.
  - Set the camera to the aperture priority setting.
  - Set aperture to a small F-stop setting of F-11.
  - Place the camera on a tripod; do not attempt to hold it by hand.

- Ensure that the back of the camera is parallel with the impression.
- Use a flashlight to provide very oblique lighting (very shallow angle, almost parallel with the wall surface).
- Take the photograph with and without a scale.
- If exposures are not clear enough, set the camera on manual—F-stop at F-11, shutter speed of 6 seconds. Take the photograph and bracket by adjusting shutter speed to 9 and 3 seconds. Bracket using varied light angles if necessary to increase contrast.

LIGHTING

4-68. Improper lighting can reduce the quality of a photograph and can render photographs useless. Many lighting techniques can be used to enhance the photographic image. A flash should be used when exposing photographs inside a building, at night, or whenever there is a general lack of light. Indoor lighting may appear adequate to the human eye but will not be sufficient for photography without the aid of a flash. Indoor photography, day or night, generally requires use of a detachable flash. Pop-up flashes are not recommended. The best flash settings for most photographs (excluding close-ups) are F-8, shutter speed 1/125th of a second, ISO 200 to 400, and TTL. TTL is a flash setting which can be adjusted on the flash unit. It allows the camera to detect automatically when sufficient light has been captured. A tripod is generally not required when these settings are used.

4-69. Flashes are also useful when photographing items outdoors when the sun is bright but the item may be shaded, such as a weapon found underneath a bush or a car. A good technique in these situations is to set the camera on manual with an F-stop of 16 and a shutter speed of 60 (1/60th of a second). Remove the flash from the camera, place on manual setting and set at half power. Hold the flash away from the camera and aim at the evidence. The flash should be attached to the camera with a flash cable. Take the photograph. If necessary move the flash closer or further away to adjust the amount of light illuminating the evidence until the appropriate exposure is obtained.

Alternate Light Sources

4-70. At times alternate light sources (ALSs) may be required to identify and observe evidence at a crime scene that is not observable under normal lighting conditions. These ALSs can be used to illuminate the fluorescence of specific types of evidence. ALSs are useful in locating and photographing blood, nonblood bodily fluids, fiber, and trace evidence. Several ALSs are at the disposal of investigators and examiners. A good ALS is small, lightweight, and portable. It should be battery operated and be equipped with a variety of interchangeable filters. The use of these ALSs and photography techniques to capture images visualized by these light techniques requires training and practice; adequate results can be obtained by using a tripod, slow shutter speeds, and appropriate filters. ALSs can be detrimental to the naked eye. Everyone in the room who is exposed to ALS should wear protective goggles.

4-71. Infrared (IR) light can be useful in locating and photographing GSR or variations on documents, and it can reveal writing on burned documents. IR light photography requires specialized film (for film photography) or modified cameras (for digital photography). Because of the special equipment requirements, IR photography is most commonly used in a laboratory setting rather than during crime scene processing.

4-72. Laser light sources typically emit a high-intensity green light. This light source is capable of illuminating a wide variety of evidence to include fingerprints, fibers and other trace evidence, body fluids, bone fragments, and narcotics residue. Laser light sources can be expensive and are therefore typically available only to laboratory personnel.

Note. Blood evidence absorbs UV light making it appear black. While UV light is very useful in finding and photographing other types of evidence, it is not a good method for identifying blood.

4-73. Evidence observed under long wave UV, laser, and forensic light sources regularly used on crime scenes can be photographed using filters over standard lenses. These filters and their uses include the following:

- **Yellow filter.** Evidence illuminated by UV light can be photographed by using a yellow filter attached to the lens; there are also lens filters specifically constructed for UV photography.
- **Orange filter.** Evidence observed under a blue light source, emitted by a laser or other forensic light source, can be photographed using an orange filter.
- **Red filter.** Evidence observed under a green light source, emitted by a laser or other forensic light source, can be photographed using a red filter.

Diffused and Bounced Lighting

4-74. At times the lighting either from natural sunlight, a camera flash, or another source may be too intense when allowed to directly impact the evidence being photographed. Camera flash may create a "white out" effect. In these instances, the flash can be placed on the manual setting and a diffusion technique applied. Diffusion is obtained by placing a material between the light source and the target of the photograph. Some easy diffusion techniques include using a finger over the flash or placing a tissue over the flash. When photographing outdoors, a white sheet can be held between direct sunlight and the evidence being photographed. Some cameras have built-in plastic diffusing components that cover the flash to diffuse the light.

4-75. A diffusing effect can also be obtained by bouncing the light off of a surface rather than aiming the light source directly at the target object. The flash or other light source can be bounced off of the ceiling or another surface such as a sheet or white poster board. Any of these or other diffusion techniques will tend to spread out the light and reduce glare and hot spots.

Oblique Lighting

4-76. One of the most common lighting techniques is oblique lighting. Oblique lighting may be required for photographing impressions, trace evidence, and other small items. Oblique lighting provides the greatest amount of contrast by casting shadows in the target impression or other target evidence, thus capturing better details. This is critical when the photographic evidence will be analyzed by examiners at the USACIL. Oblique lighting can be provided by camera flashes, flashlights, or other external light sources. To obtain the oblique lighting (and shadowing) required, place the light source at about a 45-degree angle and about 3 to 5 feet to one side of the target evidence or area. The angle of the light may be increased or decreased to obtain the best results. For example, the deeper an impression, the greater the angle should be to obtain optimum shadowing and clarity of the impression; the more shallow the impression, the more oblique the angle.

4-77. Photographs should be taken with the flash or other light source held at four different directions from the impression. North, south, east, and west directions will provide sufficient shadow variances to yield the best details. A shadow indicator, such as a thumbtack, an ink pen, or a golf tee, should be positioned in the shot to allow the examiner to determine the direction the light is coming from; this aids the examiner in his comparison work. If suitable conditions do not exist in the ambient light of the scene (such as too much direct sunlight), a shadow should be cast over the target evidence with a large piece of cardboard or other suitable material and then illuminated by using an electronic flash.

SPECIFIC CONSIDERATIONS

4-78. Some crime scenes require specific considerations due to their sensitivity or unique nature. These scenes may require a specific type of photograph or a specific method to take the photograph. Specific considerations are required for arson scenes, death scenes, autopsies, vehicle crime scenes, and surveillance activities.

Arson Scenes

4-79. Arson scenes will be either active or inactive. At an active fire, caution must be exercised when photographing the scene due to the many dangers present. All Army LE personnel must follow the orders of the fire chief or the senior fire fighter on scene. Never attempt to enter the structure during an active fire; document an active fire scene by—

- Photographing the fire in progress using a tripod from all accessible angles or sides.
- Photographing in color. The color of the flame and smoke may provide information regarding the accelerant and the temperature of the fire.
- Photographing the entire fire at intervals, keeping note of times. This will show the speed of progression.
- Photographing the crowd in small segments so that faces are identifiable. Many times arson suspects will remain at the scene to watch the fire.

4-80. At an inactive fire scene, the investigator must use caution and coordinate with the fire chief before entering the scene. Many hazards may be present within a burnt structure including chemical hazards and weakened structures that may be prone to collapse. At an inactive fire scene—

- Photograph the exterior from all sides and the interior using 360-degree overlapping photographs.
- Be aware that when photographing burned areas, the exposure may need to be reduced by two to three extra F-stops. Dark, charred areas do not reflect a great deal of light, so extra exposure is required to show the charred patterns. Take a reading with the camera on automatic, then switch it to manual and decrease the exposure by two to three F-stops (decrease the shutter speed or increase the aperture setting). Always use a flash and a tripod to photograph all fire scenes.
- Have the fire chief, a senior fire official, or a trained fire investigator point out the suspected point of origin. Photograph that area and its relationship to the rest of the area or building.
- Photograph anything of possible evidentiary value, such as cans, bottles, strings, wires, or matches.
- Photograph any suspected points of entry.
- Photograph areas that are adjacent to the fire scene to show the proximity of other structures, if present.
- Photograph any voided areas where items such as, collectibles, televisions, or stereos could have been removed. This may indicate arson by the owner.
- Photograph electrical junction boxes and the main electrical box in the building.
- Watch for trail patterns where an accelerant could have been used.

Note. Many of the same techniques are applied when photographing explosive scenes.

Death Scenes

4-81. All death scenes should be photographed in color. The photographer should—

- Take an integrity photograph before entering the area where the deceased is located. This records the area before anyone enters and disturbs the scene. This action is secondary to rendering first aid to a living victim.
- Photograph the area of the deceased with 360-degree overlapping photographs.
- Photograph the deceased from all four sides.
- Take several identification photographs of the individual's face.
- Photograph all wounds, abrasions, or other marks on the deceased. Photograph with and without rulers. These photographs should include both mid-range establishing shots and close-ups.
- Photograph the overall scene and establish close-up photographs of all potential evidence, such as weapons or pill bottles.
- Photograph livor mortis patterns, if present, before the deceased is moved.

- Photograph all bloodstains on the skin and clothing of the victim, with and without a ruler, before removal. Movement of the deceased can alter the bloodstain patterns.
- Photograph all signs of gunshot powder stippling or tattooing or the lack of it in all firearm-related deaths. Much of the powder pattern can inadvertently be washed off during the autopsy.

Autopsies

4-82. Always photograph autopsies in color. When using a scale in close-up photographs, use white, gray, or a combination of both to allow the person printing the photographs to balance the lighting. This also reduces the green color that is usually obtained when shooting film under fluorescent lights. The photographer should—

- Photograph any seals or identification tags that may be located on body bags used for transporting the body. There may also be seals or tags on refrigeration storage units used to store the body or on the body itself. Photograph all seals, tags or other identifying markers showing how the markers are affixed and any identifying information on the seal or tag.
- Take overall shots to record the entire body from all angles, to include the front and back. The use of a wide-angle lens may be required.
- Photograph the body both before and after the body is undressed and cleaned up.
- Photograph the face to include the front, profile, and any unique facial or dental features. Take several photographs of the face straight on using a normal focal length lens (50-millimeter) to avoid distortion. A ladder may be required to accomplish this.
- Photograph both hands, particularly the palms. Evidence located there, such as blood, soot, or discoloration, can diminish over a short period of time.
- Photograph old scars (including those as a result of operations or previous injuries), identifying marks, and tattoos. Scars, tattoos, and identifying marks should be photographed both with and without scale.
- Photograph wounds by taking evidence-establishing and close-up photographs with and without a ruler. The ruler must be parallel with the camera back so that the photographs can be printed life-size, if necessary. This is especially important if impressions from belt buckles, threaded pipes, or bite marks are present.
- Photograph internal injuries by taking orientation and close-up photographs.
- Photograph projectiles while still in the body and once they are removed.
- Photograph anything noted by the pathologist as being out of the ordinary or anything that proves or disproves the facts or witness testimony. Use the photographs to substantiate and document the findings, both pathological and investigative.

Note. Most ME offices, including the AFMES, have their own forensic photographers and can supply photographs to investigators. It is important that investigators request any specific photographs required for the investigation.

4-83. Take all necessary identifying photographs of the genital area as soon as possible. If no defects exist in and around the genitalia, investigators should then cover that area with a small cloth for any remaining photographs. When photographing organs or objects removed from the body, ensure that the item is wiped off and there is a clean "field" behind it. A clean cloth works best. Bloody objects, such as a table, clothes, or other items in and around the area being photographed, are distracting and can confuse the viewer.

Vehicles

4-84. A systematic approach should be used to document vehicle crime scenes. These photographs should include the exterior of the vehicle; all interior compartments; any obvious damage; and anything commonly used to identify a specific vehicle such as the VIN, the license plate number, and any other serial-numbered window stickers.

4-85. Begin at a logical point such as the front of the vehicle. Try to back up far enough to use a normal lens. Avoid wide angle lenses if at all possible; wide angle lenses will tend to distort the image. General steps for taking photographic documentation of vehicles include the following:

- Take overall photographs of all sides of the vehicle (the front, the driver's side, the passenger side, and the rear).
- Take evidence-establishing photographs of the interior compartments of the vehicle. Use a normal focal-length lens if possible; this may require the photographer to back up to increase the distance from the vehicle. Be sure to—
  - Take interior photographs of the front and rear passenger areas from both sides of the vehicle (drivers and passengers).
  - Take photographs of the interior of open doors. Do this by opening each door and photographing individually from the rear of the vehicle.
  - Take photographs of the interior compartments such as glove and console compartments.
- Photograph the open trunk area. Interior compartments of the trunk, such as the spare tire and tool compartments, may also require documentation. Multiple angles may be required.
- Photograph the engine compartment as required. Multiple angles may be required.
- Take close-up photographs of any identified evidence in the vehicle including bodies, contraband, weapons, trace evidence, or latent prints. Use close-up photographs to document identifying data on the vehicle including license plates and VINs. VINs may be located in several locations including—
  - A VIN plate mounted on top of the dash. Use a flashlight to side light the VIN from inside the vehicle while taking the photograph through the windshield.
  - A data plate in the engine compartment with the VIN number on it. Side lighting the data plate can increase detail.
  - A data plate inside the driver's side door jamb.

Surveillance

4-86. In surveillance photography, a longer length lens, such as 200- to 500-millimeter lens, is almost always required. Select the lens remembering that generally to obtain a recognizable image of a face, 2 millimeters of lens focal length is required for each foot of distance between the camera and the subject. A 200-millimeter lens will give a recognizable facial image at 100 feet.

4-87. Use a tripod and a cable release. A long lens magnifies movement. If the camera or lens is not stable, the photographs will show movement and will result in blurry images. If no tripod is available, brace the lens against a wall or tabletop. In a vehicle, a side window can be rolled partway down with the lens resting on the top edge of the window. Ensure that the vehicle engine is turned off to avoid any vibration. Remember to always use a shutter speed that is faster than the length of the lens; for example, if using a 200-millimeter lens, use a 1/250th second shutter speed. Besides obtaining a facial image on the film large enough to identify, the most important consideration is to have a fast shutter speed, usually 1/250th second or faster to top motion.

4-88. The depth of field is less important when doing surveillance photography than the shutter speed. The lens can be opened to the widest aperture in order to gain a faster shutter speed. Focus carefully because the depth of field (range of acceptable focus) will be very shallow at wider apertures, such as F-2.8 or F-4. Shoot several exposures of each subject and/or transaction.

VIDEOGRAPHY

4-89. In addition to photographing and sketching a crime scene, investigators should consider video recording the scene. Videography is not a replacement for still photography of the crime scene but rather a supplement. Do not rely on video to record fine details. Videography should be well planned and follow the same basic principles as still photography (movement from the general to the specific). This will result in fewer mistakes and allow a smooth transition from one area of the crime scene to the next. A tripod or monopod can help steady the camera and provide a smooth video.

4-90. Before taking a video camera to the crime scene, verify that there is extra videotape, recordable CDs, DVDs, or other recording medium; ensure that the batteries are fully charged and that extra batteries are available. If using tape, play the tape for approximately 10 seconds before beginning the recording to prevent recording on the tape leader and possibly losing the first few seconds of the recording. Turn off or disable the audio record capabilities. This eliminates the possibility of making erroneous statements or picking up extraneous comments. When video recording the scene—

- Identify the subject matter at the beginning of the recording, such as case number, investigator's name, or scene. This should be done before turning off the audio record capability.
- Plan each shot in advance to provide sufficient recorded information and prevent confusion.
- Do not record anything that is not of potential evidentiary value and do not delete anything.
- Use the video light if the light levels are low.
- For recordings on tape, use standard play mode to record. Image quality quickly degrades when using other than standard play.
- Try to leave the focus of the camera on normal to wide angle and move in closer to the subject for close-ups. Avoid use of the zoom—this can be distracting and it magnifies movement.
- Be consistent and establish a routine recording pattern. Always pan from the same direction (right to left or left to right).

4-91. Do not reset, rewind, or view the recording at the scene. Wait until leaving the scene when no additional recording is required. After video recording the scene, always—

- Make a master copy or working copy to use in making duplications and for viewing. Repeated playback of fragile media such as tape can result in physical damage to the media with resulting loss of data.
- Place the case number on the media and preserve it the same as other photographic evidence.
- On tapes punch out or break the antierase tabs.

SKETCHES

4-92. Crime scene sketches are a critical element in the overall documentation of a crime scene. They are especially important for major and complex crime scenes. Sketches help to recreate the crime scene by depicting the location of evidence, the victim's body, points of entry and exit to a crime scene, and other details. The two primary types of crime scene sketches are the rough sketch and the finished sketch.

ROUGH SKETCHES

4-93. A rough sketch is hand drawn while at the crime scene and must portray information accurately. A rough sketch may be drawn to scale, but it usually is not drawn to scale. Scale drawings are typically produced after the fact using the rough sketch (not drawn to scale) to develop a finished scale drawing. Regardless, the sketch must show accurate distances, dimensions, and relative proportions. When a sketch is drawn—

- To scale—
  - Allot more time for the sketch. A sketch drawn to scale is much more time consuming than one not drawn to scale. Distortion is avoided that may be present in a sketch not drawn to scale.
  - Use graphing paper.
  - Identify the longest item being drawn and place it in the sketch first. This item will be used to establish the scale.
  - Assign each square a specific measurement such as 1 block equals 1 foot (based on the item selected in the previous bullet). Ensure that the scale is documented on the sketch.
- Not to scale—
  - Place items in the diagram by approximating their size in relation to the overall sketch.
  - Understand that some distortion may be present, although drastic distortion should be avoided.

■ Mark the sketch clearly as "not to scale."

4-94. Each sketch should include the critical features of the crime scene and the major, discernible items of physical evidence. Each sketch should have a caption or title that identifies the illustration. For example, a caption might read "flat-projection rough sketch showing room C-33, building 3203, troop billets." Each sketch must have a—

- Legend that explains any symbols, numbers, and letters used to identify objects on the sketch. Numbers are used to explain items of interest and letters are used to explain items of evidence. Standard military symbols are used where practical.
- Compass orientation showing north.
- Scale designation for scaled drawings.
- Sketch title block containing the—
    - Incident report number, such as an MPR, USACIDC sequence number, or ROI number.
    - Scene portrayed, citing the room number, the building number, and the type of building (such as the Post Exchange, commissary, family housing, or troop billets).
    - Location citing the complete name of the installation or city, state, and zip code.
    - Time and date the sketch was started.
    - Name and rank or title of the person who drew the sketch.

4-95. Too much detail in a sketch can make the sketch difficult to understand. The sketch must be completed with enough detail to be completely understandable to a viewer without a detailed study. The sketch must be balanced so that enough data is provided to make the sketch useful while not including so much data that the sketch becomes confusing. Sketch notes should be taken to accompany sketches. Additional detail that may be required can be annotated in the sketch notes but not placed on the sketch itself. This ensures that any necessary detail is documented while keeping the sketch uncluttered by excessive detail. Sketch notes should also record weather and environmental data associated with the sketched scene. Height measurements are taken and annotated in the notes even though they are not reflected on most flat projection sketches. All measurements should be documented in the sketch notes.

4-96. To eliminate excessive detail in a sketch, especially for complex crime scenes, more than one sketch may be drawn of the same area with each drawing portraying a different element or aspect of the scene. This may be necessary to provide adequate detail and minimize confusion. For example, one sketch may be devoted to the position of the victim's body and one or two of the more critical evidence items. Other sketches might show the lay of evidence items with respect to the point of entry or to other critical points. Several types of sketches can be used to depict a specific aspect of the crime scene. These include—

- **A flat projection or overview sketch.** A flat projection sketch consists of a top down view or floor plan sketch of the scene portrayed on a horizontal plane. This is the most common type of sketch. See figure 4-1 for an example of a flat projection or overview sketch.
- **An elevation sketch.** An elevation sketch portrays a vertical plane such as a wall. It is typically used to show evidence on vertical surfaces such as walls or cabinetry. Elevation sketches can be useful for showing blood spatter patterns, projectile evidence, or bullet holes through windows.
- **A cross-projection or exploded view sketch.** A cross-projection sketch is a combination of the previous two sketches. The walls, windows, and doors in a cross-projection sketch are drawn as though the walls had been folded out flat on the floor with the surface projected up. See figure 4-2, page 4-30, for an example of a cross-projection sketch. Measurements in cross-projection have length, not height.
- **A perspective sketch.** The perspective sketch depicts the scene or object in three dimensions. The perspective sketch is the least used and most difficult to draw; it requires a higher level of artistic skill to produce.

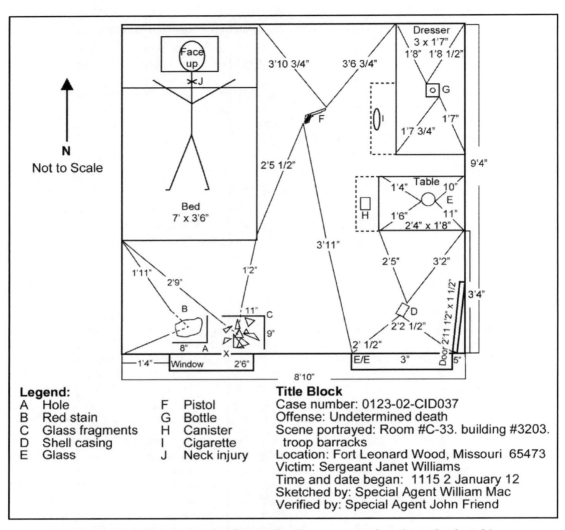

Legend:

A	Hole	F	Pistol
B	Red stain	G	Bottle
C	Glass fragments	H	Canister
D	Shell casing	I	Cigarette
E	Glass	J	Neck injury

Title Block
Case number: 0123-02-CID037
Offense: Undetermined death
Scene portrayed: Room #C-33. building #3203. troop barracks
Location: Fort Leonard Wood, Missouri 65473
Victim: Sergeant Janet Williams
Time and date began: 1115 2 January 12
Sketched by: Special Agent William Mac
Verified by: Special Agent John Friend

Figure 4-1. Example of a flat projection or overview (rough sketch)

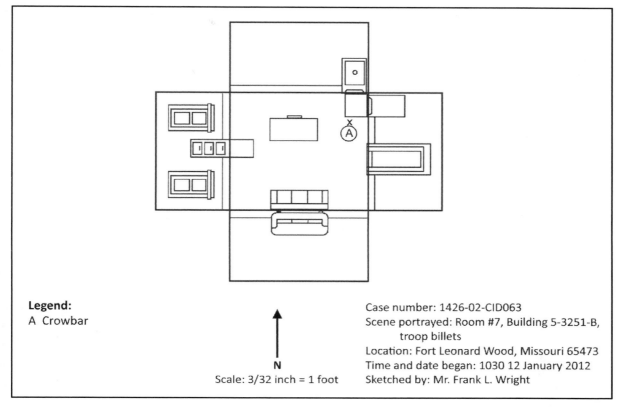

Legend:
A Crowbar

N
Scale: 3/32 inch = 1 foot

Case number: 1426-02-CID063
Scene portrayed: Room #7, Building 5-3251-B,
    troop billets
Location: Fort Leonard Wood, Missouri 65473
Time and date began: 1030 12 January 2012
Sketched by: Mr. Frank L. Wright

Figure 4-2. Example of a cross-projection sketch

FINISHED SKETCHES

4-97. A finished sketch is simply a more professional and carefully drawn version of the rough sketch. In some cases an experienced draftsman should draw the finished sketch, especially for complex or serious crimes. The finished sketch does not need to be produced by the same individual that drew the rough sketch, but the individual that produced the rough sketch must verify the accuracy of the finished sketch. The name of the person who drew the finished sketch should be reflected on the report and on the sketch. A copy of the finished sketch is attached to each copy of the investigation report. Finished sketches are often drawn to scale from information in the rough sketch. If a finished sketch is drawn to scale, the numbers showing distances may be omitted. If the finished sketch is not drawn to scale, all distances must be shown. See figure 4-3 for an example of a finished sketch drawn to scale.

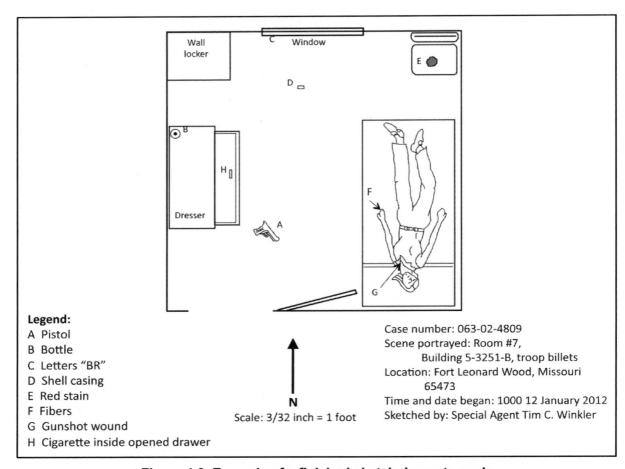

Figure 4-3. Example of a finished sketch drawn to scale

PREPARATION OF A ROUGH SKETCH

4-98. Any kind of paper may be used for a rough sketch. However, bond or graph paper is best. It can be placed on a clipboard large enough to form a smooth area for drawing. At a minimum, the following items are required to prepare a rough sketch:

- Writing implements to include—
  - Soft lead (number 2) pencils.
  - Colored pencils. A sketcher may choose to use red pencils to denote bloodstains, and other colored pencils to mark different types of evidence on the sketch.
- A 100-foot tape and a 25-foot tape. Other measuring devices that may be helpful include a laser range finder, a measuring wheel, or a total station.
- A GPS (may be useful in documenting points within an outdoor scene).
- A straightedge ruler.
- A weight, several thumbtacks, or tape to hold one end of the steel tape down when you are working alone.
- A magnetic compass.
- Crime scene templates.
- A clipboard.

4-99. The measurements shown on the sketch must be as accurate as possible and should be made and recorded uniformly. Steel tapes are the best means of taking accurate measurements and should be used if at all possible; less precise measurement methods such as counting paces should not be used unless absolutely unavoidable. It is important to verify the measurement with a tape measure or laser range finder. A measurement error on a sketch can bring the entire crime scene search into doubt. If one aspect of a sketch is inaccurate, such as the dimensions of a field in which a body was found, and the position of an object within the field is only roughly estimated, the distortion introduced renders the sketch relatively useless. Evidence must be shown using accurate measurements of the crime scene. Several items of information are considered essential in a crime scene sketch. The sketch should include—

- Dimensions of—
  - Rooms (length, width, and height). Measurements are made from corner to corner.
  - Furniture (length, width, height, depth, and thickness).
  - Doors (width, height, and thickness).
  - Windows (height and width).
  - Fields and open areas. These should be documented using observable landmarks if at all possible; GPS coordinates may be used if no useable landmarks exist.
- Distances between objects, persons, bodies, entrances, and exits.
- Measurements showing the location of evidence. Each object should be located by documenting measurements from the evidence to two fixed items, such as doors, walls, posts, or trees. In large open areas, a transecting baseline method may be used; GPS coordinates may be used when fixed objects are not available for measurement. A photograph sketch (used to document camera position during crime scene photography) must show camera positions and distances to focus points.

4-100. It is important that the distances documenting an item in the sketch are measured in the same manner. For example, one coordinate leg of the victim should not be paced and the other measured with a tape measure. It is also a mistake to pace off a distance and then show it on the sketch in terms of feet and inches. This implies a far greater degree of accuracy than the measurement technique could possibly produce. If the point arose in court, such imprecision could greatly detract from the value of the sketch.

Creating the Sketch

4-101. Before beginning a sketch, walk the crime scene to obtain a thorough understanding and view of the scene. Determine the limits of the sketch, including what to include and exclude from the sketch. If the scene is large or extremely complex, a very rough sketch with notes should be produced during the walk through. Initial rough sketches can then be used for planning and completing more detailed rough sketches. Specific areas that are complex or that require greater detail can be reproduced as separate drawings to provide the required clarity. The first step in drawing the rough sketch is to identify a baseline and document the measurement. Establish the baseline and perimeter boundaries of the sketch by—

- Identifying and laying down a baseline. The baseline of the sketch normally corresponds to the longest uninterrupted side of a room. Outdoors it could be a curb, street, building line, or an imaginary line between two fixed points.
- Measuring the established baseline and marking it on the rough sketch.
- Taking other measurements of the periphery of the scene or area being sketched. Work off of the baseline, initially, until all perimeter boundary lines and measurements have been established. Then add them to the baseline.

4-102. Once the perimeter has been established, measured, and documented on the sketch, objects and structures within the perimeter can be added. All measurements should be written down on the sketch, in the sketch notes, or both. Critical measurements should be verified by at least two people.

Establishing Evidence Location on a Sketch

4-103. Various sketch methods may be used to show evidence location and other important items at the scene. The simplest form of a sketch is a two-dimensional presentation of a scene as viewed directly from above. Evidence location is shown on this type of sketch by using triangulation or rectangular coordinates. Triangulation and rectangular coordinate measurements can be used for both indoor and outdoor sketches having fixed reference points. Inhabited outdoor areas usually have easily defined, fixed reference points such as buildings, edges of roads, and sidewalks. When these are present, the triangulation method can be used to establish the location of objects. In some cases, especially in uninhabited or remote areas that may not have easily defined, fixed points within close proximity, a transecting baseline may be a better option. When no fixed objects are available a global positioning system device may be required to fix locations. All these methods require precise measurements to fixed points. In general, when making measurements to establish evidence location do not—

- Triangulate evidence to evidence.
- Make measurements under or through evidence.
- Take a line of measurement through space. Measure the line along a solid surface like a floor, wall, or tabletop.

Triangulation

4-104.   The triangulation method documents the location of a specific object or point by creating a triangle of measurements from a single, specific, identifiable point on an item to two fixed points within the crime scene area. The distance between the two fixed points should also be measured and documented. All measurements are taken on the same plane (along the floor, a wall, a door, or another flat plane). The angle of triangulation measurements should be kept between 45 and 90 degrees on the sketches. Ensure that the measurements in the notes and sketches do not conflict. The following two triangulation methods are typically used to document an object's location:

- **The V method**. Irregular-shaped items may be fixed by creating a single triangle of measurements from the approximate center of mass of the item to two fixed points on the same plane at the scene. The longest and widest dimensions of the item are also measured. This is commonly known as the 1-V method of triangulation. The V method is also useful in outdoor areas where fixed objects in close proximity to an object may be limited. Take care when measuring not to disturb evidence. Measuring tape should not be laid across evidence. Measure from a fixed point to the edge of the object, irregular stain, or other evidence; estimate the remaining distance to the center of the evidence by taking half of the appropriate dimension measurement and adding it to the first measurement to get the total distance from fixed point to center mass of the item or evidence. Figure 4-4, page 4-34, shows an example of the 1-V method of triangulation.
- **The 2-V method.** Regular-shaped items are fixed by creating two separate triangles of measurements. Each originates at opposite points on the item and ends at two fixed points on the same plane at the scene. This is commonly known as the 2-V method of triangulation. Figure 4-5, page 4-35, shows an example of the 2-V method of triangulation.

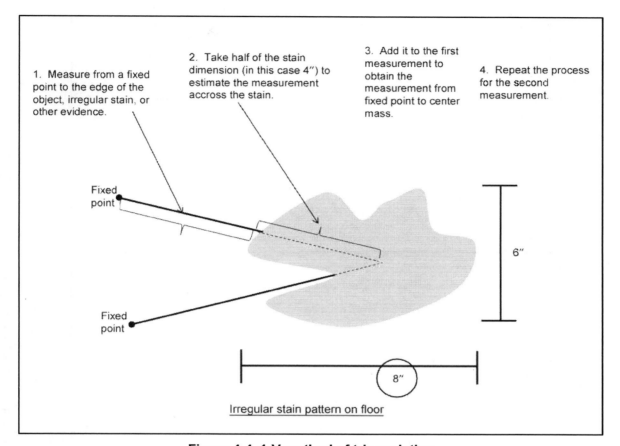

1. Measure from a fixed point to the edge of the object, irregular stain, or other evidence.

2. Take half of the stain dimension (in this case 4″) to estimate the measurement accross the stain.

3. Add it to the first measurement to obtain the measurement from fixed point to center mass.

4. Repeat the process for the second measurement.

Fixed point

Fixed point

6″

8″

Irregular stain pattern on floor

Figure 4-4. 1-V method of triangulation

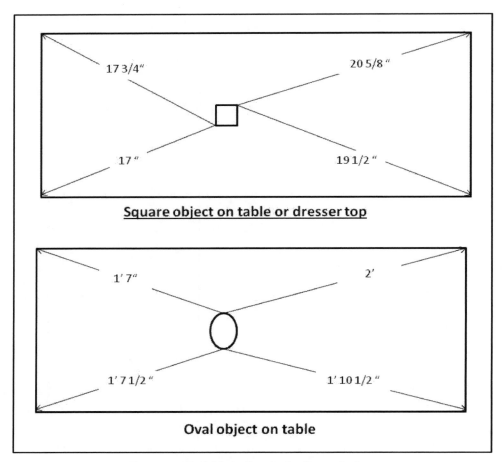

Figure 4-5. 2-V method of triangulation

Transecting Baseline

4-105.   The transecting baseline method is especially useful in large, irregularly shaped outdoor areas. Once the transecting baseline is established, multiple items of evidence can be associated with the baseline. Figure 4-6, page 4-36, shows an example of the transecting baseline method. To measure using the transecting baseline method—

- Transect the crime scene by laying down a tape measure or string or other straight line between two fixed identifiable points. The line should cross the entire area. A long tape is typically best for laying the line because measurements along the line will be required.
- Document the location of the transecting line in the sketch.
- Locate objects in the crime scene by measuring the distance from the established baseline to the evidence; the measurement must be at a 90-degree angle (right angle) to the baseline.
- Record the distance (along the baseline) from one of the fixed points to the point on the baseline from which the evidence measurement was taken. This provides the two measurements needed to locate the object.

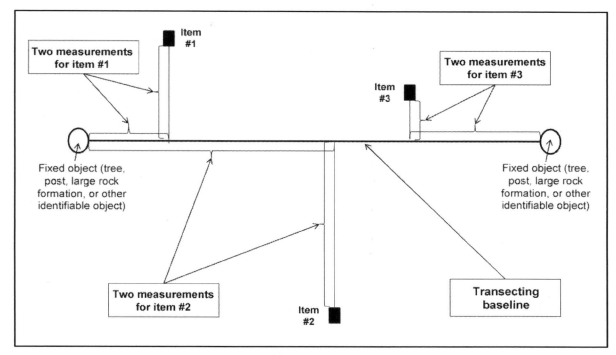

Figure 4-6. Transecting baseline method

4-106. Upon completing a sketch and all associated measurements, the investigator must recheck the crime scene against his notes and sketch to verify that all items have been consistently identified and recorded. If new evidence is discovered, it must be described, photographed, measured, and annotated on the appropriate sketch.

AUTOMATED TECHNOLOGY

4-107. Computer-based programs are available to produce both rough sketches and finished diagrams of crime scenes. These programs are typically computer-aided design based programs that can be loaded on portable notebook computers. They can be used at the scene to record measurements and generate accurate sketches on-site or to generate professional finished products from rough sketches that were hand drawn at the crime scene.

4-108. Portable devices can also be used to automatically scan the crime scene and capture details of the scene. These devices can be mounted on a tripod and conduct a 360-degree scan of the scene. These devices record high-resolution images that can then be processed to document distances between points in the scene and produce color 3-dimensional models for both investigative and courtroom purposes. The device can be positioned to capture the scene from various vantage points.

INITIAL RESPONSE

4-109. Typically military police patrols are the first to arrive at a crime scene during LE activities in support of bases and base camps. In relatively stable operational environments where U.S. forces are supporting or working in conjunction with HN LE efforts, the first responders may be military police patrols, civilian police, or military personnel. In cases where investigators are required due to the type or complexity of the incident, the senior military police patrol maintains control of the scene until an investigator arrives and control can be transferred. Military police first responders brief MPI or USACIDC SAs upon their arrival.

Note. In contingency operations, especially when the threat remains high, the first responders will likely be Soldiers or civilians that have minimal if any training on evidence collection and site preservation. This can create challenges for follow-on military police or USACIDC SAs responding after the fact, either in a direct LE capacity or as part of a site exploitation team.

4-110. The senior Army LE person on-site should take charge, plan, and direct the activities of other responding or supporting personnel; this may be military police patrols, MPIs, or USACIDC SAs, depending on the specifics of the incident. Initially the number of Army LE personnel may not be enough to perform all tasks required. Many times the priority of work for first responding LE elements is limited until additional patrols and LE investigators arrive at the scene. First responding military police should initially focus on—

- Observing and assessing the scene.
- Ensuring the safety of personnel.
- Establishing and maintaining control of the scene.
- Documenting actions and observations at the scene.
- Transferring control of the scene to investigators (as required).

Note. Critical incident support should be made available to any LE personnel exposed to death scenes, major trauma scenes, or any other incidents that can cause stress-related reactions. The Critical Incident Peer Support Program is a program that uses unit personnel trained in critical incident peer support by the USAMPS in conjunction with behavioral health professionals to assist military LE personnel and first responders to prepare for and understanding the impact of stress and related emotional trauma associated with exposure to critical or traumatic incidents. See ATTP 3-39.10 for more information.

OBSERVE AND ASSESS THE SCENE

4-111. No two crime scenes or incident sites are the same. First responding Army LE personnel should treat every incident as a crime scene until the situation can be assessed. The assessment after arrival of Army LE may be that no crime has been committed. Some cases are relatively simple and can be handled by routine military police patrol personnel; however, many cases require LE investigators to assume control of the case and conduct deliberate criminal investigations.

4-112. It is important for the first responder at the scene to be observant when approaching, entering, and exiting a crime scene. This initial assessment of the scene is typically conducted by responding military police patrols. If a crime scene exists, preservation of the scene with minimal contamination and disturbance of physical evidence is critical. Each crime scene or site must be evaluated by responding personnel based on the type of incident, environmental conditions, personnel involved, and the threat (or other hazards) to responding personnel, witnesses, victims, and the general population. Potential evidence should be identified; any evidence identified by patrols should be protected by collection and preservation or by establishing cordons or other measures to protect the evidence. Initial observation and assessment of the scene by first responders should include—

- Noting and documenting dispatch information, such as the address or location, the time, the date, the type of call, and parties involved.
- Maintaining awareness and noting any individuals or vehicles leaving the crime scene.
- Approaching the scene cautiously, scanning the entire area thoroughly to assess the scene, and noting any possible secondary crime scenes. Assume that the crime is ongoing until it is determined otherwise.
- Looking for any individuals and vehicles in the vicinity that may be related to the crime.
- Remaining alert and attentive.
- Requesting additional resources as required including emergency medical personnel, fire department personnel, and additional LE support. Once additional patrols and/or LE

investigators arrive, a division of labor can be established to prioritize and accomplish tasks required to safeguard personnel and control and protect the scene.

ENSURE SAFETY OF PERSONNEL

4-113.   The safety and physical well-being of military police and other individuals in and around the crime scene is the first priority of the first responding military policeman. The identification and control of physical threats will ensure the safety of military police and others that are present. LE patrols must quickly identify immediate or potential threats and take appropriate actions to ensure that persons at the crime scene or incident site (to include LE personnel) are safe. Continuously observe (look, listen, and smell) to assess the scene and ensure that the area is safe before proceeding, being cognizant of the presence of potential threats including people, chemicals, explosive devices, or other threats. Military police arriving at the scene should identify and control any dangerous situations or individuals by—

- Identifying and taking action to mitigate immediate threats to all responders by scanning the area for sights, sounds, and smells that may represent a threat. Possible threats include—
  - Violent or volatile personnel.
  - Environmental hazards. This can be weather conditions (such as high winds, lightning, or flash flooding) or physical hazards (such as downed power lines, downed trees, or vicious animals).
  - Hazardous material or conditions. This may include gasoline; natural or propane gas; explosives; dangerous chemicals; or unreliable structures compromised by fire, earthquake, or partial demolition. If responders identify a confirmed or suspected clandestine drug laboratory, biological weapon, or weapon of mass destruction, secure the scene and contact the appropriate personnel or agency before entering the scene.
- Notifying supervisory personnel and calling for backup and other appropriate assistance. Ensure that any identified threats are communicated to the military police desk for dissemination to all affected personnel or agencies.

4-114.   After controlling any dangerous situations or individuals, military police should ensure that medical attention is provided to injured or sick individuals while minimizing contamination of the scene. They should assist, guide, and instruct medical personnel during the care and removal of individuals requiring medical attention to diminish the risk of contamination and loss of evidence. Upon arrival and identification of individuals requiring medical attention, first responding LE personnel should—

- Assess the victim(s) for signs of life and any medical needs, provide immediate medical attention, and call for medical personnel.
- Guide medical personnel to the victim to minimize contamination or alteration of the crime scene.
- Point out potential physical evidence to medical personnel, and instruct them to minimize contact with the evidence. For example, ensure that medical personnel preserve all clothing and personal effects without unnecessary damage to evidence (such as cutting through bullet holes or knife tears). Document any movement of individuals or items by medical personnel.
- Instruct medical personnel not to "clean up" the scene and not to remove or alter items originating at the scene.
- Obtain the name, unit, and telephone number of attending personnel as well as the name and location of the medical treatment facility where the victim(s) is transported.
- Attempt to obtain a "dying declaration" if there is a chance that the victim may die.
- Document any statements or comments made by the victims, suspects, or witnesses at the scene.
- Send a military police patrol to accompany the victim or suspect to a medical treatment facility; ensure that any evidence is preserved and any comments made by the victim or the subject are documented. If military police patrols are not available to accompany the victim or suspect, ask medical personnel to preserve evidence and document any comments made by the victim or suspect.

ESTABLISH AND MAINTAIN CONTROL OF THE SCENE

4-115. Army LE personnel should establish control of the scene as soon as possible upon arrival. They should quickly identify all individuals at the scene and determine the victims, witnesses, and potential suspects. Any bystanders should also be identified and directed away from the scene; all bystanders should be quickly interviewed to ensure that they are not witnesses or are otherwise involved with the incident. Any identified witnesses, suspects, and any victims not requiring medical attention should be segregated from one another to prevent collaboration of their stories. All movement within the identified crime scene should be restricted; if possible move them to an area away from the actual scene. Any persons not required at the scene should be restricted from entering.

4-116. Military police must exclude unauthorized and nonessential personnel from the scene. This includes military police not working the case, commanders, media, and other "interested" parties. Emergency medical and other first responder personnel should be directed into and out of the scene over a specified path; designating a specified path into and out of the scene helps to mitigate potential destruction of evidence.

4-117. As soon as possible the boundaries of the crime scene should be established and cordoned. Crime scene tape, rope, or other field-expedient means can be employed. Identifying perimeter boundaries assists in the protection of the scene and can be a critical factor in maintaining the integrity of evidentiary material. The perimeters of a crime scene may be easily defined when an offense is committed within a building. When the perpetrator takes the fruits of his crime away from the crime scene to another area, the perimeter becomes more difficult to establish. If an offense is committed in the open, such as in the desert, the perimeter of the offense becomes even more difficult to definitively identify. Many crimes will have multiple crime scenes at different locations.

4-118. All personnel who are not essential to processing a scene should stay outside the established cordon area to prevent the contamination or destruction of evidence. Leadership should be briefed outside the crime scene or incident site by the senior military police or LE investigator. During contingency operations, the senior leader in charge of the site may be nonmilitary police or USACIDC personnel. Incidents involving chemical, biological, radiological, nuclear, and high-yield explosive, regardless of the environment, may require specially trained hazardous material, CBRN, or EOD personnel to control the inner cordon until the area is rendered safe. See ATTP 4-32 and FM 3-11.21 for more information.

4-119. The initial patrols on the scene should establish an initial cordon around the crime scene based on their observations and understanding of the incident and the impacted area. Crime scene boundaries should be established beyond the initial scope of the crime scene. Boundaries can be collapsed as required as more detail is discovered; expanding a crime scene boundary is difficult to effectively accomplish. The first responding Army LE element at the scene should conduct an initial assessment to establish and control the crime scene and its boundaries. Guidelines for establishing and controlling crime scenes include the following:

- Identify and segregate victims, possible subjects, and witnesses to the crime or incident.
- Establish the boundaries of the scene. Start at the focal point of the crime or incident and extend outward to include—
    - Any location(s) where a crime occurred.
    - Potential points and paths of the exit and entry of suspects and witnesses.
    - Places where the victim or evidence may have been moved. Military police must be aware of and protect trace and impression evidence while assessing the scene.
- Set up physical barriers to include ropes, cones, crime scene barrier tape, available vehicles, personnel, or other equipment. Existing boundaries, such as doors, walls, and gates can be used.
- Document the entry and exit of all individuals entering and leaving the scene once the boundaries have been established. Maintain a log of each individual's name, rank, social security number (SSN), unit, and telephone number.
- Control the flow and path of individuals and animals entering and leaving the scene to maintain the integrity of the scene.

- Protect identified items of evidentiary value. Implement measures to preserve and protect evidence that may be lost or compromised due to the elements (rain, snow, or wind) or footsteps, tire tracks, sprinklers, and such.
- Document the original location of any victim or objects that are being moved. If possible, insist that the victim and objects remain in place until the arrival of the investigative team.
- Consider rules of evidence regarding search and seizure to determine when obtaining consent to search and/or obtaining a search warrant is required. If the evidence is in no danger of damage or compromise, protect the evidence and leave it in place until investigators arrive and assume control.
- Ensure that no one—
  - Smokes.
  - Chews tobacco.
  - Uses the telephone or the bathroom.
  - Eats or drinks.
  - Moves any items (including weapons) unless it is necessary for the safety and well-being of individuals at the scene.
  - Adjusts the thermostat or opens windows or doors (maintain the scene as it was found).
  - Touches anything unnecessarily (note and document any items moved).
  - Repositions items, litters, or spits within the established boundaries of the scene.

DOCUMENT ACTIONS AND OBSERVATIONS

4-120. Responding Army LE personnel must produce clear, concise, notes documenting their actions and observations at the crime scene. This is especially important for the first LE personnel on the scene who are making the first investigative observations after the event occurs. Preservation of this early information is vital in shaping initial investigative considerations that will impact the case over the course of the investigation. All notes must be maintained as part of the permanent case file. First responding military policeman should document—

- Response to, and observations of, the incident to include—
  - Physical characteristics and the layout of the crime scene or incident site including location of persons and items within the crime scene.
  - The appearance and conditions of the crime scene upon arrival, including smells; the presence of ice, liquids, or other substances; furniture; weather conditions and temperature; and personal items in the area. Note whether the lights are on or off; the shades are up, down, open, or closed; or the doors and windows are open or closed.
  - Actions and behavior and the general demeanor of victims, subjects, witnesses, and bystanders.
- Victims, witnesses, and potential subjects.
- Results of initial interviews and investigations conducted by responding military police patrols including personal information, statements, or comments from witnesses, victims, and suspects.
- Identified evidence, including evidence physically collected and protected, but still in place.
- Physical locations and established boundaries of secured crime scenes.
- All LE actions taken at the scene.

TRANSFER CONTROL OF THE SCENE

4-121. Most crime scenes will be processed by a MPI or USACIDC SA. At major or complex incident sites or crimes scenes full investigative teams will be required to process the site. Military police patrol personnel assume a support role to the investigative team with all actions conducted under the supervision of a MPI or USACIDC SA. Upon arrival of MPI or USACIDC SAs, the senior military police LE patrol should thoroughly brief the senior investigator using the documentation guidelines discussed above.

4-122.   Following the brief, the senior military police patrol should coordinate directly with the senior investigator on scene to determine any support requirements. These will typically be crime scene security requirements to restrict foot or vehicle travel through the site; however they may be tasked to conduct canvas interviews of the area, assist in crime scene searches, or assist with other crime scene processing requirements.

CRIME SCENE PROCESSING

4-123.   Crime scene processing by Army LE personnel follows a general process that is valid regardless of the environment or type of scene. Many factors including the severity of the crime, the type of crime, the number of crime scenes, and other factors influence the specific activities within the process. Typically, crime scene processing will include—

- Assessment of the crime scene to include—
    - An initial observation and assessment.
    - An initial crime scene walk through.
    - Planning evidence collection and preservation.
- Documentation of the crime scene to include—
    - Notes.
    - Photographs.
    - Sketches.
- Collection and processing of evidence.
- Completion of final activities and site inspection.

4-124.   The senior investigator in charge of the scene has many responsibilities. This will typically be an MPI or USACIDC SA. The senior investigators responsibilities include—

- Determining team composition including the number of personnel required and how responsibilities will be assigned.
- Establishing contamination control measures and guidance.
- Documenting the scene.
- Searching for and prioritizing evidence collection.
- Preserving, inventorying, packaging, transporting, and submitting evidence.
- Assigning key tasks to include—
    - Maintaining site security.
    - Maintaining documentation of chronology of events, chain of custody, and other key requirements.
    - Sketching the scene and key evidence.
    - Photographing the scene and key evidence.
    - Searching for, identifying, and collecting evidence.

ASSESSMENT OF THE CRIME SCENE

4-125.   The investigator's initial observations and assessments are critical in the development of the overall plan for processing the crime scene. An initial assessment of the crime scene or incident site allows the investigator in charge to determine the type of incident to be investigated and the level of investigation to be conducted. The investigator in charge identifies specific responsibilities, shares preliminary information, and develops investigative plans for the coordinated identification, collection, and preservation of physical evidence and for the identification of witnesses.

Initial Observation and Assessment

4-126.   Initial observations and assessments are typically conducted from a perspective external or on the periphery of the crime scene, before the initial walk through of the scene. They include obtaining status briefs and background information from initial LE patrol personnel, making general observations of the scene, and identifying initial requirements. The investigator in charge should—

- Receive a brief from the first responding LE personnel regarding the incident, their activities, and observations. The investigator should seek information to understand—
  - Who is involved—subjects, victims, and witnesses?
  - What occurred—the incident(s) and LE actions?
  - When did the incident(s) and key activities occur?
  - Where did the incident(s) occur?
  - How was the crime committed?
  - Why was this type of crime, victim, and location involved?
- Evaluate threats and safety issues including—
  - Any remaining violent or unstable individuals that have not been placed under control.
  - The presence of blood-borne pathogens.
  - The presence of any chemical or explosive hazards that may affect personnel entering the scene.
- Ensure that witnesses to the incident are identified and separated by—
  - Obtaining a valid identification and contact information from each individual.
  - Ensuring that the surrounding area is canvassed for additional witnesses, victims, or suspects and the results documented.
- Evaluate search and seizure issues to determine the necessity of obtaining consent to search and the requirement of obtaining a search warrant.
- Evaluate the initial scene boundaries and cordon. Be sure to—
  - Make adjustments to the cordon as required.
  - Evaluate and establish a path of entry and exit to the scene to be used by authorized personnel such as medical responders, hazardous material personnel, and other LE agencies (if not already accomplished).
  - Document the entry and exit of authorized personnel to prevent unauthorized access to the scene.
- Determine and prioritize the number and size of scenes.
- Establish a command post to—
  - Maintain communication with the military police desk and the appropriate USACIDC headquarters element.
  - Establish and maintain communication to personnel at related crime scenes when multiple scenes exist.
- Establish support areas by—
  - Establishing a secure area within close proximity to the scenes for the purpose of consultation and equipment staging.
  - Establishing a secure area for temporary evidence storage according to the rules of evidence and chain of custody.
  - Establishing an area that is close (but outside the critical area) for a trash collection point (for trash generated during crime scene processing) to mitigate the chance of contaminating the scene. This area may also the designated break area for police personnel.
- Determine team composition requirements and request additional investigative resources as required based on the type of incident and the complexity of the scene. Document team composition by name and assignment. Investigators should consider—
  - Forensic requirements. Request the assistance of forensic specialists and equipment.
  - Skilled personnel. Coordinate for personnel to perform specialized tasks such as photography, crime scene sketches, lifting latent prints or impressions, and other specialized collection tasks.

- Support personnel. Ensure that coordination is conducted to maintain required support for scene security and administrative support.
- Legal support.
- Multiple crime scenes and locations of interest or large numbers of witnesses, victims, or suspects. Multiple crime scenes or large numbers of personnel requiring interviews must be considered to ensure adequate LE support is available.
- Other agency support. Notify and request any personnel or equipment support required from local, state, or other federal agencies.
- Ensure that the preliminary documentation is complete. Documentation such as notes, photographs, and sketches of persons or evidence may be lost if not immediately recorded. The initial photographs should include any injured individuals and vehicles involved in the incident.

Initial Crime Scene Walk-Through

4-127. The scene should be considered unstable and fragile in the sense that the evidentiary value of items can be easily degraded or lost. The investigator in charge conducts a careful walk-through of the scene with the individuals who are responsible for processing the scene. The safety of on-site personnel is of primary importance during a walk-through. Special attention should be placed on identifying potential hazards. The walk-through provides the investigator in charge with an overview of the entire scene. It also provides the first opportunity to identify valuable and fragile evidence, determine initial investigative priorities and procedures, identify any threats to scene integrity, and to develop a general theory of the crime. It facilitates a systematic examination and documentation of the scene. Considerations during the initial walk-through include—

- Determining the extent of the scene, the required search area, and whether the initial cordon requires expansion or reduction to best protect evidence or provide hazard mitigation.
- Using a designated path of entry and travel to avoid contaminating the scene.
- Identifying the location for an evidence collection point.
- Identifying additional equipment or special skills, outside the capabilities of the team, required to adequately process the site.
- Evaluating and prioritizing evidence. Evidence evaluation, based on observations from the initial assessment and walk through of the scene, helps investigators determine what evidence is likely to be present and the priority for collection beginning with the most transient or fragile evidence and working to the least volatile material. This enables the investigator to develop a comprehensive evidence collection plan.
- Preparing preliminary documentation of initial observations using notes, sketches, and still or video photography to brief the team and to document the condition of the site as it was initially observed.

Planning Evidence Collection and Preservation

4-128. The timely and methodical identification, preservation, and collection of evidence require deliberate planning and execution. The investigator in charge should determine the order and manner in which evidence is collected. In many investigations multiple crime scenes must be processed including multiple sets of witnesses, victims, and potential suspects. There are several considerations when determining collection priorities to include—

- Ensuring a careful and methodical evaluation to consider all physical evidence possibilities such as biological fluids, latent prints, and trace evidence.
- Assessing the environmental and other factors that may affect the evidence. Identify and protect fragile and perishable evidence that should be collected immediately or protected from environmental conditions such as wind, rain, and snow; the presence of crowds or hostile environments (chemicals, explosives, and such); or inadvertent destruction by team members.
- Using PPE and other safety and contamination control measures.
- Using evidence markers (large numbers on tent-shaped markers) by placing them adjacent to evidence.

- Selecting the appropriate progression of processing and collection methods as follows:
  - Implement a collection sequence so that initial collection techniques do not compromise subsequent methods. Conduct the least intrusive methods before conducting more intrusive processing and collection methods.
  - Determine which items are small enough to collect and which items require on-site processing such as latent prints, trace evidence, or impressions.
  - Concentrate on the most transient (fragile) evidence and work toward the least transient.
  - Focus on identified evidence (especially fragile evidence) on easily accessible areas that are in open view, then proceeding to the out-of-view areas.
- Selecting appropriate systematic search pattern(s) to locate and collect evidence based on the size and location of the scenes.
- Coordinating with laboratory examiners, MEs, and other technicians. The coordination involves the lateral sharing of information discovered as it pertains to a crime. A delay in the sharing of information may affect the successful recovery of physical evidence, contribute to damage or degradation of evidence, or delay the identification and apprehension of a suspect.

DOCUMENTATION OF THE CRIME SCENE

4-129. A well-documented scene ensures the integrity of the investigation and provides a permanent record for later evaluation. It also assists in the final written report and court testimony. Documentation begins with a narrative of the crime scene compiled by the investigator documenting initial observations and the walk-through of the scene and continues throughout the duration of crime scene processing and the investigation. All notes taken by responding military police patrols and investigators are included in the documentation of the crime and crime scene. Documentation of the site provides context to the evidence, spatial references between evidence and other objects or features of the site, and the identification of specific physical aspects of the site itself.

4-130. A narrative of the investigator's findings should begin with initial observations and initial walk-through of the scene. Record anything that catches the investigator's attention; nothing should be considered too insignificant to record. Under most circumstances, evidence is not collected during documentation of the initial narrative. Photographs and sketches of the scene and specific evidence are completed and used to supplement the narrative documentation. Notes, photographs, and sketches will be discussed in greater detail later in this chapter. Initial documentation of the scene should include—

- The arrival time at the scene.
- The case number, date, time, and location.
- Weather and lighting conditions at the scene.
- Any unusual smells or sounds.
- The condition and position of observed evidence.
- Assignments of support personnel.
- Any actions, observations, and departures from normal procedures as well as the reason for the change in procedure such as traffic, safety concerns, or other factors.

4-131. Typically, one person will be responsible for compiling all the documentation of the scene. This may be a single investigator for relatively minor cases and scenes or a designated investigator from the team for complex cases and crime scenes. The initial assessment of the scene should result in a determination of what type and extent of documentation is needed. Documentation must be coordinated to conduct and gather all notes, photographs, sketches, videos, and measurements.

COLLECTION AND PROCESSING OF EVIDENCE

4-132. The integrity of a crime scene must be maintained. Evidence at crime scenes should be protected from contamination or other harmful change. Established techniques must be followed to prevent contamination of evidence and to ensure the safety of personnel processing the scene. These techniques are implemented to ensure the welfare of all individuals at the scene and maintain the integrity of the evidence.

During the processing of the scene, evidence should be appropriately packaged, labeled, and maintained in a secure, temporary manner until final packaging and submission to a secured evidence storage facility or the USACIL. See chapter 2 for more information. The handling of physical evidence is one of the most important factors of the investigation; therefore, the team members must—

- Maintain scene security throughout processing until the release of the scene.
- Collect each item identified as evidence. Use the following techniques:
  - Identify and secure evidence at the crime scene using appropriate packaging materials; label, date, and initial any evidence container.
  - Avoid excessive handling of evidence.
  - Transport and submit evidence items for secure storage.
- Obtain standard and elimination reference samples from the scene.
- Properly document the collection of evidence by—
  - Recording detailed notes documenting the location of the evidence, the name of the person who collected it, and the time and date of collection.
  - Photographing the location of the evidence in relation to the scene.
  - Establishing and maintaining the chain of custody for each piece of evidence.

Determine Search Methods

4-133.   Many items of evidence will be plainly visible and apparent to Army LE personnel. Locating some items of evidentiary value may require a search of the area to locate them. A successful crime scene or incident site search demands attention to detail. It produces a comprehensive and nondestructive accumulation of all available physical evidence within a reasonable period of time. The search method is determined based on the intent of the search and the area to be covered. The search method selected should provide complete coverage of the target area, with minimal traffic and disturbance of evidence. Typical search methods include—

- Circle or spiral search.
- Strip or line search.
- Grid search.
- Zone or sector search.

4-134.   All searchers must be thoroughly briefed. They should be provided a description of any evidence being sought, where or how it will likely be found, and what actions to take if evidence is found. While specific items of evidence may be the intended target, other evidence may be identified during the search. Ensure that searchers do not overlook any items of potential evidence they may identify. When search personnel encounter potential evidence, they should—

- Not touch or move the item.
- Mark the item with an evidence marker, being careful not to touch or disturb the actual evidence.
- Immediately notify the investigator in charge of the search.
- Protect the area until an investigator arrives and the evidence can be processed.

Note. If circumstances do not allow for the searcher to wait for an investigator to arrive, the searcher should preserve or protect the evidence.

Circle or Spiral Search

4-135.   A circle or spiral search is completed by searching ever increasing search rings around a central point until the entire target area is searched (outward spiral). It can also be conducted by reversing the pattern and starting at the point out from the central point and searching ever decreasing rings around the center (inward spiral) until the area is searched and the center point is reached. Figure 4-7, page 4-46, shows an example of the circle or spiral search method. In large outdoor areas, using a stake at the center of the search area with a string or twine tied to the stake can be helpful to ensure uniform distance is maintained and that the entire area is covered. This type of pattern is typically used in rooms, buildings, and small outdoor areas; it can be useful when searching for items known to have been projected from a known point such as shell casings from a fired weapon, an object thrown by a subject, or other similar incidents.

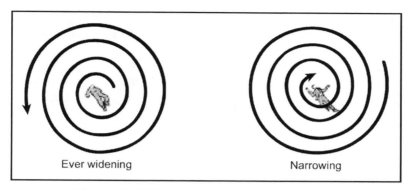

Figure 4-7. Circle or spiral search method

Strip or Line Search

4-136.   A strip or line search is commonly used to search large outdoor areas or the interior of large open buildings such as warehouses. It is useful when searching for relatively large items of evidence. The line search is normally conducted with several individuals spaced evenly apart in a line although it may be conducted by a single individual. If a group is available, searchers proceed in the same direction across the target area as depicted in the upper portion of figure 4-8. This can be a good technique to employ when there are inexperienced or untrained individuals assisting in the search; the movement can be controlled by an experienced investigator providing guidance and instruction as the group moves online. If a single individual conducts the search, the individual proceeds in one of the outer most lanes, reversing direction and moving to each of the subsequent lanes until the area is completely searched as depicted in the lower portion of figure 4-8. Stakes and string or twine can be employed to create strips or lanes to ensure coverage of the entire area and to limit overlap; a four foot width for each lane is generally adequate.

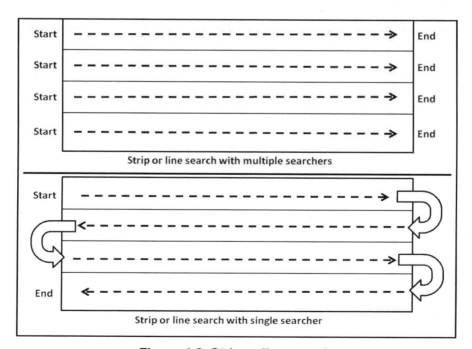

Figure 4-8. Strip or line search

Grid Search

4-137.   A grid search is one of the most thorough searches conducted; it is also more time consuming than a strip or line search. A grid search can be conducted over large outdoor areas or indoors within relatively confined areas. The grid is established by marking lanes similar to the strip or lane search; however the lanes are marked in two directions offset at 90 degrees to each other to form a grid of squares as shown in figure 4-9. The search can be conducted either by a single individual or by a group. Multiple searchers line up on one edge of the grid and move in the same direction across the target area while staying within their lane; they then line up again and move across the target area at 90 degrees to their previous movement.

4-138.   An individual searcher begins at one corner of the grid area and moves down one of the outer lanes, reversing direction and moving to each of the subsequent lanes until the area is completely searched, in the same manner as in the strip or line search described above. The individual then starts at the same grid square again, moving in a direction 90 degrees to the previous movement. The searcher moves down one lane, then reverses direction and moves to each of the subsequent lanes until the area is completely searched. Once the grid search is complete, every grid square will have been searched twice while moving in different directions.

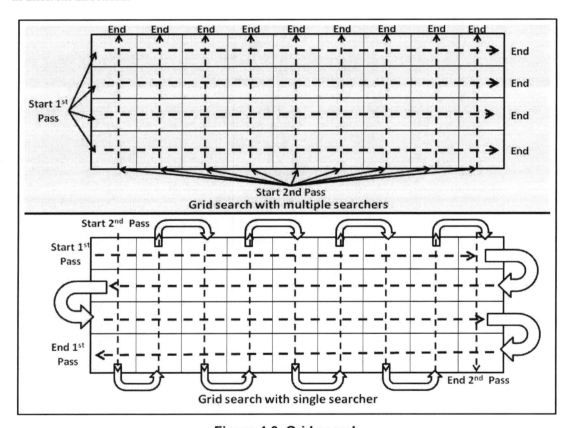

Figure 4-9. Grid search

Zone or Sector Search

4-139.   A zone search can be used to search both interior and exterior crime scenes. It is very useful when the search area is irregular and/or cluttered, making line searches more difficult. Zone searches enable the investigator to divide the search area into separate smaller areas or "zones" that can be more easily managed. Each zone is then focused on separately and systematically. Figure 4-10, page 4-48, shows an example of a zone or sector search.

4-140.   Buildings may be separated by rooms with each room being a designated zone; large rooms may be further subdivided into multiple zones within the room, if required. Vehicles may be separated into the front passenger compartment, the rear passenger compartment, the trunk, under the hood, and so forth to organize the search. Exterior areas around structures can also be zoned to enable a more systematic search. Within a zone, especially inside a room or structure, the area may also be separated into elevation zones that focus the search at specific heights within the area, each being searched sequentially. Elevation zones may be designated from floor to waist, waist to head, and head to ceiling; if there is a false or drop ceiling, this area should be designated as a search zone as well.

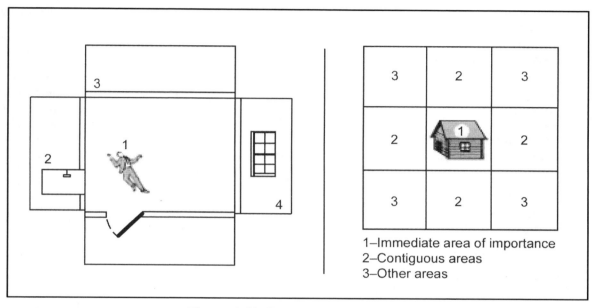

Figure 4-10. Zone or sector search

4-141.   The extent and nature of the scene determines the amount of time required on that scene. The lead investigator must assess the scene throughout the process to determine when the probability of finding additional evidence has diminished to a point that termination of the search is required.

Document Collected Evidence

4-142.   An evidence collection point should be established to ensure that evidence is properly collected, packaged, and documented. Position the collection point near the site entrance where it is easily accessible and visible, but not where it will interfere with site-processing activities. A collection point can be established inside a building that is being searched; ensure that the area has been completely searched and cleared before establishing the collection point.

4-143.   All evidence received at the evidence collection point should be checked to ensure that all documentation is complete and that the evidence is packaged properly for transport. Evidence should be screened and organized. Activities to ensure required documentation and packaging of evidence include—

*   Ensuring that evidence is correctly tagged with a DA Form 4002, *Evidence Property Tag*.
*   Ensuring that chain-of-custody documentation is properly completed (DA Form 4137, *Evidence/Property Custody Document*).
*   Conducting quality control checks to ensure that evidence is properly packaged, marked, and documented. All items of evidence should be properly marked with the initials of the collector and the time, date, and location of collection. See AR 195-5 for more information.
*   Preparing evidence for transfer. An original and three copies of DA Form 4137 must be completed and updated every time custody changes for any piece of evidence. The original and the first two copies will be submitted to the evidence custodian. The third copy will be placed in the official case file.

● Initiating a laboratory request using Department of Defense (DD) Form 2922, *Forensic Laboratory Examination Request,* if required.

FINAL ACTIVITIES AND SITE INSPECTION

4-144. Based on the specifics of the crime, the scene, and other factors, the senior investigator will decide when processing activities have reached a culminating point. The investigator in charge should conduct a debriefing of personnel processing the crime scene and supporting the investigation. A final walk-through and survey of the crime scene should also be conducted and all documentation compiled for the case file.

Conduct a Crime Scene Debriefing

4-145. A crime scene debriefing provides an opportunity for LE personnel and other responders to discuss their actions and observations, and share information regarding particular scene findings before releasing the scene. It can be a valuable tool for identifying additional tasks to be completed or to confirm that crime scene processing is complete. The crime scene debrief provides an opportunity for input regarding follow-up investigation requirements, special requests for assistance, and assignment of tasks and responsibilities for the ongoing investigation.

4-146. The investigator in charge determines which personnel participate in the debriefing. Personnel typically participating in the debriefing include—

● Investigators supporting the case.
● Crime scene technicians or SMEs (including photographers, evidence technicians, forensic computer specialists, or other experts).
● Military police personnel that—
    ■ Initially responded to the scene.
    ■ Assisted in canvass interviews.
    ■ Provided security of the crime scene.
    ■ Controlled and/or assisted victims, witnesses, and suspects.
    ■ Collected evidence.
● Dispatch and emergency service personnel (medical, fire, search and rescue).

4-147. The investigator in charge should facilitate the debriefing. Similar to an after action review conducted following a training or operational event, the debriefing should result in participants providing information based on their observations and perspective; the facilitator should not dominate the discussion. During the crime scene debriefing, the investigator in charge should facilitate a review of—

● Observations by initial response and follow-on personnel.
● Instructions provided to military police and investigators.
● Actions taken by military police and investigators.
● Evidence collection, to include—
    ■ Evidence that was collected.
    ■ Evidence documentation.
    ■ Any remaining evidence or areas still requiring action.
● Preliminary scene findings with the team members.

4-148. The results of the crime scene debriefing should be documented. Immediately following the debriefing, the investigator in charge assigns tasks and initiates any actions that were identified and are required to complete crime scene processing, consulting with superiors or any technical support elements as required. Upon completion of any remaining tasks a final walk-through of the crime scene is conducted.

Conduct a Final Walk-Through

4-149. After all processing activities are completed, including the debriefing, a final walk-through should be conducted to ensure that all evidence has been collected and the scene has been completely processed before release. During the final walk-through the investigator in charge ensures that—

- Each area identified as part of the crime scene is visually inspected.
- No area has been overlooked and no evidence remains uncollected.
- All evidence collected at the scene is accounted for including a review to ensure that reports and documentation are complete.
- All equipment and materials generated by the investigation are removed or disposed of including—
  - Disposable supplies.
  - Used PPE.
  - Other trash.
- Any dangerous materials or conditions are reported and addressed.
- The crime scene is secured or released as appropriate. Some crime scenes may be released immediately, others may remain under LE control until released by LE or by appropriate legal authority at the conclusion of the investigation or judicial proceedings as appropriate.

Compile the Case File

4-150. Reports and other documentation pertaining to the investigation are compiled into a case file by the investigator in charge. This file is a record of the actions taken and the evidence collected at the scene. This documentation allows for independent review of the work conducted. The crime scene case file should include—

- First responding military police patrol documentation.
- Emergency medical personnel documents.
- Entry and exit control logs.
- Photographs and videos.
- Crime scene sketches and diagrams.
- Evidence documentation including DA Form 4002 and DA Form 4137, DD Form 2922, and any other appropriate documentation.
- Documentation of other responders.
- A record-of-consent or search warrant.
- Reports, such as forensic or technical reports (added to the file as they become available).

4-151. AR 190-30 provides guidance on the composition of investigative case files. Case files are maintained in two parts; each part is maintained on separate sides of the physical case file. Part I of the case file contains working information relative to the case and is secured on the left side of the case folder. Part I consists of the following documents:

- DA Form 7569, *Investigator Activity Summary,* which includes a well-written chronology of investigative activity.
- The draft report to include the DA Form 3975, *Military Police Report.*
- Any DA Forms 3881 collected.
- Any DA Forms 2823 collected.
- Interview work sheets.
- Related police reports.
- Autopsy reports.
- Photographs.
- Evidence vouchers.
- Case notes completed by the investigator.
- Other supporting documents.

4-152. Part II of the case file contains final reports and supporting documentation and is secured on the right side of the folder. Part II consists of the following documents:

- DA Form 7570, *Investigator Data Form.*

- Final DA Form 3975 with enclosures.
- DA Form 4833, *Commanders Report of Disciplinary or Administrative Action.*
- Supplemental DA Form 3975.
- Requests for assistance and responses received in support of such requests.
- Authorization documents (Privacy Act release statements).
- External correspondence.

CRIME SCENE ANALYSIS AND RECONSTRUCTION

4-153.   Crime scene analysis and reconstruction includes the collection and analysis of all available evidence and the subsequent interpretation of the information derived from that evidence and analysis to develop an understanding of the events that occurred during the crime or incident. These interpretations are formed by using deductive and inductive reasoning. There are numerous academic publications that provide the framework and methodology for crime scene analysis and reconstruction. While these publications offer somewhat differing language to describe the methodologies involved in crime scene analysis and reconstruction, there are some identifiable similarities that are threaded throughout most all of the texts.

4-154.   The conduct of crime scene analysis and reconstruction involves a comprehensive approach by all elements of Army LE. Crime scene analysis includes the evidence collection and forensic analysis activities addressed earlier (as well as any information obtained through interviews and LE interrogations or other LE activities). These activities are relevant (at some level) to most crime scenes or incident sites where Army LE personnel respond. Crime scene reconstruction provides an objective, holistic view of the entire body of evidence relevant to the crime scene, applying a deliberate analytical approach to determine the cause and sequence of events at a crime scene or incident site. While crime scene analysis (collection and analysis of specific evidence) is supported by Army LE personnel and civilian support technicians across a wide range of tasks, reconstruction of the crime scene is conducted by investigator(s) viewing the evidence as a whole. Crime scene reconstruction is both time and resource intensive.

4-155.   Not all crime scenes are conducive to a deliberate crime scene reconstruction, although mentally, all investigators reconstruct the events of even the most simplistic crime. The availability of physical evidence, the type of crime or incident, and the severity of the crime will determine the level of reconstruction effort. Crime scene reconstruction is defined by the Association for Crime Scene Reconstruction as the use of scientific methods, physical evidence, deductive and inductive reasoning, and their interrelationships to gain explicit knowledge of the series of events that surround the commission of a crime.

4-156.   Subjective areas are typically avoided in crime scene reconstruction. For example, the motive of the perpetrator can be an important element in a criminal investigation; however, motive can be extremely subjective and is normally not addressed during the reconstruction process. Crime scene reconstruction focuses on objective data and logical reasoning to determine the actions that occurred in an incident. Reconstruction can determine that nine rounds were fired from a pistol in a specific direction, impacting a person and other identified objects, and that the perpetrator fired from a specific location in the room; why the perpetrator fired has no effect on the activities and is not considered during the reconstruction.

4-157.   Crime scene reconstruction attempts to determine what happened and how it happened and the sequence in which the events comprising the incident took place. The process of crime scene reconstruction often results in definitive understanding of specific actions that occurred at a scene. For example, trajectory analysis can determine the position of a victim and a shooter based on analysis of the projectiles recovered at a crime scene; blood spatter can reveal the direction of movement, the location of the victim, and other key details. Deductive and inductive reasoning applied to the compilation of numerous pieces of evidence and subsequent analysis, holistically, can result in a logical understanding of the probable actions and sequence of events that make up the incident as a whole.

4-158.   Investigators must understand the limitations of crime scene reconstruction. Short of discovery of a recording of the scene from multiple angles with full audio, it is impossible to determine with absolute certainty what events took place in an incident when direct observation of the incident did not occur. A reconstruction may be able to show the position of a victim and suspect at certain times during the crime as well as show certain paths of travel, but other relevant aspects as they moved through the scene including observations made by the individual, state of mind, and other influences and indicators cannot generally be ascertained. Investigators must be careful not to make conclusions that cannot be supported by science or the evidence.

4-159.   Evidence recovered from a scene is the result of activities and events that occurred at that scene. There will always be slightly different actions and events that could have produced similar results. The greater the amount of relevant evidence obtained at a specific scene, the higher the probability that an accurate theory can be developed based on objective evaluation of the evidence; however, 100 percent surety can never be obtained. Maintaining objectivity and avoiding subjective assumptions is important to reduce the probability of error in the final reconstruction theory.

4-160.   The process for conducting crime scene analysis and reconstruction is a deliberate method for gathering, analyzing, and interpreting evidence to develop a plausible theory that explains the events at the scene. Crime scene analysis and reconstruction subjects all available evidence to scrutiny by applying logical reasoning based on objective interpretation of the evidence available. The process is not linear but a continuous process that occurs throughout the investigation. As new evidence is obtained, hypotheses may be negated and require revision. Each new piece of evidence must be evaluated, assessed, and applied to the reconstruction to either corroborate or refute existing evidence and understanding of the events that have taken place. Crime scene analysis and reconstruction includes—

- Documenting all activities, analysis, and reasoning (occurs throughout the process).
- Recognizing the evidence.
- Collecting the evidence.
- Evaluating the evidence.
- Reconstructing the crime or incident to include—
    - Organizing the evidence.
    - Forming a hypothesis.
    - Testing the hypothesis by applying logic.

DOCUMENTING

4-161.   Documentation occurs throughout the process. It begins with documentation of evidence and maintaining chain of custody and includes documentation of all forensic analysis conducted on collected evidence. Documentation continues through hypothesis development, deductive and inductive reasoning used to test the hypothesis, and the final reconstruction of the crime or incident. Thorough documentation ensures that the theory developed to explain the events involved in the incident stand up to scrutiny.

4-162.   All evidence and reasoning applied to formulate and test hypotheses and to develop the final reconstruction of events should be documented, including those items of evidence that may not support the conclusions made by the investigator. Documentation of the reconstruction and supporting analysis must be documented in the investigative report. The documentation should be clear and concise and contain all relevant factors concerning the process including how the evidence supports or refutes the various hypotheses.

RECOGNIZING AND COLLECTING EVIDENCE

4-163.   Recognizing and collecting evidence provides the raw material the investigator and forensic experts use to develop the initial associations and linkages required for hypothesis development and testing. Chapter 2 and the previous portions of chapter 4 have covered recognition and collection of physical evidence. Testimonial evidence was covered in chapter 3. All evidence collected must be evaluated by investigators and considered during the reconstruction process. Some evidence may be evaluated in its raw form while many items of evidence require forensic analysis by USACIL laboratory examiners, MEs, or USACIDC SAs with specialized training such as USACIDC FSOs.

EVALUATING THE EVIDENCE

4-164.   Evaluation of the evidence begins upon the initial view of the crime scene and continues throughout the process. Evidence may be evaluated in its raw state, it may require analysis by laboratory examiners, or it may require on scene analysis by USACIDC FSOs or other trained personnel. Evidence evaluation should include a determination of the reliability and the credibility of the evidence as described in the following bullets:

- Reliability of evidence at a crime scene is most threatened by contamination or some level of destruction. Investigators should also be observant for signs that evidence was staged by a perpetrator to alter the conclusions of LE personnel. A staged scene obviously affects the reliability of any staged material as it does not reflect the reality of an investigated incident. Witness testimony must likewise be vetted, considering any motives the witness may have for falsifying or withholding information.

- Credibility of the evidence collected must be determined. Evidence is credible if an evaluation of the evidence reflects an action or incident that is possible based on its form, location, or other factors. Investigators should seek other evidence to corroborate existing evidence to enhance credibility. If contradictory evidence is found, the contradictions must be explained through other evidence and logical reasoning or the credibility of the initial evidence is in question.

4-165.   Physical evidence is often evaluated to identify the item or material by general class characteristics and may be examined to attempt to individually associate the evidence with a specific individual or another piece of evidence. Identification of an item of evidence by class characteristics can prove that the questioned item or substance is like or consistent with some other comparable standard but cannot produce a conclusion that the evidence is uniquely identifiable (a positive match) with that source.

4-166.   While identification by class characteristics does not lead to a positive match to another person, item, or material, depending on the degree of similarity, an increased probability of association may be deduced. For example, blood evidence may be determined to be of a specific species (human); this alone does little to identify an individual suspect. If the blood sample is identified as human and to be an AB negative blood type, the pool of suspected persons can be narrowed. There is a higher probability that a specific individual with AB negative blood deposited the questioned blood sample, but positive association of the suspect to the evidence is still not possible.

4-167.   Direct individual association is generally conducted by forensic science examiners and shows that a sample or piece of evidence is uniquely associated with a comparable standard beyond general class characteristics. DNA typing and fingerprint comparison are examples of evaluations that may produce results that individualize a specific item of evidence.

4-168.   Evidence may also be evaluated to determine critical information such as the position of subjects and victims, the direction of travel, or the number of persons at the scene. This type of information can be deduced from impression evidence left at the scene, video and/or audio recordings documented during the incident, blood spatter analysis, trajectory analysis, eyewitness reports, and a myriad of other methods. The sources of information are limited only to the investigators skills of observation and ingenuity.

RECONSTRUCTING AND ASSESSING THE CRIME OR INCIDENT

4-169.   Once evidence is collected and evaluated, the process of reconstructing the crime scene or incident site can take place. Reconstruction involves organizing the evidence into useful categories, forming hypotheses, and testing those hypotheses against the available evidence using deductive and inductive reasoning.

4-170.   A useful method for conducting reconstruction and assessment of a crime scene is proposed in *Blood Pattern Analysis with an Introduction to Crime Scene Reconstruction* written by Tom Bevel and Ross Gardner. The method includes breaking the scene into manageable pieces for conducting an analysis of the evidence, hypothesis formulation, and hypothesis testing. Each crime scene can be identified by—

- **Incidents.** This is the crime or incident as a whole. It includes all actions related to the crime, incident, or situation.

- **Events.** Events are elements or portions of the incident. These events are defined by specific related actions or items of evidence. Each crime scene or incident site may have several events such as entry into the residence, assault of the victim, and exit from the scene. The number of distinct events is dependent on the specifics of the individual incident being investigated.

- **Event segments.** Event segments are distinct individual movements or actions within an identified event. Examples of event segments within an event identified as entry into the residence may include—subject breaks the window, subject enters through the window, subject cuts hand on window glass, and subject leaves bloody print on the window sill. See figure 4-11 for an example of an incident broken into events and event segments.

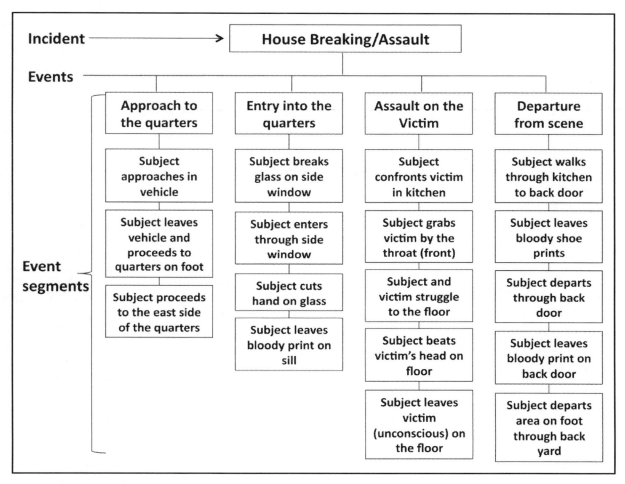

Figure 4-11. Incidents, events, and event segments

4-171. Sequencing is also an important element in reconstructing the crime scene. Sequencing involves placing the events and event segments in a chronological order based on the evidence and logical reasoning. The chronology or timeline is typically relative (the order of events and event segments are sequenced, but exact times may not be known); however, absolute chronology (exact times for an event or event segment are known) may be possible for all or part of a sequenced incident through eyewitness accounts, recorded media (time stamps on video or still photography), and evidence obtained via digital media (cell phones, computers, or other electronic devices). The differences in evidence available will likely result in timelines that may be very precise for some events and very general for others.

4-172. The identification of specific events and associated event segments, along with the formation of a sequence for those events, can help investigators gain an understanding of the probable actions as they occurred across the entire incident. It can also help investigators focus their investigation by enabling identification of gaps in the information that prevent understanding of key events or that leave periods of time unaccounted for in the timeline.

Organizing Evidence

4-173.   All evidence applicable to the crime or incident should be organized to enable timely and orderly assessment. Organizing the evidence based on the separate events and event segments specific to the incident in question can help investigators break large amounts of evidence into manageable chunks. This compartmentalization helps focus the investigator's attention on items related to a specific event without creating confusion by mixing evidence related to other events within the incident.

Forming a Hypothesis

4-174.   A hypothesis is simply a plausible theory to explain specific events. The investigator(s) conducting crime scene reconstruction must develop an educated and plausible explanation of what happened during the incident in question. The hypothesis may be relative simple and consist of a single or multiple hypotheses, each requiring a full analysis regarding likelihood of occurrence. Each hypothesis will drive the development of predicted actions or occurrences that should be present; these actions or occurrences will, in turn, require that evidence is present to support the assertion that the action took place. These hypotheses and associated actions are developed through application of the investigator's experience, overall knowledge, and understanding of the specific crime or incident. The hypothesis should not be a guess but a realistic solution that will be tested against the evidence to determine its validity.

Testing the Hypothesis

4-175.   The hypothesis developed by the investigator reconstructing the scene is tested by applying all investigative evidence and information. This information is assessed to either support or negate the hypothesis. All relevant evidence should be analyzed and determinations should be made regarding how the evidence supports or refutes each hypothesis. Throughout the process the reasons for identifying information as supporting or negating specifics of the investigators hypothesis should be documented. If enough evidence contradicts the proposed hypothesis, especially if the contradictions cannot be logically and objectively explained, the hypothesis must be modified or eliminated and another hypothesis proposed.

4-176.   Contradictory evidence does not necessarily negate a proposed hypothesis. If evidence exists that does not fit the understood sequence of actions and events, it may have been deposited before the incident in question or it may have been deposited by a third party that has yet to be identified. Sometimes contradictory evidence may support multiple hypotheses or timelines. Close examination of the specific events and event segments can reveal an area where investigators should focus their efforts to find evidence or logical deductions that can eliminate one or more hypothetical timelines and increase the likelihood that a single hypothesis is correct.

Chapter 5

Physical Surveillance

In support of LE activities, surveillance refers to the covert and systematic observation of individuals, places, or objects for the purpose of gathering information for production of criminal intelligence. Army LE personnel employ surveillance techniques in support of LE and security activities in all environments. Surveillance techniques are often used to identify criminal activity associated with terrorism, organized crime, drug and contraband trafficking, and serious crimes against individuals.

SURVEILLANCE OBJECTIVES

5-1. Army LE personnel may be required to conduct surveillance focused on observing specific criminal or threat targets and gathering required information. LE surveillance may be required to confirm suspected criminal activity, establish association of a suspected criminal in terms of time and place, and confirm association between persons, groups, or entities. Surveillance may be physical observation of a person or location, visual surveillance by remote video equipment, or audio surveillance via a myriad of technologies employed to intercept audio evidence. Information obtained through surveillance activities can directly support specific criminal investigations and can be used to support police intelligence activities and the subsequent development of criminal intelligence to support broader investigative objectives. In operational environments, information resulting from surveillance activities can be fed into the operations process to support information requirements of operational commanders. See ATTP 3-39.20 for more information.

5-2. LE surveillance is typically associated with specific criminal investigations and may be employed for a variety of criminal investigative requirements. LE surveillance is especially effective in support of drug investigations. However, it may also be performed to conduct assessments such as traffic studies, physical security assessments, or other security and protection requirements. See ATTP 3-39.10, ATTP 3-39.20, ATTP 3-39.32, and ATP 3-39.35 for more information regarding these and other surveillance requirements. Surveillance is conducted to meet specific objectives that support criminal investigations including—

- Collecting detailed information not available by other means.
- Developing leads and information received from other sources.
- Corroborating (or refuting) information collected from other assets or sources.
- Observing and collecting evidence of a crime.
- Collecting information supporting probable cause for requesting search warrants.
- Locating subject individuals through observation of their places of activity and their associates.
- Monitoring the activities of informants to determine reliability.
- Determining the location of hidden property or contraband.
- Preventing the commission of an act of crime or apprehending a suspect in the commission of a crime.
- Obtaining information for later use during interviews and LE interrogations.
- Monitoring and providing protection for Army LE personnel performing undercover activities, such as drug suppression. Only experienced investigators should be assigned surveillance activities designed to protect undercover personnel. Failure to maintain observation can result in unnecessary risks to the undercover investigator.

5-3. Most surveillance is covert, but overt efforts are sometimes used. An overt surveillance is used when it is useful to let the subject know he is being observed. For instance, a nervous subject, made aware that he is being followed, may become anxious and contact his superiors while being observed. This can lead to identification or verification of other persons involved in the investigated criminal activity.

5-4. Risk management is an integrated part of mission planning. The assessment of risk and the subsequent development of measures to mitigate those risks begin at the earliest stages of the planning process and continue throughout planning and execution of a surveillance mission. Mitigation measures are identified and employed to enable completion of the mission and attainment of stated objectives without unnecessary risk to surveillance personnel, resources, and the investigation. Risk assessment matrixes and risk mitigation worksheets should be used as tools to enable identification of risks and risk mitigation measures. See ADP 5-0 and ADRP 5-0 for more information on the operations process. See FM 5-19 for more information on risk management.

PLANNING CONSIDERATIONS

5-5. Surveillance activities require deliberate planning and coordination. LE surveillance missions can be relatively simple, requiring a single investigator and minimal equipment requirements to conduct the surveillance activities. They can also be complex involving teams of several personnel and relatively extensive equipment and logistical requirements. A tactical plan should be developed, outlining support requirements, the duties of each individual on the surveillance team, specific information requirements, event triggers that require specific actions by surveillance personnel, and alternative courses of action plans. Planning alternative courses of action enables surveillance personnel to adapt smoothly to changing situations.

Note. While surveillance by a single individual is possible and may be necessary due to the specific situation single-individual surveillance is not generally recommended.

5-6. In some cases, the investigation and supporting surveillance activities may require interagency participation and coordination. This is common when task forces are formed to address a criminal threat that crosses the jurisdiction of multiple LE agencies.

SELECTING PERSONNEL

5-7. Army LE personnel should be selected for surveillance activities based on their skill, experience, and resourcefulness. They must have well-developed observation skills as well as the ability to accurately describe those observations in detail. Personnel conducting surveillance should possess a great deal of patience and be able to endure long, tedious hours of observation. Surveillance personnel should not stand out within their environment; LE personnel selected should typically be of average height, weight, and physical features.

5-8. The ability to blend in with their surroundings is extremely important; unique physical features or physical size that is either larger or smaller than average can draw unwanted attention from the public or individuals being watched. Personnel may be selected for their ethnicity or language qualifications when the surveillance activity is targeting an area populated by persons of a specific ethnic background. The type of surveillance and the area where it will take place are important factors to consider when selecting a surveillance team.

5-9. The number of surveillance personnel is dependent on the environment, the specific surveillance mission, and the identified risk. Regardless of the size of the surveillance mission, one of the initial tasks in LE surveillance planning is the designation of the investigator in charge. This should be the most experienced investigator on the surveillance team. The investigator designated to lead the mission is responsible for executing the surveillance plan, maintaining communications with the team and higher headquarters, and directing actions of the surveillance team. Individual team members may be assigned specific tasks (especially for large and/or long-term missions) supporting the overall surveillance mission.

GATHERING INFORMATION

5-10. A successful surveillance activity is dependent on the surveillance personnel obtaining all the background information possible on the subject. This information should include the subject's habits, contacts, friends, and places he may frequent. If the focus of the surveillance is an individual or group, the surveillance team should have an accurate, detailed understanding of the subject and the environment in which the subject operates. If the focus of the surveillance is a place, locate entrances, exits, and vantage points as well as the general character of the area being observed. These details will enable surveillance personnel to blend in with the environment.

5-11. Information is generally obtained from existing information collected through previous investigations, observations, or data from interagency coordination. Some details require a reconnaissance of the target area and specific individuals to provide additional detail and to verify existing information.

Existing Data

5-12. Before initiating surveillance, team members should review all available information relating to the target of the surveillance. The more information that is known, the more likely the surveillance team can predict activities and risks in the target area and specific actions, activities, and movements of subjects. Gather and review all available information about the subject from case files, other investigators, and other LE agencies that may have information on the specific location or subject. Information to obtain may include—

- **General information.** This may include—
  - Any pertinent information received through interagency coordination.
  - Feedback resulting from the reconnaissance of the area where the surveillance will take place.
- **Information on individual persons.** This may include—
  - The names and aliases used by the subject(s).
  - The subject's characteristics and mannerisms.
  - Any known or suspected weapons as well as knowledge of the subject's propensity to use weapons.
  - The subject's habits and normal daily routine.
  - The subject's known criminal activity.
  - The subject's work and neighborhood environment.
  - A full description of vehicles that the subject may use.
  - The subject's known contacts or associates (including a description, names, and known aliases) and his history with weapons, if known.
- **Locations.** This may include—
  - A description of the area (residential, commercial, industrial).
  - A physical layout of the area such as known ingress and egress routes, main traffic routes, obstructions, and vantage points.
  - Known traffic patterns (both vehicular and pedestrian).
  - Activities (both legal and illegal) known to occur in the area.
  - Known persons of interest that frequently come and go from the location.

5-13. When the surveillance objective is focused on persons suspected of crimes under investigation, each member of the surveillance team should know the scope and extent of crimes and activities in which the subjects are involved. For example, a drug dealer may also be involved in a fencing operation; he may be trading guns in exchange for drugs. They must also know the elements of proof of the various crimes to know when a suspect has committed an offense that warrants apprehension. Knowledge of all these activities will better prepare the team and greatly increase the success of the activity.

Note. Surveillance teams should not be too quick to apprehend suspects. They should keep the suspect under surveillance until the crime is completed unless it would cause bodily harm to a victim, significantly impair national security, or adversely impact the readiness or capability of a military unit, vessel, aircraft, or weapon system. Continuing the surveillance, even after all elements of a crime have been committed, can also lead to other criminal information. The decision to continue the surveillance after a crime has been committed must be approved by the senior member of the surveillance team.

Site Reconnaissance

5-14. A reconnaissance of the neighborhood should be performed to supplement file information. This may start with a map reconnaissance including the use of geospatial products of the target area prior to conducting a physical reconnaissance. Someone who is familiar with the subjects should point out the subjects to the surveillance investigators. A physical reconnaissance should be made to study the areas where the surveillance will take place and identify vantage points that are suitable for surveillance of the target. Similarly, traffic conditions can be observed and the investigators can become familiar with the names and locations of streets in the area including locations of dead-end streets that may be used by the subject to spot surveillance investigators. The reconnaissance will also yield information on the neighborhood and its inhabitants that would not be in police files.

5-15. Regardless of the scope of the surveillance, a reconnaissance of the target area should be conducted before execution of any surveillance mission. Coordination should be conducted with other LE agencies (including local PM offices) when the surveillance will be conducted in their AO or other agency assistance is required. Reconnaissance of the surveillance site(s) enables Army LE personnel to understand the environment including specific risks associated with the area(s) where the surveillance may occur. This information enables LE personnel to—

- Verify previous information.
- Determine appropriate dress, appearance, and cover stories to explain their presence (if required).
- Determine equipment requirements.
- Determine communication requirements.
- Identify appropriate locations for positioning surveillance personnel and equipment.
- Identify potential ingress and egress routes.
- Determine the appropriate surveillance techniques and methods.

CONSIDERING APPROPRIATE DRESS AND COVER STORIES

5-16. As part of the surveillance preparation, the investigators must consider their appearance. This is especially true when the surveillance cannot be conducted from a covert fixed location. They must dress and adopt the demeanor of local inhabitants in order to blend into the setting. The type of clothing worn by surveillance personnel will determine if the concealment of weapons will be a problem. Items, such as caps, jackets, and glasses, should be readily available to make quick changes in appearance, if required. They should carry sufficient money to pay for meals, transportation, or other routine expenses incurred during the surveillance; a reserve fund should be considered to cover unexpected events requiring funds or for use in emergency situations.

5-17. Appearance considerations for surveillance personnel should include details beyond clothing. Surveillance personnel should be aware of habits that may expose them as LE officers. Do not wear rings or other jewelry that denotes status or club membership. If a distinctive ring is normally worn, it may be important to replace it with another to hide a ring mark on the finger. If a coat or pocket bulges, it may reveal a weapon or communications device.

5-18. The plan may include a cover story for each person. Explanations for being at a particular place at a particular time may be developed in case a subject (or even area bystander) approaches and accuses the surveillant of following them or asks the surveillant what he is doing. If a cover story is used, make sure it fits the dress, speech, and mannerisms of the individual. It should be easy to remember and not so far from an investigator's experiences that it becomes difficult or impossible to recall. Be resourceful when a cover story must be used. If confronted by the subject, do not offer information; he may try to check the information and possibly expose you. If a cover story requires that the surveillant possess specific equipment, ensure that the equipment is on hand (for example a meter reader should have a ticket book and an appropriate uniform, a road survey crew member should probably have a clipboard with believable forms or documents and measuring or other survey equipment). Paramount to any cover story is that it is believable within the environment where the surveillance is being conducted.

ESTABLISHING COMMUNICATIONS

5-19. A prearranged, secure system of communicating with headquarters or superiors and central coordination must be established. Surveillance activities must be planned with a primary and alternate means of communications. Two-way radio contact is vital, especially with vehicle surveillance. Secure LE radios should be used when possible. Nonsecure communications equipment can be used, although care must be exercised. These communications may be intercepted easily by the subject or other persons in the area. If unsecure communications are required, the development and use of code words or phrases can help mitigate this risk.

5-20. Cell phones can be used effectively for all types of surveillance activities; however, there are some risks to consider. Cell phone conversations can be intercepted by relatively inexpensive off-the-shelf technology. Ringing phones can alert the subject or other persons to the surveillance team's presence; set the ring volume to a low setting or to vibrate mode to avoid drawing attention.

5-21. Suitable signals for communicating information between surveillance personnel should be developed and thoroughly understood by all participants. These signals are extremely important for mobile foot surveillance and static surveillance where surveillance personnel are outside on foot and in clear view of the public. Surveillance personnel should rehearse communication techniques under the same conditions that the surveillance will be conducted in order to become familiar with what methods work best. What works best in one situation may not work in another. The type of information that might be communicated through such signals may include the following:

- Take the lead.
- The subject has stopped.
- The subject is moving.
- The subject has made a contact or a drop.
- Countersurveillance has been identified. Countersurveillance refers to persons observing the surveillance team.
- The subject has spotted the surveillance.

5-22. Radio use during surveillance activities is kept to a minimum. Static surveillance radio traffic should include updates that are typically less frequent than for mobile surveillance missions. During mobile surveillance, the lead surveillance element should have radio priority and should provide regular status specific to the surveillance. For foot surveillance focusing on an individual, these updates may include locations of the subject and his direction of travel or activity. Mobile surveillance updates may also include the street or highway on which the subject is traveling, their approximate speed, and their lane of travel as the surveillance moves from one point to another. In areas unfamiliar to the surveillance team, the subject's locations may be given by reference to area landmarks such as businesses, schools, manufacturing plants, and service stations.

5-23. The subject's location must be given often enough so that the trailing surveillance vehicles feel comfortable about their positions. The frequent transmissions provided by the lead vehicle enable the other vehicles to determine how fast they should be traveling and whether they need to change their direction of travel. The following vehicles should not have to request the subject's location. There is a tendency for team members, other than the lead vehicle, to periodically transmit their locations as the surveillance progresses. This is not necessary or helpful, unless a particular situation has developed where the lead vehicle needs the information. Generally, there should only be brief radio traffic, and it should be from the lead vehicle to the other surveillance vehicles as the subject's location is given. Other radio traffic should be kept to a minimum.

SELECTING SURVEILLANCE EQUIPMENT

5-24. A wide variety of equipment can greatly enhance the ability of surveillance personnel to effectively monitor a specific location or subject. As technology continues to advance, improved surveillance systems are becoming more readily available. Equipment used to enhance surveillance capabilities can be relatively low technology such as binoculars, telescopes, and cameras equipped with telephoto lenses. In some cases, more advanced equipment such as night vision devices, satellite-tracking systems, amplified listening equipment, or other tracking and observation devices may be used. Audio and video recording devices may also be employed in some cases. The use of computers for virtually all aspects of daily life has resulted in a wide variety of capabilities to monitor electronic communications within networks and over the internet.

5-25. The selection of surveillance equipment should be based on the environment and specific surveillance requirements. Mobile surveillance, especially when conducted on foot, severely limits the selection of appropriate surveillance equipment. Mobile surveillance requires equipment that is easily employed and concealed. Devices that are difficult to operate or hard to hide should not be selected. Static surveillance activities may allow the selection of larger and more cumbersome equipment that could not be easily concealed during mobile surveillance. Static surveillance missions, especially those that are conducted over longer time frames, allow more complicated or fragile equipment to be set up and employed because it can be emplaced and left for longer periods of time. These may include cameras, closed-circuit television systems, or audio surveillance devices.

5-26. The use of audio, video, and other recording devices to intercept wire, oral, or electronic communications must be employed only within specific legal and regulatory limits. Always obtain advice from the servicing JA before using electronic surveillance equipment and receive approval for its use from the appropriate headquarters to ensure that the gathered evidence is legal and admissible. Additional guidance on wire, oral, and electronic communication interceptions is included in 18 USC 2510-2522, AR 190-53, and internal USACIDC publications.

MAINTAINING SURVEILLANCE LOGS

5-27. Whether the surveillance is mobile, fixed, or a combination of the two, it is extremely important that the surveillance team maintain a log. Much like an investigator's notes, the surveillance log records the subject's activities. The notes also document the significant activities of the surveillance teams. Some activity considered insignificant or unrelated to the surveillance at the time it is observed may become important later. It is then difficult, without notes, to recollect or reconstruct such events. Inadequate or improper notes can result in failure to successfully prosecute offenders due to insufficient evidence or documentation.

5-28. Surveillance teams should document in the following information in the surveillance log: the identity or detailed descriptions of individual subjects; descriptions of locations and vehicles; the activity observed; and the date, time, and place of occurrence. In addition, the investigators should include the weather conditions, the location and distance between observation posts and the site of the activity, and other factors affecting the surveillance. These notes should be so accurate and complete that the team can refer to them months later and recall in detail the activity observed.

SURVEILLANCE METHODS AND TYPES

5-29. There are three basic surveillance methods: loose, close, and a combination of the two. Loose surveillance can be used to spot-check a specific individual; it can also be used to compile long-term information on a subject. Loose surveillance is broken if the subject seems to suspect that he are being observed. Close surveillance involves constant observation by the surveillance team; continued alertness on the part of the surveillance team is required. If direct observation or knowledge of a subject's location is lost, close surveillance must be continued under an alternate plan once the location of the subject is determined.

5-30. Usually, a combination of the methods works best. Surveillance teams may need to move from a loose to a close surveillance because of an act or contact made by the subject. If a place, such as a known crack house is under close surveillance, loose surveillance may be required at the same time on some of the individuals who frequent the location. Table 5-1 describes loose, close, and combined surveillance methods.

Table 5-1. Surveillance methods

Loose	Close	Combined
The subject is not continuously observed; required information can be gained by monitoring one facet of the subject's activities.	The subject is under constant observation; required information must be obtained through observation of a wide range of the subject's activities. Constant surveillance is required.	Loose and close surveillance is conducted concurrently on separate subjects or in sequence on one subject (depending on circumstances and specific information requirements) to gain more information.

5-31. There are two general types of surveillance: fixed (or stationary) and mobile. A fixed surveillance is commonly known as a stakeout. It is used when the subject is stationary or when all of the important information can be learned by observing activity at one place. During a fixed surveillance, the surveillance personnel may move from one stationary vantage point to another for closer observation of the area or the subject. A mobile surveillance is commonly known as tailing or shadowing. A mobile surveillance can be conducted on foot, in a vehicle, or a combination of the two. The choice depends on the subject's specific movements and mode of travel.

5-32. In some cases, a combination of fixed and mobile surveillance may be employed. Surveillance personnel in fixed overwatch positions can provide critical support to mobile surveillance personnel, typically when conducting foot surveillance. The overwatch personnel can help maintain contact with subjects and can provide early warning of potential risks to surveillance personnel on the ground.

FIXED SURVEILLANCE

5-33. A fixed surveillance is conducted to observe a home, building, or other fixed location; it may be conducted to obtain evidence of criminal activity, identify suspected offenders, verify source information, or fulfill other information requirements. The primary consideration for beginning a fixed surveillance is whether the observation position affords the surveillance team a necessary vantage point to observe significant activity in detail without being observed. The position selected must give the team the opportunity to make close observations, allow them to see the details of any activity, and provide the ability to identify the subjects involved. Depending on the specific surveillance activity, one or multiple fixed observation points may be established.

5-34. The team's entrance and exit routes should afford them the ability to come and go undetected. Adequate surveillance locations and ingress and egress routes should typically be identified during presurveillance reconnaissance of the area. Subjects and their associates will likely be cautious and suspicious of any strangers in the surveillance area. In rural areas, investigators may have to walk a considerable distance in the dark with their supplies and equipment in order to avoid being detected. Surveillance personnel perform fixed surveillance either by establishing an observation post or by assuming a surface undercover role.

OBSERVATION POST

5-35. An observation post may be occupied when a suitable position can be identified that provides a good view of the subject or location and relative concealment from the public or personnel being observed. Once inside the observation post, the team must not make any unnecessary noise or do anything that will draw the attention of anyone else in the area. An isolated observation post in a rural area requires that the team be very restricted in movement and have great patience and endurance. Surveillance teams can establish observation posts in—

- **Parked vehicles.** Usually a utility van or a pickup truck equipped with a camper shell (sometimes referred to as a peek truck) can provide a level of concealment for the surveillance team. This form of stationary surveillance has been used effectively in some areas, but the placement of the vehicle must be considered with respect to the type of activity in the area. There should be an obvious reason for where the vehicle is parked, such as because of a breakdown. The selection of a truck or van marked with slogans or advertisements work best. Unattended parked surveillance vehicles may create suspicion or become the target of criminal activity.
- **Buildings or other structures.** This is the preferred method when available. The observation post can be established inside an office, an apartment, or another suitable room within the building that provides adequate observation of the target area. At times, a rooftop vantage point that offers an unobstructed view of the area or person being observed may be used.
- **Concealed positions outside.** This is typically employed in rural areas where roadways and structures are limited or nonexistent.

SURFACE UNDERCOVER ROLE

5-36. A surface undercover role is used when an activity is in an area that does not readily lend itself to the use of a concealed observation position for a stationary surveillance. Surveillance is conducted from an open position, and the team's identity is kept hidden by assuming a role. In urban areas where strangers are more likely to be identified, it may be necessary to assume a surface undercover role in order to ensure the security of the surveillance team's identity, even when an observation post is located in an apartment or home. Possible undercover roles include a—

- Power company lineman.
- Telephone repairman.
- Meter reader.
- Road survey crew.
- Road repair crew.
- Door-to-door salesman.

MOBILE SURVEILLANCE

5-37. There are two primary methods of mobile surveillance: by foot and by vehicle. A mobile surveillance is commonly known as tailing or shadowing and can be conducted entirely by foot, entirely by vehicle, or by a combination of the two. The technique used varies, based on the circumstances such as the amount of traffic congestion, whether the surveillance is conducted in a rural or urban setting, and the method of movement of the subject. Foot surveillance is used when close observation of specific individuals and activities is required for the investigation to gather detailed information on their movements, contacts, and activities. Foot surveillance can also be useful when an investigation is reaching a critical point where suspect apprehensions are required. Vehicle surveillance is good at providing more general surveillance to gather information or to observe movements, contacts, and activities of individuals when those individuals are moving in vehicles over longer distances.

5-38. In some situations, it may be possible and desirable to use a vehicle in conjunction with foot surveillance. This method is used most often in city or urban areas where traffic is light and the vehicle can be quickly moved from one street to another. One or two investigators in a vehicle provide support to surveillants conducting the foot surveillance. If two investigators are in the vehicle, one can act as a reserve foot surveillant to assume a position as a member of the foot surveillance team when a position change is required. The driver stays alert to the subject's location and acts as additional eyes for the foot surveillants.

5-39. A vehicle in this type of surveillance can give the foot surveillant an important advantage—the ability to cover several blocks very quickly. This is particularly important when observation of the subject is lost. The driver must be careful to stay out of the subject's view. Another important advantage of having a vehicle available during foot surveillance is that the surveillants will be assured of transportation if the subject should board a bus, a taxicab, or any other form of transportation.

FOOT SURVEILLANCE

5-40. There are three primary types of foot surveillance: the single-surveillant foot surveillance, the two-surveillant or AB foot surveillance, and the three-surveillant or ABC foot surveillance. Any of these methods may be used in a given situation, but the ABC foot surveillance is considered the most effective and is used most often. These methods can be supported by personnel in fixed surveillance locations as well.

Single Surveillant

5-41. Successful foot surveillance by a single surveillant is extremely difficult to accomplish. This technique should be avoided if possible; however, there are situations that will suddenly require the initiation of a foot surveillance by a single surveillant. These are typically cases where the subject acts unexpectedly and there is a spontaneous requirement for observation. The number of people in the area, characteristics of the area, and the subject's actions will dictate the distance between the surveillant and the subject. With no one to provide assistance observing the subject, the distance between the subject and the surveillant is usually either too far or too close.

5-42. If the subject and the surveillant are on the same side of the street, the subject should be kept in view at all times. It is necessary to be close enough to immediately observe the subject if he enters a building, turn a corner, or make any other sudden move or direction change. Foot surveillance by a single surveillant offers few options. It has a much higher likelihood of failure due to the constraints inherent with only one person observing and moving with the subject while reacting to the subject's actions, the environment, and the people in the area. Unlike surveillance conducted by multiple personnel, the single surveillant has little flexibility, and the likelihood of losing the subject or being compromised is high. If a foot surveillance must be conducted by a single surveillant, there are several techniques the surveillant can employ. These techniques include—

- Being cautious when on the same side of the street as the subject to avoid detection while maintaining visual contact.
- Staying to the rear and varying the distance to the subject. Set the distance according to physical conditions like the number of other persons, the number of exits or obstructions in the area, and the subject's actions.
- Continuing across the street if the subject turns a corner, keeping the subject in view.
- Operating from across the street and choosing a position behind, to the front, or to the side of the subject that will provide the best observation vantage point.
- Staying abreast of the subject, if he turns a corner, in order to quickly observe whether he stops and turns around, makes a contact, enters a building, or engages in some other activity. This enables the surveillant to make a timely and appropriate reaction to the subject's action.

Two Surveillants (AB)

5-43. The use of at least two persons working as a team to conduct surveillance greatly increases the chances of success because the second team member provides added flexibility. With two surveillants, the position of the team member directly behind the subject can be changed frequently and allows for relatively close positioning behind the subject when required. The use of two surveillants affords greater security against detection and reduces the risk of losing the subject.

5-44. Normally, both team members are on the same side of the street with the subject, with the first person positioned fairly closely behind the subject. The second surveillant is positioned behind the first with more distance between them. On streets that are not crowded, one member of the surveillance team may walk on the opposite side of the street. The following is a description of the AB technique:

- The person right behind the subject has the A position. The other member of the surveillance team has the B position. When using the AB technique, A follows the subject and B follows A. B may be on the same side of the street as A or he may be on the opposite side of the street.
- When both A and B are on the same side of the street, and the subject turns a corner to the right, A continues across the street. Then he signals B what action to take. The subject's actions may

require B to take the A position, and A to take the B position. Signals between A and B should attract as little attention as possible.

- When B is across the street and the subject turns the corner to the right (away from B), B crosses and takes the A position. This step should be prearranged so that no signals are needed.
- When B is across the street and the subject turns the corner to the left (crosses toward B), B drops back to avoid contact. B then waits for a signal from A before making the next move. B may take the A position or A may continue behind the subject. If A continues behind the subject, B can be directed to fall in behind A or cross the street and continue on the opposite side.

Three Surveillants (ABC)

5-45. The ABC foot surveillance is more resource intensive but provides better coverage and reduced risk. It should be used whenever possible. The use of three investigators greatly reduces the risk of losing the subject. A third team member provides greater flexibility for the surveillance team and allows a team member, who thinks that he has been identified or "burned," to discontinue his surveillance without affecting or having to stop the surveillance.

5-46. The main advantage of the ABC technique is that it lets you cover the subject from two sides. The standard ABC formation requires team member A to follow behind the subject and B to follow A (same as the AB technique above). The additional team member takes up position C across the street and just to the rear of the subject. Besides tailing the subject from the rear on foot, one agent observes him from the opposite side of the street. The subject is thus bracketed, and the agents are provided with strategic positions from which to observe, especially when the subject turns a corner or reverses direction. Figure 5-1 shows the basic positions for the ABC foot surveillance.

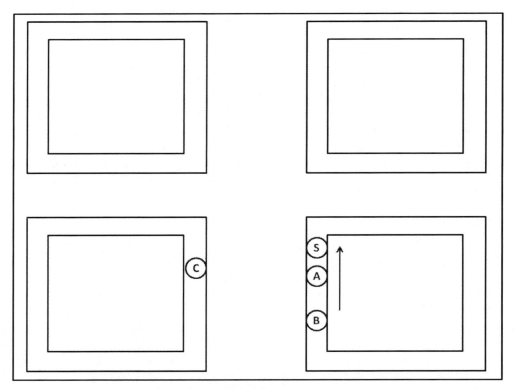

Figure 5-1. ABC surveillance example 1

5-47. The ABC technique allows several variations that can be employed, depending on the specific conditions. The following examples are provided:

- There are few people on the street. Two surveillants may be on the opposite side of the street, usually designated as surveillant B and surveillant C. Surveillant A remains to the rear of the subject, but surveillant B remains to the rear of surveillant C. Surveillant B concentrates on keeping surveillant A and surveillant C in view. This variation is depicted in figure 5-2.

- On very crowded streets, surveillant C's position is on the same side of the street as surveillant A and surveillant B and all surveillants are close to the subject. In this variation, surveillant A should follow the subject very closely. Surveillant B concentrates on keeping surveillant A in view. Surveillant C concentrates on keeping surveillant B in view. This variation is depicted in figure 5-3, page 5-12.

- In situations where the surveillants are confident that the subject is likely to follow a particular route for a period of time, the leading surveillance method may be used. The basic ABC method is employed except that in this variation one surveillant walks in front of the subject along the route that the subject is expected to take. This can be very effective in that the subject in most cases is not suspicious of individuals in front of him and walking in the same direction. See figure 5-4, page 5-12, for an example of this variation.

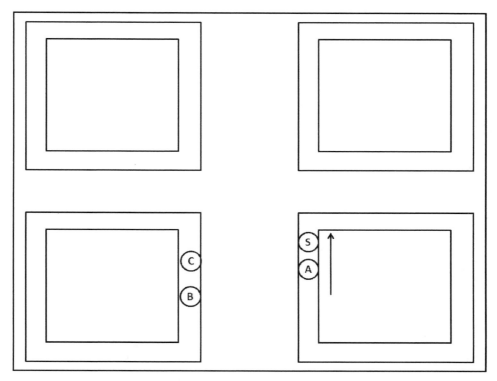

Figure 5-2. ABC surveillance example 2

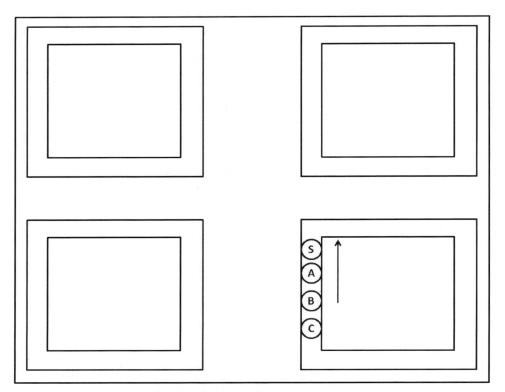

Figure 5-3. ABC surveillance example 3

Figure 5-4. ABC surveillance example 4

5-48. A frequent change in the ABC positions of each surveillant should be made to increase the probability of a successfully surveillance. These changes generally occur when the subject turns a corner at an intersection. Position changes are conducted to maintain a fluid movement and to reduce the chance of a subject recognizing the surveillance personnel. The following are two recommended techniques for changing positions:

- **Technique 1 (right turn).** The surveillance team proceeds in a normal ABC configuration as depicted in figure 5-1, page 5-10. Use the following steps:

  - **Step 1.** As the subject approaches the intersection, C (on the opposite side of the road) leads the subject and reaches the intersection first. C pauses at the intersection and turns toward the subject; C observes and signals to A and B the subject's actions. This movement is shown in figure 5-5.

  - **Step 2.** Assuming that the subject continues to walk after turning right, A crosses the intersection to the opposite side of the street. C crosses the intersection and walks in the same direction as the subject and on the same side of the street. B turns right (as the subject did) and walks in the same direction and the same side of the street as the subject. This movement is shown in figure 5-6, page 5-14.

  - **Step 3.** A (now across the street from the subject) assumes surveillant C's position and responsibilities. B assumes surveillant A's position and C (now on the same side of the street and walking behind the subject) follows behind and assumes surveillant B's position. This movement is shown in figure 5-7, page 5-14. In some cases, surveillant C may be required to cross the street and assume the A position with surveillant B turning and continuing on in the same position.

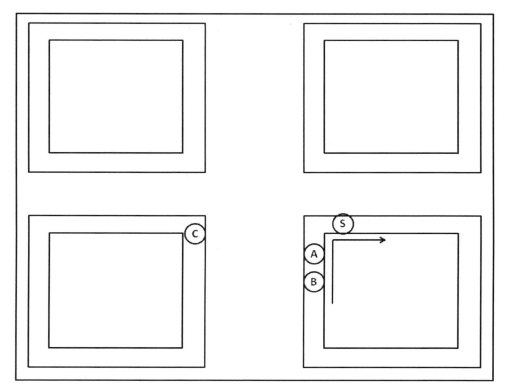

Figure 5-5. ABC position shift (right turn) example 1

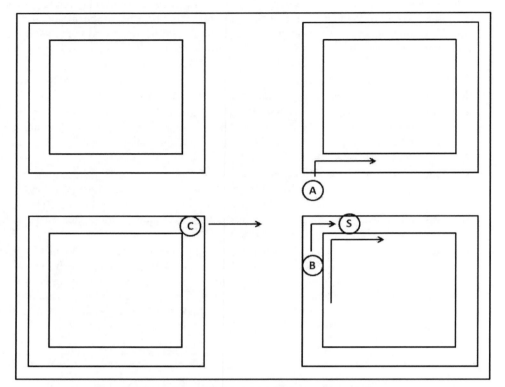

Figure 5-6. ABC position shift (right turn) example 2

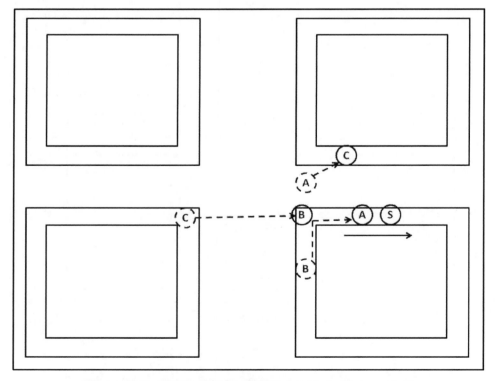

Figure 5-7. ABC position shift (right turn) example 3

- **Technique 2 (left turn).** The surveillance team proceeds in a normal ABC configuration as depicted in figure 5-1, page 5-10. Use the following steps:
  - **Step 1.** As in the previous example, the subject approaches the intersection and surveillant C (on the opposite side of the road) leads the subject and reaches the intersection first. Surveillant C pauses at the intersection and turns toward the subject to observe. This movement is shown in figure 5-8.
  - **Step 2.** The subject turns left and crosses the street toward C. C drops back and allows the subject to pass. This movement is shown in figure 5-9, page 5-16.
  - **Step 3**. A continues across the street, turns in the direction of the subject and assumes position C. B turns behind the subject and assumes position A; C moves into trail behind A and assumes position B. This movement is shown in figure 5-10, page 5-16.

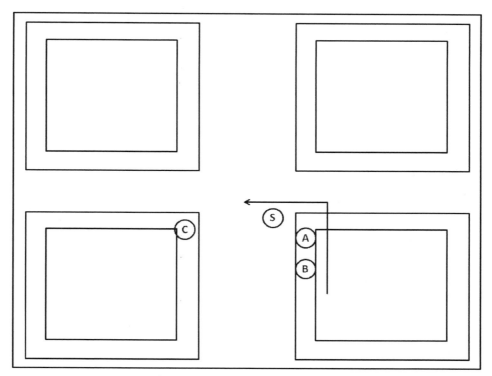

Figure 5-8. ABC position shift (left turn) example 1

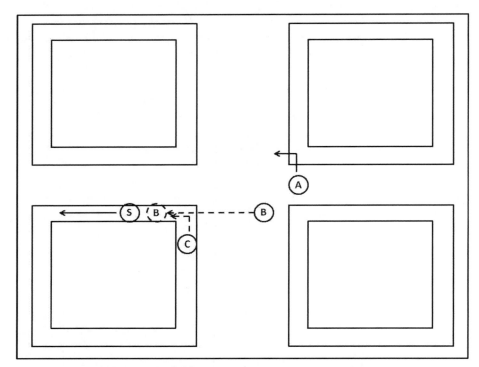

Figure 5-9. ABC position shift (left turn) example 2

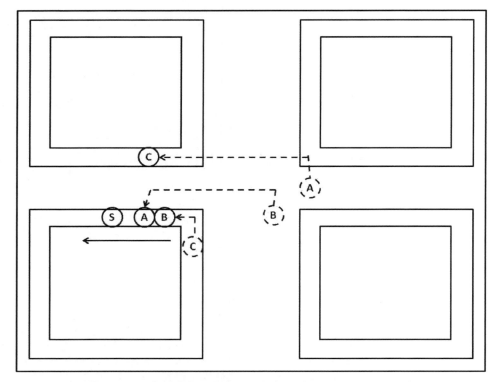

Figure 5-10. ABC position shift (left turn) example 3

Progressive Surveillance

5-49. Another surveillance technique is referred to as progressive surveillance. Progressive surveillance works best when the subject's route of travel is known and relatively consistent. The subject's predictable movements allow assignment of multiple surveillance personnel at locations along the route. Surveillance personnel can be on foot or in a static location where they can observe the subject moving along his route. On surveillant observes the subject's movements through a designated route segment. As the subject passes into the next segment of the route, the first surveillant passes the subject to the next surveillant and the first surveillant breaks contact. This is repeated through the entire route, allowing the surveillance team to observe the subject's entire route and associated activities without subjecting any one surveillant to a high risk of compromise.

Avoiding Detection

5-50. The best way to avoid detection during surveillance is to limit the exposure of any one member of the surveillance team. The longer the surveillant is in contact with a subject, the greater the risk that the subject will notice the surveillant. If manpower constraints allow, surveillance personnel should be rotated often to avoid prolonged exposure.

5-51. Sudden movements, especially unnatural actions, can attract unwanted attention. At times, a suspicious subject will test to see if he is being observed. He may quickly change course or enter a public vehicle or building. Surveillance personnel must react quickly, but naturally, to these movements. It may be better to lose sight of the subject for a moment than to cause increased suspicion.

5-52. Direct eye contact with a subject should be avoided. Direct eye contact between a surveillant and a subject can increase the subject's chances of recognizing the surveillant later. Sometimes close proximity to a subject makes direct eye contact difficult to avoid; surveillants should be cautious not to be obvious when avoiding eye contact as this can raise the subject's suspicion.

5-53. When a subject enters a confined space, such as public transportation, restaurants, hotels, or other areas, close contact may be unavoidable. These situations require caution. A few general considerations for these circumstances include the following:

- Carry enough money to pay for bus or cab fare, meals, or telephone calls.
- Enter facilities behind the subject and take position where the subject can be easily observed. Ensure that the position is a natural one for the surroundings (for example, do not stand and observe in a restaurant; if the subject sits to eat, choose a table where the subject can be observed and order a meal).
- Choose a meal that will be ready quickly if entering a restaurant and ordering a meal is required to maintain cover. Be sure the meal can be eaten easily and hastily without being unnatural and drawing attention.
- Do not press a floor button when following a subject into an elevator. This allows surveillance personnel to exit behind the subject on his floor without raising suspicion.

5-54. During foot surveillance, the subject may not be conscious of any surveillance and follow a normal route and routine; however, the subject may be either tail conscious or so suspicious of a surveillance that evasive action is taken to prevent surveillance personnel from following. He may take evasive action during his entire movement from one place to another, or he may attempt to detect the surveillance only occasionally when he feels threatened, watched, or is committing a criminal action.

5-55. Surveillance personnel should be alert to the methods a subject uses to detect and elude surveillance; however, they must understand that not all of the subject's actions associated with surveillance detection measures necessarily indicate that the surveillance has been compromised. Some of the same actions used to indicate countersurveillance by the subject may be coincidence and merely a normal reaction to some other activity or event. Regardless, when a subject takes such action, the surveillance team should be alert and even more cautious to avoid being recognized. Common methods used by a subject to detect a foot surveillance include—

- Stopping abruptly and looking to the rear.

- Looking around casually.
- Reversing course suddenly.
- Stopping abruptly after turning a corner.
- Watching for reflections in shop windows.
- Entering a building and leaving immediately by another exit.
- Walking slowly and then rapidly at alternate intervals.
- Dropping a piece of paper to see if anyone retrieves it.
- Stopping to tie their shoestrings while looking around.
- Using an associate or friend in a business to watch for surveillance.
- Boarding a bus and riding a short distance or exiting just before it starts.
- Circling the block in a taxi.

5-56. Once a subject has detected surveillance, he may use a variety of techniques to elude the surveillance. Subjects taking evasive action may use a single technique but will likely use multiple techniques to ensure successful evasion of the surveillance team. Typical techniques to evade foot surveillance include—

- Exiting a bus or subway just as the doors are about to close.
- Leaving a building through a rear or side exit.
- Entering a large crowd.
- Entering a theater and leaving immediately through an exit.
- Using a decoy.
- Using a side street or alley.
- Making a sudden turn and moving rapidly away, possibly making additional turns.
- Crossing at a street corner just as the traffic light switches to block the surveillance team's movement.

VEHICLE SURVEILLANCE

5-57. Vehicles may be used in the surveillance of premises, but their primary use and value is the surveillance of other vehicles. Foot surveillance can go with the subject only so far; if the subject transitions to vehicular travel, then the surveillance team must also transition to vehicle surveillance. Investigators must feel as confident with the techniques of vehicle surveillance as they do with foot surveillance. General considerations that enable successful vehicle surveillance include—

- **The vehicle's appearance.** The vehicle that is used on surveillance should be particularly suited for the purpose, both in appearance and speed. Consider the following:
  - The vehicle should be inconspicuous in appearance with no noticeable features that would draw attention to the vehicle. It is preferable that the vehicle be a subdued color such as dark blue or brown. Avoid bright colored vehicles such as yellow, red, or any other color scheme that draws attention; tail-conscious subjects are more apt to notice bright-colored surveillance vehicles. The color of the vehicle may often be further subdued and made indistinguishable at a distance by allowing road dirt and dust to accumulate on it.
  - Official papers, manuals, handcuffs, clipboards, and communications equipment should be removed from areas of the vehicle that are openly visible including seats, dashboards, or the rear window shelf.
  - The inside dome light should be made inoperative by taping or disconnecting the doorpost switch to avoid accidentally illuminating the vehicle's interior at night.
  - The vehicle should be in good running order. Ensure that all scheduled maintenance has been performed and the vehicle is running properly.
- **The number of surveillants per vehicle.** Two surveillants per vehicle are generally recommended for any mobile surveillance for the following reasons:
  - A second surveillant allows the driver to focus his full attention to driving while the partner operates the radio, makes notes of the subject's activities, and observes the subject.

- During any vehicle surveillance, circumstances may arise that require foot surveillance to adequately observe the subject and his activities. When this need arises a second surveillant is important. If the subject leaves his vehicle to complete some activity that the investigators need to observe, the second surveillant should leave the surveillance vehicle to continue observing the subject. The surveillant's actions while on foot must not be so unusual that he draws unwanted attention.

- The driver remains in the vehicle and maintains radio contact with the dismounted surveillant to provide immediate mobility when the subject's actions require it.

- **Driving skill.** An important factor contributing to successful vehicle surveillance is the ability to drive skillfully under all traffic conditions. This is particularly true in heavy city traffic where a moment's hesitation could result in the loss of the subject. The driver must constantly anticipate traffic conditions ahead, especially for left turns, and keep the vehicle in the correct position behind the subject. The surveillant must make quick and correct decisions to counter any evasive tactics by the subject. Army LE personnel that may be required to conduct vehicle surveillance should train on vehicle surveillance techniques under realistic conditions. This training reduces the risk of losing a subject during surveillance and also reduces the risk of collision due to rapid vehicle maneuvers sometimes required during vehicle surveillance activities.

- **Police intervention.** During the course of any type of surveillance, particularly vehicle surveillance, the surveillants may be stopped or questioned by local police. The surveillants must identify themselves and briefly explain their presence. Normally, it is not necessary for the investigators to explain the nature of their investigation. Most interventions can be prevented through coordination conducted during surveillance planning.

- **Traffic laws.** The safety of the surveillants, pedestrians, and other road users is the first priority in surveillance activities. Surveillants are required to operate vehicles in a safe and lawful manner. Deliberate violation of traffic rules and regulations is prohibited without exigent circumstances. Good judgment must be exercised at all times. For example, if proceeding through a red light is required, the surveillants must first stop and then proceed only when it is safe to do so.

- **Nighttime surveillance.** Nighttime surveillance presents unusual problems to surveillance teams. One problem is that headlights on the surveillance vehicle may alert the subject that he is being followed. Another is that the subject can use the darkness to elude surveillants by turning off his lights and driving onto a side road. Under medium traffic, the surveillants usually have the advantage (especially when tailing a lone subject). A lone subject's field of vision is restricted to the rearview mirror, and he may be unable to distinguish objects clearly because of the glare of the headlights. If available, vehicles used for surveillance should be equipped with control switches for the headlights, taillights, and brake lights. These controls enable the surveillance team to alter the vehicles appearance by turning off or changing the brightness of the lights. If the subject turns the corner, the tailing vehicle may alter one of its headlights before it turns the corner and appear to look like a different vehicle to the subject.

- **Detection avoidance.** Surveillants must be aware that a tail-conscious subject will routinely check for surveillance before departing a location. The following countersurveillance techniques may be conducted regardless of the subject's start point (home, work, or hangout):

  - Before departing a location, the subject may check for surveillance by driving or walking around several blocks in the immediate area in an attempt to identify surveillance personnel. A surveillance team may need to place personnel on foot in a hidden location several blocks away with binoculars or use a disguised vehicle such as a truck or van in order to initiate the surveillance without being detected.

  - When a subject is near his destination, he may make routine checks again by observing vehicles behind him. He may make several approaches to his destination before stopping. Surveillants must carefully position their vehicles to observe the subject, deploy strategically, and avoid detection by the subject.

- **The distance from the subject.** The distance between the subject and the lead surveillance vehicle is important and will vary with traffic conditions. The distance between them should increase as the subject's speed increases, such as on highways, and should decrease when the subject's speed decreases, such as in city traffic. Weather and light conditions must also be considered. Poor weather and darkness require the surveillance vehicles to close the distance between the surveillance team and the subject; this may require reduction in the number of cover vehicles. Bright, clear days typically force the surveillance team to increase the distance between the surveillance team and the subject; this may enable the use of more cover vehicles.

- **Cover vehicles.** Once behind the subject, the lead surveillance team must use every means possible to avoid any prolonged viewing of their vehicle by the subject in his rearview mirror. This can be accomplished by keeping one to two unrelated vehicles, referred to as cover vehicles, between the subject and the lead surveillance vehicle. Cover vehicles are vehicles that are not a part of the surveillance team, but that are on the roadway travelling in a manner that they can be used to shield the subject from observing the surveillance team. The use of cover vehicles varies depending on conditions and the type of road being travelled. The decision to use one or multiple cover vehicles between the subject and the lead surveillance vehicle is made based on a variety of factors. The more cover vehicles used, the less chance there is that the subject will become aware of the surveillance; too many cover vehicles may result in the loss of the subject. Use the following guidelines:
  - Open highway situations with fast moving traffic allow for two or more cover vehicles with few problems. In open highway situations two cover vehicles are usually sufficient to keep the subject from being alerted and prevent the surveillance team from losing the subject. Using only one vehicle as cover on the highway may not be enough if the subject is tail conscious. If no other cover vehicles are available, allowing more distance between the surveillants and the subject can alleviate this situation.
  - City traffic presents problems that are different from those found in highway traffic. The surveillance team may vary the number of cover vehicles used, depending on how heavy traffic is and the type of streets (inner city, residential, suburban). Typically no more than two cover vehicles are used between the surveillance vehicle and the subject in city traffic; one cover vehicle is often better. As traffic becomes more congested or traffic patterns are more difficult with extensive traffic lights, using two vehicles for cover can cause serious problems. Multiple cover vehicles can cause the surveillance team to lose the subject in heavy traffic, especially if a suspicious subject employs evasive action.

5-58. Usually the surveillance will begin in the area where the subject's vehicle is parked. The surveillance team leader should be in a position where the subject's vehicle can be observed with the other surveillance vehicles deployed in the area covering anticipated routes of travel. When a subject leaves his location, the team leader directs the appropriate car (possibly the team leader's vehicle) to assume the lead position behind the subject. The other cars will take up positions to the rear in a caravan style or on the paralleling streets, depending on the situation and directions from the team leader.

ONE-VEHICLE SURVEILLANCE

5-59. The use of only one surveillance vehicle should be avoided if at all possible. It is difficult to achieve a successful surveillance with only one vehicle; surveillance using one vehicle greatly increases the chances of detection by the subject. If the situation demands that a lone surveillance vehicle be used, all available traffic cover must be used to avoid the subject detecting the surveillance. In heavy traffic, the surveillance vehicle must remain very close to the subject to maintain observation; this increases the risk of being identified. On rural roads and highways, greater distance must be allowed, even to the extent of losing sight of the subject at times.

5-60. The surveillants should make every effort to alter the appearance of their vehicle so that it does not present the same image to the subject each time it is in view. Changing the appearance of the surveillance vehicle is especially important in one-vehicle surveillance; however, the same principles can be applied during prolonged multiple-vehicle surveillance. The vehicles appearance may be altered by—

- Changing seating arrangements within the surveillance vehicle.
- Donning and removing hats, coats, and sunglasses.
- Changing vehicle license plates.

- Emplacing and removing magnetic signs, flags, or other items that change the details of the vehicle.
- Turning into side streets or roads, and then returning back into traffic to resume the tail.

5-61. In one-vehicle surveillance, a second surveillant from the vehicle may be required to travel on foot many times to take up a position of observation such as when the subject has turned a corner or parked. From this position on foot, the second surveillant can give further directional signals (by hand or radio) to the driver based on the subject's activity.

MULTIPLE-VEHICLE SURVEILLANCE

5-62. Multiple-vehicle surveillance provides much greater flexibility and probability of success for the surveillance team. Frequent change of the lead surveillant vehicle position is an important factor in determining the success of the surveillance. Because this position is immediately behind the subject, it should be changed often to avoid detection of the lead surveillance team.

5-63. Once surveillance begins, the surveillance vehicles are positioned behind the subject as vehicle 1 (lead vehicle) and vehicles 2, 3, and 4. The surveillants must be continually aware of the need to switch the position of the lead vehicle. The initial positions may be in line or caravan style with all vehicles on the street or highway behind the subject or one or more vehicles may be situated on parallel streets.

In-Line Surveillance

5-64. One of the most common surveillance methods is for the surveillance vehicles to position themselves in a line behind the subject vehicle. This technique is especially effective on highways when traffic is moving at a high rate of speed. It enables easy rotation of surveillance vehicles to prevent detection. It is also conducive for using cover vehicles to shield the surveillance vehicles from view. At least one cover vehicles will typically be placed between the lead surveillance vehicle and the subject. More cover vehicles may be employed, depending on traffic conditions, the type of road, and the speed of travel. Cover vehicles may also be placed between the lead surveillance vehicle and follow-on surveillance vehicles. A two-vehicle in-line surveillance is shown in figure 5-11, page 5-22.

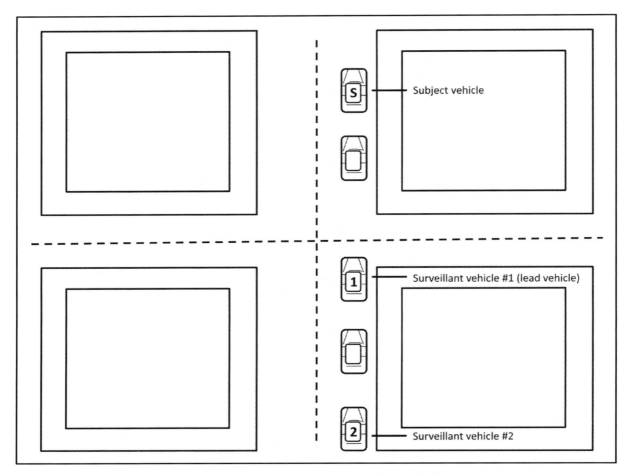

Figure 5-11. Two-vehicle surveillance in-line

Parallel Surveillance

5-65. When the subject's route of travel is fairly well established and can be anticipated for short periods of time or if the surveillance is being conducted in the city or in an urban area, parallel surveillance may be used. As the name implies, surveillance vehicles travel on streets that are parallel to that of the subject. It is a useful technique for shielding surveillance vehicles from the subject's view on streets with little or no traffic and gives flexibility to the surveillants in the paralleling vehicles when the subject turns (see figure 5-12).

5-66. Paralleling vehicles should arrive at cross streets at about the same time or shortly before the subject. This method is most effective in residential areas where the traffic is light. A lead vehicle positioned behind the subject maintains observation on the subject and maintains communication with the parallel surveillants. This vehicle should be farther behind the subject than in a normal in-line surveillance. If the subject stops, slows down, or increases speed, the timing of the paralleling vehicles may be disrupted and the subject may be lost. Communication from the lead vehicle provides the required direction to the parallel vehicles enabling them to react appropriately. If the subject turns at a cross street, each surveillance vehicle will adjust its position according to the subject's action. The appropriate parallel vehicle can assume the lead position and the remaining vehicles adjust according to the circumstances and the direction of the surveillance team lead. The surveillance team can adjust to assume another parallel surveillance or assume an in-line surveillance. A three-vehicle parallel surveillance is shown in figure 5-12.

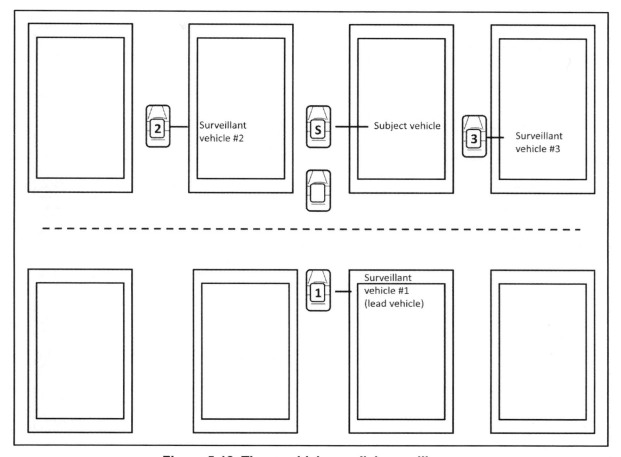

Figure 5-12. Three-vehicle parallel surveillance

Vehicle Leading Surveillance

5-67. In many cases a subject may proceed down predictable routes. The surveillance team may have knowledge of the subject's normal routes and activities based on previously obtained reliable information or based on the subject's indicated actions during surveillance. In these cases, a vehicle leading surveillance technique may be used. The technique is similar to variant of the ABC technique used in mobile foot surveillance. This technique cannot be used in all surveillance situations. It can be used only when the surveillant can anticipate the subject's travel route. In some situations, such as a subject driving at a very slow speed, the leading surveillance method is the most effective technique.

5-68. This technique employs one surveillant in front of the subject. This surveillance element leads the subject for a period of time as surveillance proceeds. The surveillants leading the subject should have at least one cover vehicle between themselves and the subject. When the subject is led in this manner, the surveillants in the vehicle behind the subject should not follow as closely as when using other surveillance techniques. When this method can be used, it is very effective. Its effectiveness can be traced to the subject's natural reaction about being concerned with who is behind him and not who is in front of him. A three-vehicle leading surveillance is shown in figure 5-13, page 5-24.

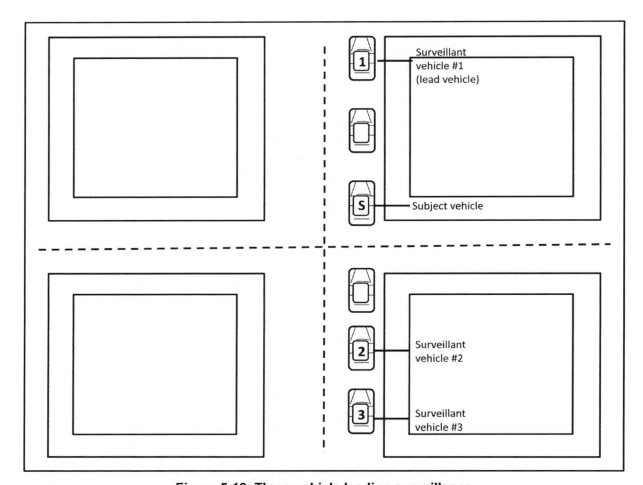

Figure 5-13. Three-vehicle leading surveillance

Progressive Surveillance

5-69. Some criminal activities do not lend themselves to being penetrated by routine surveillance methods. If a subject is extremely wary or tail conscious or if his activities are conducted very late at night or early in the morning and involve traveling considerable distances, routine surveillance is likely to be compromised. Several surveillance methods may be considered in these situations, such as using some type of electronic surveillance device (or using aircraft or unmanned aerial surveillance when possible) that allows the suspect vehicle to be tailed from a great distance. However, the best method is probably using the progressive surveillance technique. The progressive surveillance technique can be time consuming and more resource intensive than other techniques. It requires that the subject's route of travel is generally known to investigators. It is best if the surveillance team knows that the subject makes regular trips to the same destination along the identified route. Progressive surveillance can be particularly effective when the subject's route of travel takes him away from the city to more urban or rural areas.

5-70. This method involves stationing surveillance vehicles at various points, preferably at intersections along the suspected or known route. Surveillance vehicles (or surveillants on foot) are positioned at the intersections or established checkpoints. As the subject passes each surveillance position, the surveillance team reports the subjects passing and any observed activity. If the subject fails to reach a particular intersection after passing an earlier observation position, it is possible to determine where he turned off. The surveillance is then resumed from that point.

5-71. Due to the time-consuming nature of this type of surveillance, its use is limited to those occasions where it is known that the subject makes regular trips to the same destination. In another version of this method, the surveillance vehicles may tail the subject for a short distance after he passes their position. The surveillance must be done with caution or surveillance personnel risk being detected. It is best to use experienced investigators who are familiar with the area and experienced in conducting surveillance.

Subject Actions and Surveillant Counteractions

5-72. During the surveillance of a vehicle, the subject may turn left or right or make a U-turn. The turns may be legal or prohibited by law. Some turns will be normal movements for the route that the subject is traveling. They may also be used as part of routine driving patterns to make any possible surveillance difficult, detect possible surveillance, or lose a suspected tail. When subjects make a turn as a detection maneuver, they will be looking behind to see if a particular vehicle turned as well. If the same vehicle is observed on several successive turns, the subject will likely be convinced that he is under surveillance.

5-73. Regardless of a subject's motivation for his actions, surveillance personnel must be prepared to execute appropriate counteractions to maintain the surveillance. As a general rule, when a subject makes a turn, vehicle 1 (lead vehicle) should continue straight if at all possible. This procedure cannot be followed with every turn but should be used whenever it is practical. Some movements and evasive tactics commonly used by the subject include—

- Left or right turns.
- U-turns.
- Turning at an intersection and immediately stopping.
- Stopping just beyond a curve or hill crest.
- Turning into an alley.

Left or Right Turns

5-74. Right or left turns at intersections are approached with the same general techniques. When the subject makes a turn at an intersection, serious problems can arise for surveillants, even when the subject is making no effort to lose them. Intersections can present problems that may result in the loss of the subject if handled incorrectly. This is particularly true with left turns crossing traffic. Generally, right turns by subjects can be handled relatively easily by surveillants; however, left turns present more problems. If the suspect performs a turn, the general counter technique is as follows:

- The lead vehicle notifies the other vehicles of the subject's action and continues through the intersection.
- Vehicle 2 turns at the intersection behind the subject and assumes the lead vehicle position.
- Vehicle 1 does a U-turn or makes successive turns to get back into a surveillance position.
- If more than two vehicles are involved in the surveillance, the other vehicles have an option of turning at the intersection where the subject turned or turning in the same direction on paralleling streets, depending on traffic conditions and their distance from the subject. See figures 5-14 and 5-15, pages 5-26 and 5-27, for examples of left and right turns.

5-75. The actions of the surveillants during left turns are dictated by traffic conditions, including traffic lights. Left turns are made from a variety of situations and present numerous possibilities for the subject. They may be executed from highways or streets wide enough for two lanes of traffic or from a divided four-lane highway or street. They may also be made from a left-turn-only lane or from any turn lanes (against oncoming traffic). Left turns are made with or without traffic lights.

5-76. These traffic situations present potential problems for the surveillance team and, if not handled correctly, may result in loss of the subject and compromising surveillance. Vehicle 1 (lead vehicle) surveillants must be especially alert and use their best judgment in making the decision of whether to relinquish their position to vehicle 2 at left-turn situations. Ideally, the turn presents an opportunity to shift lead vehicles; however, if traffic is heavy, the delay created when the lead vehicle continues straight and vehicle 2 attempts to close the gap and negotiate the left turn across heavy traffic and assume the lead position can result in loss of contact with the subject.

5-77. The key to success in handling left turns is for vehicle 1 (lead vehicle) to maintain its position until it is sure that vehicle 2 is able to assume the lead position and follow the subject through the left turn. If it is apparent to the surveillants in vehicle 1 that vehicle 2 would be unable to follow the subject through the left turn because of traffic conditions, vehicle 1 should hold its position and delay making the change until after the turn is made.

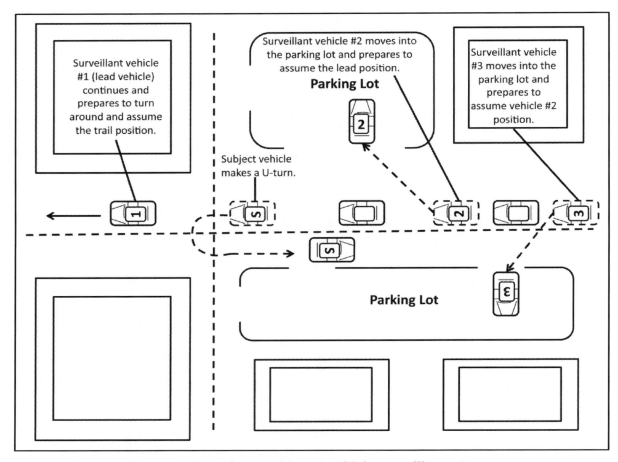

Figure 5-14. Left turn with two-vehicle surveillance team

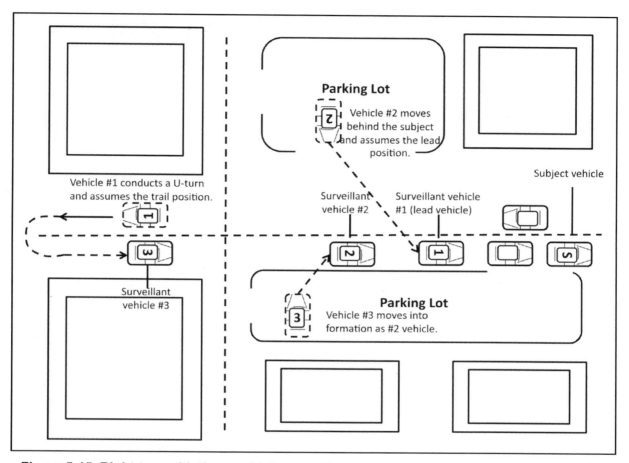

Figure 5-15. Right turn with three-vehicle surveillance team assuming a parallel surveillance

U-turns

5-78. U-turns conducted by a subject can cause immediate problems for the surveillance team. The key to successfully dealing with U-turns is to make quick decisions and smooth execution of the counteraction to maintain contact but not draw unwanted attention. If the suspect performs a U-turn in the street—

- Vehicle 1 (lead vehicle) notifies the other vehicles of the subject's action and continues through the intersection.
- Vehicle 2 responds by driving into a parking lot or an off-street area and prepares to assume the lead vehicle position behind the subject after the subject has completed the U-turn and has passed. See figure 5-16, page 5-28, for an example of a surveillance team reaction to a subject's U-turn.
- The remaining vehicles (including vehicle 1) perform a U-turn when it is safe to do so or make successive turns to get back into a surveillance position, either as vehicle 2, 3, or 4 as depicted in figure 5-17, page 5-29.

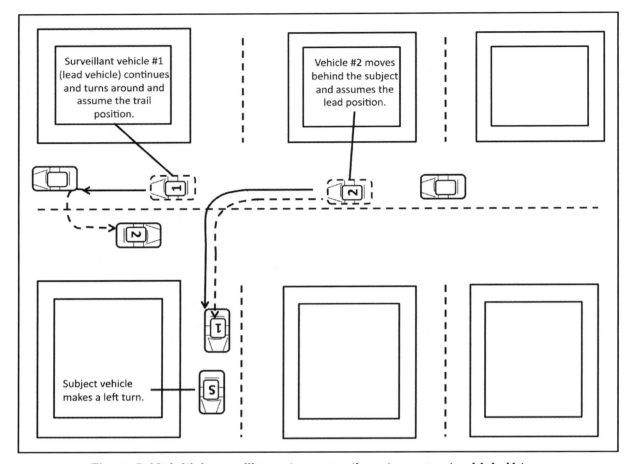

Figure 5-16. Initial surveillance team reactions to suspect vehicle U-turn

Turns and Stops

5-79. In some cases, the surveillance team may be faced with a situation where a subject turns at an intersection, but instead of proceeding the subject immediately stops. These situations can be addressed in the following manner:

- Vehicle 1 (lead vehicle) observes the subject as he drives through the intersection and notifies the other vehicles of the subject's action.
- Instead of vehicle 2 turning at the intersection behind the subject, vehicle 2 stops at the intersection and a member of the surveillance team dismounts and proceeds on foot to continue observing.
- Vehicle 1 has the option of making a U-turn and coming back to the intersection or making successive turns and getting into position for the subject's expected route of travel when the subject continues.
- When the subject does continue, vehicle 2 assumes the lead vehicle position. Other vehicles involved in the surveillance use this opportunity to take up positions to either parallel the subject or change to a closer surveillance position in anticipation of assuming the lead position at the next stop.

Note. In one-vehicle surveillances, the subject should not be followed around the corner (especially if traffic is sparse). The observer should dismount and travel on foot to the corner to observe the subject's actions. This procedure should also be followed in multiple-vehicle surveillance when a drive-by is not possible or practical, such as in a 90-degree blind turn in rural or isolated areas where the subject makes an abrupt turn and is suddenly out of sight.

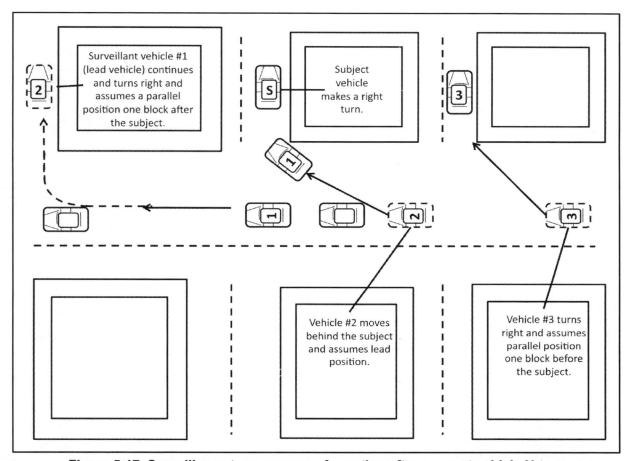

Figure 5-17. Surveillance team resumes formation after suspect vehicle U-turn

Stops Beyond a Curve or Hill Crest

5-80. In rural or isolated areas, subjects may stop just beyond a curve or hill crest. This is typically done to check for possible surveillance on their movements. If a subject stops just beyond a hill crest, use the following techniques:

- Vehicle 1 (lead vehicle) notifies vehicle 2 of the subject's actions and drives on by.
- Vehicle 2 stops and pulls off the road or onto a side road before cresting the hill or moving through the curve.
- A member of the surveillance team dismounts from vehicle 2 and proceeds on foot to observe the subject's activities.
- Vehicle 1 stops out of sight of the subject and dismounts a member of the surveillance team from the vehicle to observe the subject from the side opposite of vehicle 2. Surveillance team reaction when a subject stops beyond a curve is depicted in figure 5-18, page 5-30.

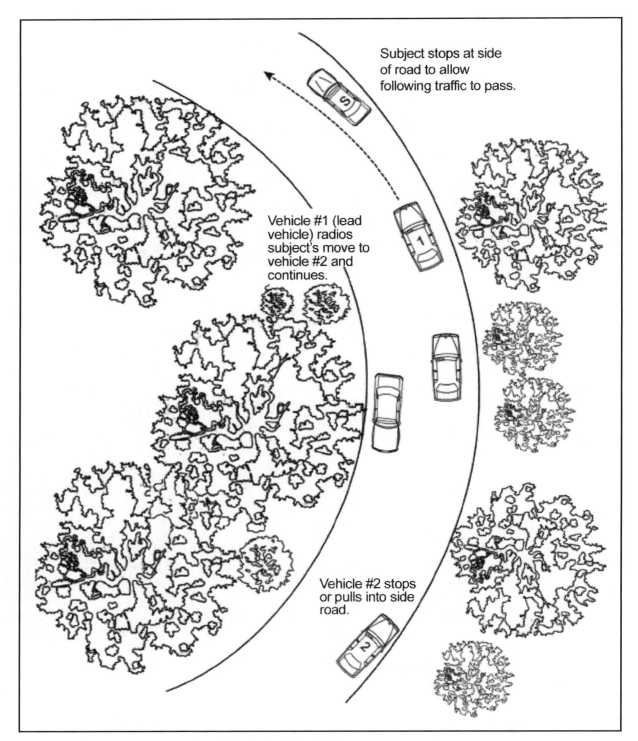

Figure 5-18. Subject stops beyond a curve

Turns Into an Alley

5-81. When a subject turns into an alley, the constraints of the alleyway create additional problems for the surveillance team. The reaction to an alley turn may appear to be a simple right or left turn; however, it requires a different approach. Use the following general guidelines for dealing with a subject that turns into an alley:

- Vehicle 1 (lead vehicle) must stop before reaching the alley or the next intersection. Stopping before the alley or the next intersection keeps vehicle 1 in position in case the subject backs out of the alley instead of proceeding through the alley.
- A member of the surveillance team dismounts from vehicle 1 and proceeds on foot to observe the subject.
- Vehicle 2 holds its position until the surveillant in vehicle 1 can determine the subject's next move. A drive-by will be ineffective in establishing the subject's intentions in this situation because of the limited or restricted visibility inherent in most alleyways. Figure 5-19 depicts a surveillance team reaction when a subject turns into an alley.

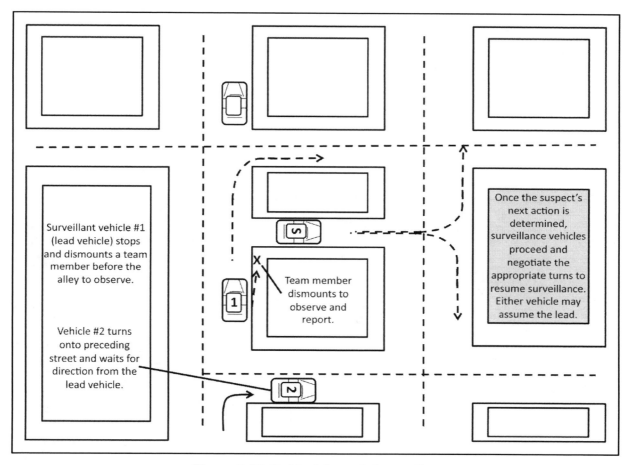

Figure 5-19. Subject turns into an alley

Chapter 6

Undercover Missions

Undercover missions are used as an investigative technique to gain police information when other efforts have proved impractical or have failed. They can be essential to the detection, prevention, and prosecution of criminal activity affecting Army programs and operations. Investigators are undercover when they leave their official identity and take on a role to gain needed information. Undercover investigators may associate with persons or become part of a group believed to have critical police information. These activities inherently involve an element of deception and may require cooperation with persons whose motivation and conduct are open to question.

PURPOSE

6-1.   The primary purpose of an undercover mission is to obtain evidence or information concerning violations of laws investigated by USACIDC SAs when required evidence or information is unattainable through conventional investigative means. Each mission should be designed to determine if criminal activity exists that affects the Army or its programs. The desired end state of an undercover mission is to identify criminal activity and obtain evidence against parties participating in criminal activity that will result in criminal prosecution. Undercover missions may also result in information that can identify and eliminate the potential for future weaknesses, detect systemic weaknesses, and recommend improvements to Army operations and programs. Undercover techniques may be required when—

- Information or evidence cannot be readily obtained using traditional overt investigative techniques.
- Continued overt investigation activities are likely to be unsuccessful.
- An undercover mission will reduce time and expenses involved in the completion of an investigation.

6-2.   USACIDC SAs may engage in undercover missions when appropriate to carry out their LE responsibilities. When there is a clear Army interest and the matter under investigation is within the investigative responsibility of USACIDC, undercover activities may be conducted jointly with other federal (including other DOD military criminal investigative organizations), local, state, or HN LE agencies. Undercover activities may be conducted during preliminary investigative inquiries or for general criminal investigations including drug investigations and economic crimes investigations.

6-3.   Undercover missions during preliminary inquiries may be required to determine the existence and extent of criminal activity and to determine whether a full investigation is warranted. In all criminal investigations, undercover methods may be used to further the investigative objectives of gathering evidence to solve crimes, prevent further criminal activity, and prosecute criminal offenders. Undercover activities are especially effective when used to investigate crimes involving drugs, stolen goods, fraud, contraband, and black marketing.

PLANNING CONSIDERATIONS

6-4.   Each undercover mission is different and should be planned in detail. An undercover approach can produce accurate, timely, and reliable results when properly planned and supported. However, failure to conduct careful planning and support preparation significantly increases the risks involved in execution of undercover activities.

6-5. Undercover missions must be planned and executed with specific objectives and end state; the objectives and end state must be specified before planning and resourcing the mission. The general objectives of an undercover mission are to obtain information, observe criminal activity, and collect evidence relevant to a specific person or group. These objectives must be clear and the degree of risk to the investigator must be assessed. Undercover missions are dangerous and should be used only when absolutely necessary and supported by a surveillance team. The appropriate USACIDC special agent in charge (SAC) must be informed of any undercover mission within his area of responsibility; the USACIDC SAC conducting the undercover mission should consider briefing the PM if necessary for operational purposes. The PM or USACIDC SAC is responsible for advising appropriate leaders within the command of the activity. Coordination with the servicing JA should be conducted before the mission, especially for complex or long duration undercover activities.

6-6. If a mission is conducted off a military installation, it should be coordinated with civil authorities who may have an interest in the mission or who may have other covert personnel conducting similar activities in order to deconflict and potentially synchronize LE activities in the area. Coordination with local police is routine in all cases involving the civilian community. However, coordination should make as few people as possible aware of the mission. Only those individuals whose consent is needed and those who can distinctly add to the investigation should be informed.

OBJECTIVES AND MISSION CONSIDERATIONS

6-7. When the decision to conduct undercover activities has been made, all personnel must understand the objectives of the mission. Clear objectives for the mission must be established and understood early to ensure appropriate planning and risk assessment. Failure to establish clear objectives increases the risk to undercover personnel and potential for failure of the mission. Objectives for an undercover mission may include—

- Obtaining information.
- Obtaining evidence.
- Determining if—
    - Criminal activity exists that warrants further investigation.
    - A crime is being planned.
    - A crime is being committed.
- Identifying individuals involved in criminal activity.
- Identifying witnesses and informers.
- Proving association between individuals involved in criminal activity.
- Checking the reliability of informants.
- Locating contraband and stolen property.
- Determining the most advantageous time to make arrests or execute search warrants.

6-8. An undercover mission can prove to be too costly in both resources and funding to justify the mission. There are many factors that should be considered before committing personnel and resources to undercover activities. Before making the decision to initiate an undercover mission, investigators and supervisors should consider the—

- Extent of the criminal activity and the results that will be achieved.
- Time and resources required.
- Complexity of the preparation involved. Complexity increases the risk to personnel; this risk must be balance with the results likely to be achieved.
- Sophistication of the subjects compared to the capabilities of investigative personnel.
- Suitability of U.S. Government participation in the type of activity that is expected to occur during the mission.
- Potential legal concerns and determination whether the activities comply with law and regulations.
- The risks associated with the specific mission including—

- The potential for personal injury, property damage, financial losses to persons or businesses, damage to reputations, or other adverse affects.
- The risk of civil liability or other loss to the U.S. Government.
- Privacy concerns including interference with privileged or confidential relationships, and any potential legal concerns.
- The potential that LE personnel engaged in an undercover mission may become involved in illegal conduct.

Note. The purchase of a larger quantity of drugs (for example, a kilogram of cocaine) is typically easier and carries less risk than the purchase of a small user quantity (such as a dime bag of crack). Individuals and organizations selling larger amounts of drugs conduct their operations as a structured business; while they may know the customer, they are more detached and less prone to violence at the point of sale. Buyers and sellers at this level are rarely users of their product. Dealer selling small amounts to users are dealing with customers who are just as likely to steal from them as buy from them; they are more likely to use violence than those trafficking in the larger amounts. User-level purchases also increase the chance that the undercover investigator may have to simulate the use of drugs. Street dealers may offer a sample to "the user;" it is unheard of for a drug abuser to refuse anything offered for free.

TYPES OF UNDERCOVER ACTIVITIES

6-9.   The nature of undercover work can vary widely. An undercover mission may require the investigator to be in several different settings and situations that will test his resourcefulness, adaptability, and endurance. The types of undercover assignments vary based on the approach, the time required, and other factors specific to the investigation and the investigator's objectives. The various types of undercover activities include—

- **An impromptu assignment.** This type of undercover mission is relatively short in duration. It occurs when an investigator conducting an open investigation is placed into an assumed role for the purpose of making inquiries. An example would be an investigator posing as a salesperson when calling on a third party or unwitting source.
- **A one-time assignment.** This is one in which the investigator has received information that illegal activity may be taking place at a given location, and an undercover visit to the subject's location will assist in determining if the information is worthy of further investigation.
- **An extended assignment.** An extended assignment may last from a few days to several months. The majority of assignments received by an undercover investigator will fall within this category.
- **A penetration.** A penetration mission is one that requires extensive planning and preparation. It involves the use of an undercover investigator over a period of several months or longer. This type of assignment is geared to the eventual penetration of a criminal organization or criminal group.
- **A sting.** Sting activities are designed to record criminal activities through direct observation and or participation. Most of these activities involve selling crimes, such as prostitution, narcotics, black marketing, or the sale of stolen property. In these activities, the investigator will generally act as a purchaser of the illicit service or product.
- **A reverse-sting.** This type of undercover mission is also designed to document criminal activities through direct observation and or participation. However, in these activities, the covert member assumes the role of the person providing the service or selling the illicit items. These activities require the approval of the USACIDC commanding general or other designated officials.
- **A storefront.** These activities are generally used to purchase items that are likely stolen. Storefronts can take the form of a pawn shop or an underground fencing operation. These activities require the approval of the USACIDC commanding general or other designated officials.

SELECTING AND PREPARING PERSONNEL

6-10. Undercover assignments test an investigator's adaptability, resourcefulness, and endurance. Only the most experienced investigators should be selected for undercover missions. No one set of qualifications or attributes will enable an investigator to be successful in all types of undercover missions. Personnel should be selected based on the type and specific circumstances of each mission. Personnel conducting undercover activities should—

- Be able to adjust their personality to fit the role they assume for the mission.
- Be skilled observers and possess the ability to make sound decisions under stressful and sometimes unpredictable environments. They must have the self-confidence to endure through hard and uncertain situations.
- Possess a highly developed ability to recall information. It is often too risky to take notes during a mission; instead, they must commit facts to memory and record them at a later time.
- Be well versed in the elements of proof.
- Be resourceful enough to work for extended periods of time without guidance.

6-11. MPIs, nonagent military personnel, or civilian employees may be used in undercover activities when necessary. The role of personnel other than USACIDC SAs should be limited; these individuals should also be closely supervised by USACIDC SAs assigned to the mission.

> *Note.* MPI and other nonagent personnel normally will not participate in sensitive undercover activities as outlined in CID Regulation 195-1, chapter 18. Guidelines for undercover activities that may require an individual to conduct activities that are illegal under normal circumstances are also outlined in CID Regulation 195-1, chapter 18. Otherwise illegal activity must be coordinated with appropriate federal, state, or local LE agencies and prosecutors before participation by USACIDC SAs or supporting personnel is approved.

6-12. The personnel selected to conduct an undercover investigation (including both undercover and support personnel) must have a thorough understanding of the objectives and the desired end state for the mission. Undercover investigators will use the stated objectives and end state to plan and prepare for their undercover role.

SELECTING AN IDENTITY AND COVER STORY

6-13. The process of building a false identity, or cover, will vary with the nature of the case. In some cases an adequate false identity may be gained just by changing rank insignia and name; in other cases, an elaborate identity must be planned. A means of communication with support personnel, including reporting procedures, duress signals, and other communications requirements, must be identified and resourced.

6-14. Depending on the extent and complexity of the case, this information may include false identification documents, police reports, and references or other documents to add credibility to the cover story. Cover stories are seldom, if ever, wholly fictitious. It is best to have the story conform to the undercover person's actual history. This helps add credibility to the story by providing background knowledge that would be unavailable if the story were completely fictitious. The story should be modified in ways that will gain the confidence of the subject. Establish a background in a city where the investigator is familiar, but do not use a locale that is the home city of the subject. Arrange to have key persons in the cover history support your statements in case the subject calls to check on you.

> *Note.* When assuming a fictitious undercover identity, investigators may assume short-term or long-term roles based on the operational plan; however, there are three occupations that may not be assumed by investigative personnel. These three occupations are attorneys, members of clergy, and medical personnel. Consequently, if an investigation is initiated within a legal office, a religious or chaplain's office, or a medical treatment facility, a role must be developed that will allow the covert team member access and credibility without violating these prohibitions.

6-15. Clothing and personal items must fit the cover role of the investigator in quality, price, age, fit, and degree of cleanliness. No detail is too small to consider. Considerations for clothing and appearance include the following:

- Clothing should have laundry marks (if needed) that are consistent with the cover story.
- Belts should have no stretch marks caused by a holster.
- Wallets, watches, rings, tokens, suitcases, stamps, miscellaneous papers, brands of tobacco, matches, letters, sums of money, and all personal items should support the fictitious role. The undercover investigator should be able to explain naturally and logically how each item came into his possession. A working wallet is recommended for use when undercover. This wallet should contain only items (identification cards, club cards, and other documents) supporting the cover identity; no real documents should be in the working wallet. This eliminates the chance that the undercover investigator might produce something with a name other than his cover name.
- Documents or identity cards should show wear. The USACIL can "age" documents if required.
- Handicaps should not be faked. Faked handicaps can be dangerous because it is hard to consistently maintain the ruse for extended periods of time.
- A weapon should be carried only if it fits your background story.

6-16. Normally, the undercover person does not work alone or independent of other investigators. A surveillance or cover team should be planned. The primary focus of the surveillance team is to protect the undercover investigator and to record his actions. See chapter 5 for information on surveillance activities.

6-17. All equipment requirements must be resourced before the mission. Equipment and communication systems should be carefully selected, and resources should include a primary and alternate means of communication. Communications plans must be established to include a means for the undercover investigator to communicate with the cover team. Signals must be arranged for the undercover person to signal his anticipated moves, contacts, and actions to the surveillant. This enables the surveillant to react appropriately and provide help, if it is needed, to protect the life of the undercover person.

GATHERING MISSION INFORMATION

6-18. Undercover personnel must have a thorough knowledge of the subject or group being investigated. Gather and review all available information about the subject from case files, other investigators, and other LE agencies that may have information on the subject and specific locations of interest. Mission checklists can be helpful when gathering information in preparation for a mission. These checklists help ensure that key information and mission requirements are not omitted during planning and preparation. Information useful to the investigation is assembled and reviewed by the undercover investigator and members of the surveillance team.

6-19. The nature, habits, interests, and routines of the targeted subject(s) must be studied. If an organization is the target, the purpose of the group and the names of group members must be known. Inadequate background information can place undercover investigators at a considerable disadvantage. They must study the mannerisms, gestures, and speech of those that they will be dealing with during the mission. No details are too small; small details like a subject's taste in food or music, favorite sports teams, or personal biases can be extremely important during the course of an undercover investigator's mission.

6-20. The team should gather as much information as possible relevant to the targeted subject or group and locations where the undercover activities will take place. Information to obtain may include—

- **General information.** This may include—
  - Any pertinent information received through interagency coordination.
  - Feedback resulting from the reconnaissance of the area where the surveillance will take place.
- **Specific information about individual persons.** Specific details of an individual subject's character and history should be thoroughly investigated. The following list is some of the information about a suspect or group that an investigator should learn before entering an undercover role:

- ■ *The full names and aliases used by the subject(s).* This should include the full name and any aliases or nicknames. This also includes any titles in relation to a job or public office which the suspect may hold.
- ■ *Addresses.* This should include past and present residential and business addresses.
- ■ *Vehicles.* A full description of vehicles that the subject may use.
- ■ *Physical description.* This should include the basic description of the individual and any unusual traits and peculiarities. A photograph of the suspect should also be obtained. If a subject frequently changes his look through clothing, accessories, beard and hair growth, or other means, these details should be gathered as well.
- ■ *Family and relatives.* This will assist the undercover investigator in his overall knowledge of the suspect.
- ■ *Contacts and associates.* This includes the subject's known contacts or associates (including a description, names, and known aliases) and his history with weapons, if known. This knowledge is essential to an understanding of the suspect's activities and can help identify other individuals that may pose a threat to undercover personnel or increased risk to the mission.
- ■ *Character, mannerisms, and temperament.* The strength and weaknesses of the subject should be known. Likes, dislikes, and prejudices are particularly helpful.
- ■ *Vices*. This should include vices such as drug addiction, alcohol, and gambling.
- ■ *Hobbies, habits, and routines.* This knowledge could help the undercover investigator in developing an acquaintance with the subject. A common interest of this nature can help create a strong bond between the investigator and the subject.
- ■ *Occupation and specialty.* Knowledge of the subject's work as well as his neighborhood environment may allow the investigator to establish a possible meeting ground with the subject. These are also indicative of the character of the subject.
- ■ *Propensity for violence.* Information received from sources, background information from past arrest records, and personal observations made by investigators will help identify a subject's possible violent nature. The investigator should make every attempt to know about any known or suspected weapons as well as the subject's propensity to use weapons or violence by other means.
- ● **Specific information about locations.** This may include—
  - ■ A description of the area (residential, commercial, industrial).
  - ■ The physical layout of the area such as known ingress and egress routes, main traffic routes, obstructions, and vantage points.
  - ■ Known traffic patterns (both vehicular and pedestrian).
  - ■ Activities (both legal and illegal) known to occur in the area.
  - ■ Known persons of interest that frequently come and go from the location.

APPROACH SELECTION

6-21. The objective of the undercover investigation will generally dictate the type of approach an investigator will use. If the target is an individual subject, the investigator will have to be accepted by the subject. This can be accomplished through the use of a source or by the investigator becoming acquainted in the places the subject frequents (cold contact). If the target is a group of people, investigators must determine a strategy that enables them to join the group or at least become accepted by the group as an associate. Gaining access to a group can take considerable time and resources; the use of a source may be a necessary. The best method to approach the target subject is through an introduction by a source. The source and target already know each other; therefore, the "trust" from source to target is being transferred or given to the undercover investigator. A cold contact takes time to develop; it is also as likely to be unsuccessful as it is to be successful. Cold contacts should be avoided unless there is no other option.

6-22. The investigator may consider frequenting establishments used by the subjects and establishing a rapport with them, enabling the investigator to gain their confidence. In some cases an undercover investigator can gain the confidence of an unwitting source familiar with an individual or members of a group and subsequently obtain an introduction. Any one or a combination of these approaches may be used. Whether the subject accepts the investigator or not depends on the investigator's ability to assume a believable role.

RISK MANAGEMENT

6-23. Risk management is an integrated part of mission planning. The assessment of risk and the subsequent development of measures to mitigate those risks begin at the earliest stages of the planning process and continue throughout planning and execution of an undercover mission. Mitigation measures are identified and employed to enable completion of the mission and attainment of stated objectives without unnecessary risk to undercover personnel, resources, and the investigation. See ADP 5-0 and ADRP 5-0 for more information on the operations process.

6-24. Risk management for undercover missions must consider a variety of risks. These risks include relatively standard risks surrounding planning time, equipment, communications, and mission preparation. Undercover activities by LE personnel also have unique considerations including the—

- **Amount of money involved.** Typically the more money the greater the risk. Larger amounts of money increase the potential payoff to a criminal and increase the chance that the money will be stolen.
- **Amount and type of drugs involved.** Large quantities of drugs increases the risk, some types of drugs carry greater risk than others.
- **Experience and organization of the offender.** Experienced and more organized offenders typically have procedures in place to vet outsiders and shield themselves. This increases the risk of detection for the mission.
- **Use of countersurveillance.** The use of countersurveillance by the target increases the risk that support personnel will be detected.
- **History of subjects.** A previous arrest history typically increases the risk; an individual that has a previous criminal history will likely be more aware of police tactics and techniques and are therefore more wary.
- **Location of the mission**. The location of the mission can increase the risk. A public place is not as risky as a private setting where cover surveillance is difficult.

6-25. Risk assessment matrixes and risk mitigation worksheets should be used as tools to enable identification of risks and risk mitigation measures. See FM 5-19 for more information on risk management. These tools are designed to aid investigative personnel in developing measures that will reduce the risk factors identified during the risk management process. A completed risk assessment enables investigators and approval authorities to decide whether identified risks are worth the potential gain. Command policies should identify the approval authority required for missions designated as low, moderate, or high risk.

MISSION APPROVAL

6-26. The approval authority for an undercover mission ranges from the SAC up through the USACIDC operations staff officer (G-3), depending on duration, cost, and sensitivity of the proposed mission. CID Regulation 195-1 provides detailed guidance and documentation requirements for the respective approving authorities. The SAC of a CID Office may approve an undercover mission—

- Not expected to exceed two months in length.
- Not expected to exceed $1,500 in appropriated funds (including .0015 funds).
- That is not sensitive in nature.

6-27. USACIDC battalion commanders, the CCIU Director, and the Fraud Field Office SAC may approve an undercover mission—

- Not expected to exceed six months in length.
- Not expected to cost more than $7,500 in appropriated funds (including .0015 funds).

- That is not sensitive in nature.

6-28. The USACIDC Headquarters G-3 is the approval authority for an undercover mission—
- Expected to exceed six months in length.
- Expected to exceed $7,500 in appropriated funds (including .0015 funds).
- Considered sensitive in nature. CID Regulation 195-1 provides a list of undercover investigations that are considered sensitive, requiring USACIDC G-3 approval.

EXECUTION

6-29. Execution of an undercover mission requires patience and skill on the part of the undercover investigator and the associated support personnel. While surveillance personnel supporting the mission can observe, the success or failure of the mission rests almost entirely on the undercover investigator and his ability to establish rapport and gain the confidence of the subjects being targeted.

6-30. The manner in which an undercover investigator makes initial contact with a subject varies based on the specific circumstances of the investigation and the parties involved. Initial contact may be through a source a direct rapport developed by the investigator, a deliberate means, or by chance. Regardless of how the contact is made, the undercover investigator must gain the subject's confidence to develop information for the crime he is investigating.

USING SOURCES

6-31. A witting source is a source that furnishes information to an investigator knowing full well his capacity as an investigator. The witting source may agree to accompany the undercover investigator during an initial contact with the subject of an investigation. The source then uses his association with the subject to provide a means for the investigator to meet the subject. This approach is the quickest and surest way to establish contact. The degree of success, however, is contingent on the amount of confidence the subject has in the source and the source's reliability. See appendix E for more information.

6-32. Before meeting the subject using a witting source, establish the cover story of the undercover investigator with the source. Allow the source to do most of the early talking with the subject; do not try to engage the subject in conversation that would require extensive use of your cover story. For example, in drug investigations subjects are usually not interested in a purchaser's background. When undercover agents talk a lot about themselves, they only cast doubt in the mind of the subject. Most dealers tend to believe that buyers will not bring unreliable persons to them.

6-33. An unwitting source provides information to investigators without knowledge that he is providing the information to a LE official. Unwitting sources may be chance contacts or persons developed by investigators while operating under their cover identity. Use of unwitting sources can be successful but are inherently riskier for the undercover investigator.

MEETING THE SUBJECT (CHANCE ENCOUNTER)

6-34. In some cases, a chance encounter with a subject may present itself to an undercover investigator. A chance encounter between the undercover investigator and the subject may occur unexpectedly when an unplanned opportunity (for both the investigator and the subject) to meet occurs. These encounters can also be well-planned maneuvers (on the part of the investigative team) while appearing to be unplanned to the subject. Either scenario must appear to the subject as a natural chain of events. Generally, this type of meeting causes little suspicion on the part of the subject and provides the initial contact that the undercover investigator needs. During a chance meeting with a subject, undercover investigators must conduct themselves in a manner that does not cause the subject to feel uneasy or believe that the investigators' motives are suspect. The investigator's actions will determine his acceptance or rejection by the subject.

GAINING THE SUBJECT'S CONFIDENCE

6-35. After the initial contact, the undercover investigator should be constantly aware of any indications by the subject that he is suspicious of the investigator. The investigator's conduct and reactions must always be calculated to avoid suspicion. This can be a delicate balance for the undercover investigator. Many things can raise the suspicion of a subject including—

- Using a cover story that is not credible. This includes clothing, knowledge, or other factors that do not match the cover story.
- Acting too eager or friendly.
- Using language that is not consistent with the cover or that indicates his LE background.
- Failing to remove identifying jewelry such as fraternal or organizational rings, pins, or necklaces.
- Interacting with LE personnel in a manner that raises suspicion.
- Having chance encounters with someone that knows the investigator's true identity.

6-36. The subject's initial attitude will likely be suspicious and skeptical. The subject may attempt to throw the investigator off balance by suddenly accusing the investigator of being a police officer or belligerently calling him a source. This does not necessarily mean that the subject is aware of the investigator's true identity, but only that he is trying to read the investigator's reaction or flush out a betrayer. A well-prepared undercover investigator anticipates such emergencies and immediately puts the subject on the defensive, possibly by using counteraccusations. To dispel the subject's suspicions and gain his confidence, the undercover investigator may—

- Pretend disgust or anger with the subject for questioning him.
- Appear as though he does not trust the subject anymore than the subject trusts him.
- Arrange to be arrested, questioned, or searched by other LE officers where the subject can observe the action.

6-37. As the mission progresses, the investigator may have to appear to be the subject's friend, a business associate, or other ruse. The investigator may have to participate in some of the subject's activities; in these cases the investigator must depend almost entirely upon his own judgment while ensuring that he does not violate the law, participate in unapproved activities, or violate other ethical restrictions.

DEVELOPING INFORMATION FROM THE SUBJECT

6-38. An undercover investigator's greatest asset is his ability to listen and observe. If he does all the talking or takes the lead in conversations, the subject will not have the opportunity to talk. Occasionally, the investigator may have to initiate a conversation, especially about criminal activity. In this instance, the investigator should talk about activities other than those currently under investigation and eventually guide the conversation toward the current activity being investigated.

6-39. The undercover investigator should listen carefully to learn everything possible about the subject and his counterparts in criminal activity. He should attempt to determine who the subject does business with and from whom the subject receives instructions or orders. If the subject is in a position to have information about persons in higher echelons of the criminal organization, the investigator should attempt to persuade the subject to arrange an introduction to those individuals. This requires persistence and resourcefulness on the part of the investigator.

PRECAUTIONS AND COMMON PITFALLS

6-40. An investigator cannot assume that he can conduct an undercover mission on his own; he should use a cover detail when possible. Undercover investigators cannot assume that all behavior is acceptable in order to "fit in." They should also be aware of how to, and how not to, interact with the opposite gender and when it is appropriate to consume alcoholic beverages. Failure to understand the risks and common pitfalls associated with undercover activities could expose the investigation and cost him his life. Undercover personnel must take precautions to avoid pitfalls and mitigate known risks including—

- **Using a cover detail.** In many situations other investigators or LE personnel are required to observe the activities of an undercover investigator during the course of their undercover activities. These LE personnel are referred to as a cover detail. A cover detail is used for the safety of the undercover investigator and to corroborate testimony documenting the undercover activity and associated transactions. The investigators comprising the cover detail should be provided with all available information pertinent to the mission so that they may adequately perform their tasks and be of maximum help to the undercover investigator. The cover detail must be used discreetly and may employ cover identities to avoid detection or suspicion. If employed too long or indiscreetly, the cover detail may be discovered or suspected and seriously hinder the undercover mission.

- **Interacting with opposite gender associates.** An undercover investigator must be aware of the possible consequences that could result from being overly friendly with opposite gender associates of the subject. The investigator's relationship with opposite gender relatives and friends of the subject should be such that he gains their cooperation in obtaining the subject's confidence, but should never extend to the point of provoking the subject. The investigator should avoid situations which would lead to accusations of improper or intimate relationships.

- **Using alcohol or drugs.** Generally, an investigator is prohibited from consuming alcoholic beverages while being armed. Investigators are also generally prohibited from using or simulating the use of drugs unless they are under duress (unless otherwise specified by regulation or policy). The battalion commander or appropriate policy authority may make exceptions for undercover activities when prudent evidence exists that a mission could be jeopardized as a result of the policy and the risks are warranted to maintain the investigation. When an exception to policy is approved, the investigator is held accountable for his actions and is expected to exercise mature, responsible judgment and professional behavior. The operational plan and risk assessment for undercover activity must address the conditions under which the investigator may consume alcohol or simulate the use drugs and any risk mitigation measures in place. If alcohol or drugs are used during the conduct of undercover operations (within the constraints of the risk assessment and formal plan), a medical evaluation of personnel involved in the activity should be conducted following the mission to ensure the safety of undercover personnel.

SPECIAL CONSIDERATIONS

6-41. There are numerous circumstances and risks that must be considered during an undercover mission. Many undercover activities require the undercover agent to use funds to buy (or prove the ability to buy) drugs, stolen merchandise, or other products of criminal activity. Undercover investigators may be required to act in a manner that in a normal circumstance would be considered questionable; they may even be confronted with possibly illegal activity. Accusations of entrapment are a common defense used against LE personnel when employing undercover techniques. These and other special considerations are discussed below.

FUNDS

6-42. Fronting of funds is defined as providing the subject with money before the planned exchange of illicit items, such as narcotics or stolen property. As a general rule, investigators should not front funds; however, this may be done on a case-by-case basis with appropriate approval. The fronting of funds should only be done when the risk of loss is minimal and the action is likely to produce a substantial investigative gain. In many cases, a mid-level dealer may not have the money to obtain drugs or other items and may request the funds be fronted. A front of funds in these cases should only be done when the person to whom the funds will be fronted is fully identified and can be picked up at a later time, should he manage to evade investigators and steal the money. If funds are fronted, the investigator should impose a reasonable time limit that will require the subject to go directly to his supplier to make the purchase. The investigative gain that justifies the front money in this situation is the ability to identify the source of the supply. Supporting investigative personnel must be in place to follow the subject to his source, thus mitigating the risk of loss of the front money and providing observation of the supply source.

6-43. When making high-dollar purchases, an investigator may have to show the subject that he actually has the money to make the deal (flashing funds). In cases where flashing funds is required, there are several techniques designed to safeguard both the money and the investigator. These techniques include—

- Never revealing in advance the location of the money. This reduces the risk that the money may be stolen by the subject or an associate.
- Making displays of money in a manner that is unsuspected by the subject. The subject should have no prior knowledge that the funds will be "flashed."
- Moving with the subject to a location away from other parties when showing him something (such as money).
- Ensuring that a third party is present to display the money; the third party should immediately depart the area with the subject watching. This ensures that the subject knows the money is no longer with the undercover investigator, thereby leaving the subject with no reason to attempt to steal the money.

PERSONAL CONDUCT

6-44. An investigator must know the limits of his personal conduct when attempting to gain a subject's trust. Sometimes an undercover investigator may act unruly or be disrespectful toward a LE officer in an attempt to make the subject more comfortable with him. However, a subject may request that an undercover investigator commit a crime to earn the subject's trust or prove that he is not a LE officer. This is generally prohibited unless the investigator is under duress. In some cases, criminal acts can be faked to make the subject believe that the investigator committed a crime, even though no crime was committed. However there may be no means to stage a crime; in these cases the investigator may not commit acts for which he can be criminally culpable.

ENTRAPMENT

6-45. While undercover, beware of any actions that could be criticized by the courts as going too far toward facilitating the commission of a crime. The most common defense used subsequent to an undercover mission is an entrapment defense. An entrapment defense can negate the results of the entire undercover mission if upheld by the courts. It is important for investigators to fully understand and appreciate what constitutes entrapment.

6-46. Entrapment exists when an agent of the government entices someone to commit a crime that he was not predisposed to commit. For instance, merely soliciting drugs from a subjected drug dealer is not entrapment when he demonstrates that he could readily produce the drugs. An example of entrapment is when a government agent approaches an individual on the street that is not suspected of trafficking drugs. If the undercover investigator offers the individual a large amount of money to make a buy, tells him where to get the drugs, and the individual subsequently produces the drugs (even though he was not predisposed to commit the offense), the investigators actions would constitute entrapment.

6-47. An investigator should render as little active assistance to his "associates" as circumstances will permit when he is undercover. Using cover details to observe undercover activities is an important measure to mitigate the risk of an entrapment accusation. Investigators observing the activities can corroborate the actions of the undercover investigator. CID Regulation 195-1 provides guidelines for approval authorities to help mitigate the risk of a successful entrapment defense.

ARREST

6-48. Arrest of the target following a drug buy or other criminal event always creates danger for the undercover investigator. This danger comes from the target subject who may think he has been double crossed or from local police that are unaware that an undercover mission is in place. A subject that has just committed a crime, triggering an arrest by other LE personnel overwatching the mission, is just as likely to think he is being robbed as arrested. Once the subject realizes that LE personnel are closing in for an arrest, the undercover investigator or source may be in significant danger.

6-49. The fact that an undercover mission has been coordinated with other LE agencies does not eliminate the chance of an undercover investigator being arrested by local LE personnel. An undercover investigator may have money and drugs on his person at any time. Local police that are not aware of the mission may stop and frisk the undercover investigator and find the contraband or they may stumble upon a drug buy purely by chance. If arrested by civil authorities while undercover, an investigator should use his best judgment regarding actions required. When an official within the arresting agency was briefed on the mission and the name of the official is known to the undercover investigator, he should refuse to make a statement except to that official. There may be circumstances where divulging the identity of an undercover investigator to local police may jeopardize the investigation or create a dangerous environment for the undercover individual. If there is any reason why the undercover investigator believes he should not reveal his identity to the local police, the undercover investigator may refuse to make a statement except to a federal agent such as a U.S. Marshal or an FBI Agent. When the federal officer arrives, the undercover investigator should disclose his identity to the federal officer and request to speak with the federal agent in charge of the local office.

Chapter 7

Death Investigations

Close liaison must be made between investigative, medical, and related forensic personnel to have an effective death investigation. Matters of mutual interest include jurisdiction, investigative responsibilities, local agreements with the civil authorities, SOFAs, and legal issues to be considered by military police, USACIDC, and medical personnel—primarily pathologists and MEs. The term pathologist will be used to identify both a pathologist and an ME, although there is a variation in training and expertise.

RESPONSIBILITIES

7-1. Many organizations have inherent responsibilities regarding death investigations. Simultaneous investigations into the death of an individual are likely in most cases. Organizations and individuals that have an investigative role in incidents involving death can include pathologists associated with the AFMES, safety officers and professionals at the Army or unit level, and line-of-duty investigators at the unit level.

ARMED FORCES MEDICAL EXAMINER SYSTEM

7-2. The AMFES provides support for death (and other) investigations to military criminal investigative organizations as required by the investigating agency. The AFMES provides comprehensive services in forensic pathology, forensic toxicology, DNA technology and identification, and mortality surveillance for the DOD. The Division of Operations is the center of medical-legal investigations for the AMFES. Working closely with investigative arms of the branches of the military, forensic investigations of crime scenes are conducted upon request. Operational deployment can be accomplished worldwide within 4 to 48 hours, depending on location, with support from board-certified forensic pathologists, forensic anthropologists, medical-legal death investigators, photographers, and histotechnicians. Teams provide a complete, multifaceted forensic investigation.

7-3. The Division of Forensic Toxicology laboratory remains the DOD's centralized laboratory which performs routine toxicological examinations for accidents involving fatalities, selected military autopsies, biological specimens supporting criminal investigations from USACIDC and other military criminal investigative organizations, blood for legal alcohol and drug tests in DUI and DWI medico-legal determinations, and selected cases of national interest. The Armed Forces DNA Identification Laboratory provides worldwide scientific consultation, research, and education services in the field of forensic DNA analysis to the DOD and other agencies and provides DNA reference specimen collection, accession, and storage of United States military and other authorized personnel.

PROVOST MARSHAL

7-4. The USACIDC, supported by the PM, is responsible for obtaining all facts pertinent to death investigations. Death investigations are within the purview of the USACIDC; the USACIDC element providing support for the area where the death occurred will lead any U.S. Army death investigation. The PM provides support as required to the USACIDC element. All available evidence, information, and circumstances concerning the death must be accurately developed to ensure that the facts support the conclusive manner of death.

MEDICAL OFFICERS

7-5. The pathologist is responsible for conducting a medico-legal (forensic) autopsy of the decedent and for completing official certificates of death. It is important to understand that there are several components of the autopsy. This autopsy is a joint venture in which the investigator and the pathologist must work together.

7-6. The investigator's direct responsibilities during the autopsy include photographing pertinent identifying data, injuries, and anomalies identified by the pathologist. The investigator is responsible for collecting and preserving postmortem major case prints and other physical evidence and samples discovered during autopsy (such as hair, biological fluids, or fingernail clippings) for subsequent forensic examinations. Investigators are encouraged to set up a liaison with the pathologist who performs the autopsy. Investigators must provide the pathologist with the known facts of the death and the initial investigative findings before the autopsy. This should include a detailed account of all circumstances known; often, crime scene photographs are useful to the pathologist. This enables the pathologist to select the proper ways to determine the cause of death and to give an opinion about the manner of death. The purpose of the medico-legal autopsy is to determine—

- The cause(s) of death.
- The manner of death.
- The mechanism of death.
- Whether drugs or alcohol were in the decedent's system at the time of death.
- The identification of the decedent.
- If the decedent was moved after death and before discovery.
- The identification or presence of physical evidence. If such is present, it should be collected.

CRIMINAL INVESTIGATORS

7-7. USACIDC SAs are responsible for the investigation of all unattended noncombat deaths within the purview of USACIDC to determine if criminal activity was involved. USACIDC SAs will conduct the criminal investigation to collect evidence, identify the responsible parties, and support criminal prosecution. The appropriate USACIDC element will investigate all deaths occurring on Army military bases and base camps except for those attended by medical personnel.

7-8. If a death is determined to be the result of a criminal act, USACIDC SAs conduct the criminal investigation. They are responsible for collection, preservation, and analysis of all physical and testimonial evidence pertinent to the investigation. They work closely with prosecutors to support criminal prosecution of identified suspects.

LINE-OF-DUTY AND SAFETY OFFICERS

7-9. The line of duty investigating officer determines the duty status and personal conduct of the deceased; the line of duty officer has no jurisdiction with the criminal investigation. The safety officer's focus is on protection of personnel and property from identified hazards. Safety officers are responsible for identifying unsafe conditions, violations of safety procedures, and potential risk mitigation measures to prevent future damage or injury. The safety officer's responsibilities are limited to safety-related issues and hazard mitigation according to AR 385-10. The safety officer has no criminal investigative authority or responsibility. When criminal activity is involved and an accident investigation is required, it will be secondary to the criminal investigation by USACIDC and supporting military police.

INTELLIGENCE OFFICER

7-10. The intelligence officer is responsible for security measures. The intelligence officer's main concern is to ensure that classified material is not compromised. Liaison with the appropriate intelligence agency is required and directed by AR 195-2 in the case of a breach of classified information. USACIDC SAs should check to determine if the victim possessed or had access to classified information. If possession or access to classified information is determined, the nearest intelligence agency should be notified. This enables the appropriate intelligence officer to determine if any classified material is missing or compromised and to take appropriate action.

DESCRIPTIONS OF CRIMES RESULTING IN DEATH

7-11. It is important that investigators know the legal descriptions for crimes resulting in death of an individual. This ensures that the investigator understands the legal elements of the crime when determining what, if any, crime has been committed. The following paragraphs provide a general description of the crimes and their associated elements. The UCMJ is the primary reference and should be referred to for detailed discussion of each crime. See the MCM for more information.

MURDER

7-12. In general, killing a human being is unlawful when done without justification. The circumstance surrounding the killing of an individual determines whether the death is characterized as murder or a lesser offense. A suspect may be charged with murder if the killing is committed with premeditation, the killing is the result of actions by the suspect committed with intent to kill or inflict great bodily harm, the death was the result of actions inherently dangerous to another, or if the death occurs during the commission of another serious crime (listed below).

Premeditated Murder

7-13. A murder is premeditated when the thought of taking life is consciously conceived and the act or omission required to commit the act was intended. The requirements for premeditation are met—
* After the formation of a specific intent and consideration of the act intended to kill someone.
* When a fixed purpose to kill has been deliberately formed. It is not necessary that the intention to kill was entertained for any particular or considerable length of time; it is immaterial how soon afterwards the actions are taken.

7-14. When an accused with a premeditated design attempts to unlawfully kill a person but, by mistake or inadvertence, kills another person, the accused is still criminally responsible for a premeditated murder. The premeditated design to kill is transferred from the intended victim to the actual victim. The elements required for premeditated murder are that—
* A certain named or described person is dead.
* The death resulted from the act or omission of the accused.
* The killing was unlawful.
* At the time of the killing, the accused had a premeditated design to kill.

Murder Without Premeditation

7-15. An unlawful killing without premeditation is also murder when the accused had the intent to either kill or inflict great bodily harm. It may be inferred that a person intends the natural and probable consequences of their purposeful actions. If a person commits an intentional act likely to result in death or great bodily injury, it may be inferred that death or great bodily injury was intended. The intent is not required to be directed toward the person killed, and there is no requirement that the intent exist for any particular time before commission of the act. The elements required for murder without premeditation are that—
* A certain named or described person is dead.
* The death resulted from the act or omission of the accused.
* The killing was unlawful.
* At the time of the killing, the accused had the intent to kill or inflict great bodily harm upon a person.

7-16. "Great bodily harm" means serious injury; it does not include minor injuries such as a black eye or a bloody nose, but it does include fractured or dislocated bones, deep cuts, torn members of the body, serious damage to internal organs, and other serious bodily injuries. It is synonymous with the term "grievous bodily harm."

Inherently Dangerous Acts

7-17. Murder may also be committed when a person intentionally engages in an act inherently dangerous to another. No intent to kill or cause bodily harm is required; the act may constitute murder if it shows wanton disregard of human life. Such disregard is characterized by disregard for the probable consequences of the act or omission, or indifference to the likelihood of death or great bodily harm. The accused must know that death or great bodily harm was a probable consequence of the inherently dangerous act. Such knowledge may be proved by circumstantial evidence. An act that is inherently dangerous to another must meet the following elements:

- A certain named or described person is dead.
- Death resulted from the intentional act of the accused.
- The act was inherently dangerous to another and showed a wanton disregard for human life.
- The accused knew that death or great bodily harm was a probable consequence of the act.
- The killing was unlawful.

Death Resulting From the Commission of a Crime

7-18. The commission or attempted commission of any of the offenses listed in the fourth bullet below is likely to result in homicide. When an unlawful killing occurs as a consequence of the commission (or attempted commission) of one of these offenses, the killing is murder. Under these circumstances, it is not a defense that the killing was unintended or accidental. The elements required for a murder under these circumstances are that—

- A certain named or described person is dead.
- The death resulted from the act or omission of the accused.
- The killing was unlawful.
- At the time of the killing, the accused was engaged in the perpetration or attempted perpetration of burglary, sodomy, rape, rape of a child, aggravated sexual assault, aggravated sexual assault of a child, aggravated sexual contact, aggravated sexual abuse of a child, aggravated sexual contact with a child, robbery, or aggravated arson.

MANSLAUGHTER

7-19. Manslaughter may be characterized as voluntary or involuntary. A death by voluntary manslaughter requires intent on the part of the accused. Involuntary manslaughter requires an unintentional but negligent act that results in the death of an individual.

Voluntary Manslaughter

7-20. The crime of voluntary manslaughter is committed when an individual, with intent to kill or inflict great bodily harm, unlawfully kills a human being in the heat of sudden passion. An unlawful killing, although done with an intent to kill or inflict great bodily harm, is characterized as voluntary manslaughter if committed in the heat of sudden passion caused by adequate provocation. Heat of passion may result from fear or rage. A person may be provoked to kill in the heat of sudden passion caused by the provocation. Manslaughter occurs under these circumstances when the killing is not necessary in defense of life or to prevent bodily harm, but a fatal blow is struck before self-control has returned. Although adequate provocation does not excuse the homicide, it does preclude conviction of murder.

7-21. The provocation must be adequate to excite uncontrollable passion in a reasonable person, and the act of killing must be committed under and because of the passion. If sufficient cooling time elapses between the provocation and the killing, as judged by the standard of a reasonable person, the offense is murder. The provocation must not be sought or induced as an excuse for killing or doing harm. Examples of acts which may constitute adequate provocation include the unlawful infliction of great bodily harm, unlawful imprisonment, and the sight by one spouse of an act of adultery committed by the other spouse.

Insulting or abusive words or gestures, a slight blow with the hand or fist, and trespass or other injury to property are not generally considered adequate provocation. The elements required for voluntary manslaughter are that—

- A certain named or described person is dead.
- The death resulted from the actor omission of the accused.
- The killing was unlawful.
- At the time of the killing, the accused had the intent to kill or inflict great bodily harm upon the person killed.

Involuntary Manslaughter

7-22. Involuntary manslaughter occurs when a death is caused by the culpable negligence of an individual; no intent to kill or cause bodily harm is required. Culpable negligence is a degree of carelessness greater than simple negligence. The basis of a charge of involuntary manslaughter is the negligent act or omission, which might foreseeably result in the death of another (when viewed in the light of human experience), even though death would not necessarily be a natural and probable consequence of the act or omission.

7-23. Acts which may amount to culpable negligence include negligently shooting in the direction of an inhabited house within range, pointing a pistol in jest at another and pulling the trigger taking reasonable precautions to determine that the pistol was empty, and carelessly leaving poisons or dangerous drugs where they may endanger life. The elements required for involuntary manslaughter are that—

- A certain named or described person is dead.
- The death resulted from the act or omission of the accused.
- The killing was unlawful.
- The act or omission of the accused constituted culpable negligence or occurred while the accused was perpetrating or attempting to perpetrate an offense directly affecting the person that was killed other than those crimes required for murder (burglary, sodomy, rape, rape of a child, aggravated sexual assault, aggravated sexual assault of a child, aggravated sexual contact, aggravated sexual abuse of a child, aggravated sexual contact with a child, robbery, or aggravated arson).

NEGLIGENT HOMICIDE

7-24. Negligent homicide is any unlawful homicide which is the result of simple negligence. Simple negligence is a lesser degree of carelessness than culpable negligence; it is the absence of due care. Simple negligence is an act or omission of a person which exhibits a lack of care for the safety of others, which a reasonably careful person would have exercised under the same or similar circumstances.

7-25. The intent to kill or injure is not required. The elements required for negligent homicide are that—

- A certain person is dead.
- Death resulted from the act or failure to act of the accused.
- The killing by the accused was unlawful.
- The act or failure to act by the accused which caused the death amounted to simple negligence.
- Under the circumstances, the conduct of the accused was to the prejudice of good order and discipline in the armed forces or was of a nature to bring discredit upon the armed forces.

DETERMINING THE MANNER OF DEATH

7-26. The initial objective of a death investigation is to determine the manner of death. The manner of death is generally classified as natural, accidental, suicide, homicide, or undetermined. If the death is determined to be a homicide, the objective of the investigation shifts to identifying and obtaining a conviction for the guilty party. The process and techniques involved in investigating any violent death are the same regardless of the environment in which they occur. The circumstances, conditions, and events before the death, the event surrounding the death itself, and those events following the death are investigated. Learning and tracing the events and actions involving a victim before their death, and the events and actions of possible suspects before and after the death, can provide information that enables investigators to determine the manner of death.

7-27. Accidental deaths and sometimes suicides may occur under circumstances that are not always readily apparent. Many of these deaths will look violent but will lack evidence supporting a criminal act. Circumstances and evidence may show a logical reason for the presence of a weapon at the scene of an accidental death. Or they may indicate death by suicide, regardless of what appears to be a dramatic and violent scene that initially appeared to support a struggle. Death investigations require us to look beyond the carnage and identify the indicators, such as prior suicide attempts or earlier written or oral statements of intent. Homicide is often identified by conditions and events leading to and following the death. A disturbed scene, forced entry, defense wounds (wounds to hands and forearms), no weapon at the scene, signs of a struggle or fight, or signs of attempted flight or surprise are all factors that can indicate a homicide.

7-28. Available evidence at a crime scene must be tempered with the fact that many scenes are not left undisturbed between the time the incident occurs and the first LE responder arrives. The absence of a weapon may be an indication of a homicide because an offender may have taken the weapon when he departed the scene; however, there are other possibilities. The weapon could have been moved by emergency medical responders, secreted by a family member, or removed by a witness before the scene was secured. Conversely, the presence of a weapon may simply be the murderer's attempt to stage the scene to appear as an accident or suicide. When determining a manner of death, it is very important that investigators consider all identifiable motives as well as opportunities and accessibility to the victim.

INVESTIGATIVE REQUIREMENTS

7-29. Criminal investigators shoulder great responsibility when they are presented with the investigation of the death of an individual. The death of an individual has significant and emotional impacts on the families and friends of the deceased. This is compounded when it occurs in a sudden, unexplained and/or violent manner. The impact of the investigation into a death can be profound; this is especially true when the manner of death is determined to be homicide. Investigations that are not performed thoroughly and with procedural precision can result in a failure to identify or convict the responsible party. General investigative techniques described earlier in the manual are applicable to death investigations; however, death investigations have unique aspects that must be considered.

NOTIFICATION, RESPONSE, AND ARRIVAL AT THE SCENE

7-30. On a military base, installation, or potentially a base camp, the initial LE responder to a death scene will likely be a military police patrol responding to the scene. Civilian LE agencies will be the first LE responders to incidents not on a base, installation, or a base camp. LE patrols and other first responders should follow normal protocol to render aid, identify and mitigate hazards, and secure the scene. Chapter 4 addresses initial response to crime scenes and associated responsibilities. The military police desk should be notified as soon as the military police patrol determines that a death has occurred or is likely to occur. The desk, in turn, will notify the USACIDC element of the death (or likely death) and all known information regarding the incident and scene. The military police desk will normally be contacted by local civilian LE agencies for military-related deaths requiring USACIDC response; the military police desk will immediately notify the appropriate USACIDC element. Chapter 4 discusses in detail initial response, crime scene security, and crime scene processing; this chapter will focus on those investigative aspects specific to death investigations.

7-31. Immediately upon notification the USACIDC SA responding to the scene should begin documenting details regarding the notification and known facts. The amount of information required during a criminal investigation, especially death or violent crime investigations, is large and can be overwhelming if not properly managed and tracked. Crime scene checklists can be very helpful to investigators to ensure that they capture all required information. See appendix F for a sample crime scene checklist.

7-32. Identify the incident command; if not on a military base or base camp, determine the lead criminal investigative agency. Obtain clearance or authorization to enter the crime scene from the site commander or the individual responsible for scene safety. Depending on the specifics of the scene, this may be LE personnel, fire department personnel, hazardous material teams, or others. Determine investigative, reporting, and other responsibilities of each agency. Determining the responsibilities of each agency at the scene is essential to synchronize and deconflict efforts of the various agencies. The investigator should identify specific responsibilities, share appropriate preliminary information, and establish the investigative requirements of each agency present at the scene.

7-33. Safety for all LE personnel is essential to the investigative process. Army LE personnel must also be vigilant for current and emerging hazards and ensure the safety of other persons at or near the scene including victims, witnesses, and other personnel. The risk of environmental and physical injury must be mitigated before processing the crime scene. Risks can include a present, armed, and hiding suspect; emotionally distraught family members and friends; collapsing structures; traffic; and environmental, chemical, and biological hazards, to include blood-borne pathogens and exposed medical paraphernalia. Ensure that the universal precautions described in chapter 2 are taken as appropriate. Primary actions required as the investigator arrives on scene are described in chapter 4 and include—

- Observing and assessing the scene.
- Ensuring the safety of personnel.
- Establishing and maintaining control of the scene.
- Documenting actions and observations at the scene.
- Transferring control of the scene from first responders to investigators.

7-34. Criminal investigators should participate in a scene briefing with first responders and any other organizations represented at the scene. The USACIDC SAs responding to the scene should obtain the following information from all first responders including LE personnel, fire, emergency medical personnel, hazardous material teams, EOD teams, social or child protective services, and others at the scene:

- Their response to, and observations of, the incident to include—
  - What activities transpired since their arrival, and what (if any) contaminants may have been introduced to the scene. Ensure that initial accounts of the incident are obtained from the first witnesses.
  - Physical characteristics and the layout of the crime scene or incident site including the location of persons and items within the crime scene.
  - The appearance and conditions of the crime scene upon arrival, such as smells, ice, liquids, movable furniture, weather, temperature, or personal items and whether the lights are on or off; the shades are up, down, open, or closed; or the doors and windows are open or closed.
  - Actions and behavior and the general demeanor of victims, subjects, witnesses, and bystanders.
  - Observed physical characteristics of the crime scene and the actions or behaviors of victims, subjects, or witnesses that seem odd or out of place. These observations can be helpful to LE investigators as they conduct the investigation.
- Identified victims, witnesses, and potential subjects.
- Identified hazards.
- Results of initial interviews and investigations conducted by responding military police patrols including personal information, statements, or comments from witnesses, victims, and suspects.
- Identified evidence, including evidence physically collected and protected, but still in place.
- Anything that was moved or disturbed before the investigator's arrival. Document any physical evidence that was moved or tampered with by persons at the scene. Document the original state of the evidence (as reported by the individual that moved the evidence) and the state it was in when observed by the investigator.
- Physical locations and established boundaries of secured crime scenes.
- All LE or other first responder actions taken at the scene.

PROCESSING THE SCENE

7-35. The basic techniques that are common and consistently applied when processing crime scenes and investigating criminal activity include crime scene assessment, documentation, and processing; collection and preservation of physical evidence; and collection of testimonial evidence. These techniques are described in earlier chapters of this manual. There are many requirements and considerations specific to death investigations. Most of these specific requirements pertain to the victim's body and the extraction of evidence from the body through both invasive and noninvasive means. Death investigations also require an understanding of the various causes of death and the evidence associated with those causes.

7-36. An initial walk-through of the scene is standard for the lead investigator to assess the scene, the scope of the investigation, specific processing requirements, and evidence collection priorities. The initial walk-through provides the investigator with an overview of the entire scene and the first opportunity to locate and view the body, identify valuable and/or fragile evidence, and determine initial investigative procedures providing for a systematic examination and documentation of the scene and the body. The initial walk-through is essential to minimize scene disturbance and prevent the loss and/or contamination of physical and fragile evidence. Stepping plates should be considered to avoid contamination and destruction of evidence; if not used; extreme care must be taken to prevent destruction or contamination of evidence. Chapter 4 describes the initial walk-through and subsequent actions taken by the lead investigator. In addition to the general techniques described in chapter 4, the investigator should locate and view the victim. Check for signs of life (and provide aid if needed) if not being attended by medical personnel or already pronounced dead. Once the victim is considered deceased by qualified medical personnel, move all personnel who are not directly involved with processing the scene outside the cordon designating the scene boundary. Only allow personnel working the scene to be inside the cordoned area.

DOCUMENTING AND EVALUATING THE SCENE

7-37. The process of documenting and evaluating the scene must be meticulous and timely. It includes photographing and sketching; writing descriptive documentation; collecting, preserving, and establishing chain of custody; and safeguarding property and evidence as described in chapter 2. It also includes documenting interviews or comments of witnesses at the scene as described in chapter 3.

Document the Scene

7-38. A written narrative of the investigator's findings should begin with initial observations and an initial walk-through of the scene. Photographs and sketches of the scene and specific evidence are completed and used to supplement the narrative documentation as described in chapter 4. Investigators should provide written scene documentation to serve as a permanent record that may be used to supplement and enhance photographic documentation and sketches, refresh recollections, and record observations. After photographic documentation, the investigator should record—

- The arrival time at the scene.
- The date, time, and location.
- The weather and lighting conditions at the scene.
- Any unusual smells or sounds.
- The condition and position of observed evidence to include—
  - Documenting items of evidence and their relationship to the body with any necessary measurements.
  - Describing and documenting (with any necessary measurements) blood and bodily fluid, including volume, patterns, spatter, and other characteristics.
- Assignments of support personnel.
- Any actions, observations, and departures from normal procedures (as well as the reason for the change in procedure such as traffic, safety concerns, or other factors).

Obtain Photographic Documentation

7-39. The entire scene, including specific evidence, should be photographed before moving or processing evidence. The photographic documentation of the scene creates a permanent historical record. Photographs provide detailed corroborating evidence that constructs a redundant system of documentation should questions arise concerning the report, sketches, witness statements, or the position of the evidence at the scene.

7-40. If evidence was moved before photography, it should be noted in the report. The body or other evidence should never be reintroduced or restaged into the scene in order to take photographs. The investigator should obtain detailed photographic documentation of the scene that provides both instant and permanent high-quality digital images. Before processing evidence the investigator should—

- Obtain an overall (wide-angle) view of the scene to spatially locate the specific scene to the surrounding area.
- Photograph specific areas of the scene to provide more detailed views of specific areas within the larger scene.
- Photograph the scene from different angles to provide various perspectives that may uncover additional evidence.
- Obtain some evidence establishing and close-up photographs with scales to document specific evidence.
- Obtain photographs even if the body or other evidence has been moved or removed.

Establish Probable Location of Injury or Illness

7-41. The location where the decedent is found may not be the actual location where the death occurred. It is imperative that the investigator attempts to determine the locations of any and all injuries or illnesses that may have contributed to the death. Physical evidence at any and all locations may be pertinent in establishing the cause, manner, and circumstances of a death.

7-42. The investigator should obtain detailed information regarding any and all probable locations associated with the individual's death. The investigator should—

- Document the location where the death was confirmed.
- Determine the location(s) from which the decedent was moved and how the body was moved.
- Identify and record any discrepancies in rigor mortis, livor mortis, and body temperature.
- Check the body, clothing, and scene for consistencies or inconsistencies of trace evidence and indicate the locations where any artifacts were found.
- Check for any drag marks on the body, clothes, and ground.
- Establish postinjury activity.
- Obtain any dispatch records, such as police and ambulance.
- Interview family members and associates, as needed.

Collect Evidence

7-43. The investigator should ensure that all property and evidence is identified, collected, preserved, documented, and safeguarded. Items of evidence with specific relevance to death investigations include—

- Illicit drugs and paraphernalia.
- Prescription medication.
- Over-the-counter medications.
- Money.
- Suicide notes.
- Personal valuables or property.
- Forms of identification.
- Physical signs of struggle or conflict including biological evidence (blood, hair, tissue, other bodily fluids, or bone fragments).

- Weapons (knives or firearms).
- Objects that could have been used as weapons (bats, tools, furniture, or other household items).
- Other materials such as ropes, ligatures, tape, or bindings.

Interview Witnesses

7-44. The documented comments of witnesses at the scene allow the investigator to obtain valuable information regarding the discovery of the body, witness corroboration, and terminal history. The investigator's report should include the source of the information, including specific statements and information provided by the witness. Chapter 3 provides detailed information regarding interviewing witnesses. While conducting interviews, the investigator should—

- Identify possible witnesses. Collect all available identifying data on witnesses, such as full name, address, date of birth, and work and home telephone numbers.
- Establish the relationship and/or association of the witness to the deceased.
- Establish the basis of the knowledge of the witness; for example, how does the witness have knowledge of the death?
- Note discrepancies from the scene briefing (challenge, explain, and verify statements).

Document and Evaluate the Body

7-45. Investigators must confirm that the deceased has been pronounced dead; appropriate medical personnel must pronounce the victim dead and provide a time of death. Once death has been determined, any on-going rescue and/or resuscitative efforts cease and medico-legal jurisdiction can be established. It is vital that a pronouncement of death occurs before a ME or coroner assumes any responsibilities. Identify and document the name of the individual who made the official determination of death (include the date and time of the determination).

7-46. The process of documenting and evaluating the body is intricate and demands the attention of the investigator to ensure that every detail is documented. Carefully document details of the body through detailed notes, sketches (with measurements), collection of physical evidence on the body, and photography.

7-47. The photographic documentation of the body at the scene creates a permanent record that preserves essential details of the position, appearance, and identity of the deceased. Photographs allow the sharing of information with other agencies investigating the death.

Conduct an External Body Examination

7-48. Conducting the external body examination provides the investigator with objective data regarding the single most important piece of evidence at the scene, the body. This documentation provides detailed information regarding the decedent's physical attributes; its relationship to the scene; and the possible cause, manner, and circumstances of death.

7-49. The investigator should properly and thoroughly document the body before it is moved. Documentation includes photographing and making detailed notes concerning the condition and location. Before moving the decedent, the investigator should do the following (without removing the decedent's clothing):

- Photograph the scene. Include the decedent as initially found and the surface beneath the body after the body has been removed.
- Photograph the decedent with and without measurements, as appropriate. Include a photograph of the decedent's face.
- Document the decedent's position with and without measurements, as appropriate.
- Document the decedent's physical characteristics including—
  - The presence or absence of clothing and personal effects.
  - The presence or absence of marks, scars, and tattoos.
  - The presence or absence of petechiae, injury, or trauma.

- Evidence of any treatment or resuscitative efforts.
- Document any foreign objects on or in the body (weapons, ligatures, tape, bindings, or other objects that may be relevant).
- Document the presence or absence of any other items immediately adjacent to the body.
- Determine the need for further evaluation or assistance of forensic specialists (such as pathologists and/or odontologists) based on the findings.

Preserve Any Evidence on the Body

7-50. The photographic and written documentation of evidence on the body allows the investigator to obtain a permanent historical record of that evidence. To maintain a chain of custody, evidence must be properly collected, preserved, and transported. All of the physical evidence visible on the body should be collected using approved techniques described in chapter 2; all evidence including blood and other bodily fluids that are present must be photographed and documented before collection and transport. Fragile evidence must also be collected and/or preserved to assist in the determination of the cause, manner, and circumstances of death. Once evidence on the body is recognized, the investigator should—

- Photograph the evidence.
- Document any blood or other bodily fluids (such as froth, purge, or substances from orifices) found on the body. Also, document the location and pattern before transporting the body.
- Collect a sample of blood and other bodily fluids for analysis.
- Place the decedent's hands and/or feet in unused paper bags and seal with tape or rubber bands.
- Collect trace evidence (such as blood, hair, and fibers) before transporting the body.

Establish the Identification of the Decedent

7-51. The establishment or confirmation of the decedent's identity is paramount to the death investigation. Proper identification allows notification of the next of kin, settlement of estates, resolution of criminal and civil litigation, and proper completion of the death certificate. The investigator should engage in a diligent effort to establish or confirm the decedent's identity. To establish the identity of the decedent, the investigator should document and/or use the following methods:

- Direct visual or photographic identification of the decedent, if visually recognizable.
- Scientific methods, such as fingerprint, dental, radiographic, and DNA comparisons.
- Circumstantial methods, such as (but not restricted to) personal effects; circumstances; physical characteristics; tattoos; and anthropologic data such as age, sex, stature, or ethnic background.

Document Postmortem Changes

7-52. Documenting postmortem changes to the body assists the investigator in explaining body appearance in the interval following death. Inconsistencies between postmortem changes and the body's location may indicate that the body was moved and can validate or invalidate witness statements or suspect alibis. In addition, postmortem changes to the body, when correlated with circumstantial information, can assist investigators in determining the approximate time of death. The investigator should document all postmortem changes relative to the decedent and the environment. The following post mortem changes should be documented:

- Livor mortis and its location and whether it is consistent with the position of the body. Note if it is fixed or still fluid.
- Rigor mortis and whether it is consistent with the position of the body. Note if it is in the large and/or small muscles.
- Stage of decomposition (include the degree of decomposition such as putrefaction, adipocere, mummification, or skeletonization).
- Insect and animal activity.
- Scene environment and temperature. Document the method used and the time of the measurement.

- A description of the body temperature (such as warm, cold, or frozen) and the measurement of body temperature. Document the method used and the time of the measurement.

Conduct a Scene Debriefing

7-53. Criminal investigators should participate in an interagency scene debriefing. The scene debriefing helps investigators from all participating agencies to establish postscene responsibilities and investigative priorities by sharing data regarding particular scene findings. It enables interagency communication, cooperation, and education. The scene debriefing provides each agency the opportunity to share information, identify special examination requirements, verify specific postscene responsibilities, and initiate interagency requests for support. During the debriefing the investigator should—

- Determine postscene responsibilities (identification, notification, press relations, and evidence transportation).
- Determine and/or identify the need for a specialist (such as crime laboratory technicians, social services professionals, entomologists, and safety professionals).
- Communicate with the pathologist about when the autopsy is schedule.
- Share investigative data, as required, to further the investigation.
- Communicate special requests to appropriate agencies being mindful of the necessity for confidentiality.

COMPLETION OF SCENE PROCESSING

7-54. Upon completing death scene processing requirements, measures must be taken to maintain control over and release the body, perform exit procedures (final walk-through), notify next of kin, and assist the family. These measures require thorough and accurate documentation.

Provide Security and Control of Remains

7-55. Ensuring the security of the body requires the investigator to supervise the labeling, packaging, and removal of the remains. An appropriate identification tag is placed on the body to preclude misidentification upon receipt at the examining agency. This function also includes safeguarding all potential physical evidence and/or property and clothing that remain on the body. The investigator should supervise and ensure the proper identification, inventory, and security of evidence or property and its packaging and removal from the scene. Before leaving the scene, the investigator should—

- Ensure that the body is protected from any further contamination or artifactual injury (if not, document it).
- Document removal of therapeutic and resuscitative equipment.
- Inventory and secure any property, clothing, and personal effects that are on the body. Remove them in a controlled environment with a witness present.
- Identify property and clothing to be retained as evidence (in a controlled environment).
- Place identification on the body and body bag.
- Ensure that the body is placed into the body bag.
- Ensure that the body is removed from the scene.
- Secure the transportation.

Maintain Control Over the Body

7-56. Maintaining control over the body allows the investigator to protect the chain of custody when the body is transported from the scene for autopsy, specimen collection, or storage. To maintain control over the body, the investigator should use a secure conveyance to transport the body. The investigator should—

- Arrange for secure transportation of the body to a medical or autopsy facility for further examination or storage.
- Document the transportation of the body.
- Coordinate and document procedures to be performed when the body is received at the facility.

Release Control of the Body

7-57. Before releasing control of the body to an authorized receiving agent or funeral director, it is necessary to determine the person responsible for certification of the death. Information to complete the death certificate includes demographic information and the date, time, and location of death. The investigator should obtain sufficient data to enable the completion of the death certificate and the release of control over the body. When releasing the body, the investigator should—

- Determine who will sign the death certificate (such as the individual's name or the agency).
- Confirm the date, time, and location of the death.
- Document and arrange with the authorized receiving agent to reconcile all death certificate information.
- Release the body to a funeral director or other authorized receiving agent.

Perform Final Walk-Through

7-58. Closeout procedures following death scene processing activities ensures that important evidence has been collected and the scene has been processed. When scene processing requirements are complete, the lead investigator should conduct a postinvestigative walk-through of the scene. The walk-through is conducted to ensure that the scene investigation is complete, no processing requirements have been overlooked, all equipment and materials are removed, and any remaining hazards are identified for appropriate resolution. Chapter 4 contains an in-depth discussion of crime scene processing requirements and techniques, including final walk-through requirements.

Proceed With Notification (Next of Kin or Chain of Command) and Family Assistance

7-59. Every reasonable effort should be made to notify the appropriate persons as soon as possible. Notification initiates closure for the family and disposition of the remains, and facilitates the collection of additional information relative to the case. The USACIDC SAs should ensure that the appropriate individuals are notified of the death and that all failed and successful attempts at notification are documented.

7-60. DODI 5505.10 requires that the USACIDC establish a Family Liaison Program to assist families of active duty service members who are victims of a noncombat death. The USACIDC will designate an investigator (trained to perform the specified duties) to provide information and appropriate assistance to the family of the deceased active duty member, in conjunction with, or in support of, other officials responsible for family notification and assistance. In cases where the USACIDC does not have jurisdiction to conduct an investigation into the cause and manner of the noncombat death of a Soldier, liaison with the investigating LE agency should be established to enable cooperation and assistance in obtaining relevant investigative reports and other information.

7-61. The USACIDC SA should provide the family with a timetable so they can make arrangements for the deceased. When the investigator is assisting the family, it is important to provide the family with the following information:

- Any requirements for an autopsy.
- Contacts for agencies and available support services (such as victim assistance, pathologist's or coroner's office, LE agencies, social services, or support groups).
- The approximate timeline for release of the body.
- The approximate timeline for the availability of autopsy and toxicology results.
- Available reports (include information regarding any costs).

DOCUMENT DECEDENT PROFILE INFORMATION

7-62. A critical element of the ongoing investigation includes documenting the decedent's profile information. Establishing and recording the decedent's profile information provides important background data that will help investigators and pathologists definitively identify the manner and cause of death. In cases characterized as homicide, the information can lead to identification, arrest, and conviction of individuals responsible for the death. This information will help determine if the death occurred by natural means or if criminal activity was involved.

DOCUMENT DISCOVERY HISTORY

7-63. Establishing a decedent profile includes documenting the circumstances surrounding the discovery. The basic profile will dictate subsequent levels of investigation, jurisdiction, and authority. The focus (breadth and depth) of further investigation is dependent on this information. The investigator should document the history surrounding the discovery of the victim including available witnesses and apparent circumstances leading to the death. The investigator should establish and document the discovery history by—

- Establishing and recording the name of the person or persons who discovered the body.
- Documenting the circumstances surrounding the discovery (who, what, where, when, and how).

DOCUMENT TERMINAL-EPISODE HISTORY

7-64. Preterminal circumstances play a significant role in determining the cause and manner of death. Documentation of medical intervention and/or procurement of antemortem specimens helps to establish the decedent's condition before death. The investigator should document known circumstances and medical intervention preceding death. The terminal-episode history should document—

- When, where, how, and by whom the decedent was last known to be alive.
- Activity and behavior of the victim before the death.
- Complaints and/or symptoms of physical distress before the death.
- The complete records of emergency medical response and associated activities.
- Copies of relevant medical records.

DOCUMENT THE DECEDENT'S MEDICAL AND BEHAVIORAL HISTORY

7-65. The majority of deaths that are referred to the ME or coroner are natural deaths. Establishing the decedent's medical history helps to focus the investigation. Documenting the decedent's medical signs or symptoms before death assists in determining the need for subsequent examinations. The relationship between disease and injury may play a role in the cause, manner, and circumstances of death. The investigator should obtain the decedent's past medical information through interviews and reviews of the written records including—

- Medical history including medications taken, alcohol and drug use, and family medical history from family members and witnesses.
- Information from the treating physicians and/or hospitals to confirm history and treatment.
- Physical characteristics and traits (such as left or right handed, missing appendages, or tattoos).

7-66. The decedent's behavioral health history can provide insight into his behavior or state of mind of. This insight may produce clues that will aid in establishing the cause, manner, and circumstances of the death. The investigator should obtain information pertaining to the decedent's mental health history from sources familiar with the decedent. The investigator should document—

- The decedent's behavioral health history to include hospitalizations and medications.
- Any history of suicidal ideations, gestures, and/or attempts.
- The names of the decedent's mental health professionals (such as psychiatrists, psychologists, and counselors).
- Any family mental health history.

DOCUMENT THE DECEDENT'S SOCIAL HISTORY

7-67. Friends and associates of the decedent help in developing the decedent's profile. The investigator should obtain social history information from sources familiar with the decedent. When collecting relevant social history information, the investigator should document the decedent's—

- Marital or domestic history.
- Family history (similar deaths or significant dates).
- Sexual history.
- Employment history.
- Financial history.
- Daily routines, habits, and activities.
- Relationships, friends, and associates.
- Religious, ethnic, or other pertinent information (such as religious objection to an autopsy).
- Educational background.
- Criminal history.

CAUSES OF DEATH

7-68. This section describes various causes of death commonly encountered by investigators. During investigations of deaths by various means, investigators must follow accepted techniques for processing the scene to ensure that all available evidence is identified, collected, preserved, and documented for analysis. This evidence can be used to make forensic identification at the crime laboratory in further identifying a suspect. All evidence collected must be supported by supporting photographs and scene sketches.

FIREARM-RELATED INJURIES

7-69. One of the most common causes of homicide and suicide is the discharge of a firearm. Accidental death from the discharge of a firearm is also possible. These violent deaths are often not witnessed. Unlike other forms of violent or unnatural death, firearm incidents will often leave trace evidence resulting from the firearm's discharge being deposited in, on, or near the victim's body. This evidence can be scientifically compared with the weapon believed to have been used in the incident and provide information about the circumstances surrounding the death.

7-70. In a medico-legal investigation of death by firearms, physical evidence is very important. Deciding the cause of the death and solving any associated criminal investigation often hinges on physical evidence directly resulting from the discharge of the firearm. The investigator must take every precaution to ensure that this evidence is not lost. For example, whenever possible GSR should be collected from the victim's hands at the scene; residue is easily lost when a body is moved and may not be retrievable after movement. If a body must be moved, bagging the hands can protect fragile GSR. If the residue cannot be collected at the scene, it may be collected at autopsy. GSR should also be collected from anyone who had access to the decedent at the time of the shooting.

7-71. A study of gunshot wounds can tell a lot about the type of gun involved. It can identify the distance the gun was from the body when it was fired as well as the ammunition, the range of fire, and the direction and angle of fire. See chapter 2 for more information.

Suicide

7-72. In the case of a self-inflicted gunshot wound, the victim generally holds the gun close to his body. Rifles and shotguns are sometimes fired by using a stick or string hooked to the trigger guard or by pushing the trigger with a toe. The chest and abdomen are often the target when a rifle or shotgun is used. The temple, mouth, chin, and chest are common sites for a suicide with a handgun. Suicide wounds are usually single, close-range, and/or contact wounds on a part of the body that is easily reachable by the decedent. Other evidence that may indicate suicide includes—

- **Exposed body parts.** An individual who commits suicide will often expose the part of their body that they plan to shoot. For example, an individual who commits suicide may open his shirt before placing the muzzle against his chest.
- **Burns on the hand.** An individual who commits suicide may guide the gun by holding the barrel with his nonfiring hand resulting in burns caused by the flame from the muzzle and breach. The individual's hand may also have singed hairs and powder residue. Finding GSR on a

victim's hands is not in itself conclusive proof of a suicide. It must be considered in light of other facts in the case. Residue can be present on a victim's hands because they were close to the muzzle blast of a shot fired by someone else.

- **Bloodstain pattern analysis.** The lack of void patterns in impact blood spatter may eliminate the possibility of someone else being present at the time of the shooting. Often, back spatter is found on the victim.
- **The bullet path.** Trajectory analysis using trajectory rods may be helpful in positioning the victim at the scene, which may allow an investigator to rule out homicide.

7-73. All crime scene findings must be analyzed in the context of the full facts and circumstances developed during the investigation. Suicide investigations must be thoroughly investigated and should seek to clearly and positively rule out homicide and accidental deaths.

Accidental Shootings

7-74. Most accidental shootings occur because of careless handling or unfamiliarity with a firearm. Perhaps the victim was on a hunting trip or was cleaning, loading, or otherwise working on the weapon. Children and young people often become accident victims by playing with guns. The condition of the weapon can suggest the manner of death. Conditions that may suggest an accidental discharge include—

- **Functional defects.** The gun may be defective, therefore making it unsafe to fire.
- **Unsafe or improper handling.** This is common with hunting accidents and with accidents involving children. Dropping a firearm can cause it to accidentally discharge.
- **Modifications.** The weapon may have been modified in some manner that rendered it unsafe.
- **Trace evidence.** Evidence may show that the trigger caught on something, discharging it accidentally.

7-75. Laboratory examinations will be of assistance in checking the functionality and safety mechanisms of the firearm. Accidental deaths are often witnessed and reported by either the victim or the shooter. Accidental gunshot deaths that are not witnessed may look like a suicide. Further investigation should be conducted to determine whether the death was a suicide or an accident.

Homicide

7-76. Most deaths that result from multiple or distant-range gunshot wounds are likely to be homicides. Most shootings involve acquaintances and result from interpersonal or domestic conflict. Stranger-on-stranger shootings are rarer.

7-77. In some cases, the location and number of empty shell cases at the scene may indicate the number of shots fired and the relative positions of the gun and the victim. Performing thorough bullet trajectory analysis using a trajectory kit and analyzing bloodstain patterns is essential to positioning victims and suspects, as well as garnering a more complete understanding of the entire incident. A gun may have been fired close to, or while resting on, a surface. A gun fired on or in close proximity to a surface will deposit GSR on the surface and may show the position from which the gun was fired; surfaces near the location of the weapon as well as the bullet hole must be considered for possible collection of GSR.

7-78. The surface areas of weapons, shells, and magazines should be checked for fingerprints, trace evidence, or DNA. When bullets or shell casings are recovered at a crime scene, the investigator must record the exact details to include—

- The location and condition of the bullet or casing.
- Irregularities in the size and shape of the bullet and the approximate angle of impact.
- Any other information that may help the laboratory examiner.
- The crime scene sketch documenting the point at which each discharged bullet or shell casing was found.

7-79. Bullets and other products from the discharge of a weapon have characteristic effects on skin and clothing. These effects can indicate the distance from which the gun was fired. At the laboratory, powder residue on evidence is tested chemically and microscopically. Bloodstains, hairs, fibers, and similar trace evidence are identified and compared. The laboratory and forensic pathologist may be able to determine from soot and powder on the clothing or skin the approximate range from which the bullet was fired. Laboratory examiners can conduct comparative analysis of markings on a bullet by the bore of the weapon and marks on the cartridge case by the firing pin, breach block, chamber extractor, or ejector to match a bullet or shell case to a specific weapon. In some cases, a lead bullet impacting on cloth may receive a patterned impression of the weave of the fabric; this may be useful in proving that a particular bullet passed through the victim.

Bullet Wounds

7-80. A bullet passing through a body makes a wound with traits that can be recognized (all wounds must be medically confirmed during an autopsy). The energy of a high-speed bullet destroys tissue as the shock waves of its impact radiate away from the bullet. This makes a track of permanently disrupted tissue wider than the bullet. External determination of bullet path is difficult if a body has started to decompose or has been damaged. The uneven surface and tumbling action of ricocheting bullets may make ragged punctures. Bullets passing across a body can cut gashes that may look like knife wounds.

7-81. In some cases, inspecting marks and defects on clothing may be the best way to determine the direction of the flight of the bullet. An autopsy examination of the track of the bullet may confirm the path of travel by identifying pieces of cloth, metal, and bone fragments carried by the bullet through the wound. The nature of bone damage may indicate the travel path of the bullet. The wounds associated with bullets are—

- Entrance wounds.
- Contact wounds.
- Intermediate-range wounds.
- Distant wounds.
- Exit wounds.

Entrance Wounds

7-82. Entrance wounds are commonly round holes showing minor bleeding. An investigator can usually differentiate entry wounds from exit wounds; however, sometimes the distinction is hard to make. Often, the skin is stretched by the impact of the bullet. This makes the hole somewhat smaller than the bullet. Sometimes a narrow ring (called an abrasion ring) around the entrance shows grayish soiling from carbon and oils on the bullet and a reddish-brown abrasion collar caused by the impact of the bullet. Some bullet entry wounds are inconspicuous or hidden. Small-caliber bullets often cause such wounds. They may be hidden under clothing, in hair, in body folds or openings, or behind closed eyelids.

7-83. Identifying entrance wounds does not always correlate with the number of shots fired into the body. A single bullet can sometimes account for a number of entry wounds by piercing the body more than once. For example, a bullet may go through an arm before entering the torso. A bullet striking a bony surface at an angle may split into two or more projectiles. The multiple projectiles can cause many exit and reentry holes. Ricocheting bullet pieces may also cause several wounds from a single bullet. One of the functions of pathologists is to trace the path of the bullet and to determine if multiple wounds can be attributed to the same bullet.

Contact Wounds

7-84. Contact wounds are wounds resulting from the barrel of the weapon touching the victim at the time it was discharged. Contact wounds are categorized as either hard contact or loose contact. In a hard contact the gases exiting the muzzle all enter the wound; this may leave a pattern impression in the shape of the weapon's muzzle. In a loose contact some of the gases escape along the surface of the skin and do not enter the body. This causes searing or burning of skin outside the wound, resulting in a more irregular shape; a partial muzzle impression may be present. Entrance wounds may leave a collar or ring; however, these collars or rings may be obscured and hard to identify in contact wounds and in many intermediate wounds. Contact wounds will have little or no stippling (small burns and abrasions produced by the impact of unburned powder grains on the skin) depending on the pressure of the contact.

7-85. The explosive force of the large volume of gases from the weapon discharge tears skin and tissue around the bullet hole, producing ragged defects radiating from the hole called stellate tearing (a star-like wound caused by the lateral movement of gasses on the skin when a shot is fired from a firearm in contact with the skin). The edges of the contact wound and the bullet track may be burned; if the gun is fired through clothing, the surrounding fabric may also burn. The gas and smoke may cause a sooty, grimy halo around the wound. Most of the unburned powder and other explosive products are blown right into the bullet track.

7-86. The size of a contact wound depends on several factors including the caliber of the firearm and the location of the contact. A contact wound made when exploding gases are received and dissipated by a large body cavity (such as the chest) may not be large or irregular. On the other hand, a contact wound to the head made by a high-powered rifle may show massive bursting fractures of the skull from the explosive effect of gas forced into the skull where it has no chance to expand. Contact wounds, especially those on bony surfaces are likely to be large, ragged wounds. Contact wounds from small-caliber guns like a .25- or .22-caliber pistol tend to be smaller and less devastating than wounds from larger caliber weapons. This is because the discharge from small-caliber weapons may not be forceful enough to disrupt the surrounding tissues.

Intermediate-Range Wounds

7-87. Intermediate-range wounds occur when the muzzle of the weapon is held away from the body at the time of discharge, but close enough to deposit GSR and produce marks on the victim. The gun is fired close enough that the powder grains expelled produce "powder tattooing" or stippling of exposed skin; this stippling cannot be wiped away. Powder tattoo marks are produced by the impact of unburned powder grains on the skin, resulting in punctured abrasions. The wounds are often rounded, with minor splitting around the edges. Recognizing powder marks and residues can help distinguish entrance wounds from exit wounds. Intermediate-range wounds may not produce stippling if there is an object or material (such as clothing or papers that the victim was holding) between the muzzle and the skin; this will mimic a distant gunshot wound. In these cases, clothing or other objects between the weapon and the skin should be checked for GSR.

7-88. Powder residues and other discharge products are projected onto the victim in ample amounts when a gun is fired within 2 feet of the target. Their pattern and composition help determine the range of fire and the kind of ammunition used. The burned and tattooed area becomes larger and more dispersed as the distance between the weapon and the victim increases. Laboratory examiners can conduct precise range-of-fire tests using the questioned weapon and the same type of ammunition.

7-89. If the burned, tattooed, and abraded areas form a concentric-symmetric margin around the entry wound, the bullet probably struck the body at a right angle. A bullet striking at an angle will produce marginal bruising and abrasions at the point where the bullet first meets the surface. A bullet striking at an extreme angle may cause a shallow-furrowed wound, and powder residues will seem to spread away from the bullet hole in an uneven V-shape. The point of the V will point toward the weapon. The size of the ammunition and the type of powder also affect the nature and extent of powder residues. For example, a handgun fired at a distance of 3 to 4 feet (or further) from the victim may not produce stippling and bruising on a victim.

Distant Wounds

7-90. Distant wounds are made by muzzles held more than 48 inches from the victim. The wounds are generally round holes with a circular ring or collar caused by tissue propelling backwards and overstretching; the projectile does not abrade the skin as previously believed. There are no burns or powder tattooing. Small-caliber contact, intermediate-range wounds, and other wounds over soft-tissue areas may appear to be long-range wounds on initial observation. The characterization of these wounds can be distinguished during autopsy through examination of tissues in the bullet track and the presence of powder residues. Be aware that intermediate wounds can mimic distant wounds if there was material or an object between the weapon and the victim.

Exit Wounds

7-91. Exit wounds generally produce more damage than entrance wounds. They are ragged and rough in shape and are usually larger than the bullet. Tissues compress in front of the bullet and burst when the bullet breaks through and exits the body. The bullet is often fragmented, deformed, and tumbled by impact. This fragmentation, deformation, and tumbling causes more destruction.

7-92. A bullet may be found protruding from the skin or loose in a victim's clothing. It may also be found under the skin where it has caused swelling or bruising. If a bullet is lodged in a body, depending on its location, it may be retrieved as evidence or left if removing it may cause more damage. This decision should be made by medical personnel.

Shotgun Pellet Wounds

7-93. Shotgun wounds are very different from wounds caused by other firearms. The destructive force of a shotgun blast at close range is significant. If the wound is to the head, the shape of the head may be greatly changed, and large sections of the head or face may be destroyed. Close-range wounds of the trunk and abdomen may cause extreme trauma causing internal organs to be exposed or protrude from the body. Close-range shotgun blasts can also cause portions of the body to be detached.

7-94. When a shotgun is fired from a distance of about 10 feet or less, the shot strikes as a fairly compact mass. It produces a large central, circular hole with very ragged edges caused by the force of many single and overlapping punctures made by the shotgun pellets. This is known as the cookie-cutter effect. Scattered around the large central hole are smaller holes made by individual shot beginning to disperse in flight. When a shotgun is fired at close range, the wounds are grossly burned and tattooed. As the distance increases between the weapon and the victim, the wound shows less tattooing and no burning. Beyond 10 feet, the shot spreads in flight and strikes the body in a more scattered grouping so that no central hole occurs.

7-95. The length of the shotgun barrel, the choke, and the type of ammunition also influence the dispersion of the shot and the scattered pattern of the wound. A shorter barrel allows quicker spread. The dispersion may be cut if the shotgun is choke-bored. The slightly narrowed muzzle of a choke-bored shotgun focuses the shot and delays its dispersion. Bird shot, even when fired at close range, usually does not go through the trunk or abdomen of an adult. But when the shot load goes through a thinner portion of the body like the neck, limb, or shoulder, it makes large exit wounds. Sometimes small, ragged exit wounds are made when only some of the bird shot exits the body. At close range, buckshot (having a greater size, weight, and energy) causes wounds similar to those made by large bullets. A general rule of thumb in shotgun spread is that for every 1 yard of distance, the wound will grow by 1 inch in diameter. This can only be verified through specific firearms testing at the crime laboratory.

7-96. Unlike comparative analysis on rifled bullet projectiles, shotgun pellets cannot be linked to a certain gun by ballistics markings. However, the size of shot may be learned from printed material on the top wad or by marks left in the wadding. It can also be learned from printed information in the shell casing. The gauge of a shotgun can be determined by comparing the diameter of the wad with other wads. If the wadding has not struck an intervening zone, it can generally be found within 50 feet of where the gun was fired. If the gun is fired within 10 feet of the victim, the wadding is often carried into the body and strikes the body with the shot.

ASPHYXIA

7-97. When the body is deprived of oxygen, asphyxia occurs. Death from asphyxia may be caused by compression of the chest, occlusion (blockage) of the airway by food or foreign objects, or occlusion of the blood vessels to and from the neck. Other forms of asphyxia include displacement or inhibition of available oxygen with chemicals such as cyanide, carbon monoxide, and carbon dioxide.

Strangulation

7-98. Strangulation is asphyxiation from compression of either the jugular vein or the carotid artery in the neck, or both. Many times, when strangulation occurs, the trachea is not obstructed. Strangulation can be done manually or with a ligature like a binder, a rope, or a necktie. Hard blows to the neck may also cause a "stunning" feeling and temporary loss of blood flow.

7-99. Manual strangulation is normally a homicide as it requires continual pressure after the victim loses consciousness. In manual strangulation, the damage caused by the assailant's hands as well as the victim's attempt to relieve the assailant's pressure often causes hemorrhaging to the victim's neck and throat. This type of strangulation may result in a fracture of the hyoid bone, a U-shaped bone at the base of the tongue, and injury to nearby soft tissue.

7-100. Ligature strangulation may be homicidal, accidental and, in rare cases, suicide. Ligature strangulation by suicide would require a mechanism that would hold the ligature in place after the victim lost consciousness. A ligature is often made from something handy at the scene, such as pajamas, neckties, belts, electrical cords, and ladies' stockings. Strangulation by a garrote made of rope or wire can be used in homicidal strangulation but is actually rare. If the ligature is not found at the scene, close inspection of the marks left on the skin may provide enough information to determine what type of ligature was used. In the event the ligature is in place at the scene, it should be left in place until autopsy where it can be removed and examined. When removing the ligature, it should be separated opposite the knot (leaving the knot intact). When investigating strangulation, search the scene and the victim for signs of struggle and defensive wounds, respectively.

Hanging

7-101. Hanging is asphyxiation by strangulation using a line of rope, cord, or similar material to work against the hanging weight of the body. Hanging is most often suicidal; but it can sometimes be accidental. Homicidal hangings are rare, but still occur such as in the case of lynching. A person does not have to be fully suspended to die from hanging, as the weight only has to be sufficient to occlude the jugular or carotid, or both. At the scene of a hanging, an investigator should—

- Inspect the scene for signs of a struggle or defense wounds. Bear in mind that an unconscious victim in the throes of dying may convulse, knocking over items in the immediate area.
- Leave the knot tied when removing the body from the scene. The knot holding the rope at both ends should be cut opposite the knot, as should the knot around the neck. The knot should not be untied until it can be photographed and examined for trace evidence.
- Make a careful inspection of the groove around the neck. A close look at the edges of the groove will often show black and blue marks from minute bleeding. Ruptured blood vessels in the skin indicate that the victim was alive at the time of the hanging. Lack of these marks does not conclusively indicate that the victim was dead at the time of hanging; this should be evaluated along with other evidence. Hangings generally produce a characteristic "V" shape on the neck of the victim. The "V" shaped mark is formed by the ligature as it proceeds up to the point of suspension. Bruising is not necessarily greater in one particular area of the mark.

7-102. Accidental hanging may occur from autoerotic sexual acts using restraints like ropes, cords, chains, and handcuffs. The victim, trying to reach sexual excitation, uses these items to restrain his hands, arms, or legs and neck. When strain on the neck causes unconsciousness or when the victim loses balance during the act, an accident results. The victim is unable to release himself because of the binding on his hands, arms, and legs. Potential indications of an accidental hanging related to sexual activity include—

- A victim being found nude or partially nude.
- Cross dressing.
- A victim suspended before a mirror.
- A victim suspended in an unusual manner.
- The presence of erotic material and evidence of masturbation.
- The use of padding between the neck and the ligature.
- Evidence of repetition, such as minor damage or wear signs on the support mechanism.

7-103. Other accidental hangings often involve infants and young children. Infants can get caught in restraining devices, or they can get their clothing caught on toys or common household objects. An accidental death can occur where a child is wrapped and caught in a common household item, such as a window blind or a telephone cord. Children may also get their heads caught between crib or fence slots. Small children lack the strength or agility to free themselves, and they succumb to their own body weight and cease breathing. These are fairly common forms of accidental death but are rarely forms of homicide.

Drowning

7-104.   Drowning is asphyxiation from water or liquid being inhaled into the airways, blocking the passage of air to the lungs. When an individual drowns, water inhaled into the windpipe causes violent choking. The choking irritates the mucous membranes of the airways causing pulmonary edema; this appears as a large amount of sticky mucus. The mucus, mixed with the water and agitated by violent attempts to breathe, turns into thick, sticky foam that fills the windpipe. Drowning is a diagnosis of exclusion. Anybody left in the water long enough will eventually have water in the lungs. Investigators and MEs must eliminate all other causes of death before drowning is confirmed.

7-105.   Most drowning occurs when the victim submerges in a body of water. The victim submerges and inhaling water into the lungs. The victim may stay submerged the first time he goes under, or he may go under and surface many times until he can no longer struggle to the surface. The loss of consciousness often occurs quickly. Because the human body is denser than water, when unconsciousness occurs, the victim sinks and tends to lie at the bottom with his head down. The rate at which sinking occurs varies depending on body type and the amount of water inhaled. Breathing may continue briefly with varying amounts of water inhaled. The heart may beat briefly after breathing stops. Death by asphyxia occurs within a few minutes. Absent strong currents, a body can sink quickly. It often comes to rest at a point close to where it was last seen on the surface. A small number of "drowning" deaths among swimmers are actually caused by their hearts stopping from the shock of submersion.

7-106.   Rigor mortis may start earlier in drowning deaths because of violent muscular struggle. Postmortem lividity occurs but is often light red in color and is noted mostly in the head and upper body as the body tends to sink headfirst. The foam that forms in the airway, called pulmonary edema, may exude from the mouth and nose. Often, the victim's hands will be grasping gravel, mud, or grass. The hands and fingertips may be scratched from violent grasping efforts. The victim's palms may have cuts caused by their fingernails during the violent clenching motion of the hands. These factors are good circumstantial signs that the victim was alive when he entered the water.

7-107.   After a few hours, depending on the temperature and movement of the water, postmortem changes peculiar to submersion begin to occur. The skin, especially on the hands and feet, becomes bleached and waterlogged (commonly referred to "washerwoman's hands"). The palms develop a wrinkled condition. The constant churning of water currents or long periods of submersion may cause maceration; this is the wearing away of skin and flesh, especially of the hands and feet. Mutilation may occur from propellers of boats or contact with rocks, submerged trees, or other debris. This causes the appearance of postmortem dismemberment. Parts of the body, most notably the face, may be eaten by marine life.

7-108.   As bacteria mounts in the body, putrefaction begins. As putrefaction progresses, gases build up in the tissues, organs, and body cavities. The body becomes distended with gas. This makes the white foam (pulmonary edema) in the airway come out of the nose and mouth. As the gases build up, the body becomes buoyant. Warm water speeds putrefaction and cold water slows it. In warm water, buoyancy may occur in a couple of days. In winter, the action may be slowed for weeks or until spring. As putrefaction advances, the skin loosens from the tissues. Sections of skin, especially hands, feet, and scalp may fall from the body.

7-109.   Unless a body is heavily weighted down or firmly caught on underwater debris, buoyancy will eventually cause it to rise to the top and float. If a body is prevented from rising, the gases eventually escape; this eliminates buoyancy and the body may not surface. When a body surfaces and is exposed to the air, decomposition proceeds at a much faster rate.

7-110.   Prolonged submersion and decaying may dim or destroy the external signs of asphyxia. Signs of violence or another cause of death may also be lost. Medical evidence may show signs of asphyxia like foam in the airways and an enlarged heart. It may also show changes in the blood from water absorbed during drowning. Algae and other substances from water may be found in the stomach or airways.

7-111. Suicidal drowning in places like bathtubs is hard to distinguish from accidents unless a reason is suggested or some other means of suicide was also attempted. Check for marks that may show suicidal intent. A weighted body strongly suggests homicide; however, persons who commit suicide may weight their bodies to speed drowning and slow recovery. Weighted bodies should be inspected carefully for injuries that suggest homicide. It should be determined if the binding and weighting method was used by the victim. An assessment for self-inflicted injuries, such as cut wrists or other sign of suicide, should also be made. Homicidal drowning is rare. Unless accompanied by signs of homicidal violence or other such conditions, the autopsy shows only signs of asphyxia by drowning. There have been times when submerged bodies have shown no signs of violence but, after the body dried, bruise marks and small abrasions appeared that could not be seen when wet.

ELECTRIC SHOCKS

7-112. Electric current, even at low voltage, can cause the heart to defibrillate, while constant current is more likely to stop the action of the heart, and the brain (deprived of oxygen) ceases to function. The effect of electric shock on a person depends on many things including the individual's health, location, and the amount of moisture present (water is a good conductor of electricity). Other factors include the length and intensity of exposure.

7-113. Electric shocks often leave marks, although it is possible for a body not to show outer or inner damage. Usually, electrical shocks leave entrance and exit wounds on the body. Entrance wounds are at the point at contact, while the exit will normally be located at the lowest point of contact as the electricity seeks to ground itself. The wounds have a gray or white puckered look. High voltage exposure leaves a more pronounced mark at the point of contact when direct contact with an electrical source occurs. This contact literally burns the skin and may also fracture the bones underneath. High voltage contact does not require direct contact.

7-114. Deaths from electric shock are most often accidental. Homicide by electrocution is rare, but it is possible. When investigating a death by electric shock, an investigator must check the weather conditions, electric appliances that the victim may have been using, and the victim's location and activity at the time of death to determine if the death was accidental; consultation with an expert, such as a master electrician or electrical engineer, is advised to determine the possibility and/or likelihood of accidental shock based on physical evidence at the scene.

7-115. One form of electric shock is lightning strikes. Although lightning deaths are not common and only occur in about 40 percent of those struck, the evidence is apparent. Evidence of a lightning strike includes the presence of weather conditions conducive to lightning and the victim's appearance and location. Burn marks around metal such as jewelry, inside running shoes, or zippers may be observed. Also, "ferning" may be observable; this is the appearance of marks on the skin which resemble a fern leaf.

SHARP-FORCE INJURIES

7-116. The vital functions of the body can be fatally impaired by injuries from sharp, edged instruments. Deaths or injuries from stabbing, cutting, and chopping are hard to evaluate without extensive experience. The type of wound and the victim's personal history can help decide if death was an accident, a suicide, or a homicide.

Stabbing

7-117. A stab is a sharp-force injury that is deeper than it is long. Any object with a fairly sharp point may be used to produce stab wounds. Knives, scissors, ice picks, triangular files, or hatpins can all make stab wounds. Most stab wounds involve an object that is inserted and then removed from the body. It may or may not be left at the scene. Sometimes stab wounds look like other kinds of wounds. If examination fails to show a definitive sign of stabbing, the wound may have been made in some other way. X-rays may help to locate an unsuspected bullet or piece of a weapon, such as a knife or stiletto that may be inside the body.

7-118. The shape of the wound depends on the direction from which the weapon penetrates and the shape of the weapon. It also depends on the movement of the weapon while in the wound. The weapon is often turned slightly as it is withdrawn; this causes a wound that has a notch in one side. Pierced bony surfaces like the skull, the sternum, or the spine often show the shape of the part of the weapon that passed through the bone. Sometimes weapons break off or are left in the bone. The blade or portions of it may project from the inner part of the bone. If a blade is broken in a fatal stab wound, the part of the bone with the blade in it may be removed at the autopsy. It can be used to support the main elements of the crime, especially if the matching part of the weapon could be located and preserved as evidence.

7-119.   The shape of a fatal stab wound, fixed during an autopsy, may give a clue to the type of weapon used, such as serrated, or double- or single-edged. The track of a weapon may be very clear in fleshy areas. However, when a weapon penetrates inner organs, its track may not be accurate. Inner organs change in shape and position after death and when a body is moved. Any attempt to judge the size of the sharp-force instrument from the wounds is unreliable due to the elastic nature of skin, compression of the tissues, and the amount of "cutting" imparted to the specific injury. A strong stabbing force against a soft area like the stomach can depress the area, making the wound deeper than the true length of the weapon. Likewise, a longer blade may not penetrate its full length, making the path of the wound shorter than the blade.

7-120.   It is difficult to determine if a wound was made before or after death. A good inspection of the wound made before the body is moved is very important. If the wound was made before death, there should be evidence of vital reactions such as blood clotting, swelling, wound healing, or infection.

7-121.   Accidental stab wound deaths are rare. When they do occur, the circumstances, such as falling through a plate glass window, are apparent. Other stabbing accidents may occur when victims falls or are thrust onto sharp, pointed surfaces of tools, equipment, building materials, or vehicles.

7-122.   Suicidal persons most frequently stab themselves in the chest over the heart; however, the throat and wrists are other common locations for suicidal stab wounds. Suicidal stab wounds may be made on any area of the body that can easily be reached. Like suicidal shootings, the victim will often open up clothing or uncover the selected stab area. The suicidal person may jab the weapon into his chest a number of times, and the wounds may vary in depth. Many of them may barely penetrate the chest. These types of stab wounds are characterized as hesitation wounds and are made as the victim works up nerve to inflict a fatal injury. Suicidal persons sometimes stab themselves repeatedly in different directions, through the same wound, without completely withdrawing the weapon. This causes more stab tracks than outer wounds. Hesitation cuts on the wrist or thighs are good signs of the suicidal intent of a victim. Investigators must look at the behavioral history of the victim to support suicide as a manner of death.

7-123.   Most fatal stab wounds are attributed to homicide. Homicidal stab wounds often appear on the back, neck, and upper chest. When many wounds are present on different parts of the body, and parts of the body that would not be accessible by the victim, homicide is strongly indicated. Several stab wounds to the breasts and genitals are suggestive of a sex-related homicide. Defensive-type wounds on the hands and arms and wounds to the back or other areas not easily reached by the victim also hint of homicide. A homicidal stab wound often penetrates a victim's clothing. For this reason, investigators must exercise special care when removing and checking the victim's clothing.

Incision

7-124.   An incision is a sharp-force injury that is longer than it is deep. Incisions are made when the sharp edge of an object is pressed to and drawn over the surface of the body. Knives and razors account for almost all incised wounds. Incisions, even though they are shallow, can cause fatal hemorrhaging and infection.

7-125.   Homicidal cuttings are usually deep, clean cuts without hesitation marks. The wounds may be on various parts of the body, particularly if the assailant attacked in a fit of rage. Cuts produced during an assault are often made on exposed surfaces like the head, neck, and arms. Where many cuts are involved, particularly when they are located on the palms of the hands or the back of the forearms, they are considered defensive injuries and may indicate a homicidal attack. Homicide attacks do not always involve excessive injury and may be just a single, deep cut on the side of the face or neck. Sometimes, when a victim tries to dodge slashes, there are small, shallow cuts near larger wounds. These defensive wounds may be confused with suicidal hesitation cuts.

7-126. Suicidal cuts are often many parallel, overlapping incisions of varying length and depth. Many times they have a lot of smaller, shallow hesitation cuts on the lead edge of the injured area. Fairly shallow incisions to the throat may still result in fatality due to the number of blood vessels close to the surface of the neck. Other common areas for self-inflicted cuts are the groin, thighs, ankles, knees, and the inside of the forearm at the elbow. Suicidal cuts on the limbs are often not fatal but are frequently found on individuals who have killed themselves some other way. They support a judgment of death by suicide.

7-127. Accidental incised wounds are rarely fatal. They occur most often, like with stabbings, from broken glass or contact with moving machinery or sharp tools. Most of the time, the situation clearly shows the accidental nature of the injury.

Chopping

7-128. A chopping wound is a deep wound often involving fractures of bone. The wound is usually made with a heavy instrument such as a cleaver, a machete, a hatchet, or an ax. The shape and size of chopping wounds often resemble the shape and size of the weapon. Because of this, a pathologist may be able to determine the type of weapon that was used by examining the depth, width, and appearance of the wound and the amount of tissue damage. This may enable investigators to link the injuries to a suspected weapon. It may even be possible to take toolmark impressions of the weapon from bone or cartilage.

7-129. Death from chopping wounds may come from shock, hemorrhaging, or the interruption of vital bodily functions. Most chopping wounds are homicidal. They are usually made on the head, neck, shoulders, and arms, and there may be multiple injuries. Defensive wounds may include total or partial loss of fingers, hands, or arms. Fatal accidental chop wounds sometimes occur from propeller blades of fans, boats, or planes. Suicide by chopping is rare.

BLUNT-FORCE INJURIES

7-130. Blunt-force injuries result in damage to the skin and tissues under the skin. The four types of blunt force injuries are—

- Abrasions or scrapes.
- Avulsions or forcible tearing away of a body part.
- Contusions or bruises.
- Lacerations or cuts.

7-131. Abrasions are surface injuries to the outer layer of the skin at the point of impact. An abrasion may duplicate the surface appearance of the impacting object. For example, it may look like a threaded pipe or the treads of an automobile tire. Abrasions normally are caused by direct violence from hands, blows of a weapon, or collision with a vehicle. They may also be caused when a body falls and strikes a surface.

7-132. Avulsion injuries occur when a part of the body is forcible ripped or torn away. These are commonly encountered in vehicle accidents but can occur any time sufficient blunt force is applied. Common avulsion injuries involve ears, eyelids, and teeth.

7-133. A contusion is a hematoma or bruising of tissue in which capillaries and sometimes venules are damaged by an impact trauma. The contusion may appear at the point of impact, or it may appear in a peripheral area to the impact site depending on the area on the body where the victim is struck, the force that is used, the angle, and the individual's response. It is not possible to give a precise estimate of the age of the contusion. Blood will often travel under the skin for a distance (generally associated with gravity) and then appear. Bruises may also be larger or smaller than the object used to inflict an injury. The size of a bruise may indicate the degree of violence, but not always. Females tend to bruise easier than males. A light blow to soft tissues like the eyelid or genitalia may cause extensive bruising, while a heavy blow to dense, fixed tissue like the scalp may cause only mild bruising. Bruises occur more easily on individuals that are—

- Very young.
- Elderly.
- Overweight.

- Soft-skinned.
- Poorly conditioned.
- Sickly.

7-134. Lacerations are caused by a shearing force or violent depression to the skin that tears or splits tissues. Blows from fists, sticks, or hammers may cause lacerations. They may also occur from the impact of a motor vehicle or as a result of a fall. Lacerations, characteristically, are bruised and ragged. The tissues are unevenly divided and the blood vessels and nerves are crushed and torn. The crushed ends of vessels may show only slight bleeding. Lacerations may contain foreign material like soil or glass from the impacting object. Lacerations of the scalp, face, eyebrow, or skin near bone have a linear splitting effect. These may be hard to tell from cuts. Normally, it is difficult to differentiate between lacerations made at the time of death and those made shortly after death. The distinction depends on the presence or absence of vital reactions like bleeding and bruising in the wound.

7-135. Homicidal deaths may occur from either generalized or localized blunt force. Victims may be struck with fists, hit with blunt objects, thrown from heights, or crushed with heavy objects. Often deaths involving generalized blunt-force injuries are the result of impact with a vehicle (as either a passenger or a pedestrian). For hit-and-run accidents involving pedestrians, the investigator must be able to link the vehicle to the victim by trace evidence left at the scene or found on the persons or vehicles involved.

7-136. Suicidal deaths from blunt force usually involve generalized blunt force. The victim jumps from a high place or in front of a moving vehicle. Sometimes a suicidal person may ram his head into a wall or in some other way create enough impact or crushing force to cause fatal injuries. Accidental deaths from blunt force may be from falls, traffic accidents, or machinery incidents resulting in a blow to the body.

Vehicle Trauma

7-137. If circumstances suggest a hit-and-run collision or a vehicular homicide, investigators must initiate an immediate search and apprehension plan. These plans may include setting up coordinated military police patrol activities including checkpoints and roadblocks; ingress and egress points on military bases or base camps should be alerted and appropriate checks conducted. Increased patrolling of parking lots, service stations, residential parking areas, motels, taverns, bar rooms, garages, and body repair shops may be initiated. If a military vehicle could be involved, it should include alerting and checking motor pools. If the suspect vehicle is believed to have moved off of a military base or base camp, coordination with civilian LE agencies may be conducted.

7-138. Investigations into incidents involving vehicular deaths are a coordinated effort with TMCIs. The criminal investigator will assume the lead in the investigation; the TMCI supports by conducting a thorough collision investigation. The investigators must synchronize and coordinate their investigative activities to ensure that all relevant evidence is identified, collected, preserved, and documented. Chapter 13 discusses collision investigations. At the scene, the investigators—

- Look for evidence supporting the crime and linking the vehicle and victim.
- Check for and document all skid marks to help determine the speed of the vehicle, the alertness of the driver, and verification of the accuracy of the driver's and witnesses' statements. Photograph all skid marks with and without a measuring device.
- Collect samples of dirt from under the vehicle to link it to the point of impact and use for future comparison.
- Photograph and cast tire tracks before they are disturbed.
- Record the bumper height measurements to match them to the victim's injuries. This may help determine if the vehicle at the time of impact was braking, maintaining its speed, or increasing its speed.
- Collect material from the scene and from the victim or the victim's vehicle that may have come from the offender's vehicle including—
  - Broken glass.
  - Vehicle parts.
  - Trim.

- Paint chips.
- Other evidence that may identify the suspect's vehicle type and that may be compared with a suspect's vehicle. The laboratory may be able to recover glass fragments, paint chips, or other material from a victim's (pedestrian's) clothing that originated from the suspect vehicle.
  - Seize trace evidence from the victim like blood, body tissue, hairs, and textile fragments.
  - Check vehicles suspected of having been involved for signs of impact and traces of the victim or victim's clothing.

7-139.   The victim's clothing often leaves patterned rub marks in hit-and-run collisions. The pattern may show in the chassis paint. It may also show on grease and mud on the undercarriage. Likewise, hand, finger, and even lip prints of the victim may be left on the vehicle. Hair, tissue, bone fragments, fabric, fibers, and other trace evidence of the victim may be stuck to the suspect's vehicle. Blood of the victim, often found on the undercarriage, must be typed with a sample from the victim.

7-140.   In cases where a suspect is not known, follow-up investigations may include—
  - Checking on individuals with a history of speeding and reckless or drunken driving.
  - Checking with insurance agents, vehicle sales, and transfers of registration.
  - Contacting the press, radio, and television for coverage to help seek out the perpetrator.
  - Conducting a thorough canvass interview.
  - Contacting medical treatment facilities to see if anyone has sought medical attention after a collision.
  - Checking stolen vehicle reports. A driver of a hit-and-run vehicle may report that the vehicle was stolen. Likewise, a hit-and-run driver may file a false report to cover the actual collision.

Note. The sobriety of the victim at the time of death must be determined through toxicology tests.

Beatings

7-141.   Beatings involve localized blunt force. Death from a beating is usually not planned. Beatings leave extensive bruises on a body. Autopsies often show ruptured vital organs and brain hemorrhaging. When a weapon is used in a beating, it often leaves distinct pattern injuries that may disclose the type of weapon used. When a person is kicked or stomped, the shoe often leaves impressions and clear-cut marks on the clothing or body.

7-142.   Sometimes in a beating death the body may be moved and another incident staged to cover up the beating. This can be a staged fall by throwing the body from an elevated location, a simulated vehicle accident, or a vehicle may be driven over the body to stage a hit-and-run collision. A staged incident may be discounted because an autopsy may show that the injuries are not consistent with a staged event, there may not be a viable point of impact for the staged traffic accident, or a thorough search of the area may show evidence inconsistent with a collision.

EXPLOSIVES

7-143.   It is imperative that in any investigation involving explosives, the EOD detachment responds to the crime scene and renders the area safe before any investigation. It is important to note that an explosion, whether it is large or small, will create similar injuries. The injuries will only vary in magnitude.

7-144.   In an explosion, the victim may be crushed or hurled against a hard surface, causing blunt-force injuries. They may receive many cuts and punctures from pieces of the explosive device and fragmentation of objects as a result of the blast force. The victim may also be burned by a thermal blast, flames, chemical exposure, or steam. Compression injuries may occur in the lungs and elsewhere from swelling gases. Foreign material in the body must be examined at the autopsy to help determine the nature of the explosion and the explosive device used. Extended searches for explosive evidence are paramount to the successful recovery and forensic testing of explosive devices.

7-145.   An obvious characteristic of a high or low explosive is the presence of a crater at the area of origin of the blast. Loose soil, debris, and objects near the area of origin should be recovered and submitted for forensic testing for the presence of explosive residues. Materials near the scene or blown away from the scene should be recovered as they may contain traces of explosive. Porous substances are especially good sources for this type of evidence, but nonporous substances, such as metal, should not be overlooked. The entire area should be thoroughly searched for evidence of the detonating mechanism or other components of the device. A mesh screen is useful for sifting through debris.

FALLS

7-146.   Deaths from falls are usually accidental. A person may be pushed or thrown from a height; however, such events are rare. Suicides by jumping from a high point are also rare. The victim may be under the influence of drugs or alcohol; toxicology of the victim's blood can determine the presence (or absence) of drugs or alcohol in his system. An investigator must consider the height from which the victim fell and the distance from the base of the object to the point of impact. Do not overlook the fact that a victim found at the very base of an object may have been rendered unconscious by an assailant and rolled over the edge. An inspection of the body's point of departure may provide a great deal of information. The totality of the circumstances must be considered when making a determination of accident, suicide, or homicide.

THERMAL DEATHS

7-147.   Most deaths by fire are accidental; however, the death and the cause of the fire may show that a homicide is involved. The fire may have been the cause of death or it may have been used to try to cover up a crime. The investigator must take steps to investigate for arson. Sometimes a person who commits a homicide with a firearm will try to hide the crime by setting fire to the scene. The investigator should seek assistance from trained SMEs (such as fire investigators or fire marshals). In cases of death by burning, request that the remains be x-rayed. This may show the presence of a bullet in the body. If the victim was alive at the time of the fire, he will usually die as a result of asphyxiation due to the smoke as opposed to death caused by burns.

7-148.   The two most difficult facts to establish in a death by fire are the victim's identity and a connection between the death and the cause of the fire. Investigating a death by fire is difficult. The fire may have mutilated the victim or the scene of the fire may have been (as is often the case) unavoidably disturbed by firefighting activities. Identifying unknown victims requires the help of pathologists. Pathologists can check skeletal remains for size, race, and sex distinctions. They can also compare the remains to dental records and x-rays.

7-149.   The investigation of a death from fire depends greatly on the pathologist's report of the cause of death. If the victim was alive at the time of burning, the autopsy will show inhaled smoke particles in the lungs and airway or carbon monoxide in the blood. The presence of these suggests life at the time the fire started, but their absence does not support death before the fire. A body is rarely burned to the point that a meaningful autopsy is not possible. Even if death occurs some time before the fire is brought under control and the body is badly charred, the inner organs are usually preserved well enough. The cremation of a body takes 1 1/2 hours at 1600 to 1800 degrees Fahrenheit. Even then, bone fragments are seen.

7-150.   The investigator must rely on the pathologist to identify wounds on a burn victim. There are many types of burn injuries that are misleading at first glance. The body may be in a pugilistic attitude, which means the fists and arms are drawn up into a boxer's stance from contracting muscles and skin. Bones fracture in an odd, curved way when cooling begins. Skull fractures may be present. The cracks, radiating from a common center, are made by the release of steam pressure rather than from a blunt force. See chapter 10 for information on arson investigations.

DEATHS INVOLVING TOXIC SUBSTANCES

7-151.   Death from toxic substances may occur if substances that are safe only for external use are taken internally. Death from toxic levels of substances safe for internal use may occur if the substances are taken in amounts greater than the body can support. In either case, the death may be an accident, a suicide, or a homicide.

Poisonings

7-152. The term poison is relative when describing a toxic substance. A poison is any agent that causes a detrimental or destructive effect when introduced into a living organism. Accidental deaths may result from industrial, home, or food poisoning. Although homicide by poisoning is fairly rare, it must not be ruled out without a thorough investigation. Murder by poison can often be made to look like suicide or accidental death.

7-153. Investigation of the crime scene is of special importance in the case of poisoning because postmortem detection of poison may be difficult if its presence is not suspected. Medical personnel may require knowledge of the type of poison suspected to perform a test that will detect the substance in the victim. When death is suspected to be the result of poison, it is important to give the pathologist performing the autopsy as much information as possible about the circumstances of the death, the on-the-scene investigation, and the type of poison suspected. This information, provided before the postmortem examination, enables the pathologist to use the appropriate autopsy methods and to keep adequate specimens for toxicological tests.

7-154. The autopsy may identify the specific poison that caused the death, its concentration in the body, and the period of time the poison was in contact with the soft tissue before and after death. In some cases, the specific poison may be unidentifiable because the dose was too small to detect or the materials in the compound were the same as natural body products.

7-155. The pathologist must be asked to obtain specimens of the victim's blood, bile, gastric contents, and urine. All toxicology specimens should be sent to the Division of Forensic Toxicology, Office of the Armed Forces Medical Examiner, Armed Forces Institute of Pathology, Washington, DC. Do not send toxicological evidence to USACIL for examination. Remember that body fluids found on a floor are likely to be contaminated. They are of little use in toxicological tests for poisons. An investigator must—

- Take samples of food, medicines, beverages, narcotics, fuels, and chemicals that the victim may have consumed.
- Check sinks, pipes, drain traps, garbage cans, cupboards, and refrigerators for possible evidence of the poison. Poison can also be easily hidden in spices, sugar, flour, baking soda, and other food items.
- Collect soiled linen or clothing that may contain traces of poison in stains from food, liquid, vomit, urine, or other matter. Submit these samples, despite an admission or confession, in any case that may involve criminal charges.
- Collect containers that could have held a substance consumed by the victim. Include cups, glasses, and utensils that may have been used to prepare or serve food or drink.
- Check medicine containers for prescription numbers and the name of the dispensing pharmacy. In difficult cases, it may be necessary to take the contents of the medicine chest to search for materials that might have been taken in amounts large enough to cause toxic effects.
- Seize any items like hypodermic needles and syringes that could introduce poison into a victim's body.

7-156. Identification and analysis of the poison may help locate its source. Many common retail products not often thought of as poison are toxic under some conditions. These materials will be easily accessible to the perpetrator of an intentional poisoning. Their ready availability may make them easy to overlook. Household sprays, paint and paint solvents, pesticides, liquid fuels, patent medicines, many antiseptics, and some cosmetics contain poison.

7-157. To learn the source of a poison, consider its availability and who would have the easiest access to it. An individual using poison usually uses a poison they know. Their familiarity with a substance can come from their occupation, hobbies, or past experience. Poisonous substances are readily available in—

- Hospitals, dispensaries, laboratories, and pharmacies.
- Illicit narcotic channels.

- Offices, homes, and grocery stores that use cleaning substances, rodent and insect poisons, and medicines that may be toxic.
- Depots, warehouses, storage areas, farms, and similar places that use rodent and insect poisons.
- Motor pools, fuel depots, and other places that store fuels and fluids with alcoholic bases, cleaning substances, and solvent compounds.

7-158. Locating the source of the poison and determining its availability may suggest the mode of poisoning. Knowing that a poison was contained in a food or beverage may help you ascertain where the victim ate the food or drank the beverage. The place where a poison takes effect is not always the place where the victim consumed the poison.

7-159. There are rarely witnesses to an act of poisoning. Consequently, you must gather as much physical evidence as possible to find out if a crime was committed and, if so, who committed it. Such evidence is not limited to the poisonous substance. Complete a background check on the victim and his activities to learn key information about the poisoning. Conduct an interview of the individuals who may have—

- Witnessed the act of poisoning.
- Known about a suspect's utterances or actions that could establish a motive for the crime.
- Known what the victim ate or drank within the time he probably received the poison.
- Sold drugs or medicines to the victim or suspects.
- Known of the victim's movements before they were stricken.
- Been familiar with the victim's eating and drinking habits, use of drugs or medicines, and attempts at self-medication or treatment from sources outside military medical channels.
- Been familiar with the victim's financial status, family background, social life, or business associates.

Overdose

7-160. A preliminary inquiry into a death may suggest that a victim died from an overdose of drugs. Victims ingest and therefore may overdose by a variety of means. General observations of the crime scene, the victim, and the victim's clothing, or information about the victim's lifestyle may support an overdose suspicion. Identify the presence and quantity of any illicit drugs or paraphernalia that are present at the scene. Note the quality and quantity of food and liquor supplies. Also identify and note the presence of prescription medications and their quantities. These clues may clarify the circumstances of the death or at least give explicit information concerning the victim and his lifestyle.

7-161. Frequently, in cases where a drug death is acute and related to intravenous drug abuse, the abuser will not have time to conceal his drug cache or paraphernalia before he collapses. Sometimes a tourniquet or other constrictive device may be dropped after a victim collapses. Syringes are commonly still at the injection site or grasped in the hand. Other evidence of illicit drug use includes—

- Cellophane envelopes.
- Balloons or paper packets.
- Syringes and needles.
- Bottle caps or other devices used as cookers.
- Cotton balls, matches, and cigarette lighters.

7-162. The pathologist will check the body for needle marks and scars, sometimes referred to as tracks. Most intravenous drug injections are made with very small needles that are designed for intradermal injection. There is no difficulty in detecting the tracks in most chronic addicts. In addition to the linear scars of intravenous drug use, flat-ovoid or circular scars from lesions caused by unsterile injections given immediately under the skin can sometimes be detected. Chronic addicts may conceal punctures by injecting at unusual anatomic sites. They often inject in and around the genitalia, the nipples, the tongue, the mouth in general, between fingers and toes, and the scalp. Some addicts may use the jugular vein in the neck to inject; these are typically addicts that are so far into their addiction that they no longer take precautions to hide their tracks.

7-163. Homicide by overdose is rare; the more common problem confronted is distinguishing between suicide and accident. If the cause of death appears to be accidental and there are no signs of criminal acts or negligence, document any evidence supporting that judgment. Sometimes an accidental death from drugs does not lend itself to early, clear resolution. Rule out all aspects of other-than-natural causes. Ensure that there was no motive for murder found and that no threats could be learned. Investigate individuals who may have had the opportunity and means to cause ingestion of the lethal dose, either by force or trick. Exhaust all leads until sufficient evidence exists that there is no credible indication that death was other than accidental.

7-164. Toxicology results from an autopsy will be critical in understanding the level of drug presence in the body. Sometimes toxicological results support a finding of suicide, such as extremely high levels of a drug in the blood or numerous undigested pills in stomach. In some instances, levels may to indicate recreational use. A full analysis of the person's habits and medical/psychological history must be completed in an effort to distinguish accidental and suicidal overdose deaths. All medications should be seized and retained for potential scientific identification. Investigators should consider consultation with a toxicologist or pharmacologist to document a drug's pharmacology and effects.

DEATHS INVOLVING CHILDREN

7-165. Investigations of deaths of infants and children are particularly complex, and great caution must be exercised. The investigation must be fully coordinated with medical personnel, social welfare agencies, and the servicing office of the SJA. Suspicious deaths that involve infants and children can be grouped into three types: those resulting from battered child syndrome, infanticide, and Sudden Unexpected Infant Death (SUID), previously referred to as Sudden Infant Death Syndrome (SIDS).

BATTERED CHILD SYNDROME

7-166. Battered child syndrome occurs in cases of child abuse. It accounts for a number of deaths of young children under violent conditions. Assigning criminal liability for deaths due to child abuse is often difficult. Recognizing and documenting the indicators of battered child syndrome in a family unit where a battering has occurred is a key step in a battered child death investigation. Chapter 8 discusses battered child syndrome in greater detail.

7-167. Suspicious deaths of children resulting from battered child syndrome differ from other child deaths due to the pattern of abuse leading up to the death. Other forms of suspicious child death are generally caused by more short-term circumstances and events, possibly resulting from a single outburst of anger or even an unintended injury inflicted upon the child.

INFANTICIDE

7-168. Infanticide is the killing of an infant. Sometimes newborns are left to die of neglect in garbage cans, furnaces, restrooms, secluded places, and public dumps. Sometimes they are simply allowed to die at home or in a car in the expectation that they will be disposed of later. The cause of death in cases like these is usually a combination of acute congestion of the respiratory system, dehydration, and lack of basic life-sustaining care.

7-169. Sometimes parents actively kill their infants. They may choke the baby with the umbilical cord, cup a hand over its mouth and nose, drown it in a bathtub, exert a deadly blunt force on the baby, or drop it into a river or sewer. Sometimes, however, infants are stillborn or die soon after unattended births. In these cases the only criminal actions are failure to report the birth and illegally disposing of the body.

7-170. Determining that a death is a case of infanticide is often difficult, especially when the death is due to asphyxia that can also occur from natural and accidental conditions. Criminal infanticide is indicated when there are indications that the death occurred from strangulation, another form of direct violence; circumstances pointing to criminal abandonment or disposal with criminal intent also support a conclusion of infanticide. The following three factors must be determined in a suspected infanticide case:

- Did the infant breathe after birth? A pathologist must conduct an autopsy to determine if the infant was breathing after birth. Normally there is a distinct difference between the lungs of a stillborn baby and a live birth; however, sometimes the signs are not conclusive. Finding food in the stomach is the only positive proof of life after birth.

- Would the infant have lived if given proper care? The pathologist medically assesses the completeness of the infant's prenatal development and checks for specific vital changes that occur immediately after birth. The general health of the infant is considered, and any congenital defects and injuries received at birth are evaluated. From these findings, the pathologist makes a determination regarding the infant's viability (whether or not the infant could have lived) if given minimal care. The military standard for a fetus to be considered viable is a gestation of 28 weeks.
- What was the cause of death? The pathologist assigns a cause of death based on findings during the autopsy.

7-171.   Identifying the victim may be impossible without finding the mother. The body of an abandoned infant usually has no identity. Identifying the mother is not easy because she probably hid the pregnancy and birth. However, a suspect may be found if she seeks medical attention after the birth. She can be medically identified as the mother of the victim if her physical condition is compatible with the birth of the dead infant. Blood tests can show close blood grouping. At all autopsies of abandoned infants, blood samples are taken and analyzed for future comparison.

7-172.   If a baby has died from injuries, the child's medical record must be checked to see if the injuries were treated or hidden. An investigator must investigate whether the mother showed signs of mental depression after the birth of the child. Cases of postpartum depression can render a mother capable of seriously or fatally injuring the child or even herself. The behavioral history of the father should also be investigated. Medical personnel, neighbors, and friends of the parents can provide information about the temperament of the family. Military or civil police will have records of any complaints or past investigations of the parents.

SUDDEN UNEXPECTED INFANT DEATH

7-173.   SUID is the sudden, unexpected, or unexplained death of a child under the age of one. This diagnosis cannot be made without a thorough investigation of the death. This investigation must include a complete crime scene examination, thorough interviews and canvasses, a review of the medical history of the child, and a complete autopsy. SUID is a medical finding where no criminality is involved. As such, it is imperative that the investigator conduct a complete investigation.

7-174.   Many cases of accidental or intentional suffocation by parents have historically been misdiagnosed as SUID cases as investigators relied upon medical personnel and not the crime scene examination. A SUID investigation at the crime scene must be viewed as any other suspicious death, and all investigative avenues must be pursued. SUID can only be concluded by the elimination of all other potential causes of death. A complete toxicological examination must be conducted to exclude poisoning, an autopsy must be conducted to look for signs of smothering, and a crime scene examination must be conducted to exclude possible accidental smothering by way of sheets, blankets, pillows, or stuffed animals. Doll reenactments are recommended and should be used by investigators to help understand the exact positions in which the infant was last seen alive and how he was put to sleep. Often by clarifying these factors, MEs are better able to understand the dynamics of the scene and thus reduce the likelihood of a misdiagnosis of SUID. The Sudden Unexpected Infant Death Investigation report/checklist, available through the Center for Disease Control is an excellent guideline for the investigation and must be attached as an exhibit to the final report.

Chapter 8

Assault and Robbery Investigations

Assault is among the most serious and feared criminal offenses because it involves threatened or actual violence to the victim. This offense occurs more frequently than either rape or homicide. Many assault victims suffer serious injuries ranging from broken bones to life-threatening gunshot or knife wounds. This chapter discusses assault investigations (except those of a sexual nature) including the crimes of maiming and robbery. Sex assault investigations are covered in chapter 9.

LEGAL CONSIDERATIONS

8-1.   It is important that investigators know the legal descriptions for crimes against persons. This ensures that the investigator understands the legal elements of the crime when determining what, if any, crime has been committed. The following paragraphs provide a general description of the crimes and their associated elements. The MCM is the primary reference and should be referred to for a detailed discussion of each crime including legal definitions and elements for each crime.

ASSAULTS

8-2.   Article 128 UCMJ identifies basic assaults. Army LE personnel must understand the terminology used to describe assaults. These terms are used to describe the elements of proof required for an offense to be characterized as an assault. See the MCM for a more detailed description and exact legal wording. These terms include—

- **Assault.** An assault is an attempt or offer with unlawful force or violence to do bodily harm to another, whether or not the attempt or offer is consummated. It must be done without legal justification or excuse and without the lawful consent of the person affected. "Bodily harm" means any offensive touching of another, however slight.
- **Attempt-type assault.** An attempt-type assault requires a specific intent to inflict bodily harm, and an overt act. An attempted assault requires more than mere preparation; it requires an overt action to effect the intended bodily harm. An attempt type assault may be committed even though the victim had no knowledge of the incident at the time. For example, if individual A swings a fist at individual B's head intending to hit individual B but misses, individual A has committed an attempt-type assault. This is true even if individual B was not aware of the attempt.
- **Offer-type assault.** An offer-type assault is an unlawful demonstration of violence by either an intentional or a culpably negligent act or omission. The act or omission must create in the mind of another a reasonable apprehension of receiving immediate bodily harm. Specific intent to inflict bodily harm is not required. Examples of attempted and offered assaults include the following:
  - Individual A swings a bat in the direction of individual B's head (either intentionally or as a result of culpable negligence). Individual B sees the blow coming, causing apprehension of being struck. Individual A has committed an offer-type assault whether or not individual A intended to hit individual B.
  - Individual A swings at individual B's head, intending to hit individual B, and individual B sees the blow coming and is thereby put in apprehension of being struck. Individual A has committed both on an offer- and an attempt-type assault.

- Individual A swings at individual B's head simply to frighten individual B, but without any intent to actually strike individual B. If individual B does not see the action of individual A and is not placed in fear, then no assault of any type has been committed.
- **Battery.** A battery is an assault in which the attempt or offer to do bodily harm is consummated by the infliction of actual physical contact and harm. The force applied in a battery may have been directly or indirectly applied. Thus, a battery can be committed by inflicting bodily injury on a person through striking the horse on which the person is mounted causing the horse to throw the person, as well as by striking the person directly. Examples of battery can include—
  - Landing a direct physical blow on a person.
  - Spitting on another person.
  - Pushing a third person against another person.
  - Unleashing a dog to attack another person.
  - Cutting the outer clothing that a person is wearing, even if the person is not directly touched and there was no intent to touch the person.
  - Shooting or using any other type of weapon or object on a person.
  - Poisoning a person.
  - Driving an automobile into a person.
  - Using excessive force, even though a more minimal level of force is justified.
  - Throwing an object into a crowd may be a battery if the object hits anyone.
- **Dangerous weapon.** A weapon is dangerous when used in a manner likely to produce death or grievous bodily harm.
- **Grievous bodily harm.** Grievous bodily harm means serious bodily injury. It does not include minor injuries, such as a black eye or a bloody nose, but does include fractured or dislocated bones, deep cuts, torn members of the body, serious damage to internal organs, and other serious bodily injuries.
- **Other means or force.** The phrase "other means or force" may include any means or instrumentality not normally considered a weapon. When the natural and probable consequence of a particular use of any means or force would be death or grievous bodily harm, it may be inferred that the means or force is "likely" to produce that result. The use to which a certain kind of instrument is ordinarily put is irrelevant to the question of its method of employment in a particular case. Examples of other means or force include the following:
  - A bottle, a glass, a rock, a piece of pipe or wood, or boiling water may be used as weapons in a manner likely to inflict death or grievous bodily harm.
  - An unloaded pistol, when presented as a firearm and not as a bludgeon, is not a dangerous weapon or a means of force likely to produce grievous bodily harm, whether or not the assailant knew it was unloaded.

8-3.   Assaults are generally characterized as assaults, assaults consummated by battery, and aggravated assaults. A person who attempts or offers with unlawful force or violence to do bodily harm to another person (whether or not the attempt or offer is consummated) is guilty of assault. A person who commits an assault with a dangerous weapon or other means or force likely to produce death or grievous bodily harm or who commits an assault and intentionally inflicts grievous bodily harm (with or without a weapon) is guilty of aggravated assault.

8-4.   There are two types of aggravated assault. The first is an assault with a dangerous weapon or another means of force likely to produce death or grievous bodily harm. It is not necessary that death or grievous bodily harm be actually inflicted. The second type of aggravated assault is that in which grievous bodily harm is intentionally inflicted with or without the use of a weapon.

8-5.   In cases of aggravated assault in which the victim has been badly injured, the investigator will normally follow many of the same techniques used to investigate a homicide. When it is difficult to determine the actual degree of assault (aggravated or simple), consult with the servicing JA for advice.

8-6. The UCMJ allows for increased punishments for specific categories of assault victims. Assaults permitting increased punishment based on the status of the victim include—

- Assault upon a commissioned officer or a warrant, noncommissioned, or petty officer.
- Assault upon a sentinel or lookout in the execution of duty or upon a person in the execution of LE duties.
- Assault consummated by a battery upon a child less than 16 years of age.

8-7. Aggravated assault or assault in connection with other crimes generally warrants the expertise of an investigator. When investigating an assault, the investigator must also be aware of techniques involved in investigating other crimes and offenses. These cases include assaults perpetrated with the intent to commit murder, voluntary manslaughter, rape, arson, burglary, housebreaking, or other crime. Assaults committed with the intent to commit certain other crimes are usually determined during the investigative process of the intended crime. An assault with the intent to commit an offense is not necessarily the equivalent of an attempt to commit the intended offense.

MAIMING

8-8. Maiming, Article 124 UCMJ, is committed when someone intentionally causes disfiguring or disabling injuries to another individual. A disfigurement does not necessarily mean that an entire member is mutilated; it may merely affect (perceptibly and materially) the victim's appearance. Maiming is a specific intent crime and can only be associated with attempt-type assaults. It only requires intent to injure, not intent to maim. An accused can be guilty of maiming if he intends only a slight injury but in actuality causes injury consistent with the elements of maiming.

8-9. For example, if someone is seriously disfigured in a traffic accident, where there was no intent to cause injury to another, maiming cannot be associated with the incident. However, if two people engage in a fistfight and, during the course of the altercation, one of the parties bites off the ear or knocks out a tooth of the other party, this could constitute maiming. Infliction of the following type of injury on a victim may support an inference of the intent to injure, disfigure, or disable:

- Putting out an eye.
- Cutting off a hand, foot, finger, or other appendage.
- Knocking out a tooth.
- Cutting off an ear.
- Scarring a face with acid.
- Causing other similar injuries that would destroy or disable any members or organs mentioned above or cause serious disfigurement.

ROBBERY

8-10. Robbery, Article 122 UCMJ, is a serious offense that may be carried out by a variety of means. Robbery occurs when an item of value is deliberately taken from a victim. The item could be taken from the victim's presence and against their will by the use of force or violence or by instilling fear. The victim's fear can be of immediate or future threat of injury to their person, property, or the person or property of a family member or anyone in the victim's company at the time of the robbery. Because larceny or attempted larceny is an important element of robbery, it is essential for the investigator to be familiar with the elements of larceny and related offenses.

Note. For a robbery to be committed by putting the victim in fear, no actual force is needed. Rather, there must be a demonstration of force or menace placing the victim in such fear that the victim is warranted in making no resistance. The fear must be a reasonable apprehension of present or future injury, and the taking must occur while the apprehension exists.

INVESTIGATING ASSAULTS

8-11. In serious assault cases, especially maiming incidents, obvious physical evidence in the form of injury to the victim will be apparent. Investigators should be aware that while the presence of physical injuries indicates some form of physical violence, this evidence alone does not necessarily prove assault. Injuries can be staged by the victim for a variety of motives. A thorough investigation must be conducted to ensure that all elements of the crime are met. Investigators conducting an assault investigation should—

- Interview the victim. The investigator must substantiate the allegation and determine who the complainant was (if other than the victim).
- Process the scene. Identify the crime scene and conduct required activities to identify, preserve, and collect physical evidence.
- Interview witnesses, to include medical personnel and other first responders.
- Interview suspects.

INTERVIEW THE VICTIM

8-12. Investigators must interview the victim to determine if the elements of proof for an assault are included in the victim's account of the incident. For example, if the installation emergency room notifies the military police station that it is treating an individual who was struck by a baseball bat, this does not necessarily substantiate that an assault occurred. Upon interviewing the victim, it may be determined that the individual was accidentally struck with a bat during a friendly baseball game. Because there was no intent to do bodily harm, there is no assault.

8-13. During the interview record, as chronologically as possible, the events that took place. Many victims provide inaccurate information during initial interviews. This does not indicate that they are not victims; even individuals who are legitimate victims frequently lie about some aspect of the incident. Feelings of guilt, embarrassment, or the attempt to hide other facts from the investigator may cause a victim to lie. Investigators who learn to appreciate what can cause victims to omit information or lie to avoid embarrassment will likely gain greater cooperation from victims than those who make conclusions about conflicting information. Use discretion in cases where a victim has been substantially traumatized or injured. Assist the victim in seeking professional counseling from a member of the clergy or social work services.

8-14. In unknown subject cases or complex investigations, it may be necessary to interview the victim on multiple occasions. A victim may recall more information as time is spent in reflection of the incident. This is especially true when the victim has consumed excessive amounts of alcohol before the assault. Information received in the initial interview may be hazy and unclear. A second interview conducted a day or two later may produce additional details that the victim did not initially recall. In later interviews with the victim, information from previous interviews should be revisited. Refer to chapter 3 for a complete discussion of interview and LE interrogation techniques.

8-15. To avoid lengthy initial questioning of the victim, the investigator should prepare questions based on the information provided by first responding military police patrols. This action assists in conducting a timely crime scene search and may assist in the identification and capture of the assailant (if at large). If there is a possibility that the injuries are life threatening, an effort must be made quickly to obtain as much information and detail about the incident as possible. Interviews of a dying victim must be conducted with the cooperation of medical personnel and should be recorded, both audio and video. The victim should be notified before conducting a recorded interview. A dying declaration consists of the utterances of a dying person and can be used in court as an exception to the hearsay rules of evidence. Investigators should question the victim of an assault to determine—

- The victim's activities leading up to the assault.
- The victim's activities after the assault.
- Any confrontation or meeting with the assailant before the assault.
- Any relationships with the assailant.
- Any witnesses to the assault.

8-16. Investigators must ask a victim other relevant questions to establish their actions leading up to the assault. If the assailant used a weapon, ask the victim to describe it. During the initial interview, victims may be able to identify the assailant and provide insight as to the motivation of the assailant. In cases where the assailant is unknown to the victim, the investigator must obtain a composite sketch as soon as possible. It is extremely rare that a victim cannot provide some insight into the motivation of a known assailant; most assaults result from the escalation of a verbal argument or affray.

8-17. If questioning a victim fails to identify the assailant, check the victim's background, associates, and activities. Check police and personnel records to see if the victim has been involved in previous incidents. Question relatives, members of their military unit, neighbors, and so forth. An investigator may find that the victim has a motive for withholding information, such as his involvement in drug or other illicit activities, which may have spawned the attack. Telling the police about these activities would likely incriminate the victim in other offenses. Information gleaned through this process may aid the investigator in a reinterview of the victim to help reveal additional details of the reported offense.

Collect Victim Evidence

8-18. In physical assault cases, the investigator should have the victim examined by a physician. This examination ensures the physical well being of the victim and also facilitates the collection of physical evidence from the victim. Investigators should—

- Seize any evidence recovered during the examination.
- Collect fingernail scrapings and the results of a head hair combing.
- Collect blood from the victim for comparison with blood at the scene or on clothes.
- Collect clothing worn by the victim at the time of the attack. Use the following techniques:
    - Arrange for a change of clothing for the victim.
    - Have the victim disrobe while standing on paper or a hospital sheet.
    - Place each item of clothing into separate paper bags and properly seal.
    - Be sure to collect the paper or sheet as evidence, taking care to fold in up with the relevant surface on the inside.
    - Air-dry any bloodstained clothing at the office in an area separate from the suspect's clothing. Do not use a fan or similar method of speed-drying.
- Obtain the victim's consent to take photographs of visible injuries. Photography techniques are described in chapter 4. Use the following techniques:
    - Take photographs (with and without a ruler) of the injuries. Use discretion. Have medical personnel take any photographs of areas that may embarrass the victim.
    - Take photographs of individual injuries with the camera parallel to the body surface.
    - Take all close-up photographs with and without a scale.
    - Photograph injuries at intervals of 24, 48, and 72 hours, since injuries sometimes become more observable as time passes.
- Obtain swabs of locations on the body where transfer of body fluids or skin cells from the suspect could have occurred.
- Ask the doctor what type of weapon might have caused the injuries and determine if the injuries are consistent with the victim's account of the assault.
- Obtain a copy of all the associated medical reports.

Document Medical Treatment

8-19. When a victim receives medical treatment, the investigator should obtain copies of the victim's treatment record. The treatment record provides documentation of the physical injuries and the victim's accounts of how the injuries were sustained as observed by the attending physician. An interview of the physician should be conducted to record observations, the treatment provided, the prognosis, recommended follow-up treatment, and other information the physician may have obtained during the treatment process. When possible, especially in cases of severe injury, obtain a sworn statement from the attending physician.

This statement can be of great assistance to the investigation, but may not always be practical due to the pace of the emergency room.

8-20. Ask the physician if any of the injuries can be approximately dated. The treating physician should be able to determine if the injuries sustained were consistent with the accounts of the sequence of events provided and be able to articulate how the injuries logically occurred. The physician may also provide an opinion regarding the type of weapon that could have caused the injuries.

PROCESS THE CRIME SCENE

8-21. After questioning the victim, a thorough search of the crime scene should be conducted as described in chapter 4. Determine if the scene has been disturbed and identify who was in the scene before, during, and after the incident (to include medical and LE personnel). Determine if the victim knows the type of weapon used or if other specific items were touched or disturbed during the commission of the crime; Army LE personnel should attempt to locate these items. If the suspect took the weapon when he departed, get a complete description of the weapon for follow-on searches.

8-22. Basic techniques that are common and consistently applied when processing crime scenes and investigating criminal activity including crime scene assessment, documentation, and processing. These techniques are described in earlier chapters of this manual. The crime scene should be secured, and the number of personnel in the crime scene must be kept to a minimum. Witnesses and suspects should be removed from the crime scene and secured in another location for later questioning. The witnesses and suspects must be separated from one another so that they cannot confer with each other.

8-23. After the crime scene is secured the investigator should conduct an initial walk-through. The walk-through allows the investigator to assess the scene, identify valuable and/or fragile evidence, and determine initial investigative requirements. A return to the scene at the same time of day and on the same day of the week as when the incident occurred can sometimes be helpful. This allows investigators to make observations about lighting, traffic, deliveries, trash collection, and so forth.

8-24. The investigator must document the scene of the alleged assault. Begin with initial observations and an initial walk-through of the scene. Photographs and sketches of the scene and specific evidence may be required to supplement the narrative documentation, depending on the scope and severity of the assault. See chapter 4 for information on crime scene photography. The investigator's documentation should include—

- Initial observations and data. This should include—
  - The arrival time at the scene.
  - The date, time, and location.
  - Weather and lighting conditions at the scene.
  - Any unusual smells or sounds.
  - The condition and position of observed evidence.
  - Activities of any first responders or support personnel.
- Photographs of the scene and any relevant evidence.
- The identity of the location(s) of the assault and any other key events.
- Information on evidence collection. Chapter 2 addresses collection of physical evidence. The investigator should ensure that all property and evidence is identified, collected, preserved, documented, and safeguarded. Evidence of activities leading up to an assault can be critical in determining what events transpired leading up to the assault. This can be signs of a domestic altercation, indications of other criminal activity, or evidence of alcohol or drug use. Evidence at the scene can help in the identification of potential suspects when a suspect is not known. Investigators should look for—
  - Evidence of other criminal activity such as illicit drugs and paraphernalia, contraband, or other evidence.
  - Signs of alcohol consumption.
  - Physical signs of struggle or conflict including biological evidence (blood, hair, tissue, other bodily fluids, or bone fragments).

- Weapons (knives, firearms).
- Objects that could have been used as weapons (bats, tools, furniture, or other household items).
- Other materials such as ropes, ligatures, tape, or bindings.
- Personal valuables or property.
- Forms of identification.

INTERVIEW WITNESSES

8-25. Investigators must identify all potential witnesses and suspects in an assault. The identification of witnesses and suspects may result from interviews with the victim or other witnesses. Additionally, analysis of evidence and consideration of potential motive and opportunity may lead to possible suspects. Investigators must locate and question potential witnesses to an assault as soon as possible. Witness interviews must be conducted separately because each witness will see different aspects of the same event and will report them differently. Other witness accounts can skew the true observations of each individual. The investigator must—

- Conduct each witness interview independently.
- Allow each witness to describe what they saw. Ensure that the information they provide is the result of their personal observations and not what they were told by another witness.
- Ask the same questions of each witness pertaining to events leading up to, during, and after the assault to determine the credibility of the victim and/or witnesses.
- Determine what attracted the attention of the witnesses to the event. This will aid in developing a chronological account of the assault based on what people saw and when they made their observations.
- Explore any gaps or differences in the description of events in an attempt to separate fact from speculation.
- Conduct canvass and witness interviews as soon as possible after the event. Human memory will fade rapidly with the passage of time.
- Determine if any of the witnesses knew the parties involved and, if so, the nature of their relationship.
- Obtain full, physical descriptions of the individuals that the witnesses observed in the event (to include other potential witnesses). This includes the individuals' names (if known), what they were wearing, scars, tattoos, and other individualities.
- Record personal information of the witnesses (to include contact numbers) for follow-up interviews, as necessary.

8-26. In almost all instances, witness accounts will differ to some degree. This does not necessarily indicate that any of the witnesses are lying, but that their perspective of the event is different. In some cases, witnesses who have actually observed an attack will be reluctant to come forward out of fear. Others who were not present may come forward in support of a friend or relative. Those who attempt to describe events differently than they actually occurred will stand out with time and can be refuted through supporting evidence. Unlike a true eyewitness, those who did not actually observe the event, but attempt to assert information, will not be able to provide specific detailed information about the event. The lack of detailed information should alert investigators to use caution when trying to piece the incident together. The detailed and specific chronological event timeline developed by the investigator will help in corroborating or eliminating witness statements.

INTERVIEW SUSPECTS

8-27. An investigator can interview a suspect after a proper rights advisement. Investigators should base their questions on information and evidence developed throughout the investigation. Investigators conducting suspect interviews should consider both the direct testimonial evidence and gaining information that supports collected physical evidence and leads to potential physical evidence. The investigator should attempt to determine if the suspect—

- Had motive.
- Had opportunity to commit the assault.
- Was in the area at the time of the assault.
- Had access to the type of weapon used in the assault.
- Can be tied to the evidence.
- Has an unsupportable alibi.

8-28. Consideration should be given to conducting a photographic, physical, or voice lineup of the suspect with the witnesses and victims if there is any uncertainty regarding the involvement of a suspect in an assault. Lineups are discussed in chapter 3. Once it is determined that a suspect is likely the assailant, he must be processed. Obtain a sworn statement, fingerprints, and photographs from the suspect as well as any possible evidence. This will likely require an examination of the suspect.

8-29. The need to examine the suspect will depend on the possibility of finding incriminating evidence and the amount of needed corroborating evidence. When an examination of a physical assault suspect is necessary, the investigator should—

- Obtain legal authorization, as necessary.
- Look for any injuries on the suspect and any blood transferred from the victim.
- Photograph any—
  - Cuts and abrasions.
  - Identifying marks or characteristics (scars, tattoos, birthmarks).
- Recover the suspect's clothing.
- Consider blood alcohol and drug tests.
- Collect DNA swabs and blood and hair samples for comparative laboratory analysis.
- Search for (and collect if found) weapons used in the crime, considering patterned injuries on the victim as an indicator.
- Search for other evidence (including trace evidence) that might link the suspect to the crime scene.

ASSAULT UPON A CHILD

8-30. Investigations of assault of infants and children are particularly complex. These investigations must be conducted with great caution as they can be emotionally challenging to all involved; investigators must maintain their objectivity throughout the investigative process. These investigations must be fully coordinated with medical personnel, social welfare agencies, and the office of the SJA, and must include a clinical history, a physical examination of the victim, adequate processing of the scene, and radiologic information. An autopsy is required in the case of a child's death when an assault or pattern of abuse is suspected. Death investigations are covered in chapter 7. Clues which may raise the suspicion of child abuse or neglect include—

- Inconsistency of the events as they are provided by the caregiver regarding the injuries identified by the clinical examination.
- Statements by the caregiver that the child had been engaging in behavior that annoyed or aggravated him, making the issue more about himself than the injured victim.
- Evidence of a lack of bonding or outright fear by a victim's behavior or reaction in the presence of the abusive parent, guardian, or caregiver that indicates a pattern of violence or abuse.
- Injuries which cannot be explained by accidental or natural phenomena.

INDICATORS

8-31. Investigators must consider many indicators at the scene of a potential child abuse. When conducting a child abuse investigation, it is important to follow the fundamentals required to process any crime scene as discussed in see chapter 4; however, the following additional indications of abuse should also be considered:

- **Conditions of the scene.** The home should be examined not only for evidence of a crime but also its state of repair, degree of cleanliness, presence of food and other provisions that are age appropriate to the child, heating, and bug or rodent activity or infestation. All observations should be documented in written reports and through photography of the scene.
- **Evidence (or lack of same) that the child is nurtured and loved.** For example, are there photographs of the child displayed in the house? Are there age appropriate toys and supplies available?
- **Suspicious objects.** Objects that may have been used to inflict suspected injuries may be present but not always apparent. Any potential instruments of the abuse should be collected. Because child abuse is typically an emotional act when a parent or caregiver loses control, the weapon is typically a weapon of opportunity. Also, because children are so small and fragile, what may cause little or no injury to an adult may cause substantial injury to a child. Objects that are more common in child assault cases include—
  - Belts.
  - Rods.
  - Sticks.
  - Extension cords.
- **Other suspicious objects.** Any items that may indicate abuse should be identified. These include items such as weapons or drug paraphernalia; all identified items should be documented and seized.
- **The observance of pattern injuries.** Pattern injuries may assist LE personnel in identifying the wounding object. Any object at the scene that may have been used to make the patterned injuries should be seized. Be aware that bruises are particularly difficult to match as they produce different patterns depending on the force, location, angle, and individual response to blunt-force trauma.
- **Bodily fluids and tissue.** Any biological matter such as blood, semen, urine, saliva, nails, or vomitus should be collected. Such bodily fluids may be found in the victim's bed or room.
- **Trash cans.** Both indoor and outdoor trash receptacles should be searched for discarded items that may provide evidence and further the investigation.

ADDITIONAL CONSIDERATIONS

8-32. Evidence of child assault and abuse can take many forms. In some instances the signs of "suspected" abuse may prove to be unsubstantiated. The causes of injury to the child may be determined an accident or the result of ignorance on the part of a parent or caregiver that requires education or counseling but do not rise to the level of criminal conduct. In other cases deliberate physical or emotional assaults on a child may be substantiated. Investigators must maintain an objective viewpoint when conducting investigations into potential child abuse.

Burns

8-33. Physical abuse of children includes burns, both contact and immersion burns. These burns can cause serious medical problems, especially if left untreated. A significant amount of burns are deliberately inflicted. The skin of a child younger than five is thinner and therefore more susceptible to burn injuries. In general, infant and young children sustain second and third degree burns in less than one second in water at or about 140 degrees Fahrenheit. At 131 degrees Fahrenheit, it takes two seconds. The younger the child the more quickly the burn will result.

8-34. Immersion burns are caused when the body (or a part of the body) is placed into liquid at a high enough temperature to cause burns to the skin. The liquid is usually water, although cooking oil or other forms of liquid can cause immersion burns. When investigating possible immersion burns, it is important to look at indicators such as the condition of the bathtub and sink, as well as determine the setting of the hot water heater. Thermostat settings may exceed what is considered acceptable, particularly in overseas areas. Investigators should obtain temperatures of the water out of the faucet as well as in the tub or sink. Immersion burns are the most common type of intentionally inflicted burns. Statistically, the majority of intentional immersion burns are a "disciplinary response" to what the caregiver considers inappropriate behavior, such as bedwetting or failure to potty train. Immersion burns cause straight, horizontal lines of injury on the buttocks, thighs, and waist. The line of injury is consistent with the depth of the water.

8-35. Contact burns involve solid objects and generally result in second or third degree burns. The shape of the burn is important, as it may be indicative of the object used to inflict the injury. Typically, contact burns made with lit cigarettes or cigars leave a circular burn with a crater like lesion. Contact burns made with appliances such as the stove, an iron, or a radiator leave a patterned injury. Investigators must consider the depth and extent of the injury. Intentionally inflicted injuries are typically more extensive than accidental injuries. In an accidental burn, the heat and pain would cause the victim to recoil away from the heat source; an intentionally inflicted injury is indicated by a deeper burn where the abuser intentionally placed a part of the child's body on a hot object and forced them to leave it there for a sustained period of time.

Radiologic Findings

8-36. Radiologic findings provide information of the most recent injury, but also every pre-existing trauma from acute injuries that may have gone undetected and unreported. When a child is being evaluated for abuse, a skeletal survey consisting of a series of x-rays should be exposed at the initial evaluation and two weeks following the initial examination. Healing fractures produce a callus and are easier to detect then fresh injuries. X-rays exposed at varying angles can help to ensure that minor fractures are not overlooked. Other diagnostic tools, such as magnetic resonance imagery (MRI), bone scans, and computed tomography (CT) scans are sometimes employed by medical personnel and can also provide evidence of injury.

Munchausen by Proxy Syndrome

8-37. Munchausen by proxy syndrome is a form of abuse where fabricated or induced illnesses are reported to others, including medical personnel, by a caregiver. The purpose of the ruse is believed to be a need for attention by the caregiver. The caregiver is typically so convincing that the child and others, including medical providers, believe the child is sick. It is most successful when the victim is a young child that cannot speak for themselves; this allows the caregiver to talk for the child, relaying symptoms and medical issues to health care providers that do not exist. In older children the symptoms may be induced.

8-38. The most common symptoms include seizures, bleeding, apnea, diarrhea, vomiting, fever, and rash. As stated, these symptoms may be fabricated by the addition of blood to the child's secretions, overheating the body, falsifying thermometer readings, suffocation to induce apnea symptoms, or they may be induced through a drug (such as a laxative to induce diarrhea). What makes diagnosing Munchausen so difficult is that the abuser appears to be a caring and concerned parent. Looking past the ruse can be challenging and requires the help of medical personnel.

Sudden Unexpected Infant Death

8-39. SUID, previously referred to as SIDS, is a sudden, unexpected, or unexplained death of a child under the age of one. The diagnosis must be supported by a thorough investigation that includes a complete crime scene examination, thorough interviews and canvasses, and a review of the medical history of the child. An autopsy is also required. The final determination of SUID is a medical finding based on the autopsy and the elimination of other possible causes of death. Death investigations, including SUID, are discussed in chapter 7.

Battered Child Syndrome

8-40. Battered child syndrome is a broadly applied term referring to injuries sustained by a child as a result of physical abuse. The abuse is normally inflicted by a parent or adult caregiver. Battered child syndrome also encompasses other forms of abuse such as shaken baby syndrome. The victims are most often small children under three years old. If they are still alive, they are usually unable or unwilling to describe what happened.

8-41. In households with multiple children, one child in the family may be singled out as the main target of abuse. This child may be the product of an unwanted premarital pregnancy or the child may be unwanted for other reasons. The home may be basically clean and the remainder of the children in it well cared for, fed, and clothed. It should be noted that financial and social status are not discriminators in battered child syndrome; many times the family is financially well established, well educated, and socially oriented. Other indicators include—

- **Generational abuse.** Many times battering parents were targets of abuse in their childhood. A statement such as, "If you think he is mistreated, you should have seen the way my old man kicked me around," shows a trend of child abuse from generation to generation. Parents may raise their children the way their own parents raised them, because they know no other way. A battering parent often shows signs of emotional immaturity and mental and environmental stress.
- **Family competition and stress.** Another factor that may be recognized is the presence of an extreme sense of competition between the parents. This competition can cause resentment that is taken out on the child. In most abusive families, there is a constant stress of one kind or another.
- **Emotional outlook.** Most parents feel some degree of guilt even though their children have been injured accidentally. They make statements like, "I shouldn't have bought him such a big bike," or "Why didn't I watch him more closely?" or "Why did I let his bath water run so hot?" Emotional outbursts from aggravation or frustration are common in many abusive deaths. The battering parent, on the other hand, often shows anger and a hostile, argumentative outlook. They may cry harassment on the part of an investigator.

8-42. An investigator must assess the parents to try to detect undue frustration, belligerence, or nervousness when child abuse is suspected. Do not overlook the possibility that a brother or sister beat the child. A small child 18 months and older may think and feel that their position in the family has been invaded by the arrival of a new baby. Parents may unthinkingly talk of the new baby in a way that the older child will resent. A child has many toys and objects at hand that can be used to cause battering injuries.

8-43. Living battered children may be difficult to identify. This child may appear at a medical treatment facility with a broken arm, a cut lip, a black eye, or extensive bruises. Parents easily explain these injuries. A fall or toys thrown by an older child are often the excuses used by battering parents. Only repetitive injuries of this type can alert the doctor to a battered child. To avoid discovery, the parent will take the child to a different doctor or hospital each time.

8-44. Some battered children show no outer signs of injuries. Others show extensive injuries. There may be deep bruises of the face and arms. Deep cuts are rare. They are probably only seen when a blunt object is used to strike a child on the head or face. Cuts on the inside of the mouth are more common, caused by the child biting themselves when hit. UV photography can be used to visualize faint bruises or those which have healed.

8-45. Almost all children have one or two scars from falls, but multiple scars on a small child show a pattern lending evidence to abuse. Most "normal" childhood injuries take place on the bony prominent features of the child such as the forehead, nose, eye brows, chin, elbows, knees, and such. Injuries not normally observed from accidents and child play should draw suspicion. Small, round burn scars may indicate cigarette or cigar burns. The caregiver that describes the onset of symptoms (such as crying or lethargy) was likely either present when the injury was inflicted or the offender.

8-46. Sometimes a parent will bite a child. The bite often leaves a pattern of human teeth marks on the child. An investigator must remember to document bite impressions in his notes and report. Additionally, the investigator must photograph the impressions with and without a measuring device. The investigator should consult with a forensic odontologist (dentist) to make a cast of the impression. The photographs and impressions can be used for elimination and suspect identification purposes. See chapter 2 for more information.

8-47. Most of a battered child's internal injuries occur in the head or the stomach. The face and scalp may not show outer signs of abuse, but heavy hemorrhaging may be present under the skull. Subdural hematomas, common among battered children, are caused by severe force. They can occur when a child is beaten repeatedly on the head or when a child is being held by the ankles and swung against a wall. They may also occur from a child being dropped down a staircase. Blunt-force injury to the stomach often causes a lacerated, torn, or ruptured spleen spilling into the peritoneal cavity. The small and large intestines may be perforated, causing feces to enter into the body cavity. Pancreatic substances or bile may be sent to the stomach by injuries to the liver or pancreas. All of these injuries will cause much pain, crying, listlessness, shock, and finally a coma. Because the lining of the stomach is soft, these injuries may not be apparent. One clue to an intra-abdominal injury in the absence of obvious skin injury is a swollen stomach. A careful investigation, including medical examinations, will usually result in findings that such injuries were not accidental.

DOMESTIC VIOLENCE AND ABUSE

8-48. Domestic violence (also referred to as intimate partner violence) and domestic abuse are two terms that have often been used interchangeably by LE personnel with little thought to what difference exists between them. LE personnel should recognize that domestic violence is included within the definition of domestic abuse. Generally speaking, domestic abuse is a broader term that includes the emotional or psychological aspect of violence directed toward a person, while domestic violence is the use, attempted use, or threatened use of the physical aspect of violence.

8-49. Domestic abuse is defined as domestic violence or a pattern of behavior resulting in emotional or psychological abuse, economic control, and/or interference with personal liberty that is directed toward a person who is a current or former spouse, a person with whom the abuser shares a child in common, or a current or former intimate partner with whom the abuser shares or has shared a common domicile. Domestic abuse can take place without any physical violence or with only minor physical implications. When there is no complaint or evidence of any physical violence, LE personnel must investigate the matter with the same thoroughness as they would a physically violent act.

8-50. Domestic violence is defined as an offense under the USC, the UCMJ, or state law involving the use, attempted use, or threatened use of force or violence against a person or a violation of a lawful order issued for the protection of a person who is a current or former spouse, a person with whom the abuser shares a child in common, or a current or former intimate partner with whom the abuser shares or has shared a common domicile.

8-51. The criminality of domestic abuse can to be more difficult to prove when there is neither a complaint of physical violence nor any physical evidence that physical violence has occurred. LE personnel must therefore seek to discover a history or pattern of psychological abuse by investigating earlier allegations. This investigative process can be extremely useful for family advocacy personnel in establishing a pattern of behavior consistent with the definition of abuse for intervention for both partners. Some disputes between spouses or intimate partners do not reach physical violence early in the cycle; these domestic disputes involve verbal altercations that may result in a pattern of behavior that is emotionally and psychological abusive, and without intervention have been shown to escalate to physical violence.

INVESTIGATIVE CONSIDERATIONS

8-52. When responding to the scene, it is important to understand the nature of intimate partner violence. While some emotionally abusive relationships do not involve physical abuse, all physically abusive relationships contain some emotional abuse. Actions can be abusive, such as controlling access to money, displaying intense jealousy, isolating partner from friends and family, causing sleep deprivation, taking possessions, and using manipulation.

8-53. LE personnel should also consider the potential of sexual assault. Sexual assault is one of the most under-reported crimes and can take many forms in intimate partner violence. Often the assault does not leave any visible marks or injuries. It can range from rape to forcing one to participate in unwanted sexual activities. Sexual assault can also be used as a power and control tactic. See chapter 9 for more information on sex crime investigations.

8-54. LE personnel may respond to a domestic disturbance call where the initial investigation reveals there is no physical violence but a verbal altercation. In these cases the abuse may be emotional and/or psychological. Emotional abuse is more difficult to define than physical abuse; however, it is an integral part of the investigation. Emotional abuse may be indicated by the use of words, tone of voice, action, or lack of action meant to control, hurt, or humiliate another person. Emotionally abusive relationships often involve repeated hurtful exchanges with disregard for the partner's feelings. Emotional abuse leaves no physical bruise, but does leave a tremendous amount of psychological pain. The signs and symptoms of this abuse are inclusive with the evidence that the LE personnel are looking for when conducting the victim interview.

Victim Interviews

8-55. While conducting victim interviews, LE personnel should obtain evidence of any physical abuse. They should also ascertain from the victim if their partner committed any type of the following verbal abuse: threats to life or limb; threats to children; threats to family members, friends, or pets; belittling; name calling; or harassment. The following information should be documented during the investigation and victim interviews:

- The victim's emotional condition and observable injuries. Ensure that the victim is offered and receives any required medical treatment.
- The victim's relationship to the suspect.
- Any history of abuse. This can be obtained from the victim, witnesses, and police reports.
- Any temporary restraining or other court orders.

8-56. The investigator should physically separate the victim and the suspect in different rooms; this increases the likelihood that a victim may be willing to talk to LE personnel by reducing the intimidation and fear created by the presence of the suspected abuser. Investigators should use the following guidelines when interviewing the victim:

- Ask only one question at a time, and wait for the answer.
- Listen carefully to the victim's answers, and do not interrupt.
- Allow the victim to describe the incident in his own terms, and then ask clarifying questions.
- Acknowledge the victim's emotional state if he is shaking or crying. Be prepared for the victim to be angry as well.
- Remember that victims may often use minimizing language to describe extreme acts of violence, so be sure to follow up by asking them to expand on what they just said.
- Ask the victim about any history of abuse, whether it was reported or not. Remember that victims may not remember all instances of abuse; they are more likely to remember the first, the last, and the worst incidents.
- Be patient and reassuring, and try to avoid unnecessary pressure. The victim may feel a combination of both fear and loyalty to the suspect.
- Do not judge victims; listen with impartial feedback.
- Try to avoid making assumptions about the situation or the victim's experience.
- Resist giving your personal opinion about what the victim should do.
- Reassure the victim that he is not to blame and that help is available.
- Ask the victim whether he has injuries that are not apparent.
- Ask an open-ended question if necessary, such as, "Where did he put his hands?"
- Establish victim confidence by showing awareness of the risks the victim is taking by sharing his story.
- Demonstrate an investment in protecting the victim from further harm. Unless this confidence is established, it may be impossible to obtain an adequate victim statement and the victim will likely withdraw from being fully cooperative.

8-57. Because of the nature of intimate partner violence, obtaining a complete and thorough victim statement is a fragile process. LE personnel must engage the victim as a 'partner' in developing case evidence by obtaining thorough and significant information from the victim. Due to the uniquely intimate nature of these crimes, sharing the details of the crime is usually full of intense emotional pain. Because of the control the perpetrator may exert on every aspect of the victim's life (children, housing, and finances), he risks losing it all by reporting the abuse or consenting to an interview. LE personnel must understand these features of violence against victims and make a conscious effort to mitigate these fears during the investigation. This will enhance the chances of obtaining an honest and complete statement from the victim.

8-58. When practical, the victim should be asked how his injuries were sustained. If an individual states that he were choked, LE personnel must ascertain from the individual by statement or demonstration what he means when he states that he was choked. If any statement of strangulation or choking is made, medical personnel should be notified immediately. Serious injury or death could occur several weeks after a choking incident, due to the lack of oxygen to the brain. There are usually three types of strangulation—hanging, ligature, and manual. Manual strangulation is the most common type often seen in domestic violence.

Suspect Interviews

8-59. Before conducting an interview with the suspect, the investigator should obtain as much background information from the victim and witnesses as possible. It is important to not make accusatory statements or confront the suspect with contradictory information. Ask open-ended questions and allow the suspect to tell his story. Acknowledge that the suspect may be feeling frustration, anger, and concern, but do not justify or excuse the behavior. Do not express sympathy with his explanations for the violence. The following information should be documented during the suspect interviews:

- Any statements or admissions made by the suspect.
- The suspect's emotional and physical condition.
- Any observable injuries on the suspect.
- Evidence of substance or chemical abuse by the suspect, including alcohol.

Interviews of Children

8-60. There are seldom witnesses to intimate partner violence for several reasons. Typically, the assault occurs in the home, behind closed doors, and the assailant prefers to have no witnesses to the incident. If there are witnesses, they are usually the couple's children. Although they will still need to be interviewed, care should be taken, as they are also victims of the emotional turmoil exhibited in their home. Use the following guidelines when conducting interviews of the children:

- Do so outside the presence of their parents.
- Conduct the interview in a place that is comfortable for the child.
- Attempt to place yourself on the child's level by sitting or kneeling.
- Begin the interview with nonthreatening questions and avoid suggesting responses to questions.
- Understand that children may feel responsible for what happened or guilty about telling the police about the incident.
- Reassure children that you only want to help and that they would not be doing anything wrong by talking about what happened.

FAMILY ADVOCACY

8-61. Family advocacy and LE agencies have similar objectives in assisting, protecting, and defending the lives of victims of abuse, but they pursue those objectives in different ways. Family advocacy activities are relationship driven, while LE is process driven. LE activities are punitive in nature, while family advocacy activities are rehabilitative in nature. Both must coexist because many cases will never make it to family advocacy without LE initiating a report.

8-62. It is extremely important for LE personnel to thoroughly document what transpired; this information is then passed on to family advocacy counselors. They can then respond with a type of intervention most suitable for the situation. The following four intervention techniques should be considered when responding to intimate partner violence:

- **Mediation.** Mediation allows LE personnel to further explore the allegations. LE personnel's use of mediation is an information gathering process where the responding military police patrol and/or MPI facilitates a discussion between the two disputants and should be used when there is no violence. This method of intervention empowers disputants to work collectively to resolve their problem or to see where counseling may be valuable to the relationship. Mediation is never conducted when there is evidence of physical assault, because you cannot mediate violence. The results of any mediation efforts should be document in the appropriate police reports.

- **Referral.** Referral is applicable if disputants cannot resolve the problem. LE personnel can recommend the disputants to appropriate agencies and/or service providers. Army Community Service provides services to Soldiers and their families for family life education, parent education, new-parent support, and such. Referral also can be made to the servicing office of the SJA for legal services, the chaplain for spiritual guidance, and social work services for at-risk families. Any referrals should be documented.
- **Separation.** Separation is conducted when and where command policy dictates that the service member be separated from the spouse for whatever length of time is deemed necessary or until the Family Advocacy Office deems it safe.
- **Apprehension.** Apprehension is conducted when there is probable cause to believe that a crime has been committed, such as an assault.

INVESTIGATING ROBBERY

8-63. Robbery is a serious crime that occurs when an item of value is deliberately taken from a victim. It encompasses elements of an assault (discussed earlier) and a larceny, which is discussed in chapter 10. Thus, if the elements of proof do not support a charge of robbery, they may support a charge for either assault or larceny (lesser offenses). For instance, someone steals the property of another and is subsequently observed by the owner of the property. The owner confronts the thief who then assaults the owner and flees the scene. This would warrant both larceny and assault charges but would not support the charge of robbery.

8-64. The types of robbery investigated most frequently by military investigators are muggings and planned robberies of post facilities. The principles and techniques used to investigate these robberies also apply to vehicular, bank, and other robberies that are encountered less often. The elements of proof for the offense of robbery remain the same regardless of the type of robbery being investigated.

8-65. The most common commercial robberies involve shoppettes, gas stations, liquor stores, cab drivers, and other businesses or activities that operate during the evening hours and involve cash transactions. Other robberies include—

- Street robberies.
- Vehicular robberies.
- Bank robberies.
- Robberies in schools.

8-66. Normally, robberies are reported soon after they are committed, and LE response is quick. The likelihood of locating the offender of a robbery depends on how long it takes to obtain a description of the assailant and broadcast it to responding patrols.

8-67. Frequently, mugging-type robberies are committed by people who live on the street or who are involved in drug-related activities. Consequently, patrols responding to a robbery scene may drive past a suspect who fled the immediate area, then continued walking away from the area to avoid raising suspicion. Rapid dissemination of the suspect's description can aid responding patrols in detaining potential suspects who may not otherwise be identified.

8-68. An investigator who responds to a robbery should observe areas for possible assailants while en route to the scene, such as a person running or driving recklessly away from the scene. Upon arrival at the scene, the investigator follows the basic steps in crime scene processing as described in chapter 4. A thorough investigation must be conducted to ensure that all elements of the crime are met. Similar to other assault investigations, investigators conducting a robbery investigation should—

- Interview the victim. The investigator must substantiate the allegation and determine who the complainant was (if other than the victim).

- Process the scene. Identify the crime scene and conduct required activities to identify, preserve, and collect physical evidence.
- Interview witnesses including any medical personnel and other first responders.
- Identify and interview suspects.
- Review any available video from surveillance systems to attain possible videos of the suspect.

INTERVIEWS

8-69. First and foremost, the investigator should quickly obtain a detailed physical description of the assailant and any accomplices. Remember that a detailed description should begin with what unique or uncommon features were most memorable, not "height, weight, clothing," as these are the most common, easily misconstrued and, in the case of clothing, easily altered. Instead, ask about the assailant's voice, mannerisms, jewelry, tattoos, scars, and distinguishing features. Investigators must understand that assailants can be difficult to identify. Many robberies, especially muggings, occur after dark or under conditions that make the assailant's features hard to see. Even when the assailant directly confronts his victim, the victim may not able to provide an accurate description because of his emotional state.

8-70. The investigator should get as much descriptive information from victims and witnesses as possible while it is still fresh in their minds. Investigators should attempt to obtain the following information from all witnesses and victims:

- A description of the assailant.
- Whether the assailant had any accomplices and, if so, a description of the accomplices.
- The movements of the victim and others.
- A detailed description of the methods and actions used by the assailant and any accomplices to the crime. This includes—
  - Weapons used. Obtain a description of the weapons used.
  - Vehicles used. Obtain a description of the vehicles used and the route used when the assailant departed.
  - Any conversations or communication between the assailant and accomplices.

8-71. Due to the nature of the crime, identifying and interviewing witnesses are critical to solving robberies. Military police or other investigators must help get the names of every person in the facility or area. They must check for witnesses beyond the actual scene who may have observed the assailant flee. The witnesses should be interviewed separately.

8-72. The victim of a robbery should be interviewed more than once. The initial interview may focus more on obtaining an initial description of the assailant and his actions in an attempt to locate and apprehend the perpetrator. At a later interview, the victim may recall details not remembered initially or thought to be unimportant during the initial interview. The investigation can benefit even if the victim recalls only a few details about the assailant. The victim interview should focus on—

- Identifying any injuries to the victim. If the victim is injured, request permission to take photographs of the observable injuries, preferably during a medical evaluation with an investigator or military police person of the same gender present. Follow the same photographing techniques used when photographing an assault victim. See chapter 4 for additional techniques for photographing injuries.
- Describing the assailant and any accomplices.
- Describing any verbalizations by the assailant and any communications between the assailant and any accomplices. Communications between the assailant and his accomplices may be verbal or through gestures. Carefully document the wording of verbal threats or demands uttered by the assailant. Retain and examine written threats and demands.
- Identifying where the victim was immediately before the attack and what he was doing at the time of the attack. Try to determine what type of approach the assailant used and whether he "blitzed" the victim or used a pretense, such as asking for the time or directions.
- Providing a detailed description of the items taken and their reported value.

CRIME SCENE PROCESSING

8-73. Depending on the nature of the robbery, physical evidence may be minimal. When considering a robbery on the street, the event occurs so quickly, there is very little exchange or deposit of physical evidence by the assailant. Remember that injuries to the victim, particularly abrasions, may glean some evidence and should be processed for DNA.

8-74. The scene, although it may simply be a spot on the sidewalk, should be searched for possible evidence. The assailant may have dropped a personal item containing identifying trace evidence. He may have left footwear impressions or tire impressions or marks from a vehicle. If the robbery occurred near a structure, the assailant may have touched a window or glass door with an ungloved hand, leaving latent print evidence. If there was a physical confrontation, the assailant could have been injured, leaving biological evidence at the scene. If the assailant was scratched by the victim, biological evidence may be retrieved from the victim's fingernails. If the assailant was injured badly enough, he may require medical attention; a check of local medical treatment facilities could result in identification of the assailant. Surveillance video from systems in the area may have captured relevant images of the perpetrator.

IDENTIFYING SUSPECTS

8-75. A composite sketch based on multiple victim and witness accounts can be an effective means to identify a suspect. Information from multiple victim and witness accounts allows for the integration of key features provided by different individuals who observed several different aspects of the assailant. If the composite can be developed in sufficient detail, prepare and distribute CID Form 88, *Wanted Poster*. Disseminate copies of the wanted poster to local LE and resident federal agencies. Post them on the installation and around the area where the offense was committed.

Note. Even if a composite drawing is not an accurate rendition of the assailant, it can be beneficial by putting the community on alert. This creates awareness that the robbery has occurred, causing community members to be more alert for both potential suspects and further robbery attempts.

8-76. A few days after posting the wanted posters, return to the area where the offense occurred to determine if they have been removed. If the posters are being removed, a surveillance mission may be an effective means to identify who is removing them; the individual removing the posters may be the suspect. On occasion, the post and local newspapers and local TV stations may be used as other means of publicizing the poster. Investigators should consider if requesting and offering a reward is warranted.

8-77. There are many people and places that an investigator can seek out to gain more information and develop leads to a robbery. Investigators must use their experience, intuition, and imagination to identify and develop information leading to the identification and apprehension of a robbery suspect. Investigators should check—

- **Known or suspected drug addicts.** Addicts are often desperate for money to support their habit and are compelled to rob others as a rapid means in which to obtain more drugs.
- **Pawn shops.** Check pawn shops periodically for items taken in robberies. Many addicts are careless as to how they exchange stolen items for cash and are quick to make exchanges without hiding their identity.

Note. In some cases, it may be beneficial to have the victim check pawn shops a reasonable distance from the incident, particularly if the item stolen was not serial numbered and can be more easily identified by the victim. This not only assists in the investigation, it is also more efficient in that the victim is more likely to recognize the item than anyone else.

- **LE databases.** LE databases should be checked for—
  - Vehicles similar to those used in the crime (when automobiles have been involved). If similar vehicles are identified, the victim should be asked to view the photographic identification file.

■ Persons with convictions or suspected history of similar crimes. If photos are on file, these may be included in a photo lineup for the victim.

8-78. A diligent review of police intelligence data bases and networks may produce investigative leads. Sometimes victim, witness, or canvass interviews do not provide adequate leads or identification of a suspect. This can be compounded by a scarcity of physical evidence typical of many robbery scenes. Common patterns may be identified across multiple crime scenes. Crime pattern analysis examines all of the characteristics of the crime and compares it to characteristics of other crimes that have occurred before and after the current incident. Comparisons of this nature uncover patterns and 'hot spots' for crime trends and may even result in surveillance that catches an offender in the act. See ATTP 3-39.20 for more information.

Modus Operandi Identification

8-79. Because robbery is a recidivistic crime, the techniques and mannerisms of an assailant are clues to his identity. Investigators should recognize that most people who develop methods that are successful for a specific activity will by nature continue to use those methods. This action solidifies a modus operandi (MO) and will assist investigators in linking crimes that may have been committed by the same individual or group of individuals. Investigators should note facts pointing to a certain MO. Matching the MO of an unsolved robbery with cases from other police agencies may lead to identifying and apprehending the responsible parties. Investigators should—

- Consider if the target was observed by perpetrators weeks in advance.
- Determine if there was a detailed timetable of activities. Did the suspect appear to be monitoring or calling out time? This may be evidence of a plan, rehearsals, and an MO.
- Note the number of individuals used to commit the robbery and how their tasks were split. Sometimes one person directs the activity and others perform the actual work of the robbery. Tasks may be handled by roles, such as a driver, a gunman, a lookout, and an inside man.
- Check the techniques used and how individuals were positioned during the robbery. Did they use verbal commands, written or verbal demands, and/or visual signals? What did they call the other team members when issuing directions?
- Establish what kind of equipment was used and the types of facial disguises were used.
- Attempt to capture the conversations between the suspects in each witness interview. Determine if the conversations provide any insight into the robbery and the suspect's escape plan.

8-80. Both positive and negative actions may have influenced the suspect's plans. Investigators should—

- Consider whether fewer employees worked on the day of the crime because of lighter patronage. This factor may have entered into the suspect's planning. Habitual movements by employees could also have been used to the suspect's advantage.
- Identify indicators that the suspect was familiar with the crime target. The level of familiarity the assailants had of the location robbed may indicate that—
  - They received assistance from an employee.
  - They expended a significant amount of time in learning the routines and weaknesses of security personnel and security procedures.
  - They may know or be related to an employee based on their level of "inside information."
  - They may be a former employee.
- Review surveillance tapes for several weeks before the robbery to detect suspicious activity of suspects that was not noticed during surveillance activities.

8-81. In the commission of some robberies, especially those of convenience stores and gas stations, the suspects may not have taken the time to extensively plan and observe their target location. In the vast majority of robberies involving banks and other cash facilities, it likely that suspects reconnoiter the target location to determine when and how cash is moved, what the security protocols are, and how they can be defeated. Whenever a robbery occurs at the peak of cash flow periods or while funds are being moved, there is an extremely high likelihood that extensive planning preceded the robbery.

Crime Analysis

8-82. Activities, associations, and events pertinent to crimes committed by the same perpetrators tend to have identifiable and characteristic patterns. Crime pattern analysis can be helpful in identifying patterns of activity, association, and events. Crime pattern analysis looks at the components of crimes to discern similarities in the areas of time, geography, personnel, victims, and MO. Investigators should identify and analyze details of the current and previous similar crimes for—

- The use of the same or similar locations. Perhaps there is a pattern of using parking lots, parade grounds, or stairwells.
- The types of weapons were used, if any.
- The methods of approach and the number of assailants involved in each attack.
- Any opening statement to the victim. Any conversation or communications between the victim and the assailant or among the accomplices. Determine consistencies in what was said.
- Any identified peculiarities about the assailant's accent or pronunciation of certain words.
- Any violence that was used against the victim. Specifically, note how and where an injury may have been inflicted.

8-83. When an assailant is identified, obtain legal authorization to search him. Search the suspect for injuries and items transferred from the victim or the scene. Recover the suspect's clothing and collect known samples of hair and blood, if appropriate. Consider searching the suspect's home and possessions, such as his car and storage areas, for evidence that links him to the victim or the scene. Interview the suspect using techniques described in chapter 3.

STRONG-ARM ROBBERY OR MUGGINGS

8-84. Assailants who mug others are often the least professionals of all assailants; they generally use strong-arm tactics or other unsophisticated means of committing their crime, such as using a gun or weapon to overcome potential resistance. Most muggings occur out of necessity and opportunity. Assailants who mug do not generally know their targets nor can they control other factors, such as who passes by or who may witness the attack. The actions of an inexperienced assailant who mugs someone may be based only on a need for money and a sudden chance to victimize a person who is alone. Due to these factors, they are likely to commit one or more careless mistakes or complacently walk into a nearby establishment subsequent to the attack.

8-85. Individuals who take wallets, purses, or other items (which can be linked to the victim) generally do not want to possess them any longer than they have to. They will frequently flee the immediate area and hide where they believe they will not be discovered. Once in hiding, perhaps behind a shrub or garbage dumpster, they will sort through the items taken and discard the items they do not want. Conduct canvasses and a crime scene examination that includes a search beyond the scene. Look for discarded items and review surveillance tapes of local area establishments (such as liquor stores, gas stations, automated teller machines, and so forth) to help identify the assailant. Frequently, latent fingerprint impressions will be deposited on discarded items, because it is cumbersome to rifle through the contents of a wallet or purse while wearing gloves. The recovery of these items may prove to be valuable evidence.

8-86. Experienced individuals who mug often plan their actions or use the same methods to identify their target. They may enlist the aid of others to serve as watch outs or helpers in the attack. Those who mug normally try to select individuals who are alone or will not likely be able to defend themselves and are believed to have a large sum of money. They select locations that are free of witnesses and that will provide the advantage of surprise. The patterns or MOs associated with these assailants can aid investigators in predicting additional attacks and can be used to proactively thwart these crimes.

ROBBERY OF MONEY-HANDLING FACILITIES

8-87. Criminals who commit robbery of money-handling facilities tend to plan their actions ahead of time. Rapid response by LE personnel is the best defense against these types of robberies. Military police responding should be observant while en route for persons or vehicles that may be fleeing the scene. Prior planning and drills involving military police and facilities ensure that the response is adequate. This enables military police to respond in a preplanned, rehearsed manner, which leads to the successful blocking of avenues of escape in an actual robbery.

8-88. All victims and witnesses should be interviewed to obtain as much descriptive information as possible regarding the perpetrators and their actions. In most post facilities where high-dollar amounts of money are handled, there are video-recording devices inside and outside. Investigators should obtain these vital pieces of evidence and analyze them for clues to identify the assailants. The video should be viewed away from the victims of the robbery and then compared to the interviews of the victims to prove or disprove the account of the robbery.

VICTIM AND WITNESS ASSISTANCE

8-89. Army LE investigators are required to inform victims and witnesses of the services available to them. Particular attention should be paid to victims of serious and violent crimes, including child abuse, domestic violence, and sexual misconduct. This information can be viewed on-line at <www.DOD.mil/vwac/> or a copy of the policy can be obtained by writing to Department of the Army: Criminal Law, Office of the Judge Advocate General, 2200 Army Pentagon Washington, DC 20310-2200.

8-90. DODD 1030.01 and DODI 1030.2 implement statutory requirements for victim and witness assistance and provide guidance for assisting victims and witnesses of crimes from initial contact with offenders through investigation, prosecution, and confinement. Together, the directive and instruction provide policy guidance and specific procedures for all sectors of the military to follow for victim and witness assistance.

8-91. The directive includes a bill of rights that closely resembles the federal crime victims' bill of rights. DOD officials are responsible for ensuring that victims of military crimes enjoy these rights. Victim's rights include the following:

- The right to be treated with fairness and respect.
- The right to be reasonably protected from the offender.
- The right to be notified of court-martial proceedings.
- The right to be present at court-martial proceedings.
- The right to confer with the government attorney.
- The right to available restitution.
- The right to know the outcome of an offender's trial and release from confinement.

8-92. DOD victim and witness assistance programs cover the entire military justice process from investigation through prosecution and confinement. In providing services and assistance to victims, DOD programs emphasize an interdisciplinary approach involving the following:

- LE personnel.
- Criminal investigators.
- Chaplains.
- Family advocacy personnel.
- Family service center personnel.
- Emergency room personnel.
- Equal opportunity personnel.
- JAs.
- Unit commanding officers.
- Corrections personnel.

8-93. DOD victim and witness assistance programs use the following forms to advise victims and witnesses of their rights during all stages of a case:

- DD Form 2701, *Initial Information for Victims and Witnesses of Crime*. This form provides notice to victims and witnesses about their rights and information on the military justice system.

- DD Form 2702, *Court-Martial Information for Victims and Witnesses of Crime* and DD Form 2703, *Post-Trial Information for Victims and Witnesses of Crime*. These forms provide notice to victims about their rights during court-martial proceedings and information about the court-martial process.
- DD Form 2704, *Victim/Witness Certification and Election Concerning Prisoner Status* and DD Form 2705, *Victim/Witness Notification of Prisoner Status*. These forms provide information to victims about the offender's sentence, confinement status, clemency and parole hearings, and release from confinement.
- DD Form 2706, *Annual Report on Victim and Witness Assistance*. This form provides statistical information about assistance rendered to victims and witnesses.

8-94. An Interdisciplinary DOD Victim and Witness Assistance Council provides a forum for the exchange of information and the coordination of policy recommendations. The council helps to foster the implementation of consistent and comprehensive policies and procedures to respond to crime victims and witnesses in all of the military services. A senior program specialist with the U.S. DOJ, Office for Victims of Crime, serves as a liaison member.

Chapter 9

Sex Crime Investigations

Investigators may be required to investigate the alleged commission of sex offenses contained in the MCM. The DOD established the Sexual Assault Prevention and Response Program to eliminate incidents of sexual assault through training and education. In an effort to minimize revictimization, it further provides investigators and commanders with training and guidance on the requirements for response, victim advocacy, confidentiality, and confidential reporting. When called upon, an investigator must conduct a complete, thorough, and impartial investigation.

REQUIREMENTS

9-1. Alleged sex offenses may be reported to authorities by any person, not just the victim. The response must be tactful and discreet, regardless of gender and age. The goals of the investigation must include creating a climate that encourages victims to report incidents of sexual assault without fear, ensure sensitive and comprehensive treatment to restore a victim's health and well-being, ensure that leaders understand their roles and responsibilities regarding response to sexual assault victims, and thoroughly investigate allegations of sexual assault and take appropriate action.

9-2. Every sex offense is different. When arriving at the scene, the investigator must first offer the victim access to an advocate. Rape is perhaps the most serious crime, excluding homicide, that an investigator will encounter. The trauma of rape can be a long-lasting one. It is essential that investigators who are assigned rape cases have a special knowledge and understanding of rape victims and suspects.

9-3. The reporting of an alleged commission of a sex offense can create public pressure to identify and apprehend a suspect and prevent future offenses. This pressure may hurt a suspect's right to a complete and fair investigation of the charges. Because of the nature of sex offenses, an investigator must work quickly during the preliminary investigation. Investigators must avoid hasty or rash conclusions during this phase of the investigation because they can cause innocent individuals to be falsely branded as sex offenders. An investigator conducting a sex offense investigation must—

- Report all incidents of sexual assault to the SARC immediately (see Victim Advocacy Program below).
- Escort the victim from the scene when requested by the victim, chain of command, or USACIDC.
- Ensure the physical safety of the victim and determine if the alleged assailant is still nearby
- Advise the victim of the need to preserve evidence (by not bathing, showering, or washing garments).
- Direct the investigative effort toward finding out if an offense did occur, the specific nature of the offense, and who committed the offense. This effort includes—
    - Collecting evidence to prove or disprove facts of the offense.
    - Maintaining records so that the chain of custody can be shown at a trial by court-martial or can support administrative action.
    - Treating each reported sexual assault incident seriously by following proper guidelines and policies.
    - Directing the investigation toward apprehending the suspect.
    - Allowing legal and medical authorities to determine the disposition of the suspect according to their professional analyses.

Note. In sexual assault cases, particularly those that involve children, the investigator must act in the best interest of the victim, ensuring that he is protected during the investigative and prosecutorial process.

CONFIDENTIAL REPORTING

9-4.   Confidential reporting gives Soldiers access to medical care, counseling, and victim advocacy without initiating an investigation. To request restricted reporting, a Soldier must report the assault to a SARC, a VA, a health care provider, or a chaplain. Note that restrictive reporting is only an option for Soldiers and does not apply to civilians, dependents, children, or retirees. Further guidelines on restrictive reporting can be found in AR 600-20.

VICTIM ADVOCACY PROGRAM

9-5.   A victim's use of advocacy services is optional; however, commanders must ensure that victims have access to a well-coordinated, highly responsive sexual assault victim advocacy program that is available 24 hours a day, seven days a week, both in garrison and deployed environments. There are various echelons of VAs for both environments, starting with the installation SARC who implements the program. The VAs work directly for the SARC; within military units the VAs are Soldiers or civilians who are trained to provide limited victim advocacy as a collateral duty. In a deployed environment, deployable SARCs are Soldiers trained in sexual assault prevention and response and are responsible for managing the program within the unit and ensuring that reporting requirements are met. They are assigned to each brigade and higher echelon while the VAs are assigned to each battalion-sized unit.

ADULT PRIVATE CONSENSUAL SEXUAL MISCONDUCT

9-6.   Adult private consensual sexual misconduct includes sexual acts in violation of the UCMJ between consenting adults, conducted in private, and regardless of whether the acts were on or off a military installation. It does not include any sexual act or acts that involve allegations of force, coercion, or intimidation; abuse of position or rank; fraternization; persons under the age of 16; or conduct that relates directly to applicable security standards for access to classified information.

9-7.   Current DA and DOD policy mandate that military LE agencies will not conduct an investigation of adult private consensual sexual misconduct when it is the only allegation involved. Such allegations are investigated only if approved by the Commander, USACIDC. Allegations of adult private consensual sexual misconduct received by Army LE personnel will normally be referred to the commander of the military member for appropriate disposition. LE personnel may consult with trial counsel on these types of issues.

Note. Due to relatively frequent changes in policy, investigative personnel must remain vigilant in their review of DODI 5505.8 and AR 600-20. Allegations of adult private consensual sexual misconduct received by Army LE personnel will normally be referred to the commander of the military member for appropriate disposition.

9-8.   It is important for LE personnel to obtain elements of proof and the age of the victim in order to determine the appropriate offense. LE personnel must understand the legal descriptions of specific terms used to describe sex crimes. Crimes associated with sexual misconduct cover a wide range of activity from rape and sexual assaults to pandering and prostitution. The definitions and elements of these crimes are revised frequently by congressional action; investigators must stay current with changes as they occur. The MCM (and any published updates) should be referenced for the exact legal terminology and elements for each crime.

INVESTIGATING SEX OFFENSES

9-9.   The initial response to a reported sexual offense is critical. Specific guidance regarding physical evidence collection is covered in chapter 2; crime scene processing is discussed in chapter 4. When called to investigate a sex offense, the investigator should—

- Document the—
  - Time of notification.
  - Arrival time on the scene.
  - Person making the report.
  - Weather conditions, environment, and unusual odors.
- Obtain as many details as possible from those who reported the sex offense; questions such as who, what, when, where, and how should be answered quickly and clearly to establish jurisdiction.
- Coordinate with required agencies and those that may assist in the investigation.
- Ensure that the VA has been notified.
- Locate and interview witnesses, particularly those that can support or refute an alibi (if one was provided).
- Notify trial counsel.

9-10.   Victims may delay reporting a sexual assault incident for days, months, or even years. Furthermore, it is possible that victims may never discuss the incident with anyone, including family and close friends. It is imperative that investigators discuss the delay in reporting with the victim and document the reasons for a delayed report; however, investigators should not construe the fact that a delay in reporting exists as evidence that the incident did not occur.

VICTIM INTERVIEWS

9-11.   During the initial contact with the victim, the investigator must instill confidence in the victim that he is qualified to investigate the offense. An investigator's interest in the victim and a concern for the victim's welfare are important factors affecting the victim's sense of safety and also helps in ensuring future cooperation. Avoid using multiple investigators to interview the victim. Whenever a sexual assault victim is interviewed, the victim will be asked if he desires to have a VA or some other support person present (personal friend, chaplain, or other professional); if an advocate is requested, the interview should not proceed until that support person arrives. The only time a support person or advocate will be removed is if they interfere with the interview process. Consider that a family member or friend may be inappropriate, particularly if the victim is a child and the incident occurred in the home or with family members or friends.

9-12.   When conducting an interview with the victim, it is helpful to explain what is being done and why, particularly during the initial stages. When there is enough information to enable other personnel to begin crime scene processing, the victim must be taken quickly to the nearest medical treatment facility for a thorough examination (the victim must consent to a medical examination). Explain that the clothing worn during the attack must be examined for evidence, and make arrangements for the victim to obtain a change of clothing.

9-13.   The interview of the victim should be accomplished using the FETI technique. This technique can significantly enhance the quality of the interview and reduce the risk of a victim changing or recanting his story. It can also increase victim cooperation and participation and significantly improve the chances of successful prosecution. The FETI technique is introduced in chapter 3 and outlined in appendix C. Multiple interviews may be required to fully get through the incident with the victim. Multiple interviews, while sometimes necessary, should be kept to a minimum as each additional interview retraumatizes the victim. A victim's reaction to the assault may vary; however, it is common for a victim not to remember all the details regarding the incident. Certain memories of the incident may become clearer over time, which underscores the need for follow-up interviews.

9-14. The victim may feel ashamed, guilty, or embarrassed and believe he may have placed himself into a situation that resulted in the incident. Victims frequently feel as though the incident was their fault. As a result, the victim may be unable or unwilling to provide details that are embarrassing, which could make him appear as though he is hiding something. A victim may also withhold significant information, not knowing that the information is critical to the outcome of the investigation. When questioned about certain details regarding an incident, a victim may become "hostile" or "defensive" and may be unwilling or unable to cooperate further with the investigation in order to avoid discussing sensitive or embarrassing details regarding the incident. Investigators should expect that a victim will be reluctant to describe extremely unpleasant events and facts.

9-15. Interviews of victims of child sexual assault are extremely sensitive and subject to considerable scrutiny. Additionally, after an interview in which a child implicates an adult, there may be pressure on the child to recant his statement. Care must be taken to ensure these victims are put into the care of a supportive adult, which may ultimately be through Child Protective Services, depending on the support of the non-offending parent.

9-16. Most victims know the alleged suspect before the incident. It is important to obtain as much information as possible to determine the full extent of the victim's relationship with the perpetrator. During the interview, the investigator should—

- Attempt to determine how and under what circumstances the victim and the suspect met.
- Identify the frequency and nature of the contact between the victim and the suspect (before and after the alleged assault).
- Identify if the victim previously engaged in sexual acts with the suspect, and were these acts consensual or nonconsensual?

9-17. Many investigations involve the issue of whether or not the victim consented to the activity in question. In determining whether or not consent was absent, investigators should conduct a detailed interview with the victim to determine—

- If physical or verbal resistance was presented by the victim. Simple gestures such as clenching fists, looking away, ducking a head, or hugging oneself can often be signs of nonconsent. The investigator must identify and report such behavior.
- Information pertaining to the location and the environment in which the assault occurred.
- Details regarding how the victim felt and what he was thinking during the incident.
- The presence of any perceived threats to the victim, either before the incident, at the time of the incident, or subsequent to the incident.
- If force (or threats of force) were used by the suspect during the incident.
- The size and strength of the subject.
- The existence of previous and postoffense consensual activity between the suspect and the victim.
- Whether the victim experienced previous traumatic events such as prior sexual assaults, assaults, or robberies as an adult or child. Many adults undergoing trauma often respond to current traumatic events in a way akin to how they reacted during previous similar traumas.

9-18. Investigators should keep in mind that previous or postassault consensual sex acts do not preclude the possibility that a sexual assault occurred. The investigator should make every attempt to determine what was different between the consensual and nonconsensual incidents. Investigators should obtain or determine the following:

- What were the emotional and physical experiences of the victim before, during, and after the incident?
- What were the thought processes of the victim before, during, and after the incident?
- What were the physical and emotional effects of the incident on the victim?
- What were the behavioral and physical changes experienced by the victim following the incident?
- Was the victim or the suspect menstruating?

- How was the suspect behaving (before, during and after the incident)? This may include—
  - Grooming behaviors of the suspect (behaviors that "set up" the victim for the assault).
  - Documentation of the specific acts committed and whether any acts were repeated.
  - A description of the suspect's sexual, physical, and emotional behavior.
  - Whether the suspect said anything before, during, or after the assault?
- What was the level and use of force, the perception of force, the threat of force, or the lack of force?
- What were the movements and activities of the suspect at the crime scene? This may include answers to the following questions:
  - How did the suspect enter and exit the crime scene?
  - What did the suspect touch?
  - Did the suspect steal anything? (The item taken does not necessarily have to be something of value but could have been taken as a trophy or souvenir.)
- Were restraints used (rope, clothing, bedding, tape, belts, and such)?
- Were any foreign objects or aids used (pen, stick, bottle, condom, lubricant, and such)?
- Can the suspect be described in detail using an interview worksheet? Ask the victim if he can—
  - Provide enough description for a composite sketch.
  - Identify the suspect in a physical or photographic lineup.
  - Recognize the suspect's voice.
  - Identify the suspect's clothing.
  - Identify items of clothing the suspect removed from himself.
  - Identify what items of the victim's clothing were removed. Did the suspect remove any of the victim's clothing? Did the victim remove any of his own clothing?
  - Recall any unusual anatomical markings or tattoos on the suspect.
- How soon after the sexual assault did the victim report the crime? To whom?
- Were there any potential ear and/or eye witnesses?
- Were there any individuals who interacted with the victim before, during, or after the incident. This includes friends, neighbors, relatives, co-workers, or law enforcement, medical, and other professionals.
- Were there any individuals who interacted with the suspect before, during, or after the incident. This includes—
  - Friends.
  - Neighbors.
  - Relatives.
  - Coworkers.
  - LE, medical, and other professionals.
- Were there any witnesses who can place the suspect and the victim together before or after the attack, or at the location of the assault?
- Has the victim talked to the suspect since the incident? If so, what was said and who initiated the conversation?

CONSENT DETERMINATION

9-19. Do not assume from a victim's occupation, associates, habits, or appearance that the victim is promiscuous and most likely consented. Do not infer consent from the fact that the victim has associated with the accused. Very few rapes can be categorized as "stranger" rapes, and the likelihood that the victim knew his assailant, even remotely, is high. The courts decide whether or not consent was given. Always consult with trial counsel. Never ignore physical or other evidence of sexual activity just because the accused admits it. All available evidence is collected and probative evidence will be forwarded to the USACIL for examination.

9-20. Statements and accusations that the victim is known to participate in lewd conduct, habits, or associations or has engaged in specific sex acts with the suspect or other individuals may be admissible evidence. These points should be checked in detail. Although these points may be true, such individuals can be bona fide victims of sex offenses. In many cases, the offender considers them easier targets as they have a reputation and are less likely to be believable as victims.

9-21. Investigators must be alert for attempts by an accused to make up untrue stories of past sex acts with the victim. A suspect may produce other individuals who claim such experiences. On the other hand, check on efforts by relatives or friends to provide the victim with a good reputation that is not deserved. It is important to remain unbiased, gather all of the facts, and remain vigilant in the pursuit of the truth.

9-22. When there is no dispute that the act of sexual intercourse occurred, but there is dispute over whether the victim consented or not, collect and review all evidence for possible examination. Generally for adult sexual assault investigations where consent is the only issue, sexual assault evidence will not be submitted for DNA examination. In these cases sexual assault evidence will be submitted for DNA examination if—

- The suspect recants his statement.
- The suspect's confession is anticipated to become inadmissible.
- Charges have been preferred for court-martial or civilian court, and the trial counsel or local civilian prosecutor requests it and is needed for trial.

CRIME SCENE PROCESSING

9-23. Security and control of the crime scene must be established quickly. Physical evidence at a sexual assault crime scene is fragile; special care must be taken to identify and protect physical evidence associated with the incident. Investigators should process the scene consistent with techniques outlined in chapter 4. Investigators should—

- Ensure that required search authorizations are obtained.
- Make photographs and sketches of the scene.
- Gather and process items of evidence.
- Collect the clothing worn by both the victim and the suspect if discarded and located at the scene.
- Search for seminal stains, blood, fiber, and hair using varying techniques, such as oblique and alternate light source.
- Check entrance and exit points when the incident occurred indoors, and look for items left by the assailant.
- Make a thorough search of the area that the victim declared in the initial interview to be the exact point of the attack.
- Search the bathroom if the attack was made in a residence. Many sex offenders will use the bathroom after committing a sex offense.
- Check the kitchen, such as the refrigerator and trash cans that the assailant may have used to discard any evidence.
- Ensure that if a condom is retrieved and still wet, swab both the exterior and interior with separate swabs before air-drying for shipment.

9-24. Investigators must be aware that in a sexual assault investigation, the victim and the suspect possess a great deal of evidence on their bodies and clothing. Many times the victim will feel the need to "cleanse himself" of the event, destroying physical evidence. Urge the victim to refrain from discarding, destroying, or attempting to wash away any physical evidence.

Note. In some cases, the suspect is still at the scene. Ensure that the victim and the suspect are separated and not transported in the same vehicle or interviewed in the same office. Not only does it retraumatize the victim, it also risks cross contamination of trace evidence.

9-25. One investigator, at a minimum, should be assigned the responsibility of conducting a crime scene examination of the actual scene. A different investigator should be responsible for escorting the victim and obtaining physical evidence at the hospital. The suspect (once identified and apprehended) should be processed by a third investigator; the suspect's body will hold physical evidence just as the victim's body does. This will prevent cross contamination of the three areas where evidence will be located and collected. Medical personnel will conduct collection from the victim and the suspect unless the suspect or the victim has changed clothes since the offense occurred, in which case clothes will be collected where they are located.

9-26. Medical personnel must examine all victims and suspects as soon as possible to avoid the loss or degradation of physical evidence. Medical personnel qualified to conduct an examination and collect evidence can include an attending physician, a nurse practitioner, a sexual assault nurse examiner, or a physician's assistant. Detailed questioning of the victim can be done later, but enough information should be obtained initially to locate the suspect, if possible. Avoid multiple investigators questioning the victim. One investigator should be tasked to interview and obtain any additional information from the victim. This will prevent redundancy and retraumatizing the victim. Obtain as much information from the initial responder as possible to avoid the same issue.

9-27. General evidence collection and crime scene processing techniques are discussed in detail in chapters 2 and 4, respectively. Requirements for collection and preservation of evidence in sexual assault cases are addressed in DODI 6495.02, AR 600-20, and relevant USACIDC policy. There are several evidence considerations that require specific attention or consideration during the investigation of sex crimes. These are discussed in the following paragraphs.

Alternate Light Source

9-28. Frequently, there is evidence present on the victim that is not visible to the naked eye. The victim should be examined using an alternate light source. Bite marks, bruises, seminal fluid, and fiber evidence which may not be evident become obvious when viewed under a light source. To conduct the examination, first ask the victim where to look for evidence; some victims may require a search beyond where they have indicated. To conduct the examination, activate the light source, put on the appropriate goggles, and slowly examine the area. Different substances will fluoresce at different light wavelengths and may be readily visible with the goggles. Any potential evidence discovered should be photographed and documented. If evidence is present, collect it as outlined in chapter 2.

Hair and Fiber Samples

9-29. Foreign hairs and fibers on the body must be collected as evidence from both victims and suspects. The method most often used on homicide victims is combing with a new, fine-tooth pocket comb. It is the best way to find loose hairs and fibers. Pack the teeth of the comb with absorbent cotton along the comb's base where the teeth meet the spine. Use separate combs for the head and pubic areas. Use transparent tape to collect fibers from other areas. Do not pull or comb pubic hair from a victim.

9-30. Pack each hair sample in a white, sealable envelope or paper bag. Carefully label each sample and identified it with the initials of the doctor or investigator who took the samples. Send the samples to the appropriate crime laboratory for examination.

Saliva, Urine, and Blood Samples

9-31. Collect and test saliva, urine, and blood samples for venereal diseases and the presence of alcohol, narcotics, and poisons. Toxicology examinations pertaining to "date rape" drugs or other controlled substances are conducted by the Division of Forensic Toxicology laboratory within the AFMES. When a toxicology examination is needed in conjunction with a sexual assault investigation, urine is the preferred bodily fluid; however, blood can be obtained and tested. If a date rape drug is suspected, toxicology testing must be performed promptly as these drugs dissipate quickly. Consult trial counsel and Division of Forensic Toxicology immediately. Collect the sample as soon as possible from the victim. Document evidence collected for toxicology examination by the Division of Forensic Toxicology laboratory on a separate evidence voucher and submit it directly to the Division of Forensic Toxicology laboratory using AFMES Form 1323.

Fingernail Scrapings

9-32. Medical personnel should take fingernail scrapings from each finger. Right-hand scrapings, along with the tool used to scrape underneath the fingernails, must be kept separate from left-hand scrapings and the scraper. The scrapings, properly packed and marked, should be sent to the crime laboratory. This is especially critical if the victim or the subject has been scratched. Hands and fingers should then be swabbed using a sterile swab in cases involving digital penetration.

Clothing

9-33. The clothing the victim worn during the crime is needed as evidence. The investigator must legally and promptly obtain the victim's clothing. The victim's family may destroy valuable evidence in an effort to clean or dispose of the garments. Even if a garment has been cleaned, it still may contain valuable evidence and should be secured.

9-34. Mark each item for identification. Package clothing in separate paper containers for shipment to the laboratory. If a garment is wet or has damp blood or seminal stains, dry it at room temperature without a fan or artificial heat. The garment must not become contaminated while it is being dried or stored; do not allow it to come in contact with any other clothing. Package and seal clothing as soon as possible in order to preserve any evidence present. Deliver these items to the evidence custodian in a sealed package pending shipment to the laboratory for examination. If the offense is committed in a bed, mark all bed linens for identification. Packaging and storage requirements for bed linens are the same as clothing.

Victim Photographs

9-35. Take photographs to preserve injuries as they appear on the victim. The photographs can show bruises and cuts that may heal or disappear by the time a suspect is brought to trial. Both bruises and cuts will change over a period of time and should be taken initially and again over the next several days, normally four times with 24 hours of separation (initial, 24 hours, 48 hours, and 72 hours later). Changes in color and shape of injuries may reveal various patterned injuries that may be important in determining the nature of the incident.

9-36. Photographs of living victims taken by LE personnel should be limited to those parts of the body normally visible when the victim is clothed. Photographs may be needed of the genitalia to substantiate and illustrate medical testimony. Photographs may not be taken of these parts of the victim's body except with their written consent. It is best if these photographs are taken by competent medical personnel. If the victim is a minor, consent must be received from the victim's parents or guardians before taking the photographs (unless the parent or guardian is the offender). The photographs of these areas of any victim should only be made under the supervision of the examining medical personnel. Ensure that a witness of the same sex as the victim is present during the photography process; for example, a female must be present when a female is photographed. LE personnel may photograph the bodies of deceased victims without permission of the next of kin.

9-37. If the victim of an alleged sodomy is an animal, it needs to be examined by a veterinarian for bruises, cuts, scrapes, human semen, blood, hair, and clothing fibers. Hair and blood samples should be taken and swab samples should be taken from body openings. If the animal is to be destroyed, take a picture of it first (showing evidence of the assault). If the animal is dead, the veterinarian should do a complete necropsy. The veterinarian can give expert testimony in court concerning the results of the examination.

Evidence Obtained From Suspects

9-38. The suspect must be examined for bruises, cuts, or scrapes. These may have been caused by the victim's struggle or from an act of forced sex. Search the entire body, particularly the genitals and pubic area, for blood, semen, hair, feces, vaginal debris, or other matter from the victim. For sodomy suspects, examine the oral and anal areas as well. Evidence is collected to compare with materials from the victim's body or the crime scene. Collect hair, blood, saliva samples, and fingernail scrapings from the suspect. Properly seal and mark all evidence, and send it to the crime laboratory.

9-39. Suspects do not have the legal right to refuse to have their photograph taken. Wounds on the suspect should be photographed. As with victims, bruises and cuts should be photographed four times with 24 hours of separation (initial, 24 hours, 48 hours, and 72 hours later). An offender sex crimes kit, with search warrant or consent, should be performed in every case.

MEDICAL EXAMINATIONS

9-40. The victim's body is the crime scene, and it may conceal evidence of a crime. From this evidence, the examining medical personnel can give expert testimony. Wounds, bruises, cuts, abrasions, and irritations may help to show penetration, violence, or resistance. These should be described in the doctor's notes, reports, and testimony. This evidence may provide leads to the type of suspect and the weapons used. Photographic records are quite helpful to the prosecution. Remember that evidence collection is followed "per the condition and needs of each victim." Use sexual assault forensic evidence (SAFE) kits to collect evidence of a sexual assault. See DODI 6495.02 for more information.

9-41. Victims and suspects who are subject to the UCMJ are examined by medical officers at the nearest military or civilian medical treatment facility. Before the examination, the investigator should provide the examining medical personnel with details about the victim, the subject, and the crime scene. This will facilitate a more comprehensive examination of the individual to ensure that required items of evidence are obtained for a successful resolution and prosecution of the investigation. It should never be assumed that the victim has communicated all aspects of the assault, particularly during the initial interview. Some of the aspects of the assault may be too humiliating or degrading to discuss. In light of this, an examination should be as thorough and comprehensive as the victim will allow and the medical personnel feels is prudent.

9-42. The examination must be done in a reasonable way for both the victim and the suspect. If possible, obtain the consent of both parties. If the victim or the suspect will not consent to the examination and collection, a legal search authorization must be obtained. Such searches are allowed if they are not unreasonable or morally reprehensible. Consult with both supervisor and trial counsel before obtaining a search authorization for a victim. A search of any part of the body not normally open to public view may be made without an individual's consent if it is incident to a lawful apprehension. Use only the degree of force needed to conduct the search, and ensure that a complete chain of custody is kept for all collected evidence. The victim may opt for a strictly medical examination where the evidence may be collected and retained by the medical treatment facility for a period of time but not released. At any point the victim requests to pursue the offense, the items can be released to the appropriate investigative agency.

9-43. Individuals not subject to the UCMJ may choose to be examined by either a civilian doctor of their choice or a medical officer. They cannot be forced to submit to an examination by a medical officer. The fact that the suspect is military or that the military is investigating the offense does not alter a civilian's right to choose an examining doctor or to refuse a military examination.

9-44. If the victim indicates that he is sexually active and has had sex recently, hair and blood standards should be collected from the victim's sexual partner for elimination purposes. The attending medical personnel or sexual assault nurse examiner should be able to determine whether or not this is necessary. Trial counsel should be consulted in these cases. Send all physical evidence such as hair, blood, and foreign materials taken from the body of the victim or suspect and comparison samples to the laboratory immediately.

SEXUAL CRIMES INVOLVING JUVENILES

9-45. Obtain written permission from a parent or guardian before a child is examined or treated by a medical officer. A parent or guardian should be with the child and present during the examination. Explain very tactfully that an examination is needed for the investigation. Advise them that it should be shown by medical opinion that the offense did take place.

Note. In cases where the parent or guardian is the offender, written permission from the parent or guardian suspected is not required. In these cases, an advocate will be assigned to the victim. The parental authority may also be circumvented if the investigator believes the nonoffending parent's refusal is to protect the offending parent from prosecution. Consult with trial counsel in such a case. A judicial order may be required.

9-46. All evidence should be collected and evaluated for submission based on the elements on the incident. Consideration will be given to the age of the victim and the child's potential as a witness in a court. When warranted, use SAFE kits for collecting evidence of sexual assault. Facilities that perform or could perform examinations on alleged sexual assault patients maintain SAFE kits within the facility at all times. Medical examination of juveniles should be performed by medical personnel trained in child sexual assault examinations. In most cases, colposcope photography is highly recommended.

IDENTIFYING SUSPECTS

9-47. One of the objectives of a criminal investigation is to solve the crime by finding evidence that proves the suspect and the victim were both at the crime scene at a particular point in time. This, coupled with the ability to answer who, what, where, when, why, and how, will result in a successful investigation. When checking leads, keep in mind that sex crimes do not just have one type of suspect. Anyone can commit a sex offense. Whoever had the chance to commit the crime can be suspect. This is in spite of an excellent reputation, a law abiding past, being an "excellent" Soldier, or a high station in life.

9-48. The first steps in apprehending a suspect often relates to whether the victim or witnesses know or can identify the person. If the suspect is known or if a description is available, send this promptly to military police patrols to make the apprehension. Use all resources to identify, search, and apprehend the suspect. Descriptions of individuals recently apprehended by military police may be matched with the description of the wanted suspect.

9-49. Think about what the victim or witness said the suspect wore. Make a detailed visual examination of the suspect's clothing. Examine it for evidence of the offense, physical contact with the victim, and presence at the crime scene. Collect and air-dry clothing if necessary, then package and seal it as soon as possible in order to preserve any evidence present. These items should be delivered to the evidence custodian in a sealed package and remain that way until the evidence is examined at the laboratory. An investigator must be particularly attuned to all types of physical evidence. Trace evidence is minute and easily overlooked as it is frequently not seen at all with the unaided eye.

9-50. Sometimes items belonging to friends or associates of a suspect should be examined. This is done if there is evidence that the suspect has loaned, borrowed, or exchanged clothing. Search places where the suspect may have disposed of incriminating evidence. Many sex offenders take items of clothing or personal items from their victims. Physical objects symbolic of sex and obscene literature and photographs are often found in the possession of suspects. Because some suspects will not want these items left around their homes, the investigator should get permission to search a suspect's place of work. Other items that might give a clue to the identity of a sex offender are tape recordings of previous sexual acts or letters from friends discussing his shared participation in unusual sexual activity.

9-51. Medical personnel can help identify and locate the suspect. They may be asked to identify persons recently seeking treatment for injuries that may be associated with a sexual assault. They may also be able to account for the activities and recent whereabouts of patients who may be suspects. There are special considerations with regard to privileged medical information.

9-52. If leads do not develop elsewhere, check databases and sex offender files for offenses with similar MOs. Identify individuals who have committed similar crimes or who have used similar criminal methods. Accurate and detailed records of unrelated sex crimes can lead to early detection of a sex offender. A check of these individuals and their recent activities may result in leads. Check assault records as assaults are sometimes sex related. Remember that rape, although a sex crime, is not about having sexual relations but rather about control and domination.

Chapter 10

Crimes Against Property Investigations

Property crimes require extensive investigative skill and diligence to effectively investigate. This chapter will cover those crimes associated with thefts, wrongful appropriation, and unlawful entry as well as arson investigations. LE investigators must overcome the effects of delayed or false reporting, undocumented ownership, disturbed or staged crime scenes, improperly secured property, poor descriptions of property, and a lack of witnesses. Crimes involving fire and explosions present many difficulties to investigators, most significantly the destruction of physical evidence associated with fires. General investigative approaches and techniques are common across all criminal investigations. These investigative approaches and techniques are covered in previous chapters. Chapter 2 covers collection of physical evidence, chapter 3 covers collection of testimonial evidence, and chapter 4 covers crime scene processing. This chapter will address investigative considerations specific to crimes against property.

DESCRIPTIONS OF PROPERTY CRIMES

10-1. It is important that investigators know the legal descriptions of the possible crimes against property. This ensures that the investigator understands the legal elements of the crime when determining what, if any, crime has been committed. The following paragraphs provide a general description of the crimes and their associated elements. The MCM is the primary reference and should be referred to for detailed discussion of each crime including legal definitions and elements for each crime.

BURGLARY

10-2. Burglary, Article 129 UCMJ, is the breaking and entering of a dwelling of another in the nighttime (hours of darkness) with the intent to commit an offense punishable under Articles 118 through 128, except Article 123a, whether the intent is carried out or not. Burglary is primarily an offense against the security of habitation. The break-in may be perpetrated by using physical force or by false pretenses, such as posing as a utility worker. The breaking can be physical or constructive, meaning the actual physical "breaking" of a door or window is not required; the only requirement is the breaking of the "barrier," whether it be opening a closed door or completely opening a partially opened window.

10-3. Any person subject to the UCMJ who, with the intent to commit these offenses, breaks and enters the dwelling of another in the nighttime (hours of darkness) is guilty of burglary. A dwelling includes outbuildings within the common enclosure, farmyard, or cluster of buildings used as a residence. As soon as any part of the body is inserted into the dwelling, the requirement of "entry" is met. Inserting an object into the dwelling to extract property also qualifies as "entry." It is immaterial whether the intended offense at the time of breaking and entering was committed or even attempted, but the intent to commit the act is essential to the proof of burglary.

HOUSEBREAKING

10-4. Housebreaking, Article 130 UCMJ, is similar to burglary. The elements required for a housebreaking are that the accused unlawfully entered a certain building or structure a certain person and that the entry was made with the intent to commit a criminal offense within the building or structure. The intent to commit a criminal offense is an essential element of housebreaking and must be alleged and proven in order to support a conviction of this offense. There are several major differences between a housebreaking and a burglary. The offense of housebreaking is broader than burglary: the place entered is not required to be a dwelling; it is not necessary that there be a breaking; the entry may be either in the nighttime or the daytime; and the criminal offense intended need not be to commit one of the offenses made punishable under Articles 118 through 128 of the UCMJ.

UNLAWFUL ENTRY

10-5. Unlawful entry, Article 134 UCMJ, is closely related to housebreaking. It is an entry on land or into a structure on that land, affected peacefully and without force, accomplished without consent or authority. Unlike housebreaking, the intent to commit an offense within the place entered is not necessary to constitute this offense.

LARCENY AND WRONGFUL APPROPRIATION

10-6. Larceny, Article 121(a)(1) UCMJ, is when a person wrongfully takes, obtains, or withholds by any means, the property of another including money, personal property, or articles of value of any kind. The taking of the property must include the intent to permanently deprive or defraud the victim of his property. The crime of larceny often results from burglary or housebreaking. However, other forms of larceny may include frauds against persons, larcenies involving safes, larceny of motor vehicles, and shoplifting.

10-7. Wrongful appropriation, Article 121(a)(2) UCMJ, is the same as larceny except that the intent is to temporarily, rather than permanently, deprive or defraud the owner or any other person of the property. Intent may be proved by circumstantial evidence. If a person secretly takes property, hides it, and denies knowing anything about it, intent to steal may be inferred; if the property was taken openly and returned, this would tend to negate such intent.

10-8. The crime of larceny includes common-law larceny, false pretenses (fraud), and embezzlement. A wrongful acquisition, assumption, or exercise of control over the property of another is what each of these crimes has in common. Each contains the proof of intent of the accused to permanently deprive the owner of the property. These included offenses are described as—

- **Common-law larceny.** This offense requires the taking (by trespassing) and felonious carrying away of property belonging to another with the intent to deprive him of that property permanently. This includes shoplifting and pilferage.
- **False pretenses (fraud).** This offense contains all the elements of proof for larceny, but the property is obtained by a misrepresentation of an existing fact or condition that the victim relied on.
- **Embezzlement.** This offense occurs when an individual who lawfully is in possession or control of the property of another through a position of trust intentionally and unlawfully withholds or diverts it; for example, if a bank teller receives money to pay customers, retains part of the money, and then alters records to cover up the amount taken.

ARSON

10-9. Arson, Article 126 UCMJ, is separated into two separate offenses of arson—aggravated arson and simple arson. Simple arson applies to any person who willfully and maliciously burns or sets fire to the property of another person. Aggravated arson occurs when a person willfully and maliciously burns or sets fire to an inhabited dwelling or other structure with knowledge that another person is inside the structure. Intent is a critical element of proving arson, but motive is not.

10-10. In aggravated arson, danger to human life is the essential element; in simple arson, it is injury to the property of another. In either case, the fact that no one is injured is immaterial. It must be shown that the accused set the fire willfully and maliciously. Arson cannot be the result of negligence or accident; for both simple and aggravated arson, it must be proven that the act was willful and malicious.

10-11. Burning with intent to defraud, Article 134 UCMJ, is a form of arson motivated by monetary gain. The primary element of burning with intent to defraud is that the accused willfully and maliciously burned or set fire to certain property owned by a certain person or organization and that such burning or setting on fire was with the intent to defraud a certain person or organization and that, under the circumstances, the conduct of the accused was to the prejudice of good order and discipline in the armed forces or was of a nature to bring discredit upon the armed forces.

INVESTIGATING BURGLARY, HOUSEBREAKING, AND LARCENY

10-12. Evidence from a burglary or housebreaking investigation usually leads investigators to other crimes, such as larceny. The investigative techniques for larceny often apply to both burglary and housebreaking. The investigator's goal is to identify and apprehend the offenders and recover stolen property. Crimes against property are investigated using the same techniques described in chapter 4. Those techniques include—

- Measuring, photographing, video recording, and sketching the scene.
- Searching for evidence.
- Identifying, collecting, examining, marking, protecting, and storing physical evidence.
- Questioning victims, witnesses, and suspects.
- Documenting all statements and observations in notes.

10-13. Burglary, housebreaking, and larceny are among the most tedious and difficult to investigate for even the most seasoned investigators. Although property crimes are among the most common crimes reported, many more larcenies go unreported. If a victim feels responsible for the lack of effective security, believes the property lacks enough value to investigate its loss, doesn't realize his property has been stolen, or feels LE personnel won't seek diligently to recover the property or identify the perpetrator, the theft will likely go unreported.

10-14. Physical evidence in property crimes is similar to that in crimes against persons and includes fingerprints, foot and tire impressions, toolmarks, trace and serological evidence, and objects left at the crime scene. The collection of evidence in property crimes is no less important than evidence collected in crimes against persons. Investigators have been rewarded with unexpected recoveries of property and the apprehension of subjects by thoroughly processing crime scenes and pursuing unlikely investigative leads. The following tips are provided to assist an investigator when conducting an investigation of a burglary or housebreaking:

- Establish who had the means, opportunity, and motive to commit the offense.
- Eliminate individuals who had no access to the stolen property.
- Use the crime scene examination to determine how access was gained, how many people were involved, and the time frame of the occurrence. The presence of excessive damage may be indicative of juvenile involvement.
- Establish what the suspect and victim did before and after the offense. This will aid in eliminating them as suspects or in establishing their ability or opportunity to participate in the crime.
- Conduct canvass interviews of the people who live, work, and spend time in the area where the crime was committed to determine who might know the victim or suspect.
- Pursue property—not people. Make timely entries of stolen property into the National Crime Information Center files. Expeditiously check pawnshops, flea markets, and other sources used for quick resale of property. Also canvass internet sale sites for resale activity.
- Conduct polygraph examinations earlier in the investigation, rather than as a last resort.
- Send the evidence to the USACIL.

PROCESSING THE SCENE

10-15. The initial notification begins the investigative process. Obtain as much detail as possible during this phase of the investigation. Fully identify the caller and get detailed information about how the caller discovered the crime and what action the caller took at the crime scene. Inform the caller to avoid rearranging items and to prevent others from entering the area. In many cases, the caller may have been notified of the crime by a third party. If so, identify the third party for later questioning. Use this information to develop a preliminary plan.

10-16.   Look for evidence in areas outside the immediate crime scene, such as parking lots, sidewalks, or footpaths. Consider having the military police record the license plate numbers of vehicles parked in the area. Observe the general condition of the crime scene.

10-17.   During the initial observation, determine if a crime was committed and, if so, what type. Larceny is the offense most often involved during the investigation of a housebreaking or burglary. Get a detailed description of the missing property and record the exact location from which the item was taken. Get the location of all parties initially thought to be involved in the crime and the details concerning how the property was secured. Find out where the owners or occupants were at the time of the crime. If there is more than one victim, interview each victim separately. Take note of inconsistencies in their accounts of the incident.

10-18.   Proof of ownership must be established early in the investigation. Obtain the names and addresses of individuals who can verify ownership or possession of the stolen item. The owner may be able to provide documents or photographs to help establish ownership, possession, and the value of the stolen property. If military property was involved, obtain hand receipts and any other accountability documents. If the stolen property was insured, determine the amount, policy number, name and address of the insuring company, and the names of beneficiaries of the policy. Insurance companies record detailed information on insured items.

10-19.   Check for holes sawed or hacked through walls, floors, partitions, or ceilings. The size, shape, and location of openings are important clues in the investigation. Note the height of the openings from the ground or from where the offender stood. If possible, determine if entry was made bodily or with an instrument. Investigate the possibility that someone from inside the building assisted in the crime. Look carefully to see if evidence was destroyed. In an attempt to mask a crime, offenders often wipe off fingerprints, wear gloves, deface toolmarks, or try to obscure footprints and tire tracks. In many instances, larcenies are crimes of opportunity where a suspect may take an item left unattended and unsecured. This may be considered a more difficult crime to solve as there is less physical evidence available; however, consider the mindset of the suspect as it is likely someone who has observed this item over a period of time and identifies is as "easy pickings." In this event, you would want to consider those who observe the stolen item based on how long it has been viewable and left unsecured.

COLLECTING EVIDENCE

10-20.   The circumstances of a case must guide the actions of the investigator when processing a crime scene. However, developing a system for searching a crime scene reduces the chances of making mistakes. Evidence usually common to breaking and entering includes—
- Glass.
- Cigarette butts.
- Fingerprints.
- Dust prints.
- Shoe prints.
- Fabrics.
- Paint.
- Blood.
- Hair and fiber.
- Saliva
- Soil.
- Tape.
- Tire tracks.
- Toolmarks or impressions.

10-21. Physical evidence must be protected and processed according to AR 195-5. Fragile evidence must be protected from the elements, animals, and people. If possible, all evidence must be photographed, sketched, preserved, collected, and recorded. Upon collection, the investigator must properly mark the evidence with his initials and the time and date of the recovery on each item. See chapters 2 and 4 for more information on protecting and processing evidence.

10-22. Determine points of entry and exit where evidence is often discovered. Check locks or fasteners for evidence of tampering. Ask the victim to assist in the crime scene search by pointing out where items have been disturbed or removed. Once points of entry and exit have been determined, inspect the ground surrounding the entry and exit points for signs of footprints or other impressions. Examine broken windows for clothing fibers, blood, other trace evidence, and the method used to break or force the window open. Ask the victim when the dwelling or structure was last known to be secure. Look for cut locks in and around the crime scene. Check dumpsters for discarded tools or evidence.

10-23. Look for fingerprints and other evidence at points where the offender was likely to be within the overall crime scene. Such evidence may suggest how much time an offender spent on the premises, his skill, or his familiarity with the location. Determine if the offender's search was systematic, thorough, selective, or haphazard. The manner of search may reveal the crime to be the work of either a professional or an amateur.

10-24. Examine garbage containers and nearby dumpsters for food items identified by the victim as missing from the refrigerator or kitchen. These items may have fingerprints or bite marks from the offender. Canvass the neighborhood to identify witnesses.

10-25. Evidence obtained through the questioning of people or by other means must be verified; a confession does not negate the need for evidence that supports the confession. Look for evidence (such as fingerprints, palm prints, footprints, or identifiable tire tracks) that places the suspect or his vehicle at the scene of the crime. Match soil or rock samples from the suspect's clothing or vehicle to samples taken from the crime scene to help place the suspect at the scene. Evidence may lead to finding stolen property in the possession of a suspect or in a place under his control. Finding the item or evidence of the item in the possession or control of the suspect is not, by itself, enough to convict him of theft. The investigator must show the suspect knowingly and illegally deprived another of possession of the item.

10-26. To develop leads, inquire at pawnshops in the area. Provide shop owners with a full description of the stolen items. If such items were pawned, coordinate with local police agencies to have the items seized or a "police hold" placed on them. Also check internet sales sites to see if stolen items are being offered for sale.

CONDUCTING INTERVIEWS

10-27. General considerations and techniques for conducting interviews and LE interrogations are covered in detail within chapter 3. The following paragraphs describe considerations specific to interviews relevant to burglary, housebreaking, and larceny.

10-28. Interview the victim and obtain a sworn statement as soon as possible. Obtain full details concerning potential suspects and a full description of the missing property. Identify potential witnesses; interview neighbors, individuals who frequent the area, and coworkers of the victim. Compare details contained within the statements to other physical and testimonial evidence to identify inconsistencies or issues requiring further inquiry.

10-29. During the interviews the investigator should focus on determining who had the motive, means, and opportunity to commit the offense. Motive is the least important factor to consider in determining who committed the crime; however, the means is very important. Determine if the suspect had the means and if he was mentally and physically capable of committing the offense. Determine if the suspect can be placed at the scene of the crime and if an alibi can be proven false.

10-30. Once a potential suspect has been identified, conduct an interview and obtain a sworn statement. Have the suspect describe his actions before, during, and after the crime. Address elements of proof of the suspected crime during the interview. Obtain proper legal authority and search the suspect's residence, vehicle, and other areas within their control.

ANALYZING CRIME PATTERNS

10-31.   Crime pattern analysis is the process of identifying patterns of activity, association, and events. A basic premise is followed when using this technique: activities, associations, and events occur in identifiable and characteristic patterns. Crime pattern analysis looks at the components of crimes to discern similarities in the areas of time, geography, personnel, victims, and MO. Crime pattern analysis examines all of the characteristics of the crime and compares it to characteristics of other crimes that have occurred before and after the current incident. Comparisons of this nature uncover patterns and 'hot spots' for crime trends and may even result in surveillance that catches an offender in the act. See ATTP 3-39.20 for more information.

10-32.   If no suspects emerge from victim, witness, or canvass interviews or through the examination of physical evidence, a diligent review of police intelligence databases and networks may yield important investigative leads. The investigator should consider the types of items stolen, methods of entry or access, presence of footprints or fingerprints, location of the crime, or time of day of the crime. Common patterns may be identified across multiple crime scenes.

CONSIDERING OFFENDER TYPOLOGIES

10-33.   The motivation for committing housebreaking and burglaries are as varied as the offenders themselves and the methods they employ. Trends among offenders are influenced by a number of factors including drug abuse, economic strain, and the relative security of a community. Although military communities are oriented toward a higher level of security as it relates to protection of persons and property, it doesn't override the motivation of offenders to take things from others.

10-34.   Offenders can be considered in three broad categories—those who commit housebreaking and burglary using organized methods, serial offenders who target potential victims and commit crimes not necessarily oriented toward financial gain, and unorganized offenders who conduct a general targeting of homes or businesses looking for easy targets.

10-35.   Organized offenders are more professional and deliberate than other types of offenders. They are more likely to choose targets where the payoff is worth the risk. Organized offenders avoid residences where they are likely to encounter a homeowner. They look for targets such as retail establishments, military storage facilities, construction sites, and units storing high-value items. They are also more likely to choose places where the crime will go undetected until the offender is long gone. Organized housebreaking and burglary crimes of this type often remain unsolved as the offender is careful to use methods that thwart investigative efforts.

10-36.   Serial offenders who commit housebreaking and burglaries may target victims over a long period of time and are not always motivated by financial gain. Statistically, a high number of victims are revictimized because a perpetrator sees them as "easy targets." The thief may have seen property during a previous criminal act and is motivated to return for the desired property. Some offenders may break into homes for the psychological thrill or sexual satisfaction. They tend to take small personal items such as underwear or jewelry and use the items for psychological or sexual gratification at a later time. In military communities, serial offenders may build up courage by stealing underwear from laundry rooms until they are confident enough to break into barracks rooms or homes. This type of offender may graduate to breaking into homes when people are present and even further to violent sexual crimes such as rape.

10-37.   Most housebreakings and burglaries are committed by unorganized offenders who loosely target homes and businesses. Unorganized offenders will also target family, friends, and coworkers in the pursuit of quick money. Unorganized offenders are also responsible for 'smash and grabs' of both people and businesses. Their crimes normally yield small high-value items that can be quickly pawned or resold. They often graduate to bigger crimes where they find a more deliberate approach is more profitable. Both drug users desperate for money and juveniles are known to commit unorganized housebreaking and burglaries.

For housebreakings and burglaries to occur, three conditions must be present—a motivated offender, a suitable target, and the likelihood of committing the crime without being caught.

INVESTIGATING ARSON AND EXPLOSIONS

10-38. Similar investigative techniques are used to investigate arson and explosive incidents. The investigator must determine the nature and cause of the incident. Initially, he must distinguish between an accidental fire or explosion and one produced intentionally or by criminal negligence. Crimes involving fire and explosions present many difficulties, paramount among which is the partial or total destruction of evidence. Although the usual investigative steps are followed at the crime scene, great care must be taken in handling items of evidence and interpreting the pattern suggested by their location. Police intelligence gathered as a result of these investigations is reported and shared with other federal, state, local, and HN police agencies.

10-39. Except in the most obvious cases, the determination of the origin and cause of a fire or explosion may be a complex and difficult undertaking that requires specialized training and experience as well as knowledge of generally accepted scientific methods of fire and explosion investigation. The investigator must either have the appropriate expertise or call on the assistance of someone with that knowledge. This is especially true in cases involving deaths, major injuries, or large property losses. Knowledgeable resources may include local fire marshals and alcohol, tobacco, and firearms investigators trained in arson and/or explosion investigation.

ARSON INVESTIGATION

10-40. Arson investigation is a difficult field for the investigator. Arson frequently involves the use of an accelerant (a material used to spread or increase the rate of burning). Typical accelerants include ignitable liquids such as gasoline, mineral spirits, kerosene, and similar materials. The presence of such materials, if there is no legitimate reason for their presence, may indicate arson. It is extremely important that evidence or debris is not moved before careful examination to enable reconstruction of the cause of the fire.

10-41. Fires, by their destructive nature, consume evidence of their ignition. LE investigations are often compromised, and evidence is often further damaged or destroyed by the actions of firefighters whose primary objectives are preservation of life and protection of property.

10-42. During a fire involving an accelerant, the accelerant will undergo change. The more volatile components will be lost to a much greater extent than the components of lower volatility, and those that remain may be absorbed into the wood or carpeting of the structure. Laboratory analysis can determine if an ignitable liquid is present in any evidentiary samples collected at the scene. The volatility range and general chemical composition can also be determined. There will be situations in which one sample may disclose the presence of an ignitable liquid and another will not, even though the samples were taken from areas quite close together.

10-43. There are four categories of fires—natural, accidental, incendiary, and undetermined. Natural fires occur due to naturally occurring conditions such as lightning strikes. Most fires are accidental, caused by persons with no intent to cause damage. Incendiary fires are those that are deliberately set. To prove it was an incendiary fire, it must first be proven that it was not accidental or natural. To determine if a fire was accidental or incendiary, investigators must understand the basics of fire chemistry and behavior and the associated evidence left by fires.

Understanding Fire Chemistry

10-44. Fire is a chemical reaction that takes place when fuel, heat, and oxygen combine in the correct proportions to produce an uninhibited chain reaction. Fire can only exist when all of these factors are present. Remove any one of the elements and the fire goes out because the continuing chemical reaction has been stopped. Fires produce heat, flame, smoke, and gases. These combustion by-products may or may not be readily seen. Flame includes both an open flame and a smoldering glow. Smoke is composed of very fine solid particles and condensed vapors.

10-45.   In a fire only gases burn; solid and liquid fuels must be heated until they become vapor (gas) before they can burn. Heat chemically decomposes a fuel into its gaseous elements. This decomposition is known as pyrolysis. For example, when wood is heated, it pyrolyzes to form hydrogen, oxygen, ethane and methane gases, and methyl alcohol. It is these highly flammable vapors that burn. Fuel in vapor form in its normal state, like natural gas, does not need to be pyrolyzed.

10-46.   Most fuels are compounds of carbon, hydrogen, and oxygen along with traces of mineral matter. When the fuels burn completely and freely in air, the carbon reacts with the oxygen to form carbon dioxide and the hydrogen combines with the oxygen to form water vapor. The mineral matter remains behind as ash. As the oxygen in the fuel is used up, oxygen is drawn from the air to continue the reaction. That is why drafts and air supplies directly affect the behavior of a fire. A fire started in a completely enclosed space soon dies. It uses up all of the available oxygen and generates noncombustible gases that smother it. On the other hand, the rate of burning is greatly increased if a chimney effect exists when the hot gases and flame contact combustible material. Disastrous fires result in large buildings where elevator shafts or stairways served as chimneys to direct the up-rushing flames and gases.

10-47.   Heat is required to ignite the fuel and start the chemical reaction. Once ignition has taken place, the reaction (fire) produces its own heat and becomes self-generating as long as fuel and oxygen remain present in the appropriate amounts. Fuels do not need to be touched by flame to begin burning. They simply need to be heated above their ignition points. It is for this reason that heat, not flame, is the greatest cause of fire spread. Heat can be transferred from one place to another by—

- **Convection.** Convection occurs when heat is transferred by a circulating medium like air or water. Heat convection by circulating air is the most common method of fire spread.
- **Conduction.** Conduction transfers heat by contact. Often, heat from a fire in one room is conducted throughout the structure by pipes or electrical conduit. If combustible material in another room is in contact with the pipe, it can become heated above its ignition point and start a second fire. Metal objects are the most frequent conductors of heat. Sometimes, even brick walls can conduct enough heat to cause a second fire.
- **Radiation.** Radiation transfers heat in the form of energy waves through space. Heat radiates through any transparent medium like air, glass, or even water. No physical contact is needed. This is how the heat of the sun is transferred through the vacuum of space to the earth. Often, a fire in one building radiates enough heat to start a fire in another building, even though a curtain of water is sprayed between the buildings.

10-48.   The composition of fire gases emitted by the burning materials depends on the chemical makeup of the burning material, the amount of oxygen available during burning, and the temperature of the fire. Most fire gases are highly toxic. They are the biggest cause of fire deaths. The biggest single killer is carbon monoxide—not because it is the most toxic, but because it is the most abundant. When large quantities are breathed in, carbon monoxide causes unconsciousness and eventually death. At less than lethal concentrations, it causes disorientation and confusion, subjecting victims to other hazards present in the fire. The second most dangerous gas produced by a fire is carbon dioxide. While not toxic in itself, a 2 percent increase in carbon dioxide in the air causes a 100 percent increase in a human's breathing rate. This doubles a victim's intake of other toxic gases.

Understanding Fire Behavior

10-49.   The term fire behavior describes the magnitude, direction, and intensity of fire spread. Fires behave according to well-defined principles of burning to include the following:

- Fire burns up and out. It leaves a V-shaped char pattern on walls and vertical structures. A fire that is hot and fast at the point of origin will leave a sharp V pattern. A slow fire will produce a shallow V pattern. If fire meets an obstruction, such as a ceiling, it will burn across the obstruction looking for a place to go up.
- Fire travels with air currents. It never travels into the wind unless the entire fire load (the combustible material or fuel in an area) is on the windward side of the fire. If this happens, the fire slowly eats into the fire load as its tendency to follow the wind is overcome by its attraction for fuel.

- Fire seeks oxygen. Because fire consumes great amounts of oxygen, it is always drawn toward new sources of oxygen when burning occurs indoors. It is not unusual to see a char pattern going up a wall to the ceiling and across the ceiling toward an open window. It is also common to find deeper charring and evidence of higher heat on window frames and doorways.

10-50. These principles of burning account for most of the fire and char patterns seen during and after a fire. In some cases, patterns may indicate conditions known as a flashover or backdraft. These are natural conditions which only occur during fires when specific conditions exist. These two conditions are described as follows:

- **Flashover (also referred to as a rollover).** A flashover occurs when flames instantaneously erupt over the entire surface of a room or confined area. Once a fire starts, it produces gases that rise and form a superheated gas layer at the ceiling. As the volume of this gas layer increases, it begins to move down to the floor, heating all objects in the room regardless of their proximity to the flaming objects. In a typical contained fire, the gas layer at the ceiling can rapidly reach temperatures in excess of its autoignition point. If there is enough existing oxygen, a flashover occurs and everything in the room becomes involved in an open flame all at once. This sudden eruption into flames generates a tremendous amount of heat, smoke, and pressure with enough force to push beyond the room of origin through doors and windows. This combustion process will accelerate more now because it has a greater amount of heat to move to objects.
- **Backdraft.** A backdraft occurs when a structure burns with all doors and windows closed and the fire uses up all of the available oxygen. It then turns into a slow smoldering fire, generating huge amounts of superheated carbon monoxide gas. The hot gases rise to the top of the room and stay there. Because carbon monoxide is a flammable gas and is heated above its ignition point, it only needs more oxygen to burst into flames. Oxygen entering around cracks in doors and windows keeps the fire smoldering. This produces more and more superheated carbon monoxide. When a door is opened or a window melts out, the in-rushing oxygen combines with the superheated carbon monoxide, causing an explosive fire.

10-51. Flashovers and backdrafts result in an explosive ignition of combustible material. Windows may blow out, and the explosion may be strong enough to damage the structure of the building. Damage caused by a backdraft may look similar to that caused by a low explosive. A backdraft produces an unusual char pattern; most of the burn damage will be at the extreme top of the room. There will also be a rather sharp line of demarcation at the bottom of the char pattern on the wall. Accelerant residue may not be present.

10-52. When wood burns, it chars a pattern of cracks that looks like the scales on an alligator's back. The scales will be the smallest and the cracks the deepest where the fire has been burning the longest or the hottest. Most wood in structures chars at the rate of 1 inch in depth per 40 to 45 minutes of burning at 1400 to 1600 degrees Fahrenheit (the temperature of most house fires). However, no specific time of burning can be determined based solely on the depth of charring since most fires vary in intensity and fuel load. A room fire chars only the upper one-half to two-thirds of the room. Ceiling damage in a normal structural fire is usually at least five times that of the damage to the floor. Sometimes a char pattern has a sharp line of demarcation on one side. This indicates that the fire quit spreading in that direction when a draft entered and blew it back.

10-53. When glass is exposed to fire, it begins to melt at about 1200 degrees Fahrenheit. It becomes runny at about 1600 degrees Fahrenheit. A lot can be learned about a fire from the glass at the scene. All glass at the scene should be examined; conclusions should not be made based on the appearance of one glass sample. As a general rule, glass that contains many cracks indicates a rapid heat buildup. Glass that is heavily stained indicates a slow, smoky fire. Bright metals, like the chromium on toasters, turn colors when heated. These colors may remain after the fire and indicate the temperature of the fire at that location.

Investigating the Fire Scene

10-54. The National Fire Protection Association (NFPA) 921 was developed as a consensus document based on the knowledge and experience of fire, engineering and legal and investigative experts from throughout the United States. The guide is considered to be a benchmark tool for fire investigations.

10-55.   Before investigating a fire scene ensure that search authorization is obtained to perform a search of the area. Investigators arriving at a fire scene should observe and mentally note the conditions and activities and, as soon as conditions permit, initiate permanent documentation of the information (such as notes, voice recordings, photographs, or videotapes). Investigators should document the following:

- The presence, location, and condition of victims and witnesses.
- Vehicles leaving the scene, bystanders, or unusual activities near the scene.
- Indicators that arson may have been the cause of the fire including—
  - The presence of accelerants (flammable liquids) including empty containers.
  - Indications of pooling or streamers that may have been used to start or spread the fire.
  - The presence of timing devices or other ignition devices.
  - Signs of explosion.
  - Evidence of multiple points of origin.
  - Signs of tampering to electrical outlets or appliances.
  - Signs of tampering with the sprinkler or other fire suppression systems.
- Flame and smoke conditions (the volume of flames and smoke; the color, height, and location of the flames; and the direction in which the flames and smoke are moving).
- The type of occupancy and the use of the structure (such as a residential occupancy being used as a business).
- The condition of the structure (lights turned on; fire through the roof; walls standing; open, closed, or broken windows and doors).
- Conditions surrounding the scene (blocked driveways, debris, or damage to other structures).
- Weather conditions.
- Any unusual characteristics or circumstances of the scene (the presence of containers, exterior burning or charring on the building, the absence of normal contents, unusual odors, or fire trailers).
- Fire suppression techniques used (including ventilation, forcible entry, and utility shutoff measures).
- The status of fire alarms, security alarms, and sprinklers.

10-56.   Before entering the scene, responding investigators should identify and introduce themselves to the incident commander (IC). They should determine who has jurisdiction and authorization (legal right of entry) and to identify others at the scene, such as LE, firefighting, EOD, emergency medical services, hazardous material, and utility services personnel.

10-57.   Information obtained from the IC and first responders will help the investigator determine the level of assistance required and whether additional investigative personnel are needed. Before entering the scene, determine initial scene safety by using observations and coordination with first responders. Consider environmental as well as personnel safety concerns, and assess changes in safety conditions resulting from suppression efforts.

10-58.   Investigators should perform a preliminary scene assessment to provide for the safety and security of personnel and to protect the evidence. They should determine the area in which the site examination will be conducted and establish or adjust the scene perimeter. To determine the boundaries of the scene, the investigator should—

- Make a preliminary scene assessment to identify areas that warrant further examination, being careful not to disturb evidence. The preliminary scene assessment is an overall tour of the fire scene to determine the extent of the damage, proceeding from areas of least damage to areas of greater damage.
- Inspect and protect adjacent areas, even areas with little or no damage that may include nonfire evidence, such as bodies, bloodstains, latent prints, toolmarks, or additional fire-related evidence (such as unsuccessful ignition sources, fuel containers, or ignitable liquids).
- Mark or reevaluate the perimeter and establish or reassess the procedures for controlling access.

10-59. Investigators should take steps to protect evidence from further damage or loss to the extent possible. These measures are discussed in detail in chapters 2 and 4. Investigators should document any conditions effecting evidence or scene integrity including—

- Fire suppression activities which may wash away or dilute evidence or destroy fire patterns.
- Salvage activities which involve removing potential evidence.
- Medical treatment of victims.
- Witnesses and victims leaving the scene.
- Vehicles moved across the scene which may introduce fluids of other materials.
- Power tools or equipment which may introduce contamination from external sources.
- Changing weather conditions which may destroy potential evidence.

10-60. Investigators should determine the condition of the building and/or the vehicle before the fire (abandoned, occupied, intact, and/or secured). They should also determine if the intrusion alarms and/or fire detection and suppression systems were operational at the time of the fire. This information helps to establish factors, such as ventilation conditions, possible fire development timelines and scenarios, and whether vandalism of the property or systems occurred before the incident. To determine the status of security at the time of the fire, the investigator should—

- Ask first responders where entry was made, what steps were taken to gain entry, and whether systems had been activated when they arrived at the scene.
- Observe and document the condition of doors, windows, and other openings. Attempt to determine whether they were open, closed, or compromised at the time of the incident.
- Observe and document the position of timers, switches, valves, and control units for utilities, detection systems, and suppression systems, as well as any alterations to those positions by first responders.
- Determine if the security or suppression systems were available and contact the monitoring agencies to obtain information and available documentation about the design and functioning of the systems.

Identifying and Interviewing Witnesses at the Scene

10-61. Persons with information about the scene, activities before the incident, the incident, and its suppression are valuable witnesses. Determine the identities and locations of witnesses and make arrangements to conduct interviews. To develop a witness list, the investigator should—

- Contact the IC, identify first responders and first-in firefighters, and arrange to document their observations either in writing or through recorded interviews.
- Determine who reported the incident, and secure a tape or transcript of the report if available.
- Identify the owner of the building or scene, any occupants, and the person responsible for property management.
- Identify who was last to leave the building or scene and what occurred immediately before his departure.
- Identify and interview other witnesses (such as neighbors, bystanders, people injured during the incident, or public agency personnel arriving later) and record their statements.

Documenting the Scene

10-62. Based on the preliminary scene assessment and an analysis of fire patterns and damage at the scene, the investigator should identify a distinct origin (the location where the fire started) and an obvious fire cause (an ignition source, the first fuel ignited, and circumstances of the event that brought the two together). If neither the origin nor the cause is immediately obvious, or if there is clear evidence of an incendiary cause, the investigator should conduct a scene examination according to recognized national guidelines such as those of the NAFI or the NFPA.

10-63. Written descriptions of the scene, along with accurate sketches and measurements, are invaluable for focusing the investigation. Written scene documentation recreates the scene for investigative and scientific analysis and judicial purposes, and correlates with photographic evidence. Photographic documentation creates a permanent record of the scene and supplements the written incident reports, witness statements, or reports on the position of evidence. The investigator should create and preserve an accurate visual record of the scene and the evidence before disturbing the scene. Additional photography or video recording should occur as the investigation progresses.

10-64. Chapter 4 describes the techniques for notes, photographs, and sketches. The scene should be photographed before the disturbance or removal of any evidence and throughout the scene investigation. The investigator (or other individual responsible for documenting and collecting evidence) should—

- Photograph and/or videotape the assembled crowd and the fire in progress.
- Remove all nonessential personnel from the background when photographing the scene and evidence.
- Photograph the exterior and interior of the fire scene (consider walls, doors, windows, ceilings, and floors) in a systematic and consistent manner. (Video recording may serve as an additional record but not as a replacement for still photography.)
- Photograph any points or areas of origin, ignition sources, and first material ignited. Remember that fire scenes tend to absorb the light and result in photographs with little detail. Consider over exposing photographs to obtain better light and detail.
- Photograph any physical reconstruction of the scene.
- Maintain photograph and video logs.
- Determine whether additional photographic resources are necessary (aerial photography, infrared photography, stereo photography).

10-65. Written documentation of the scene provides a permanent record of the investigator's observations that may be used to refresh recollections, support opinions and conclusions, and support photographic documentation. The investigator should—

- Prepare a narrative, written descriptions and observations (to include assessments of possible fire causes).
- Sketch an accurate representation of the scene and its dimensions, including significant features, such as the ceiling height, fuel packages (combustible contents of the room), doors, windows, and any areas of origin.
- Prepare a detailed diagram using the scene sketches, preexisting diagrams, drawings, floor plans, or architectural or engineering drawings of the scene. This may be done at a later date.

Collecting Evidence

10-66. Preventing contamination during evidence collection protects the integrity of the fire scene and the evidence. Fuel-powered tools and equipment present potential contamination sources and should be avoided. When it is necessary to use these tools and equipment, the investigator should document their use. The investigator should ensure that access to the fire scene is controlled after fire suppression and that evidence is collected, stored, and transported in a manner that will prevent contamination as described in chapter 2.

10-67. Like any other crime scene, the investigator should ensure that evidence collectors identify and properly document, collect, and preserve evidence for laboratory analyses, further investigations, and court proceedings. To optimize the recovery and evaluation of physical evidence, evidence collectors should—

- Take normal precautions to prevent contamination and cross contamination.
- Document the location of evidence using written notes, sketches, photographs, photograph and video logs, an evidence recovery log, evidence tags, and container labels. When evidence is excavated, additional photographs may be of value.
- Take special care to collect evidence in any areas of origin (such as the first fuel ignited and ignition source) in cases where the fire is not accidental.
- Place evidence in labeled containers for transportation and preservation. Evidence collected for laboratory identification of ignitable liquids must be immediately placed in clean, unused vapor-tight containers (clean, unused paint cans; glass jars; or laboratory-approved nylon or polyester

bags) and then sealed. Package evidence according to the policies and procedures of the laboratory.

● Collect and preserve comparison samples. Comparison samples are comprised of the same kind of materials or substances as the samples that are taken from possible points of origin for ignitable liquid analysis. These samples are not always available.

● Recognize the presence of other physical evidence, such as bloodstains, shoe prints, latent prints, and trace evidence. Use proper preservation and collection methods or seek qualified assistance.

Note. In cases where the fire appears to be accidental, evidence should not be needlessly disturbed, but the property owner or insurer should be notified to avoid continued damage to property.

10-68.   Preventing changes in the condition of a sample after it has been collected ensures the integrity of the evidence and requires controlled packaging and transportation. The investigator should ensure that packaging, transportation, and storage procedures are followed to prevent any destructive changes in the condition of the samples. To minimize changes in the condition of samples, the personnel responsible for packaging and transport should—

● Take precautions to prevent contamination.
● Package fragile items carefully.
● Freeze or immediately transport items containing soil to the laboratory.
● Transport all volatile samples to the laboratory in a timely manner.
● Comply with shipping regulations.

10-69.   The investigator should ensure that the scene is not released until reasonable efforts have been made to identify, collect, and remove all evidence from the scene for further examination and all physical characteristics of the scene have been documented. In addition, before releasing the scene to the receiving party, associated legal, health, and safety issues must be articulated and reported to public safety agencies, if necessary. Doing so minimizes the risk of any further incident or injury and the potential liability of the authority releasing the scene. The investigator should complete the necessary tasks before releasing the scene including—

● Performing a final walk-through as detailed in chapter 4. Verify that all scene documentation has been completed. This can be accomplished using an incident documentation checklist.
● Discussing preliminary scene findings with team members. This may include the following:
   ■ Discussing post-scene issues, including forensic testing, insurance inquiries, interview results, and criminal histories.
   ■ Assigning post-scene responsibilities to LE personnel and other investigators.
   ■ Addressing legal considerations.
   ■ Addressing structural, environmental, health, and safety issues.
● Decontaminating equipment and personnel.
● Documenting the following information:
   ■ The time and date of release.
   ■ The receiving party.
   ■ The authority releasing the scene.
   ■ The condition of the scene at the time of release (structural, environmental, health, and safety issues). The investigator may want to consider photographing and/or video recording the final condition of the scene.
   ■ The cautions given to the receiving party on release (safety concerns, conditions, evidence, and legal issues).

10-70.   Detailed fire information is collected, integrated, and disseminated through national and state databases. This data assists authorities in identifying fire trends, developing techniques, and procuring equipment. The responsible agencies must file incident reports with the correct authorities for input into the appropriate databases.

EXPLOSION INVESTIGATION

10-71. Bomb threats (written or telephonic), bombings, and other explosive incidents on military installations are immediately reported to local police, fire, USACIDC, the Bureau of Alcohol, Tobacco, and Firearms, FBI, and other appropriate agencies. The examination of an explosion scene is generally conducted in the same manner as an arson investigation. In some cases, an explosion may lead to a subsequent fire. Like arson scenes, it is extremely important that evidence or debris is not moved before careful examination. The relationship between the various pieces may be critical to reconstructing the cause of the explosion.

Understanding Characteristics of Explosives

10-72. An explosive is a substance that, through chemical reaction, violently changes into a gas, creating pressure and liberating heat. Explosives are divided into the following two classes:

- **Low explosives.** In a low-order explosion, the rate of change to a gaseous state is relatively slow and must be in a compressed or enclosed state to explode. Low-order explosions tend to produce large chunks of debris. Examples of low explosives are black powder, smokeless powders, volatile flammable liquids, and flammable gases. These explosives can also be called deflagration agents. A dust or grain explosion can also be considered a low-order explosion.
- **High explosives.** In a high-order explosion, the rate of change to the gaseous state is extremely rapid. They tend to pulverize everything nearby. Compressing or enclosing the explosive is not required. Such an explosion is said to detonate. High explosives include dynamite, military explosives, trinitrololuene (TNT), pentaerythrite tetranitrate (PETN), composition B (CB), composition 4 (C4), and mixtures of ammonium nitrate and fuel oil.

10-73. The effects of the two classes of explosives are different. Low-order explosions tend to "push" rather than shatter. Large chunks of debris can usually be found. Twisting and tearing of objects tend to occur. High-order explosions tend to shatter and fragment material near the center of detonation, and there is much evidence of impact by small, high-velocity missiles near the center of detonation. The resulting debris is in small fragments.

Investigating Explosion Scenes

10-74. Investigators should interview all first responders (LE officers, firemen, EOD personnel, and hazardous material teams) and all possible witnesses at scene to document initial observations and events surrounding the incident. Initiate a canvass of the area for witnesses. Ensure that the list includes injured persons who were taken to a hospital or rescue workers who have departed from the scene. All persons at the explosion scene should be identified and the crowd and vehicles in the immediate area should be photographed.

10-75. During witness interviews investigators should attempt to obtain descriptions and times of any sounds, colors of the smoke, and any odors noticed by the witnesses. Witnesses should be questioned regarding general activity at the scene before the explosion including any activities that seemed unusual or out of place. Obtain information pertaining to any observations concerning unidentified packages, items, persons, or vehicles.

10-76. Investigators should determine the owner of the property, victims of the explosion, and if any persons were injured in the blast; obtain names and gain accountability of any persons who are normally on the premises, such as employees, watchmen, or janitors. Initial observations and witness statement will help investigators develop their investigative plan.

10-77. The scene of an explosion must be carefully processed after it has been rendered safe by qualified EOD personnel. The scene may be very large with significant debris scattered over a wide area. Debris and soil close to the point of detonation are likely to bear residue from the explosive; soil samples should be collected and all debris in close proximity to the blast documented and collected for analysis as described in chapter 2. Search teams may be divided into close-in search teams to focus on the immediate area of the blast and general-area search teams to search the outlying areas of the blast scene. Evidence of components used in the explosion may be found; information from examination of these components can be valuable to the investigation. Any containers or material foreign to the scene should be collected. Some examples of explosive components include—

- Fragments of blasting caps.
- Safety fuse fragments.
- Wire.
- Matches.
- Match folders.
- Fuse lighters.
- Batteries or other sources of electric current.
- Fragments of a timing device.
- Delay mechanisms.
- Switches.

10-78.   The entire site should be checked for—

- Fingerprints.
- Footprints.
- Tire tracks.
- Toolmarks.
- Unusual odors.

10-79.   The scene should be processed using the techniques outlined in chapter 4. Investigators should seek the assistance and expertise of USACIDC SAs or other personnel that have attended a postblast investigation course. Within the military, EOD personnel and Weapons Intelligence Course graduates are trained in postblast investigation. These personnel provide the best technical and tactical assessment of a scene where an explosive event has taken place. Disturbing an explosion scene or a blast crater, or collecting explosive-related material without consulting personnel trained in postblast investigation may result in loss of evidence and understanding regarding techniques used by the perpetrator.

10-80.   Investigators and other first responders must stay alert for structural hazards, secondary devices, and entrapment devices before and after entering the blast area. The magnitude of some explosion scenes can be daunting and requires significant thought, prioritization of effort, and task assignment. The ultimate determination of how to handle an explosive incident must be made by the investigating team and the senior investigator responding to the scene. Availability of time, personnel, and other resources greatly influences the course of action to choose. When it is safe to enter the blast scene, investigators should—

- Search the area for evidence from the explosion. Document the blast effect and glass breakage in the surrounding area.
- Divide the scene into areas for search. A review of area maps can be helpful to assess ingress and egress routes and select a methodical search pattern for processing the area. Determine the appropriate search pattern and conduct a methodical search; normally the search team starts at the seat of the explosion and moves outward. Adjust the outer perimeter of the search pattern as necessary.
- Measure and record the size, depth, and shape of any crater or damage. Coordinate with the sketch artist and photographer before disturbing the crater or immediate blast area.
- Determine whether any delivery vehicles or personnel were in the area before the explosion. Make a list of their names and addresses for follow-up interviews.
- Canvass business premises that may support ingress and egress; for example, all-night service stations, cafes, taverns, and toll bridges.
- Check sources of device components and/or materials recovered at the crime scene.
- Prepare a suspect list with necessary facts relating to the investigation. Document descriptions of suspects, suspect vehicles, and suspect premises for follow up investigation.

- Photograph the scene and associated evidence. Take photographs of—
  - The immediate and general area including the victims, crowd, and vehicles.
  - Team activities.
  - The blast seat (center of the blast) and damage showing the measurements.
  - Evidence as it was found on the scene.
  - The immediate and general area from an aerial perspective.
  - Known or potential suspects.
  - Additional requirements identified by scene investigators.
- Sketch the scene. The capabilities of a schematic sketch artist may be required. Detailed sketches should be produced to document—
  - The immediate blast area.
  - The general area.
  - Evidence found by indicating the assigned evidence numbers on the evidence control sketch showing the location where the evidence was found.
  - Evidence and associated locations with appropriate measurements (heights, lengths, and widths).
  - An artist's conception of the scene before the blast with the help of witnesses showing where furniture was arranged or how the structure was before the explosion.
  - All evidence.
- Search the scene for, and collect, evidence. Ensure that all evidence is photographed, measured, and sketched before movement. Search personnel should—
  - Conduct a methodical search using the search pattern designated by the team lead. Search from the seat of the explosion outward.
  - Locate the seat of the explosion or the point of origin of the fire.
  - Collect samples from the blast seat, and retains the necessary control samples.
  - Search and sift the seat of the explosion for device components.
  - Record and package (individually) the evidence found, and follow routine procedures with the photographer, the sketch artist, and the evidence technician.
  - Check all surrounding buildings, vehicles, and objects for damage by projectiles from the explosion, and mark them for the photographer and the sketch artist.
  - Search the area of ingress and egress for associative evidence, such as footprints, tire tracks, torn clothing, blood, hair, fingerprints, or other evidence that may relate to a suspect.
  - Search rooftops and trees or other high places that may have caught debris from the explosion.
  - Identify the outer limits of the outer perimeter of thrown projectiles and evidence. Indicate these findings to the sketch artist, the photographer, and explosives experts.

10-81. Some scenes may warrant laboratory personnel on-site. The deployment of laboratory examiners capable of conducting forensic chemical analysis is determined by the size and damage associated with the explosion. Laboratory examiners on-site—

- Assist the lead investigator in evaluating the situation and discuss the method of approach.
- Assist in the scene search where appropriate.
- Coordinate with off-site laboratory personnel, as appropriate.
- Act as technical advisors for all laboratory-oriented questions arising at the scene.
- Conduct field tests, where appropriate.

Chapter 11

Fraud and Economic Crime Investigations

Fraud is an economic crime involving intentional deception to cause an individual or entity to give up property, benefit, privilege, allowance, consideration, or some other lawful right to which the offender is not entitled. It differs from theft in that fraud uses deceit, surprise, trickery, cunning and unfair practices rather than stealth or force to obtain goods or an unfair advantage. Fraud is committed in many ways, including identity theft, checks and credit card fraud, contract fraud and forgery and is limited only by the imagination of the person perpetrating the fraud.

DESCRIPTION OF FRAUD

11-1. There are three methods by which a person or entity may be relieved of their property—force (robbery), larceny, and fraud. Fraud is the most complicated method as it involves a more complex MO; therefore, it requires more complex investigative techniques. Adding to the complexity is the fact that the crime of fraud is most often leveraged against an organization rather than an individual, and the offense of fraud is only revealed when actively sought through an audit or investigative process.

11-2. Army LE investigators are most often involved with frauds involving the U.S. Government. With an entity as large as the U.S. Government, the opportunity for fraud is infinite. Other crimes falling within the category of fraud include—

- Violations of public trust such as bribery, graft, conflict of interest, unauthorized employment, or violations of the Uniform Trade Secrets Act.
- Fraud and false statements including making false official statements, submitting false claims, altering documents, forgery, false certifications, false vouchers, and deceiving by either suppressing the truth or misrepresenting fact and perjury.
- Contract fraud and false claims, contracting or obligating funds in excess of appropriations, insufficient delivery of products or services, product substitution, or kickbacks.
- Obstruction of justice, racketeering, and violations of the Sherman Anti-Trust Act.
- Conspiracy to commit any of the above listed offenses.

11-3. As investigators begin the complex and laborious task of conducting a fraud investigation, the following critical issues should be considered:

- What is the suspected crime?
- Who is the victim?
- Can a loss be documented?
- Who has primary jurisdiction for investigation?
- Who has primary responsibility for prosecution?

11-4. By answering these questions the investigator can determine whether the investigation should be initiated and, subsequently, whether the investigation falls within the purview of the investigator's organization or agency. Many fraud investigations expand into the purview of the Defense Criminal Investigative Service, the Army's MPFU, the U.S. Secret Service, The U.S. Postal Service, another Defense Criminal Investigative Organization, or the FBI. The investigation of any economic crime is complicated and requires precise identification of jurisdiction and specialized skills and experience. An investigation improperly conducted from its onset may be permanently jeopardized.

FRAUD AGAINST THE GOVERNMENT

11-5. The USACIDC and the FBI have concurrent jurisdiction over persons who are subject to the UCMJ and commit fraud against the U.S. Government. When fraud against the government is committed outside military installations and involves a person subject to the UCMJ, it may be investigated by the FBI or USACIDC. A memorandum of understanding (MOU) between the FBI and the military criminal investigative organizations in 1984 established guidelines to determine investigative priority for certain cases, including fraud. The first step in any investigation of a fraud against the United States is to review the MOU between the Justice Department and the DOD on the Investigation and Prosecution of Certain Crimes (a copy of the MOU is in DODI 5525.07) to determine if the case should be referred to the FBI.

11-6. When fraud against the government is committed on a military installation and involves persons subject to the UCMJ, it is investigated by USACIDC to determine the nature and extent of the crime. If the fraud is determined to be a minor offense as defined by AR 27-10, the investigation may be continued by the military. If the fraud is a serious offense, prompt notification is made to the FBI. The military maintains authority to investigate, apprehend, and detain persons subject to the UCMJ; the investigation is continued unless the DOJ assumes investigative responsibility and notifies the military commander to withdraw from the investigation. Even then, the military commander may make inquiries for administrative action related to the offense as long as no action is taken that would interfere with the FBI investigation and subsequent prosecution of the case.

11-7. USACIDC may conduct or participate in investigations of persons not subject to the UCMJ if the military has a substantial interest in the investigation when there is a reasonable basis to believe that a suspect may be a civilian employee of the DOD or a DOD contractor who has committed an offense in connection with his or her assigned contractual duties which adversely affects the Army or the Army is the victim of the crime. In occupied territory, USACIDC may investigate any fraud against the U.S. Government. In liberated areas, USACIDC investigates fraud committed against the U.S. Government by persons subject to the UCMJ. In liberated countries or in countries in which U.S. Armed Forces are present as guests, investigations by USACIDC of fraud committed by nationals of those countries against the U.S. Government are conducted according to the agreements between the United States and the host country.

11-8. USACIDC has primary investigative responsibility for investigating allegations of fraud involving—

- A contract and procurement action awarded by the U.S. Army regardless of what organization administers the contract.
- Allegations of fraud involving DFAS where they pertain to the DFAS providing services for a post, camp, and station hosted by the U.S. Army.
- Activities of the Defense Reutilization and Marketing Service and defense distribution depots outside the United States in which the U.S. Army is providing support facilities to the host installation.
- Allegations of fraud against TRICARE or other intermediary health care providers by anyone entitled to TRICARE benefits that have made claims or received services under such programs or operations.
- Construction contracts funded by the U.S. Army.
- All DOD dependent schools outside of the United States and hosted by the U.S. Army.
- Army combatant commands.
- All Defense Energy Support Centers activities outside the United States, where the U.S. Army has an interest.
- All North Atlantic Treaty Organization (NATO) projects and expenditures by DOD in connection with NATO projects or activities where the U.S. Army has an interest.
- Allegations of bribery of a U.S. Service member or civilian employee.
- All matters regarding the Army and Air Force Exchange Service on Army installations and all nonappropriated fund activities on Army installations.

COORDINATING FRAUD OFFENSES INVOLVING CLAIMS

11-9. The crime of defrauding the U.S. Government by the claims process is illusive. It is strongly recommended that any investigation involving fraud be closely coordinated with the servicing office of the SJA. This legal advice can help the investigator avoid many of the pitfalls inherent in establishing the existence of offenses in this highly technical area of criminal investigation.

MAKING AND PRESENTING FALSE AND FRAUDULENT CLAIMS

11-10. There are two common elements of proof needed to substantiate the offense of making and presenting false and fraudulent claims. The investigator must show the false or fraudulent nature of the claim and show proof that the accused knew of the dishonest or fictitious character of the claim in question. For example, a false or fraudulent claim is made against the government when a person files a claim for property lost in military service knowing that the articles were not lost. Making a false or fraudulent claim, by its very nature, requires the claimant to personally make a false statement. Presenting a claim for payment when the claimant knows that it has been paid or that he is not authorized to present the claim does not require him to make a false statement.

MAKING OR USING A FALSE WRITING OR OTHER PAPER WITH A CLAIM

11-11. Making or using a false writing or other paper in connection with a claim is fraud against the government. The offense of making a false writing for the purpose of obtaining an allowance, payment, or approval of a claim is complete with the writing of the paper, whether or not the writer attempts to use the paper or to present the claim. Common examples of false paper includes false receipts, false marriage certificates, and false lease agreements. If a person makes or uses a false writing in connection with a claim and if the false writing contains statements intended to mislead government officials considering or investigating the claim, the claimant has committed a criminal offense.

MAKING A FALSE OATH WITH A CLAIM

11-12. Proof that a fraud against the government has been committed by means of a false oath requires evidence that the accused knowingly made a false oath to a fact or to a writing to obtain an allowance, payment, or approval of a claim. For example, a claimant filing a sworn statement requesting quarters for a person to whom he is not married is making a false oath to support his claim.

FORGING A SIGNATURE WITH A CLAIM

11-13. Under the UCMJ, forgery of a signature in connection with a claim constitutes a separate offense from the crime of forgery. Any person subject to the UCMJ who, with intent to defraud, falsely makes or alters any signature to, or any part of, any writing which would, if genuine, apparently impose a legal liability on another or change his legal right or liability to his prejudice; or utters, offers, issues, or transfers such a writing, known by him to be so made or altered; is guilty of forgery according to Article 120 UCMJ. The offense is complete once it can be demonstrated that the accused forged an individual's signature or knowingly used a forged signature for the purpose of obtaining an allowance, payment, or approval of a claim.

INVESTIGATING PAY AND ALLOWANCE FRAUD

11-14. The fact that an individual receives U.S. Government funds to which he is not entitled and forms the intent to steal the property is sufficient to prove the offense of larceny. The intent to steal can be inferred if the individual retains funds in spite of knowing he was not entitled to them. An investigation does not need to demonstrate an affirmative misrepresentation by the recipient concerning the entitlement of payment. The investigation must prove intent by the recipient to fraudulently convert the funds to his own use while knowing that he was not entitled to the funds (spending the funds). Upon receipt of credible information that an individual received military pay and allowances to which he was not entitled, a criminal investigation will be initiated by USACIDC.

INVESTIGATING A CLAIMS FRAUD

11-15. To investigate a fraudulent claim against the government, make a discreet inquiry into the circumstances surrounding the allegation of fraud to determine if an offense has been committed. This should be accomplished without endangering any sources of information or placing suspects on their guard. If it is determined that a fraud has been committed, continue the investigation to learn the extent of the offense and the identity of the individuals involved.

11-16. Learn the specific transactions by which the fraud was committed, identify the roles of the suspects in the alleged fraud, and check for jurisdictional problems. Based on these findings, estimate the technical skills needed to establish the offense and the identity of the offenders. Also look for probable types and locations of evidence of the fraud. Carefully question individuals who—

- Prepared or submitted the claim.
- Received and approved the claim at local or intermediate levels of command.
- Witnessed or attested to the circumstance on which the claim was based.
- May have been in collusion with the suspect to prepare or justify the claim.
- Witnessed or knew of any motive, incident, or circumstance that may point toward the fraudulent nature of the claim.
- Witnessed conversations or observed correspondence between the individuals involved in making, justifying, or approving the claim.

11-17. The investigator may need to audit many pieces of documentary evidence to find those that bear on suspected fraud. Claims, applications, travel vouchers, receipts, business and finance reports, audits, bank deposits and withdrawals, and records of monetary conversions and transmittals can all be used to substantiate this form of fraud against the government. Guided by the elements of proof required for the specific offense, the investigator should search for documents to substantiate the allegations of a claims fraud.

11-18. Take action early to secure cooperation from other organizations, and refer undeveloped leads to the appropriate investigative agencies. This will expedite the investigation and give other agencies time to comply with requests. If there is a need for more information or additional documents on the fraudulent actions under investigation, coordinate with any other agencies involved in the investigation. Try to do this without disclosing the results of the preliminary investigation. While awaiting replies or action, check every available local source of information. Make careful use of selected sources, and seek out reliable individuals who possess information material to the investigation.

11-19. Arrange the evidence to point directly to the elements of proof of the specific alleged offense. The final case report for a fraud must be specific in its allegations and in its information. When undeveloped leads are to be checked by investigators in other fields of study, provide them with information allowing them time to proceed logically in their work.

INVESTIGATING SUPPLY FRAUD

11-20. Fraud in the supply system of the U.S. Army, commonly called supply diversion, is the most frequent crime occurring within logistics channels on military installations. Supply diversion ranges from ordering self-service items for personal use or resale to requesting supplies to be shipped by rail and then routing the railcars to areas of low-density traffic to steal their contents.

Common Supply Frauds

11-21. Common supply frauds include ordering items under the wrong national stock number (NSN) or a false document number and ordering unauthorized items. This is often accomplished when an offender puts the wrong NSN of the item in the stock number block on the request form while putting a correct item description in the description block. The automated system issues and ships the NSN item, not the description item. When the perpetrator receives the requested item, he diverts it for his own private gain. To spot the diverter, use the document number and trace the document from the requestor to the issuing activity and back to the receiver obtaining copies of all requests and receipts.

11-22.   If a perpetrator places an order under a false document number, trace the audit trail to establish the diversion pattern and find the perpetrator. If a perpetrator is ordering unauthorized items, trace the complete audit trail. Take statements from key witnesses, and then compare a copy of the table of organization and equipment (TOE) or table of distribution and allowances against the property book.

Investigative Approach

11-23.   The first step in investigating supply fraud is to identify the supply system in which the fraud or theft occurred. Then determine if the system is at the retail (installation or organization) or wholesale (depot or manufacturer) level of the U.S. Army logistical system. Determine if the system is manual or computer-automated. Manual and automated systems use the same forms, but their operational principles differ at the local level. The manual system uses a property book reflecting TOE and table of distribution and allowances equipment on individual property pages. The automated system uses computer listings reflecting all authorized and on-hand equipment on a single printout.

11-24.   After determining the system from which a supply item is missing, review the supply transaction register, called a document register, and see which unit or organization requested the item. Obtain the document number of the requisition. Then carefully follow it through the audit trail. Check each level of the supply system furnishing material to the supply activity that has physically issued and shipped the item to the requestor. Obtain a copy of the request at each step of this initial investigative path for backup. Then begin following the issue trail that leads from the supply activity that was the issuer to the requestor or user. The points along the path of issue will reflect at what point the item was taken from U.S. Army control. Obtain copies of all requests for issue, issue documents, shipping reports, or such. When all of these documents are collected, continue the investigation as if investigating a larceny.

11-25.   Not all supply frauds occur as diversions from a supply system. Many items are reported stolen from a storage area. To investigate the loss, obtain the supply documents verifying that the items were physically present at the activity reporting the loss. Determine the inventory procedures of the activity. Then establish the time frame extending from the date when the items were last seen at the activity to the date when the loss was noted. If the items were last present at an inventory, apply larceny investigative techniques to identify the offender. If the items were known to be missing before the last inventory and they were carried on the inventory as being on hand, the provisions of AR 735-5 apply. The property book officer must initiate a financial liability investigation of property loss. Be aware that inventory shortages are often reported as supply larcenies. This is done in an attempt to cover poor supply management techniques and to generate a criminal investigation instead of a financial liability investigation of property loss.

INVESTIGATING PETROLEUM DISTRIBUTION FRAUD

11-26.   Fraud in the petroleum distribution system can be minor pilferage or systematic theft. It can also be falsification of multimillion dollar orders by a purchasing conspiracy among contracting officials and oil companies. A study of AR 70-12 and FM 10-67-1 should give the investigator the knowledge of petroleum activities needed to investigate most petroleum fraud. Investigations of extremely large losses from conspiracies are usually outside the Army LE purview.

11-27.   Pilferage may occur in "nickel-and-dime" losses of petroleum in amounts as low as 5 or 10 gallons a day. The methods of pilferage may range from recording the wrong amounts on DA Form 3643, *Daily Issues of Petroleum Products*, to siphoning gas from a vehicle tank. Investigators can discover these losses by simply monitoring the amount of gas used and then comparing that amount with the amount stated on the form. If pilferage is discovered, use the gasoline theft detection kit and undertake surveillance to catch the offenders.

11-28.   Larger, systematic losses are usually from theft by a supplier. Suppliers may use false tanks. They may trap petroleum in buckets inside the delivery vehicle or add air or heat to the delivery line just before it connects to the meter. They may also conspire with a government attendant to leave some of the petroleum in the delivery vehicle. Large-scale theft usually means the government attendant is not making the checks required by AR 70-12 or is conspiring with the supplier. In the latter case, a fluid is usually mixed with the petroleum to cover the shortage.

11-29. Sometimes paperwork is falsified to cover a loss. It is easy to cover shortages by adding gallons to those a driver signs for on the DA Form 3643 or by falsifying entries on the form. The driver, for example, may be receiving 10.2 gallons and signing for 11 gallons. At a large issue point, several hundred gallons a week can be lost by this method. Use surveillance and cross-check the logbook against the DA Forms 3643 to help prove the fraud.

INVESTIGATING CONTRACTING FRAUD

11-30. Contracts embrace all types of agreements to procure supplies or services. The investigation of crimes like fraud and bribery involving government contractors is within the purview of the FBI. However, under AR 27-10, which implements the MOU between the FBI and DOD, the investigation may be conducted by military investigators depending on whether federal statutes were violated. In cases where it appears that a government employee has violated a departmental regulation involving standards of conduct but has not violated any federal statutes, military investigators normally conduct the inquiries. They investigate to obtain the detailed information which the commander needs to base any action. An investigation of this nature, while mainly of administrative interest, may be conducted concurrently with a criminal investigation.

11-31. All suspected criminal conduct and noncompetitive practices related to contracting must be reported. Reports of possible fraud or violations of antitrust laws must contain a certified statement of the facts of the dereliction. The reports must include affidavits, depositions, records of action (if applicable), and other relevant data. This reporting may require preliminary investigation of allegations of a criminal nature for referral to the DOJ and the FBI for determination of prosecutorial interest. It may include supplying details for consideration of debarring persons or firms from participating in procurement contracting. It may include furnishing information to a commander to help him decide whether or not to take administrative or disciplinary action in connection with procurement.

11-32. Government personnel engaged in contracting may violate statutory prohibitions and administrative regulations by accepting gratuities or conspiring to defraud the government. Their wrongful act and malfeasance in the performance of duty, when established as fact, may be criminally, civilly, and administratively actionable. Government contracting personnel may perform a lawful act in a manner prohibited by regulations or perform the act in a manner not directed by regulations. Their malfeasance would be administratively actionable. Their actions violate the UCMJ and other federal criminal code. Government contracting personnel who fail to follow procedures required by acquisition regulations are guilty of nonfeasance. Even if the omission is not a part of a scheme to defraud the government, it is nevertheless actionable. In an effort to 'keep the system moving,' government contracting personnel may attempt to excuse noncompliant government contractors by explaining their malfeasance as a misunderstanding or as a result of complicated government procedures. It may be difficult to obtain cooperation from government contracting personnel who do not consider wrongful acts by contractors as criminal.

Standards of Conduct and Ethics

11-33. Regulatory standards of conduct and ethics apply to contracting officers and all military or civilian personnel engaged in contracting actions and related processes. In contracting, many decisions are largely a matter of personal judgment. Contracting is necessarily carried on, to a great extent, through personal contacts and relationships. Thus, high ethical standards of conduct are essential to protect the interests of the government. The standards of conduct for government civilians and military personnel are set forth in Part 1, Title 48, Code of Federal Regulations (48 CFR Part 1) and DODD 5500.07-R.

11-34. Any act that compromises or impairs confidence in government relations with industry or individuals must be avoided. Violations of regulatory standards of ethics and conduct may involve such variable factors as judgment, previous experience and relationships, and individual interpretation of ethics. Whatever the circumstances, the ethical standards of all individuals charged with the administration and expenditure of government funds must be above reproach and suspicion in every respect and at all times.

Investigative Approach

11-35.   An investigator should be familiarized with the contracting process and the laws and regulations that apply before conducting an investigation. Irregularities often occur in the contracting process due to the complexity of statutory provisions, administrative regulations, and departmental or agency procedures. The investigator must be reasonably familiar with these laws, regulations, and procedures to recognize deviations from normal contractual processes.

11-36.   Discovering contracting irregularities requires continuous scrutiny of each step of the process from the inception of the contract to its termination. Identification of the exact spot where an irregularity has occurred is a rarity. An extensive study of a contract and the regulations pertaining to it must be conducted before the investigator can expect to successfully undertake a contract investigation. The investigator's familiarity with these matters is a basic tool for exploring the causes of, and contributing factors to, contract irregularities.

11-37.   Begin the investigation by methodically and carefully separating pertinent issues and completely reviewing all related records, regulations, and procedural requirements. Approach contractors, government contracting personnel, and others connected with the issues in question on an informed basis. Appropriate curiosity is essential to a definitive investigation. Check and confirm verification information, statements, time sequences, and observations. Seek corroborative evidence. Exhaust all leads as quickly as possible to clear up matters not fully understood. Delays may permit suspects to develop collusive measures or cover stories to alter or substitute records.

11-38.   Most of the human sources of information are likely to have only a general suspicion or a fragmentary knowledge of an alleged irregularity. However, some people may be able to supply enough information to permit a rapid and thorough evaluation of the situation. The investigator should get full information on any allegations. This information may indicate which individuals and processes are suspect. If allegations are in writing, contact the writers to seek more information. Often, they can provide names, dates, or places not initially reported. Check their motives for making the allegations. Anonymous allegations are often unfounded and made for ulterior motives. Investigate all such allegations to confirm or refute them.

Current Government Employees

11-39.   Some of the most valuable sources of information will be government employees. They have a basic obligation to report suspected wrongdoings. Nurture their confidence and trust; if an investigator receives information with a stipulation of confidence, he must honor that confidence.

Former Employees

11-40.   Former employees are often willing to become involved in an investigation, especially if they feel they have been treated unfairly during their employment or in connection with their separation from government service. Review records of employees separated from government service to find those who may have observed a questioned action during their employment. Former employees of government contractors may also be willing to cooperate as long as nondisclosure agreements do not create a legal liability.

Trade Groups

11-41.   A discreet inquiry among trade groups can often produce revealing information as to whether or not procurement actions involving a particular agency or firm are "clean." Perhaps the most willing, if not the most knowledgeable, sources of information will be disgruntled, unsuccessful bidders.

Preaward Inspections

11-42.   Preaward survey inspections may have been inadequate or reports of inspection of the contractor's facilities may be false or misleading. Inspectors may have failed to inspect contractor products or they may have permitted the contractor to use inferior materials. Inspectors may have allowed contractors to meet weight specifications by adding unauthorized materials or they may have allowed contractors to deviate from weight or density specifications. Determine if the contract administrator failed to document actions in the contract file that could result in savings to the contractor or that could be detrimental to the government.

11-43. Check the preaward activities of contractors. Learn if gratuities were given to a government employee or if other favors were established pursuant to contract award. Determine if frequent visits or telephone calls to government employees may have resulted in information creating a more favorable position for the contractor. Determine if the contractor presented false data or incorrect information before the award of a contract.

11-44. Specifications can be slanted to favor the product or services of a particular contractor. Sole-source contracts must be checked to ensure that individuals in engineering, supply, maintenance, or such have not inserted specifications for their own interest or that create a noncompetitive environment.

INVESTIGATING BLACK MARKETING

11-45. Black marketing provides an opportunity for a seller to make money and a buyer to possess an item that is restricted from his possession. By definition, black marketing is the illegal business of buying or selling goods in violation of restrictions or price controls. Black marketing is punishable under the UCMJ, but because of its financial appeal, many Soldiers, their family members, U.S. Government employees, and other personnel participate in its illegal activities. Both the seller and buyer are typically aware of the legal consequences associated with participating in black marketing activities.

11-46. Black marketing thrives when goods commonly available in developed nations are imported into developing nations on a restricted basis. The potential for black market activities exists whenever U.S. forces are located in a HN. U.S. forces introduce, through supply and commercial exchange channels and by HN allowances of tax-exempt mail and baggage, many items that are not available to the HN populace through commercial markets. Many of these items have a potential or an actual black market value.

11-47. The impact of black market activities on the economy of a HN can be devastating. The cost to the United States of replacing military supplies and equipment that have been diverted to the black market is expensive. Mission performance can be greatly reduced when needed supplies and equipment are not available to commanders. Illegal trafficking of legally purchased items or issued supply items is a constant problem. This type of trafficking can be harder to stop than cargo diversions. Legal or authorized access to these items by host countries and third-country nationals makes it difficult to stop black marketing. Cases involving negotiable-dollar instruments on the black market need special attention because these instruments can cause a direct-dollar loss to the United States.

11-48. Black market activities contribute to the commission of other crimes. Black marketing can promote fraud, the stealing and selling of government property, counterfeiting, forgery, and drug offenses. It may also promote the violation of foreign currency exchange laws, import laws, tax laws, and SOFAs. Black market operations may be the result of an organized group or an individual's efforts. They are often the result of a combination of the two.

Black Market Rings

11-49. One type of black market organization and operation is the black market ring. While the type of contacts may change from one ring to another, the basic organization and its operation stay much the same. The leader and suppliers are the most essential members in a ring. The supplier discovers a supply source, which may be an Army facility or activity that stores, handles, or uses the item. The supplier gets the item through purchase or theft. He may be a military person, a civilian employee, or an acquaintance of someone who will get the item for him. After the supplier gets the item, he takes it to the operator of a temporary storage point or uses a transporter to deliver it. The transporter may or may not be a regular member of the ring. The item is then passed, on demand, to the retailer. Sometimes a wholesaler may act for the leader and have a transporter get the item from the storage point and take it to the retailer, or the retailer may get it directly from the warehouse. The retailer then sells the item to the consumer.

11-50. The ring leader may have any number of suppliers, transporters, warehousemen, wholesalers, and retailers. If he has more than one wholesaler, each will normally handle only one type of item. Most often, the only individuals in the ring who have direct contact with or know the leader are the suppliers and the wholesalers.

11-51. A means to breaking up a black market ring is to trace commodities found on the black market. Examining these items may help an investigator find the supply source. When an Army facility is among the supply sources, a check of the facility records can show if items are being removed illegally. Enlisting the aid of the commander of this facility will expedite this action. Surveillance may be used to detect the supplier or the transporter; if either one is seen, they may be placed under surveillance to find other members of the ring. Investigators should also check on personnel or activities at the military depot or warehouse to identify ring members or individuals being exploited as suppliers.

11-52. Transporters may be spotted when items in bulk storage are being removed. Investigators may buy information from transporters, especially if they are not members of the ring. The pay for their work may be small, and they may be willing to tell what they know for a small fee or other consideration. Information may also be gained in the operation of the ring by planting would-be transporters. Individuals like taxi drivers work well as plants in black market areas. A retailer may approach a plant for a onetime job. A retailer, wholesaler, or warehouse representative may be found in this manner. Other ways of making contacts with retailers is by purchasing items or stationing personnel in black marketing locations to watch for transactions. When a retailer is spotted, maintaining surveillance may reveal other members of the ring.

11-53. Large-scale diversions and inventory shortages are major signs of organized rings of black marketers. Good security controls over black marketable items in supply channels can reduce these rings. Screening reports of supply shortages or thefts may yield important information. These documents may consist of police reports, financial liability of property loss investigations, inventory adjustment reports, and such. Because federal employment requires frequent relocation of personnel, these reports must be screened promptly. Any leads should be checked out as soon as possible. Experience will show which missing supplies are likely to go on the black market.

Sources of Information

11-54. People working at commissaries and post exchanges may detect irregularities on the part of fellow employees. They may spot the sale of black marketable items to certain individuals. Merchants often know about commodities that are being procured for the black market. The black market is competition for the merchants' businesses so they may provide the names of individuals who have competing commodities for sale. Gate guards and taxi drivers are often good sources for black marketing information. Gate guards can answer questions regarding who is taking a lot of controlled items off an installation and can identify the items in demand on the local black market. Taxi drivers, by virtue of the nature of their work, often come in contact with many people. They too, may know what items are in demand. Personnel assigned to a ration control office can also be good sources of information.

11-55. Persons who are engaging in black marketing activities may also be engaging in other illegal activities. They may spend their money for drugs or patronize prostitutes. Special consideration should be given to known narcotic addicts. They may engage in black marketing for money in order to buy drugs or to obtain drugs in exchange for their services. Prostitutes, drug dealers, or other low-level criminals, by association with these individuals, may pick up information. If they can be persuaded to talk, they may provide tips on persons who have money in excess of normal amounts. They may also provide tips on actual black marketers and their operations.

11-56. Civil affairs personnel deal with the economy of a HN area. They may be able to help trace black market transactions. For example, if the problem is big enough to affect the country's economy, they may be able to pinpoint where this activity exists. Such pinpointing can help investigators concentrate their efforts in these areas.

Locating Supply Sources

11-57. If an investigator suspects that an item on the black market is coming from a specific source, other like items at that source may be marked for future tracing. One of several inks or powders may be used for this purpose. These inks and powders are invisible unless developed by specific reagents or exposed to IR or UV light. The price of commissary or exchange items may be marked in special ink or like substance.

11-58. With petroleum products, an identification reagent (an additive) can be added at petroleum, oil, and lubricant (POL) storage and supply facilities. The reagent can be detected by chemical testing after the seizure of suspected petroleum products. This is normally done under the supervision of USACIDC personnel. USACIDC is responsible for local administration and control of operations where the reagent will be added. They also set the type and quantity of fuel to be identified. Normally, the additive is blended in with the POL products as the storage tanks are being filled. The proper ratios for blending are discussed in the appropriate Army materiel command technical bulletins. If the additive is blended as prescribed, there should be no interference in the operation of a motor. These approved additive reagents can be requested on an as-needed basis. One field-expedient reagent is 2 2/3 ounces of phenolphthalein in one pint of alcohol added per 1,000 gallons of gasoline. This should be coordinated with POL technical personnel.

11-59. If there is reason to believe a certain place has black market items, an investigator may wish to have it raided. Contact the office of the SJA to ascertain what authorities have jurisdiction in a given location. Civilian police may have to conduct the raid. Jurisdiction, for this purpose and with respect to the apprehension and search of individuals found there, is affected by applicable treaties, laws, or other directives.

Identifying Suspects

11-60. Certain acts or conditions may indicate black market involvement. A person may be suspected of black market activity based on the presence of these indicators; the indicators do not prove black market activity but may present cause for further investigation. Indicators of persons engaging in potential black market activity can include—

- Having more money than would normally be expected for someone of that rank or position.
- Spending more money than legally received or spending large amounts of money on friends.
- Purchasing unusually large quantities of items.
- Purchasing items not normally used, such as a light smoker who buys large quantities of cigarettes or a male soldier who frequently buys quantities of perfume or lipstick.
- Carrying a lot of goods off the compound on a regular basis.

11-61. Once enough information about a suspect is gathered, an investigation should be initiated. If it is believed that a suspect has unusual amounts of money, make inquiries with the post and finance offices. In response to an official request, postal officials may provide information on the purchase of money orders. The dollar amount purchased may show that a buyer had more money than he or she might be expected to have. This information may provide grounds for further investigation. The finance office may be able to disclose information regarding military personnel who have exchanged large amounts of money at its location. Travel agencies may also be a source of information for potential black marketing activities. They keep records of the trips they arrange for people, which may show frequency of travel and consistency in the destination of individuals.

11-62. Investigators must make contact with a suspect's associates. The contacts may provide pertinent information on the suspect and may disclose other members of the group. An investigator should study a suspect's habits and customs to learn about his character. This may help determine whether the person would or would not engage in unlawful activities. Other checks an investigator must make of a suspect include—

- **Personnel records.** Check personal records for anything of evidentiary value.
- **Bank accounts.** These may show if he has deposited more money than he is known to have received legally. For military personnel, this check should include the Soldier's deposits and other authorized investments.
- **Private property.** It may show income that exceeds what he is known to have obtained legally.

11-63. Federal, state, local, and HN LE agencies may be contacted in the investigation of a suspect. Local agencies often keep records that may be of value to the investigation. These records may show that a suspect had money in excess of what he should have legally or may indicate involvement in related activity investigated by other agencies. Civilian police records may provide information leading to a suspect, especially if he is a local civilian or has been residing in the area for a while.

11-64.   A suspect may be put under surveillance to complete the investigation. The investigator may choose to use that suspect in gaining new information by letting him lead the investigator to others engaged in black marketing. A surveillant may be placed at banks, finance offices, or other places that convert money instruments into dollars to watch for suspects who make monetary transactions.

IDENTITY THEFT

11-65.   The DOJ prosecutes cases of identity theft and fraud under a variety of federal statutes. In the fall of 1998, for example, Congress passed 18 USC 1028 which created a new offense of identity theft. This legislation prohibits knowingly transferring or using, without lawful authority, a means of identification of another person with the intent to commit, or to aid or abet, any unlawful activity that constitutes a violation of federal law or a felony under any applicable state or local law. In the military, most offenses involving identity theft are investigated and prosecuted as larceny.

11-66.   The Internet has been a catalyst for commerce to take place electronically and anonymously, thereby facilitating the crime of fraud by minimizing direct risk to offenders and blurring jurisdictional boundaries. Jurisdiction is much more complicated with the Internet because the offender and the victim rarely share the same jurisdiction. With so many service members in transit or serving outside of the continental United States, crimes of this type are difficult to investigate.

11-67.   The person whose identity is stolen is the primary victim; however, once a credit card company, bank, or other business has assumed liability for the loss, they become the primary victim. Many companies do not seek the investigation and prosecution of offenders; they are more likely to put money into deterrence and detection.

11-68.   The Fair and Accurate Credit Transactions Act of 2003 has a number of provisions to protect victims of identity theft. As a result many credit card companies, banks, and businesses require a police report in order to absolve a victim of financial liability when a fraud has occurred. That requirement forces victims to report crimes they may otherwise not have reported; this represents a large number of complainants who just want a report and not necessarily the 'hassle' of cooperating with an investigation.

11-69.   Criminals may steal an individual's identity by co-opting their name, social security number, credit card number, or some other piece of personal information for their own use. In short, identity theft occurs when someone appropriates personal information from another individual, without that individual's knowledge, to commit fraud or theft. Methods used by identity thieves include—

- Opening a new credit card or services account using another individual's name, date of birth, and social security number. A military identification card is particularly desirable to thieves because it represents credibility and a source of income to businesses who may accept it as proof of both identity and employment.
- Opening a bank account in another individual's name and writing bad checks on that account.
- Establishing Internet purchasing accounts for everything from online gaming to online auctions.
- Establishing online identities for the purpose of confidence schemes.
- Using a military identification card for discounts.

11-70.   Identity theft often has a devastating effect on members of the military and their families. Victims must act fast to minimize the damage to their credit and financial status. Army LE personnel assist victims by providing them with information designed to help them take the appropriate action to prevent further loss and to recover from identity theft. The following information should be provided to the victims of identity theft when there is reason to believe that these conditions exist:

- If keys were taken, change or rekey the locks that need to be changed for protection of the keyed asset.
- If checks or credit cards were taken, notify the bank. Get "fraud alert" placed on affected accounts so that new credit will not be issued without appropriate authorization. Do this by

reporting the loss to the major credit reporting bureaus. The primary credit reporting agencies include—
- Experian.
- Trans Union.
- Equifax.

● If a social security card was taken, call the Social Security Administration fraud hotline to notify it of the loss and get information on how to get a duplicate card. Contact the Social Security Administration fraud hotline at 1-800-269-0271 or <www.ssa.gov>.

● If a driver's license was taken, apply for a new driver's license as soon as possible and ask if anyone has applied for a replacement license since the theft using the stolen license number. If required, the victim can be referred to an investigator.

● If new checks or cards have been mailed to a different address, call the local office of the U.S. Postal Inspection Service to report the situation and follow their guidance.

● If stolen checks or cards have been used, contact the banks and/or businesses that accepted the checks or cards to notify them of the fraud and offer to sign any affidavits of forgery, as needed. Encourage the banks and businesses to pursue pressing charges against any suspects identified.

● If someone has stolen an identity to get new credit, report the crime to any LE agencies with jurisdiction over the area where the fraudulent application was made. The Federal Trade Commission identity theft hotline (1-877-438-4338) can also be called to report the incident and get advice on how to proceed. To report fraud other than identity theft to the Federal Trade Commission, call 1-877-382-4357.

CHECK FRAUD

11-71. A significant amount of check fraud is due to counterfeiting through desktop publishing and copying to create, chemically alter, or duplicate an actual financial document, which consists of removing some or all of the information and manipulating it to the benefit of the offender. Victims include financial institutions, businesses that accept and issue checks, and the consumer. In most cases, these crimes (including forgery) begin with the theft of a financial document. It can be perpetrated as easily as by someone stealing a blank check from a home or vehicle during a burglary, searching for a canceled or old check in the garbage, or removing a check mailed to pay a bill from a mailbox. Types of check fraud include—

● **Forging signatures.** This generally involves stolen legitimate checks where the offender has forged the signature of the payer.

● **Forging endorsements.** This generally involves stolen legitimate checks where the offender has forged the signature of the payee.

● **Counterfeiting.** Counterfeiting can either mean wholly fabricating a check by using readily available desktop publishing equipment consisting of a PC, a scanner, sophisticated software, and a high-grade laser printer or by simply duplicating a check with advanced color photocopiers.

● **Altering.** This involves using chemicals and solvents, such as acetone, brake fluid, and bleach to remove or modify handwriting and information on the check. When performed on specific locations on the check such as the payee's name or amount, it is called "spot alteration." Spot alterations are almost always related to the increase of the check's amount or changing the name of the payee. When an attempt to erase information from the entire check is made, it is called "check washing."

● **Paperhanging.** This problem primarily has to do with people purposely writing checks on closed accounts (their own or others).

● **Check kiting.** Check kiting is opening accounts at two or more institutions and using "the float time" of available funds to create fraudulent balances. This fraud has become easier in recent years due to new regulations requiring banks to make funds available sooner, combined with increasingly competitive banking practices.

11-72. There are several signs that may indicate a bad check. One sign on its own does not guarantee a check to be counterfeit; however, the greater the number of signs, the greater the possibility that the check is bad. Bad check indicators include the following:

- The check lacks perforations. Many checks produced by a legitimate printer are perforated and have at least one rough edge. However, many companies are now using in-house laser printers with magnetic ink character recognition (MICR) capabilities to generate their own checks from blank stock. These checks may have a microperforated edge that is difficult to detect.
- The address of the bank is missing.
- The payer's address is missing.
- The check number is either missing or does not change from one check to the next.
- The check number is low on personal checks (numbers 101 through 300) or on business checks (numbers 100 through 1,500).
- The type of font used to print the payer's name looks different from the font used to print the address.
- There are additions to the check such as phone numbers written by hand.
- There are stains or discolorations on the check possibly caused by erasures or alterations.
- The numbers printed along the bottom of the check (called MICR coding) are shiny. Real magnetic ink is dull and nonglossy in appearance. Some forgers lack the ability to encode the bank and customer account information on the bottom of a check with magnetic ink. They will often substitute regular toner or ink for magnetic ink. If a counterfeit MICR line is printed or altered with nonmagnetic ink, the sorting equipment at the bank will not be able to read the MICR line, thus causing a reject item. Unfortunately, the bank will normally apply a new magnetic strip and process the check. This works to the forger's advantage because it takes additional time to process the fraudulent check, reducing the time the bank has to return the item. Banks cannot treat every non-MICR check as a fraudulent item because millions of legitimate checks are rejected each day due to unreadable MICR lines.
- The MICR coding at the bottom of the check does not match the check number.
- The MICR numbers are missing.
- The MICR coding does not match the bank district and the routing symbol in the upper-right corner of the check. The nine-digit number between the brackets on the bottom of a check is the routing number of the bank on which the check is drawn. The first two digits indicate in which of the 12 Federal Reserve Districts the bank is located. It is important that these digits be compared to the location of the bank, because a forger will sometimes change the routing number on the check to an incorrect Federal Reserve Bank to buy more time.
- The word "void" appears across the check.
- Notations appear in the memo section listing "loan," "payroll," or "dividends." Most legitimate companies have separate accounts for these functions that eliminate a need for such notations.
- The check lacks an authorized signature.

CREDIT CARD FRAUD

11-73. Many laws cover larceny or fraudulent use of credit cards. The elements of proof for the offense of larceny by credit card are: possessing a credit card obtained by theft or fraud, using the card to obtain services or goods, and signing the cardholder's name. Investigating credit card fraud normally requires obtaining samples of handwriting from sales slips signed by the suspect. The increase in commerce over the Internet where neither signatures nor proof of identity are required has made credit card fraud much more difficult to investigate and prosecute.

11-74. When investigating crimes where an actual credit card was used, examine the credit card for alteration of the cardholder's name, signature section, and the numbers on the card. Merchandise listed on the sales receipts found in the suspect's possession could also provide evidence of illegal credit card use. Potential witnesses include sales clerks, food service personnel, airline and hotel employees, and car rental personnel. Consider email accounts as a location where electronic receipts for credit card purchases may be stored. Increasingly, digital evidence and computer forensics are required to produce required evidence.

11-75.   If investigators suspect that the U.S. mail system was used in credit card fraud, they should contact the local office of the U.S. Postal Inspection Service. The U.S. Postal Inspection Service has primary jurisdiction in all matters infringing on the integrity of the U.S. mail.

Chapter 12

Drug Crime Investigations

Military LE personnel investigate criminal drug activities, including their use, sale, manufacture, and distribution. Investigators employ surveillance, use informants, and operate undercover to identify those involved in illegal drug activity. They execute search warrants to seize illegal drugs, confiscate money derived from the sale of drugs, and apprehend those involved. Investigators also collect and analyze criminal intelligence gathered during drug investigations. Investigators help reduce the criminal threat to U.S. and friendly forces by sharing criminal intelligence with other federal, state, local, and HN police agencies.

INVESTIGATIVE RESPONSIBILITY

12-1. The USACIDC is charged with overall responsibility for investigative activity involving controlled substances violations in accordance with AR 195-2. The USACIDC investigates use, possession, manufacture, or distribution of controlled substances described in the Controlled Substances Act (CSA) (21 USC 812). When appropriate, the investigation of drug offenses on an installation may be conducted by a joint USACIDC and installation LE team. This approach fosters better coordination and is encouraged when deemed in the best interest of the overall drug suppression effort.

12-2. Illicit drug activity includes the nonmedical use and abuse of controlled prescription drugs (CPDs). The threat posed by the use of CPDs, primarily pain relievers, is the fastest growing drug threat in the United States. The abuse of CPDs has also contributed to the number of drug-related fatalities throughout the United States.

12-3. As a result of physical and psychological injuries sustained by Soldiers involved in combat, the number of CPDs prescribed to Soldiers has created a high-risk environment for their nonmedical use and abuse. LE investigators are challenged with identifying the alteration, abuse, and wrongful possession and distribution of CPDs.

LEGAL CONSIDERATIONS

12-4. The CSA is the legal foundation of the government's fight against the abuse of drugs and other substances. This law is a consolidation of numerous laws regulating the manufacture and distribution of narcotics, stimulants, depressants, hallucinogens, marijuana, anabolic steroids, and chemicals used in the illicit production of controlled substances.

12-5. The CSA regulates the manufacture and distribution of all legal and illegal drugs and places all substances regulated under existing federal law into one of five schedules. This placement is based upon the substance's medicinal value, harmfulness, and potential for abuse or addiction. Schedule I classification is reserved for the most dangerous drugs that have no recognized medical use, while Schedule V classification is used for the least dangerous drugs. The act also provides a mechanism for substances to be controlled, added to a schedule, decontrolled, removed from control, rescheduled, or transferred from one schedule to another.

12-6. Article 112a UCMJ, interprets the CSA in terms of military justice. Schedules I, II, and III have maximum punishments of 5 years for possession and 15 years for distribution. Schedules IV and V have maximum punishments of 2 years for possession and 10 years for distribution. Marijuana has specific penalties. Possession of less than 30 grams has a maximum punishment of 2 years. Possession of 30 grams or more has a maximum punishment of 5 years. Possession of any amount with the intent to distribute it has a maximum punishment of 15 years.

ELEMENTS OF PROOF

12-7. The elements for wrongful possession, use, distribution, manufacture, or introduction of a controlled substance are very simple; they are that the accused possessed, used, distributed, manufactured, or introduced a certain amount of a controlled substance and that the possession, use, distribution, manufacture, or introduction by the accused was wrongful.

12-8. Wrongful possession, manufacture, or introduction of a controlled substance with the intent to distribute it is more complex in that circumstances must support the intent to distribute. The possession, manufacture, or introduction must be wrongful to begin with, but then the intent to distribute must be inferred from circumstantial evidence. Examples of evidence which may tend to support an inference of intent to distribute are: the possession of a quantity of substance in excess of that which one would be likely to have for personal use; the market value of the substance; the manner in which the substance is packaged; and that the accused is not a user of the substance. On the other hand, evidence that the accused is addicted to or is a heavy user of the substance may tend to negate an inference of the intent to distribute.

LEGAL TERMS

12-9. Army LE personnel must understand the legal terminology used to describe drug crimes. The following terms are used in describing the elements of proof required for an offense to be criminal:

- **Controlled substance.** Controlled substance means amphetamine, cocaine, heroin, lysergic acid diethylamide (LSD), marijuana, methamphetamine, opium, phencyclidine (PCP), and barbituric acid, including phenobarbital and secobarbital. Controlled substance also means any substance which is included in Schedules I through V established by the CSA.

Note. In addition, AR 600-85 prohibits using the following substances for the purpose of inducing excitement, intoxication, or stupefaction of the central nervous system. This provision is not intended to prohibit the otherwise lawful use of alcoholic beverages. Violations of this regulation are a punitive violation of the UCMJ. The prohibited substances include: controlled substance analogues (designer drugs); chemicals, propellants, or inhalants (huffing); dietary supplements that are banned by the U.S. Food and Drug Administration; prescription or over-the-counter drugs and medications (when used in a manner contrary to their intended medical purpose or in excess of the prescribed dosage); and naturally occurring substances (to include but not limited to Salvia Divinorum, Jimson Weed, and such).

- **Possess.** Possess means to exercise control of something. Possession may be direct physical custody like holding an item in one's hand or it may be constructive, as in the case of a person who hides an item in a locker or car to which that person may return to retrieve it. Possession must be knowing and conscious. Possession inherently includes the power or authority to preclude control by others. It is possible, however, for more than one person to possess an item simultaneously, as when several people share control of an item. A suspect may not be convicted of possession of a controlled substance if he did not know that the substance was present and under his control. Awareness of the presence of a controlled substance may be inferred from circumstantial evidence.
- **Distribute.** Distribute means to deliver to the possession of another. Deliver means the actual, constructive, or attempted transfer of an item, whether or not there exists an agency relationship.
- **Manufacture.** Manufacture means the production, preparation, propagation, compounding, or processing of a drug or other substance, either directly or indirectly. Manufacturing can also be accomplished by extraction from substances of natural origin, or independently by means of chemical synthesis or by a combination of extraction and chemical synthesis. Manufacture also includes any packaging or repackaging of such substance or labeling or relabeling of its

container. Production, as used in this context, includes the planting, cultivating, growing, or harvesting of a drug or other substance.

12-10. To be punishable under Article 112a of the UCMJ, possession, use, distribution, introduction, or manufacture of a controlled substance must be wrongful. Possession, use, distribution, introduction, or manufacture of a controlled substance is wrongful if it is without legal justification or authorization. Possession, distribution, introduction, or manufacture of a controlled substance is not wrongful if such act or acts are done pursuant to legitimate LE activities, by authorized personnel in the performance of medical duties, or without knowledge of the contraband nature of the substance; for example, a person who possesses cocaine, but actually believes it to be sugar, is not guilty of wrongful possession of cocaine.

INVESTIGATING DRUG CRIMES

12-11. A successful investigation involving the wrongful possession, use, distribution, manufacture, or introduction of drugs is largely dependent upon reliable intelligence. Drug offenders have become very adept at avoiding detection and protecting illegal drug activities. For this reason, it is very important for LE investigators to methodically follow all investigative leads regardless of how trivial they may seem.

12-12. Developing investigative leads that evolve to the highest levels of seizures and apprehensions of drug offenders is a daunting task due to the lack of complaining witnesses. In a military environment, the DOD Urinalysis Program generates the bulk of investigative leads, along with a continuous analysis of criminal intelligence, reviews of USACIDC and military police reports, and liaison with local and federal LE agencies.

12-13. Most drug investigations overlap jurisdictional boundaries—more so in a military environment where distinctions must be made between what USACIDC investigates and what installation LE activities investigate as well as the distinction between civilian and military offenders. The continuing criminal conduct of a drug investigation may have suspects moving between jurisdictions throughout the course of the investigation. DODD 5525.7, AR 195-2, and CID Regulation 195-1 outline investigative and reporting responsibilities.

12-14. Once a drug investigation has been initiated, the investigator must rely upon fundamental principles of drug investigation—intelligence, surveillance, the use of confidential informants, and undercover activities. Because of the overlap of jurisdictional boundaries, these efforts must be coordinated carefully throughout the investigation. Physical surveillance is discussed in detail in chapter 5 of this manual, undercover activities are discussed in chapter 6, sources are discussed in appendix E, and drug identification is detailed in appendix G.

12-15. The success or failure of an investigation often is determined by small procedural and legal details. It is in the best interest of the investigator to coordinate with the prosecutor early and throughout the investigation to minimize legal problems.

DEPARTMENT OF DEFENSE URINALYSIS PROGRAM

12-16. DOD laboratories test over 60,000 urine samples each month. All active duty members must undergo a urinalysis at least once per year. Members of the Guard and Reserves must be tested at least once every two years. There are several protections built into the system to ensure accurate results.

12-17. Urine samples undergo an initial immunoassay screening (using the Olympus AU-800 Automated Chemistry Analyzer). Those that test positive for the presence of drugs at this point undergo the same screen once again. Finally, those that come up positive during two screening tests are put through a much more specific gas chromatography/mass spectrometry test. This test can identify specific substances within the urine samples. Even if a particular drug is detected, if the level is below a certain threshold, the test result is reported back to the commander as negative.

12-18. Every sample gets tested for the specific component or metabolite of marijuana, cocaine, and amphetamines, including ecstasy. Some drugs metabolize quickly; therefore, testing must be conducted quickly. Results from drug testing may be discussed with a toxicologist or other expert to determine what drugs were ingested, and other investigative questions related to the suspected drug use may also be addressed.

12-19.   Commonly available substances such as Goldenseal® and Lasix® are often touted as magical substances that can mask drugs in urine. In fact, they can make drugs easier to detect. These substances are diuretics, so if they're taken before giving a urine sample they flush chemicals out of the body and right into the collection cup. Drugs are often more concentrated in the urine after a Soldier takes one of these substances. In an effort to avoid detection, some Soldiers drink vinegar or bleach. Neither of these will defeat the urinalysis test.

12-20.   Over-the-counter cold medications and dietary supplements can cause a screening test to produce a positive result, but more specific secondary testing would positively identify the medication. In this case, the report that goes back to the commander says negative.

12-21.   The legal use of drug test results depends upon the reason for the urinalysis test. Urinalysis testing may be conducted for—

- **Random testing.** Each military member must be tested at least once per year. Reserve Soldiers must be tested at least once every two years. This is done by means of "random testing." A commander can order that either all or a random-selected sample of the unit be tested at any time. Results of random testing can be used as the basis for judicial and nonjudicial punishment. Soldiers do not have the right to refuse random testing. However, commanders cannot order specific individuals to take a "random" test. Those selected must be truly "random."
- **Probable cause.** If a commander has probable cause that a person is under the influence of drugs, the commander can give LE personnel search authorization to obtain urine or blood evidence. Results of urinalysis tests obtained through search authorizations can be used as the basis for judicial and nonjudicial punishment and involuntary discharges to include service characterization. Soldiers cannot refuse to provide a urine sample which has been authorized by a military search warrant.
- **Consent.** If a commander does not have probable cause, he can ask the Soldier for "consent to search." If the Soldier grants consent, the results of the urinalysis may be used as the basis for judicial and nonjudicial punishment and involuntary discharges to include service characterization. Under this procedure, Soldiers do not have to grant consent.
- **Commander-directed.** If a member refuses to grant consent and if the commander does not have enough evidence to warrant a probable-cause search warrant, the commander may order the Soldier to give a urine sample anyway. However, commander-directed urinalysis results may not be used for court-martial or Article 15 purposes. The results may be used as a reason for involuntary discharge, but they may not be used to determine service characterization.

PRELIMINARY IDENTIFICATION OF DRUGS

12-22.   A major challenge to LE personnel is the identification of drugs found at a crime scene or in a suspect's possession. Because of the number of drug types, colors, sizes, and street names, the aid of a pharmaceutical reference book is often necessary. An excellent reference source for drug identification is the Physician's Desk Reference. When the Physician's Desk Reference cannot assist an investigator in the identification of a drug, a preliminary identification of the drug by using a chemical-reagent field test kit (also known as presumptive testing) can be conducted. There are several drug identification kits available. Each kit contains vials of reagent-grade chemicals that a qualified chemist uses when testing substances in a laboratory environment. The presumptive test shows a color reaction. Although the color reactions are valuable, they have the following limitations:

- The tests are qualitative and not quantitative (the drug percentage will not be known).
- The tests are only precursory and presumptive (a chemist's testimony as to a scientific analysis is the most valid evidence).
- A negative test does not necessarily preclude the presence of a drug, nor does a positive test guarantee the presence of a drug.

CONDUCTING PRESUMPTIVE TESTS

12-23.   The first rule an investigator must adhere to when testing suspected drug substances is to never taste or try the substance in any fashion. Secondly, the investigator must remember to use only the amount of the suspected substance needed to conduct the presumptive test and to preserve enough of the substance for laboratory testing. Instructions are provided with all test kits and should be followed. Users of the kits should receive training in their use and must be aware that the reagents can give both false-positive and false-negative results. Investigators should also be aware that there is no presumptive screening test available for synthetic drugs.

12-24.   Investigators will be required to test drugs in powder, solid, or liquid form. Drugs found in powder form can be mixed with other substances and contained in capsules. If suspected drugs are found in capsules, open one capsule to pour some of the powder into a test vial to conduct a presumptive test. When encountering solid forms of suspected drugs, such as tablets, either crush the tablet into powder form or break the tablet in half and scrape powder from the inside of the tablet into the test vial. For vegetable material, such as marijuana or hashish, a few flakes of the crumbled substance can be put into the test vial. When suspected liquid drugs are found, only add the necessary amount to the vial to receive a reading from the test kit. Use care when extracting a testable amount of the suspected drug to avoid sample contamination. At the time of the test, the ambient temperature should be between 50 degrees Fahrenheit and 104 degrees Fahrenheit; the relative humidity should be between 10 percent and 90 percent.

12-25.   Upon completion of the test, use the neutralizing agent that comes with the kit. Kits contain reagent-grade chemicals and are considered hazardous waste. As such, they require proper disposal. Every investigator should identify where hazardous material can be discarded on the installation. These kits are not to be disposed of in office trash receptacles.

SAFETY

12-26.   Safety is an important consideration who conducts preliminary drug identification tests. The chemicals are sometimes caustic and can cause burns or irritate the body. Some commercial tests are manufactured in glass vials and, when opened, small fragments of glass may scatter. Wear rubber gloves when available; when they are not available wash your hands as soon as possible after conducting the test. Always wash your hands before eating, drinking, or smoking if you have been handling suspected drugs. In addition to wearing gloves, wear protective goggles and use the presumptive test kits in a well-ventilated area.

DOCUMENTING PRESUMPTIVE TESTING

12-27.   Presumptive field tests must be confirmed by laboratory analysis. In the event there is not enough of the suspected drug to be field tested and sent to the laboratory, the investigator must decide which choice is imperative for the investigation.

12-28.   When an investigator conducts a field test, he must document the results using CID Form 36, *Field Test Analysis on Non-Narcotic Substances*. CID Form 36 allows documentation of what the suspected drug was, what type of field test kit was used, and the results of the test and is an important aspect of the investigation. CID Form 36 must accompany DA Form 4137; both forms document the chain of custody of the suspected drugs. CID Form 36 is used to document that a portion of the suspected drug was consumed for testing, and this information will be recorded on DA Form 4137 in the chain of custody portion.

CLANDESTINE LABORATORIES

12-29.   The Drug Enforcement Administration (DEA) defines a clandestine drug laboratory as "an illicit operation consisting of a sufficient combination of apparatus and chemicals that either has been or could be used in the manufacture or synthesis of controlled substances." Clandestine laboratories are known to cause serious injury or death to the laboratory operator and to the investigator. Fire and explosions from organic solvents and reactive material remain a serious threat. However, the silent killers are deadly gases and by-products emitted from the process.

12-30. The methamphetamine manufacturing or "cooking" process results in five to seven pounds of chemical waste for each pound of methamphetamine manufactured. The chemical waste by-products are considered hazardous waste; therefore, extreme caution must be taken when LE personnel respond to a reported clandestine laboratory setting. In addition, the aftermath clean-up is subject to hazardous waste laws. Responding to a reported methamphetamine laboratory can be extremely dangerous due to the nature of the chemicals used in the manufacturing process. LE personnel who respond to a reported methamphetamine laboratory scene are trained to follow specific safety guidelines as part of their normal LE duties. In most instances, specialized response teams are formed and trained to deal with the initial hazards associated with a first response.

12-31. Some of the safety hazards associated with an initial response to a methamphetamine laboratory include exposure to flash-fires and exposure to hazardous chemicals. Skin and respiratory exposure to chemicals are two key components that require special training in order to prevent potential serious injury during an emergency response. Training includes educating responders about the importance of safety, including the need to wear the appropriate personal protective equipment for the hazardous conditions normally present in a methamphetamine laboratory.

12-32. The precursor chemicals used in clandestine drug laboratories are continually changing and vary from state to state. The local hazardous material team, fire department, or federal or state LE agency should have the latest information and technologies in dealing with clandestine laboratories for the area. The DEA and the Environmental Protection Agency (EPA) are two federal agencies that may be able to provide assistance in dismantling, removing, and cleaning up a clandestine drug laboratory.

Chapter 13

Collision (Traffic Accident) Investigations

Traffic collisions are extremely confusing events. How they occur, who or what causes them, and why they occur are factors the military police must determine. All military police Soldiers should know the fundamentals of collision investigations and how to prepare a DA 3946, *Military Police Traffic Accident Report*. TMCIs receive specialized training to enable them to conduct collision investigations. Major collisions involving death, serious bodily injury, or significant property damage should be investigated by trained TMCIs. The primary reference for this chapter is the *Traffic Management and Collision Investigations Student Study Guide and Workbook* from the Traffic Management and Collision Investigations Course at Lackland, Air Force Base.

INVESTIGATIVE REQUIREMENTS

13-1. Collision investigations (also referred to as traffic accident investigations) are a specialized investigative capability within the military police structure. The focus of collision investigations is on events that occur between a vehicle and another object. The second object can be another vehicle, a person, a structure, or any other natural or manmade obstacle.

13-2. Military police and TMCIs responding to a vehicle collision employ many of the same investigative principles as criminal investigators. A collision investigation is the process of observation, collection and documentation of evidence (including physical measurements of objects, markings, and vehicles), analysis, preparation, and presentation of evidence (both physical and testimonial) to determine the cause or causes of a collision or mishap involving a vehicle. A collision investigation is a fact finding, not a fault finding, process. Investigators must establish the facts related to the incident and allow those facts to guide their conclusions.

13-3. Vehicle collisions can be extremely complex with multiple factors contributing to the event; TMCIs and military police investigating a collision should avoid any temptation to blame any single component for the cause of the collision. Impartiality is critical. The investigator processing the collision scene must maintain an impartial approach and not take sides while conducting an investigation. This can be difficult in some cases (especially cases involving death or serious injury) and requires discipline, maturity, and focus on the part of military police and TMCIs working the collision scene. They must at all times remain calm and guard against injecting personal opinions and emotions while investigating.

13-4. A properly conducted collision investigation should answer the essential investigative elements including—who was involved in the incident, what happened during the incident, when the incident happened, where the incident happened, why the incident happened (contributing factors), and how the incident happened. The DA Form 3946 will answer these questions when properly completed. Depending on the severity of the collision, the DA Form 3946 may be completed as a standalone document or be supplemented by scaled diagrams, photographs, statements, results of breath analysis, and other evidence. See appendix D for a sample filled-out DA Form 3946.

13-5. DA Form 3946 should be thorough and concise. The report may be used in civil or judicial proceedings and reflects the professionalism and capabilities of the military police Soldier or TMCI who prepared the report. Readers of traffic accident reports seldom know the writer; therefore, opinions are often formed on the basis of the report. The credibility of the report may be compromised based on the initial impression of the audience. Poorly written reports can make the most professional military police

Soldier or TMCI appear incompetent and unprofessional. Military police who prepare collision reports should strive for—

- **Accuracy, brevity, and clarity.** Plan and write reports so that they clearly and accurately state the essential elements of the case.
- **Objectivity and impartiality.** To conduct a thorough investigation, the investigation must be objective and impartial. Never take sides.
- **Completeness.** Ensure that reports contain all information essential to the investigation. The report should answer the following questions:
  - What took place? Include all known actions leading up to and including the collision.
  - Who was involved? Include all persons surrounding the incident—drivers, victims, pedestrians, and witnesses.
  - When did the collision occur? Include the date, day, and time (for example, 25 March 2011, Friday, 1400).
  - Where did the collision occur? Describe the exact location, and include any diagrams.
  - How did the events occur? List the collision sequence of events in chronological order.
  - What elements were involved? Include all vehicles, persons, buildings, traffic control devices, characteristics of the roadway, and other environmental factors.
  - Why did the collision occur? This is a statement that includes the military police Soldier's or TMCI's conclusion, based on the operational and conditional factors of the incident.

13-6. AR 190-5 and local policy provide guidance on the level of detail required for the specific collision investigations. Regulatory and policy guidelines are used to determine the required depth of an investigation and can provide for the maximum effective use of military police and TMCI resources for investigating traffic incidents. A detailed investigation is generally mandated for incidents including those involving—

- Government vehicles.
- Damage to government property.
- Fatalities or personal injury.
- Evidence of a serious offense (for example, driving under the influence, hit and run incidents, reckless driving, or vehicular assault).
- Extensive damage to privately owned vehicles.
- Incidents as prescribed within applicable SOFAs.

13-7. The environment associated with collisions involving vehicles creates unique challenges for responding LE personnel. Military police and TMCIs responding to a collision should be equipped with a wide variety of materials and equipment required to process the incident scene, provide safety for all personnel at the scene (including LE personnel and other first responders), and to render assistance to victims of the incident. Equipment and materials required may include—

- Investigative equipment and materials to include—
  - DA Form 2823, DA Form 3881, DA Form 3946, and DA Form 4137.
  - 100-foot (30-meter) and 300-foot (90-meter) metal-reinforced fabric measuring tapes or plastic-coated fiberglass measuring tapes. Ensure that steel pins, nails, or weights with hooks or clips are available for securing the ends of the measuring tapes when making measurements.
  - A collision investigator's template.
  - Paper and ruler.
  - Binoculars.
  - A digital SLR with camera bag, telephoto and 50-millimeter lenses, flash, and tripod.
- Drafting equipment to include—
  - A drafting compass with lead—0.5 millimeter is recommended.
  - An engineer's scale.
  - Mechanical pencils—0.5 millimeter.

- White gum erasers.
- An eraser shield.
- Two clipboards or posse box containers.
- A flexi-curve.
- A scientific calculator.
- A carrying case for equipment.
- A drafting template.
- Protective and first aid equipment to include—
  - An emergency response guidebook.
  - Blankets.
  - Flashlights with cones and extra batteries.
  - Red signal flares or fusees. A fusee is a type of flare that burns for an extended period (up to 60 minutes). Fusees are commonly referred to as road flares and are used to indicate obstacles or advise caution on roadways during limited visibility.
  - A portable reflector or flashing lights.
  - A portable public address system such as a bullhorn.
  - Portable light systems for area illumination.
  - A portable spotlight.
  - Warning flags and stanchions.
  - Engineer tape.
  - Reflectorized vests.
  - A first aid kit.
  - Traffic cones.
  - A dry chemical fire extinguisher.
  - Safety glasses.
  - Latex or nitrile gloves.
  - Leather work gloves.
- Tools to include—
  - A pinch bar.
  - A heavy scissor-type jack.
  - A 25-foot (8-meter) tow chain or cable.
  - A shovel.
  - An axe.
  - A hammer or mallet, nails, and stakes.
  - Crescent wrenches.
  - Socket sets.
  - A variety of screwdriver types and sizes.
  - Pliers.
  - Wire cutters.
  - Vise grips.
  - A continuity tester or voltmeter.
  - A magnifying glass.
  - A tire pressure gauge.
  - A tire tread depth gauge.
  - A 36-inch crow bar.
  - Bolt cutters.
  - A seatbelt cutter.

- A window breaking punch tool.
- A pocketknife.
- Additional flashlights.
- A roller measuring wheel.
- A 15- to 25-foot steel tape measure.
- A stopwatch.
- A 48-inch carpenter's level.
- Chalk.
- Lumber crayons.
- Spray paint in aerosol cans for marking roads—yellow or orange is best.
- A drag sled.

13-8. Crime scene kits may be required if there are serious injuries or fatalities or if there is evidence of criminal activity or negligence that may result in a criminal prosecution. Basic evidence collection materials should be carried in the vehicle of all military police patrols. Crime scene kits for more extensive evidence processing are typically provided by responding MPI or USACIDC SAs. All LE personnel must understand and abide by the rules of evidence during collection of physical and testimonial evidence; these are addressed in chapters 2 and 3.

13-9. MPIs or USACIDC SAs may assume investigative responsibility for criminal activity in collisions in which evidence of other criminal offenses is discovered at the collision scene, including those that contributed to or resulted from the collision. Military police will notify the supporting USACIDC element whenever a traffic accident involves a fatality or an offense within USACIDC investigative responsibility as described in AR 195-2. In these cases, military police and TMCIs will complete the investigation of the facts pertinent to the actual collision and provide a copy of the report to the USACIDC element.

13-10. Advanced equipment may be available to the TMCI for processing complex collisions. These items can be costly, and their availability is dependent on local command budgets and priorities. Portable traffic signals can be used to aid in traffic control at the site of the collision. Software and specialized computers are also available to aid the investigator in producing collision diagrams and making required calculations. Crash data recorder or event data recorder retrieval tools are available that can download pre- and postcrash data on some late-model vehicles. This data can provide valuable information to the investigator enabling a more thorough understanding of specific data characteristics of the vehicle at critical moments surrounding a collision event. Total station measuring devices with associated software can be valuable tools for making accurate measurements of distance and slope critical to collision investigations.

FACTORS AND STAGES OF A COLLISION

13-11. Collision investigators must understand the factors that directly contribute to traffic incidents and the stages of progression leading up to a collision. The ability to understand the factors that contribute to a traffic incident enables collision investigators to understand the collision based on a cause and effect standpoint. An understanding of the stages or phases of a collision allows the investigator to analyze the incident in event segments that enable the investigator to compartmentalize the factors involved into separate event segments.

FACTORS

13-12. Factors that contribute to collisions can be aligned within two categories: operational factors and conditional factors. An operational factor is one that the driver can control or change. It is a behavior, action, or negligence (lack of action) by a driver that contributes directly to a collision. Operational factors are influenced by many factors including an individual's actions before driving such as amount of sleep and whether the driver has been drinking or taking legal or illegal medications. The driver's mental state can also contribute to operational factors causing collisions; if the driver is preoccupied due to stress at work or problems at home, this can reduce the drivers attentiveness and focus on the task at hand (safe driving).

Driving habits of the individual, such as speeding, multitasking, and general failure to observe traffic laws, can be a major operational factor resulting in traffic collisions. Operational factors may include—

- **Speed.** Speed greater or lesser than a safe normal speed can contribute to collisions by—
  - Making it impossible to negotiate a curve.
  - Reducing the ability of the driver to take successful evasive action from hazards on the roadway.
  - Presenting surprise to other traffic elements.
  - Creating unsafe braking distances.
- **Behavior.** Behaviors by drivers contribute to collisions by—
  - Unusual or reckless action such as skidding or spinning out.
  - Illegal actions such as driving under the influence or driving on the wrong side of the road.
  - Hazardous actions such as excessive lane changing.
  - Inattentiveness such as talking or texting on mobile phones, eating, or reading.
- **Delayed perception.** This is a failure to perceive and safely respond to the impending danger of a possible collision, caused by inattention or distraction.
- **Faulty actions.** These are evasive actions taken when the road user reacts to a hazard after the perception of the danger. Faulty actions can include—
  - Slowing.
  - Braking or stopping.
  - Swerving.
  - Backing.
  - Accelerating.
  - Turning.

13-13. Conditional factors are factors over which the driver has no control or cannot change. These are conditions that contribute to, or compound, operational factors. There may be one or more factors, such as excessive speed and skidding on a curve (operational factors) and slippery pavement (a condition factor). Conditional factors may include—

- **Other people—driver and/or pedestrian.** These people can introduce conditional factors outside the drivers control through a variety of means including—
  - Driving under the influence of drugs or alcohol. Other drivers operating vehicles or pedestrians can create a wide variety of hazards for other drivers.
  - Physical impairments. Physical impairments can affect both other drivers and pedestrians making their actions unpredictable. These impairments can range from vision limitations to sudden and unexpected medical conditions that cause loss of control.
  - Inattentiveness. Lack of attention by pedestrians and other drivers is a major conditional factor beyond the control of drivers. Persons transiting a roadway are often distracted. These distractions can be due to internal distractions such as preoccupation with issues other than their current activity—work, relationship issues, or other distractions—or through their attention being directed away from their primary activity—cell phones, music players, reading material, or other distractions.
  - Reckless behavior. This includes any intentional actions by others that create a hazardous environment for other persons in the roadway.
- **Roads.** Conditional factors of the roadway include—
  - Road conditions such as potholes, construction, soft shoulders, or other road characteristics.
  - Weather.
  - Poor roadway design.
  - Obstructions.
  - Traffic control measures or devices. This can include improper placement, malfunctioning, damaged, or missing traffic control measures or devices.
- **Vehicle condition.** Conditional factors related to vehicles include—

- Brakes that are not functioning properly.
- Inoperable or missing lights.
- Steering malfunction.
- Defective or worn tires.
- Cracked or broken windows that limit the operator's field or vision.

13-14.   A road with severe potholes is a conditional factor; if a vehicle has bald tires (a conditional factor) and hits a pothole, the major contributing factors are conditional. Operational and conditional factors can combine to compound the effect. If a driver swerves into the opposite lane to avoid a pothole and collides with an oncoming vehicle, the pothole is a conditional factor and the swerve is an operational factor.

STAGES

13-15.   Each collision has a number of stages or sequential events that make up the collision incident. These stages are shown in figure 13-1. There are five major events of a collision. These events are sequential throughout the incident; however, not all events are present in every collision incident. Identifying the points where the events occurred can help investigators measure or calculate speed at specific points in the sequence and calculate distances between events (see appendix J). These events include the—

- **Point of possible perception.** The point of possible perception is the position or point where a normal driver could possibly have perceived the impending hazard. This point will be present in all collisions and may be approximated with adequate investigation. A walk-through of the entire collision scene is generally required to identify the point of possible perception.
- **Point of actual perception.** The point of actual perception is the point where the driver actually recognizes the hazard. This point comes after the point of possible perception; the perception time is the period of time between these two points. Additionally, —
  - This can be identified by combining skid marks with reaction distance to show the driver's estimated point of reaction. This point does not exist in all cases, such as when a driver falls asleep at the wheel. It is possible that the driver will not see a hazard, even up to the primary point of impact.
  - A reaction is a person's response, either voluntary or involuntary, to an external stimulus, in this case a traffic hazard. A normal reaction time between perception of the hazard and a physical reaction to that hazard is 1.6 seconds; this reaction time can be slowed significantly in cases of physical impairment. Reaction distance is that distance the vehicle traveled during these 1.6 seconds.
- **Point of no escape.** The time and place, after which the collision cannot be avoided. It may occur before or after the point of actual perception. The point of no escape is present in all collisions but can be difficult to locate, depending on the circumstances of the collision.
- **First harmful event (point of initial impact).** The first harmful event is the first contact between two vehicles, a vehicle and another object, or a vehicle and a highway surface during an overturn. It marks the first occurrence of damage or injury; this event is present in all collisions. It determines the exact time and place of the collision. The point of impact is divided into the following three subcategories:
  - *Point of primary contact.* This is the first contact between two vehicles, a vehicle and another object, or a vehicle with a highway surface during an overturn.
  - *Point of maximum engagement.* This is the point of maximum penetration or engagement by one object into another such as the maximum penetration of one traffic unit into another traffic unit or object during collision.
  - *Point of disengagement.* This is the point where two objects separate following a collision. The point of disengagement always follows the point of primary contact and maximum engagement.
- **Point of final rest (final position).** The place where the objects involved in a collision finally stop movement. Any collision following this stage should be considered as another incident. The

point of final rest may be controlled or uncontrolled, and is present in every collision. This is further explained as follows:

- **Controlled.** The driver moves the vehicle off the roadway.
- **Uncontrolled.** The vehicle continues to roll, slide, or flip after the impact. No driver control directed the final rest position.

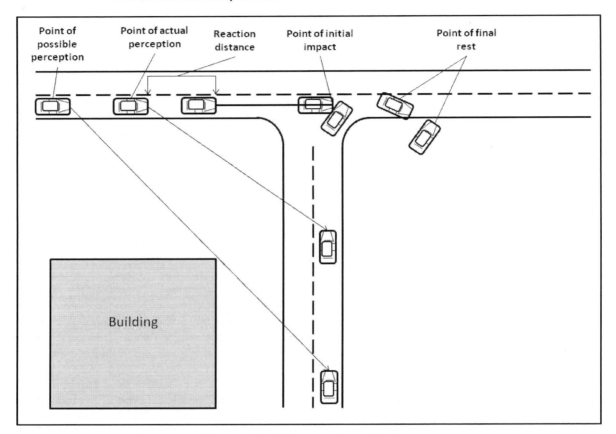

Figure 13-1. Stages of a collision

13-16.   The manner in which a driver reacts to a hazard is affected greatly by the driver's skill, training, experience, and physical state. A driver's strategy, tactics, and reactions while driving can greatly affect the outcomes in the stages of a collision. Strategy, tactics, and reaction as they relate to driving are described as follows:

- **Strategy.** Driving strategy involves the general approach a driver uses while driving and how the driver perceives potential hazards in advance of a critical point. A good driving strategy increases the likelihood that a hazard will be perceived with enough advanced warning to allow the driver to take appropriate action to avoid the hazard. This may include adjusting the line and speed taken while driving around curves, maintaining a safe following distance and speed, making safe and appropriate lane changes, and constantly scanning for potential problems and adjusting accordingly. Solid driving strategy rarely involves quick decisions.
- **Tactics.** Tactics require quick decisions and are actions taken by a driver to escape an imminent collision. These actions may include steering right or left, accelerating, decelerating, backing up, or simply doing nothing at all. Application of good driving tactics increases with experience. Advanced drivers training can also increase the driver's ability to execute successful driving tactics.
- **Reaction.** A reaction is a person's voluntary or involuntary response to a hazard. The normal time it takes from perception to reaction is 1.6 seconds. Normal reactions may be affected by age, strength of stimulus, physical conditions, habits, and perception delays. A driver's ability to

perceive and react quickly can greatly influence the outcome of an incident. Inexperience and poorly applied driving tactics can negate the benefit of good reactions.

13-17. The greater the driver's skill and experience, the higher the likelihood that a collision can be avoided or at least damage from a collision can be mitigated. This is why younger, less experienced drivers statistically have more collisions than older, more experienced drivers. Some persons may have received extensive driver training including evasive driving tactics that can increase the driver's skill level. Physical impairments and limitations resulting from medical conditions, physical disabilities, and advanced age can also affect a driver's ability to react to hazards in a manner that results in collision avoidance or damage mitigation.

LEVELS OF COLLISION INVESTIGATION

13-18. There are five levels or stages of collision investigation. The level of investigation conducted is determined by several factors including local policies, the relative severity of the collision and associated effects, and requirements for traffic or safety studies and associated statistical data. The five levels of a collision investigation include—

- Initial report and information collection.
- On-scene investigation.
- Technical evaluation.
- Professional reconstruction.
- Cause analysis.

INITIAL REPORT AND INFORMATION COLLECTION

13-19. Initial information collection begins with the initial report to military police. This initial report is typically made to military police desk personnel; however, it can occur through direct report to a military police patrol that is in the area of the incident when the collision occurs. In some instances a military police patrol or other LE personnel may witness or be involved in a collision. This level includes actions by military police desk and patrol personnel involving initial collection of information from persons reporting and/or involved in an accident or incident.

13-20. For minor collisions in which all vehicles involved are only cosmetically damaged, there is no damage to government property, and there are no physical injuries, this may be the only required level. Local policy may allow for drivers to exchange insurance and contact information without completing a full traffic accident report.

ON-SCENE INVESTIGATION

13-21. This level focuses on the on-scene assessments and actions of military police and/or TMCIs upon arrival at the scene of a collision. For relatively minor incidents a TMCI may not be required for investigations up to this level. This stage of the investigation is conducted while the scene remains relatively fresh and the roadway has not been opened for routine vehicle traffic.

13-22. The investigation activities conducted on-scene in the immediate aftermath of an incident are the most important of all five collision investigation levels. This represents urgent data collection of perishable evidence, statements, and data. During this stage the investigator examines evidence, documents the collision, and obtains physical and testimonial evidence that may not be available hours after the collision. At this point in the investigation the scene remains relatively fresh and untainted. The scene of a collision investigation, unlike a traditional crime scene, is typically in a location that cannot be preserved for extended periods. Collisions that block highways and other roadways must be cleared as soon as possible to allow normal traffic flow and prevent disruption of normal activities.

13-23. The military police patrol or TMCI conducting the investigation must make rapid and accurate observations relevant to the condition of each of the components related to collision investigations. For example, is there evidence of intoxication, was road damage or visual obstacles present, or are faulty or damaged traffic control devices a contributing factor? There are three basic components of the highway transportation system. These three components must all be considered when conducting a collision investigation. The components include—

- **People.** There may be many people involved in a collision or who may provide information about a collision. These people include—
  - *Drivers.* A driver is any person who operates or is in actual physical control of any vehicle regardless of the type(s) of vehicle(s) involved.
  - *Passengers.* A passenger includes person on or in a vehicle involved in the collision other than the driver.
  - *Pedestrians.* Any person on foot, including joggers and runners, is pedestrians. Pedestrians may be involved in the collision or may merely witness the incident.
  - *Other witnesses.* A witness can include any person at the scene other than the driver, passenger, or pedestrian involved in the collision. It is possible that the witness may not have actually seen the collision, but may have heard or seen the results of the collision.
- **Roads.** Include all highways and roads relevant to the collision.
- **Vehicles.** Include all vehicles relevant to the collision.

13-24. Military police and TMCIs should record factual information and collect physical and testimonial evidence only; they should avoid making conclusions at this stage in the investigation. Initial photographs and measurements should be taken. LE personnel conducting the investigation must ensure that they examine, collect, and record data and evidence relevant to each component. Information used to document each of the three collision components (people, vehicles, and roads) include the—

- Identification of the component involved.
- Description of the component.
- Condition of the component before to the collision.
- Results of the collision on the component.

TECHNICAL EVALUATION

13-25. This level requires trained TMCIs to conduct technical evaluations and assessments based on collected data and evidence at the scene and on follow-up evidence and data collected after the scene has been cleared for normal traffic. This level will be required for more serious collisions involving injuries to persons, major property damage, and collisions resulting in damage to government property.

13-26. A technical evaluation is a delayed evaluation; it does not occur during the on-scene investigation. It is conducted as a follow-up to the initial on-scene investigation. A technical evaluation is undertaken to address specific requirements to complete the investigation or for research and statistical purposes.

13-27. During the technical evaluation initial measurements may be verified and additional measurements taken based on specific legal and analytical requirements related to the collision. Additional photographs may be taken to supplement or add clarity to those taken during the initial on-scene investigation. The technical evaluation stage also includes preparation of documents and reports including—

- Scale diagrams.
- Damage evaluations.
- Simple speed estimates.
- Laboratory evaluations such as tire and lamp evaluations.

PROFESSIONAL RECONSTRUCTION

13-28. This level includes multidisciplinary efforts to reconstruct the events and causes of serious incidents, especially those resulting in serious injury or death and/or possible criminal liabilities. Professional reconstruction uses scientific techniques in an effort to identify/verify operational and conditional factors and determine how a collision occurred. It is resource-intensive and conducted only when there is a definite need and involves data collection beyond the scope of a technical evaluation. Like crime scene reconstruction, collision reconstruction is a deliberate method for gathering, analyzing, and interpreting evidence to develop a plausible theory that explains the events at the scene. It applies logical reasoning based on objective interpretation of the evidence available.

13-29.   Collision reconstruction involves careful analysis, calculation, laboratory experimentation and examination, and other functional applications. The results of the varied functional analyses are then fused to develop an accurate reconstruction of the events that make up the collision incident. Reconstruction of the collision events requires expert opinions, deductions, and assessments from a variety of disciplines and includes areas of—

- Vehicle dynamics.
- Vehicle system evaluations.
- Traffic engineering.
- Evaluation of driving strategy and evasive action.
- Injury evaluations.
- Autopsies.
- Scientific experimentation and/or lab examination.
- Time and distance computations.

CAUSE ANALYSIS

13-30.   Cause analysis is the final level of a collision investigation. This level is conducted after the incident to determine causes of collisions for the purpose of statistical and research applications. Cause analysis requires a great degree of speculation and inference when evaluating available data; therefore, it is generally used for research and statistical purposes.

13-31.   Individuals conducting cause analysis evaluate operational and conditional factors related to the relevant components of the collision. Investigators and other experts conducting cause analysis use deductive and inductive reasoning, based on the evidence and data available, to accurately analyze these factors surrounding the incident as a whole. The results of cause analysis may be used for traffic studies, safety analysis, or other statistical research to correct or improve the causal conditions identified through these research methods.

CLASSIFICATION OF COLLISIONS

13-32.   Collisions are described and classified based on type and severity. Collisions present themselves in many forms. Generally collisions can be described by the following types:

- Vehicle to vehicle.
- Vehicle to pedicycle (2 or 3 wheels—no motor).
- Stolen vehicle.
- Vehicle to object.
- Vehicle to railway train.
- Collision with pedestrian.
- Single-vehicle incident.
- Hit and run.
- Other.

13-33.   The severity of a collision is assigned within two categories—severity of injury and severity of damage. Classification of the severity of the injuries sustained by persons involved in the collision and property damage resulting from the collision are classified using guidance outlined in AR 190-5. A general overview of the major classifications include—

- **Severity of injury.** This includes—
  - *Fatal collision (within 12 months).* A classification of fatal is assigned when a collision results in the death of a person. If a person dies within 365 days of the collision, and that death is a result of injuries sustained in the collision, then that collision must be categorized as a fatal injury collision.

- *Incapacitating injuries.* These injuries prevent the person from walking, driving, or continuing with normal activities that person was capable of just before the collision. This can include severe cuts, broken limbs, skull or chest injuries, unconsciousness at the scene, and being unable to leave the scene without assistance.
- *Nonincapacitating injuries.* This includes injuries other than fatal or incapacitating which are evident to a person other than the injured. This can include a lump on the head, abrasions, bruises, cuts, and scratches.
- *Possible injuries.* An injury is reported or claimed, but does not meet criteria for the other injury classifications. A possible injury may include momentary unconsciousness, whiplash, limping (injury may be seen), nausea, or hysteria.
- *No injury.* No apparent or claimed bodily harm is present.
- **Severity of vehicle damage.** This includes—
  - *No damage.* The vehicle shows no signs of physical or functional damage.
  - *Other damage to the vehicle (minor damage, not unsafe).* Any damage to a vehicle that is not either disabling or functional. This type of damage typically affects only the appearance of the vehicle such as dents and scratches; damage to grills, hubcaps, or trim; or glass cracks or other minor damage that does not affect the safe operation of the vehicle.
  - *Functional damage to the vehicle (can move, but would not be safe).* This includes any damage to the vehicle (or trailer) that, though not disabling, affects the operation of the vehicle or components of the vehicle. This can include damage to fenders, trunk lids, doors, or hoods that prevents them from operating properly or broken headlights, windows, taillights, horns, or other damage that prevents the vehicle from passing an official motor vehicle inspection.
  - *Disabling damage to vehicle (cannot be moved).* This includes any damage to a vehicle that prevents the vehicle from being driven from the scene in a normal manner (during daylight hours) without causing further damage to the vehicle, personnel, or the roadway. Trailers are classified as disabled if damage prevents them from being towed without causing further damage to the trailer, personnel, or the roadway.

CONDUCTING THE INVESTIGATION

13-34. Investigators at a collision scene must be organized. They must conduct their investigation in an orderly and efficient manner in an environment that is chaotic and possibly emotional. Conducting the collision investigation begins with the initial report of a collision and subsequent response by military police, arrival at the collision scene, collecting physical and testimonial evidence, and completion of the accident report.

13-35. Like any investigation, the elements of the investigation are not linear. Many of the investigative actions may occur simultaneously. Information obtained during an investigation may require Army LE personnel to return to and reexamine a previous action. In cases where criminal activity is identified and the criminal investigation becomes the priority, collision investigators should coordinate their actions with the lead criminal investigator to ensure that all investigative activities are synchronized.

INITIAL NOTIFICATION AND RESPONSE

13-36. Prompt arrival at the scene of an accident is essential; however, safety should be emphasized at all times. Speed limits apply to all vehicles, including emergency vehicles, and should not be exceeded unless local policy permits and the situation warrants such action. Military police and TMCIs should maintain contact with the military police desk while en route to the accident scene. While traveling to the scene they should be observant of any suspicious or damaged vehicles fleeing the general area.

13-37. Responding patrols should collect as much information as possible before arrival at the scene. The basic information collection conducted during this stage of the collision investigations is intended to identify the basic details surrounding the event. These details include the—
- **Specifics of the collision.** This includes—

- The time and location of the collision.
- The time of notification.
- The identification of the reporting individual.
- The number of vehicles involved.
- General information regarding the type and severity of the collision.
- Traffic congestion and other known traffic flow concerns.

- **Persons involved.**
- **Vehicles and property involved in the incident.** This includes any vehicles directly or indirectly involved in the incident. Any property that was damaged as a result of the incident or that otherwise contributed to events surrounding the incident should be identified.
- **Resources required and whether they have been dispatched.** This includes—
  - The number of military police patrols required.
  - TMCIs required.
  - Other first responders—fire, ambulance, hazardous material response, and such.
  - Criminal investigators—MPIs or USACIDC SAs—if required.
  - Safety equipment.

ARRIVAL AT THE SCENE

13-38. Upon arrival at the scene, patrols should position their vehicles in a location and manner that does not create additional hazards or congestion. The scene and specific situation may require placement of LE vehicles as roadblocks or to aid hasty traffic control measures. At night, vehicles should be positioned so that the headlights illuminate the entire scene. During day or night, emergency lights should be on to warn approaching motorists of the hazard.

13-39. Military police dispatched to a vehicle collision must quickly assess the situation and determine priorities based on the severity of the collision, roadway blockage, injuries, environmental conditions, and many other factors. The on-scene investigation is concerned primarily with data gathering and recording. See ATTP 3-39.10 for additional information on military police first response requirements. Upon arrival at the scene, military police conduct a number of actions that include—

- **Establishing traffic control.** Traffic control is essential at a collision scene to prevent further accidents or injury. Additional military police patrols may be required. Some situations may be so hazardous that traffic control measures may be required before aiding the injured to prevent further injury to victims or injury to others. Military personnel at the scene (other than LE personnel) may be temporarily employed to help control traffic or people, or for other requirements. All other spectators or unnecessary persons should be cleared from the scene.
- **Assessing incidents for the presence of hazardous materials.** If evidence of hazardous material is identified, the area should be secured and appropriate hazardous material teams should be requested.
- **Providing aid to injured personnel.** Military police personnel determine the extent of injuries (if any) to collision victims, render first aid, and request medical assistance, if necessary. Severely injured persons should not be moved, except in circumstances where their immediate safety is in jeopardy. The position of all victims should be noted for report purposes. In cases of a fatality, appropriate medical personnel will make the final determination of death; the local USACIDC element must be notified for any fatality incidents or incidents where death of a collision victim is likely.
- **Taking actions to protect property.** The scene should be secured to protect property and preserve evidence. Personal property of collision victims must be gathered and returned to the victims or inventoried and secured until return of the property can be accomplished. Any classified documents found at the scene should be safeguarded and reported to the unit or nearest military intelligence officer.
- **Requesting additional support.** Support required can include—
  - Medical.

- Fire.
- Hazardous materials.
- Civil engineers.
- Towing services.
- Portable lighting.
- Temporary traffic control devices and personnel.
- Criminal investigators—MPIs or USACIDC SAs as appropriate—if evidence of a crime is identified.
- **Obtaining vehicle and operator information.** Military police should check the driver's license, military identification, vehicle registration, and proof of insurance of persons involved in the collision.
- **Identifying damage.** Military police should determine damage to vehicles and surrounding facilities and infrastructure and document all identified information.
- **Locating and interviewing witnesses.** Military police should identify and separate potential witnesses. When possible, all witnesses should be separated until interviews are complete to prevent discussion that may influence their perception of the events surrounding the collision. Statements should be taken when potential witnesses are identified as having significant information. All witness interviews that are not reflected on a witness statement should be documented as part of DA Form 3946.
- **Gathering required information.** Responding military police should obtain all facts surrounding the collision for inclusion in the accident report. Information should be verified by statements or physical evidence. This may include measurements for diagrams of the collision scene.
- **Completing the accident report.** Military police use all gathered data and observations to complete DA Form 3946 and supporting documentation.

13-40.   When responding to major collisions with significant property damage and/or injuries to personnel, it is best to leave vehicles in their final resting place until the scene can be processed. In some cases, factors surrounding the incident may require that vehicles to be moved. This is typically driven by requirements to—

- Provide aid to victims such as when victims are trapped and inaccessible without moving the vehicle or trapped in vehicles near a fire or hazardous material source.
- Ensure safety when traffic control measures are not adequate.
- Protect property when hazards exist such as one vehicle catching fire and endangering others.

13-41.   The decision to move a vehicle from its final position often must be made quickly by military police patrols arriving at the scene. When this is done, the positions of the wheels should be marked on the ground so that they can be relocated for investigative purposes.

COLLECTING EVIDENCE

13-42.   After securing the scene of the collision and taking appropriate measures to protect persons and property, investigators must obtain and record all available evidence required to complete their report and to arrive at logical and objective conclusions. Any fragile evidence that can be damaged, altered, destroyed or removed from the scene by any willful or negligent act must be identified and protected. Before removal, its position should be noted, sketched, photographed, and/or marked. Examples include puddles of gasoline, oil, blood, pieces of broken glass, or evidence of alcohol or drug consumption. Check the position of turn signal levers. Secure alcoholic beverage containers found inside a vehicle. Tag, mark, and secure evidence using the same techniques described in chapter 2 before removing the evidence from the scene.

13-43.   All the evidence obtained combined together will help the investigator develop an understanding of the collision and the events associated with the overall incident. Witness statements, debris or broken parts from vehicles, tire marks and skids, damage to fixed objects, and other evidence can help investigators identify the paths of the vehicles involved and the stages of the incident (point of possible perception, point of actual perception, point of no escape, point of impact, and point of final rest). Marks or traces such as skid or scrape marks help the investigator locate pertinent points accurately. All marks, puddles, bits of metal, and contents of vehicles must be located and their positions measured and recorded. Skid marks are very important since they show position and direction of travel, evasive action, or unlawful behavior. Especially note things that would help locate the point of first contact, such as changes in skid marks, chips in pavement, and damage to roadside objects.

13-44.   If a violation of law is identified, the investigator must ensure that enough evidence is gathered to prove each element of the offense. Investigators should focus on the three main components that produce the operational and conditional factors that contribute to a collision—people; roads, ground surfaces, and fixed objects; and vehicles. Interview first all individuals involved in the incident and any witnesses. This provides background information concerning the collision and the events leading up to the incident. Testimonial evidence can help investigators in their search for physical evidence that will either support or refute statements collected earlier in the investigation.

PEOPLE—DRIVERS, PASSENGERS, AND WITNESSES

13-45.   Investigators should identify the drivers of all vehicles involved in the collision. Carefully examine the driver's licenses of all operators to determine if the license is valid, all information is current, and what (if any) restrictions are required for the person to drive—eyeglasses required, daytime driving only, driving only with a licensed driver in the front seat, or other restrictions. If the driver does not possess a valid license or is operating in violation of required restrictions, document these violations and take action as appropriate. Before taking witness statements identify passengers and other witnesses. See ATTP 3-39.10 for more information.

13-46.   Interview all persons involved in the collision or others that may have information directly relevant to the collision. These individuals include drivers, passengers, and any pedestrians that were involved in the collision. Be observant and note behaviors and other evidence that may indicate the condition of persons involved in the incident that may have contributed to the collision. See chapter 3 for information regarding interviews and LE interrogation.

Interviews

13-47.   Witnesses from other vehicles, pedestrians, and inhabitants of buildings in the immediate area that may have witnessed the incident should be canvassed and interviewed as well. In some cases persons not at the scene may provide relevant information such as an acquaintance that can provide evidence that a driver was intoxicated or suffered from sleep deprivation. Identify and interview any of these categories of people that are present at a collision to determine if they can provide relevant information.

13-48.   Interviewing witnesses and victims should be done at the scene. If this is not possible, take statements as soon as possible at the Military Police Station or other suitable location. All persons who have knowledge pertinent to the investigation should be requested to make and sign written statements. Conduct interviews and LE interrogations of persons suspected of a crime in accordance with Article 31, UCMJ; these interviews may be conducted at the military police station or USACIDC element offices as appropriate.

13-49.   Witnesses, drivers and passengers should be questioned individually, out of hearing range of others. Military police and TMCIs conducting interviews should be aware that differing perspectives of the various witnesses may produce variances and discrepancies in the statements provided. Review statements on-scene to identify possible discrepancies; attempt to clarify any discrepancies identified.

13-50.   All persons interviewed should be positively identified to ensure that accurate information is available for the accident report. Military identification, driver's licenses, or other forms of official identification should be provided to the LE personnel conducting the interview. LE personnel must verify all information that is subject to change—addresses, names—and make sure that the identification provided is valid and current. Information obtained from drivers and passengers includes—

- Locations of vehicles involved at the various stages of the incident.
- Actions of pedestrians or other persons not in the vehicles involved that may have contributed to the incident.

- Reactions of persons involved at the various stages of the incident.
- The point when they first realized a collision might occur.
- Any observations regarding behavior and condition of persons involved including—
  - Driver.
  - Passengers.
  - Pedestrians.
- Any observed or known conditions that may have contributed to the collision including—
  - Road conditions.
  - Traffic control devices.
  - Obstructions.
  - Events or activities that may have created distractions and inattentiveness for the driver(s).
  - Physical or emotional impairments that may have contributed to the incident.

Observations

13-51. Army LE personnel should observe all persons involved in the collision to identify any obvious signs of injury. Most injuries are obvious to all persons present at the scene. Injuries are categorized as fatal, incapacitating, nonincapacitating, possible injury, or no injury (see paragraph 13-33). Some individuals may fake an injury to receive sympathy or to attempt to gain financial compensation. In many cases, emotions and adrenaline resulting from involvement in a collision can cause an individual to be unaware of his injuries. All individuals with obvious injuries and with claimed injuries should receive first aid and be directed to medical personnel for appropriate evaluation and treatment. Document all injuries resulting from a collision in the accident report.

13-52. During the investigation, including during the process of conducting interviews, military police personnel must be observant for any relevant information. These observations may provide evidence of possible driver distraction or impairment. These items may be seized as evidence or merely drive further questioning and investigation by investigators working the incident. Items to note include—
- Open food containers.
- Beer cans, liquor bottles, or other evidence of intoxicating beverages.
- Medications or illicit drugs.
- Open maps, newspapers, or other reading material.
- Cell phones and audio and video players.

13-53. Investigators should note observations, including information gleaned from witness statements, which provide an understanding of the driver's physical and emotional state at the time of the incident. Investigators should review all witness and passenger statements regarding the driver's condition to identify any evidence of impairment. Testimonial evidence of impairment must be corroborated with physical evidence. Many of these potential factors require laboratory examination and/or evaluation by medical personnel. Conditions that can result in temporary impairment include—
- Alcohol consumption.
- Use of illicit drugs.
- Use of prescription or over-the-counter medication
- Carbon monoxide exposure.
- Drowsiness due to sleep deprivation.
- Sudden disablement.

ROAD AND FIXED OBJECT DAMAGE IDENTIFICATION

13-54. After gaining all the information possible from all persons involved in the collision, the investigator begins to examine the physical condition of the scene and to record his observations. Collision investigators must identify critical locations on the road that are relevant to the collision. They must also document these locations in their report so that the locations may be identified at a later date, well after any physical indicators of the collision have been removed. Photograph all physical evidence before moving the evidence or clearing the scene. To ensure consistent usage in accident reports, use the following terms to describe roads and associated areas:

● **Highway.** The entire width, boundary to boundary, of the publicly maintained area that is open to the general public for travel.

● **Roadway.** The improved portion of the highway designed for vehicular travel.

● **Road.** Includes the roadway and the shoulder on either side.

● **Roadside.** That part of a highway not occupied by the road or sidewalk.

● **Median.** The portion of a divided highway that separates the roadways for travel in opposite directions.

● **Traffic way.** The entire width, boundary to boundary, open to travel by the general public including areas that may not be publicly maintained. A traffic way is similar to a highway except, while open to the public for travel, it may include private property such as shopping centers and parking lots. Figure 13-2 shows the terms used to describe the road and associated areas.

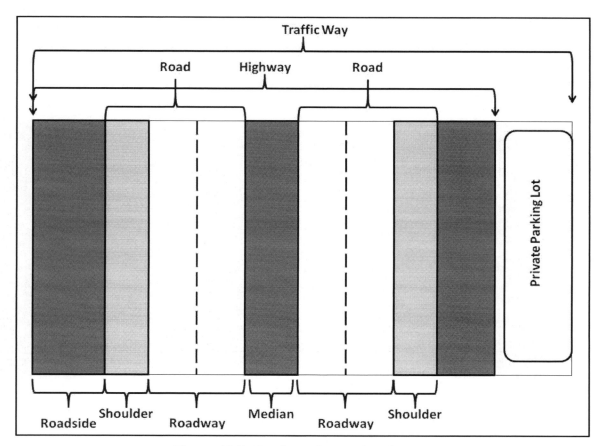

Figure 13-2. Roads and associated areas

Road and Point of Impact Identification

13-55.   The investigator should first identify and document the point of initial impact (collision location). This location must be represented on any diagrams produced in the accident report (diagramming will be discussed in detail later in this chapter). Documenting the collision locations includes—

● Locating the first harmful event (point of impact). This is usually the point of first contact between the objects involved in the collision. It is important to be exact in locating the first harmful event. The point of impact should be easily located by using the collision diagram by another person (unrelated to the collision or investigation) well after the incident to ensure that the site can be located again. The investigator's documentation must be accurate enough to enable an individual to locate the point of impact on a map within—

- One-tenth of a mile (five hundred feet) on a straight, level road and in rural areas.
- Fifty feet on curves, hills, intersections, and urban areas.

● Identifying and documenting the name of the road on which the collision occurred. Be very specific. If the road has more than one identity, use the name of the more important route. Avoid the use of local names.

● Stating the name of the city, county, or installation where the collision occurred.

● Stating the exact point on the road the collision occurred. Use landmarks when possible. There are four basic descriptors used to identify the first harmful event or point of impact location for a collision. Figure 13-3 illustrates descriptors for identifying collision locations. They are as follows:

- Intersection describes the location if the point of impact occurs within the limits of an intersection. The intersection is shown as "A" in figure 13-3.
- An intersection-related designation indicates that the collision occurred on the approach to or exit from an intersection. Intersection-related areas are depicted as "B" in figure 13-3.
- Driveway access involves a vehicle turning into or out of a driveway, parking lot, or other entrance into the roadway or crossing a roadway from one driveway to another. Driveway access locations are depicted as "C" in figure 13-3.
- Nonjunction would indicate that all traffic way collisions occurred on the road or off the road, but away from connecting roads. The designator "D" in figure 13-3, identifies a nonjunction area of the traffic way.

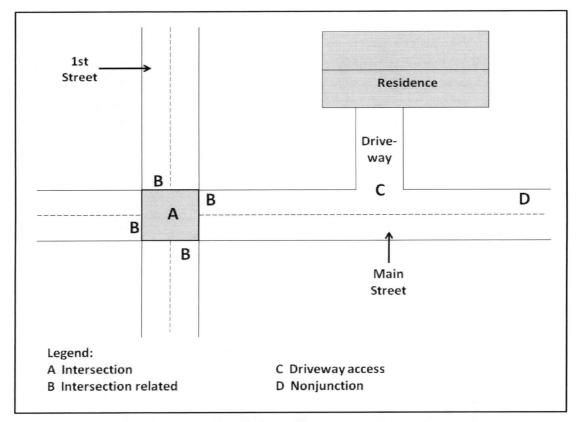

Figure 13-3. Descriptors for identifying collision locations

Road Description

13-56.   After locating the point of impact for the collision, the investigator should describe the road on which the collision occurred. The description should provide enough detail to provide persons not involved in the incident or at the scene an understanding of the characteristics of the road. Information used to describe the road include—

- The type of road component where the collision occurred; for example, interstate highway, U.S. numbered route, state numbered route, county road, or a local street.
- The identity of each lane. Traffic lanes are numbered from left to right of the road as you would drive.
- Land characteristics. Land use characteristics are typically described as urban, rural, commercial area, port, warehouse or manufacturing district, or other descriptive term.
- Special descriptions. These include describing specific features and characteristics present on the road. These descriptions may include slope/grade or curves; roadway surface material; traffic control devices such as signs, signals, and pavement markings—condition and functionality should also be referenced; and road accessories such as curbs, guardrails, medians, islands, bridges, and tunnels.

13-57.   The investigator should also describe the conditions of the road and structures, control measures affecting the road, and environmental conditions at the time of the incident. At a minimum the investigator addresses—

- **Visibility.** Conditions and objects that obstruct a driver's visibility affect the driver's ability to identify and react to potential hazards on the road. The following factors can a driver's visibility to be reduced or obstructed:
  - Weather conditions such as fog, rain, or snow.
  - View obstructions such as signs, buildings, vegetation overgrowth, or parked vehicles.
  - Glare from headlights, backlighting, fixed lights, sun glare, and reflections.
  - Varying light conditions—day, night, dusk, dawn.
- **Surface conditions.** Surface conditions contribute to a high amount of collisions. Poor surface conditions may be a result of environmental factors or road composition. Poor surface conditions can cause loss of control when the vehicle loses traction and begins to slide or skid. Loss of traction can surprise the driver and, if appropriately applied driving tactics are not employed to recover from the resulting skid, a collision is likely. Poorly constructed or maintained roads can also present hazards that can contribute to vehicular collisions. Surface conditions that contribute to loss of vehicle traction include—
  - Moisture—residue of rain or water runoff.
  - Falling rain.
  - Ice and snow.
  - Loose gravel, sand, leaves, or grass on the road.
  - Oil, grease, and excess tar.
  - Dirt or gravel roads.
  - Ruts and/or potholes in the road.
  - Low or soft shoulders.
- **Traffic control devices.** Traffic control devices are essential to maintain good traffic flow and safe conditions, especially in high-volume or heavily populated areas. These devices range from highly technical light systems and information systems to relatively simple signs and road markings. As useful as traffic control devices are to enable safe and efficient traffic flow, they can contribute to collisions if they are not properly placed or maintained. Traffic control devices can contribute to collisions when—
  - There are too many traffic control devices present. This can create confusion to a driver, especially if they are transiting an unfamiliar road.
  - The wrong type of traffic control device is emplaced.

- The device is improperly placed. Traffic control devices can be placed in areas where they are not clearly visible, they do not allow sufficient reaction time, or they are confusing to the driver when viewed in the context of the immediate surroundings.
- A traffic control device is nonoperational, absent, or obstructed. This can be due to improper maintenance of the device itself, failure to maintain the area around the device (such as failure to trim trees and shrubs that may obstruct the device), or the device may have been tampered with or removed.
- **Traffic volume and congestion.** The volume and type of traffic on the road at the time of the collision can be important factors contributing to a collision.

Collision Impacts on the Road

13-58. Investigators must identify what evidence from the collision was deposited on the road. Consistent with Locard's exchange theory, which paraphrased states that every contact between two items results in an exchange of material, every vehicle involved in a collision leaves some physical sign of what happened on the road. By studying, recording, and photographing these signs, an investigator can gather and develop valuable information to supplement witness statements and their observations. The investigator's responsibility is to identify those physical deposits and document them through photography, diagramming, notes, and collection and preservation of the evidence when possible. In their totality, these items of evidence can enable the investigator to establish the sequence of events.

13-59. The most obvious result or impact of a collision on the road is the final rest position of the vehicles or objects involved. This location should be thoroughly documented. The investigation should start where the vehicle came to its final resting point and retrace the paths of the vehicles involved. Current weather, visibility, and road conditions, traffic volume, traffic control devices (including their condition), potential obstructions, and possible causes of driver distraction should be noted. Mark and photograph all evidence relevant to the collision; evidence that can be physically collected should be collected and preserved as described in chapter 2. Evidence deposited on the road by vehicles and objects involved in the collision include—

- Tire or skid marks.
- Metal scars.
- Debris.
- Fixed objects.
- Vaults and falls.

Tire and Skid Marks

13-60. Investigators can extract a large amount of valuable data and evidence from tire and skid marks left on the road as a result of a collision. Tire and skid marks indicate points of friction between the tires on the vehicle and the road. Tire and skid marks can help determine many details about the collision including—

- The point of actual perception.
- Evasive action.
- The probable point of impact—direction of travel is suddenly changed.
- The direction of travel—very light prints slowly getting darker to the point of impact.
- If the tire is sliding and not rotating.
- The minimum speed.

13-61. Tire and skid marks occur when the tires slide or spin on the surface of the road. There are several different types of tire and skid marks. Each type of mark is indicative of a different action by the tires and/or vehicle in question and is identified by their direction and striations. The duration of a skid or tire marks will vary, depending on the type of road, the kind of mark, weather, vehicle speed, and other factors. Tire marks are the prime means of estimating the minimum speed of vehicles and the path of vehicles before, during, and after impact. The types of tire and skid marks include—

- **Acceleration marks.** These are marks left on the road surface when the power transferred to the drive wheels exceeds the ability of the tires to maintain traction with the road surface. The beginning of this mark will be very dark and lighten along its length as the tires gain traction.
- **Yaw or critical speed scuffs.** These marks indicate that the tires are still turning and the vehicle is slipping sideways or parallel to the axle. Side slipping can be caused by road configuration and vehicle weight shifting forward and sideways. Yaw marks are characterized by striations left on the pavement.
- **Skid marks.** These are generally straight, parallel marks that indicate that the brakes have been locked and the tires are not turning. Slight curving can occur in a skid due to unequal brakes or unlevel road surface such as the road sloping to one side due to a hill or bank, excessive road crowning, or other cases making the road unlevel. When all four brakes lock, the skid will cause the rear wheel marks to overlap the front wheel marks. Additionally, —
  - Front tire skid marks tend to be darker than rear tire marks due to the forward shift in weight during braking. The outside edges of the skid marks of a front tire will tend to be darker than the inside area of the skid mark.
  - Skid marks from rear tires tend to be more uniform in appearance.
  - The rear tire marks will begin a distance behind the front wheel marks that is equal to the vehicle's wheel base length.
  - The tire mark(s) will end at the same time, but the rear tire mark(s) will be a wheelbase length behind the front tire mark(s) and will be straight and parallel.
  - To obtain a true measurement of overlapping skid marks, the investigator must measure the entire length (each side) then subtract the length of the wheelbase. Do this for both sides if and when there are skid marks from both sides. If there is curvature in the skid, measure the length of the skid along the curve. Do not measure a straight-line distance from one end to the other.
- **Crook or scrub marks.** These are marks that indicate a sudden change in direction due to impact (collision). They may appear at the end of a skid that was left before impact.
- **Shadow or ghost marks.** These are marks that indicate the beginning of an impending skid. Ghost marks are lighter marks than the full skid mark caused when the brakes are applied and tire rotation is slowing but has not fully stopped turning. A shadow or ghost mark may be very difficult to locate depending on the weather, light, and road conditions. These are also known as decelerating scuffs.
- **Skip skid marks.** These marks are braking skid marks that are repeatedly interrupted at regular intervals and deposited when a locked wheel bounces on the road. They can be caused by bumps in the road, potholes, or suspension problems. This type of skid mark is common from trailers that are lightly loaded. Measure the entire length as though there were no skips. Be sure to identify the skid mark as a skip skid; a skip is usually no longer than 1 to 3 feet. Vehicles equipped with antilock brake systems are designed to stop the wheels from locking during a hard braking situation. This skid will also appear as a mark that is repeatedly interrupted at regular intervals; it will be very similar to a standard skip skid except the marks will be significantly lighter.
- **Spin marks.** These are marks that result when a vehicle rotates around its center of mass (when the rear wheels or front wheels move in a manner that causes the vehicle to spin around). They can be caused when a significant impact is applied to a vehicle at a location other than in direct line with its center of mass. They can also be caused by an excessive acceleration on a rear wheel drive vehicle if the front wheels are turned to an extreme in either direction during the acceleration. Measure the entire length of the spin skid mark as it appears on the surface; measure the mark in a straight line from the start point to the end point.
- **Gap skid marks.** An intermittent skid mark which is caused by the release and reapplication of the brakes. They can be caused by "pumping" defective brakes in an effort to stop or through driver indecision that results in application, release, and reapplication of the brakes. These marks are usually 10-20 feet in length depending on the vehicles speed and the driver's reaction time.

Measure each individual mark separately and add the measurements to get the total length of the skid.

Metal Scars

13-62.   Investigators should examine the roadway for evidence of marking or damage to the road caused from impact by the metal parts of the vehicle. A moving vehicle may be damaged in such a way that metal parts from the vehicle make contact with the road surface. This contact can produce identifiable marks in the form of surface marks (scratches) and gouges. Surface marks and gouges are described as follows:

- Surface marks are visible scrapes and scratches on the surface of the road; they cause no major damage to the road but appear as visible scrapes and abrasions on the surface of the road. They are visible but no substantial removal of surface material occurs.
- Gouges are chips, chops, grooves, furrows, or chunks of surface material that is removed from the roadway. Gouges are much deeper and wider than surface marks.

13-63.   Identification of metal scars on the road can help investigators determine the direction of travel, the point of impact, and the point of maximum engagement during the collision. In some instances, scratches on pavement made before impact can indicate a component failure on a vehicle, such as marks made by the rim of a wheel following a tire failure. Scrapes on the road surface may indicate where the vehicle initiated a rollover movement. The direction of the movement and the number of rolls may be determined by the scratches and gouges left as the vehicle continued to its point of final rest. The point of impact of a severe head-on collision may be located by identifying gouges in the road surface as the front ends of the two vehicles were driven down into the road surface by the force of the impact.

Debris

13-64.   Debris can be any vehicle parts or pieces that become separated from the vehicle. It is loose material scattered about the scene as a direct result of a collision. Debris is normally not reliable in determining the probable point of impact, but can be useful in determining a point of final rest. Debris includes—

- Vehicle fluids such as radiator coolant, engine oil, gasoline or diesel, brake fluid, battery acid, and water.
- Vehicle parts such as chrome, glass, and paint marks.
- Spilled cargo—either solid or fluid.
- Undercarriage dirt and mud dislodged and deposited on the road.
- Underbody debris, such as rust, dirt, and mud.
- Road material dislodged and spread as a result of the collision such as dirt, tar, asphalt, and rocks.

13-65.   Severe collisions involving serious injuries to persons involved in the collision can also produce biological debris. This may include body parts, body fluids, hair, skin, and other matter. Universal precautions should be taken by collision investigators when biological material is present at a collision scene.

13-66.   Debris patterns at a collision scene can be helpful in understanding the dynamics of the specific collision. Debris from vehicle cargo or broken vehicle parts can be dispersed over long distances; these distances and the dispersal direction of the debris field will be indicators of the level of impact force and the direction of movement of the vehicles involved in the collision. Fluid debris can provide valuable indicators of vehicle impact points and movement. When a fluid container is ruptured as a result of impact, the fluid is dispersed with the same velocity as the vehicle. The impact of the moving fluid on road surfaces can help determine vehicle movement at impact.

Fixed Object Damage

13-67.   Damage to fixed objects (such as bent and broken guardrails, posts, trees, buildings, the roadway, and other fixed objects) can provide an indication of the speed and position of a vehicle that contacted the object. Damage to a fixed object can be matched with damage or marks on the vehicle; this can enable investigators to positively fix the position of that vehicle at a specific point within the chain of events. Scrapes, scratches, and paint transfer can link a specific vehicle involved in a collision with a fixed object at the scene; this can be very helpful in complex scenes when multiple vehicles are involved.

Falls and Vaults

13-68. The term fall is used to describe a vehicle that has left the ground for a short time while falling or flipping. A fall may occur when a vehicle travelling at a high rate of speed hits a bump or crests a hill with a steep drop and temporarily leaves contact with the road surface. A fall can also occur when a vehicle slides sideways and squarely hits a curb or other solid object causing the vehicle to flip and leave the ground; the portion of the event where the vehicle leaves the ground is the fall. Evidence of a fall will generally be associated with marks or damage created on the ground surface when the vehicle regains contact (the end of the fall). In some cases, evidence can be found at the beginning of the fall if the event was initiated by impact with a portion of the ground surface.

13-69. Flips or vaults are caused when a vehicle, moving with sufficient force, strikes an obstruction that suddenly stops the lead wheels (a vault is an end-over-end flip). The vehicle's trailing wheels then pivots upward, leaving the ground. In cases of flips or vaults, indications of impact (tire marks) at the initial stop (take-off) and the point of final rest should be carefully identified. Vehicles that leave the roadway and enter soft ground will dig a furrow; these indicators generally make identification of the initial and final points of the flip easier to determine.

VEHICLE DESCRIPTION AND DAMAGE IDENTIFICATION

13-70. Collision investigators must also identify all vehicles associated with the collision and gather evidence associated with those vehicles. The investigator documents the identification numbers of each vehicle involved, a description of each vehicle, the condition of the each vehicle before the collision, and the results of the collision impact on each vehicle involved. All vehicles involved in the collision should be photographed to document any damages that are present. To ensure consistent usage in accident reports, the following terms are used to describe vehicles associated with a collision:

- **Vehicle.** A vehicle is any form of ground transportation used by an individual to move personnel or material on a road or traffic way.
- **Motor vehicle.** A motor vehicle is any transportation device with a motor powered by fossil fuels, electricity, or other external sources of energy, except devices moved by human power or used exclusively on stationary rails or tracks.
- **Traffic.** Traffic is defined as pedestrians, ridden or herded animals, vehicles, streetcars, or any other forms of transportation on the highways for the purpose of travel.
- **Traffic unit.** A traffic unit is a single element of traffic. A traffic unit can be an automobile, a pedicycle, an animal, a pedestrian, or another traffic element using a traffic way for travel or transportation.

Vehicle Identification

13-71. All vehicles involved in a collision must be identified. For motor vehicles the best method is to document the VIN. The VIN on most vehicles can be located on a data plate in the lower left corner of the dashboard of the vehicle (from the driver's perspective). Other locations where a VIN may be located include—

- The front of the engine block.
- On the front corner of the car frame near the fluid reservoirs for washer fluid and coolant.
- At a rear wheel well, directly above the tire.
- Inside the driver-side doorjamb on the forward area beneath the side-view mirror that is exposed when the door is opened.
- On the driver-side door post (the rear door post area where the door latches).
- In the trunk underneath the spare tire.

13-72. Serial numbers may be used for pedicycles or other similar vehicles. All vehicles should be linked to an operator; in cases where the operator is not the owner the owner should also be identified. The vehicles registration and/or information received from drivers, passengers, and other witnesses can be used to identify and contact vehicle owners.

Vehicle Description

13-73. Collision investigators must provide a general description and classification of the vehicles involved in the collision and a description of the condition of the vehicles involved. The condition of the vehicle both before and after the collision should also be documented. Vehicle description and classification should include a—

- General description to include—
  - Make—Ford, Dodge, Chevrolet, Toyota, Volkswagen, and such.
  - Model—Mustang, Ram 1500, Camaro, Jetta, and such.
  - Color.
  - Year.
- General classification to include—
  - Type—sedan, pickup truck, panel van, sport utility vehicle, cargo truck, tractor trailer, and such.
  - Use—private, commercial, or government/military.

13-74. The condition of the vehicle before the collision should be determined and documented when possible. This determination can be made through a variety of means. Witness statements can be very helpful in determining a vehicle's precollision condition. Maintenance records may also provide some indications of the vehicle's condition. One of the best methods to determine the general condition of a vehicle before a collision is through examination of the vehicle components. These observations can reveal evidence of previous damage, excessive wear, improper repairs, and missing or faulty equipment. Vehicle components that offer evidence of the precollision condition of the vehicle include—

- Wheels.
- Tires.
- Lights.
- Shocks.
- Mirrors.
- Windows and windshields.
- Brake system.
- Steering system.
- Vehicle body.

Results of the Collision

13-75. Collision investigators must observe and record the results (damage) of the collision. This will generally be determined through observation of the vehicle at its position of final rest in a serious collision. In minor collisions the vehicle may have been moved for safety reasons and to expedite traffic flow. It is extremely important that the on-scene investigator correctly categorize the amount and type of damage sustained by a vehicle. There are four basic categories used to classifying damage—no damage, other damage, functional damage, and disabling damage (see paragraph 13-33).

13-76. A careful inspection of the vehicles involved, to include component equipment and contents, is necessary. Items affecting vehicle control, such as tires, brake systems, lights, steering systems, signals, and safety equipment, should receive specific focus. In many cases examination by a qualified mechanic or laboratory examiners to verify specific conditions and potential impacts may be required. In many instances information gleaned from examining the vehicle must be evaluated along with other evidence collected to determine whether an identified condition was a conditional factor contributing to the collision or a result of the collision's impact. For example, it is important to know whether a tire was damaged as a result of the collision, or whether a tire failure was a possible contributing factor of the accident; this can be determined by analyzing skid and scuff marks along with the condition of the tire.

Note. The contents of the vehicle may also give important information concerning the identity, residence, occupation, destination, and position of vehicle occupants.

13-77. Damage to a vehicle can be characterized as contact damage or induced damage. Contact damage results from direct contact between any components of a vehicle with some other object—another vehicle, a fixed object, a pedestrian, the road surface, or another object—that results in damage to any part of the vehicle. Contact damage can appear as—

- Paint transfer.
- Scratches, rubs, or abrasions.
- Dents, buckling, or breakage.
- Tire damage.
- Road or surface damage (including material lodged within vehicle components).
- Damage to other fixed objects, such as trees, fences, buildings, and associated residue on the vehicle.
- Impressions from another impacted object on the vehicle such as poles, grill and headlight housings, or other impacted objects.
- Biological matter—human and animal remains or plant matter—deposited during the collision.
- Glass and windshield damage. Windshield contact damage leaves multiple fracture lines radiating away from the contact point resembling a spider web. There may or may not be a hole created in the glass. Clouded or discolored cracks in a windshield indicate damage that existed before the collision. Note obstruction on the glass such as dirt or frost. For side windows note position, up or down, if relevant. Position and functionality of side and rearview mirrors should also be noted.

13-78. Induced damage is caused by the force of the collision, not impact with another object. This can include damage to vehicle components directly due to physical forces associated with rapid deceleration or direction change. This type of damage can include broken or dislodged parts or glass breakage, and can cause an observable deformation in light bulb filaments. Induced damage on a windshield typically appears as a parallel or checkerboard pattern. Tempered glass (side and rear windows) shatters into small pieces and leaves no pattern when subjected to either contact or induced damage.

Assessing Exterior Damage

13-79. The investigator must evaluate and determine if the damage and other evidence gathered at the scene is consistent with his understanding of the collision. The investigator should weigh witness statements and physical evidence observed including vehicle orientation and dynamics. Collision damage on a vehicle should be carefully examined; this damage can be helpful in determining how an object was impacted. Areas of penetration and/or denting should be compared with other vehicle components, fixed objects, or other objects involved in the collision to determine what two surfaces were contacted to create the observed damage. This is easiest when analyzing damage from contact between a vehicle and a narrow object such as a pole or the end of a guardrail. Contours of two vehicles that have collided can be more difficult to analyze due to the level of damage and the broader surface areas that may have been involved. Investigators should document—

- Any points of ejection for persons or cargo.
- Gross vehicle failures. This will typically be in the form of roof separation, door separation, or other structural damage to the passenger compartment.
- Evidence of equipment failure such as tire damage or broken components not immediately attributed to impact.

Note. Investigators should check for alteration to the frame, the body, or the suspension which could have negatively affected the driver's vision or vehicle performance.

13-80. Tire damage is common in vehicle collisions. Carefully examine and document the condition of wheels and tires. The purpose of a tire examination is to determine what role the tire or wheel had in the collision. If damage to the tires exists, the investigator should attempt to determine—

- If the condition of the tire contributed to the collision.
- At what stage of the collision the tire was disabled.

13-81. When damage to tires is identified, carefully document the location of the tire in relation to the vehicle, such as right front or left rear; which vehicle the tire belonged on if there is more than one vehicle involved; and the type of tire to include the tire name, the manufacturer's name, and the tire size. The tire identification chart at figure 13-4 explains the identifying markings on a tire.

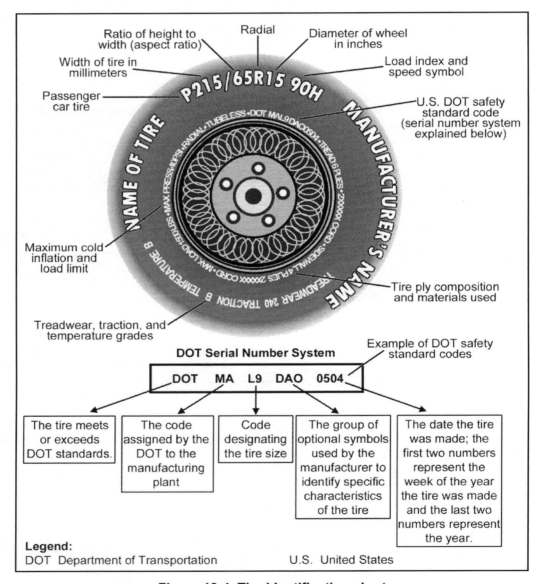

Figure 13-4. Tire identification chart

13-82. For major collisions where criminal and significant civil liabilities are likely, tires should be examined by trained laboratory examiners. The USACIL can assist in identifying the appropriate laboratory facility to conduct the examination. In a court of law, the recognized experts are laboratory personnel that examine the tires and make determinations based on that examination. The collision investigator is not recognized as an expert in these cases; the investigator's responsibility is to identify tires with damage that potentially created conditional factors that contributed to the collision. Laboratory examiners will determine what information is required, in addition to the tire evidence, to complete the examination. Examination of tires will result on one of six conclusions including—

- **No disablement.** There is no functional damage to the tire; the tire is functional.
- **Before difficulty.** The tire possessed defects that could have affected the performance of the vehicle before the collision and that may have contributed to an incident.
- **During controlled loss.** Tire disablement occurred due to forces during steering or braking, but before the collision.
- **During collision.** The tire was damaged as a direct result of impact during the collision. This is the most common time for disablement.
- **After collision or other harmful event.** The damage occurred after the initial collision.
- **Indeterminate.** There is not enough information to determine the proximate time of tire damage.

Lamp Examination

13-83. A lamp examination may be conducted to determine if the lamps (bulbs) were on or off at the time of the collision. Lamp examinations should be conducted when preliminary investigation by the investigator reveals that the condition of a lamp (headlamps, turn signal, brake lights, and such) at the time of the incident may have played a major role in the collision. Lamps to consider when investigating a collision include headlights, brake lights, and turn signals. In addition to functionality, the investigator should observe and document whether lights are obstructed by dirt, mud, abrasions, or other damage.

13-84. Examination of lamps may be warranted when witness statements indicate that lights or lack of lights were a factor in the collision. Collisions at night routinely require examination of lamps to determine their functionality and state (whether the lamps were on or off) at the time of the collision. Investigators should identify possible indicators and make preliminary assessments regarding lamps. Carefully document the location on the vehicle, the type of bulb (brake light, turn signal, taillight, and such), the position of control switches, and which vehicle the bulbs were collected from if there is more than one vehicle involved.

13-85. Determination of the functionality and state of the lamps can be especially helpful when investigating collisions at night. The collision could have been caused by the operator's vision being limited through lack of headlamp illumination or from other vehicles not seeing a vehicle with no head or tail lamp illumination. Night collisions affected by lack of lighting and reduced visibility include—

- **Head-on collisions (vehicles traveling in opposite directions).** Headlight failure or operators failing to have their headlights turned on can create poor visibility and contribute to head-on collisions.
- **Same-direction collisions.** Tail lights or turn signals either off or inoperable may be a factor in rear-end collisions.
- **Angle or right-of-way collisions.** These collisions may result if lights were off before the collision, reducing visibility.
- **Single-vehicle collisions.** Headlight malfunction or the operator driving without lights may contribute to single-vehicle collisions.

13-86. Lamp examination can be useful in hit-and-run investigations. When a suspected driver claims that the damage to his vehicle was sustained from a daytime collision, lamp examination may prove that the lights were on during the collision. This can be an indicator of a nighttime collision; if the headlights were on, investigators must determine if there was a reason for the lights to be on during daylight hours such as inclement weather or the vehicle was equipped with daytime running lights. When investigating a nighttime collision during pursuit of a fleeing subject, the driver may claim that he was not fleeing from the scene. Evidence that his headlamps and tail lamps were turned off may indicate intent to evade LE personnel. Understanding the components of automobile lamps and their basic operation help investigators identify potential indicators of the state of the bulb at the time of the collision. These components and operational requirements include the—

- **Filament.** This is a coil made of tungsten wire usually formed into a uniform coil.
- **Base.** This is normally comprised of copper; it acts as a pocket for the filament.
- **Insulator or contact.** The insulator allows for electrical flow required to illuminate the filament.
- **Glass bulb.** The bulb seals in inert gases and prevents oxygen from making contact with the filament and prevents the filament from oxidizing.
- **Electrical current.** The current heats the filament, causing it to illuminate.
- **Tungsten filament.** The filament becomes incandescent at approximately 4000 degrees Fahrenheit.
- **Pitting of the filament.** Repeated heating and cooling of the filament causes pitting, which narrows the filament, making the filament burn hotter.
- **Failure of the filament.** Pitting will increase as the filament burns hotter and will cause eventual failure of the filament—a burned-out bulb.

13-87.   Lamps that were on at the time of a collision will exhibit specific characteristics. These observable characteristics are referred to as "ON" indicators. There are also specific characteristics of a bulb that indicate that the bulb was not on at the moment of impact. These are referred to as "OFF" indicators. These indicators are further explained as follows:

- ON indicators include damage to the filament and glass including—
  - **Hot shock.** This indicates that the bulb was damaged due to impact; the result of force applied to a bulb while the filament was hot (bulb was on). Visible signs of hot shock include a stretched or distorted filament from the force applied as a result of vehicle impact during a collision. Hot shock will result in a filament with very pronounced deformation. A sagging filament is not hot shock; a bulb that has been used for a long time may have a slight (but normal) sag in the filament.
  - **Fused glass.** When this occurs the filament will appear attached to the glass bulb. This is caused by the glass softening and melting due to the heat from the hot filament (stretched and forced against the side of the bulb due to vehicle impact during a collision). The glass and filament remain attached as they both cool.
  - **Etched glass.** These are melted and gouged glass bulbs caused by hot filament stretching during impact; the filament gouges (melts) the glass but does not adhere to the glass (fused glass) creating scars on the bulb.
  - **Short circuit.** This occurs when there is more than one filament in the bulb; the force of impact causes one filament to touch or tangle with the other filament.
- OFF indicators include—
  - **Normal filament.** Like a new bulb, the filament will be relatively straight or may have a slight sag if the bulb is old. Lack of significant sag indicates that the bulb was off at the time of collision, and it was not damaged by hot shock.
  - **Broken filament.** The filament may be broken, but remains relatively straight. In this case the impact causes the filament to break off. The relative straightness of the filament indicates that the bulb was not on at the moment of impact; the bulb could have been inoperative before the impact.
  - **Normal glass.** The glass has not been damaged by contacting a hot filament; a hot filament would melt and gouge the glass bulb. This fact by itself is not a conclusive OFF indicator since the filament may not stretch all the way to the glass of the bulb during impact, but it corroborates other OFF indicators.

13-88.   In some cases a driver involved in a collision may switch his lights after the collision has occurred and then claim the lights were on the whole time. In these cases, as in previous off indicators, there will be no indication of hot shock or fused/etched glass in the lamp. In addition, a broken bulb with an even distribution of white or yellowish oxide on the filament is an indicator that the bulb was broken before the collision and could not have been working at the time of the collision. If the bulb appears intact (it is not broken, the filament looks normal, and the light may still work) and there is no indication of hot shock or fused/etched glass in the lamp, the lamp was likely off at the time of the collision.

13-89.   Just as laboratory experts may be required to evaluate tires, suspect bulbs should also be examined by laboratory experts in cases where criminal or significant civil liability may be present. The recognized experts are laboratory examiners that examine the lamps and associated hardware and make determinations based on that examination. The USACIL can conduct these examinations or direct the investigator to another laboratory facility to conduct the examination. The collision investigator is not recognized as an expert in these cases; the investigator's responsibility is to identify lamps with potentially created conditional factors that contributed to the collision or that are in an observed state that is inconsistent with a driver's statement. Laboratory examiners will determine what information is required, in addition to the lamp evidence, to complete the examination. Typically, the entire light assembly will be sent to the laboratory.

Vehicle Movement During Impact

13-90.   The force of an impact between two vehicles modifies the speed, direction, and rotation of the vehicles involved. There are several forces that can cause vehicle movement during a collision; the two primary forces are impact and friction. Investigators must consider the effects of collision forces on the vehicles, the road, persons (including pedestrians and those within vehicles), and any other objects involved in a collision.

13-91.   Friction alone is necessary for all movement. The activities of braking and turning are examples of how controlled friction forces are used to change the speed and direction of the vehicle. Impact involves force placed upon vehicles and other objects upon contact during a collision. This force can cause the vehicles and objects involved to change speed, direction, and rotation. Friction force following an impact involves the lateral motion of two objects in physical contact such as tires rubbing across pavement. Both friction and collision forces leave some kind of evidence including—

* Friction forces leave signs on the road surface in the form of skid marks. See the earlier discussion of collision impacts on the road.
* Collision forces leave signs on the object the vehicle strikes such as vehicles, marks on the road, fixed objects, and pedestrians.

13-92.   In addition to changing its speed, force may make an object rotate or spin. Rotation will depend on the strength of the force, its direction, and the point of impact upon the vehicle. The point of impact on a vehicle can be described as—

* **Concentric.** If the force on a vehicle is concentric, through center mass of the vehicle or object, there will be little or no rotation. Concentric forces during collisions are uncommon. Figure 13-5 shows a concentric impact.
* **Eccentric.** If the force on a vehicle is eccentric, the center of mass on the vehicle that is struck will not be aligned with the other vehicle. This causes both vehicles to rotate after the collision. Figure 13–6, page 13-30, shows an eccentric impact.

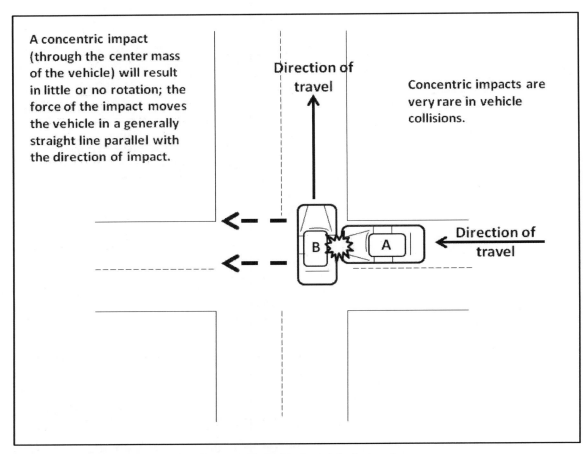

A concentric impact (through the center mass of the vehicle) will result in little or no rotation; the force of the impact moves the vehicle in a generally straight line parallel with the direction of impact.

Direction of travel

Concentric impacts are very rare in vehicle collisions.

B

A

Direction of travel

Figure 13-5. Concentric impact

CLEAR THE SCENE

13-93. Vehicles are removed safely from the scene under military police supervision. Military units will normally move their own vehicles. However, if this is not practical, military police elements should arrange for a military wrecker. Civilian vehicles normally are removed by commercial wrecker. In this case, the wrecker operator's name, the name of the firm, the time of departure, and the new location of the vehicle should be recorded, especially if further inspection of the vehicle may be necessary. Vehicles involved in incidents involving possible criminal liability may require seizure and impounding in the military police impound lot. If a vehicle must be retained as evidence, it must be securely impounded and its contents inventoried and recorded to maintain chain of custody.

13-94. Before leaving the scene the investigator should recheck the collision location for any additional marks, debris, victims, and such. If a collision occurs at night, the scene should be searched during daylight also. The reverse of this is also true. Retracing the driver's approach to the scene on the following day at the same time can reveal additional unanticipated evidence.

13-95. All statements should be taken at the scene if possible; however, it may be necessary to delay taking statements due to injury or an individual's desire for legal counsel. Ensure that all statements taken after the collision are documented on DA Form 2823. If during the course of taking a statement the investigator suspects a person of violating the law, the person must be warned of their legal rights, and DA Form 3881 must be completed.

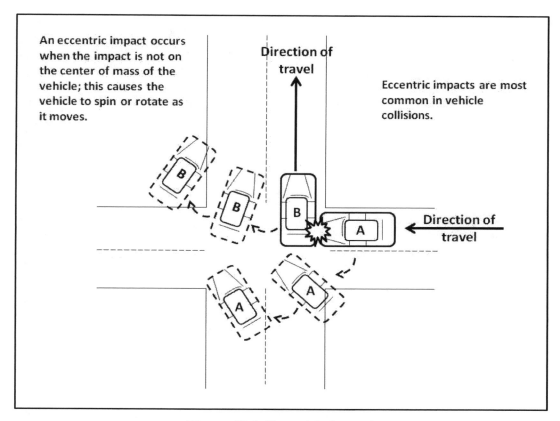

Figure 13-6. Eccentric impact

COMPLETE THE INVESTIGATION

13-96. Collision investigations must provide accurate explanations of the facts. In addition to DA Form 3946, which should include additional diagrams, statements (DA Form 2823 and DA Form 3881) and photographs, the investigator should prepare a statement (see appendix D for instructions for completion of these forms). This statement should clearly distinguish between fact and opinion. The statement should describe how the collision occurred, identifying contributing factors including condition and actions of the driver, actions of passengers and pedestrians that may have contributed to the collision, road and weather conditions, evidence (or absence of evidence) of mechanical failure, and any other identified contributing factors. All conclusions arid recommendations must be supported by fact. After completing the statement, a final check should be made to ensure that all supporting documentation is included in the case file, all evidence is secured and properly documented on a DA Form 4137, and all injury information is up to date. The completed investigation should be turned over to the desk sergeant or traffic section for review as determined by local policy.

COLLISION PHOTOGRAPHY

13-97. Photography of a collision scene requires a thorough understanding of the technical application of photography equipment. Chapter 4 provides details regarding photographing scenes under various conditions. The purpose of collision photography is to preserve information from the collision scene and to provide photographic evidence that supports investigator notes and other collected evidence. They become a permanent and accurate record of investigators' observations. While they are a very important part of a complete report, collision photographs are not a substitute for good investigator observation and notes, accurate and complete measurements, and thorough collection of evidence. Collision photographs serve many purposes including—

- **Acting as a supplement to accurate field notes.** They can—
  - Be used to verify the accuracy of scale diagrams and are an important tool in collision reconstruction.
  - Show details that might have been overlooked at the scene, such as debris, vehicle parts, body parts, and roadway damage.
  - Be useful to investigators for memory recall when preparing or completing the collision report and can be extremely useful when presenting a case in court.
- **Adding credibility to the investigation.** Specific photographs may be used in court as an aid to explain what the investigators saw and may provide details the investigator omitted in their report. They can—
  - Verify the observations and accuracy of investigator and witness statements.
  - Explain the collision scene. Photographs provide visual detail to help explain what was observed at the collision scene.
- **Serving as training tools for new and inexperienced investigators.** They can also be useful for public information and education efforts through billboards, leaflets, and handouts.
- **Supporting damage appraisals.** They can assist the investigator by providing support for damage evaluations and appraisals that will prove or disprove statements made by the individuals involved.

13-98. All photographs must be relevant to the investigation. Photographs support the testimony. They must not be inflammatory or be produced for shock value—particularly photographs of bodies or injuries to victims. Photographs of bodies in relation to the vehicles' position are not, however, considered inflammatory if relevant to support a point of testimony. Photographs alone do not substantiate facts; they must be supported by testimony or other physical evidence. The investigator or photographer must be able to testify that the photos reflect a true representation of the scene.

13-99. Collision investigators should preplan their photographs. Establish a continuous, logical procedure in order that the photographs taken are relevant and material to the collision. An established procedure followed at every collision scene increases the efficiency of the process and reduces the chance that critical evidence will be missed. Be sure to photograph the entire collision scene leaving nothing to chance. The number of photographs will vary depending on the severity and type of collision.

PRESERVING AND DOCUMENTING PHOTOGRAPHS

13-100. Collision photographs are evidence. In general, collision photographs should be preserved and documented in the same manner as crime scene photographs and as detailed in chapter 4. Investigators must ensure that the chain of custody for photographic evidence is maintained. This includes all prints, negatives, or digital files; all prints and negatives must be maintained as part of the collision report to include spoiled prints and negatives (if using film) or poor exposures (if using a digital camera). Both film and digital photography are accepted, and methods for maintaining digital photographic evidence are well established. Digital photography has increasingly become the preferred photographic medium.

13-101. Admissibility of the photographic evidence depends on the ability to preserve the images in an unaltered state. Chapter 4 discusses requirements for preserving and maintaining chain of custody and admissibility for court proceedings. In general, the following techniques must be adhered to for photographic evidence:

- Record and preserve the evidence in an unaltered form.
- Never delete an exposure from a digital medium once it has been taken.
- Write-protect original files; use duplicates or copies for working images.
- Document the evidence and maintain a chain of custody.
- Document completely any alteration or manipulation of an image—enhancement, enlargement, and such—for forensic analysis.
- Ensure that the photographer or investigator is able to testify to the credibility of the images in court.

Recording Information at the Scene

13-102. All photographs should be documented in the investigators field notes. The investigators should record the following information pertaining to photography of the scene:

- General information entries including the—
  - Date and time of the collision.
  - Location of the collision.
  - Weather conditions.
  - Identification of the photographer.
- Equipment identification including the—
  - Type of camera to include the brand name.
  - Type of lens.
  - Type of film (if applicable).
  - Accessories or special effects equipment.
- Photograph documentation including the—
  - Photograph number (written as # of total #).
  - Camera settings.
  - Camera position including the camera height, the approximate distance from the camera to the subject, and the directional view of the photograph; for example, 10 feet, viewed from west.
  - Description and purpose for taking the photograph.

Marking Photographs as Evidence

13-103. Properly marking photographs ensures that the photograph can be positively identified at a future date. Photographs submitted as evidence in court must be marked and authenticated. The investigator is required to authenticate that the photographs are a true and unaltered representation of the scene. The original photographs must not be altered. Copies of the photographs should be made for use during the investigation. Overlays may be produced to place explanatory data over the top of the photograph without altering the original.

13-104. Photographs must be appropriately marked to identify the photographer and other information pertinent to the case. Photographs should be marked on the back side of the photograph with the—

- Photograph number; for example, 1 of 10.
- Date and time of the photograph.
- Identity of the photographer including his—
  - Name (last, first, middle initial).
  - SSN.
  - Rank and/or title.
  - Unit, base, state, zip code.
- Case number (if available).

CLASSIFICATION OF PHOTOGRAPHS

13-105. The investigator must decide what photographs are necessary when photographing a collision scene. Certain photographs are nice to have, whereas other photographs are mandatory. Mandatory photographs include—

- Establishing photographs.
- Approach photographs.
- Final rest photographs.
- Damage photograph.

Establishing Photographs

13-106. An establishing photograph depicts the collision scene as the investigator first saw it upon approach. These are similar to the overall photograph taken at a crime scene. This photograph includes as much of the scene as possible such as signs, signals, traffic control devices, and all components involved. More than one establishing photograph may be required, depending on the seriousness and size of the collision scene. If more than one photograph is taken, they must overlap every 10 feet to show relationship and must include some type of identifying fixed landmark such as street name signs, numbered buildings, or telephone poles.

Approach Photographs

13-107. The approach photograph depicts the driver's and/or pedestrian's view as they approached the collision scene. An identifying landmark is not required but should be included if possible. The approach photograph should begin at the point of possible perception and must include the first harmful event such as potholes and curbs. More than one approach photograph is typically required to document the approach of multiple components from multiple directions.

13-108. If it is necessary to photograph the scene later, every effort should be made to take the photograph under the same conditions as those at the time of the collision. For example, if it was raining, snowing, foggy, or dark during the collision, attempt to take subsequent photos under similar conditions. This photograph should be taken at the same eye level as the driver or pedestrian and facing in the same direction as they were traveling. Photographs should also be taken from relatively the same position on or off the roadway and must include view obstructions, traffic control devices, road hazards, and light conditions. When taking a series of photographs, ensure that they are completed at 10-foot overlaps.

Final Rest Photographs

13-109. Final rest photographs depict the positions and locations of vehicles and bodies after the collision. A final rest photograph should show as much of the collision scene as possible and include gouges, signs, signals and the final rest of all components. These photographs are comparable to mid-range or evidence establishing photographs during crime scene processing.

13-110. More than one photograph may be required to show the relationship between the components involved in the collision. Include a 10-foot overlap when taking multiple exposures. Final rest photographs should include an identifying fixed landmark such as numbered buildings, street name signs, telephone poles, or any other permanent object or structure. This can include items on the roadway.

Damage Photographs

13-111. Damage photographs are taken to indicate the amount and type of damage sustained by the vehicles and other components, not including persons. Damage photographs may be either mid-range or close-up. Do not limit damage photographs to just vehicles. Other damage is possible and even probable. This can include damage to guardrails, trees, signs, poles, roadway surfaces, buildings, fences, and other objects or structures. These photographs may be taken during initial scene processing or at a later time. Damage photographs for vehicles are typically taken after they have been separated from other vehicles or objects and may be taken at a location away from the collision scene. There are three types of damage photographs including the—

- **Standard four-series (360-degree).** This is the most comprehensive method and provides the greatest amount of information for collision reconstruction. The standard four-photograph series depicts both sides and both ends of a damaged vehicle. Ensure that photographs are taken on the centerline of the vehicle while facing towards it. For technical purposes, this is the preferred method because it eliminates distortion caused by angles. Figure 13-7, page 13-34, illustrates a standard four-series damage exposure.
- **Two-series.** This is a series of two photographs taken from opposite corners of the damaged vehicle. Each exposure must show one side and one end of the vehicle.

- **Single photograph.** A single exposure may be taken to depict one side and one end of the vehicle. This exposure includes as much of the damaged and undamaged area as possible. This photograph should be taken only when more than one photograph would not be justified, such as when there is only minor damage to one fender. Figure 13-8 illustrates two-series and single damage exposures.

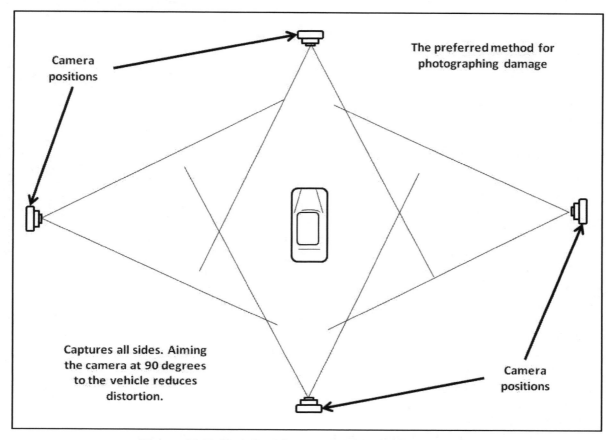

Figure 13-7. Standard four-series damage exposures

13-112. There are four types of damage that investigators may encounter. Classification of the damage types enables the investigator to accurately describe the damage to vehicles after a collision. The four categories for vehicle damage are—

- **Prior damage.** This is damage done to a component before the collision. This type of damage will be indicated by rust, body repair materials, or even paint transfers.
- **Collision damage.** Collision damage indicates that the damage to the component occurred during the collision. It includes—
  - Contact damage which results from direct contact with another vehicle or object. This is primary damage.
  - Induced damage which is other than contact damage. This type of damage is secondary damage that results from the force of impact produced subsequent to contact damage.
- **Rescue damage.** This is damage caused when attempting to remove collision victims from a vehicle. This is usually caused by tools such as crowbars or Jaws-of-Life®.
- **Removal damage.** This is damage normally caused while separating and towing vehicles from the collision scene. Vehicle damage photographs are normally taken after they have been separated from one another.

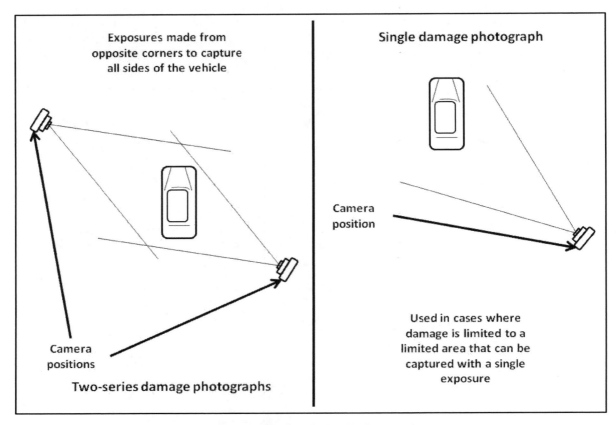

Figure 13-8. Two-series and single damage exposures

Other Optional Photographs

13-113. Some types of photographs, while not mandatory for all collision investigations, may provide additional information and detail that can enhance the overall investigation. Investigators should consider these techniques based on the specific circumstances of the collision and the availability of resources.

Close-Up Photographs

13-114. Close-up photographs are not mandatory in most collision investigations; however, they can be helpful in documenting specific details of vehicle damage. Close-up photographs are taken to enhance overall and/or mid-range exposures. Investigators must use their judgment to determine the best combination of close-up and other photographs. Overall or mid-range photographs will normally be taken first; these photographs are then supplemented with close-up photographs to capture important details of vehicle, roadway, or other damage. Close-ups are most commonly used in conjunction with approach or damage photographs. Close-up photographs can be very helpful when documenting—

- Evidence of vehicle component failure.
- Evidence of previous damage such as rust, old paint transfer, previous repair attempts.
- Lamp condition that indicates the condition or state of the lamp upon impact.
- Tire conditions.
- Road damage.
- Small but important items of debris.
- Evidence of contributing factors such as open alcoholic beverage containers or open maps in the driver's area.

Roadway Photographs

13-115. These photographs depict anything on the roadway that may have contributed to the collision such as road configuration, surface conditions, traffic control devices, and road accessories. A roadway photograph can also include results of the collision on the roadway such as tire marks, metal scars, debris, damage to fixed objects, and signs of the vehicle leaving the ground. Skid marks, scuffs, yaws, and other marks will typically require a series of photographs. If a series of photographs are needed, it is necessary to include a 10-foot overlap from one photograph to the next. This evidence indicates what may have occurred.

Aerial Photographs

13-116. Aerial photographs can be especially helpful if the collision scene is spread over a large area. They can also provide a good general view of the collision scene. They are helpful to provide overall perspective of the scene, especially for persons that were not present at the collision scene. They can also provide important information for postevent analysis of the area to identify problems and specific safety issues. Aerial photographs may be taken from any elevated vantage point; they can be taken from fixed wing aircraft, helicopters, a nearby tall building, or a camera mounted on a pole.

Appendix A

Investigations Support in an Operational Environment

Army LE personnel conduct investigations in all environments. Techniques and investigative requirements remain relatively constant regardless of where the investigation is conducted; however, investigations and related tasks conducted in support of Army operations in a deployed environment have unique challenges due to the environment in which they are conducted. USACIDC SAs conduct war crimes investigations in support of unified land operations. In addition to normal LE support to U.S. forces, military police and USACIDC SAs can support site exploitation activities.

INVESTIGATIVE CHALLENGES

A-1. Conducting an investigation in a forward deployed environment can add additional challenges to the investigator. These challenges can include language or cultural barriers, resource constraints, and environmental conditions.

LANGUAGE BARRIERS

A-2. Standard interview techniques must be modified with war crime survivors and witnesses. A very prominent problem that must be overcome in these interviews is the language barrier. The investigative team must have experienced, reliable, and competent interpreters. The interpreter must be able to convey the attitude and personality of the investigator. It is best if part of the investigative team is fluent in the languages of those being interviewed. Investigators will be able to convey their own ideas and thoughts much more clearly to the interviewees. U.S. interpreters from a military intelligence unit or the supporting unit may be used. When using interpreters, investigators must understand that most interpreters lack a LE background, investigative experience, and the ability to reflect the investigator's personality.

A-3. A less effective alternative is to use a local national. Even with good language skills, a local national may hurt the investigation. Local national interpreters are often indifferent to the outcome of an investigation. They may have no patience with very old, young, or confused witnesses. Local nationals are often unreliable or may not be loyal to the United States or the mission. Like U.S. interpreters, local nationals will likely lack any LE background and investigative experience and are often unable to reflect the personality of the investigators for whom they interpret. If U.S. or local national interpreters must be used to support an investigation, provisions for payment, billeting, and messing must be made. These personnel must be thoroughly vetted; only interpreters of the highest caliber should be selected for the mission, and an extensive background check should be considered.

CULTURAL BARRIERS

A-4. In some instances, especially within HN environments overseas, cultural and religious differences, convictions, and traditions will heavily influence how individuals within some cultures interact with investigators. Some cultures take significant time to build relationships and trust. They may require periods of small talk and general discussion before engaging in critical topics. Western societies (specifically the United States) have a tendency to get straight to the matter at hand. Many cultures see our desire to get straight to the point of business and eliminate niceties as rude. Interviewees may be fearful and apprehensive, and they may be illiterate and lack sophistication. In some parts of the world, everyday points of reference are nonexistent, such as standard units of measure, western calendars, and directional points of the compass. Consideration must be made to overcome these differences.

A-5. In some cultures, only the eldest male can speak for the group, and women may not be allowed to speak to men outside their immediate family. These situations can be significant barriers to effective communication. Investigators must understand and shape their methods of interaction to overcome cultural and religious barriers. The use of female investigative personnel may facilitate reaching some elements of the population that are otherwise unavailable to males.

RESOURCE CONSTRAINTS

A-6. Some environments may be extremely austere with limited logistical support and connectivity. Availability of protection assets can also be a concern, especially in high threat environments. USACIDC SAs in particular may be dependent on units other than military police or USACIDC for their support. Investigators must be prepared to work under these conditions. The best method for overcoming these obstacles is to identify as many potential constraints as possible and plan accordingly. Resupply of investigative tools and supplies may be extremely slow. Investigators should account for this when packing their equipment and supplies. Early coordination with supporting units can alleviate some problems by identifying requirements early in the deployment.

ENVIRONMENTAL HAZARDS

A-7. Investigators must be aware of potential environmental hazards, such as areas devastated by major combat operations. Areas may have unexploded munitions (including minefields) present or CBRN threats and hazards may be encountered. Many nations do not comply with the same environmental standards as the United States. Environmental hazards in the form of chemical contamination due to improper material handling and disposal techniques are a problem in many areas of the world. Poor sanitation can also result in biological hazards. Extreme caution should be maintained for the possibility of unexploded ordinance and/or chemical/biological material at the site. Prior coordination should be made with CBRN units to clear any site suspected of containing CBRN hazards and EOD units to clear any site suspected of containing explosive ordnance.

A-8. Enemy combatants, insurgents, or other threat elements may be operating in the area. Risk assessments to identify required personal and unit protection measures must be conducted. Investigators should coordinate for security from military police or other units in the area that are providing support to USACIDC activities. Investigators must exercise due caution in moving in and around the scene and ensure that onlookers are carefully removed from the scene for their protection as well as the protection of the investigator and any potential crime scene.

WAR CRIMES INVESTIGATIONS

A-9. War crimes are investigated by USACIDC SAs. Investigations of war crimes are conducted when they are committed by an enemy against U.S. personnel and by U.S. personnel against an enemy or upon the local population. One of the most important actions an investigator can take during the investigation of a war crime is to maintain steady communications with his chain of command. These communications keep the command informed and allow the command the precise moment of knowing if and when to pass the investigation on to another investigative agency. An example of such an investigation is that of a suspected series of murders that turns into a suspected genocide. Depending on the circumstances (such as cases where no U.S. personnel are involved), the investigation may be assumed by the United Nations (UN) or other governmental investigative organization, although USACIDC investigators may continue to support the investigation.

A-10. When investigating war crimes, investigators work closely with the servicing JA, which answers to the commander for the administration of war crime matters. Investigators also collect and report pertinent police intelligence to military intelligence, counterintelligence, and other investigative agencies of the United States and the HN. Investigators must ensure that information is shared consistent with regulatory and legal restrictions; consult the servicing JA for guidance when required.

LAWMAKING TREATIES AND CUSTOMARY LAWS

A-11. The law of land warfare, which is both written and unwritten, exists to regulate the conduct of armed hostilities. It is inspired by the desire to diminish the evils of war by—

- Protecting combatants and noncombatants from unnecessary suffering.
- Safeguarding certain fundamental human rights of individuals who fall into the hands of the enemy, particularly prisoners of war, the wounded and sick, and civilians.
- Facilitating the restoration of peace.

A-12. The laws of war are derived from the following two principal sources:

- International treaties or conventions including the Hague Conventions and the Geneva Conventions.
- The body of unwritten laws that have been established by custom and are recognized by authorities on international law.

A-13. The laws of war treaties have a force equal to that of laws enacted by Congress and must be observed by all individuals in the United States. Customary laws are binding upon the United States, its citizens, and other individuals serving the United States. The term war crime is a technical expression for violations of the laws of war by any military or civilian individual or individuals. Every violation of the laws of war is a war crime. See FM 27-10 for war crimes, lawmaking treaties, and customary laws.

A-14. The Geneva Conventions spell out the customary laws of war. In the case of armed conflict (not on an international level) in the territory of one of the high contracting parties, each party is bound to apply some basic provisions. Individuals who do not take an active part in hostilities shall be treated humanely. This includes members of armed forces who have laid down their arms and those removed from the conflict by sickness, wounds, detention, or other cause. No distinction in treatment will be made by race, color, religion, sex, birth, wealth, or any other similar criteria. The wounded and sick will be collected and cared for. Certain acts are prohibited, at any time and place, with respect to these nonparticipants. There will be no—

- Violence to life and person, murder of any kind, mutilation, torture, or cruel treatment.
- Hostages taken.
- Outrages upon personal dignity. Humiliating and degrading treatment are expressly forbidden.
- Sentences passed or executions carried out without prior judgment by a legitimate court affording all the judicial guarantees viewed as essential by civilized individuals.

IDENTIFYING WAR CRIMES

A-15. Violations of the laws of war may include conspiracy and attempts to commit war crimes. An individual may commit war crimes in which the individual and the commander or only the commander may be held accountable, or war crimes may be committed by an organization to include that of a given government. In all cases, the war crime has to be identified and investigated.

A-16. Violations of the Geneva Conventions are specific crimes of the laws of war and include—

- The willful killing of noncombatants.
- The torture or inhumane treatment of combatants and noncombatants, to include performing biological experiments that willfully cause great suffering or serious injury to the body or health.
- The unlawful deportation, transfer, or confinement of protected persons, such as a clergyman.
- The forcing of protected persons to serve in the forces of a hostile power.
- The taking of hostages and excessive destruction and appropriation of property not justified by military necessity and carried out indiscriminately.

A-17. In addition to the grave breaches of the Geneva Conventions, the following are some of the representative acts identified in FM 27-10 that constitute war crimes:

- Making use of poisoned or otherwise forbidden arms or ammunition.
- Requesting quarters by using treacherous means.

- Maltreating dead bodies.
- Firing on areas that are undefended and have no military significance.
- Misusing the Red Cross emblem or its equivalent.
- Abusing or firing on the flag of truce.
- Using civilian clothing to conceal military status during battle.
- Pillaging or purposelessly causing destruction of protected places.
- Improperly using privileged buildings (such as hospitals or churches) for military purposes.
- Violating the terms of surrender.
- Firing on hospital zones.
- Poisoning wells or streams.

A-18. In 1998, the Tribunal for the Former Yugoslavia became the first international court to determine that an individual accountable for rape was also accountable for war crimes. The Tribunal determined that rape is now inclusive of war crimes when committed under the laws of land warfare. In 2001, the Tribunal set another legal precedence when it convicted former Bosnian Serb soldiers of systematically raping and torturing Muslim females. This same court established sexual enslavement as a war crime.

A-19. The occurrence of criminal acts taking place before the declaration of war or after the termination of a war by agreement or unilateral declaration of one of the parties, by complete subjugation of an enemy before termination of war, or by termination of war or armed conflict by simple cessation of hostilities with exception are not war crimes. These criminal acts will be investigated as are crimes that are committed in time of peace. See FM 27-10 for more information.

INITIATING A WAR CRIMES INVESTIGATION

A-20. When a CID investigator receives a report of a war crime, the same investigative process should be used as when investigating any other criminal activity. The investigator initiates CID Form 28, *Agent Activity Summary*, and annotates the date, time, and details of the notification. Each time an investigator makes a related action to the case, he annotates it in detail on CID Form 28. When an investigator makes or observes significant achievements during the investigation, he annotates these results on CID Form 94, *Agent Investigation Report*. This form is compiled by the agent and is attached to the final CID report that is submitted to a suspect's commander. In addition to these two forms, the investigator maintains a daily journal in which he records, in abbreviated style, the significant operational decisions and developments of the day. See CID Regulation 195-1 for prescribed formats.

A-21. War crimes investigations are conducted using standard investigative techniques that include—

- Protecting and processing the crime scene using standard techniques documented by the investigator's notes, photographs, and sketches.
- Collecting, marking, packaging, and shipping evidence.
- Interviewing witnesses.
- Identifying suspects.

A-22. War crimes investigations can be long and tedious, requiring the investigator to interview many individuals, likely with language and cultural obstacles to deal with. In some cases, the repetitive nature of these interviews may cause the interviews to become less disciplined and systematic over time due to mental fatigue on the part of the investigator. The lead investigator can help eliminate this issue by soliciting the entire investigative team's help in preparing a comprehensive list of key questions to ask during the interviews. This list will elicit the most complete statements from the interviewees and will ensure uniformity of coverage from one interviewee to the next. Investigators should be cautious not to conform only to listed questions. If a statement made by an individual logically leads in a direction not accounted for in the prepared questions, the investigator should follow the logical flow of questions to obtain full understanding and clarity on the subject at hand. The investigator can then resume with the prepared questions at the point where the questioning was diverted.

A-23. Choosing an interview site is important to the results of the interview and can help offset some of the above problems. Interviews are best done in an atmosphere near the witnesses' homes, which allows many more witnesses, including the very young and the very old, to be questioned. USACIDC funds can be used to provide cigarettes, gum, and like items for interviewees and will also be used to supply the investigative team with the national currency. With this currency, investigators can ensure interviewees that they will be reimbursed for out-of-pocket expenses incurred incidental to the interviews.

> *Note.* Investigators will not discuss claims with potential claimants. It is advisable to have legal personnel available to answer any questions from victims and their families related to claims against the U.S. Government for injuries sustained by war crimes.

MASS GRAVESITE INVESTIGATIONS

A-24. USACIDC SAs may be required to conduct mass gravesite investigations or support mass gravesite excavation teams. Investigators must know how to secure and preserve evidence of atrocities at mass gravesites. Their investigative focus should be to determine how the victims died, how long they had been interred, and their nationality, and to conduct a forensic assessment to determine if an atrocity or war crime occurred.

A-25. Often there is tremendous pressure from the families and loved ones of the victims to recover the victims as soon as possible so that they may be given a proper, decent or religiously-correct burial. Securing a mass gravesite for an extended period of time without releasing victims may cause increased friction between the families, local authorities and U.S. forces.

A-26. The security of a mass gravesite will be difficult to maintain for any extended period of time due to the limited number of forces available to provide security. Suspected mass gravesites should be processed as quickly as possible, while maintaining site security to gather and protect sufficient physical and testimonial evidence to assist in any follow-on investigations and possible judicial proceedings.

A-27. When a suspected mass gravesite is encountered, investigators should—

- Initiate a report of investigation.
- Fix the location and size of the site. The use of a GPS receiver is recommended to ensure that the most accurate measurements are recorded. At large sites, GPS readings may need to be recorded from the four corners of the site.
- Prepare an overall sketch of the scene. If possible, supplement the sketch with aerial video and still photographs of the site. Ideally, photographs should depict the site before, during, and after the excavation and processing.
- Canvass the immediate local population including any persons reporting the site. Document all interviews to the fullest extent reasonably possible. Interview persons who claim to have knowledge of the—
    - Circumstances of the gravesite.
    - Identities of the deceased.
    - Manner in which the mass grave was discovered.
- Ascertain the approximate number of dead.
- Take video and still photographs to depict the scope of the scene and the cause of death of the victims. Document any injuries to the victims, especially signs of violent death. Take special care to document and photograph any physical evidence such as firearm projectiles and cartridge casings, bindings, blindfolds, and personal identification and effects.
- Identify and collect physical evidence. Collect any identified physical evidence such as firearm projectiles and cartridge casings, bindings, blindfolds, and personal identification and effects. A metal detector may aid in the search if available. Collect items of evidence as described in chapter 2. In the case of sites where extremely large numbers of persons are buried (generally over 100 persons), collect evidence depicting a representative sample of the injuries to the victims and characteristics of the scene, such as blindfolds or bindings.
- Employ the most competent medical personnel reasonably available to opine on the causes of death of the victims. Forensic pathologists may be the most preferred experts, but trained pathologists, surgeons, doctors, dentists, and forensic anthropologists may be used depending on

circumstances. Investigators should consider employing or contracting with qualified local national or third country medical doctors or forensic experts from nongovernmental organizations operating in the area. Coordinate with the servicing JA to ensure that any medical personnel used would be qualified to testify as expert witnesses in future judicial proceedings.

- Attempt to identify the victims. This should be accomplished to the fullest extent possible within available resource constraints. Place priority on identifying the victims' nationality, ethnic background, and status as military or civilian. Further efforts to determine sex, stature, and age may assist in identifying the victim. Retain any identification documents that are present on a victim; ensure these items are documented sufficiently to enables the documents to be traced to the victim from which they originated.

- Develop and pursue logical and realistic investigative leads. The investigation should consider the investigative and support resources available and local conditions including support or lack of support from the local population, the security environment, and available protection resources.

A-28. When a mass grave is located, the investigative goal is to secure and preserve sufficient evidence to establish leads that further the investigation. These leads may result in identification of the individuals that may have ordered or caused the wrongful deaths of the victims.

Appendix B

Electronic Devices

Electronic devices may contain data crucial to an investigation. The devices themselves and the information they contain may be used as digital evidence. Many electronic devices contain memory that requires continuous power to maintain the information, such as battery or alternating current power. Unplugging the power source or allowing the battery to discharge can result in lost data. After determining the mode of collection, collect and store the power supply adaptor or cable (if present) with the recovered device. In all cases where electronic devices and digital evidence are seized, proper search authorization must be obtained. This may be by consent or by search authorization from a magistrate.

COMPUTER SYSTEMS

B-1. A computer system typically consists of a main base unit (sometimes called a central processing unit [CPU]), data storage devices, a monitor, a keyboard, and a mouse. Computer systems are used for all types of computing functions and information storage, including word processing, calculations, communications, and graphics. A computer system may stand-alone or be connected to a network. There are many types of computer systems, such as laptops, desktops, tower systems, modular rack-mounted systems, minicomputers, and mainframe computers. Additional components include modems, printers, scanners, docking stations, and external data storage devices. For example, a desktop is a computer system consisting of a case, a motherboard, a CPU, and a data storage device with an external keyboard and a mouse.

B-2. Identifying information associated with the computer system as well and the system and its components are all potential evidence. The device itself (hardware) may be evidence of component theft, counterfeiting, or remarking. Internal hardware of specific value includes—

- The CPU. Often called the chip, the CPU is a microprocessor located inside the computer. The microprocessor is located in the main computer box on a printed circuit board with other electronic components. The CPU performs all arithmetic and logical functions in the computer. It controls the operation of the computer.
- Memory boards. Memory is information stored on removable circuit boards inside the computer. Memory boards store the user's programs and data while the computer is in operation. This data is usually not retained when the computer is powered down.
- Hard drives (discussed below).

B-3. Additional evidentiary value may exist in—

- Software.
- User documents such as data files, photos, image files, e-mail, and e-mail attachments.
- Databases.
- Financial information.
- Internet-related data such as browsing history, chat logs, buddy lists, and event logs.
- Data stored on external devices.

STORAGE DEVICES

B-4. Storage devices may contain information that can be valuable to an investigation or prosecution. They vary in size, capacity, and the manner in which they store and retain data. Army LE personnel must understand the value these devices have in an investigation. Storage devices such as hard drives, external hard drives, removable media, thumb drives, and memory cards can contain the full range of information and data produced by a computer system; their only limitation is the physical capacity of the specific storage device. They can store photographs and other image files; financial records; written documents; e-mail messages; Internet browsing history, chat logs, and buddy lists; databases; and other forms of data that can be valuable evidence in an investigation or prosecution. Evidence is most commonly found in files that are stored on hard drives and storage devices and media. Along with the primary data, there are components of files that may have evidentiary value including the date and time of creation, modification, deletion, access, user name or ID, and file attributes; Army LE personnel must understand that even turning the system on can modify some of this information. There are several types of files that may be encountered including—

- **User-created files.** User-created files may contain important evidence of criminal activity such as address books and database files that may prove criminal association, still or moving pictures that may be evidence of pedophile activity, and communications between criminals, such as e-mail or letters. Also, drug deal lists may often be found in spreadsheets. The following are examples of user-created files:
  - Audio or video files.
  - Calendars.
  - Documents or text files.
  - Internet bookmarks or favorites.
- **User-protected files.** Users have the opportunity to hide evidence in a variety of forms. For example, they may encrypt or password protect data that is important to them. They may also hide files on a hard disk, within other files, or under an innocuous name. The following are examples of user-protected files:
  - Compressed files.
  - Encrypted files.
  - Hidden files.
  - Misnamed files.
  - Password-protected files.
  - Cryptography.
- **Computer-created files.** The following are some examples of computer-created files:
  - Backup files.
  - Configuration files.
  - Cookies.
  - Hidden files.
  - History files.
  - Log files.
  - Printer spool files.
  - Swap files.
  - System files.
  - Temporary files.
- **Other data areas.** Evidence can also be found in files and other data areas created as a routine function of the computer's operating system. In many cases, the user is not aware that data is being written to these areas. Passwords, Internet activity, and temporary backup files are examples of data that can often be recovered and examined. The following are considered other data areas:
  - Bad clusters.
  - Computer date, time, and password.
  - Deleted files.
  - Free space.
  - Hidden partitions.

- Lost clusters.
- Metadata.
- Other partitions.
- Reserved areas.
- Slack space.
- Software registration information.
- System areas.
- Unallocated space.

HARD DRIVES

B-5. A hard drive is a sealed box containing an external circuit board, external data and power connections, and rigid platters (disks) capable of magnetically storing data. Hard drives can be internal to the computer system or they can be external components. Army LE personnel should understand that even hard drives designed for internal installation may be found at a crime scene separate from a computer; these drives may still hold valuable information. External hard drives increase the computer's data storage capacity and provide the user with portable data. Generally, external hard drives require a power supply and a means to connect to the computer such as universal serial bus (USB), Ethernet, or wireless connection. A hard drive is used to store information such as computer programs, text, pictures, video, and multimedia files. The device itself may be evidence of component theft, counterfeiting, or remarking or it may be valuable for the information stored on the hard drive.

MODEMS

B-6. Modems can be internal and external (analog, DSL, ISDN, and cable). A laptop computer may use a wireless modem or PC card. A modem is used to facilitate electronic communication by allowing the computer to access other computers and/or networks via a telephone line, wirelessly, or through another communications medium.

REMOVABLE MEDIA

B-7. Removable media are typically used to store, archive, transfer, and transport data and other information including computer programs, text, pictures, video, and multimedia files. The object itself may be evidence of component theft, counterfeiting, or remarking. Removable media can be tape cartridges, floppy disks, disk-based data storage devices such as CDs or DVDs, memory cards, and thumb drives. These devices help users share data, information, applications, and utilities among different computers and other devices. New types of storage devices and media come on the market frequently, so LE personnel must stay current on advances in technology to ensure that all devices are being properly checked for evidentiary value. Descriptions of these common removable media include—

- **Tape cartridges.** Tape cartridges are typically small plastic boxes that hold magnetic tape for storing information. Though not as common today as other forms of storage, these may still be encountered by investigators in some applications. These cartridges will typically require special drives and software to read and access data stored on the media.
- **Disk-based storage.** CDs and DVDs are common storage media. They are flat plastic discs with a hole in the center. They can be used to record audio, video, and data files.
- **Memory cards.** Memory cards are removable electronic storage devices that do not lose the information when power is removed from the card. They provide additional, removable methods of storing and transporting information. It may even be possible to recover erased images from memory cards. Memory cards can store hundreds of images on a very small module. They can be used in a variety of devices including mobile phones, computers, digital cameras, and personal digital assistants (PDAs).
- **Thumb drives.** Thumb drives or flash drives are small, lightweight, removable data storage devices with USB connections. They are easy to conceal and transport and can hold large

amounts of data. They can be found as an integrated part of other common items such as wristwatches, pens, pocket knives, key chain fobs, or other items.

ACCESS DEVICES

B-8. Access devices such as smart cards, dongles, and biometric scanners are commonly used to prevent unauthorized access to computer systems; these devices provide access control to computers or programs or function as encryption keys. A smart card is a small handheld device that contains a microprocessor capable of storing a monetary value, an encryption key or authentication information (password), a digital certificate, or other information. A dongle is a small device that plugs into a computer port that contains types of information similar to information on a smart card. A biometric scanner is a device connected to a computer system that recognizes physical characteristics of an individual; for example, fingerprint, voice, and retina. The ID authentication information on the card and the user, the level of access, configurations, permissions, and the device itself may be evidence.

HANDHELD DEVICES

B-9. Handheld devices are portable data storage devices that provide communications, digital photography, navigation systems, entertainment, data storage, and personal information management. These devices include tablets, electronic readers, mobile phones and smart phones, PDAs, digital multimedia (audio and video) devices, pagers, digital cameras, and GPS receivers. They can store software applications; photographs and other image files; financial records; written documents; e-mail messages; Internet browsing history, chat logs, and buddy lists; databases; and other forms of data that can be valuable evidence in an investigation or prosecution. Investigators should understand that—

- Data or digital evidence on some handheld devices may be lost if power is not maintained.
- Data or digital evidence on some devices such as mobile or smart phones can be overwritten or deleted while the device remains activated.
- Some handheld devices—especially mobile and smart phones—are loaded with software that can be activated remotely to render the device unusable and make any resident data inaccessible if the device is lost or stolen; this software can be enabled by the owner or other persons with access if the device is seized by LE personnel. Army LE personnel should take precautions to prevent the loss of data on devices they seize as evidence; contact appropriate experts for guidance.

DIGITAL CAMERAS

B-10. A digital camera is a digital recording device for images and video. Related storage media and conversion hardware make it capable of transferring images and video to computer media. Digital cameras capture images and/or video in a digital format that is easily transferred to computer storage media for viewing and/or editing. Digital cameras may provide the following potential evidence:

- Images.
- Removable cartridges.
- Sound.
- A time and date stamp.
- Video.

MOBILE PHONES

B-11. Mobile phones are used to provide wireless phone access. Most modern mobile phones include some level of internet connectivity, photographic capability, and calendar and other personal organizing options. Smart phones are a kind of mobile phone that includes computer capability; they typically have a touch screen interface. Most mobile phones are also equipped with a GPS tracking capability. Smart phones can store a wide variety of digital files including video and audio files. Smart phones will typically be loaded with various software applications. Virtually any information that can be stored on a traditional computer system can be stored or accessed via a smart phone. Mobile phones may provide the following potential evidence:

- Address and phone books.
- Call and message logs.
- Images.
- Audio.
- Video.
- Text messages.
- Voice messages.
- Appointment calendars and information.
- E-mails.
- GPS data.

PERSONAL DIGITAL ASSISTANTS AND ELECTRONIC ORGANIZERS

B-12. A PDA is a small handheld device that can be used for computing, storing information, and communicating. It is typically used as a personal organizer. A handheld computer approaches the full functionality of a desktop computer system. Some PDAs do not contain disk drives, but may contain card slots that can hold a modem, a hard drive, or another device. They usually include the ability to synchronize their data with other computer systems, most commonly by a connection in a cradle. If a cradle is present, attempt to locate the associated handheld device. Batteries have a limited life; data could be lost if they fail. Therefore, appropriate personnel should be informed that a device powered by batteries is in need of immediate attention. This may be an evidence custodian, a laboratory chief, or a forensic examiner. Handheld devices may provide the following potential evidence:

- An address book.
- Appointment calendars and information.
- Documents.
- E-mails.
- Handwriting.
- A password.
- A telephone book.
- Text messages.
- Voice messages.

PAGERS

B-13. A pager is a handheld, portable electronic device that can contain volatile evidence such as telephone numbers, voice mails, and e-mails. Cell phones and PDAs also can be used as paging devices. Pagers are used for sending and receiving electronic numeric and alphanumeric messages. Batteries have a limited life; data could be lost if they fail. Therefore, appropriate personnel should be informed that a device powered by batteries is in need of immediate attention. This may be an evidence custodian, a laboratory chief, or a forensic examiner. Pagers may provide the following potential evidence:

- Address information.
- E-mails.
- Telephone numbers.
- Text messages.
- Voice messages.

GLOBAL POSITIONING SYSTEMS

B-14. GPSs can provide information on previous travel via destination information, waypoints, and routes. Some GPSs automatically store the previous destinations and include travel logs. GPSs may provide the following potential evidence:

- Home location.
- Previous destinations.
- Travel logs.
- Waypoint coordinates.
- A waypoint name.

TABLET COMPUTERS

B-15. Tablet computers are a highly mobile type of computer. They are normally operated by using a touch screen rather than the traditional keyboard. Tablets are configured with software applications and may run adapted versions of common software applications used by traditional computer systems. Virtually any information that can be stored on a traditional computer system can be stored on a tablet computer.

NETWORKS AND COMPONENTS

B-16. A computer network consists of two or more computers linked by data cables or wireless connections that share or are capable of sharing resources and data. A computer network often includes printers, other peripheral devices, and data routing devices such as hubs, switches, and routers. Networked computers and connected devices may be evidence that is useful to an investigation or prosecution. Along with information previously discussed as being resident on computer systems and associated hardware and peripherals, the device functions, capabilities, and any identifying information associated with the computer and network system such as Internet protocol (IP), LAN, and network interface card (NIC) addresses associated with the computers and devices may be useful as evidence.

LOCAL AREA NETWORK CARD OR NETWORK INTERFACE CARD

B-17. LAN cards or NICs are indicative of a computer network. Network components are network cards and associated cables. Network cards also can be wireless. A LAN card or NIC is used to connect computers. These cards allow for the exchange of information and resource sharing. The device itself as well as the media access control address may be evidence.

ROUTERS, HUBS, AND SWITCHES

B-18. Routers, hubs, and switches are used in networked computer systems. Routers, hubs, and switches provide a means of connecting different computers or networks. They can frequently be recognized by the presence of multiple cable connections. This equipment is used to distribute and facilitate the distribution of data through networks. The devices themselves as well as configuration files for routers may be evidence.

SERVERS

B-19. A server is a computer that provides services for other computers connected to it via a network. Any computer, including a laptop, can be configured as a server. Servers provide shared resources such as e-mail, file storage, Web page services, and print services for a network. The device itself may be evidence of component theft, counterfeiting, or remarking.

NETWORK CABLES AND CONNECTORS

B-20. Network cables and connectors connect components of a computer network. Network cables can be different colors, thicknesses, and shapes and have different connectors. Differences depend on the components to which they are connected. The devices themselves may be evidence.

MISCELLANEOUS ELECTRONIC DEVICES

B-21. There are many additional types of electronic equipment that might be found at a crime scene. However, there are many nontraditional devices that can be an excellent source of investigative information and/or evidence. Some examples are credit card skimmers, cell phone cloning equipment, caller ID boxes, audio recorders, and Web television. Fax machines, copiers, and multifunction machines may have internal storage devices that may contain information of evidentiary value. The search of this type of evidence may require a search warrant.

ANSWERING MACHINES

B-22. An answering machine is an electronic device that is part of a telephone or connected between a telephone and a landline connection. Some models use magnetic tape or tapes, while others use an electronic (digital) recording system. An answering machine records voice messages from callers when the called party is unavailable or chooses not to answer a telephone call. It usually plays a message from the called party before recording the message.

B-23. Answering machines may draw power from an internal battery, an electrical plug-in, or the telephone system. Batteries have a limited life and data could be lost if they fail. Therefore, appropriate personnel should be informed that a device powered by batteries is in need of immediate attention. This may be an evidence custodian, a laboratory chief, or a forensic examiner. Answering machines can store voice messages and, in some cases, the time and date information about when the message was left. They may also contain other voice recordings. Answering machines may provide the following potential evidence:

- Caller ID information.
- Deleted messages.
- The last number called.
- Memorandums.
- Telephone numbers and names.
- Tapes.

PRINTERS

B-24. A printer is one of a variety of printing systems (thermal, laser, inkjet, and impact) connected to the computer via a cable (serial, parallel, USB, or fire wire) or accessed via an IR port. Printers are used for printing text and images from the computer to paper. Some printers contain a memory buffer, allowing them to receive and store multiple page documents while they are printing. Some models may also contain a hard drive.

B-25. Printers may maintain usage logs and time and date information, and they may store network identity information (if attached to a network). In addition, unique characteristics may allow for the ID of a printer. Printers may provide the following potential evidence:

- Documents.
- A hard drive.
- Ink cartridges.
- Network identity information.
- Superimposed images on the roller.
- A time and date stamp.
- The user's usage log.

SCANNERS

B-26. A scanner is an optical device connected to a computer. It scans a document and sends it to the computer as a file. Scanners convert documents and pictures to electronic files which can then be viewed, manipulated, or transmitted on a computer. The device itself may be evidence. Having the capability to scan may help prove illegal activity; for example, child pornography, check fraud, counterfeiting, and identity theft. In addition, imperfections such as marks on the glass may allow for unique ID of a scanner used to process documents.

TELEPHONES

B-27. A telephone is a handset either by itself (as with a cell phone), a remote base station (cordless), or connected directly to the landline system. Telephones draw power from an internal battery, an electrical plug-in, or the telephone system. Telephones are used for two-way communication from one instrument to another, using landlines, radio transmission, cellular systems, or a combination. Telephones are capable of storing information.

B-28. Batteries have a limited life; data could be lost if they fail. Therefore, appropriate personnel should be informed that a device powered by batteries is in need of immediate attention. This may be an evidence custodian, a laboratory chief, or a forensic examiner. Many telephones can store names, telephone numbers, and caller ID information. Additionally, some cell telephones can store appointment information, receive electronic mail and pages, and may act as a voice recorder. Telephones may provide the following potential evidence:

- Appointment calendars and information.
- Caller ID information.
- The electronic serial number.
- E-mails.
- Memorandums.
- Passwords.
- Telephone books.
- Text messages.
- Voice mail.
- Web browsers.

COPIERS

B-29. Some copiers maintain user access records and a history of copies made. Copiers with the scan once/print many feature allow documents to be scanned once into memory, and then printed later. Copiers may provide the following potential evidence:

- Documents.
- A time and date stamp.
- The user's usage log.

CREDIT CARD SKIMMERS

B-30. Credit card skimmers are used to read information contained on the magnetic stripe of plastic cards. Cardholder information contained on the tracks of the magnetic stripe may provide the following potential evidence:

- A card's expiration date.
- Credit card numbers.
- The user's address.
- The user's name.

DIGITAL WATCHES

B-31. There are several types of digital watches available that can function as pagers that store digital messages. They may store additional information such as address books, appointment calendars, e-mails, and notes. Some also have the capability of synchronizing information with computers.

FAX MACHINES

B-32. Fax machines can store preprogrammed telephone numbers and a history of transmitted and received documents. In addition, some contain memory that allows multiple-page faxes to be scanned and sent at a later time and incoming faxes to be held in memory and printed later. Some may store hundreds of pages of incoming and/or outgoing faxes. Fax machines may provide the following potential evidence:

- Documents.
- Film cartridges.
- Telephone numbers.
- Send and receive logs.

AUTHORIZATION TO SEARCH AND SEIZE ELECTRONIC DEVICES

B-33. Search authorizations issued by a U.S. magistrate or civilian judge at the state or federal level or the consent of the property owner is required before searching privately owned electronic devices. However, in almost all cases, courts have held a relatively high standard with regard to the specificity of computer-related search authorizations. Investigative personnel seeking search authorization must be able to articulate specific and recent information pertaining to the individual items cited on the affidavit and authorization in order to establish probable cause. Figures B-1 through B-3, pages B-10 through B-15, provide a sample DA Form 3744, *Affidavit Supporting Request for Authorization to Search and Seize or Apprehend*; figures B-4 and B-5, pages B-16 through B-18, provide a sample DA Form 3745, *Search and Seizure Authorization*. See appendix D for additional information regarding the use of DA Form 3744.

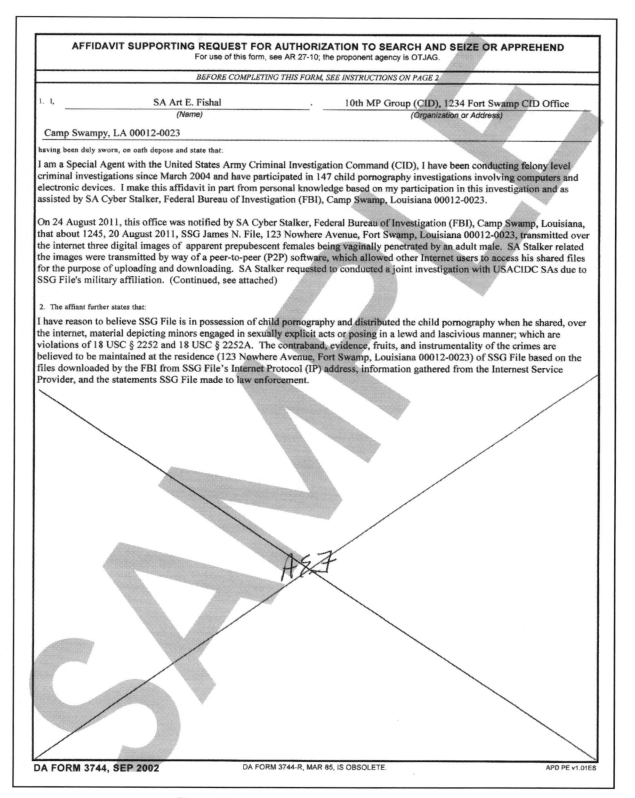

AFFIDAVIT SUPPORTING REQUEST FOR AUTHORIZATION TO SEARCH AND SEIZE OR APPREHEND
For use of this form, see AR 27-10; the proponent agency is OTJAG.

BEFORE COMPLETING THIS FORM, SEE INSTRUCTIONS ON PAGE 2

1. I, _____ SA Art E. Fishal _____ , 10th MP Group (CID), 1234 Fort Swamp CID Office
   (Name)   (Organization or Address)

Camp Swampy, LA 00012-0023

having been duly sworn, on oath depose and state that:

I am a Special Agent with the United States Army Criminal Investigation Command (CID), I have been conducting felony level criminal investigations since March 2004 and have participated in 147 child pornography investigations involving computers and electronic devices. I make this affidavit in part from personal knowledge based on my participation in this investigation and as assisted by SA Cyber Stalker, Federal Bureau of Investigation (FBI), Camp Swamp, Louisiana 00012-0023.

On 24 August 2011, this office was notified by SA Cyber Stalker, Federal Bureau of Investigation (FBI), Camp Swamp, Louisiana, that about 1245, 20 August 2011, SSG James N. File, 123 Nowhere Avenue, Fort Swamp, Louisiana 00012-0023, transmitted over the internet three digital images of apparent prepubescent females being vaginally penetrated by an adult male. SA Stalker related the images were transmitted by way of a peer-to-peer (P2P) software, which allowed other Internet users to access his shared files for the purpose of uploading and downloading. SA Stalker requested to conducted a joint investigation with USACIDC SAs due to SSG File's military affiliation. (Continued, see attached)

2. The affiant further states that:

I have reason to believe SSG File is in possession of child pornography and distributed the child pornography when he shared, over the internet, material depicting minors engaged in sexually explicit acts or posing in a lewd and lascivious manner; which are violations of 18 USC § 2252 and 18 USC § 2252A. The contraband, evidence, fruits, and instrumentality of the crimes are believed to be maintained at the residence (123 Nowhere Avenue, Fort Swamp, Louisiana 00012-0023) of SSG File based on the files downloaded by the FBI from SSG File's Internet Protocol (IP) address, information gathered from the Internest Service Provider, and the statements SSG File made to law enforcement.

DA FORM 3744, SEP 2002   DA FORM 3744-R, MAR 85, IS OBSOLETE.   APD PE v1.01ES

Figure B-1. Sample DA Form 3744, page 1

3. In view of the foregoing, the affiant requests that an authorization be issued for a search of _____ SSG File and the residence
(the person) (and)

123 Nowhere Avenue, Fort Swamp, Louisiana 00012-0023 (Continued, see attached)
(the quarters or billets) (and)

_____ and (seizure) (apprehension) of _____ (See attached)
(the automobile) (   ) *(items persons searched for)*

TYPED NAME AND ORGANIZATION OF AFFIANT	SIGNATURE OF AFFIANT
SA Art E. Fishal 10th MP Group (CID), 1234 Fort Swamp CID Office, Fort Swampy, LA	*A. E. Fishal*

SWORN TO AND SUBSCRIBED BEFORE ME THIS ___9___ DAY OF ___September___ ___2011___ AT ___1000___

TYPED NAME, ORGANIZATION AND OFFICIAL CAPACITY OF AUTHORITY ADMINISTERING THE OATH	SIGNATURE OF AUTHORITY ADMINISTERING THE OATH
John A. Doe, Captain, JA, Military Magistrate Office of the Staff Judge Advocate, Fort Swampy, LA 00012-0023	*John A. Doe*

INSTRUCTIONS FOR

AFFIDAVIT SUPPORTING REQUEST FOR AUTHORIZATION TO SEARCH AND SEIZE OR APPREHEND

1. In paragraph 1, set forth a concise, factual statement of the offense that has been committed or the probable cause to believe that it has been committed. Use additional page if necessary.

2. In paragraph 2, set forth facts establishing probable cause for believing that the person, premises, or place to be searched and the property to be seized or the person(s) to be apprehended are connected with the offense mentioned in paragraph 1, plus facts establishing probable cause to believe that the property to be seized or the person(s) to be apprehended are presently located on the person, premises, or place to be searched. Before a person may conclude that probable cause to search exists, he or she must first have a reasonable belief that the person, property or evidence sought is located in the place or on the person to be searched. The facts stated in paragraphs 1 and 2 must be based on either the personal knowledge of the person signing the affidavit or on hearsay information which he/she has plus the underlying circumstances from which he/she has concluded that the hearsay information is trustworthy. If the information is based on personal knowledge, the affidavit should so indicate. If the information is based on hearsay information, paragraph 2 must set forth some of the underlying circumstances from which the person signing the affidavit has concluded that the informant (whose identity need not be disclosed) or his/her information was trustworthy. Use additional pages if necessary.

3. In paragraph 3, the person, premises, or place to be searched and the property to be seized or the person(s) to be apprehended should be described with particularity and in detail. Authorization for a search may issue with respect to a search for fruits or products of an offense, the instrumentality or means of committing the offense, contraband or other property the possession of which is an offense, the person who committed the offense, and under certain circumstances for evidentiary matters.

DA FORM 3744, SEP 2002
Page 2 of 2
APD PE v1.01ES

Figure B-2. Sample DA Form 3744, page 2

DA Form 3744-R
Continuation Sheet
SA Art E. Fishal
9 September 2011
Paragraph 1 (continued):

On 20 August 2011, the FBI conducted a preliminary investigation which revealed the Internet Protocol (IP) address from which the images were downloaded was registered to SSG Files residence and SSG Files name was the account holder for the internet service, this information was obtained through a subpoena served to Word Tech Fios Internet Service Provider (ISP).

On 23 August 2011, the FBI telephoned (123) 555-2345 (the number listed by the Bell South Telephone Company as belonging to SSG File) to conduct a pretext phone interview. A male answered the call an identified himself as Jim File. SA STALKER interviewed SSG File, stating she was a representative from a data software corporation. SA Stalker request that SSG File participate in a survey pertaining to computer usage, to which SSG File agreed. During the interview, SSG File stated he owned two desk top computers running Windows operating systems (one of which he built himself and the other was a Dell Optiplex 7300 with upgrades he performed). SSG File stated he built the first computer about 4 to 6 months ago and has been using it on the Internet ever since. SSG File related that he has owned the second computer since he purchased it in 2008 and that both computers have been connected to the internet for the past year. SSG File stated he was extremely proficient in computer usage, construction, and on-line access (citing he has been an on-line computer user for approximately 4 years and has been using the World Tech Fios as a network service provider for the past 1 ½ years). SSG File stated he spent approximately 4 to 6 hours per day using his computers on-line for educational, business, and recreational needs. When asked how many of the occupants of his residence used on-line services, SSG File stated he had three daughters (only one of which was old enough to use the computer; however, she could not do so without his password, which she did not know). SSG File also stated his wife occasionally used the computer, but did not do so frequently or with any level of proficiency.

During the conversation with SSG File it was determined the two computers were in his possession at the time the child pornographic images were transmitted and he confirmed the computers were still in his possession located at his residence; which he verified to be 123 Nowhere Avenue, Fort Swamp, Louisiana 00012-0023.

Paragraph 3 (continued):
The residence of 123 Nowhere Avenue, Fort Swamp, Louisiana 00012-0023,
The premise is 2.17 miles east of Highway 172. The single family ranch style house is approximates 200 feet from north side of the road and has a gravel driveway. The house has white metal roof and the exterior walls are an off-white color, with a stucco type covering. There is a tall television antenna on the roof. In front of the house is a small wishing well in the front yard. There is a small portable building in front of the house. To the east of the house there is a large metal building approximately 400 square feet in size. The building has galvanized metal siding. The address is on the right hand side of the mail box. Two small American flags are placed on each side of the entrance gate.

Based upon investigations conducted thus far, I expect to find on premises of SSG File, computers of several varieties and associated peripherals; to include, but not limited to, hard disk drives, removable data storage media, portable data storage devices, cameras, photographs, movies, manuals, notebooks, papers, and computer input and output devices all of which are used either as instrumentalities of criminal offenses or as storage devices for possible evidence of criminal offenses; and are believed to contain some or all of the evidence described in the warrant and evidence contained within the hardware described as,

Page 1 of 4

Figure B-3. Sample DA Form 3744 continuation sheet

but not limited to, text, graphics, electronic mail messages, and other data including deleted files and folders, containing material related to the sexual exploitation of minors; and/or material depicting apparent or purported minors engaged in sexually explicit conduct; and data and/or information used to facilitate access to, possession, distribution, and/or production of such materials. The computers are likely to take the form either of "mainframe" computers, or of "micro" or "personal" computers, either standing alone or joined through a series of connected computers called a "network".

The term "computer" as used herein is defined as set forth in 18 U.S.C. § 1030(e)(1), and includes any electronic, magnetic, optical, electrochemical, or other high speed data processing device performing logical, arithmetic, or storage functions, and includes any data storage facility or communications facility directly related to or operating in conjunction with such device.

Computer hardware is described as any and all computer equipment, including any electronic devices, which are capable of collecting, analyzing, creating, displaying, converting, storing, concealing, or transmitting electronic, magnetic, optical, or similar computer impulses or data. These devices include but are not limited to any data-processing hardware (such as central processing units, memory typewriters, and self-contained "laptop" or "notebook" computers); internal and peripheral storage devices (such as fixed disks, external hard disks, floppy disk drives and diskettes, tape drives and tapes, optical storage devices, and other memory storage devices); peripheral input/output devices (such as keyboards, printers, scanners, plotters, video display monitors, and optical readers); and related communications devices (such as modems, cables and connections, recording equipment, RAM or ROM units, acoustic couplers, automatic dialers, speed dialers, programmable telephone dialing or signaling devices, and electronic tone generating devices);as well as any devices, mechanisms, or parts that can be used to restrict access to such hardware (such as physical keys and locks).

Computer software is described as any and all information, including any instructions, programs, or program code, stored in the form not electronic, magnetic, optical, or other media which are capable of being interpreted by a computer its related components. Computer software may also include certain data, data fragments or control characters integral to the operation of computer software. These items include but not limited to operating system software, applications software, utility programs, compilers, interpreters, communications software, and other programming used or intended for use to communicate with computer components.

Computer-related documentation is described as any written, recorded, printed or electronically stored material, which explains or illustrates the configuration or use of any seized hardware, software, or related item.

Computer passwords and data security devices are described as all those devices, programs, or data-whether themselves in the nature of hardware or software that can be used or is designed for use to restrict access to or facilitate concealment of any computer hardware, computer software, computer- related documentation, electronic data, records, documents or materials within the scope of this application. These items include but are not limited to any data security hardware (such as any encryption devices, chips and circuit boards), passwords, data security software or information (such as test keys and encryption codes), and similar information that is required to access computer programs or data or to otherwise render programs or data into a useable form.

Based on training and through my personal use of computers, I have knowledge of the method by which files are transmitted over telephone or cable lines between computers. Based on my training and knowledge I know the following:

Page 2 of 4

Figure B-3. Sample DA Form 3744 continuation sheet (continued)

a. The Internet is a worldwide network of computer network systems operated by governmental entities, corporations, other commercial entities, universities and others. To access the Internet, an individual computer user must subscribe to an Internet Service Provider or ISP, which operates a host computer system with direct access to the Internet. In the work environment, many governmental entities, corporations and universities provided employees and students with access to the Internet and with e-mail accounts. The Army provides this service for its employees to accomplish the Army's mission.

b. A device known as a modem or a Network Interface Card (NIC) allows any computer to communicate with another computer through the use of telephone lines or cable. Even "wireless" communication at some point touches a telephone or cable line. The modem may be internal or external to the computer; the NIC is generally internal.

c. By connection to the Internet, either through a commercial ISP or through access provided by a private service provider such as the government, an individual with a computer and a modem or NIC can make electronic contact with millions of computers around the world.

d. With such a computer, a user can transport a computer file to his own computer, so that the computer file is stored in his computer. The process of transporting a file to one's own computer from another is called "downloading."

e. The user can then view the file on his/her computer screen (monitor), and can "save" or retain the file on his/her computer for an indefinite time period.

f. In addition to permanently storing the file on the computer, the user may print the file.

g. The original file that was downloaded is also maintained in the originating computer.

h. The user can also send a file from the user's computer to another computer on the Internet. This process of sending a file is called "uploading."

i. The process of "uploading" is similar to the "downloading" process except the user is sending the computer file to others instead of retrieving the information from another computer. As with the process of "downloading," the original file is maintained on the originating computer.

j. A user can also use Peer-to-peer (P2P) file sharing to allow users to download media files such as images and movies using a P2P software client that searches for other connected computers. The "peers" are computer systems connected to each other through the Internet. Thus, the only requirements for a computer to join peer-to-peer networks are an Internet connection and P2P software.

Based on my training, my experience and on conversations with other law enforcement agents, I know that searching for computerized information for evidence or instrumentalities of a crime commonly requires agents to seize most or all of a computer system's input/output peripheral devices, related software documentation, and data security devices (including passwords) so that a qualified computer expert can accurately conduct the search by retrieving the system's data in a laboratory or other controlled environment. This is true for the following reasons:

a. The volume of evidence. Computer storage devices (such as hard disks, diskettes, compact disks, tapes, etc.) can store the equivalent of thousands of pages of information. Much of this information may be unrelated to the focus of the search but is commingled with relevant information in a way that does not permit it to be easily or safely separated. For example, a user may seek to conceal evidence of criminal activity by storing it in random order with deceptive file names. Forensics examiners are thus required to

Page 3 of 4

Figure B-3. Sample DA Form 3744 continuation sheet (continued)

examine all the stored data to determine which particular files are evidence or instrumentalities of criminal activity. This sorting process can take weeks or months, depending upon the volume of data stored, and it would be impractical to attempt this kind of data analysis "on-site."
b. Technical requirements. Analyzing computer systems—to include those found within pagers, wireless phones, electronic organizers, data watches and desktop computers—for criminal evidence is a highly technical process requiring expert skill and a properly controlled environment. The vast array of computer hardware and software available requires even computer experts to specialize in some systems and applications. Thus, it is difficult to know prior to the search which expert possesses sufficient specialized skills to best analyze the system and its data. No matter which system is used, however, data analysis protocols are exacting scientific procedures, designed to protect the integrity of the evidence and to recover even "hidden," erased, compressed, password-protected, or encrypted files. Since computer evidence is extremely vulnerable to tampering or destruction (either from external sources or from destructive codes embedded in the system as a "booby trap"), a controlled environment is essential to its complete and accurate analysis.

In light of these concerns, I hereby request the Court's permission to seize the computer hardware (and associated peripherals) that are believed to contain some or all of the evidence described in the warrant, and to conduct an off-site search of the hardware for the evidence described, if, upon arriving at the scene, the agents executing the search conclude that it would be impractical to search the computer hardware on-site for this evidence.

Searching the computer system for the evidence described may require a range of data analysis techniques and take longer than a search not involving a computer hard drive. In some cases, it is possible for agents to conduct carefully targeted searches that can locate evidence without requiring a time-consuming manual search through unrelated materials that may be commingled with criminal evidence. For example, agents may be able to execute a "keyword" search that searches through the files stored in a computer for special words that are likely to appear only in the materials covered by a warrant. Similarly, agents may be able to locate the materials covered in the warrant by looking for particular directory or file names. In other cases, however, such techniques may not yield the evidence described in the warrant. Criminals can mislabel or hide files and directories; encode communications to avoid using key words; attempt to delete files to evade detection; or take other steps designed to frustrate law enforcement searches for information. These steps may require agents to conduct more extensive searches, such as scanning areas of the disk not allocated to listed files, or opening every file and scanning its contents briefly to determine whether it falls within the scope of the warrant. In light of these difficulties, I request that USACIDC forensic examiners be given permission to use whatever data analysis techniques appear necessary to locate and retrieve the evidence described in Attachment B and be granted a sufficient period of time in which to conduct the search to allow for technical difficulties and backlogs related to forensic examinations.

If, after inspecting the input/output peripheral devices, system software, and pertinent computer related documentation, it becomes apparent that these items are no longer necessary to retrieve and preserve the evidence, such materials and/or equipment will be returned within a reasonable time.

Page 4 of 4

Figure B-3. Sample DA Form 3744 continuation sheet (continued)

SEARCH AND SEIZURE AUTHORIZATION

For use of this form, see AR 27-10; the proponent agency is OTJAG

TO: *(Name and Organization of the person to whom authorization is given)*
SA Art E. Fishal or any other USACIDC Special Agent or other person designated by USACIDC, 10th MP Group (CID), 1234 Fort Swamp CID Office, Fort Swampy, LA 00012-0023

(An affidavit) (A (sworn) or (unsworn) oral statement) having been made before me by ___SA Art E. Fishal___
(Name of Affiant)

10th MP Group (CID), 1234 Fort Swamp CID Office, Fort Swampy, LA 00012-0023
(Organization or Address of Affiant)

(which affidavit is attached hereto and made a part of this authorization), and as I am satisfied that there is probable cause to believe that the matters mentioned in the affidavit are true and correct, that the offense set forth therein has been committed, and that the property to be seized is located *(on the person)* *(at the place)* to be searched, you are hereby ordered to search the *(person)* *(place)* known as

123 Nowhere Avenue, Fort Swampy, LA 00012-0023 (including all vehicles and storage facilities located at the premises).

for the property described as ___(See attached continuation sheet).___

bringing this order to the attention of the *(person searched)* *(person in possession, if any, that can be found at the place or on the premises searched)*. The search will be made in the *(daytime)* *(nighttime)*, and if the property is found there, you shall seize it, issue a receipt therefor to the person from whom the property is taken or in whose possession the property is found, deliver the property to:

SA Art E. Fishal, 10th MP Group (CID), 1234 Fort Swamp CID Office, Fort Swampy, LA 00012-0023
(Name and Organization of Authorized Custodian)

and prepare a written inventory of the property. If there is no person at the searched place to whom the receipt may be delivered, the receipt will be left in a conspicuous location at the place or on the premises where the property is found.

Dated this ___9___ day of ___September___, ___2011___.

TYPED NAME AND GRADE OF AUTHORIZING OFFICIAL	DUTY POSITION OF AUTHORIZING OFFICIAL
John A. Doe Captain, JA	Military Magistrate

ORGANIZATION OF AUTHORIZING OFFICIAL	SIGNATURE OF AUTHORIZING OFFICIAL
Office of the Staff Judge Advocate Fort Swampy, LA 00012-0023	*John A. Doe*

DA FORM 3745, SEP 2002   DA FORM 3745-R, MAR 85, IS OBSOLETE   APD PE v1.02ES

Figure B-4. Sample DA Form 3745

DA Form 3745
Continuation Sheet

SA Art E. Fishal
9 September 2011

Evidence of certain activities relating to material involving the sexual exploitation of minors (18 USC § 2252) and/or certain activities relating to material constituting or containing child pornography (18 USC § 2252A), maintained within computers of several varieties and associated peripherals; to include, but not limited to, hard disk drives, removable data storage media, portable data storage devices, cameras, photographs, movies, manuals, notebooks, papers, and computer input and output devices all of which are used either as instrumentalities of criminal offenses or as storage devices for possible evidence of criminal offenses

The evidence is described as, but not limited to, text, graphics, electronic mail messages, and other data including deleted files and folders, containing material related to the sexual exploitation of minors; and/or material depicting apparent or purported minors engaged in sexually explicit conduct; and data and/or information used to facilitate access to, possession, distribution, and/or production of such materials. The computers are likely to take the form either of "mainframe" computers, or of "micro" or "personal" computers, either standing alone or joined through a series of connected computers called a "network".

The term "computer" as used herein is defined as set forth in 18 U.S.C. § 1030(e)(1), and includes any electronic, magnetic, optical, electrochemical, or other high speed data processing device performing logical, arithmetic, or storage functions, and includes any data storage facility or communications facility directly related to or operating in conjunction with such device.

Computer hardware is described as any and all computer equipment, including any electronic devices, which are capable of collecting, analyzing, creating, displaying, converting, storing, concealing, or transmitting electronic, magnetic, optical, or similar computer impulses or data. These devices include but are not limited to any data-processing hardware (such as central processing units, memory typewriters, and self-contained "laptop" or "notebook" computers); internal and peripheral storage devices (such as fixed disks, external hard disks, floppy disk drives and diskettes, tape drives and tapes, optical storage devices, and other memory storage devices); peripheral input/output devices (such as keyboards, printers, scanners, plotters, video display monitors, and optical readers); and related communications devices (such as modems, cables and connections, recording equipment, RAM or ROM units, acoustic couplers, automatic dialers, speed dialers, programmable telephone dialing or signaling devices, and electronic tone generating devices);as well as any devices, mechanisms, or parts that can be used to restrict access to such hardware (such as physical keys and locks).

Computer software is described as any and all information, including any instructions, programs, or program code, stored in the form not electronic, magnetic, optical, or other media which are capable of being interpreted by a computer its related components. Computer software may also include certain data, data fragments or control characters integral to the operation of computer software. These items include but not limited to operating system software, applications

page 1 of 2

Figure B-5. Sample DA Form 3745 continuation sheet showing a detailed property description

software, utility programs, compilers, interpreters, communications software, and other programming used or intended for use to communicate with computer components.

Computer-related documentation is described as any written, recorded, printed or electronically stored material, which explains or illustrates the configuration or use of any seized hardware, software, or related item.

Computer passwords and data security devices are described as all those devices, programs, or data- whether themselves in the nature of hardware or software that can be used or is designed for use to restrict access to or facilitate concealment of any computer hardware, computer software, computer- related documentation, electronic data, records, documents or materials within the scope of this application. These items include but are not limited to any data security hardware (such as any encryption devices, chips and circuit boards), passwords, data security software or information (such as test keys and encryption codes), and sim1ilar information that is required to access computer programs or data or to otherwise render programs or data into a useable form.

page 2 of 2

Figure B-5. Sample DA Form 3745 continuation sheet showing a detailed property description (continued)

Appendix C
Forensic Experiential Trauma Interview

Most traditional interview techniques focus on obtaining information stored using cognitive brain functions (who, what, were, why, when, and how). During a traumatic event the brain may not process this type of information. Traditional techniques may actually inhibit accurate disclosure, create false information, and damage or destroy fragile testimonial evidence. In cases involving individuals experiencing extreme stress, fear, or trauma, investigators should employ the FETI technique. The FETI technique can increase the likelihood that relevant and accurate information can be obtained from these individuals.

HUMAN INFORMATION PROCESSING

C-1. Witnesses and victims of trauma do not mentally process the experience in the same way in which they process nontraumatic events. Most interview techniques trained and used by LE personnel focus on obtaining cognitive information such as the color of shirt, a description of the suspect, the timeframe, and other important information generally required to answer the essential elements of an investigation (who, what, where, why, when, and how). These details are routinely missing from a victim's memory.

C-2. The FETI technique was originally developed for interviewing victims of sexual assault; it is most helpful when interviewing traumatized individuals that have experienced an event resulting in emotional feelings of fear, shock, anger, rage, sadness, or other base emotion. While originally designed to interview traumatized victims, the FETI technique can also be useful when employed during routine indirect interviews of individuals under less traumatic or emotional circumstances. It can also be effective in obtaining information from suspects.

C-3. Obtaining information from an individual requires some understanding of how people in general perceive and retrieve information. Without this knowledge, it is possible that an investigator may misinterpret information and direct the individual further way from the real truth.

C-4. There is a common misconception that the human mind acts like a video recorder, capturing and storing all experiences exactly as they occur. Perception, memory (storage), and recall (retrieval) of information are active mental processes. A multitude of factors within any of these three mental processes can affect a person's ability to gather the information, retrieve it, and then articulate it accurately. These processes are describe as follows:

- **Perception.** Humans do not passively record events as they occur in the environment. They actively gather and process sensory information. An individual selectively pays attention to certain elements while filtering out others, all the while actively interpreting their possible meanings and interrelationships. Perceptions become the assumed reality on which people operate. This has a number of important implications for Army LE personnel attempting to obtain information. The investigator must recognize that information received from a specific individual may not necessarily be a true representation of what happened.
- **Memory.** The memory consists of three stages. The first is sensory memory, in which stimuli are only momentarily registered to facilitate perception. The second is short-term memory, also known as active or working memory. The function of short-term memory is to hold information while it is being processed (eventually to be eliminated or transferred to long-term memory). The third stage is long-term memory.
- **Recall.** Just as human perceptions are constructed, rather than recorded, the memories themselves are "reconstructions." Event memories can be altered by information inserted or suggested during attempts to retrieve them. One proposed cause of these errors can be an

individual's difficulty or inability to distinguish the source of a given unit of information. The line between information developed internally (in one's head) and information formed externally (actual experience) is inconsistent. Stress, even at moderate levels, can impair memory recall. Additionally, trauma and stress can naturally create fragmented memories, loss of certain memories (either temporarily or permanently), and false memories.

C-5. The brain is optimized for reacting to fear and trauma by closing down the majority of the cognitive functions at the time of the event or experience; it also reduces the cognitive functions during recall of the event or experience. During the traumatic event the cognitive (thinking) brain may close down leaving the more primitive areas of the brain (the mid brain and brainstem) to control behavior and record memories. These primitive areas of the brain function at a more instinctive level; they do not record memories in the typical manner in which the thinking portion of the brain does. These instinctive portions of the brain are primarily designed for survival and focus on recording experiential information and sensations (such as sights, sounds, smells, tastes and feelings) instead of peripheral and "fact-based" information.

C-6. Due to the affects of trauma and extremely emotional events on the human memory, the FETI technique is the best and arguably only method to successfully obtain victim or witness information regarding a traumatic event. While the primitive brain is dominant during a traumatic event, it is also active during less stressful situations; this fact enables investigators to use the FETI technique very effectively when interviewing individuals who are providing information of a more routine nature.

TECHNIQUES AND CONSIDERATIONS

C-7. During a FETI, the investigator approaches the victim or witness of a crime or other event by addressing the instinctive feelings and experiences that the individual likely retained. The FETI process obtains significantly more information about the experience, enhances an individual's ability to recall his experiences, reduces the potential for false information, and allows the individual to recount the experience in the manner in which the incident was experienced.

C-8. The concept and approach of this technique can be described as a forensic physiological investigation; it is an opportunity for the individual to describe the experience of an event both physically and emotionally. This significantly enhances the quality and quantity of testimonial and associated physiological evidence obtained. These interview techniques can result in significantly more information than traditional interview techniques. They not only reduce the inacuracy of the information provided but can greatly enhance understanding of the experience. The technique also provides the individual a better avenue for disclosure, reducing the potential for defensive feelings and uncooperative behavior, which can limit the information provided to an investigator. During a typical FETI the investigator should use the following guidelines:

- Acknowledge the individual's trauma and/or pain.
- Ask the individual—
  - What he is able to remember about his experience.
  - About his thought process at particular points during his experience.
  - How this experience affected him physically and emotionally.
  - About sensory memories such as sounds, sights, smells, and feelings before, during, and after the incident.
  - What the difficult part of the experience was for him.
- Clarify other information and details.

ACKNOWLEDGEMENT OF TRAUMA OR PAIN

C-9. The investigator should not begin too rapidly. The session should begin with the investigator acknowledging the pain and emotion the individual may be suffering. This helps the investigator put the individual at ease and shows the individual that the investigator empathizes with him.

MEMORY OF THE EXPERIENCE

C-10. After acknowledging the individual's trauma or pain and allowing him some time, the investigator should ask what he is able to remember about his experience. Two key words in this question are "able" and "experience." Not all individuals are able to recall all significant information about something that happened to them, either initially or over a period of time. Using the word "able" may relieve some pressures on the trauma victim. This may calm the victim and increase the information he is able to provide. Using the term "experience" encourages the individual to describe his actual experience. It also relieves pressure that the individual may feel to try to figure out what is important to the investigator. As the individual describes his experience, the investigator gains a better understanding of what happened as the events are recounted, typically in great detail.

C-11. Following the initial open-ended prompt, employ active listening techniques allowing the individual to free-flow his description of what he remembers about his experience. The investigator can enhance this description by adding open-ended prompts such as "tell me more about that" or "tell me more about ____." This technique will enable the individual to recall even more significant information about his experience by prompting his memory in a more natural way. Open-ended prompts should include the individual's emotional and physical experiences before, during, and after the reported incident or event. Do not tell the individual to start at the beginning; this technique often inhibits trauma memory recall. Provide an opportunity for the individual to communicate his experience in the manner in which he recalls what happened. This is much more effective than initially requiring the individual to provide a chronological narrative. A sequential narrative may come to the individual later.

THOUGHT PROCESS

C-12. Ask the individual about his thought process at particular points during the experience. What was he thinking and how was he processing the experiences. This will enable investigators to better understand the actions, inactions, and behaviors of the individual before, during, and after the event. This will also reduce or even eliminate the need for the investigator to ask the individual why he did or did not do something such as intervene, fight back, kick, scream, or run. Questions of this nature have been proven to increase the anxiety of the individual, close him down, increase false information, and destroy or damage fragile trauma memories. Asking what his thought process was not only provides additional understanding of the individual's reaction and behaviors, but also increases his ability to recall additional information. For example, an individual may have been sexually assaulted, and during the sexual assault they may have "frozen." Asking him what he was thinking at the time he was being assaulted may prompt responses such as, "I thought he was going to kill me," or "I couldn't move or scream," or "I couldn't understand what was happening at that moment." This type of information not only assists the investigator in gaining a better understanding of why the individual reacted in a certain way, but also identifies significant physiological evidence that may help prove, disprove, or corroborate the reported offense.

PHYSICAL AND EMOTIONAL AFFECT

C-13. Ask the individual how this experience affected him physically and emotionally. How the individual felt before, during, and after the event under investigation is fundamentally important for the investigator to understand and collect. This is extremely important because understanding the effects of the assault will increase the investigator's understanding of the context of the individual's experience. During fear-producing and traumatic events the individual may experience the emotional feelings of fear, shock, anger, rage, sadness, or other base emotion. He may also experience reactions to the trauma including the emotional feelings combined with the physical reactions to stress such as shortness of breath, increased heart rate, dilated pupils, muscle rigidity and/or pain, light-headedness, or headache. Identifying and properly documenting these reactions to their experience are essential pieces of information that can greatly assist the investigator in understanding the context of the experience and provide significant physiological evidence.

SENSORY MEMORIES

C-14. Ask about sensory memories such as sounds, sights, smells, and feelings before, during, and after the incident. Because the brain is optimized to collect, store, and recount this information far more efficiently than peripheral information or details, this can be crucial evidence to collect. Recalling specific sensory information may also enable an individual to recall associated details that have been repressed.

MOST DIFFICULT EXPERIENCE

C-15. Ask the individual what the most difficult part of the experience was for them. Trauma victims will often repress extremely difficult to handle information about their experiences. Inquiry about the most difficult part of the experience may provide significant evidence of the trauma experience and/or crime and can increase understanding of the overall incident and circumstances.

DETAIL CLARIFICATION

C-16. The interviewer should clarify other information and cognitive details (to determine who, what, where, when, and how) after facilitation and collection of the physiological evidence. Although the mid-brain and brainstem collect, store, and recall information pertaining to the experience, the cognitive brain may have collected (or is able to retrieve from other portions of the brain) information that can be relevant to answering who, what, where, when, and how questions.

C-17. Investigators should be careful about asking specific questions pertaining to length of time and elements of distance due to the fact that fear and trauma often distorts time and distance. Few people can estimate time and distance accurately. Instead, investigators should have the witness physically show them the distance by walking it on the ground or pointing out the distance using reference points. The investigator can then measure the distance and record it. An investigator should not ask for duration unless the interview shows a specific reason the victim knows the time; for example, "I was staring at the clock on the bedside table when I heard a loud noise." The investigator should explore the additional peripheral and who, what, where, when, and how type of information in a sensitive and empathetic manner taking great care not to inhibit or change already fragile memories of the individual. By avoiding direct questions throughout most of the interview, the individual is open to respond with more detail.

Appendix D

Forms

This appendix provides examples of forms required for LE investigations. Each section includes line-by-line descriptions explaining the entries into each section of the specific form.

DEPARTMENT OF THE ARMY FORM 2823

D-1. Sworn statements are recorded on DA Form 2823. Figures D-1 through D-3, pages D-2 through D-4, provide samples of a DA Form 2823. To permit written statements to be admissible in court, they must be carefully and completely prepared. Block-by-block instructions for completing DA Form 2823 include—

- **Block 1.** Enter the geographic location; for example, the city or installation in which the statement is rendered.
- **Block 2.** Enter the date of the interview. Have the individual being interviewed initial above the date after he signs the sworn affidavit located on the last page of the statement.
- **Block 3.** Have the individual write in the time and initial above it after he signs the sworn affidavit located on the last page of the statement.
- **Block 4.** Enter the CID or military police case file sequence number.
- **Block 5.** Enter the individual's last name, first name, and middle initial.
- **Block 6.** Enter the individual's SSN.
- **Block 7.** Enter the military or civilian pay grade of the person being advised; for example E-3, O-3, GS-09, or "Civ" if there is no military affiliation. If the person is in the military, indicate his status as active duty, USAR, or ARNG.
- **Block 8.** Enter the individual's complete military or governmental organization including unit, installation, state, and zip code, Army Post Office (APO), or Fleet Post Office (FPO). If interviewing a civilian who does not have any military affiliation, enter his current home address including the city, state, and zip code, APO, or FPO.
- **Block 9.** In most cases, the statement will consist of a narrative section followed by a question and answer portion. The narrative format is where the individual provides his version of events in a logical story-based format in his own words (but not necessarily verbatim). After the entire story is laid out in the narrative format, questions and answers will be used to draw out inconsistencies, gaps, and other issues that are not clear. If the elements of proof were not adequately addressed in the narrative, they must be addressed by specific questions that will draw out these details. Seasoned investigators may use several questions to resolve one element of an offense, as opposed to formulating one question directly from the UCMJ. For example, do not ask the individual, "When you struck the man in the head with the brick, did you intend to cause grievous bodily harm or death?" because this may compel the individual to lie. Instead the investigator should ask the following:
  - "Why did you hit the man with the brick?"
  - "What did you think would happen when you hit him in the head with the brick?"
  - "Did you think that hitting him in the head could seriously hurt him?"
  - "Why didn't you just use your fist?"
  - "Did you want to hurt this man?"
  - "Do you think striking someone with a brick could kill them?"

SWORN STATEMENT
For use of this form, see AR 190-45; the proponent agency is PMG.

PRIVACY ACT STATEMENT

AUTHORITY: Title 10, USC Section 301; Title 5, USC Section 2951; E.O. 9397 Social Security Number (SSN).

PRINCIPAL PURPOSE: To document potential criminal activity involving the U.S. Army, and to allow Army officials to maintain discipline, law and order through investigation of complaints and incidents.

ROUTINE USES: Information provided may be further disclosed to federal, state, local, and foreign government law enforcement agencies, prosecutors, courts, child protective services, victims, witnesses, the Department of Veterans Affairs, and the Office of Personnel Management. Information provided may be used for determinations regarding judicial or non-judicial punishment, other administrative disciplinary actions, security clearances, recruitment, retention, placement, and other personnel actions.

DISCLOSURE: Disclosure of your SSN and other information is voluntary.

1. LOCATION	2. DATE (YYYYMMDD)	3. TIME	4. FILE NUMBER
Fort Lewis, WA	2012/01/11	1443	0033-02CID018-32656

5. LAST NAME, FIRST NAME, MIDDLE NAME	6. SSN	7. GRADE/STATUS
FISHAL, Art Vandalay	000-00-0000	SFC/AD

8. ORGANIZATION OR ADDRESS
B CO, 3/47 Infantry Battalion, Fort Lewis, WA 98433

9. I, Art V. Fishal _____, WANT TO MAKE THE FOLLOWING STATEMENT UNDER OATH:

Around 1800, 10 Sep 02, I received a telephone call from my friend, Bobby J. STELLS, (NFI), who asked me to meet him at Young's Bar and Grill, Tacoma, WA 98435. I was told there was a new disco band playing at the club and some of the band members were asking if anyone in the area had some marihuana for sale. I told STELLS that I still had plenty of marihuana to sell if they were willing to pay whatever the local price was. Around 1900, 10 Sep 02, I opened my safe and removed approximately 80 grams of marihuana and placed it inside a small trash bag. I then placed the trash bag containing the marihuana under the passenger seat of my pickup truck in order to transport it to Young's Bar and Grill. About 1945, 10 Sep 02, I departed my safe and drove directly to Young's Bar and Grill in order to meet the band members and sell them the marihuana. I was met by STELLS at the front door fo teh bar, prior to meeting any of the band members. STELLS asked me how much marihuana I brought and how much it would cost. I told STELLS that I brought enough marihuana to last the band throughout the entire week they would be in Washington, and that it would cost $500.00, which was not negotiable. STELLS told me the price was fair and the band should have no problem paying that amount. Around 2300, 10 SEP 02, I met with one of the band members who introduced himself by the name "Big Joe" (NRI). Big Joe told me that he and his other band members needed marihuana in order to continue playing, as they were starting to lose thier sanity. I handed Big Joe the trash bag containing the marihuana and he handed me a piece of paper, which indicated he would make restitution after his band completed their performance later that night. Initially, I told Big Joe that would not be acceptable; however, I felt intimidated by him and realized I should do what he said. Big Joe asked me if I wanted to go back to the dressing and smoke some of the marihuana with him and his partner prior to the concert. We waited a few minutes, but the other band members never showed up. So STELLS, Big Joe, and myself went back to the dressing room and smoked three joints, which he told me to roll. Around 0010, 11 Sep 02, Big Joe departed our company stating he needed to go do what it was he came to, which I assumed he meant to perform with the band. A few minutes later, Big Joe came back to the room and took the bag of marihuana. I stayed in the dressing room enjoying my buzz and I must have passed out. When I woke up, the police were asking me about the joint remnants in the ashtray next to me. I told them I didn't know what they were talking about. They told me they would check it for fingerprints, at which time I knew I was already in trouble and told them that it was mine. While being transported to the Police Station, I asked the officers why they were at the club, and they informed me that' an anonymous male caller had notified them that I was in the dressing room and that I was in possession of marihuana. I asked about the band, and they told me that the bar was closing when they arrived and there was no band there. It was at that time, that I realized that Big Joe had made the phone call and skipped out to avoid paying me for the drugs.

Q: What was the name of the Band "Big Joe" was playing in?
A: I'm not sure, but the sign on the door said "The Boogie Brothers" were playing live that night, so I think that was the name of Joe's band.
Q: Where is the band from?
A: Again I don't know, but I remember Big Joe saying something about New Orleans.
Q: How long were they in Washington State?

10. EXHIBIT	11. INITIALS OF PERSON MAKING STATEMENT	
	AVF	PAGE 1 OF 3 PAGES

ADDITIONAL PAGES MUST CONTAIN THE HEADING "STATEMENT OF _____ TAKEN AT _____ DATED _____

THE BOTTOM OF EACH ADDITIONAL PAGE MUST BEAR THE INITIALS OF THE PERSON MAKING THE STATEMENT, AND PAGE NUMBER MUST BE INDICATED.

DA FORM 2823, NOV 2006   PREVIOUS EDITIONS ARE OBSOLETE   APD PE v1.01ES

Figure D-1. Sample DA Form 2823, page 1

Forms

USE THIS PAGE IF NEEDED. IF THIS PAGE IS NOT NEEDED, PLEASE PROCEED TO FINAL PAGE OF THIS FORM.

STATEMENT OF Art V. Fishal   TAKEN AT Fort Lewis, W.A.   DATED 2012/01/11

9. STATEMENT (Continued)

A: I don't know, STELLS told me they were going to be here for a week, but I think that either he lied to me, or they lied to him.
Q: Do you know where they were going next?
A: I don't have any idea, but I know they're a traveling band.
Q: Describe the man you call "Big Joe".
A: He was a black male, approximately 73 inches tall, 300 lbs, short black hair, and he was around 49 years old.
Q: Did you observe any identifying marks, scars or tattoos on Big Joe?
A: Yes, he had a pierced left ear, from which he wore a trumpet earring; he had a tattoo of a really cool cross on his right hand.
Q: Do you know what Big Joe did in the band?
A: Based on the trumpet earring and a comment he made about blowing notes. I assume he played the trumpet.
Q: Describe STELLS?
A: He's a white male, approximately 71 inches tall, 180 pounds, about 2? years old. He has severe acne, a nose ring, short black hair, kind of tan, and he has a tattoo of a rat on his right shoulder. He also walks with a slight limp, I think he might have hurt himself recently.
Q: How do you know STELLS?
A: We inprocessed together at the Fort Lewis Replacement Center. We kind of became friends, and I see him downtown about once or twice a week.
Q: Where can we find STELLS?
A: He was in the Army, I think was a medic or something. I don't know exactly when he came in, but he was a private when we inprocessed together in April of 2000. I think he got chaptered out of the Army for using drugs around July of 2002. I don't know exactly where he lives, I think it is on Freak Street, but I've never been to his house.
Q: Did you ever meet any other members of the band?
A: No.
Q: It is my understanding that you took 80 grams of marihuana to Young's Bar and Grill for the purpose of selling it to a party you did not know for the amount of $500.00; that you provided the marihuana to the party in question (Big Joe), but you did not receive the money for this transaction because you passed out, he skipped out, and you were arrested. Is this accurate?
A: Yes-he got my dope, but I didn't get paid.
Q: Since you entered the Army, how many times have you consumed controlled substances?
A: I've been smoking marihuana off and on since I was about 16 years old. I would say I have smoked marihuana about twice a week for the past 10 years.
Q: Have you consumed any other types of drugs while serving in the Army?
A: Yes, I have used cocaine periodically.
Q: What do you mean periodically.
A: I would say only at parties when other people have it. Maybe once a month or so.
Q: Who do you get your drugs from?
A: I buy all my marihuana in bulk, as I sell most of it, and just use what I want. I get it from a guy by the name of Stan DELEVERS, who is a SGT in the 1/48th FA, on Fort Lewis. He has a cousing who has a plantation somewhere in Oregon. I don't have a steady source of cocaine, but I only do it with people I trust. The only ones I remember doing it with are MAJ Licks PAYNE, and SSG Les CHAPTER, both assigned to the Ranger Bat. They always provide it to me.
Q: What do you mean when you say "plantation"?
A: I mean an area where he cultivates marihuana plants, harvests them, then sells the marihuana.
Q: Do you know his cousin's name?
A: No, SGT DELVERS just calls him Johnny.
Q: Do you know where this plantation is located?
A: No, but I think it is located in the southern part of Oregon. Somewhere near Mount Ashland.
Q: Where did you get the marihuana you provided to Big Joe?
A: I got that from SGT DELEVERS about three days ago.
Q: How much marihuana did you obtain from SGT DELEVERS on this occasion?
A: He provided me with three pounds. I sell it, then give him the money before he gives me my next shipment.
Q: How often do you get shipment from him?
A: Generally about once every two weeks.
Q: How much do you pay him for these shipments. AVF

INITIALS OF PERSON MAKING STATEMENT
AVF

PAGE 2 OF 3 PAGES

DA FORM 2823, NOV 2006   APD PE v1.01ES

Figure D-2. Sample DA Form 2823, page 2, continuation page

19 August 2013   ATP 3-39.12   D-3

STATEMENT OF ___Art V. Fishal___ TAKEN AT ___Fort Lewis, WA___ DATED ___2012/01/11___

9. STATEMENT *(Continued)*

A: Unless I specify otherwise, he always gives me about three pounds. For this I pay him $4,000.00, which is the price I get from him due to our friendship.

Q: How much do you sell the marihuana for?

A: I generally sell it for $2,000.00 a pound; or about $150.00 to $300.00 per ounce, depending on if I know the person I'm selling it to .

Q: Who do you sell marihuana to?

A: I don't know many of thier names off the top of my head, but I keep a ledger in my safe which contains all of the names, dates and amounts of these transactions.

Q: Do you have any other controlled substances in your safe?

A: Yes, I have about 2 pounds of marihuana in the safe right now.

Q: Where do you keep this safe?

A: I didn't think it was safe at my house if I got raided, so being smart, I keep my safe at the storage unit I rent at World Wide Storage, located on Loser Ave, in Tacoma, WA. My storage unit is number C-76.

Q: How do you know you were providing 80 grams of marihuana to Big Joe?

A: The only thing I use my storage unit for is my drug trade. I have scales, bags, coffee and other items in there that I use to evade detection by the police. I used the scales to measure out how much I was giving to them.

Q: Who else knew you were making this transaction?

A: Nobody, I'm pretty smart and I don't talk about my business.

Q: Why did you decide to tell us the truth about your drug related activities?

A: Because I knew I was busted and I figured it was better just to lay it all out.

Q: Is there anything you would like to add or delete from this statement at this time?

A: Yes, I would like to apologize to my commander and first sergeant, I know I've let them down, but I hope they will still support me.

Q: Is there anything else you would like too add to this statement?

A: NO

///END OF STATEMENT/// AVF

AFFIDAVIT

I, Art V. Fishal _____, HAVE READ OR HAVE HAD READ TO ME THIS STATEMENT WHICH BEGINS ON PAGE 1, AND ENDS ON PAGE ___3___. I FULLY UNDERSTAND THE CONTENTS OF THE ENTIRE STATEMENT MADE BY ME. THE STATEMENT IS TRUE. I HAVE INITIALED ALL CORRECTIONS AND HAVE INITIALED THE BOTTOM OF EACH PAGE CONTAINING THE STATEMENT. I HAVE MADE THIS STATEMENT FREELY WITHOUT HOPE OF BENEFIT OR REWARD, WITHOUT THREAT OF PUNISHMENT, AND WITHOUT COERCION, UNLAWFUL INFLUENCE, OR UNLAWFUL INDUCEMENT.

(Signature of Person Making Statement)

WITNESSES: Bob C. Ozark

SA Bob C. Ozark

Fort Lewis RA CID

Fort Lewis, WA 98643

ORGANIZATION OR ADDRESS

Subscribed and sworn to before me, a person authorized by law to administer oaths, this __11__ day of ___January___, __2012__

at Fort Lewis, WA 98643

(Signature of Person Administering Oath)

SA Noel S. Jones

(Typed Name of Person Administering Oath)

ART 136 UCMJ

(Authority To Administer Oaths)

INITIALS OF PERSON MAKING STATEMENT AVF

PAGE 3 OF 3 PAGES

DA FORM 2823, NOV 2006

APD PE v1.01ES

Figure D-3. Sample DA Form 2823 page 3, affidavit or final page

D-2. The statement must specify the times and dates of specific acts and the methods used to complete the crime. During the interview and subsequent statement, investigators should attempt to—

- Identify suspects, accomplices, witnesses, and persons who knew of the crime.

- Account for stolen property and instruments used in the crime.
- Tie the evidence to the victim and/or a suspect.

D-3. The individual must be given the chance to edit the statement when it is completed. The first step in this editing process is to ask, "Is there anything you would like to add or delete from this statement at this time?" This question is repeated until an answer of "No" is received. After the last word in the body of the statement, write "End of Statement" to close it out. When preparing statements, LE personnel should use the language of the interviewee and avoid substituting their own verbiage, particularly legal or "cop" language that an interviewee would not typically understand.

D-4. If the statement will not fit on the front, back, and top of the final page of DA Form 2823, use continuation pages. A sample continuation page is shown at figure D-2, page D-3. Begin the statement on the front of DA Form 2823. Line out the reverse side with one diagonal line drawn from corner to corner if the page is not needed. Do not include the lined-out side of the form in the page count; it does not need to be initialed. Use white bond paper for your continuation pages. Each page must have a heading giving the same information as the heading of DA Form 2823 and bearing the word "continued." The bottom of each continuation page must show the initials of the person making the statement and cite the page number in relation to the total pages of the statement. Instructions for using continuation pages can be found at the bottom of page 1, DA Form 2823. Conclude the statement on page 3 (final page) where the affidavit is printed.

D-5. Before administering the oath of affirmation, the individual being interviewed must read the entire statement or have it read to him. The individual must line through and correct all misstatements, errors, and corrections as he edits his statement. It is generally an accepted practice to program several easy to identify typographical errors into the statement, which the individual should identify, correct, and initial during his review. This helps to establish that the individual read the statement before signing it and that he felt comfortable changing errors or misstatements. If a mistake is found after the statement is completed, line the word out, write the correction above the mistake, and have the individual initial the correction. Do not use correction tape or white correction fluid to correct errors.

D-6. The affidavit is the last section of DA Form 2823. It states that the information was given voluntarily and that all mistakes and corrections on the statement were corrected and initialed by the individual. It shows that the number of pages in the statement was verified. Before administering the oath, the investigator must have the individual read the affidavit out loud, which will allow the investigator to refute later claims that the individual could not read and was too embarrassed to tell the investigator. The individual could also claim that, even though he could not read, he signed the statement to avoid ridicule. The investigator should then ask the individual what the oath means to him. Having the individual state in his own words what the oath means will allow the investigator to testify to the individual's level of reading comprehension. Administering the oath is accomplished when the investigator raises his right hand and has the individual providing the statement raise his right hand and the investigator asks, "Do you swear or affirm that this statement is true and correct to the best of your knowledge, so help you God." If the individual objects to the use of the word God, the investigator deletes it from the oath and then reads the oath again.

D-7. After the individual answers the oath in the affirmative, the investigator has the individual place his initials in block 2 and write the current time in block 3 along with his initials. The investigator should also have the individual initial beside the first and last word on the page and on the bottom of each page of the statement. The individual signs the affidavit on the line above "signature of person making statement" (page 3). The investigator signs the affidavit on the line above "signature of person administering oath" (page 3). Additionally, the investigator must type or print his name on the line above "typed name of person administering oath" and the authority on the line above "authority to administer the oath." The authority for military investigative personnel to administer an oath is Article 136 (b)4 UCMJ. The authority for civilian investigative personnel, to include civilian USACIDC SAs, is 5 USC 303. The affidavit page is included in the page count of the statement even if it contains no text from the statement. It is an integral part of the statement.

DEPARTMENT OF THE ARMY FORM 3881

D-8. DA Form 3881 is used when advising military and civilian witnesses or suspects of their rights. This section describes the preparation of a DA Form 3881. A sample DA Form 3881 is provided at figure D-4 and figures D-5 and D-6, pages D-8 and D-9.

RIGHTS WARNING PROCEDURE/WAIVER CERTIFICATE

For use of this form, see AR 190-30; the proponent agency is PMG

DATA REQUIRED BY THE PRIVACY ACT

AUTHORITY: Title 10, United States Code, Section 3012(g)

PRINCIPAL PURPOSE: To provide commanders and law enforcement officials with means by which information may be accurately identified.

ROUTINE USES: Your Social Security Number is used as an additional/alternate means of identification to facilitate filing and retrieval.

DISCLOSURE: Disclosure of your Social Security Number is voluntary.

1. LOCATION	2. DATE	3. TIME	4. FILE NO.
Fort Leonard Wood, MO	12 January 2012		0012-02-CID901

5. NAME (Last, First, MI)	8. ORGANIZATION OR ADDRESS
WRIGHT, John D.	HHC, 26th Infantry Battalion

6. SSN	7. GRADE/STATUS
000-00-0000	E5/RA

Fort Leonard Wood, MO 65473

PART I - RIGHTS WAIVER/NON-WAIVER CERTIFICATE

Section A. Rights

The investigator whose name appears below told me that he/she is with the United States Army Criminal Investigation Command As A Special Agent _____ and wanted to question me about the following offense(s) of which I am suspected/accused: Robbery, Kidnapping///

Before he/she asked me any questions about the offense(s), however, he/she made it clear to me that I have the following rights:

1. I do not have to answer any question or say anything.

2. Anything I say or do can be used as evidence against me in a criminal trial.

3. *(For personnel subject to the UCMJ)* I have the right to talk privately to a lawyer before, during, and after questioning and to have a lawyer present with me during questioning. This lawyer can be a civilian lawyer I arrange for at no expense to the Government or a military lawyer detailed for me at no expense to me, or both.

- or -

(For civilians not subject to the UCMJ) I have the right to talk privately to a lawyer before, during, and after questioning and to have a lawyer present with me during questioning. I understand that this lawyer can be one that I arrange for at my own expense, or if I cannot afford a lawyer and want one, a lawyer will be appointed for me before any questioning begins.

4. If I am now willing to discuss the offense(s) under investigation, with or without a lawyer present, I have a right to stop answering questions at any time, or speak privately with a lawyer before answering further, even if I sign the waiver below.

5. COMMENTS *(Continue on reverse side)*

Section B. Waiver

I understand my rights as stated above. I am now willing to discuss the offense(s) under investigation and make a statement without talking to a lawyer first and without having a lawyer present with me.

WITNESSES (If available)	
1a. NAME (Type or Print)	3. SIGNATURE OF INTERVIEWEE
SA Josephine P. Garrett	
b. ORGANIZATION OR ADDRESS AND PHONE	4. SIGNATURE OF INVESTIGATOR
Fort Leonard Wood Resident Agency CID Fort Leonard Wood, MO 65473	
2a. NAME (Type or Print)	5. TYPED NAME OF INVESTIGATOR
	SA Regina R. Brown
b. ORGANIZATION OR ADDRESS AND PHONE	6. ORGANIZATION OF INVESTIGATOR
	Fort Leonard Wood RA, CID Fort Leonard Wood, MO 65473

Section C. Non-waiver

1. I do not want to give up my rights

☐ I want a lawyer   ☐ I do not want to be questioned or say anything

2. SIGNATURE OF INTERVIEWEE

ATTACH THIS WAIVER CERTIFICATE TO ANY SWORN STATEMENT *(DA FORM 2823)* SUBSEQUENTLY EXECUTED BY THE SUSPECT/ACCUSED

DA FORM 3881, NOV 1989   EDITION OF NOV 84 IS OBSOLETE.   APD LF v2.02ES

Figure D-4. Sample 1, DA Form 3881

RIGHTS WARNING PROCEDURE/WAIVER CERTIFICATE
For use of this form, see AR 190-30; the proponent agency is PMG

DATA REQUIRED BY THE PRIVACY ACT

AUTHORITY:	Title 10, United States Code, Section 3012(g)
PRINCIPAL PURPOSE:	To provide commanders and law enforcement officials with means by which information may be accurately identified.
ROUTINE USES:	Your Social Security Number is used as an additional/alternate means of identification to facilitate filing and retrieval.
DISCLOSURE:	Disclosure of your Social Security Number is voluntary.

1. LOCATION	2. DATE	3. TIME	4. FILE NO.
Fort Leonard Wood, MO	12 January 2012		0911-02-CID901

5. NAME (Last, First, MI)	8. ORGANIZATION OR ADDRESS
SMITH, Everett R.	A CO, 1/55th Engineer Battalion

6. SSN	7. GRADE/STATUS	Fort Leonard Wood, MO 65473
000-00-0000	E4/RA	

PART I - RIGHTS WAIVER/NON-WAIVER CERTIFICATE

Section A. Rights

The investigator whose name appears below told me that he/she is with the United States Army ___Office of the Provost Marshal as a Military Police Investigator___ and wanted to question me about the following offense(s) of which I am suspected/accused: Assault///

Before he/she asked me any questions about the offense(s), however, he/she made it clear to me that I have the following rights:

1. I do not have to answer any question or say anything.
2. Anything I say or do can be used as evidence against me in a criminal trial.
3. *(For personnel subject to the UCMJ)* I have the right to talk privately to a lawyer before, during, and after questioning and to have a lawyer present with me during questioning. This lawyer can be a civilian lawyer I arrange for at no expense to the Government or a military lawyer detailed for me at no expense to me, or both.

   - or -

   (For civilians not subject to the UCMJ) I have the right to talk privately to a lawyer before, during, and after questioning and to have a lawyer present with me during questioning. I understand that this lawyer can be one that I arrange for at my own expense, or if I cannot afford a lawyer and want one, a lawyer will be appointed for me before any questioning begins.
4. If I am now willing to discuss the offense(s) under investigation, with or without a lawyer present, I have a right to stop answering questions at any time, or speak privately with a lawyer before answering further, even if I sign the waiver below.

5. COMMENTS *(Continue on reverse side)*

Waived legal rights, but declined to initial or sign DA Form 3881. INV Metelski brought in to witness waiver.

Section B. Waiver

I understand my rights as stated above. I am now willing to discuss the offense(s) under investigation and make a statement without talking to a lawyer first and without having a lawyer present with me.

WITNESSES (If available)	3. SIGNATURE OF INTERVIEWEE
1a. NAME (Type or Print) INV Donald A. Metelski	
b. ORGANIZATION OR ADDRESS AND PHONE Law Enforcement Command Fort Leonard Wood, MO 65473	4. SIGNATURE OF INVESTIGATOR
2a. NAME (Type or Print)	5. TYPED NAME OF INVESTIGATOR INV Chance C. Davis
b. ORGANIZATION OR ADDRESS AND PHONE	6. ORGANIZATION OF INVESTIGATOR Law Enforcement Command Fort Leonard Wood, MO 65473

Section C. Non-waiver

1. I do not want to give up my rights
   - ☐ I want a lawyer
   - ☐ I do not want to be questioned or say anything

2. SIGNATURE OF INTERVIEWEE

ATTACH THIS WAIVER CERTIFICATE TO ANY SWORN STATEMENT *(DA FORM 2823)* SUBSEQUENTLY EXECUTED BY THE SUSPECT/ACCUSED

DA FORM 3881, NOV 1989   EDITION OF NOV 84 IS OBSOLETE.   APD LF v2.02ES

Figure D-5. Sample 2, DA Form 3881

PART II - RIGHTS WARNING PROCEDURE

THE WARNING

1. WARNING - Inform the suspect/accused of:
   a. Your official position.
   b. Nature of offense(s).
   c. The fact that he/she is a suspect/accused.
2. RIGHTS - Advise the suspect/accused of his/her rights as follows:
   "Before I ask you any questions, you must understand your rights."
   a. "You do not have to answer my questions or say anything."
   b. "Anything you say or do can be used as evidence against you in a criminal trial."
   c. (For personnel subject to the UCMJ) "You have the right to talk privately to a lawyer before, during, and after questioning and to have a lawyer present with you during questioning. This lawyer

can be a civilian you arrange for at no expense to the Government or a military lawyer detailed for you at no expense to you, or both."
- or -
(For civilians not subject to the UCMJ) You have the right to talk privately to a lawyer before, during, and after questioning and to have a lawyer present with you during questioning. This lawyer can be one you arrange for at your own expense, or if you cannot afford a lawyer and want one, a lawyer will be appointed for you before any questioning begins."
   d. "If you are now willing to discuss the offense(s) under investigation, with or without a lawyer present, you have a right to stop answering questions at any time, or speak privately with a lawyer before answering further, even if you sign a waiver certificate."

Make certain the suspect/accused fully understands his/her rights.

THE WAIVER

"Do you understand your rights?"
(If the suspect/accused says "no," determine what is not understood, and if necessary repeat the appropriate rights advisement. If the suspect/accused says "yes," ask the following question.)

"Have you ever requested a lawyer after being read your rights?"
(If the suspect/accused says "yes," find out when and where. If the request was recent (i.e., fewer than 30 days ago), obtain legal advice whether to continue the interrogation. If the suspect/accused says "no," or if the prior request was not recent, ask him/her the following question.)

"Do you want a lawyer at this time?"
(If the suspect/accused says "yes," stop the questioning until he/she has a lawyer. If the suspect/accused says "no," ask him/her the following question.)

"At this time, are you willing to discuss the offense(s) under investigation and make a statement without talking to a lawyer and without having a lawyer present with you?" (If the suspect/accused says "no," stop the interview and have him/her read and sign the non-waiver section of the waiver certificate on the other side of this form. If the suspect/accused says "yes," have him/her read and sign the waiver section of the waiver certificate on the other side of this form.)

SPECIAL INSTRUCTIONS

WHEN SUSPECT/ACCUSED REFUSES TO SIGN WAIVER CERTIFICATE: If the suspect/accused orally waives his/her rights but refuses to sign the waiver certificate, you may proceed with the questioning. Make notations on the waiver certificate to the effect that he/she has stated that he/she understands his/her rights, does not want a lawyer, wants to discuss the offense(s) under investigation, and refuses to sign the waiver certificate.

IF WAIVER CERTIFICATE CANNOT BE COMPLETED IMMEDIATELY: In all cases the waiver certificate must be completed as soon as possible. Every effort should be made to complete the waiver certificate before any questioning begins. If the waiver certificate cannot be completed at once, as in the case of street interrogation, completion may be temporarily postponed. Notes should be kept on the circumstances.

PRIOR INCRIMINATING STATEMENTS:
1. If the suspect/accused has made spontaneous incriminating statements before being properly advised of his/her rights he/she should be told that such statements do not obligate him/her to answer further questions.

2. If the suspect/accused was questioned as such either without being advised of his/her rights or some question exists as to the propriety of the first statement, the accused must be so advised. The office of the serving Staff Judge Advocate should be contacted for assistance in drafting the proper rights advisal.

NOTE: If 1 or 2 applies, the fact that the suspect/accused was advised accordingly should be noted in the comment section on the waiver certificate and initialed by the suspect/accused.

WHEN SUSPECT/ACCUSED DISPLAYS INDECISION ON EXERCISING HIS OR HER RIGHTS DURING THE INTERROGATION PROCESS: If during the interrogation, the suspect displays indecision about requesting counsel (for example, "Maybe I should get a lawyer."), further questioning must cease immediately. At that point, you may question the suspect/accused only concerning whether he or she desires to waive counsel. The questioning may not be utilized to discourage a suspect/accused from exercising his/her rights. (For example, do not make such comments as "If you didn't do anything wrong, you shouldn't need an attorney.")

COMMENTS (Continued)

REVERSE OF DA FORM 3881

Figure D-6. Sample reverse side of DA Form 3881

D-9. This form is filled out each time an accused or suspected person is questioned. It is best to fill out the administrative data on the form first. Block-by-block instructions for completing DA Form 3881 include—

- **Block 1.** Enter the geographic location; for example, the city or installation and the state in which the form will be executed. Do not enter specifics such as a building number or military police station.
- **Block 2.** Enter the date (day, month, and year). Have the suspect initial above the date.
- **Block 3.** Have the suspect write in the time and initial above it after he has been administered the rights warning.
- **Block 4.** Enter the CID or military police case file sequence number.
- **Block 5.** Enter the suspect's last name, first name, and middle initial.
- **Block 6.** Enter the suspect's SSN.
- **Block 7.** Enter the military or civilian pay grade of the person being advised; for example, E-3, O-3, GS-09, or enter "Civ" if there is no military affiliation. If the person is in the military, indicate their status as active duty, USAR, or ARNG.
- **Block 8.** Enter the individual's complete military or governmental organization including unit, installation, state, and zip code, APO, or FPO. If interviewing a civilian who does not have any military affiliation, enter his current home address including the city, state, and zip code, APO, or FPO.
- **Part I, Section A.** Enter the applicable organization and status of the person issuing the rights warning, such as "Criminal Investigation Command as a Special Agent" or "Provost Marshal's Office as a Military Police Investigator." A formal accusation can only be accomplished through the referral of charges. Investigative personnel will always line through the word "accused" to ensure that the suspect understands that he is merely a suspect. However, if interviewing someone subsequent to the referral of charges, the word "accused" should not be stricken. The investigator must then orient the suspect toward the nature of the offense for which he is suspected. Plain language should be used (not a statute or other citation). For example, if suspected of murder, the word "murder" would be entered in this section, not Article 118 UCMJ. After all suspected offenses have been indicated, three slashes (////) should be placed behind the last offense cited. Having the suspect draw in the slashes and initial both where the word "accused" was stricken and again following the slashes will help to show the suspect's understanding of his status in the interview and specifically what offenses he is being interviewed about.
- **Blocks 1 through 4.** Administer the rights warning advisement by reading the information, starting with number 2, that is located in the warning section on the reverse side of DA Form 3881, shown at figure D-6, page D-9. The investigator should provide the rights waiver certificate that is located on the front of DA Form 3881 to the suspect for him to follow. Upon completion of the rights warnings advisement, the investigator administers the rights waiver advisement by reading verbatim the questions in quotations that are located in the waiver section on the reverse side of another DA Form 3881. Proper use of DA Form 3881 will help investigators ensure that only knowing and voluntary waivers are obtained.
- **Block 5.** Use the comments section to record clarification questions posed to the suspect and his responses. If additional space is required, use the comments section located on the reverse side of the form. Because of the "McOmber Rule" being abolished, there is no longer a requirement to ask if the suspect has requested an attorney after being read his rights within the past 30 days. The suspect's attorney is only required to be present if the subject asks for an attorney; unless the interview is conducted after preferral of charges and the questioning concerns the matters that are related to the preferral and when the presence of counsel is otherwise constitutionally required. MRE 305(e)(2) covers postpreferral questioning.
- **Part I, Section B, Blocks 1 through 2.** All witnesses to a rights warning, which may include military police and/or investigators, parents or guardians of juveniles, and military sponsors, should print their names in the blocks dedicated to witnesses (blocks 1a or 2a). Additionally, the witness should record their unit or organization, address, and telephone number in blocks 1b or

2b. It is also a good idea to have the witness initial adjacent to their name (see figure D-5, page D-8.

- **Block 3.** If the suspect states the following: (1) I understand my rights, (2) I have not requested an attorney after being read my rights, (3) I do not want an attorney, and (4) I am willing to make a statement, he has waived his rights and should sign his name in this block (see figure D-4, page D-7. If the suspect has questions or does not answer the questions to the satisfaction of the investigator to show that he knowingly and voluntarily waived his rights, the investigator must provide clarification or ask additional questions. The investigator must do this before having the suspect sign the waiver certificate.

- **Blocks 4 through 6.** The special agent or military policeman administering the rights advisement signs in block 4 and prints or types his name in block 5. The investigator's unit of assignment should be entered in block 6.

- **Part I, Section C, Blocks 1 and 2.** If the suspect invokes their rights by requesting counsel or declines to discuss the offenses at that time, he should then check the appropriate boxes in block 1 and sign in block 2. If the suspect invokes his rights and declines to sign the document, the investigator may write, "declined to sign" in block 3 (see figure D-5). Once the suspect invokes his legal rights, the investigator must stop all discussions that are designed or likely to cause the suspect to be incriminated. If a suspect did not request an attorney, but related he did not desire to be interviewed at that time, he may be reapproached by investigators after two hours. However, if the suspect requested counsel, the investigator may not reapproach the individual until 14 days after the end of custody. In cases where a suspect requests a lawyer and the suspect remains in custody of LE personnel, the suspect may not be questioned without their lawyer present for the duration of their custody. SJA should be consulted for guidance on this or any other irregularities concerning rights waivers.

D-10. In the instance that a suspect waives his rights but declines to sign the DA Form 3881, this fact may be recorded both in Part I, Section A, block 5 (comments) and in Part I, Section B, block 3 (signature of interviewee). Whenever possible, such waivers should be witnessed by at least one other party. This can be accomplished by simply bringing a third party into the interview room and asking the suspect if he was advised of his rights, understood his rights, and is willing to discuss the offenses under investigation but did not want to sign the form. If the suspect affirms this to be true and accurate, the witness should sign his name in Part I, Section B, block 1a to confirm his presence during this portion of the interview (see figure D-4).

DEPARTMENT OF THE ARMY FORM 4137

D-11. Regardless of how evidence is obtained, Army LE personnel will inventory and account for all physical evidence on a DA Form 4137. The LE personnel who first acquired the evidence must prepare the DA Form 4137 with an original and three copies. The last copy of the signed DA Form 4137 will be provided as a receipt to the person releasing the evidence if the evidence is received from a person. If the evidence is not collected from an individual (such as evidence collected while processing a crime scene or through chance discovery) all copies of the DA Form 4137 will be turned over to the evidence custodian for processing and distribution. A sample DA Form 4137 is shown at figures D-7 through D-9, pages D-13 through D-15. Block-by-block instructions for completing DA Form 4137 include—

- **MPR or CID Sequence Number.** Enter the military police report number or CID sequence number assigned to the investigation.

- **CID ROI Number.** Enter the CID ROI number assigned to the investigation.

- **Receiving Activity.** Enter the office conducting the investigation (such as 75th Military Police Detachment [CID]).

- **Location.** Room number, building number, installation, state, and zip code of the office conducting the investigation.

- **Name, Grade, and Title of Person From Whom Received.** If the evidence is received from a person, the "Owner" or "Other" block is checked (as appropriate). If the evidence is not received from a person the "Other" block is checked and a term such as "crime scene" or "found" should be entered in this block.

- **Address.** Enter the address of the person from whom the evidence is obtained. If not applicable, write "NA" in the block.
- **Location From Where Obtained.** Enter the location of the evidence at the time it was acquired. This may include a sketch if required to accurately describe the location. If found on a person, enter the person's name, location, and, rank (if a military member).
- **Reason Obtained.** When an item is possible evidence, "evidence," "safe keeping," or "found property," may be entered as appropriate.
- **Time and date Obtained.** Use the alphanumeric format (such as 1500, 15 Sep XX or 1500-1600, 15 Sep XX).
- **Item No.** Enter the number assigned to the item (corresponding with the item number shown on the evidence tag). Each item should be assigned a separate item number. In cases when like items are found at the same place and are grouped together, one entry number is sufficient.
- **Quantity.** Each item will normally be listed by itself. When like items are grouped, you may list them under one entry (for example, 20 pills).
- **Description of Articles.** Enter a detailed and accurate description of each item of evidence. Describe the item's physical characteristics and condition, especially if the item is valuable. The value of articles is never estimated or listed, nor is the type of metal or stone in the case of jewelry or similar items, beyond stating their color, size, and shape. If the item is marked for identification, describe the mark and the mark's location. If evidence is marked, the investigator should mark it with his initials and the date and time the evidence was collected. The words "LAST ITEM" are placed in capital letters after the last item listed. These words are centered on the page, and solid lines are drawn or capital Xs placed from the words to the margin on each side of the form. A continuation page may be used if needed. Figure D-9, page D-15, shows a sample continuation page.

D-12. Chain of custody section is used to document the physical accountability of the evidence. This section of the DA Form 4137 should be completed as follows (see figure D-7 and figure D-8, page D-14):

- **Item No.** Enter the item number. If several items, you may list them all in one block.
- **Date.** Enter the date that the item was received or released. Use alphanumeric format for day, month, and year (6 Jun 11).
- **Released By. Obtain the n**ame and signature of the person from whom the property was taken. Should the person refuse or be unable to sign, his name and grade is entered with "refused to sign" or "unable to sign" entered into the block When the evidence is obtained directly from the crime scene or found by Army LE personnel, the first "released by" block should be annotated as nonapplicable or "N/A."
- **Received By.** The first entry in this block should be the Army LE person receiving the property. Each time the evidence changes possession, the chain of custody change should be documented accordingly.
- **Purpose of Change of Custody.** The purpose for the change of custody should be described briefly, such as "evaluation as evidence" or "released to evidence custodian." This procedure is followed for each custody change.

D-13. The location and document number, located at the bottom of the first page of the form, is assigned to the document by the evidence custodian. The location should be written in pencil (such as "safe 1, shelf 4"). The document number is a two-part number consisting of the sequenced number of the document for the year and the year the document was initiated. For example "1-07" represents the first evidence custody document received in the calendar year 2007; "27-10" represents the 27th evidence custody document received in the calendar year 2010.

D-14. The final disposal action section is used by the evidence custodian and the approving authority in making final disposition of the evidence (see figure D-8). Completion of this section only pertains to documents retained by the evidence custodian. The number of the item is entered on the destroy line. The name, rank, or address will be entered on line one (person to receive property). For evidence which will be destroyed, the item number and method of destruction is indicated (such as "ITEM 1 - BURN").

D-15. The final disposal authority section is completed when the evidence is of no further value. Portion number one is completed by the evidence custodian. The second portion is completed by the individual authorized to grant final disposal authority. The witness to destruction of evidence section is completed for any items of evidence that are destroyed. The witness will place his name, organization, and signature in this section.

EVIDENCE/PROPERTY CUSTODY DOCUMENT

For use of this form see AR 190-45 and AR 195-5; the proponent agency is US Army Criminal Investigation Command

MPR/CID SEQUENCE NUMBER	0038-06-CID122
CRD REPORT/CID ROI NUMBER	15378
RECEIVING ACTIVITY	75th Military Police Detachment (CID)
LOCATION	Fort Belvoir, VA 22060
NAME, GRADE AND TITLE OF PERSON FROM WHOM RECEIVED	☐ OWNER ☑ OTHER — Death Sentence
ADDRESS (Include Zip Code)	N/A
LOCATION FROM WHERE OBTAINED	White Chevy S-10 Pickup of PV2 McVeigh while parked adj. 9100 Shenandoah Road, Fort Belvoir, VA 22060
REASON OBTAINED	Evidence
TIME/DATE OBTAINED	1730-1905 06 Jan 06

ITEM NO.	QUANTITY	DESCRIPTION OF ARTICLES (Include model, serial number, condition and unusual marks or scratches)
1	1	Revovler, Colt brand, .38 cal, 2" barrel, black, with scuffed brown wooden-type hand grips, bearing manufacturers markings "Colt Firearms Div, Harford, CT USA ," and SN: 754341. Arrows are scratched on rear face of cylinder on each side of chamber which was positioned under the firing pin. Superglue fumed for latent prints and sealed in a cardboard gun box. The seals and box were marked for ID with DKS/1730/6 Jan 06. (Obtained from left hand of deceased victim in driver's seat)
2	1	Cartridge casing, .38 cal, barss in color metal-type, bearing a small indentation in the approximate center of the primer end and manufacturer's markings "Federal .38 Special" on rim of cartridge base. Superglue fumed for latent prints and sealed in a clean pill box. The seals and box were marked for ID with DKS/1801/6 Jan 06. (Extracted from item #1 above)
3	1	Bag, clear plastic, zip lock type, in a closed condition, containing three hadn rolled cigarettes filled with unknown vegetable matter. Superglue fumed for latent prints and placed in a clean plastic heat sealed bag which was sealed. The seal was embossed with a seal unique to the office and marked for ID with DKS/1820/6 Jan 06. (Obtained from crack between driver's seat and center console)
4	1	Ring, gold in color, metal-type, mounted to the ring is a diamond-like stone. Inscribed on the inside of the band is "Maria October 10, 1986 18k." THe bad is in a worn condition. Sealed in a clean pill box. The seals and box were marked for ID with DKS/1827/6 Jan 06. (Obtained from cup holder in a center console)
5	9	Pills, oval, bearing the number "205" on one side, about 1/2 inch by 1/4 wide by 1/8 inch. Placed in a clean pill box that was sealed in a clean plastic heat sealed bag which was sealed. The seal was embossed with aa seal unique to this office and marked for ID with DKS/1830/6 Jan 06. (Driver's side floor board) (Continued on page 2)

CHAIN OF CUSTODY

ITEM NO.	DATE	RELEASED BY	RECEIVED BY	PURPOSE OF CHANGE OF CUSTODY
1-7	6 Jan 06	SIGNATURE: N/A NAME, GRADE OR TITLE: DEATH SCENE	SIGNATURE: David K. Schuman NAME, GRADE OR TITLE: SA DAVID K. SCHUMAN	Evaluation as Evidence.
3	6 Jan 06	SIGNATURE: David K. Schuman NAME, GRADE OR TITLE: SA DAVID K. SCHUMAN	SIGNATURE: N/A NAME, GRADE OR TITLE: Field Test	Small unmeasurable quantity consumed in the field test. (See CID Form 36)
1-7	9 Jan 06	SIGNATURE: David K. Schuman NAME, GRADE OR TITLE: SA DAVID K. SCHUMAN	SIGNATURE: Gary B. Belcher NAME, GRADE OR TITLE: SA GARY B. BELCHER	Released to Evidence Custodian SCRCNI
		SIGNATURE: Gary B. Belcher NAME, GRADE OR TITLE: SA GARY B. BELCHER	SIGNATURE: Registered Mail NAME, GRADE OR TITLE: RA 123456789 US	Forwarded to USACIL for exam
		SIGNATURE: Registered Mail NAME, GRADE OR TITLE: RA 223456789 US	SIGNATURE: David W. Hill NAME, GRADE OR TITLE: DAVID W. HILL, GS-09	Received at USACIL for examination

DA FORM 4137, 1 JUL 1976 — Replaces DA FORM 4137, 1 Aug 74 and DA FORM 4137-R Privacy Act Statement 26 Sep 75 Which are Obsolete — LOCATION 1-3/5-7 USACIL 4 SIDL — DOCUMENT NUMBER D33-06 — APD PE v1.00

Figure D-7. Sample DA Form 4137, page 1

ITEM NO.	DATE	CHAIN OF CUSTODY *(Continued)*		PURPOSE OF CHANGE OF CUSTODY
		RELEASED BY	RECEIVED BY	
1→3 and 5-7	02 MAR 06	SIGNATURE *David W. Hill* NAME, GRADE OR TITLE DAVID W. HILL, GS-09	SIGNATURE *Federal Express* NAME, GRADE OR TITLE 4452886710	Returned to submitter
1-3 and 5-7	03 MAR 06	SIGNATURE *Federal Express* NAME, GRADE OR TITLE 4452886710	SIGNATURE *Paul W. McDonald* NAME, GRADE OR TITLE SA PAUL W. MCDONALD	Received by Evidence Custodian SCRCNI
06	10 MAR 06	SIGNATURE *Paul W. McDonald* NAME, GRADE OR TITLE SA PAUL W. MCDONALD	SIGNATURE *Donna C. Hansen* NAME, GRADE OR TITLE DONNA C. HANSEN, MAJ	Released to SJA-IC for review. Sealed container opened.
6	10 MAR 10	SIGNATURE *Donna C. Hansen* NAME, GRADE OR TITLE DONNA C. HANSEN, MAJ	SIGNATURE *Paul W. McDonald* NAME, GRADE OR TITLE SA PAUL W. MCDONALD	Returned to Evidence custodian. Item resealed.
1 and 4	16 SEP 06	SIGNATURE *Paul W. McDonald* NAME, GRADE OR TITLE SA PAUL W. MCDONALD	SIGNATURE *Registered Mail* NAME, GRADE OR TITLE RA 234567890 US	Forwarded to owner. Return receipt attached. Final disposition.
2 and 7	16 SEP 06	SIGNATURE *Paul W. McDonald* NAME, GRADE OR TITLE SA PAUL W. MCDONALD	SIGNATURE *Destroyed-Rendered* NAME, GRADE OR TITLE useless/harmless	Final Disposition
3 and 5	16 SEP 06	SIGNATURE *Paul W. McDonald* NAME, GRADE OR TITLE SA PAUL W. MCDONALD	SIGNATURE *Destroyed* NAME, GRADE OR TITLE By Burning	Final Disposition
6	16 SEP 06	SIGNATURE *Paul W. McDonald* NAME, GRADE OR TITLE SA PAUL W. MCDONALD	SIGNATURE *Released to* NAME, GRADE OR TITLE Case File	Final Disposition

FINAL DISPOSAL ACTION

RELEASE TO OWNER OR OTHER *(Name/Unit)* Items #1&4-Next of Kin (Mrs. Becky McVeigh, 123 3rd Street, Fairfax, VA 22345)

DESTROY. Items 2&7 by crushing/destroying. Items 3&5 by burning.

OTHER *(Specify)* Item 6-Case file.

FINAL DISPOSAL AUTHORITY

ITEM(S) 1 thru 7 ON THIS DOCUMENT, PERTAINING TO THE INVESTIGATION INVOLVING E-2/PV2 *(Grade)*

JAMES M. MCVEIGH _____ 232d Engr Co, 22 FSB, Fort Belvoir, VA 22060 _____ (IS) (ARE) NO LONGER
(Name) *(Organization)*

REQUIRED AS EVIDENCE AND MAY BE DISPOSED OF AS INDICATED ABOVE. *(If article(s) must be retained, do not sign, but explain in separate correspondence.)*

DONNA C. HANSEN, MAJ, Ch Crim Law _____ *Donna C. Hansen* _____ 15 Sep 06
(Typed/Printed Name, Grade, Title) *(Signature)* *(Date)*

WITNESS TO DESTRUCTION OF EVIDENCE

THE ARTICLE(S) LISTED AT ITEM NUMBER(S) 3 and 5 _____ (WAS) (WERE) DESTROYED BY THE EVIDENCE CUSTODIAN, IN MY PRESENCE, ON THE DATE INDICATED ABOVE.

SA CRAIG P. BROTT, 75th MP Det (CID), Fort Belvoir, VA 22060 _____ *Craig P. Brott*
(Typed/Printed Name, Organization) *(Signature)*

APD PE v1.00

Figure D-8. Sample DA Form 4137, page 2

EVIDENCE/PROPERTY CUSTODY DOCUMENT

For use of this form see AR 190-45 and AR 195-5; the proponent agency is US Army Criminal Investigation Command

MPR/CID SEQUENCE NUMBER
0038-06-CID122

CRD REPORT/CID ROI NUMBER
15378

RECEIVING ACTIVITY	LOCATION
75th Military Police Detachment (CID)	Fort Belvoir, VA 22060

NAME, GRADE AND TITLE OF PERSON FROM WHOM RECEIVED

☐ OWNER
☑ OTHER   Death Sentence

ADDRESS (Include Zip Code)
N/A

LOCATION FROM WHERE OBTAINED	REASON OBTAINED	TIME/DATE OBTAINED
White Chevy S-10 Pickup of PV2 McVeigh while parked adj. 9100 Shenandoah Road, Fort Belvoir, VA 22060	Evidence	1730-1905 06 Jan 06

ITEM NO.	QUANTITY	DESCRIPTION OF ARTICLES (Include model, serial number, condition and unusual marks or scratches)
6	1	Piece of paper, white lined spiral type, approximately 8 1/2" x 11", bearing the handwritten words "We are through. I have taken the kids and moved out. Do not try to find or contact me" in blue ink and in a cursive writing style on one side. No visible marks or writings on the reverse side. Sealed in a paper envelope to protect for latent prints. The envelope and seals were marked for ID with DKS/1850/6 Jun 06. (Lap of the deceased victim in driver's seat)
7	1	Bottle, brown smoked glass, 12 oz size, empty, bearing a paper label. Printed on the label was "Sam Adams...Winter Blend..." The bottle was superglue fumed for latent prints and sealed in a clean paper sack. The seals and sack were marked for ID with DKS/1905/6 Jan 06. (Passenger side floor board) //LAST ITEM//

CHAIN OF CUSTODY

ITEM NO.	DATE	RELEASED BY	RECEIVED BY	PURPOSE OF CHANGE OF CUSTODY
1-7	6 Jan 06	SIGNATURE: N/A NAME, GRADE OR TITLE: DEATH SCENE	SIGNATURE: NAME, GRADE OR TITLE: SA DAVID K. SCHUMAN	Evaluation as Evidence.
3	6 Jan 06	SIGNATURE: NAME, GRADE OR TITLE: SA DAVID K. SCHUMAN	SIGNATURE: N/A NAME, GRADE OR TITLE: Field Test	Small unmeasurable quantity consumed in the field test. (See CID Form 36)
1-7	9 Jan 06	SIGNATURE: NAME, GRADE OR TITLE: SA DAVID K. SCHUMAN	SIGNATURE: NAME, GRADE OR TITLE: SA GARY B. BELCHER	Released to Evidence Custodian SCRCNI
		SIGNATURE: NAME, GRADE OR TITLE:	SIGNATURE: NAME, GRADE OR TITLE:	
		SIGNATURE: NAME, GRADE OR TITLE:	SIGNATURE: NAME, GRADE OR TITLE:	

DA FORM 4137, 1 JUL 1976   Replaces DA FORM 4137, 1 Aug 74 and DA FORM 4137-R Privacy Act Statement 26 Sep 75 Which are Obsolete   LOCATION _____   DOCUMENT NUMBER _____   APD PE v1.00

Figure D-9. Sample DA Form 4137, continuation page

DEPARTMENT OF THE ARMY FORM 4002

D-16. DA Form 4002, shown at figure D-10, page D-16, is used to mark and identify evidence collected at a crime scene. The first DA LE officer assuming custody of evidence will mark the evidence itself for future identification. The marking will consist of the time and date of acquisition and the initials of the person who assumes custody of the evidence. Caution must be taken in order to prevent cross-contamination of evidence at all levels of evidence processing. If marking the evidence itself is not possible or practical, the evidence will be put in a container that is sealed and marked. See chapter 2 and AR 195-5 for additional information and guidance.

D-17. A self-adhesive DA Form 4002 will be attached to each item of evidence or evidence container at the earliest opportunity to identify and control it. Items that are grouped together and listed as a single item on the DA Form 4137 (for example, a box containing tools) should be tagged with only one DA Form 4002. The DA Form 4002 should be attached directly to the item of evidence or the evidence container, or affixed to a blank shoe tag and attached to the item.

Figure D-10. Sample DA Form 4002 with instructions

DEPARTMENT OF THE ARMY FORM 3946

D-18. A DA Form 3946 is prepared for all accidents reported to the military police. This form is needed to document the collision scene and associated personnel and vehicles. This form should be accompanied by sworn statements (DA Form 2823), detailed scene diagrams, notes, photographs, and other documentation as required based on the severity of the collision. Figures D-11 through D-14, pages D-23 through D-26, provide samples of DA Form 3946. DA Form 3946 is used to—

- Record information concerning collisions reported to and investigated by the military police.
- Provide information to commanders concerning collisions involving members of their commands.
- Provide information concerning collisions to those involved in the accident or their representatives.
- Provide management information for analysis, review, and development of accident prevention and safety programs.

D-19. Military vehicles are always designated "Vehicle Number 1" if a military vehicle is involved. If there are no military vehicles involved, or if all vehicles are military, then numbering is based on whatever is easier or makes sense to the person completing the form. The form is designed for one- or two-car collisions. If three or more vehicles are involved, additional continuation forms are required. If continuation forms are used, the drivers and occupants should be listed on the same form as their respective vehicles. Block-by-block instructions for completing DA Form 3946 include—

- **Block 1.** Insert the MPR number, CID ROI number (if applicable), and any other report number prescribed by the local PM SOP. If these numbers are not known, leave this space blank.
- **Block 2.** Enter the year, month, and day on which the collision occurred. For example, 30 April 2011 would be entered, "20110430."
- **Block 3.** Enter the time in hours and minutes at which the collision occurred. Use military time (such as 2350 hours). Time of collisions means actual moment of the incident, not the time the collision was reported and not the time the investigation began.
- **Block 4.** Enter the day of the week on which the collision occurred.
- **Block 5, Location of Accident.** This section provides the description for the location of the collision including—
  - **Block 5a.** Indicate with an "X" whether the collision occurred on or off a military reservation. Enter the route number and/or the name of the highway or street, road, alley, or such on which the collision occurred. Use the official name rather than some nickname.
  - **Block 5b.** If the collision occurred on a military reservation or in a city, enter the name of the reservation or city and state. If outside the United States, enter the name of the reservation, state or district, and the name of the country. If the collision occurred off a military reservation and outside a city, enter the word "outside," then the name of the nearest installation or city. Next, enter the word "in," and note the county, district, state, and country (if not in the United States) in which the collision occurred. For example, "outside Saint Robert, Missouri, in Pulaski County, Missouri."
  - **Block 5c.** If the collision occurred on a street or road, enter the street or road designation.
  - **Block 5d.** If the collision occurred within an intersection, enter the name and/or route number of the intersecting highway, street, road, alley, or such. If the collision occurred at the intersection of a highway with an entrance or exit ramp, this ramp must be accurately identified by name and/or number to permit follow-up engineering and enforcement action. If the collision occurred at the intersection of a road and a railroad, identify the railroad crossing number. "Within an intersection," means that area within imaginary lines drawn from the edges of the intersecting roads on through the intersection.
  - **Block 5e.** If the collision did not occur in an intersection or on an entrance or exit ramp, enter the descriptors of the nearest intersecting street or landmark.

- **Block 5f.** If the collision did not occur in an intersection, enter in feet the distance between the center line of the nearest intersecting street and the location of the key event of the collision.
- **Block 5g.** If the collision did not occur in an intersection, enter the direction from the intersection or landmark to the location of the collision.
- **Block 5h.** If the collision occurred off of a military installation and outside city limits, enter the approximate miles from the nearest military installation or city (identified previously). If kilometers are used, strike out "Miles" and enter "Km." Check the appropriate block that generally describes the cardinal direction of the collision from the nearest city or military installation and check whether the distance is from the city limit, installation boundary, or city center.
- **Block 5i.** Mark an "X" in the box or boxes that best describe the area in which the collision occurred. If none of those listed is appropriate, check "Other" and briefly describe it in the space after it.
- **Block 6, Type of Accident.** Mark (X) the box or boxes which best describe the incident. If a vehicle hit both an object and a pedestrian, mark only the box indicating the first impact. If "Other" is marked, explain in the space provided (for example, "Vehicle-Animal").
  - **Block 6a.** Indicate the number of people killed and the number injured in the appropriate blocks. Disposition of killed and injured personnel will be explained in the "Description of Collision" block in Part B of the form. Mark an "X" in "Property Damage Only" block if there were no human fatalities or injuries. If any person claims an injury, it will be recorded as an injury even though the person does not appear to be injured.
  - **Block 6b.** Enter the total number of vehicles involved in the collision. If more than two vehicles are involved, additional copies of DA Form 3946 must be used.
- **Block 7, Weather, Light, and Road Conditions.** Mark an "X' in appropriate blocks for each vehicle. If necessary, more than one block may be checked, especially in the "Character," "Conditions," "Defects," and "Weather" blocks. If "Other" is marked in any column, explain in the "Description of Collision" block on the other side of the form or on a continuation sheet. The blocks to be marked are to the left of the descriptions.
- **Block 8, Traffic Control.** Mark an "X" by any traffic control devices affecting either vehicle. Explain "Other" devices in the "Description of Collision" block on the other side, or on a continuation sheet. If necessary, more than one block may be marked. Again, the blocks to be marked are to the left of the descriptions.
- **Block 9, Vehicle Descriptions.** There is a section 9a and a section 9b; each section will be filled with data for a single vehicle. Enter the—
  - Registration number if it is a military vehicle. Always make sure that numbers on the hood match the data plate in the vehicle. If it is a nongovernment vehicle, enter the license number and state, district, or county.
  - Enter the make of the vehicle, for example "Dodge, Chevrolet, or Volkswagen."
  - Enter the last two digits of the vehicle's model year, such as "07," "99," or "03."
  - Describe the model and style of the vehicle, for example "Mustang, 2-door;" "1500, quad cab pickup," or "Caravan, passenger van." For common military vehicles, use "common" descriptions; for example, "HEMTT Fueler," "HMMWV cargo truck," or M1A3 Tank."
  - Enter unit bumper markings if it is a tactical military vehicle. If the military vehicle is a nontactical vehicle (commercial), enter the license plate number. If privately owned, enter the license plate number.
  - Mark an "X" in the appropriate box for privately owned or Government owned.
  - If the registered owner is the driver, enter "NA." If the owner is not the driver, enter the owner's last name, first name, middle initial. If owner is military, also include his rank and SSN. If owner is a civilian, include his SSN. If it is a government-owned vehicle, enter "U.S. Government." Enter the military address (unit or dispatching motor pool, station or location, state or district, and country if not the United States) if the owner is military; use

the current mailing address of the owner if he is a civilian. Be sure to include the zip code on all U.S. addresses.

- Enter the name of the insurance company or agent. If it is a company, the city and state will normally be all the address needed. If a private agent is given, list the complete address of the agent. No effort will be made to ascertain the limits of insurance of any of the parties. If it is a government-owned vehicle, enter "U.S. Government."

- **Block 10, Driver Information.** There is a section 10a and a section 10b; each section will be filled with data for a single driver. Use the following instructions:

  - If there was no driver in the vehicle at the time of the collision, enter "No driver" in name block. If the driver is a service member, enter his last name, first name, middle initial, rank, and military address (unit, station, state, zip code). If the driver is a family member, enter the last name, first name, middle initial, dependency status, and abbreviated unit of sponsor (such as "d/wife of CPT Harry B. Smith, 3/19 Arty"). A family member's local mailing address should also be entered here (including zip code). For civilians, list their last name, first name, and middle initial.

  - Enter the SSN for all U.S. personnel. If foreign, use their military ID number or the appropriate civilian ID number. If no number is available or known, enter "UNK."

  - Enter the driver's age in years.

  - Place an "X" in the appropriate block, "Male" or "Female."

  - If the driver is military and driving a military vehicle, enter the driver's military license number and the station where it was issued.

  - In the case of military personnel driving military vehicles and having military licenses, enter "U.S. Government" in the block for "State." For civilians, including dependents, enter the operator's license number and issuing state. If an international license, note "Inter" in the block for "State."

  - If limitations or restrictions are stated on the driver's license, mark an "X" in "Yes" block and specify. Examples of limitations or restrictions are glasses, day-time only, and such. If a military driver is operating a vehicle for which he is not qualified as indicated on his license, this is not to be entered here but should be noted on an appropriate citation and in the "Description of Collision" block. If no limitations are noted on the driver's license, put an "X" in the "No" block.

  - Enter the operator's driving experience in years. For drivers with less than one year of experience, ensure that the word "months" is placed after the number entry (for example 6 months). Unless it is clearly unreasonable, the driver's word should be accepted for this information.

  - The codes are listed by the specific categories at the bottom of the page. Select the appropriate letter within each category and place in the box it for that category.

- **Block 11, Occupants.** Information here does not include drivers. The following information should be provided:

  - For military occupants, list their last name, first name, middle initial, rank and SSN. Military unit addresses should be used for all military personnel. If the individual is a family member, enter their last name, first name, middle initial, SSN, dependency status, and abbreviated unit of sponsor (such as "d/son of SP4 Joe E. Jones, 385th Trans"). Local mailing addresses should be used for family members. For civilians, enter their last name, first name, middle initial, and SSN. Enter a married woman's name as "Johnson, Beverly S.," not "Mrs. James Johnson."

  - Enter the number to indicate which vehicle the occupant was in. If more than two vehicles were involved, the numbering should continue on additional forms. Try to list the occupants on the same form as the driver and vehicle in which the person was riding. For example, occupants in Vehicle 3 should be listed on the same additional form as the driver and vehicle description of Vehicle 3.

  - Enter the age of each individual.

  - Enter "M" or "F" for each individual listed.

- Fill in the appropriate code from the list at the bottom of the page.
- **Block 12, Pedestrians.** Enter the name and address of any pedestrian involved in the collision including—
  - **Blocks 12 a-e.** Enter the information in the same manner that "Occupants" were entered in the preceding paragraph. Also, enter the appropriate code for age, sex, category, and injury.
  - **Block 12f.** Complete in a manner that best describes exactly what the pedestrian was doing at the time of the collision. Mark "X' in the appropriate blocks. More than one condition may apply. Again, the blocks are to the left of the conditions.
- **Block 13, Witnesses.** Provide information regarding witnesses not involved in the collision. The following information should be included:
  - **Block 13a.** Enter names and addresses of witnesses in the same manner as occupants were entered previously.
  - **Block 13b.** Ensure that a current telephone number and other contact information is entered for all witnesses.
- **Block 14, Vehicle Damage.** Describe damage to each vehicle involved. The following information should be included:
  - **Block 14a.** Indicate damage to the vehicle by marking the appropriate boxes with an "X" to describe the areas of the vehicle that were damaged. Multiple boxes may be required. If a bus, motorcycle, trailer, or other vehicle (not an automobile) is involved and damaged, use the space available for sketching the type of vehicle. Shade in the areas receiving the severest damage and use arrows to indicate the direction of force at collision points.
  - **Block 14b.** Indicate the severity of damage to the vehicle by marking the appropriate box with an "X" to describe the severity of the damage.
  - **Block 14c.** If the vehicle was towed away, write in the name of the towing or wrecker service that removed it. Local wrecker companies will normally be familiar, so it will not usually be necessary to include an address. If the vehicle is towed away by a military wrecker, simply enter "military wrecker."
  - **Block 14d.** Identify the destination of the towed vehicle. For example, if a vehicle was towed by Acme Auto Repair to their garage in Waynesville, Missouri, this section would appear as: "Acme Garage, Waynesville, MO." If the vehicle is not towed away, list what its disposition was in this space ("released to operator").
  - **Block 14e.** Enter a description of damage to property other than vehicles. Make this description as concise as possible without leaving out important facts. Try to restrict description to the space allotted. In cases of severe damage to high-value items such as aircraft, supporting descriptions of damage should be attached in the form of statements and/or estimates of repair cost.
- **Collision Sketch (Block 14f).** Most collisions are relatively minor and simple. The space on the form should be sufficient for most minor collisions. Serious collisions will require more thorough diagrams attached as separate sheets. Depending on the severity of the collision, the following items should be noted on the diagram (the simpler the collision, the fewer items needed):
  - Include an arrow indicating north in the circle at the upper right.
  - Include and identify within the sketch the roadway layout, vehicles, pedestrians, objects on or off the roadway, traffic controls, skid marks, and unusual or temporary conditions (ice patch, stones, gravel, and such).
  - Locate the probable point of impact.
  - Show positions of vehicles, pedestrians, or objects at the point of impact. Use solid lines to indicate paths followed after the collision or point of impact.
  - Show probable vehicle and pedestrian paths before and after the collision. Use broken lines to indicate probable paths followed before the collision or point of impact.
- **Collision Description (Block 14g).** Provide a short, concise description of the collision. It is not necessary to repeat all of the information in this block. As with the sketch block, the space

provided here for description will be sufficient for most collisions. Serious collisions may require a continuation sheet. Indicate here what probably happened before, during, and after the collision. Include information not on the diagram or not on other parts of the form. Describe special conditions or events associated with the collision such as any vehicles on fire, vehicles immersed or submerged, or roadway lights not operating. Only the last names of persons identified elsewhere in the report need to be used in this block; these last names should appear in this section in all capital letters along with operator restrictions, disposition of injured personnel, or other pertinent details. An example of a collision description is "Vehicle 2 (SMITH) was stopped at the stop sign, waiting to cross 38th Street. Vehicle 1 (JONES) approached Vehicle 2 from the rear and was unable to stop when the brakes were applied. Skid marks were present measuring approximately 20 feet. The pavement was wet; visibility was approximately 100-150 feet. No injuries were evident at the scene."

- **Block 15, Driver's Actions Before the Incident.** Throughout this section mark "X' in appropriate blocks for drivers and vehicles. There are two columns (column 1 and column 2), one column for each vehicle. More than one block per vehicle may be marked. The blocks to be marked are to the left of the descriptions. The investigator should—

  - Mark an "X" in the block to indicate the direction each vehicle was traveling immediately before the collision.

  - Mark an "X" to indicate one or more of the actions the drivers of the respective vehicles were executing immediately before the collision. The blocks to be marked are to the left of the descriptions. In the case of parked vehicles, mark in "Other" block and enter "parked vehicle" in the space provided.

  - Identify distances and speeds for each of the items listed. For vehicle distances and speeds, enter the best estimate possible for each of the items listed. If the item is not applicable to the collision being reported, enter "N/A" in the block. If it is impossible to make a reasonable estimate, enter "UNK."

- **Block 15b, Contributing Circumstances.** Throughout this section mark "X' in appropriate blocks for drivers and vehicles. There are two columns (column 1 and column 2), one column for each vehicle. More than one block per vehicle may be marked. The blocks to be marked are to the left of the descriptions. The investigator should—

  - Check one or more of the listed contributing factors.

  - Indicate whether drugs or alcohol are involved. Any time alcohol appears to be involved, a DD Form 1920, *Alcoholic Influence Report*, must be completed and attached to the form. "Drugs Involved" may be marked only when this determination has been made by medical authorities. If pedestrian action contributed to the collision, such as disregarding a traffic signal or being under the influence of alcohol, it should be noted in the "Description of Collision" block.

  - Enter whether chemical tests were given and whether they were refused. If blood alcohol tests were given, enter the resulting blood alcohol content in the space provided.

  - Indicate whether defective brakes, headlights, or tires are observed.

- **Block 16, Military Police Activity.** This section records actions by the responding military police and includes the following information:

  - **Block 16a.** Enter the last name, first name, and middle initial of all personnel charged with any offense in connection with the collision. If their names do not appear elsewhere on this form, enter all information required in the "Name and Address" portion under the heading "Occupants" discussed earlier in this appendix.

  - **Block 16b.** List charges for each individual charged. For example, if one driver was charged with going 50 miles per hour in a 35 mile per hour zone, this entry would read "speeding, 50/35."

  - **Block 16c.** List the report number for each person charged. If cited on a DA Form 3975, *Military Police Report,* this will normally be the same MPR number that appears at the top of that form. If the individuals are cited on a Central Violation Bureau (CVB) Form, *United* *states District Court Violation Notice* or DD Form 1408, *Armed Forces Traffic Ticket,* enter the sequential number of the form in this block.

- **Block 16d.** Enter the time the military police were first notified (whether first notification was made to the desk or directly to a patrol). Entry will be in military time (for example, 1:00 p.m. is entered as 1300).
- **Block 16e.** Enter the time the first military police personnel arrived at the scene of the collision. Entry will be in military time. Should on-duty military police patrols be involved in the collision, local policy will determine the need for a separate investigative unit.
- **Block 16f.** Enter the location of places other than the collision scene or the provost marshal's office where statements were taken or the investigation was continued; for example "El Paso, Police Department" or "Johnson Army Community Hospital."
- **Block 16g.** Enter the names of other agencies participating in the investigation. If another agency did the entire investigation and the information on the form is based on that report state, "All information supplied by El Paso, Police Department." When another agency conducted most of the investigation, attach a copy of that agency's report.
- **Block 16h.** Operators of military vehicles are required to exchange completed DD Form 518, *Accident – Identification Card.* Mark an "X" to indicate whether or not these forms were exchanged. Forms need not be exchanged when only privately owned vehicles are involved.
- **Block 16i.** Military operators of military vehicles are also required to complete Standard Form (SF) 91, *Operator's Report of Motor Vehicle Accident.* Mark an "X" to indicate if the forms were completed. The SF 91 is to be turned into the operator's unit by the operator; it is not to be taken by the military police.
- **Block 16j.** Place an "X" to indicate if this DA Form 3946 was completed from an investigation at the scene of the collision. If it was not, explain why. Example: "completed from witness reports, scene within hostile fire area."
- **Block 16k.** Enter the date this form is completed and signed by the investigator.
- **Block 16l.** Enter the name of the person who actually observed the collision scene and supplied the information for completion of this form. If more than one person assisted, enter the name of the senior investigator. List any additional investigators on the DA Form 3975 that will accompany this form in distribution.
- **Block 16m.** The signature of the person whose name appears in the preceding block, and his grade, if applicable, is entered here.
- **Blocks 16n through q.** The final "approval" line should be completed as required by local policy.

MILITARY POLICE TRAFFIC ACCIDENT REPORT
For use of this form, see AR 190-45; the proponent agency is PMG.

PRIVACY ACT STATEMENT

AUTHORITY:	Title 10 USC Section 301; Title 5 USC Section 2951; E.O. 9397 dated November 22, 1943 *(SSN)*.
PRINCIPAL PURPOSE:	To provide commanders and law enforcement officials with means by which information may be accurately identified.
ROUTINE USES:	Your social security number is used as an additional/alternate means of identification to facilitate filing and retrieval.
DISCLOSURE:	Disclosure of your social security number is voluntary.

1. PM ACTIVITY CODE/REPORT NO.	2. DATE OF ACCIDENT *(YYYYMMDDD)* 2011/10/30	3. TIME OF ACCIDENT *(Use 2400 hour)* 2315	4. DAY OF WEEK OF COLLISION *(Sunday, Monday, etc.)* Sunday

5. LOCATION OF ACCIDENT

a. MILITARY RESERVATION [X] YES [ ] NO	b. NAME AND LOCATION OF MILITARY RESERVATION *(Include City and State, etc.)* Fort Leonard Wood, MO

c. ROAD OR STREET ON WHICH ACCIDENT OCCURRED Main Street	d. NAME OF INTERSECTING STREET IF AT INTERSECTION 2nd Street

e. NAME OF NEAREST INTERSECTING STREET, HIGHWAY, OR OTHER PERMANENT IDENTIFYING LANDMARK IF NOT AT INTERSECTION N/A	f. NO. OF FEET N/A	g. DIRECTION N/A

h. IF ACCIDENT OCCURRED OFF MILITARY RESERVATION, AND OUTSIDE CITY LIMITS, INDICATE:
_____ MILES [ ] N [ ] S [ ] E [ ] W FROM [ ] CITY LIMITS [ ] CENTER OF CITY OR TOWN

i. KIND OF LOCALITY	[ ] Troop Billets [X] Residential	[ ] Mfg or Industrial [ ] Open Country	[ ] School or Playground [ ] Business	[ ] Other *(Specify)*

6. TYPE OF ACCIDENT

[X] Vehicle-Vehicle [ ] Vehicle-Pedicycle [ ] Stolen Vehicle	[ ] Vehicle-Object [ ] Vehicle-RR Train [ ] Vehicle-Pedestrian	[ ] Single Vehicle *(Non Collision)* [ ] Hit and Run [ ] Other *(Specify)*	a. SEVERITY	
			NO. KILLED 0	NO. INJURED 0

b. TOTAL NO. OF VEHICLES INVOLVED 2	[X] PROPERTY DAMAGE ONLY

7. WEATHER, LIGHT, AND ROAD CONDITIONS

VEHICLE 1 2	DRIVING LANES	VEHICLE 1 2	CHARACTER	VEHICLE 1 2	SURFACE	VEHICLE 1 2	WEATHER
	One	[X][X]	Straight		Concrete		Clear
[X][X]	Two		Curve	[X][X]	Black Top	[X][X]	Rain
	Three or More	[X][X]	Level		Brick		Fog
	Divided Highway		On Grade		Gravel		Snowing
	Other		Other		Other		Other

VEHICLE 1 2	CONDITIONS	VEHICLE 1 2	DEFECTS	VEHICLE 1 2	LIGHT
	Dry		Holes, Ruts, Bumps. etc.		Daylight
[X][X]	Wet		Loose Material on Surface		Dawn
	Mud		Defective Shoulder		Dusk
	Snow	[X][X]	No defects	[X][X]	Dark, Street Lights
	Other		Other		Dark, No Street Lights

8. TRAFFIC CONTROL

VEHICLE 1 2		VEHICLE 1 2		VEHICLE 1 2		VEHICLE 1 2	
	Stop and Go Signal		Flashing Light		Warning Sign		One way Street
[X][X]	No Traffic Signal		Officer or Watchman		Solid Center Line		Stop Sign
	Other *(Explain)*						

DA FORM 3946, DEC 1998   DA FORM 3946, SEP 73, IS OBSOLETE   Page 1 of 4
APD PE v1.02ES

Figure D-11. Sample DA Form 3946, page 1

9a. VEHICLE NO. 1				9b. VEHICLE NO. 2			
USA REGISTRATION OR LICENSE NO. CRB-847 (GA)	MAKE Chev	YEAR 4	BODY TYPE 2 door Camaro	USA REGISTRATION OR LICENSE NO. EA-7326 (MO)	MAKE Ford	YEAR 9	BODY TYPE 4 door Fusion
UNIT MARKINGS/DECAL NO. None		✓ Privately Owned ☐ Government		UNIT MARKINGS/DECAL NO. None		✓ Privately Owned ☐ Government	
REGISTERED OWNER (If not driver) (Last, First, MI) N/A				REGISTERED OWNER (If not driver) (Last, First, MI) N/A			
ADDRESS OF OWNER				ADDRESS OF OWNER			
NAME AND ADDRESS OF INSURANCE COMPANY OR AGENT Quick Insurance Podunk, GA 31905				NAME AND ADDRESS OF INSURANCE COMPANY OR AGENT Speedy Insurance Backwoods, MO 65583			

10a. DRIVER NO. 1		10b. DRIVER NO. 2	
NAME (Last, First, MI), Grade and Address Percy, Helen 306 Any Road Podunk, GA 31905	SSN 000-00-00000 AGE 18 ☐ Male ✓ Female	NAME (Last, First, MI), Grade and Address Brown, Harvey G. 4237 Red Road Backwoods, MO 65583	SSN 000-00-00000 AGE 36 ✓ Male ☐ Female
DRIVER'S LICENSE/PERMIT NUMBER 0-43861524	STATE GA	DRIVER'S LICENSE/PERMIT NUMBER B-34357332	STATE MO
LIMITATIONS ON LICENSE/PERMIT ☐ NO ✓ YES (Specify) Corrective Lenses	YEARS' DRIVING EXPERIENCE 6 months	LIMITATIONS ON LICENSE/PERMIT ✓ NO ☐ YES (Specify)	YEARS' DRIVING EXPERIENCE 20
CODES	CAT (1) F / INJ (2) A / SEAT BELT (3) C / SEAT POS (4) 1	CODES	CAT (1) B / INJ (2) A / SEAT BELT (3) C / SEAT POS (4) 1

11. OCCUPANTS

NAME AND ADDRESS	VEH NO.	AGE	SEX	CAT (1)	INJ (2)	SEAT BELT (3)	SEAT POS (4)
Brown, Sally S. (same as driver #2)	2	34	F	F	A	C	3

CODES

(1) CATEGORY	(2) INJURY CLASS	(3) SHOULDER/LAP BELTS	(4) SEAT POSITION
A. Army Officer B. Army Enlisted C. Other Service Officer D. Other Service Enlisted E. Civilian F. Dependent O. Other	A. No Injury B. Dead at Scene C. Dead on Arrival D. Died in Hospital E. Incapacitating Injury F. Non-incap (evident) Injury G. Possible Injury H. Injury Unknown	A. Lap Belt Used B. Shoulder Harness Used C. Both Used D. Not Used E. Not Installed F. Lap Belt Failed G. Shoulder Harness Failed H. Both Failed U. Unknown	1. Front Left 2. Front Center 3. Front Right 4. Back Left 5. Center Back 6. Back Right 7. Other Position (Bus-Motorcycle) 8. Position Unknown

DA FORM 3946, DEC 1998

Page 2 of 4 / APD PE v1.02ES

Figure D-12. Sample DA Form 3946, page 2

12. PEDESTRIAN

a. NAME AND ADDRESS	b. AGE	c. SEX	d. CATEGORY	e. INJURY
N/A				

f. PEDESTRIAN WAS GOING [ ] N [ ] S [ ] E [ ] W [ ] ALONG [ ] ACROSS [ ] INTO STREET, ROAD OR HIGHWAY,
FROM (NW to SW corner, or east to west side, etc.) TO

[ ] Crossing With Signal	[ ] Crossing No Signal	[ ] Standing on Roadway	[ ] Walking in Road Against Traffic
[ ] Crossing Against Signal	[ ] Hitching on Vehicle	[ ] Coming From Behind Parked Car	[ ] Walking in Road With Traffic
[ ] Crossing Not at Intersection	[ ] Playing on Roadway	[ ] Pushing or Working on Vehicle	[ ] Other

13. WITNESSES

a. NAME AND ADDRESS	b. TELEPHONE NUMBER
Smith, Harry Q. Co B.,3/60th Engineer BN, Fort Leonard Wood, MO	(573) 734-6410

14. VEHICLE DAMAGE

a. DAMAGED VEHICLE NO. 1		DAMAGED VEHICLE NO. 2		DAMAGED TRAILER, MOTORCYCLE ETC.
[X] Right Front of Car	[X] Left Front Door	[ ] Right Front of Car	[ ] Left Front Door	(Sketch Damage)
[X] Right Front Fender	[X] Left Front Fender	[ ] Right Front Fender	[ ] Left Front Fender	
[ ] Right Front Door	[ ] Left Front of Car	[ ] Right Front Door	[ ] Left Front of Car	
[ ] Right Rear Door	[X] Hood	[ ] Right Rear Door	[ ] Hood	
[ ] Right Rear Fender	[ ] Roof	[X] Right Rear Fender	[ ] Roof	
[ ] Right Rear of Car	[ ] Trunk	[X] Right Rear of Car	[X] Trunk	
[ ] Left Rear of Car	[ ] Undercarriage	[X] Left Rear of Car	[ ] Undercarriage	
[ ] Left Fender	[ ] Overturn	[ ] Left Fender	[ ] Overturn	
[ ] Left Rear Door		[ ] Left Rear Door		

b. SEVERITY OF DAMAGE VEHICLE NO. 1		c. SEVERITY OF DAMAGE VEHICLE NO. 2		SEVERITY OF DAMAGE OTHER VEHICLE	
[X] Disabling Damage	[ ] Other MV Damage	[ ] Disabling Damage	[ ] Other MV Damage	[ ] Disabling Damage	[ ] Other MV Damage
[ ] Functional Damage	[ ] No Damage	[X] Functional Damage	[ ] No Damage	[ ] Functional Damage	[ ] No Damage

c. TOWED BY	TOWED BY	TOWED BY
Happy's Towing	Released to Owner	

d. TOWED TO	TOWED TO	TOWED TO
Honest John's Garage, St Robert, MO		

e. DAMAGE TO PROPERTY OTHER THAN VEHICLE

f. SKETCH OF COLLISION. (1) Identify roadway and roadway features, vehicles, pedestrians, objects on/off roadway, traffic controls, skidmarks, unusual/temperature conditions (ice patch, construction areas, etc.). (2) Locate probable point of impact. (3) Show vehicle, pedestrian or object positions at impact. (4) Show probable vehicle or pedestrian paths before and after collision.

g. DESCRIPTION OF COLLISION. Indicate what probably happened before, during, and after the crash; include information not on sketch, e.g., driver disability, reduced visibility, pedestrian clothing color, construction or repair work, etc.

Vehicle #2 (BROWN) was slowing at the approach to 2nd Street. Vehicle #1 (Percy) was approaching behind vehicle #2 (BROWN). The driver of vehicle #1 (PERCY) failed to notice vehicle #2 (BROWN) slowing and could not stop in time to avoid a collision. Skid marks were deposited (approximately 10 feet). Pavement was wet and visibility was good.

DA FORM 3946, DEC 1998

Page 3 of 4
APD PE v1.02ES

Figure D-13. Sample DA Form 3946, page 3

15a. DRIVER'S ACTION BEFORE ACCIDENT					

15a. DRIVER'S ACTION BEFORE ACCIDENT

DIRECTION HEADED	DRIVER *(Check one or more)* 1 2	DRIVER *(Check one or more)* 1 2 Other *(Specify)*	VEHICLE *(Specify Feet/MPH)* 1	2	
VEHICLE 1 ☐ N ☐ S ☒ E ☐ W VEHICLE 2 ☐ N ☐ S ☒ E ☐ W	Backing ☒☒ Going Straight Ahead Making Left Turn Skidding Making Right Turn Making "U" Turn Overtaking or Passing Avoiding Veh/Obj ☒ Slowing or Stopping Stop in Traffic Lane		12 Feet		Estimated Distance When Danger Was First Noticed
			35 MPH		Estimated Speed When Danger was First Noticed
			15 MPH	10 MPH	Estimated Speed at Impact *(MPH)*
			10 Feet	10 Feet	Distance Traveled After Impact *(Feet)*
			35 MPH	35 MPH	Lawful Speed *(MPH)*

b. CONTRIBUTING CIRCUMSTANCES

DRIVER *(Check one or more)* 1 2	DRIVER *(Check one or more)* 1 2	DRIVER *(Check one or more)* 1 2	
Exceeding Speed Limit ☒ Speed Excessive for Conditions Failed to Yield Disregarded Stop Signal Vision Obstructed Following Too Close Improper Overtaking No or Improper Signal Disregarded Traffic Signal Improper Turn Unknown Other *(Specify)*	Alcohol Involved Drugs Involved Ability Impaired Ability Not Impaired Unknown See attached DD Form 1920 *(Alcoholic Influence Report)* VEHICLE *(Check one or more)* 1 2 Defective Brakes Defective Head Lights Tires Worn or Smooth Tires Punctured or Blown Other *(Specify)*	Chemical Test Given Chemical Test Refused TEST RESULTS	
		DRIVER NO. 1 % BAC	DRIVER NO. 2 % BAC

16. MILITARY POLICE ACTIVITY

a. NAME OF PERSON(s) APPREHENDED	b. CHARGES	c. REPORT NUMBER
	Speed excessive for conditions	CVB Form 1805 A 665175

d. TIME MILITARY POLICE NOTIFIED *(Hour)* 2321	e. TIME MILITARY POLICE ARRIVED AT ACCIDENT *(Hour)* 2327		YES	NO
f. WHERE ELSE WAS INVESTIGATION MADE? N/A	h. DID MILITARY OPERATOR COMPLETE DD FORM 518 *(Accident Identification Card)?*		☐	☒
g. IF OFF MILITARY RESERVATION, WHO ELSE CONDUCTED AN INVESTIGATION? *(If other agency conducted complete investigation, so indicate)* N/A	i. DID MILITARY OPERATOR COMPLETE SF FORM 91 *(Motor Vehicle Accident Report)?*		☐	☒
	j. WAS FORM COMPLETED FROM ON SCENE INVESTIGATION? *(If not, explain)*		☒	☐

k. DATE 30 Oct 2011	l. TYPED OR PRINTED NAME AND GRADE OF INVESTIGATOR Joe M. Smart, SGT	m. INVESTIGATOR'S SIGNATURE AND GRADE *Joe Smart, SGT*
n. DATE APPROVED 3 Nov 2011	o. APPROVED BY *Burke S. Smith* MAJ, MP, DEPUTY PROVOST MARSHAL	p. ENCLOSURES Statements (4) q. DISTRIBUTION

DA FORM 3946, DEC 1998

Figure D-14. Sample DA Form 3946, page 4

DEPARTMENT OF DEFENSE FORM 2922

D-20. A DD Form 2922 must accompany all evidence submitted to the USACIL for analysis. Samples of DD Form 2922 are provided at figures D-15 and D-16, pages D-28 and D-29. The form is used to establish priority for processing, provide specific background surrounding the case and collection of the evidence, and provide an item-by-item list of all evidence submitted. Block-by-block instructions for completing DD Form 2922 include—

- **Block 1.** Check the default address for the Director, USACIL. There is no need to specify a specific branch within the USACIL. If the evidence is sent a laboratory other than the USACIL, check the "Other" block and list the name and address of the appropriate laboratory.
- **Block 2.** Enter the address of the investigator submitting the evidence; a physical street address is preferred.
- **Block 3.** Enter the address to which the evidence should be returned after conclusion of examination; a physical street address is preferred.
- **Block 4.** Check "Routine" unless expeditious examination is required. If an expedited examination is required, "Expedite" should be checked as well as the reason for the expedited processing.
- **Blocks 5 and 16.** Laboratory use only.
- **Block 6.** Enter the case number applicable to the evidence submitted.
- **Block 7.** Enter the type of offense.
- **Block 8.** Provide information regarding any previous evidence submitted for this case including the date submitted, the method of delivery, the lab case number assigned, and any suspects in the case.
- **Block 9.** List the last, first, and middle names of any suspects for this evidence.
- **Block 10.** List the last, first, and middle names of any victims for this evidence.
- **Block 11.** Provide a brief synopsis of the facts of the investigation. Ensure that you provide sufficient detail for USACIL examiners to determine the best way to process and examine the evidence. Supporting documentation such as initial case reports and crime scene photographs may be included to ensure understanding by USACIL examiners.
- **Block 12.** List evidence numerically. Organize the evidence in a clear and logical manner with consideration given to the type of examination requested (for example, group evidence by type of examination such as questioned documents, serology evidence, firearms, and so forth). Describe the evidence in sufficient detail for laboratory examiners to correctly identify the specific item of evidence; for clarity the document and item number from the evidence custody document may be used.
- **Block 13.** Describe the examinations required; only request specific examinations necessary to address investigative requirements. Investigators may also request "other examinations as appropriate" to enable laboratory examiners appropriate latitude to conduct additional examinations (based on their experience and expertise) to address investigation requirements. Provide any additional information not included in block 11 which the investigator feels may help the examiner and aid in processing the evidence.
- **Block 14.** List the primary and alternate investigator contact information.
- **Block 15.** Enter the date, typed or printed name, signature, and contact information for the submitter.

FORENSIC LABORATORY EXAMINATION REQUEST

1. TO:	2. FROM:	4. EXAM PRIORITY	5. LAB USE ONLY
Director USACIL [X] 4930 N. 31st Street Forest Park, GA 30297-5205 ☐ Other *(Specify)*:	Special Agent in Charge 75th MP Det (CID) Bldg 1457, 6104 3rd Street Fort Belvoir, VA 22060-5592	⦿ ROUTINE ◯ EXPEDITE ☐ Trial/Article 32/39A (*) ☐ Subject in pre-trial confinement ☐ Subject pending PCS/ Separation/Reenlist (*) ☐ Other (Specify in Block 13) *Date _____	a. LAB CASE # b. METHOD OF RECEIPT c. RECEIVED BY/DATE
	3. RETURN EVIDENCE TO: Special Agent in Charge 75th MP Det (CID) Attn: Evidence Custodian Bldg 1457, 6104 3rd Street Fort Belvoir, VA 22060-5592		

6. SUBMITTING AGENCY CASE NUMBER	7. TYPE OF OFFENSE
0001-06-CID122-19999	Aggravated Sexual Assault

8. PREVIOUS EVIDENCE SUBMITTED

DATE: MAIL METHOD: LAB CASE #:   SUSPECT(S):

9. SUSPECT(S) [*Last, first and middle name(s)*]	10. VICTIM(S) [*Last, first and middle name(s)*]
Jones, Larry E.	Smith, Missy M.

11. BRIEF DESCRIPTION (SYNOPSIS) OF CASE FACTS THAT MIGHT ASSIST THE LABORATORY IN EXAMINING OR EVALUATING THE EVIDENCE OR ADDITIONAL DOCUMENTATION ATTACHED (*e.g., Summary of investigation, crime scene sketches/photographs, statements*)

Investigation determined Smith, and acquaintance of Jones (Co-worker), after drinking several alcoholic beverages, lost consciousness in her barracks room after attending a party at a nearby room. Jones attended the party, and was seen dancing and flirting with Smith. Smith woke up the next morning in her bed and felt soreness in her vaginal area, and stated she felt as though she had sexual intercourse, though she could not recall doing so. She also found an opened and empty condom package in her trash can inside her room. A search with an ALS detected a possible biological stain on a sheet on Smith's bed. Witnesses observed Jones leave the party, walk to Smith's room, and enter. The witnesses, however, did not hear or see Jones having sexual intercourse with Smith. Jones waived his legal rights and stated he went to Smith's room to determine if she was okay. He denied having sexual intercourse with her, removing her clothing, or engaging in any type of sexual activity or intimate contact with her. Jones denied any knowledge regarding the condom wrapper. Jones did state that he danced with Smith and made flirtatious comments to her while at the party. There are no indications Smith and Jones have had previous sexual contact. Smith, Jones, and witnesses have stated Jones has visited Smith in her room on several prior occasions, always with friends. See Initial Report, AIRs, photographs, and sketches for additional details. ⊞

12. EVIDENCE SUBMITTED

a. EXHIBIT	b. DESCRIPTION OF EXHIBIT
1	SAFE Kit of Smith, (Item 1, VO 001-06).
2	SAFE Kit of Jones, (Item 1, VO 002-06).
3	Undergarments of Smith worn during incident (Item 1, VO 003-06)
4	Underwear of Jones, (Item 1, VO 004-06)
5	Sheet from bed of Smith, (Item 1, VO 005-06)
6	Condom wrapper from Smith's room (Item 2, VO 005-06)
7	Major case prints of Smith.
8	Major case prints of Jones.

DD FORM 2922, JUL 2006   REPLACES DA FORM 3655, AF FORM 1880, AND NCIS FORM 5580/29, WHICH ARE OBSOLETE.   Adobe Designer 7.0

Figure D-15. Sample DD Form 2922, page 1

12. EVIDENCE SUBMITTED *(Continued)*	
a. EXHIBIT	b. DESCRIPTION OF EXHIBIT

13. EXAMINATION(S) REQUESTED *(Briefly furnish any information or instructions that might assist the laboratory in examining the evidence)*

DNA Branch: Please examine exhibits 1-5 (SAFE kits, clothing, and sheet) to establish a link between Smith and Jones. Please examine Exhibit 6 (condom wrapper) to obtain touch DNA. If obtained, compare with Smith's and Jones' DNA samples.

Trace Evidence Branch: Please examine exhibits 1-6 to establish intimate contact between Smith and Jones. Also, please examine exhibits 1-5 for the presence lubricants and compare to exhibit 6 to determine if a condom was used. Note that exhibit 6 was found at the crime scene.

Latent Print Branch: Please examine exhibit 6. Compare any prints with Exhibits 7 and 8. Please check databases if applicable.

14.a. INVESTIGATOR AND ALTERNATE POC *(Typed or Printed) (Mandatory Information)* SA Lee D. Investigator/SA B. A. Cupp	b. TELEPHONE *(Primary/Alt)*: 999-000-0000/0001
	c. DSN *(Primary/Alt)*: 111-000-000/0001
	d. Fax: 999-000-0012
	e. E-Mail: lee.d.investigator@us.army.mil

15. I CERTIFY EVIDENCE HAS NOT BEEN SUBMITTED TO ANOTHER LABORATORY FOR THE SAME EXAMINATION			
a. DATE	b. TYPED/PRINTED NAME OF REQUESTOR SA Lee D. Investigator	d. TELEPHONE *(Primary/Alt)*: 999-000-0000/0001	
2012-05-30	c. SIGNATURE	e. DSN *(Primary/Alt)*: 111-000-000/0001	
		f. Fax: 999-000-0012	
		g. E-Mail: lee.d.investigator@us.army.mil	

	16. LAB USE ONLY
	LAB CASE #

DD FORM 2922 (BACK), JUL 2006

Figure D-16. Sample DD Form 2922, page 2

DEPARTMENT OF THE ARMY FORM 3744

D-21. Authorizations to search and seize or search and apprehend may be issued on the basis of a written or oral statement, electronic message, or other appropriate means of communication. Information provided in support of the request for authorization may be sworn or unsworn. MREs 315 and 316 address requirements for request and issue of search and seizure and search and apprehension authorizations. Sworn information is generally more credible and often carries greater weight than information not given under oath. Sworn affidavits are generally preferred when requesting authorization to search and seize or search and apprehend. DA Form 3744 is used to submit sworn information to a competent military authority authorized to approve the request. A sample completed DA Form 3744 is shown at figure D-17.

D-22. Authorizations to search and seize or search and apprehend may be issued orally or in writing by the appropriate authority. An inventory of the property seized is made at the time of the seizure or as soon as possible following the seizure of the evidence. A copy of the inventory is provided to the person from whose possession or premises the property was taken; DA Form 4137 may be used for this purpose. After execution of the authorization, the authorization document (if provided in writing) and a copy of the inventory are returned to the issuing authority. All documents and papers related to the search or seizure are maintained in the investigator's case file. See AR 27-10 for additional information.

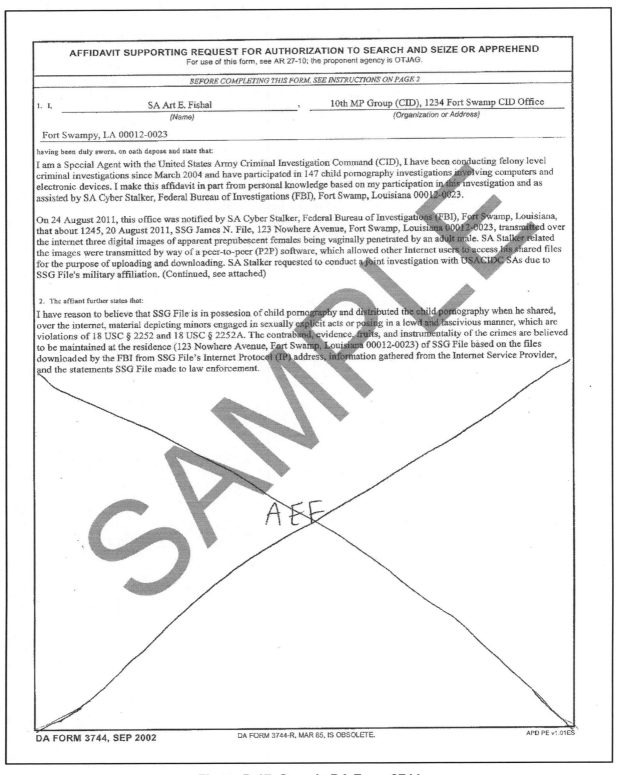

AFFIDAVIT SUPPORTING REQUEST FOR AUTHORIZATION TO SEARCH AND SEIZE OR APPREHEND
For use of this form, see AR 27-10; the proponent agency is OTJAG.

BEFORE COMPLETING THIS FORM, SEE INSTRUCTIONS ON PAGE 2

1. I, _____SA Art E. Fishal_____ , _____10th MP Group (CID), 1234 Fort Swamp CID Office_____
   (Name)   *(Organization or Address)*

Fort Swampy, LA 00012-0023

having been duly sworn, on oath depose and state that:

I am a Special Agent with the United States Army Criminal Investigation Command (CID), I have been conducting felony level criminal investigations since March 2004 and have participated in 147 child pornography investigations involving computers and electronic devices. I make this affidavit in part from personal knowledge based on my participation in this investigation and as assisted by SA Cyber Stalker, Federal Bureau of Investigations (FBI), Fort Swamp, Louisiana 00012-0023.

On 24 August 2011, this office was notified by SA Cyber Stalker, Federal Bureau of Investigations (FBI), Fort Swamp, Louisiana, that about 1245, 20 August 2011, SSG James N. File, 123 Nowhere Avenue, Fort Swamp, Louisiana 00012-0023, transmitted over the internet three digital images of apparent prepubescent females being vaginally penetrated by an adult male. SA Stalker related the images were transmitted by way of a peer-to-peer (P2P) software, which allowed other Internet users to access his shared files for the purpose of uploading and downloading. SA Stalker requested to conduct a joint investigation with USACIDC SAs due to SSG File's military affiliation. (Continued, see attached)

2. The affiant further states that:

I have reason to believe that SSG File is in possession of child pornography and distributed the child pornography when he shared, over the internet, material depicting minors engaged in sexually explicit acts or posing in a lewd and lascivious manner, which are violations of 18 USC § 2252 and 18 USC § 2252A. The contraband, evidence, fruits, and instrumentality of the crimes are believed to be maintained at the residence (123 Nowhere Avenue, Fort Swamp, Louisiana 00012-0023) of SSG File based on the files downloaded by the FBI from SSG File's Internet Protocol (IP) address, information gathered from the Internet Service Provider, and the statements SSG File made to law enforcement.

DA FORM 3744, SEP 2002   DA FORM 3744-R, MAR 85, IS OBSOLETE.   APD PE v1.01ES

Figure D-17. Sample DA Form 3744

AEF

3. In view of the foregoing, the affiant requests that an authorization be issued for a search of __SSG File and the residence__
(the person) (and)

123 Nowhere Avenue, Fort Swamp, Louisiana 00012-0023 (Continued, see attached)
(the quarters or billets) (and)

_____ ___ and (seizure) (apprehension) of _____ (See attached)
(the automobile) ( ) *(items/persons searched for)*

TYPED NAME AND ORGANIZATION OF AFFIANT	SIGNATURE OF AFFIANT
SA Art E. Fishal	A. E. Fishal

SWORN TO AND SUBSCRIBED BEFORE ME THIS __9__ DAY OF __September__ __2011__ AT __1000__

TYPED NAME, ORGANIZATION AND OFFICIAL CAPACITY OF AUTHORITY ADMINISTERING THE OATH	SIGNATURE OF AUTHORITY ADMINISTERING THE OATH
John A. Doe, Captain, JA, Military Magistrate Office of the Staff Judge Advocate, Fort Swampy, LA 00012-0023	John A. Doe

INSTRUCTIONS FOR
AFFIDAVIT SUPPORTING REQUEST FOR AUTHORIZATION TO SEARCH AND SEIZE OR APPREHEND

1. In paragraph 1, set forth a concise, factual statement of the offense that has been committed or the probable cause to believe that it has been committed. Use additional page if necessary.

2. In paragraph 2, set forth facts establishing probable cause for believing that the person, premises, or place to be searched and the property to be seized or the person(s) to be apprehended are connected with the offense mentioned in paragraph 1, plus facts establishing probable cause to believe that the property to be seized or the person(s) to be apprehended are presently located on the person, premises, or place to be searched. Before a person may conclude that probable cause to search exists, he or she must first have a reasonable belief that the person, property or evidence sought is located in the place or on the person to be searched. The facts stated in paragraphs 1 and 2 must be based on either the personal knowledge of the person signing the affidavit or on hearsay information which he/she has plus the underlying circumstances from which he/she has concluded that the hearsay information is trustworthy. If the information is based on personal knowledge, the affidavit should so indicate. If the information is based on hearsay information, paragraph 2 must set forth some of the underlying circumstances from which the person signing the affidavit has concluded that the informant (whose identity need not be disclosed) or his/her information was trustworthy. Use additional pages if necessary.

3. In paragraph 3, the person, premises, or place to be searched and the property to be seized or the person(s) to be apprehended should be described with particularity and in detail. Authorization for a search may issue with respect to a search for fruits or products of an offense, the instrumentality or means of committing the offense, contraband or other property the possession of which is an offense, the person who committed the offense, and under certain circumstances for evidentiary matters.

DA FORM 3744, SEP 2002 Page 2 of 2
APD PE v1.01ES

Figure D-17. Sample DA Form 3744 (continued)

Appendix E

Sources

Anyone who provides information of an investigative nature to LE personnel is a source. A source may provide an investigator with specific information about a particular case or background information that is useful in a number of investigations. The use of registered sources within the context of Army LE activities is governed by USACIDC policy. Military LE personnel must comply with all applicable laws and regulations governing the collection of information and/or intelligence on individuals to include common law, 18 USC 1385 (The Posse Comitatus Act), the law of war, DOD and DA directives and regulations, and SOFAs.

CATEGORIES OF SOURCES

E-1. Sources generally fall into one of the following four groups:
- U.S. and HN citizens.
- Police, security, and other LE personnel.
- Mentally or emotionally challenged individuals.
- Criminals and their associates.

UNITED STATES AND HOST NATION CITIZENS

E-2. People within a community are often aware of criminal behavior. They may live in a high-crime area or have recently been a victim of crime. Others gain knowledge of criminal activity through their employment. A short list of some potential sources in the community includes the following:
- Bartenders.
- Cab drivers.
- Barbers.
- Beauty shop operators.
- Hotel managers and employees.
- Insurance and other private investigators.
- Postal carriers.
- Public utility employees.
- Airport and railway personnel.
- Rental agency clerks.

E-3. Normally, citizens do not seek out the police to report criminal activity; however, they may confide in an officer they know and trust. Police officers should cultivate these contacts at every opportunity. The importance of citizens in fighting crime cannot be overstated.

POLICE AND SECURITY PERSONNEL

E-4. Police and security officers usually exchange information with fellow officers. Investigators should take every opportunity to meet as many federal, state, local, and HN officers as possible and establish a professional relationship with them. Sharing of police information and criminal intelligence greatly enhances the ability of an organization to identify threats and interdict criminal activity.

MENTALLY OR EMOTIONALLY CHALLENGED INDIVIDUALS

E-5. Often, mentally and emotionally challenged individuals will try to provide information to LE personnel. Sometimes criminals will say or do something incriminating in the presence of these individuals because they do not consider them a threat to their criminal activity. With experience, an investigator can identify these individuals whose information can often be attributed to newspapers, gossip, or hallucinations. Information from such individuals must be corroborated through an independent source.

CRIMINALS

E-6. The most valuable source is often the person who is a violator or has been associated with the criminal element. This person is usually in a better position to have substantive information regarding criminal activity.

E-7. A source that is closely associated with criminals is often difficult to control. Dependability and reliability are usually not characteristic of the criminal element. Therefore, it is critical that the investigator maintain firm control and management of the source. The legal, moral, and safety considerations of an investigation are the responsibility of the investigator, not the source. Sources who disregard the investigator's guidelines should be severed from further association with the investigation before major problems or violations occur.

SOURCE SELECTION AND EMPLOYMENT CONSIDERATIONS

E-8. The most important consideration in selecting sources may be reliability. The investigator must evaluate both the source and his information to arrive at the facts. Source information must be tested for consistency by checking it against data from other sources. To test a source's reliability, an investigator should ask the person being evaluated about data known only to the LE organization. This allows for a tentative degree of reliability to each source.

E-9. Investigators must maintain a good liaison and a friendly working relationship with investigators in their unit and in other LE agencies. This will help them in developing quality sources. Sometimes, newer investigators will be referred sources by the more experienced investigators as a result of their being transferred or because they have more sources and investigations than they can effectively work.

E-10. Investigators may consider every individual that is arrested or detained as a potential source. Some investigators may work an entire career by developing sources only from individuals arrested in cases that they have investigated. This technique is generally recommended for source development.

E-11. When considering an individual for selection, the investigator should review the prospective source's mental and physical health, age, education, and personality traits. An individual's experience, work record, financial status, and presence or lack of a criminal background should all be checked. Failing to look at the whole person can waste time and money.

E-12. A skillful investigator can develop a sense of gratitude in a potential source. In return for providing some ethical assistance, the source may show their thanks by giving information. Sometimes simple concern for the source's welfare may create a sense of gratitude.

SOURCE MOTIVES

E-13. Most investigators readily accept the tenet that sources are fundamental in LE work. An investigator must understand what motivates a person to become a source, especially criminals or their associates. A source's motivation is a key factor in determining their reliability. The investigator should attempt to find out what motive a person has for informing. A source gives information for any number of reasons.

Citizens and Law Enforcement Personnel

E-14. Motivation for average citizens and LE personnel is usually easily recognized. The average citizen source ordinarily supplies information or performs a service because of his civic duty and a desire to see justice done. LE personnel are motivated by the same basic factors as the average citizen plus their professional responsibility as sworn officers to enforce the law and investigate violations.

Mentally or Emotionally Challenged Individuals

E-15. What motivates a mentally or emotionally challenged person to become a source is very complex and difficult to determine. In a majority of instances, these individuals give useless information and should not be used as sources. When mentally or emotionally challenged individuals possess valuable information or are able to provide a necessary service, they are usually inspired by one motive or a combination of motives associated with the criminal or associate source.

Criminals and Their Associates

E-16. The investigator often uses criminals and their associates as sources. These sources present many legal, ethical, and moral problems for the investigator that are not usually associated with the other three classifications of sources (civilians, LE personnel, and mentally or emotionally challenged individuals). If an investigator is to properly instruct, control, protect, and effectively use sources and evaluate information, it is critical, in every instance, that he knows the source's motivation.

E-17. Many investigators have allied sources for life, even after a source's case has been adjudicated or the revenge motive situation no longer exists. By treating a source honestly and fairly, the source will sometimes continue to provide information or service because of his appreciation or gratitude. Investigators must be careful not to misinterpret a source's motivation. There are many instances where individuals have supplied information to LE personnel for purely unselfish reasons and then were completely "turned off" when offered money by an investigator. The following paragraphs describe the most common motivations of sources. These motives are not necessarily all-inclusive.

- **Fear.** It is said that self-preservation is the first law of nature. Therefore, many individuals turn to LE personnel with a desire to cooperate when they are afraid of something. Probably the most typical of this situation is the person who has been arrested for an offense and is afraid of going to jail. Since man is social by nature and does not like to live alone, they will sometimes cooperate with LE personnel in return for a consideration of leniency by the court regarding pending charges. Telling a potential registered source that his cooperation will be brought to the attention of the appropriate authority is acceptable. However, any speculation or promises by the investigator relative to the disposition of the charges pending against the source is beyond the authority of the investigator and must be avoided. Additional examples of individuals motivated by fear are victims of rackets or swindles and those afraid of criminal associates for a variety of reasons.

- **Revenge.** The person who is motivated by revenge is usually overwhelmed with a desire for retaliation and often has little concern about openly testifying in court or his identity being publicly exposed. The typical revenge-motivated source is a person who wishes to settle a grudge because someone else informed on him, took advantage of him or, in some manner, injured him. This type of source may exaggerate or make a report that is completely erroneous in an effort to accomplish his goal. A desire for revenge may arise from factors other than criminal activities, such as jealousy and quarrels over lovers, causing close friends to become bitter enemies.

- **Monetary gain.** Some individuals provide information or render a service to LE personnel strictly for a fee. They want to sell what they know for the highest price. Their information is usually good but may backfire when too much reliance is placed on the mercenary motive or the reward payments. Investigators must be cautious not to let financially motivated sources needlessly extend an investigation. Some, especially those on a continuous pay status during an investigation, will attempt this tactic by providing frivolous information knowing that payment will stop when the investigation is over.

- **Egotism or vanity.** Within the average citizen category of sources, these individuals usually subconsciously or consciously want to be LE personnel but for various reasons cannot qualify for LE employment. The benefit of these individuals to LE personnel should not be too quickly discounted. Since a willingness to assist LE personnel is a positive characteristic of any source, these individuals can often be of substantial benefit if directed and motivated properly by a competent investigator.

- **Advantage over competition or adversary.** Characteristic of this type of motivation is the source that makes a disclosure hoping for some unusual advantage. This motivation is prevalent in the areas of vice and/or contraband crimes when a source earns his living by questionable means and informs LE personnel with the desire to eliminate his competition. The source provides trivial or worthless information while attempting to learn investigative techniques, the identities of undercover agents, or to direct attention away from himself.
- **Repentance or reform**. Occasionally, a source will cooperate with LE personnel because he wants to repent for his wrongdoing, he has a desire to make restitution, or he wants to break criminal alliances. A source may decide to cooperate for money, but subconsciously convince himself that he is cooperating with LE personnel for altruistic reasons. When this type of source is properly managed, he can become an excellent continuing source of police information.

E-18. For whatever reason sources volunteer information, they should never be cut short. Investigators should give them the chance to tell their story and then ensure that it is checked out. There is always that one chance that the information could be the missing link in an important case.

SOURCE INTERVIEW TECHNIQUES

E-19. One key to developing and gaining the cooperation of most sources is proper interviewing techniques. Most criminals or their associates do not readily offer information or agree to cooperate with LE personnel. However, an investigator who is a good listener and can communicate clearly and effectively can often gain their cooperation.

E-20. A criminal or his associate often has two principal concerns that must be addressed before he will seriously consider cooperating. First, they are concerned about their identity being registered. Secondly, they are concerned with whether the investigator or organization will address their specific motivation, such as monetary payments. Therefore, the investigator must be prepared to discuss these concerns with the potential source to gain cooperation. If most of the following questions can be answered by a source or potential source, an investigator should be able to objectively evaluate the source and the information the source has provided. The following are questions that an investigator should attempt to find the answers to when interviewing a source or potential source:

- What is the source's motivation?
- Has the source been reliable in the past?
- How intelligent is the source?
- How does the source know about the violation?
- Does the source have a personal interest?
- Does the source have direct knowledge relative to the information?
- Does the source have access to additional related information?
- Does the source have reason to be vengeful toward the violator?
- Does the source have enough experience to report the information accurately?
- Is the source withholding some of the information?
- Has the source fabricated information in the past?
- Is the source willing to testify in court?

SOURCE IDENTITY PROTECTION

E-21. Every USACIDC SA and MPI has a professional and ethical obligation to safeguard the identity of sources to the maximum extent provided by the law. Failure to fulfill this obligation may result in the death, injury, or intimidation of the source or his family. Reprisals against a source due to improper investigator techniques weigh heavily on the investigator's conscience and undermine the total LE effort. As a general rule, an investigator should not place a source in a situation where the source's identity could be exposed unless the investigator has previously explained to the source that this could happen as a result of his cooperation.

E-22. The names of sources are privileged information as supported by the source privilege doctrine. This doctrine allows the government to withhold the identity of the source under most circumstances. The rationale for this privilege is twofold—it ensures a constant and continuing flow of information regarding illegal activities to LE authorities and it protects the source of information from reprisals or revenge.

E-23. Confidentiality must be furnished to all sources that have provided LE personnel with information concerning the criminal activities of others, regardless of the source's motive. Restricting the release of the source's identity, exercising appropriate security measures regarding communications between the source and the handler, and using caution in documenting the source's activities can normally provide confidentiality. Additional measures may include providing physical protection and transferring an individual to another location.

SOURCE CONTROL AND HANDLING

E-24. The investigator, not the source, directs and controls the investigation. This is not as basic as it may sound, especially for the inexperienced investigator who wants to do a good job and establish his reputation. Investigators could fall prey to a perversely motivated source. There is nothing wrong in asking the source for suggestions or showing appreciation for quality information. In fact, these techniques are encouraged. However, the investigator must control the interaction and be the decisionmaking authority.

E-25. Investigators must avoid promising inflated monetary payments or making other promises to a source that cannot be kept or that are outside their authority. Source payments are not within the sole discretion of a case agent or investigator and are contingent upon such factors as supervisory approval, budget, or unit and organization guidelines. Sources may be told that monetary payments are available and general payment guidelines. Inflated promises of payment or rewards may stimulate a source one time, but a source is not likely to assist in future investigations once a promise has been reneged upon. Advising a source of anticipated judicial disposition of a charge pending against him or indicating that a source will receive probation or a reduced sentence because of his cooperation are examples of commitments that are beyond the authority of an investigator.

E-26. To maintain proper control of the source and the direction of the investigation, the investigator must maintain frequent personal contact with the source. When personal contact is not possible, telephonic contact should be used. Personal meetings between the investigator and source are the best atmosphere for debriefing the source, developing a rapport, and issuing instructions. Prearranged, secure meeting places should be established. Using government buildings, police departments, and other official buildings to meet a source should be avoided to reduce the risk of exposing the source.

E-27. It is generally recommended that a second witnessing investigator be present at these meetings. The second investigator serves to corroborate anything said or done at the meeting. This could become important at a later time if the source makes incriminating accusations against the controlling investigator. Exposure of a second investigator to the source will make the transition of the source to another investigator easier, such as when the controlling investigator transfers or retires. Although some organizations do not make it mandatory for two investigators to meet with a source, they do recognize that meetings between investigators and sources of the opposite sex and meetings where sources are paid money are obvious situations that dictate the presence of two investigators.

E-28. A good rapport and mutual trust between an investigator and a source greatly enhance the likelihood of accomplishing the mission. Initially, creating this type of atmosphere may be difficult especially when dealing with a fear-motivated source that has recently been arrested. Generally, if the investigator is truthful and fair with the source, a solid professional relationship will eventually develop. An investigator must conduct personal and criminal background checks on a source and attempt to corroborate the source's information through independent means.

SOURCE TESTIMONY

E-29. The confidentiality of a source's identity is a limited privilege recognized by military law. Rule 507 of the MCM provides that a source's identity is normally privileged against disclosure. Communications with these individuals are also privileged to the extent necessary to prevent disclosure of their identity. This privilege, however, is not absolute and is subject to various exceptions. Legal considerations in this area are both complex and subject to change.

E-30. At the trial, all disclosure orders made by a military judge will be complied with fully. However, in an appropriate case, such as where disclosure may jeopardize an important ongoing investigation, a recess to petition the convening authority to terminate the current judicial proceedings may be requested through the trial counsel by USACIDC personnel.

ENTRAPMENT

E-31. The defense of entrapment exists when the design or suggestion to commit the offense originated in the government and the accused had no predisposition to commit the offense. The "government" includes agents of the government and individuals cooperating with the government, such as informants. The fact that individuals acting for the government afford opportunities or facilities for the commission of an offense does not constitute entrapment. Entrapment occurs only when the criminal conduct is the product of the creative activity of LE officials. Therefore, one of the first things discussed with a source is the law regarding entrapment. The investigator must ensure that the source understands the difference between providing an opportunity for a suspect to violate the law and providing the inspiration for such a violation.

Appendix F

Investigations Checklists

Investigations checklists are compiled to provide Army LE personnel with a planning and execution guidelines addressing specific requirements. Crime scene predeployment checklists provide a general list of required equipment and materials adequate for processing most crime scenes. The crime scene checklist outlines tasks that should be conducted or considered when investigating a crime.

CRIME SCENE PREDEPLOYMENT CHECKLIST

F-1.   Army LE managers must plan for short-notice deployments by preparing crime scene kits. Table F-1 provides an equipment list that is intended to be a guide. In addition to this list, planners should also consider special tools and equipment required for the specific situation and environment. Every deployment will present different challenges. Many of the items necessary for crime scene processing are not available in remote locations. Supervisors and planners must consider their transportation and lift capabilities. Predeployment kits are organized for a single lift.

Table F-1. Equipment list for a crime scene deployment kit

General Supplies	
Hand sanitizer/disinfectant	Plastic trash bags
Distilled water	Portable lighting
Flashlights (with extra batteries)	Knife
Handheld magnifying glass	Tape, rubber bands, string
Evidence markers	Crime scene tape
Extension cords	Compass and/or Global Positioning System (GPS)
Camera kit	Measuring instruments to include— • Steel tape. • A ruler. • A surveyor's measuring wheel. • Laser rangefinders/measuring devices.
Tool kit	
Paperwork and Supplies	
Crime scene sketch kits	Drawing templates
Notebooks and folders	Tape
Pens, pencils, paper, and erasers	Envelopes (various sizes)
Accordion files (preferably tabbed)	Necessary forms to include— • CID Form 36. • CID Form 44. • DA Form 2823. • DA Form 3881. • DA Form 4002. • DA Form 4137. • DD Form 2922.

Table F-1. Equipment list for a crime scene deployment kit (continued)

Personal Protective Equipment (Universal Precaution)	
Nitrile gloves	Surgical masks
Eye protection	Shoe covers (booties)
Disposable hooded protection suits	Face shields
Disinfectant	

Collection and Packaging Supplies	
Swabs	Wire bundle/cable ties
Sturdy cardboard boxes (various sizes)	Paper bags
Evidence collection bags (various sizes)	Evidence labels and tags
Alternate light sources	Specimen containers (for evidence items and toxicology specimens)
Questioned documents holders	Blood collection tubes, syringes, and needles
Evidence tape	Antistatic bags
Bubble wrap and other packing materials (Avoid materials that can create static electricity such as polystyrene peanuts.)	Packing tape
Drug field identification kits	Primer/gunshot residue collection kits
Casting kit	Dental stone
Shovels and trowels	Trace evidence kit

Fingerprint Kits	
Fingerprint cards	A fingerprint dusting kit
Ink and rollers	Palm print lifters
Gel and hinge lifters	Portable fuming equipment
Fingerprint tape	Dust print lifters

Additional Resources for Death Scene Investigations	
Chemical luminescent	Paper bags with sturdy rubber bands (for deceased hands and feet)
A clean sheet (stored in a plastic bag) **Note.** Just sheets, unless they are brand new out of the bag, have the potential to cross contaminate if the plan is to put them over the body. Shrouds are accessible through medical supply channels. Like sexual assault kits, they can be order in advance and kept on hand.	Medical equipment (scissors, forceps, rubber coated tweezers, exposure suit, scalpel handle with blades, a disposable syringe, large gauge needles, cotton tipped swabs)
A thermometer	A presumptive blood test kit
Evidence seals	

Additional Resources for Arson and Explosives Investigations	
Clean unused evidence containers (cans, glass jars, and nylon or polyester bags)	Decontamination equipment (buckets, pans, and detergent)
Heavy work gloves	Rakes, brooms, and spades
Marker cones or flags	

Legend:
CID   criminal investigation division
DA   Department of the Army
DD   Department of Defense

CRIME SCENE CHECKLIST

F-2. Criminal investigation and crime scene processing can be complicated. There are a number of important and detail-oriented activities that need to be completed within the first 24 to 48 hours. Keeping accountability of these tasks can be a daunting mission, made more arduous when the incident involves a violent crime and an entire team is involved in completing them. The following 12-step checklist, shown at table F-2, is an investigative tool that can guide the investigator through the key requirements pertaining to most crime scenes. It is meant to be used as a guideline and some portions may not apply to all crimes. Revisions to this checklist are encouraged to improve the tool. Checklists may already exist at the local level.

Table F-2. 12-step crime scene checklist

	Requirement	Action or Area of Focus
	Step 1: Receive initial notification/receipt of the complaint	
	Detail the initial notification	Record the time and date and how the MPI or USACIDC SA receives the complaint.
	Determine the purview	Determine the UCMJ offense and purview of complaint (within MPI or USACIDC purview).
	Detail the complaint received by military police	Record the time and date and how the incident was first reported to military police.
	Determine details of the discovery	Record the time, date, location, and type of incident or the details pertaining to its initial discovery and who, what, when, where, why, and how as specified in the complaint.
	Identify all related persons	Obtain the full identification, address, and telephone number of all persons related to the incident (desk sergeant, complainant, military police, victim, witness, and so forth).
	Summarize the complaint	Prepare a summary of the incident specified in the complaint.
	Note military police response	Record available information of military police patrols dispatched to crime scene.
	Detail the notification of SAC/MPI/ operations	Record the time and date the SAC, MPI, or operations section was notified. Note details of SAC, MPI, or operations guidance.
	Step 2: Arrive at the crime scene	
	Verify the crime scene	Note the room number or name and general location within the building to include which floor.
		Include the building number and/or name.
		Note the color of the building (include multiple colors).
		Note the type of construction.
		Note the number of floors (stories) within the building.
		Note the principal use of the building (troop barracks, officer's quarters, warehouse, offices, and such).
		Note the geographical location of the building on the installation.
	Document the weather conditions	Note the sky conditions (for example, overcast, clear skies, raining, snowing, or sleeting).
		Note the wind factor (for example, calm, mild, strong, or gusting from the SW).
		Note the humidity factor (for example, moderate, high, or approximate 50 percent).
		Note visible air pollution (for example, smog, dust, or pollen).

Table F-2. 12-step crime scene checklist (continued)

	Requirement	Action or Area of Focus
	**Step 2: Arrive at the crime scene (continued)**	
	Document the weather conditions (continued)	Note the approximate temperature in degrees Fahrenheit for both inside and outside the crime scene.
		Include any odors (out of the ordinary) detected or not detected.
		Note the moisture content of the grass and ground area around the crime scene.
	Identify persons met at the scene	Obtain full identification, address, telephone number, and status of persons at the crime scene. This will include military police, emergency medical personnel, firemen, victims, commanders, unit leadership, and supervisors.
		Note the time and date of their arrival at the crime scene.
		Obtain information from military police at the scene regarding their observations and actions upon arrival at the crime scene.
		Note the time and date scene security was established, the persons used, where they were posted, and specific instructions.
	Identify altered evidence	Determine if any evidence has been touched or moved or if the crime scene has undergone physical changes as the result of weather or other actions since their arrival.
	Establish/adjust security	Note the names of persons used to secure the crime scene, where they were posted, and specific instructions. Determine if crime scene security is sufficient and make adjustments as necessary.
	Establish a VIP briefing point	Note the name of the person used to establish a VIP briefing point, where he posted, and specific instructions.
	Coordinate for additional assistance	Note any additional investigative or security assistance required and list who you coordinated with.
	Identify personal protective equipment requirements	Don the appropriate personal protective equipment.

Note. If injured persons are on the scene, the first military police or USACIDC SAs to arrive must render first aid, obtain their identification if possible, and arrange to have them evacuated to the nearest medical treatment facility as soon as possible. Suspects, witnesses, and complainants must be identified, separated, not allowed to talk to each other, and removed from the area as soon as possible. **Human life is primary! When in doubt, move them out!**

	Requirement	Action or Area of Focus
	Establish a pathway	Establish a pathway to the victim.
	Check for signs of life/describe observations of death	Check for a pulse or respiration.
		Determine if skin is cold to the touch.
		Determine if fingernail beds remain in a blanched condition after finger pressure is applied and withdrawn.
		Determine if movement or sounds are made.
		Determine if a bullet wound (or other apparent injury) is present on the body.
		Determine the extent of bleeding and the color of the blood.
		Determine if rigor mortis is present and, if so, the location on the body.
		Determine if livor mortis is visible and, if so, the location on the body.

Table F-2. 12-step crime scene checklist (continued)

	Requirement	Action or Area of Focus
		Step 2: Arrive at the crime scene (continued)
	Evaluate the victim for injuries/evidence	Check the victim for visible wounds or fragile evidence.
	Identify fragile evidence	Identify evidence requiring immediate attention or the absence thereof.
		Conduct gunshot residue test immediately if a weapon is involved.
	Document the arrival of the medical doctor	Document the time and date of arrival of the medical doctor.
		Obtain the full identification, address (unit), and telephone number of the doctor.
		Obtain the specific time and date the doctor pronounces the victim dead.
		Obtain the doctor's opinion regarding the estimated time and date of death as well as possible cause and manner of the victim's death.
		Obtain the time, date, and location of the autopsy.
		Arrange with the doctor for a copy of the death certificate.
	Note transportation arrangements	Identify the driver and ambulance transporting the victim to the hospital morgue.
	Identify the medical treatment facility	Obtain the name and location of the medical treatment facility where the victim is to be taken upon removal from the crime scene.
	Note the departure of the medical doctor	Document the departure time and date of the doctor from the crime scene.
	Coordinate with the commander	Arrange with the commander or other responsible person to view the victim to confirm identification upon the release of the body from the scene.
	Obtain a search authorization	Obtain appropriate search authorization from— • The military magistrate. • The unit commander. • The U.S. Magistrate (for a federal search warrant). • The owner (consent to search).
		Step 3: Photograph the crime scene
	Establish the method of search	Determine the method of search before beginning photography to ensure consistent and progressive photographs that demonstrate the scene as found by law enforcement. Once the investigator is ready to expose the photographs, he must have decided on the search and the processing method to be used (circle, strip, grid, zone, or sector).
	Expose images	Begin photographing the scene and detailing photographs on the photograph log as appropriate. The log should document the camera type and serial number, the photograph number, what the photograph depicts, and the type of photograph (360, establishing, close-up).
	Follow the sequence of photography	Take outside establishing photographs that include— • Cross streets. • Building numbers.
		Take outside 360-degree overlapping photographs of the scene.
		Take outside entrance/exit photographs to inside scene location.
		Take scene identification photographs.

Table F-2. 12-step crime scene checklist (continued)

	Requirement	Action or Area of Focus
	Step 3: Photograph the crime scene (continued)	
	Follow the sequence of photography (continued)	Take Initial entry photographs.
		Take inside 360-degree, overlapping photographs of the scene.
		Take physical evidence establishing photographs.
		Take photographs of evidence close-up (macro) including— • Without scale. • With scale.
	Identify fragile evidence discovered	Describe any fragile evidence requiring immediate attention or the absence thereof during photography. Refer to step 2 as applicable.
	Identify equipment/technical information	Describe the technical history of the camera, equipment, and the data for each photograph recorded on the log. The log should document the camera type and serial number, the photograph number, what the photograph depicts, and the type of photograph (360, establishing, close-up).
		Describe camera positions, the photograph number, and the distance to the focus point; include this information on the log.

Notes.

1. An integrity photograph of the crime scene supports the investigator's initial observations. However, at a personal injury or death scene, the investigator must be able to justify the time required to expose the photograph before rendering first aid or checking dead victims for signs of life.

2. If injured persons are on the scene, the first military police or USACIDC SAs to arrive must render first aid, obtain their identification, and arrange to have them evacuated to the nearest medical treatment facility as soon as possible. Suspects, witnesses, and complainant must be identified, separated (not allowed to talk to each other), and removed from the area as soon as possible. **Human life is the primary concern! When in doubt, move them out!**

Step 4: Document the crime scene	

Note. Use the following 8-step method of description (in order) as applicable in documenting the scene and evidence:

- **Step 1. Identify quantity.** Identify how many of each item.
- **Step 2. Identify the item.** Identify the common name; for example, pistol, bottle, bag, stain, glass fragments.
- **Step 3. Describe the location.** Document the orientation and position as appropriate. For example, right side of pistol lying on the floor, 2 feet from northwest base corner of entrance/exit (abbreviated NWBC of E/E).

Note. Upon collection, when documenting on DA Form 4137, *Evidence/Property Custody Document,* note the location as floor.

- **Step 4. Color.** Include multiple colors.
- **Step 5. Construction.** What does the item appear to be made of?
- **Step 6. Size.** Document the length, width, height, depth, and thickness or standard size if applicable.
- **Step 7. Features.** Document the serial number, brand name, labels, and such.
- **Step 8. Condition.** Document if items are soiled, dirty, scratched, rusty, torn, and such.

Table F-2. 12-step crime scene checklist (continued)

Requirement	Action or Area of Focus
Step 4: Document the crime scene (continued)	
Describe indoor scenes	Describe each of the following as applicable: • The room. • The floor. • The walls. • The ceiling. • The entrance/exit way and door (opened or closed). • The window (opened or closed; curtains, blinds or shades). • The lighting conditions. • The light fixture and control switch (control switch up or down, lights on or off, and such). • Appliances and/or utilities. • Containers and their visible contents (ashtrays, trash cans, and such). • Visible personal items of clothing and equipment. • Unusual damage to property and/or equipment. • Each item of furniture (drawers open or closed). • Each visible item of physical evidence.
Describe human remains	Describe the following as applicable: • The position and orientation. • Wounds or injuries. • Dress. • Gender, race, skin tone (light, medium, dark), hair color, eye color, approximate age, and height/weight. • Physical evidence on or near the body.

Describe outdoor scenes	Describe the following as applicable:
	• Observation of the overall scene to include—
	  ▪ The relation to geographical area, buildings, and roadways.
	  ▪ Visible personal items of clothing and equipment.
	• Concealed or protected areas from view to include—
	  ▪ Foliage.
	  ▪ Groundcover.
	• Obstructions or obstacles to the scene (natural or manmade).
	• The key significance of the scene and the primary use of the area—rural, urban, industrial.
	• Avenues of approach—vehicular and/or pedestrian.
	• Visible physical evidence to include—
	  ▪ Tire or shoe impressions.
	  ▪ Personal items of clothing and/or equipment.
	  ▪ Fluids (including bodily fluids)
	  ▪ Weapons.
	  ▪ Other.

Table F-2. 12-step crime scene checklist (continued)

Requirement	Action or Area of Focus
*Step 4: Document the crime scene (continued)*	

Describe outdoor scenes (continued)	• Unusual damage to the scene to include—
	  ▪ Fire.
	  ▪ Flood.
	  ▪ Animal activity.
	  ▪ Other.

Describe vehicle scenes	Describe the following as applicable:
	• The vehicle to include the—
	  ▪ Make.
	  ▪ Model.
	  ▪ Year.
	  ▪ Vehicle identification number.
	  ▪ License plate number (including issuing state or agency).
	  ▪ Color.
	• The exterior and interior of the vehicle.
	• Visible physical evidence.
	• Unusual damage to the vehicle including fire and/or impact damage.

Describe factors pertinent to entry/exit	Describe the probable routes of entry to or exit from the scene; including any other specific information of interest.
*Note.* Normally documentation is appropriate even if it is similar to, "Being an open area, access could be gained from any direction." It is important, however, to report only objective observations. Speculation such as, "Apparently entrance was gained through the office's window," should be avoided unless supported by specific facts that eliminate other possibilities (for example a broken window, footprints on window ledge, and such).	
Describe negative (absence of) evidence	Identify the absence of evidence. This includes noting evidence which should be present, based on the initial complainant; for example,— • There is a broken window but no glass fragments on the floor. • There is a report of a violent altercation but there were no signs of a struggle at the reported location.
Describe information factors	The presence of evidence or information not offered in the initial complainant; for example, there is no mention of a weapon from the complainant and there is one at the scene.
*Step 5: Measure the scene and evidence (flat projection)*	
Make a flat-projection sketch	Supplement the investigative notes with a rough sketch depicting evidence, measurements, and triangulation. Prepare all sketches in pencil.
*Note.* Height measurements are not shown on a flat-projection (two-dimension) room sketch although height is annotated in notes.	

Table F-2. 12-step crime scene checklist (continued)

	Requirement	Action or Area of Focus
	Step 5: Measure the scene and evidence (flat projection) (continued)	
	Make a flat-projection sketch (continued)	Take minimum required measurements to include the— • **Room.** Include the length, the width of the floor, and the height of the walls. • **Entrance/Exit.** Include the width and height—fixing the measurement. • **Door.** Include the width, height, and thickness. • **Window.** Include the width and height—fixing the measurement using a plumb bob. • **Furniture.** Include the length, width, height, and depth—fixing the measurement if not flush with two walls in the room corner or flush with a wall and fixed item of furniture).
		Triangulate the evidence as follows: • Regularly shaped items require two separate triangles of measurements (2-V method). • Irregular-shaped items require one triangle of measurement and a pattern size. Measurements are taken from the approximate center of mass to a fixed location.
	Note. Always fix an item from an "unknown" (unfixed) to "known" (fixed) location. Never measure under, over, or through the evidence or space.	
	Step 6: Measure the scene and evidence (cross projection)	
	Note. Cross projection in sketching is required when evidence items or locations of interest are on or in the wall or ceiling surfaces as well as elsewhere in an enclosed space. The walls, windows, doors, and/or ceiling are drawn as though they had been folded flat on the floor with the inside (or outside, if appropriate) surface projected up.	
	Make a cross-projection sketch	Supplement the investigative notes with a rough sketch depicting evidence, measurements, and triangulation (inside surface of the appropriate wall or ceiling). Prepare all sketches in pencil.
		Ensure that the minimum required measurements include— • **Wall or ceiling.** Measure length and width as appropriate. • **Reference points.** Identify/designate reference points on the wall's edge(s) as needed. • **Entrance/exit.** Measure length and width, fixing measurements as appropriate. • **Window.** Measure length and width, fixing measurement as appropriate. • **Light Switch.** Measure length and width, fixing measurements.
		Triangulate the evidence as follows: • Regularly shaped items require two separate triangles of measurement (2-V method). • Irregular-shaped items require one triangle of measurement and a pattern size. Measurements are taken from the approximate center of mass to a fixed location.

Table F-2. 12-step crime scene checklist (continued)

	Requirement	Action or Area of Focus
		Step 7: Perform first recheck (visual search) of the scene
	Conduct a visual search	Conduct a visual search of the scene for evidence and record the results (to include negative results).
		If evidence is discovered (overlooked earlier), it must be described, photographed, triangulated (if appropriate), and entered in the photograph log, and flat-projection or cross-projection sketches prepared as appropriate.
		Step 8: Preserve and collect evidence
	Protect an item for later collection	Check for additional and/or trace evidence and record the results.
		Cover and protect the evidence with a suitable clean device.
		Secure the device with appropriate material to protect and preclude cross contamination.
		Mark for protection with the time, date, and your initials.
	Mark an item for identification (per AR 195-5, Chapter 2-1)	Check for additional and/or trace evidence and record the results.
		Record additional marks and/or features not previously identified in the overall description and where they are located on the item.
		Mark the item with the time, date, and initials and annotate where the item was marked.
		Record the item on DA Form 4002, *Evidence Property Tag,* and place it on evidence.
		Record the item on DA Form 4137.

Notes.

1. The first LE officer assuming custody of the evidence will mark the evidence itself for future identification. The marking will consist of the time and date of acquisition and the initials of the person who assumes custody of the evidence. Annotate where markings are placed in the investigator's notes and on the DA Form 4137. Caution must be taken to prevent cross contamination of evidence at all levels of evidence processing.

2. Package all evidence per AR 195-5.

	Requirement	Action or Area of Focus
	Containerize evidence	When evidence is packaged, the investigator— • Checks for additional and/or trace evidence and records the results. • Records additional marks and/or features on the item that were not previously identified in the overall description and where they were located on the item. • Places item into a suitable container and seals the container with paper packing tape or evidence tape. The investigator marks the container with his initials, date, and time of collection, and includes initials on the remaining tape and package. • Records the item on DA Form 4002 and places the form on the container. • Records the item on DA Form 4137.

Table F-2. 12-step crime scene checklist (continued)

Requirement	Action or Area of Focus
Step 8: Preserve and collect evidence (continued)	
Heat seal evidence	When evidence is hot-sealed, the investigator— • Checks for additional and/or trace evidence and records the results. • Records additional marks and/or features on the item that were not identified in the overall description and records where the marks are located on the item. • Places the evidence in a clean, plastic heat-seal bag and heat seals the container per procedures provided with the equipment. The investigator affixes a self-adhering DA Form 4002 that includes his initials and the date and time of collection to the outside of bag away from the heat-seal strip. He embosses the heat-seal strips in the upper right hand corner with a raised seal unique to the submitting agency. • Marks the heat-seal strip with his initials and the time and date the evidence was obtained, then seals the bag. • Record the item on DA Form 4137.
Note. When completing the DA Form 4137, the following statement should be used: Placed in a clean heat-seal bag, heat sealed, and marked for identification across the heat-seal strip with the time, date and initials.	
Use sampling/forensic kits	When sampling/forensic kits are used, investigators— • Check for additional and/or trace evidence on the area where the evidence was located and record the results of the item and its sample. • Follow the instructions of forensic kits (as applicable) in collecting evidence and document steps completed and the results. • Swab the evidence with a clean cotton swab or suitable device, if wet <u>or</u> if dried, add two drops of distilled water to the swab and then swab the stain. • Record additional marks and/or features on the item that was not visible in the overall description and where it was located on the item. • Place and seal the sample in a container per procedures provided with the equipment or forensic kit. • Place the item into a suitable container and seal the container with paper packing tape or evidence tape. • Mark the container with your initials and the date and time of collection, and mark your initials on the remaining tape and package. • Record the item on DA Form 4002 and place it on the container. • Record the item on DA Form 4137.

Table F-2. 12-step crime scene checklist (continued)

Requirement	Action or Area of Focus
Step 8: Preserve and collect evidence (continued)	

Notes.

1. If you consider doing a swabbing, this should be your first item of collection to allow for the swab to dry completely before containerization. As applicable, follow the instructions of forensic kits in collecting evidence and document steps completed and results.

2. Prepare a memorandum for record on the evidence custody document as appropriate, detailing discrepancies or changes to evidence such as air-dried swabbing or fuming item for latent prints. Place the item into a suitable container and seal the container with paper packing tape or evidence tape. Mark the container with your initials and the date and time of collection, and mark your initials on the remaining tape and package. Affix the completed DA Form 4002 to the outside of the package.

Requirement	Action or Area of Focus
Coordinate with the commander or responsible personnel	Coordinate with personnel who are responsible for equipment or facilities of which items of evidence will be collected and possibly altered or destroyed.
Conduct external coordination	Contact appropriate subject matter experts including facility and installation engineers, logistics officers, explosives ordnance disposal personnel, or fire department personnel to respond with the proper equipment/tools to assist the investigator/agent in removing evidence. Brief the building manager or unit commander.
Coordinate with emergency room or appropriate medical treatment facility	Contact emergency room (or appropriate medical treatment facility) to have an ambulance assist in the transport of the victim to the morgue.
Coordinate for USACIDC support	Contact the supporting CID element to have a supporting USACIDC SA assist by escorting the body from the scene to the morgue.

Notes.

1. Items such as small amounts of powders, hairs, fibers, small paint chips, or flakes will not be placed directly in plastic bags; such items will adhere to the inside of the bag because of static electricity. Instead, put them in paper wrappings or druggist fold, cardboard containers, plastic vials, or glass vials. Plastic bags may be used after the evidence has been placed in a druggist fold.

2. Evidence to be submitted for serological tests will not be sealed in any type of plastic container. There is no requirement to seal nonfungible evidence; however, it may be sealed if desired. When sealed, it will be handled the same as fungible evidence.

Requirement	Action or Area of Focus
Step 9: Perform a second recheck of the crime scene	
Ready the body for release (if applicable)	Check the victim's hands and feet for additional and/or trace evidence and record the results. Collect evidence found on the body such as gunshot residue, hairs, or fibers (as applicable).
	Resecure clean paper bags over the hands and feet (if bare); if gloves and shoes are present, collect them.
	Conduct a visual search of the body; check around and under the body, the bed surface, and the immediate area for additional and/or trace evidence and record the results. Collect evidence found under the body as applicable.
	Record signs of other external injuries on the body or the absence thereof.
	Photograph the victim's back and its relation to the bed surface; enter the photograph in the photograph log.

Table F-2. 12-step crime scene checklist (continued)

Requirement	Action or Area of Focus
Step 9: Perform a second recheck of the crime scene (continued)	
	Wrap the victim together with the bed linen in a clean sheet and place it in a clean body bag.
	Ensure that the commander or another responsible person confirms identification of the victim.
	Release the victim to the ambulance driver (obtain the full identification of the driver and the vehicle identification number).
	Record the identification of the USACIDC SA or senior military police Soldier accompanying the body to the morgue and any specific instructions given to that escort.
Search for latent prints	Attempt to develop latent prints, noting the method used, the equipment used, locations processed, and the results.
Conduct an exploratory search	Conduct an exploratory search of the crime scene (furniture drawers, tables, containers, under bed, and such) and record the results.
Process evidence from the search	Process and collect any newly discovered evidence as you have done to previous evidence found earlier.
Step 10: Perform a third recheck of the crime scene	
Conduct another search of the scene (recheck)	Conduct a third recheck (search) of the scene and record the results. Continue rechecks of the scene until the results are negative.
Process evidence from the search	Process and collect any newly discovered evidence as you have done to previous evidence found earlier. Refer to previous steps as needed.
	Process and collect evidence you have protected earlier that required special assistance or equipment in order to collect. Ensure that full identification of any persons or special equipment used is recorded. Refer to step 8 if necessary.
Step 11: Search beyond the immediate crime scene	
Conduct an outer scene search	Conduct a thorough search beyond the scene and record the results.
	If evidence is found, expand scene security as appropriate. Refer to step 8 to collect and process evidence.
Evaluate security	Determine if additional crime scene security is needed and, if so, set it up; describe how it is to be maintained, and record specific instructions.
Expose images	Take photographs as appropriate of newly discovered scene observations during such as the following: • Signs of forced entry. • Points of entry or egress of perpetrators. • Newly discovered evidence.
Note. The sequence of this step is determined by your evaluation on the scene, security requirements, and weather conditions to include possible changes in the weather forecast.	

Table F-2. 12-step crime scene checklist (continued)

Requirement	Action or Area of Focus
Step 12: Release or maintain crime scene security	
Determine whether to release or maintain the scene	If the determination is to release the scene, record the full identification of the responsible person who will assume the scene and release scene security.
	Consult with the servicing JA for guidance if necessary.
Describe continued security requirements	If security of the crime scene is to be maintained, describe how and why security is to be maintained.
	Obtain the personnel roster, the security log, and the access list.
Coordinate with military police	Coordinate release of the scene to appropriate authority such as Provost Marshal Operations staff or the military police duty officer for security personnel.
Coordinate with the commander	Coordinate with the unit commander or other responsible person in the unit regarding the retention or release and security of the scene.
Release any support personnel no longer required	Release any personnel providing support and/or subject matter expertise.

Legend:

AR	Army regulation	SAC	special agent-in-charge
CID	criminal investigation division	SW	southwest
DA	Department of the Army	U.S.	United States
JA	judge advocate	USACIDC	United States Army Criminal
LE	law enforcement		Investigation Command
MPI	military police investigator	UCMJ	Uniform Code of Military Justice
SA	special agent	VIP	very important person

Appendix G

Commonly Abused Drugs

Drug suppression activities are routinely conducted by USACIDC SAs and supporting military police personnel. All Army LE personnel conducting LE activities may encounter persons in the possession of or under the influence of illicit drugs. This appendix describes some of the common drugs that may be encountered by Army LE during the conduct of their LE duties.

MARIJUANA AND ITS DERIVATIVES

G-1. Cannabis sativa L. (from the genus Cannabis and the family Cannabinaceae) is the botanical name for a tall, annual, woody shrub commonly known as marijuana. The Federal law definition, Part A, Subchapter I, Chapter 13, Section 802, Title 21, USC (21 USC 802), of *marijuana* is as follows: "The term 'marihuana' means all parts of the plant Cannabis sativa L., whether growing or not; the seeds thereof; the resin extracted from any part of such plant; and every compound, manufacture, salt, derivative, mixture, or preparation of such plant, its seeds or resin. Such term does not include the mature stalks of such plant; fiber produced from such stalks; oil or cake made from the seeds of such plant; any other compound, manufacture, salt, derivative, mixture, or preparation of such mature stalks (except the resin extracted therefrom); fiber, oil, cake, or the sterilized seed of such plant which is incapable of germination."

G-2. Marijuana and hashish are derivatives of the cannabis plant that has been cultivated for centuries for its fiber, oil, and psychoactive resin. There are two varieties of the cannabis plant. One is resin producing and the other is fiber producing. Delta-9-tetrahydrocannabinol (THC) is found most abundantly in the upper leaves, bracts, and flowers of the resin-producing variety.

G-3. Marijuana and hashish products contain cancer causing elements (carcinogens), just like cigarettes. Marijuana is seldom smoked with the same frequency as tobacco, but it can lead to upper respiratory problems such as those caused by cigarette smoking. Chronic, heavy users of marijuana and hashish products often show memory and concentration impairments. However, these effects generally disappear several weeks after use stops. Some people can become tolerant to the effects of marijuana with long-term, heavy use, needing larger doses to achieve the same effect. Psychological dependence is also possible, particularly for young people.

MARIJUANA

G-4. Marijuana is a commonly abused illicit drug in the United States. It is a dry, shredded green and brown mix of flowers, stems, seeds, and leaves derived from the hemp plant Cannabis sativa L. The main active chemical in marijuana is THC.

G-5. The flowering tops, leaves, and small stems are gathered and dried. Marijuana is usually smoked as a cigarette (joint) or in a pipe. It is also smoked in blunts, which are cigars that have been emptied of tobacco and refilled with marijuana. Since the blunt retains the tobacco leaf used to wrap the cigar, this mode of delivery combines marijuana's active ingredients with nicotine and other harmful chemicals. Marijuana can also be mixed in food or brewed as a tea. As a more concentrated, resinous form it is called hashish, and as a sticky black liquid, hash oil. Marijuana smoke has a pungent and distinctive, usually sweet-and-sour, odor. High doses of marijuana can produce an acute psychotic reaction; in addition, use of the drug may trigger the onset or relapse of schizophrenia in vulnerable individuals. Although symptoms vary by user, the most common signs and symptoms associated with marijuana use include—

- Pinpoint pupils.
- A sense of relaxation and happiness.

- A heightened sense of visual and auditory perception.
- A heightened sense of taste perception.
- Poor memory.
- Increased blood pressure and heart rate.
- Red eyes.
- Decreased coordination.
- Difficulty concentrating.
- Increased appetite.
- Slowed reaction time.
- Psychological addiction.
- Panic.
- Paranoia.
- Persistent anxiety.
- Impaired learning skills.

HASHISH

G-6. Hashish consists of the THC-rich resinous material of the cannabis plant, which is collected, dried and compressed into a variety of forms such as balls, cakes, or cookie-like sheets. Pieces are then broken off, placed in pipes, and smoked. It is logical to assume that the potency of THC content within the hashish is directly related to the marijuana from which it was extracted. However, a basic rule is that hashish is 8 to 10 times stronger than commercial- grade marijuana on the average. A general range in THC content would be 0.5 to 22 percent.

G-7. Hashish oil is concentrated cannabis; it is sometimes called "marijuana oil" or "honey oil." This substance is an illicitly manufactured form of what was formerly known in the pharmaceutical and medical professions as tincute or extract of cannabis, a lawful product once used for medicinal purposes. In general, hashish oil is about 3 to 4 times stronger than hashish and 30 to 40 times stronger than commercial-grade marijuana. It appears on the street as a very thick liquid and is many times so thick that it must be heated to allow it to flow. It varies in color, but can generally be found in amber, dark green, brown, or black. Many users smoke hash oil by adding it to a marijuana cigarette or a commercial cigarette. Some users take hash oil by mouth, such as adding it to food preparations or liquids like hot teas.

G-8. A hash pipe or a regular pipe is normally used when it is smoked. It can be eaten as is or used in cooking. The most common signs and symptoms of hashish use include—
- Dilated pupils.
- Intense euphoria.
- Peacefulness.
- Empathy.
- Sympathy.

STIMULANTS

G-9. The two most prevalent stimulants are nicotine (found in tobacco products) and caffeine (the active ingredient of coffee, tea, and some bottled beverages). When used in moderation, these stimulants tend to relieve fatigue and increase alertness. They are an accepted part of our culture. There are, however, more potent stimulants that, because of their dependence-producing potential, are under the regulatory control of many countries. These controlled substances are available by prescription for medical purposes. They are also clandestinely manufactured in vast quantities for distribution on the illicit market.

G-10. Stimulants are compounds that affect the central nervous system by accelerating its activities. Stimulants are either natural (such as epinephrine, nicotine, or caffeine) or synthetic (such as amphetamine, dextroamphetamine, or methamphetamine). Some stimulants may be mixed compounds such as Yaba which is a mixture of methamphetamine and caffeine. In terms of illicit use, amphetamine, dextroamphetamine, and methamphetamine are the focus for LE personnel.

AMPHETAMINE

G-11. Amphetamines are stimulants to the central nervous system. Their chemical structures are so similar that it is difficult for users to tell the difference. Amphetamines generally increase alertness, attention, and energy. Amphetamines are used medically as an aid in treating narcolepsy, some forms of depression, and attention deficit hyperactivity disorder in children (in children amphetamines can have a calming effect instead of the stimulant effect they exhibit in adults). Due to the potential for abuse and addiction, other treatments are used more frequently. While there are numerous legitimate uses for amphetamines when taken under the supervision of medical personnel, they are commonly obtained, distributed, and used for illicit purposes. Legitimate medical amphetamines are produced under several brand names including—

- Adderall®.
- Ritalin®.
- Desoxyn®.
- Dexedrine®.
- Destrostat®.

G-12. There are many symptoms of stimulant abuse. They include—

- Excessive activity.
- Irritability.
- Nervousness.
- Paranoia.
- Argumentativeness.
- Excessive sweating.
- Excitability.
- Talkativeness.
- Trembling hands.
- Dry mouth.
- Overreaction to normal stimuli.
- Flushed skin.
- Headache.
- Tremors.
- Euphoria.
- Dilated pupils.
- Increased blood pressure or pulse rate.
- The ability to go long periods without eating or sleeping.

METHAMPHETAMINE

G-13. Crystal methamphetamine (crystal meth), commonly called glass or ice because of its appearance, is a colorless, odorless, large-crystal form of d-methamphetamine. When it is produced, it is reported to have a skunky odor. Crystal meth is most often produced by slowly recrystallizing powder methamphetamine from a solvent such as water, methanol, ethanol, isopropanol, or acetone to remove impurities.

G-14. Crystal meth is typically smoked like crack cocaine—using a glass pipe, an empty aluminum can, a piece of aluminum foil, or a broken light bulb. The effects of crystal meth are similar to those of powdered methamphetamine. Typically crystal meth has a high level of purity and the effects can last 12 hours or more. The availability of crystal meth has increased in recent years because of the relative ease with which it can be produced. This has enabled widespread production and distribution by small-level criminals across the United States. It is also a popular drug for distribution by criminal groups from Mexico.

G-15. Methamphetamine can be smoked, snorted, injected, or taken orally. Immediately after smoking the drug or injecting it intravenously, the user experiences an intense rush or "flash" that lasts only a few minutes and is described as extremely pleasurable. Snorting or oral ingestion produces euphoria—a high, but not an intense rush. Snorting produces effects within 3 to 5 minutes, and oral ingestion produces effects within 15 to 20 minutes.

G-16. Methamphetamine is highly addictive; heavy users exhibit progressive social and occupational deterioration. Psychotic symptoms (paranoia, delusions, and mood disturbances) can sometimes persist for months or years after use has ceased. Over time, methamphetamine appears to cause reduced levels of dopamine, which can result in symptoms like those in Parkinson's disease, a severe movement disorder. The most common signs and symptoms of methamphetamine users include—

- Dilated pupils.
- Dry mouth.
- Euphoria.
- Decreased appetite.
- Rapid speech.
- Irritability.
- Restlessness.
- Depression.
- Nasal congestion.
- Insomnia.
- Weight loss.
- Increased heart rate.
- Increased blood pressure.
- Increased temperature.
- Lack of interest in food or sleep.
- Degradation in personal hygiene.
- Argumentative nature.
- Nervousness.
- Violent nature.
- Paranoia.

YABA

G-17. Yaba is Thai for "crazy medicine." Yaba tablets have overwhelmed Southeast Asia, but availability in the United States and other areas of the world is limited. Yaba tablets are manufactured with varying amounts of methamphetamine and caffeine and are often stamped with the logos "wy" or "r." Generally they are no larger than a pencil eraser and are sold in different colors and flavors. They taste like candy and are marketed to a younger audience, particularly at raves and parties where ecstasy has already been established.

G-18. Yaba is typically ingested orally, although it can be crushed into a powder and snorted or mixed with a solvent and injected. Another common method of ingestion is "chasing the dragon." The user places the tablet on aluminum foil, heats it, and inhales the vapors.

COCAINE

G-19. Cocaine is a white crystalline alkaloid that is chemically synthesized using the leaves of the coca plant (erythroxylon coca) and acts as a stimulant to the central nervous system. The coca plant is an evergreen that is native to South America—particularly the countries of Peru, Bolivia, Brazil, Chile and Columbia—and should not be confused with the cocoa plant from which chocolate is made. Although the coca plant is natural to South America, it has been successfully cultivated in Java, West Indies, India, and Australia.

G-20. There are two forms of cocaine—powdered cocaine and crack. The powdered, hydrochloride salt form of cocaine can be snorted or dissolved in water and injected. Crack has not been neutralized by an acid to make the hydrochloride salt. This form of cocaine comes in a rock crystal that can be heated and its vapors smoked. Cocaine is the most potent stimulant of natural origin and is one of the oldest identified drugs. The pure chemical, cocaine hydrochloride, has been an abused substance for more than 100 years.

G-21. There is great risk whether cocaine is ingested by inhalation (snorting), injection, or smoking. It appears that compulsive cocaine use may develop even more rapidly if the substance is smoked rather than snorted. Smoking allows extremely high doses of cocaine to reach the brain very quickly and brings an intense and immediate high. The user experiences a high in less than 10 seconds. This rather immediate and euphoric effect is one of the reasons that crack became enormously popular in the mid 1980s.

G-22. The effects of cocaine can be divided into what goes on in the central nervous system, the brain, and the rest of the body. The effects of the drug vary greatly, depending on the route of administration, the amount, its purity, and effects of the added ingredients. The effect also varies with the user's emotional state while taking the drug. This is based on the user's attitude toward the drug, the physical setting in which the drug is being used, the user's physical condition, and whether or not the person is a regular user. Cocaine affects every organ system, from the brain to the skin. The street names for cocaine are coke, snow, nose candy, flake, blow, big C, lady, snowbirds, and white. The most common signs and symptoms of cocaine use include—

- Dilated pupils.
- Hyperactivity.
- Euphoria.
- Irritability.
- Anxiety.
- Excessive talking.
- Depression or excessive sleeping.
- Weight loss.
- Dry mouth and nose.
- Paranoia.
- Disturbance of heart rhythm.
- Chest pain.
- Heart failure.
- Respiratory failure.
- Strokes.
- Seizures.

OPIATES AND OPIATE DERIVATIVES

G-23. Initially, opium and its derivatives were considered an acceptable analgesic (a drug that alleviates pain without resulting in unconsciousness), but very little was known of their pharmacological affect or toxicity. Certain individuals began to glamorize the stupefying effects of the drugs and, shortly thereafter, large numbers of people began to abuse the drugs. Through continuous promiscuous use, the numbers of addicts began to swell in countries throughout Europe.

G-24. Opiates refer to any drug derived from the opium poppy (papaver somniferum). The opium poppy is indigenous to many climates, growing from the southernmost tip of Africa to as far north as Moscow, with the largest quantities coming from the area known as the Golden Triangle (Laos, Burma, and Thailand), the area known as the Golden Crescent (Afghanistan, Pakistan, and Iran), and Mexico. Opium and opium derivatives have both legitimate medical and illicit uses.

G-25. There are many legitimate medical opiates in use today including morphine and codeine. Legally produced morphine and codeine are available and necessary drugs that are extensively used throughout the medical world. They are used to reduce severe pain, quiet nervous individuals, and arrest heart disease, among many other additional uses. They are also highly addictive and can be abused when not properly monitored. While morphine and codeine are subject to abuse and illicit use, they are not the most commonly abused opiates. The most common illicitly used opiates are described below.

HEROIN

G-26. Heroin is an opiate drug that is synthesized from morphine, a naturally occurring substance extracted from the seed pod of the Asian opium poppy plant, categorizing it as a semisynthetic. It is three times more potent than morphine and penetrates the blood-brain barrier faster, resulting in an intense rush. Heroin usually appears as a white or brown powder or as a black sticky substance, known as "black tar heroin."

G-27. Heroin is usually injected, sniffed, snorted, or smoked. Injection continues to be the prominent method of heroin use among addicted users, although there has been an increase in sniffing and smoking as a method of heroin use. Intravenous use provides the greatest intensity and the most rapid onset of euphoria (7 to 8 seconds) while intramuscular produces a relatively slow onset (5 to 8 minutes). When sniffed or smoked, peak effects are usually felt within 10 to 15 minutes.

G-28. After an intravenous injection of heroin, users report feeling a surge of euphoria ("rush") accompanied by dry mouth, a warm flushing of the skin, heaviness of the extremities, and clouded mental functioning. Following this initial euphoria, the user goes "on the nod," an alternately wakeful and drowsy state. Users who do not inject the drug may not experience the initial rush, but other effects are the same. Heroin is metabolized to monoacetylmorphine and morphine within 45 minutes of being administered.

G-29. With regular heroin use, tolerance develops, in which the user's physiological (and psychological) response to the drug decreases, and more heroin is needed to achieve the same intensity of effect. Heroin users are at high risk for addiction—it is estimated that about 23 percent of individuals who use heroin become dependent on it. The common signs and symptoms associated with heroine abuse include—
- Pinpoint pupils.
- No response of pupils to light.
- A rush of pleasurable feelings.
- Cessation of physical pain.
- Lethargy.
- Drowsiness.
- Slurred speech.
- Shallow breathing.
- Sweating.
- Vomiting.
- A drop in body temperature.
- Sleepiness.
- Loss of appetite.

HYDROCODONE

G-30. Hydrocodone is a legal opiate prescribed for pain that has qualities similar to morphine. There are over 200 medications that contain hydrocodone, and in the United States, over 20 tons of hydrocodone are used annually. Hydrocodone is available in pill and syrup forms. Vicodin (hydrocodone with acetaminophen), is one of the most commonly abused forms of hydrocodone. Not only is hydrocodone dangerous and addictive, high doses of acetaminophen can severely damage the liver.

G-31. Hydrocodone's analgesic potency is from two to eight times that of morphine, but it is shorter acting and produces more sedation than morphine. Hydrocodone is sought after by narcotic addicts who dissolve and inject the tablets as a substitute for heroine. Hydrocodone is marketed under several brand names including—
- Anexia®.
- Dilaudid®.
- Hycodan®.

- Hycomine®.
- Lorcet®.
- Lortab®.
- Tussionex®.
- Tylox®.
- Vicodin®.
- Vicoprofen®.

G-32. While hydrocodone can cause feelings of joy and euphoria, it is not safe to use on a regular basis. It is extremely addictive, and side effects can include permanent liver and kidney damage, skin rashes, chest pain, nausea, flu symptoms, and difficulty breathing.

G-33. Most people who abuse Vicodin® and other hydrocodone products cannot quit on their own, especially if they have been using them for a long time or using in large amounts. Withdrawal is not pleasant and can, in rare cases, cause sudden death or coma if the person tries to quit without professional help. Even if the person manages to get through physical withdrawal, it can be very hard to overcome the psychological dependency upon this drug. Hydrocodone allows people to disengage from everyday life and to live in a kind of pain-free state of bliss. They usually need help coming back to normal life with goals, responsibilities, and healthy relationships with others. The most common signs and symptoms of hydrocodone abuse include—

- Dilated pupils.
- Nausea.
- Drowsiness.
- Impaired coordination.
- Weakness.
- Confusion.
- Relaxed muscles.
- Lowered blood pressure.
- Lower heart and respiratory rate.

OXYCODONE

G-34. Oxycodone is a narcotic prescribed to relieve pain and is twice as potent as morphine. There are many variations of oxycodone products. It is reportedly crushed (to break down the timed-release component) and then snorted or injected. Used as a substitute for heroin, abusers use the drug to relieve pain, alleviate withdrawal symptoms, and gain euphoric effects. The street names for oxycodone are OC, OX, Oxy, Oxycotton, Hillbilly heroin, and Blue. Brand names of oxycodone include—

- Oxycontin®.
- Roxicodone®.
- M-oxy®.
- ETH-Oxydose®.
- Oxyfast®.
- OxyIR®.

G-35. The common signs and symptoms associated with oxycodone abuse include—

- Pinpointed pupils.
- Dry mouth.
- Sweating.
- Headache.
- Rash.
- Constipation.
- Nausea.

- Drowsiness.
- Impaired coordination.
- Weakness.
- Confusion.
- Muscle relaxation.
- Lower blood pressure.
- Lower heart and respiratory rate.

HALLUCINOGENS

G-36. The term "hallucinogens" refers to a group of drugs that affect the central nervous system and produce perceptual alterations, intense and varying emotional changes, ego distortions, and thought disruption. Most of these substances have no medical use and are taken simply because of the subjective effect they produce. They are not considered to be addictive, although they can and do produce psychological dependence. Hallucinogens are exotic drugs that have received considerable attention from the media and drug abuse educators.

G-37. Hallucinogens (also called psychedelics) are capable of provoking alterations of time and space perception, illusions, hallucinations, and delusions. The results are variable because the same person may experience a "good trip" or a "bad trip" on different occasions. Many drugs will cause a delirium accompanied by hallucinations and delusions when taken by individuals who are hypersensitive to them. Extraordinarily large amounts of other types of drugs may also produce hallucinations because of their direct action on brain cells. Because of the potentially adverse effect of hallucinogens on the human body, these drugs pose special dangers to anyone handling them. Moreover, since very small quantities (micrograms in some cases) may have great potency, Army LE personnel must be extremely careful in how they handle and package hallucinogens seized as evidence. Under no circumstances should an investigator taste this or any other type of drug or narcotic. Equally important, investigators must avoid any direct physical contact with the suspected drug. Drugs categorized as hallucinogens include LSD; PCP; psilocybin and psi l ocyn; 3,4-methylenedioxymethamphetamine (MDMA), and mescaline.

G-38. The symptoms of hallucinogens and dissociative drug abuse vary depending on the particular drug. Drugs with street names like acid, angel dust, and vitamin K distort the way a user perceives time, motion, colors, sounds, and self. These drugs can disrupt an individual's ability to think and communicate rationally or even to recognize reality, sometimes resulting in bizarre or dangerous behavior. Hallucinogens such as LSD cause emotions to swing wildly and real-world sensations to seem unreal, sometimes with frightening aspects.

LYSERGIC ACID DIATHYLAMIDE

G-39. The most powerful and possibly the most widely used of the "mind-expanding" drugs is LSD, a semisynthetic alkaloid substance extracted from a fungus that grows on rye, wheat, and other grains. It is an extremely potent drug, requiring only a small amount to induce a "trip." The affects of an average dose (about 100 micrograms) usually last for 6 to 12 hours. One ounce is enough to provide 300,000 doses. LSD is encountered as a liquid or a powder. In its original state, it is colorless, odorless, and tasteless. It is often put on or in things, such as sugar cubes, toothpicks, aspirin, crackers, postage stamps, or bread.

PHENCYCLIDINE

G-40. PCP, is known on the streets as "angel dust" and numerous other exotic names. The affects of PCP vary widely. In small doses, it causes sedation like most depressants. In moderate doses, analgesic and anesthetic symptoms occur, characterized by sensory disturbances. In large doses, PCP may produce convulsions and a coma leading to death. Most persons using PCP experience a confused state characterized by feelings of weightlessness, unreality, and hallucinations. Reports of difficulty in thinking, poor concentration, and preoccupation with death are frequent. Other effects include—

- Nausea.
- Vomiting.

- Profuse sweating.
- Involuntary eye movements (nystagmus).
- Double vision.
- Restlessness.
- Increased rates of fetal loss, chromosome breakage, and decreased fertility.

PSILOCYBIN AND PSILOCYN

G-41. Psilocybin occurs naturally in several species of mushrooms. Psilocybin is relatively unstable and upon ingestion is converted to psilocyn by the enzyme, alkaline phosphatase. Therefore, it seems likely that psilocyn is actually responsible for the drug effects accredited to psilocybin.

METHYLENEDIOXYMETHAMPHETAMINE

G-42. MDMA (3, 4-methylenedioxymethamphetamine), also known as Ecstasy, is a synthetic drug with both stimulant and hallucinogenic qualities. MDMA is sometimes referred to as a designer drug. A designer drug is one that is a copycat of another drug or a synthetic compound of two or more drugs. MDMA is a synthetic compound. For a time, MDMA use was on the decline, but use has risen again in recent years.

G-43. MDMA is most often available in tablet form and is usually ingested orally. It is also available as a powder and is sometimes snorted and occasionally smoked, but rarely injected. Its effects last approximately four to six hours. Users of the drug say that it produces profoundly positive feelings, empathy for others, elimination of anxiety, and extreme relaxation.

G-44. MDMA is also said to suppress the need to eat, drink, or sleep, enabling users to endure two- to three-day parties. Consequently, MDMA use sometimes results in severe dehydration or exhaustion. MDMA is classified by Federal regulators as a drug with no accepted medical use.

G-45. Studies have revealed that former users suffered damage to the neurons in the brain that transmit serotonin, an important biochemical involved in a variety of critical functions including learning, sleep, and integration of emotion. Recreational MDMA users may be at risk of developing permanent brain damage that may manifest itself in depression, anxiety, memory loss, and other neuropsychotic disorders.

MESCALINE

G-46. Mescaline is a hallucinogen obtained from the small, spineless peyote cactus. Mescaline is also found in certain members of the Fabaceae (bean family). From earliest recorded time, peyote has been used by natives in northern Mexico and the southwestern United States as a part of traditional religious rites. The top of the cactus aboveground, also referred to as the crown, consists of disc-shaped buttons that are cut from the roots and dried. These buttons are generally chewed or soaked in water to produce an intoxicating liquid.

G-47. The hallucinogenic dose for mescaline is about 0.3 to 0.5 grams (equivalent to about 5 grams of dried peyote) and lasts about 12 hours. While mescaline produced rich visual hallucinations which were important to the native peyote cults, the full range of effects served as a chemically induced model of mental illness. Mescaline is used primarily as a recreational drug and is also used to supplement various types of meditation and psychedelic therapy.

G-48. Users typically experience visual hallucinations and radically altered states of consciousness—most often experienced as pleasurable and illuminating. But these experiences are occasionally accompanied by feelings of anxiety or revulsion. Other effects include—

- Open- and closed-eye visualizations.
- Euphoria.
- A dream-like state.
- Laughter.
- A psychedelic experience.

OTHER SUBSTANCES

G-49. A multitude of other substances may be used to achieve an intoxicating effect. Some of these substances are controlled under the CSA. The use of these substances to achieve an intoxicating affect is prohibited by AR 600-85 and can result in a punishment under the UCMJ. They can include a wide range of substances including bath salts, inhaling aerosols, and other substances. One of the more common is synthetic cannabis or K2.

G-50. K2 is synthetic cannabis. "K2" or "spice" is a mix of herbs and a chemical compound that's sold as incense at essentially the same price as real marijuana. Even though K2 is a synthetic form of cannabis, it can produce strong hallucinogenic effects. It is reported to be 10 times as potent as THC, the active ingredient in marijuana. K2 has been responsible for severe hallucinations in teenagers who acquire it. In addition to the "potent psychotropic drug," the mixture is likely contaminated with an unknown toxic substance that is causing many adverse effects. The most common signs and symptoms (none of which are associated with marijuana) of K2 use include—

- Increased heart rate.
- Increased blood pressure.
- Agitation.

Appendix H

Environmental Crimes

Environmental crimes are not new. However, recent national events have caused increased emphasis on LE agencies training to conduct investigations in a hazardous or contaminated environment. Investigating an environmental crime or a crime with an environmental impact is very similar to investigating any other crime. A crime scene examination, evidence collection, and interviews are still required. Environmental crimes do not consist of just an intentional dumping of hazardous material. They are also criminal investigations with an environmental impact that include things such as a package delivered with suspected anthrax, a fatal collision involving a tanker truck, or a clandestine drug laboratory. These crimes could easily encompass or be part of other crimes, such as fraud, arson, or assault, and could involve the use of computers or other electronic records, such as hazardous material disposal records. Even the most common investigation could involve environmental concerns.

BACKGROUND

H-1. The EPA and state, local, and even foreign agencies (depending on the applicable SOFA) hold military installations responsible for environmental damage that they cause, even though the majority of this damage is caused by the military's main peacetime mission, which is training. Because of excessive environmental fees (9.9 million dollars between 1992 and 1994) assessed to Army installations, the Army has developed a strict policy to protect the environment) with specific guidelines for vehicle maintenance during field operations. Therefore, investigators are charged to thoroughly investigate the intentional dumping of used motor oil, parts-cleaning solvent, and other hazardous material. See AR 200-1 for more information on environmental protection.

H-2. Other concerns include conservation areas on military installations. Many installations border or encompass national forest lands, historic sites, landmarks, wildlife refuge areas, or parks. U.S. law requires the preservation of these areas. Although training in these areas may be forbidden or severely restricted, activities (such as noise, pyrotechnics, or dust from heavy vehicle movement) in adjacent areas could have a negative impact on the environment.

H-3. Generally, the major significant difference between a crime with an environmental impact and any other crime is the contamination of the crime scene. Traditionally, fire department personnel have controlled these scenes. This is primarily due to their specialized training on working in protective clothing within a hazardous environment and their responsibility to contain, control, and clean the area to prevent the spread of contamination. As with any arson investigation, the techniques used to contain and control these scenes are very destructive and not conducive to the preservation of physical evidence. Therefore, the investigator should respond to the scene (either with or at the same time as fire and medical personnel) as a member of the hazardous-incident integrated response team.

IDENTIFYING ENVIRONMENTAL CRIMES

H-4. Before defining an environmental crime, it must be determined what is meant by "environment." An environment is conceptual and encompasses anything (including circumstances, conditions, and other elements) that affects the existence and development of an individual, an organism, or a group. The environment of an organism is made up of everything around it. Sunlight, temperature, air, soil, minerals, water, and other living things are all elements of the environment of an organism. An environmental crime is any crime that has, or possibly could have, a negative impact on any specifically protected element of the environment.

H-5. Not all actions that cause a negative impact on an environment are crimes. A person who cuts down a tree in the woods behind his house is damaging the environment of that tree, other trees, animals, and every organism in the area of the tree, but that would not usually be a crime. If the same individual chose to dump a significant amount of poison into the soil around that same tree and the poison not only killed the tree but also washed over to his neighbor's property and seeped down into the water table, then a criminal act might have taken place. A violation of the law must occur before an incident can be considered an environmental crime.

H-6. U.S. Army installations and activities do not develop environmental laws. They develop regulations and policy guidelines to comply with the statutes. Although all federal laws apply to the U.S. Army, each individual installation must be aware of, and comply with, other laws and regulations in its area. The following are sources of laws that may apply to U.S. installations and activities:

- **Federal law.** The Federal Facility Compliance Act (FFCA) of 1992 requires military installations to comply with environmental laws. The FFCA allows regulating agencies to impose civil fines on other federal agencies, like the DA, for violations of the Resource Conservation and Recovery Act. Congress expanded the concept of federal facility compliance to other U.S. environmental laws, including the Clean Water Act. Changes to the FFCA now require federal agencies (including military installations) to comply with state, regional, county, and local laws; allow for the imposition of fines for violations of these laws; and allow these governmental bodies or even individuals to sue U.S. Army installations.
- **State law.** Each state has its own regulatory agencies charged with developing and implementing environmental regulations. All state regulations should at least parallel federal regulations. Some federal statutes allow states to set standards that are more stringent than the federal requirements. When the EPA approves a state program, that state has "primacy" for that particular environmental program.
- **Regional, county, and local law.** Local laws and ordinances address the concerns of the local community. Generally, these ordinances will be based on state and federal laws. However, each municipality or community may place restrictions that are more stringent on certain activities, such as noise restrictions during certain hours of the day and restrictions on pollution, which require car pool lanes in major cities. Although regional and county ordinances could affect installations within their boundaries, it is unlikely that local or municipal ordinances will apply since most installations are not within municipal boundaries. However, the potential for conflict exists when installations are located along a border with cities or towns.
- **Host nation law.** While serving in areas outside the continental United States, individuals and installations are required to maintain cooperative relationships with regulatory agencies of the HN and comply with their environmental control standards. SOFAs that permit or require standards other than those of the host country are considered part of the environmental abatement standards that apply to the military in the HN or its jurisdiction.

Note. Investigators should consult with SMEs trained in environmental law and regulations before beginning an environmental investigation. These experts can include the servicing office of the SJA and state and federal government environmental stakeholders (including the EPA office responsible for the area of focus for the investigation).

HAZARDOUS INCIDENT RESPONSE

H-7. Hazardous incidents are uncontrolled, illegal, or threatened releases of hazardous substances or hazardous by-products of substances. When the Superfund Amendments and Reauthorization Act (SARA) was passed in 1986, it regulated the storage, transportation, use, and disposal of hazardous material into the environment. Within the SARA, Title I and Title III were established to provide specific guidance for responding to hazardous incidents.

H-8. Title I of SARA mandates that the Occupational Safety and Health Administration (OSHA) and the EPA establish regulations on training, emergency response, safety, and associated hazardous material activities. Within this title, 29 CFR 1910.120 for OSHA and 40 CFR 311.1 for EPA were established. These federal regulations outline training standards and mandate written SOPs for hazardous material incidents.

H-9. Title III of SARA sets requirements for industries to report materials used or stored in the workplace. These reports supply emergency responders with an inventory of what chemicals may be found in an industrial setting. Part of the reporting includes a requirement to supply a material safety data sheet for certain substances, based on their particular level of toxicity or danger.

GENERAL CONSIDERATIONS

H-10. Investigators must meet OSHA training and medical requirements before entering potentially hazardous sites. The base bioenvironmental offices and military public health offices should be contacted to determine and arrange for necessary training and medical monitoring. Investigators are not first responders to environmental crime scenes. They should enter potentially hazardous sites only under the guidance and supervision of environmental regulatory or emergency response personnel. Do not risk exposure. Responsible environmental management personnel make safety determinations and specify the use of protective gear. The investigator must follow their instructions. Never direct an investigator to enter potentially hazardous sites or handle potentially hazardous material unless he is specifically trained and experienced in operating in a hazardous environment.

H-11. Gather as much information about the hazardous substance as possible through interviews and document reviews. The investigator should determine the following:

- The products involved, the types of containers, and the extent of the discharge.
- The potential offenders, the ownership of the materials, and the property involved.
- Any ongoing dangers posed by the discharge.
- The circumstances surrounding the discovery of the incident.

H-12. Once the scene is determined to be safe and released to investigators, decide on a search technique and assign a search team to conduct an area search. The search team should look for any—

- Discoloration of soil, water, and vegetation.
- Distress or absence of vegetation.
- Sheen on the water.
- Dead or sick wildlife.
- Unusual odors.
- Residue on hoses, storm drains, grates, and so forth.
- Drums and other containers.
- Tanks (aboveground and belowground).
- Recent soil movement.
- Tire tracks and footprints.
- Labels on the containers.
- Paperwork associated with the incident.

H-13. Aerial photography can document visible water, soil, and vegetation contamination and changes due to discharges of hazardous material. Special films can show a variety of conditions (temperature changes due to the presence of chemicals, bacterial growth, and vegetation discoloration).

Appendix I

Investigator Testimony

The final and most severe test of an investigator's efficiency is often as a witness before a court of law. The effectiveness of the evidence can be directly affected by the impression the investigator makes as a witness. Testimony is only effective when it is credible. Credibility is established when the investigator articulates his testimony with sincerity, knowledge of the facts, and impartiality. Although the substance of his testimony is of great importance, equal significance is attached to his conduct on the stand and to the manner in which he presents the facts discovered during the course of the investigation.

PREPARATION

I-1.   The final result in bringing a successful investigation to a close is often the investigator's testimony in the courtroom. The investigator must prepare carefully and ensure that all known case facts are in order. Whenever the investigator is preparing for trial, he should coordinate with the counsel who is calling him as a witness, in order to prevent misunderstandings and surprises. The investigator should develop a close working relationship with the trial counsel (TC) so that both parties will clearly understand the questions that will be asked and the answers that will be provided. The investigator must be professional in every way and never give the impression that he is attempting to conceal information from the court. The accused has the right to a fair trial regardless of the investigator's opinion.

I-2.   For an investigator to be better equipped to provide testimony, he should—
- Acquire a general knowledge of what is occurring in the courtroom.
- Ask trial counsel about protocol or local court rules about carrying a firearm into the courtroom.
- Understand what the defense and prosecuting attorneys are trying to achieve through a particular strategy.
- Recognize relevant and material evidence with an understanding of the rules as they apply to hearsay, confessions, polygraph results, and documents. See the MCM for more information.
- Testify only to the facts that he acquired firsthand, through his own senses. This means that he cannot be prompted to provide an opinion unless he is recognized as an expert witness. It also means that it is permissible for him to pause before providing a seemingly inadmissible answer, which allows the opposing counsel an opportunity to object.

COURTROOM TESTIMONY

I-3.   Military police training seldom devotes sufficient time to trial preparation and testimony. A good police witness must be truthful, positive, and firm in answering all questions. Military police and investigators must be taught to defend against the tactics used by lawyers in the courtroom. They must use intelligible and understandable language when talking to the panel or members of the court. Military police have been trained to recognize that providing good first impressions and giving solid concluding statements in testimony give them an advantage in the courtroom.

FIRST IMPRESSIONS IN THE COURTROOM

I-4.   Impressions that the investigator first gives in a courtroom are critical to his testimony. The following guidelines will assist the investigator in setting a good first impression with the members of the court:

- Know what to do when entering the courtroom. This may require you to report ahead of time to become familiar with the layout of the room.
- Walk confidently. You should appear secure without looking cocky or arrogant.
- Do not carry notes or reports to the witness stand. Leave them with the trial counsel who called the LE investigator.
- Stand straight and face the administrator of the oath with the palm of your right hand facing that person.
- Answer the question, "Do you swear to tell the truth, the whole truth, and nothing but the truth, so help you God?" in a clear, firm voice. You should not look at anyone other than the administrator of the oath.
- Sit in the chair with your back straight when instructed to take the stand, but be comfortable. Keep your hands folded in your lap or rested on the arms of the chair. Avoid becoming rigid, fidgeting in the chair, or swiveling the chair around. This is distracting to the testimony and may be perceived as indications of deceit or anxiety.
- If you cannot recall or are unsure of an answer, it is acceptable to say, "I do not recall." This will trigger a legal procedure the lawyers may use to refresh your recollection, including a review of your notes if necessary. The trial counsel may show the investigator the notes or report, have him read it silently, and after reviewing the document, ask the question again.

INVESTIGATOR'S TESTIMONY

I-5.   The prosecutor will ask the investigator for his full name, SSN, unit, and duty position. Before appearing in court, the TC and the investigator should discuss whether the investigator will be requested to disclose his military rank and, if so, what the appropriate response should be. Additionally, depending upon the nature of the offense, the investigator may be requested to provide a summary of his investigative training relating to the investigation that he intends to testify about. The investigator must be cognizant of inadmissible statements which include information related to—

- Privileged communication.
- Hearsay.
- Polygraph results or declinations.
- Opinions (unless the investigator is a qualified and recognized expert in the related field of questioning).
- Statements about the character and reputation of the defendant, to include a past criminal record (unless the statements establish a pattern of conduct).

I-6.   The investigator testifies only to what he saw, heard, or did. He does not testify to what he thinks or believes, heard about, or was told about unless the information falls within one of the exceptions to the hearsay rules of evidence as described in the MCM. The manner in which the investigator expresses himself verbally can impact the way in which the testimony is received by persons in the courtroom. Consider the following when providing courtroom testimony:

- Speak slowly and deliberately, with expression, and loud enough to be heard. Do not use profanity or vulgarity unless asked to provide the exact words of the suspect, victim, or witness. If profanity or vulgarity is present in those words, forewarn the court.
- Pause briefly to form answers before answering each question. If an opposing counsel makes an objection, stop speaking until the court rules on the objection. Never blurt out answers to a question objected to by the counsel.
- Answer questions from either counsel in a polite, courteous manner. When a question is not understood, ask that it be repeated or clarified. If you do not know the answer to a question, respond with, "I do not know" or "I do not recall." Never speculate or guess at an answer.

I-7.   Nonverbal physical appearances and actions by the investigator are equally important to the success of an effective testimony. The following nonverbal factors should be considered:

- **Appearance.** Present a clean and well-kept appearance, dress in appropriate business attire, and ensure that personal grooming standards are according to AR 670-1, unless an exception for ongoing covert activities is authorized. In such instances, ensure that the TC is aware of this authorization before any anticipated testimony. If an exception to policy is authorized, the investigator's appearance should still be neat and professional.

- **Posture.** Present a comfortably straight posture when standing and sitting. Refrain from slouching, as this may suggest contempt or a lack of confidence.
- **Gestures.** Use meaningful gestures to emphasize what is being stated, but avoid waiving and using excessive hand movements.
- **Eye contact.** Make eye contact with the person for whom the information is intended. The investigator must be aware that the primary audience of his testimony is the panel. It is appropriate for the investigator to look at the counsel who is asking the question while it is being asked, but he may look at both the counsel and the panel when he provides his response. Common sense must be used when answering a series of short questions.
- **Rate and tone of speech.** The rate at which the investigator speaks may have an effect on the panel's perception of his credibility. If he gives his testimony too quickly, the panel may not hear him.
- **Movement.** Avoid movements that are annoying and distracting.

AGGRESSIVE DEFENSE COUNSEL

I-8. During examination by the defense counsel (DC), it is not uncommon for the DC to become overbearing or aggressive. The DC may demand "Yes" or "No" answers to complex questions or to questions that present parts that could be answered "Yes" while other parts could be answered "No." The best approach for investigators dealing with a DC who employs these tactics is to turn to the judge and advise him that he cannot accurately respond to the question with a "Yes" or "No" answer, and seek his guidance and intervention. In most cases, the judge will ask the DC if he wants the question answered and then issue instructions to him on how to resolve the conflict.

I-9. It is paramount that investigators never take an adversarial tone with the DC. If the DC is hostile while the investigator is calm and composed, the loss of credibility and respect will impact the DC, not the investigator. Conversely, if the investigator loses his temper or becomes hostile, his professionalism and credibility are diminished in the eyes of the panel.

CROSS-EXAMINATION

I-10. The most difficult part of testifying is usually the cross-examination. The investigator must remain calm during cross-examination and avoid arguing. The DC will use a variety of questioning techniques to establish possible inconsistencies or prejudice. He may attempt to cast doubt on the investigator's testimony in an attempt to get an acquittal. It is important for the investigator to remember that the DC is merely doing his job the best way he can and that such attacks are not personal; they are merely a tactic used to create doubt. The investigator must be familiar with the methods of attack for cross-examination to avoid falling prey to such tactics. These tactics include the following:

- Acting overly friendly or brutal.
- Attacking the investigator's skills or knowledge of investigative procedure.
- Using rapid-fire questioning.
- Employing the silent treatment after the investigator's response.
- Demanding a simple answer to a complex question.
- Asking leading questions.
- Misquoting the investigator and declaring him incompetent or inconsistent. The investigator should not become defensive, but may merely restate his previous testimony in correcting the perception of inconsistency. Investigators should not argue with the DC.
- Attempting to force contradictions. The DC repeats the question using slightly different verbiage in an attempt to create disparity in the investigator's answers. The investigator should merely say, "As I previously stated," and repeat his earlier response.

TESTIMONY CONCLUSION

I-11. When the investigator has completed his testimony, he should not let his guard down. He must maintain the same presence that he had when he entered the courtroom. He should leave the stand when directed to do so. While leaving the stand, he should not direct his attention to the DC, the defendant, the prosecutor, the judge, or panel members. The investigator should—

- Determine if he has been temporarily or permanently excused. If he has been permanently excused, he may observe the remainder of the proceedings or leave the court building and return to work. If he has been temporarily excused, he should return to the waiting area until he is permanently excused.
- Show neither approval nor disapproval of a verdict rendered to a defendant.
- Not discuss testimony with anyone other than the TC until the case has been adjudicated.

Appendix J
Collision Diagramming

Collision investigations require the collision investigator to develop rough sketches, also known as field sketches, and scale diagrams of collision scenes. Depending on the type and severity of the incident, the requirement for sketches and diagrams can range from a simple sketch recorded on the DA Form 3946 (for minor collisions with minimal damage) to detailed, scaled drawings requiring multiple sheets (for major collisions resulting in death, serious injury, or extensive property damage). An accurate diagram of the collision scene ensures that persons not at the scene can understand clearly the results of the collision.

PURPOSE

J-1.   Collision sketches and scaled diagrams are completed using many of the same techniques as those applied to crime scene sketches and described in chapter 4; see paragraph 13-7 for a list of drafting equipment required to complete collision diagrams. Rough sketches are made by military police and TMCIs to document the collision based on observation and measurements at the scene. The resulting rough sketch is used to develop scaled diagrams for the case file and any legal requirements. These sketches support testimonial and physical evidence identified and collected at the scene; they provide clarity to the responding patrol's original notes and photographs from the scene. Rough sketches provide necessary detail to—

- Help explain the collision.
- Help the investigator reveal facts.
- Pinpoint specific locations and evidence at the scene.
- Support investigator notes and photographs of the scene.
- Serve as the basis for accurate scale drawings.
- Enable accurate reconstruction of the scene, when necessary.

J-2.   Scaled diagrams are produced after the scene investigation using the investigators scene sketch and notes. They are a more professional and carefully drawn version of the rough sketch. In some cases, an experienced draftsman should draw the finished sketch, especially for complex or serious collisions with potential criminal liability. The following information must be placed on sketches and scaled drawings:

- The time of the collision to include the date and hour.
- Names of roads. If on a rural highway, show the distance to the nearest identifiable landmark.
- The direction of north.
- Names, SSNs, and units of LE personnel making measurements and drawings.
- The report or case number.
- References to photographs taken.

PREPARATION OF THE ROUGH SKETCH

J-3.   The measurements shown on the sketch must be as accurate as possible and should be made and recorded uniformly. It is important that the distances documenting an item in the sketch are all measured and reflected on the diagram in the same manner. Do not document one measurement in meters and another in feet and inches. Pick one consistent measurement scale and reflect all measurements to the same degree of accuracy; for example, if one measurement is documented in feet and inches, all measurements should reflect feet and inches.

J-4. Before beginning a sketch, walk the collision scene to obtain a thorough understanding and view of the scene. Determine the limits of the sketch, including what to include and exclude from the sketch. If the scene is large or extremely complex, a preliminary sketch with notes can be made during the walk through; this preliminary sketch can be used for planning and completing more detailed rough sketches. Areas that are especially complex or require greater detail can be reproduced as separate drawings to provide the required clarity. The basic steps for completing a collision scene rough sketch are outlined below.

IDENTIFY THE BASELINE AND REFERENCE POINTS

J-5. The first step in drawing the rough sketch is to identify a baseline, also referred to as a reference line, and any required reference points. The baseline of the sketch normally corresponds to the edge of the roadway, although curbs, sidewalks, building lines, or an imaginary line between two fixed reference points may be used to represent the baseline.

> **Note.** If no easily identifiable baseline is present, such as a roadway, sidewalk, or other linear reference, reference points must be identified to establish an "imaginary" baseline. Reference points are discussed below.

J-6. Reference points must be identified before any measurements can be made. Always attempt to use the minimum number of reference points possible to cause less confusion. Draw reference points on the sketch. These are those points used in making measurements by the triangulation or coordinate method (see paragraph J-13). Once these points have been identified, measurements can be made from the reference points to the item of evidence.

J-7. Reference points are fixed points from which measurements will be made. Each reference point should be assigned a designator such as RP1 or RP2. The exact number of reference points depends on the number of objects and the method of documenting evidence locations. Reference points can be—

- **Permanent fixed points.** These are the best choice when available due to their enduring presence at the collision scene. Permanent fixed points can include utility poles, fire hydrants, mileage markers, road sign posts, manhole covers, or buildings. Identify permanent objects by using numbers, letters, and symbols. This enables them to be located at a later date, preferably up to 12 months.
- **Imaginary fixed points.** Items such as the apex of a curve or corner, the center of the intersection, or any point established along a reference line, such as a road edge, can be an imaginary fixed point. Since all measurements are conducted from reference points, it is necessary to mark these points.

J-8. Measurements are made from the place where the reference point meets the ground. If large cylindrical objects such as telephone poles are used, the exact reference point should be marked with a nail or paint. If permanent objects are not available, reference points can be established by—

- Driving wooden stakes into the dirt at the edge of the roadway.
- Driving nails into the asphalt or other road surface.
- Marking the reference point with paint.

J-9. Next, draw the roadway, shoulder, and other areas of the scene which are pertinent to the investigation. Include any physical characteristics which may constitute contributing factors to the cause of the collision or which will be used as base points. The baseline and each established reference point must be measured and marked on the rough sketch.

IDENTIFY AND DOCUMENT EVIDENCE

J-10. The investigator must identify the evidence and other elements of the scene that need to be included in the sketch. These items should be identified, marked, and documented in the investigator's notes. Evidence that should be documented on the sketch includes—

- The position of vehicles where they made initial impact, first landing (if any), and final rest. Include vehicle dimensions. This may include cars, trucks, motorcycles, or bicycles.

- The position of dead or injured persons. Include the point of impact, first landing, and final rest of the body. This includes drivers and passengers ejected from a vehicle.
- Gouges, chips, chops, or grooves on the road surface.
- Scratches, scrapes, or scars on the road or ground surface.
- Tire marks such as skid marks, scuff marks or tire impressions, related to the collision that are found on the pavement, shoulder, or other locations.
- Debris of various kinds related to the collision.
- Objects on or near the road, which were damaged as a result of the collision.
- Other items at the collision scene that may have had an impact on the collision including—
  - Traffic control devices. Any traffic control signs or signals that have a direct impact on the collision.
  - Pavement markings. These include crosswalks, warning markings, or directional markings.
  - Obstructions. This includes anything that may have impaired the vision or blocked the view of traffic control devices at the scene.
  - Anything else that could have had an effect on the collision.

J-11. The next portion of the sketch should show the final position of all vehicles, occupants, and objects involved in the collision. Indicate on the sketch all damage to the vehicle and other property. Enter this information in the narrative portion of the investigation.

J-12. Complete the sketch by including information on vehicle marks and debris at the scene. Vehicle marks include skid and scuff marks, scratches, scrapes and gouges of the pavement and marks left from yaws. These marks will be used in determining speeds of the vehicles involved. Debris is useful in determining the point of first contact. Include in the sketch an outline of the areas in which debris has come to rest; also document points where debris concentration is greatest. Debris is usually spread in an elongated pattern in the direction of travel. Notes should be made if there appears to be two or more separate debris areas. After entering identifying information on the sketch, recheck the sketch at the scene to ensure that all pertinent evidence is captured. Ensure that the legend and all administrative data are included on the sketch.

MEASUREMENT REQUIREMENTS

J-13. Measure all evidence at the scene if it is believed to be a result of the collision. Investigators do not need to know an object's significance when identifying evidence for inclusion in the sketch. If uncertainty exists regarding whether to include a piece of potential evidence in the sketch, mark, measure, and include the item in the sketch. After deciding what evidence will be included, determine the number of required measurement points on each object. Considerations for determining the number of required measurement points include the following:

- **Measure using one point.** One point will adequately locate relatively small objects such as—
  - Gouges, or groups of gouges, in an area less than 3 feet across. Measure to the center of the group.
  - Grooves and tire marks less than 3 feet across. Measure to the center of the group.
  - Small scrapes or dents to guardrails or damage to posts and trees. Measure to the center of the mark.
  - Spatter areas and puddles less than 3 feet across. Measure to the center of the area.
  - Small debris areas. Measure to the center of the area.
  - Vehicle parts, such as wheels that have become detached. Measure to the center of the item.
- **Measurements with two points.** Use two points to locate items including—
  - Vehicles. Ordinarily, locate the tires on the undamaged side of the vehicle. The ends of the vehicle on the undamaged side can be used to locate the vehicle. Do not locate corners on the same end, such as the two front corners or two rear corners, because they are too close together and do not allow for proper directional placement.

- Human bodies. Locate the center mass of the body and the center mass of the head. If a body part is amputated, locate the center mass of the body part.
- Straight tire marks. Locate the beginning and end of each mark.
- Curved tire marks more than 3 feet long, but less than 8 feet long. Locate both ends.
- Straight grooves more than 3 feet long. Locate both ends.
- Long sections of railings or fences scraped or damaged. Locate both ends of the damage.
- Dribble path. Locate both ends.
- **Measurements with three or more points.** Three or more points are required to locate—
  - Curved tire marks, especially yaw marks. Locate each end and point where the tire mark crosses a roadway edge, lane line or centerline.
  - Straight marks with angles, crooks, gaps, or other irregularities in them. Locate both ends of each mark and the angle or other irregularity.
  - Large debris areas. Locate three to six points on the perimeter of the area. Include only substantial deposits of debris, not all widely scattered debris.

J-14. Measurements of the roadway are necessary for the investigator to produce a scale diagram of the scene including documentation of the exact placement of physical evidence identified during the investigation. The location of all evidence in relation to the roadway and each other must be documented. Identification of the actual location of the roadway itself is not required, although the availability of GPS makes this a relatively easy task. Specific characteristics of the roadway at the collision site must be documented to enable the production of accurate scaled diagrams and reconstruction of the collision. This enables investigators or other persons to reconstruct the roads and all evidence associated with the collision. These measurements include—

- The width of the roadway.
- The width of each lane.
- Road markings. This includes painted lines as follows:
  - Where centerlines begin in all directions of the intersection (normally using coordinate measurements).
  - The distance of intermittent lines and gaps between each of these lines.

J-15. There are two primary methods for documenting the location of a point or piece of evidence at a collision scene—the triangulation method and the coordinate method. The triangulation method for documenting the location of evidence at a collision scene is conducted using the same basic methods as for a crime scene. Chapter 4 addresses crime scene processing. This method documents the location of a specific object or point by creating a triangle of measurements from a single, specific, identifiable point on an item of evidence to two fixed reference points at the scene. The distance between the two fixed points should also be measured and documented. The coordinate method uses the same techniques as the transecting baseline method discussed in chapter 4. Once the baseline is established, the positions of multiple items of evidence can be documented by measuring from the evidence to the baseline.

J-16. Regardless of the method selected, it is imperative that investigators take accurate and concise measurements of all evidence. The investigator making measurements of the scene should take time to evaluate the collision scene and plan how to measure with the highest degree of accuracy, ease, and safety.

Coordinate Method

J-17. The coordinate method is preferred of the two methods of measuring evidence locations at a traffic collision. This method is best used on roadways with well defined edges and when measurements are to be made within 25 feet (7 to 8 meters) of the roadway edge. The coordinate method involves establishing a baseline and reference points and documenting a straight-line distance (measurement 90 degrees to the baseline) coupled with a direction. It is the most accurate method for establishing the location of an object. The direction component of the measurement does not have to be a cardinal direction (north, south, east, or west). It may be a nominal compass direction such as northwest or southeast. A nominal direction is applied to provide a general direction of the roadway when the—

- Roadway curves at the scene of the collision.
- Roadway runs more or less between compass directions.
- Exact compass direction at the scene of the collision is unknown.

J-18. The coordinate method provides two important advantages at the scene of a collision. All measurements along the edge of the roadway can be made on the shoulder of the roadside, limiting exposure of LE personnel to potential traffic hazards. The straight lines and 90-degree angles used for this method are easier to draw to scale than the angles involved when using triangulation method.

J-19. The first step is to identify a reference point along the baseline. As discussed earlier, the baseline is a straight line that normally corresponds to the edge of the roadway; it could also be defined by curbs, sidewalks, building lines, or an imaginary line between two fixed points. Once an acceptable reference point is identified and marked, the investigator must—

- Secure a tape measure at the designated reference point and extend it along the baseline; this can be the roadway edge or other identified line.
- Lay another tape measure from the item of evidence being documented to the baseline, intersecting the baseline at a right (90-degree) angle.
- Record the distance and direction from the reference point to the point intersecting line from the evidence.
- Record the distance and direction from the baseline to the evidence; the direction recorded is in relation to the reference point.
- Take at least two measurements from the reference point and the baseline to different points on the object. At least two measurements must be obtained to pinpoint the location of an item of evidence Record the measurements. Figure J-1, page J-6, provides an example of the coordinate method of measurement.
- Record measurements on the rough sketch and the investigator's notes. For large and complex scenes with many measurement requirements, a chart or table may be useful to record the measurements for each item of evidence. The table can then be attached to the appropriate diagrams and reports.

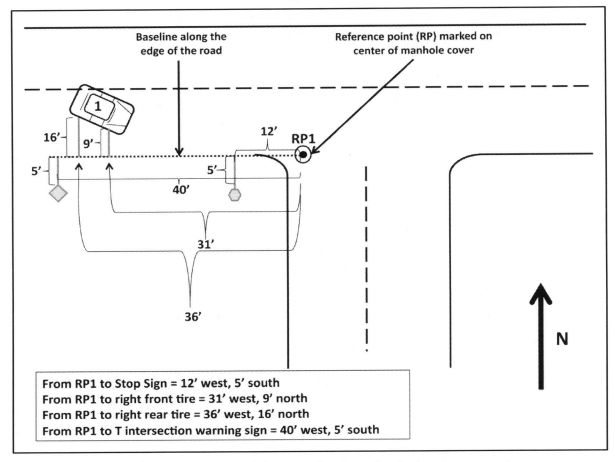

Figure J-1. Example of the coordinate method of measurement

Triangulation Method

J-20. The triangulation method of measurement may be used if the coordinate method is not practical. The triangulation method should be considered in lieu of coordinate measurements when—

- Roadway edges are not conducive to establishing a usable baseline such as when—
  - There are no clear roadway edges for reference lines. The edges of the roadway may be difficult to locate, covered with vegetation or other material, broken and in disrepair, or nonexistent. Problem areas may be rural roads, construction sites, gravel pits, large parking lots, or open fields.
  - Roadway edges are irregular such as in traffic circles and some complicated junctions.
- Points to be located are more than 30 feet off the roadway.
- Objects are off the road in woods or swamps.
- Some obstacles, such as a building, pond, bank, or trees, prevent making the shortest direct distance measurements.

J-21. The first step required to locate an object by triangulation is to identify two reference points. The two reference points should be no less than 20 feet apart and no more than 50 feet apart from each other. These minimum and maximum distances prevent having a triangle that is too acute or too obtuse. Document the distance between the two reference points.

J-22. Next measure the straight-line distance from each reference point to at least two points on the object, such as the right rear and right front tires of a vehicle. This distance is a straight-line distance from the reference points to the object and does not require a compass direction. Record the measurements on the sketch and investigator notes. Figure J-2 provides an example of the triangulation method of measurement. The procedure is repeated for each item of evidence.

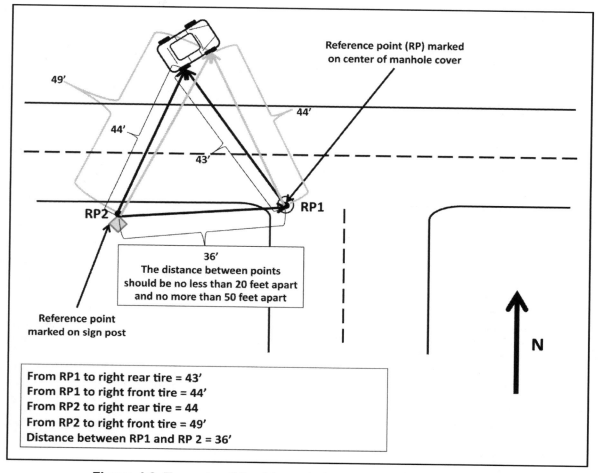

Figure J-2. Example of the triangulation method of measurement

SPECIAL DIAGRAMMING CONSIDERATIONS

J-23. Relatively straight roads and intersections that converge at 90-degree angles are relatively simple to diagram. Unfortunately not all roads meet at a 90-degree angle or maintain a uniform traffic way.

OFFSET ROADWAY EDGES

J-24. At some intersections or road junctions, the roadway may be wider on one side, or the roadways may be offset at the intersection. In either case, the roadway edges do not line up. The investigator may use his line of sight to determine if the intersection is offset. When measuring a roadway junction, the investigator should position himself about 50 to 75 feet away from the intersection on the edge of the road. A visual line of sight down the edge of the road and through the intersection is generally sufficient to determine if the roadway edges go straight through the intersection.

J-25. If the visual inspection indicates that the roadway edges are offset, the amount of offset must be determined to ensure an accurate scale diagram. Using this measurement, the roadway can be drawn accurately. The offset can be determined by—

- Extending a tape measure from one roadway edge across the intersection. Make sure that the measuring tape is kept aligned with the initial (near side) road edge.

● Measuring the difference between the roadway edges. The tape, aligned against the road edge on the near side of the intersection, will extend either on the shoulder or on the road surface on the far side of the intersection. The distance between the tape and the road edge is measured to record the offset.

● Recording the information on the sketch and investigators notes.

IRREGULAR ROADWAYS

J-26. Irregular roadways present challenges when diagramming to scale. An irregular road is one that intersects with another road at other than a 90-degree angle. When irregular roadways exist at the collision scene, the investigator must use the following procedure to accurately diagram the collision scene:

● Identify the apex of the roadway edges (reference lines) at the corner, and designate as reference point 1. This is the base reference point.

● Identify a second and third reference point on each reference line, one on each roadway edge. It is best that the reference points be no less than 20 feet apart and no more than 50 feet apart. Use the same distance from reference point 1 to the other two reference points. This creates an isosceles triangle; an isosceles triangle has two equal sides (the third side is different). Having two equal sides simplifies the calculations.

● Determine the straight-line distance between reference point 2 and reference point 3.

● Determine the measure of the angle at reference point 1. Draw the triangle to scale on paper and then use a protractor to determine the approximate angle. This triangle drawn to scale is the base for drawing the road junction to scale. Use the following steps to draw the triangle to scale:

■ **Step 1.** Identify the base reference line and reference point 1 on the baseline by drawing a straight line on the paper and marking the first reference point as shown in figure J-3.

■ **Step 2.** Use a compass to identify reference point 2. Open the compass to the correct distance using the scale on the traffic template. This is the distance designated and measured at the scene from reference point 1 to reference point 2. Place the pivot of the compass on reference point 1 and make an arc across the base reference line; ensure that the arc extends a distance long enough to go beyond the estimated point for reference point 3. This arc identifies reference point 2 where it crosses the baseline created in step 1. This step is depicted in figure J-3.

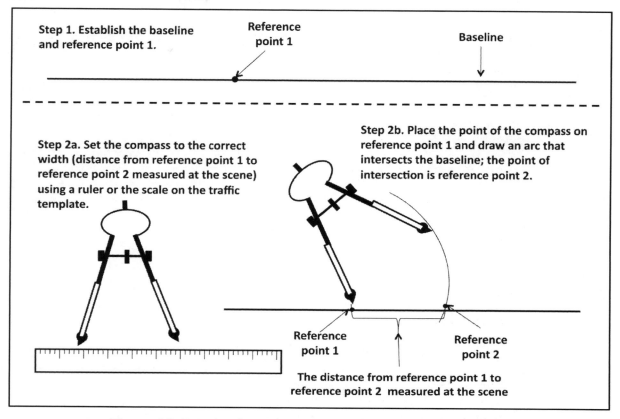

Figure J-3. Drawing irregular roadways to scale (steps 1 and 2)

- **Step 3.** Identify reference point 3 by making an arc from reference point 2 that crosses the first arc. Open the compass to the correct distance using the scale on the traffic template. This is the distance measured on the scene from reference point 2 to reference point 3. Place the pivot of the compass on reference point 2 and make an arc that crosses the first arc; this arc identifies reference point 3 where it crosses the first arc created in step 2. This step is illustrated in figure J-4, page J-10.

- **Step 4.** Connect reference point 1 and reference point 3 with a straight line. Use a straight edge, such as the traffic template or a ruler, and draw the line between the two points as shown in figure J-5, page J-11. The roadway is now drawn to scale; a protractor can be used to determine the angle at the road junction.

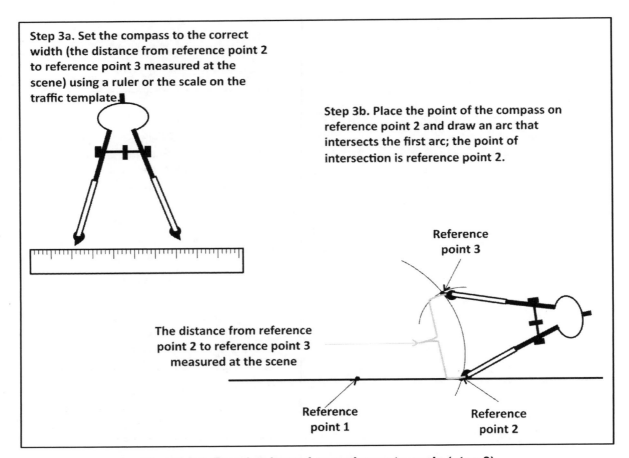

Step 3a. Set the compass to the correct width (the distance from reference point 2 to reference point 3 measured at the scene) using a ruler or the scale on the traffic template.

Step 3b. Place the point of the compass on reference point 2 and draw an arc that intersects the first arc; the point of intersection is reference point 2.

Reference point 3

The distance from reference point 2 to reference point 3 measured at the scene

Reference point 1

Reference point 2

Figure J-4. Drawing irregular roadways to scale (step 3)

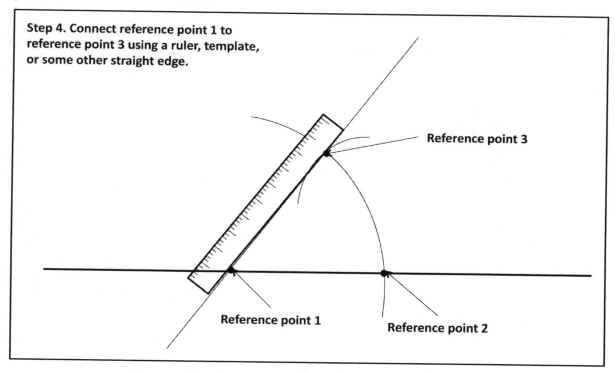

Figure J-5. Drawing irregular roadways to scale (step 4)

J-27. Road widths are added by placing parallel lines to represent the far sides of the roads based on road-width measurements to produce the entire road junction. Figure J-6, page J-12, illustrates an irregular road drawn to scale. Fixed objects, vehicles, and other evidence can now be added to the diagram.

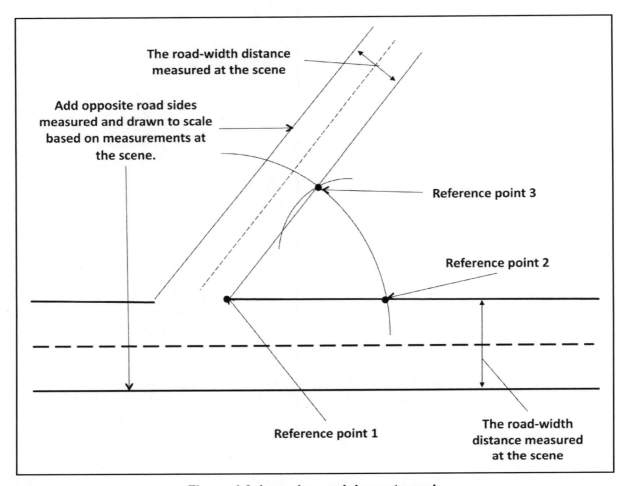

Figure J-6. Irregular road drawn to scale

Appendix K

Collision Calculations

Collision investigations require investigators to conduct calculations to determine a variety of factors contributing to vehicle collisions. The primary reference for this appendix is the *Traffic Management and Collision Investigations Student Study Guide and Workbook* from the Traffic Management and Collision Investigations Course at Lackland Air Force Base.

SKID CALCULATIONS

K-1. Collision investigators use skid marks together with other factors to estimate the speed of a vehicle involved in a collision. Calculations based on a vehicle's skid marks can be used to determine the vehicle's minimum traveling speed; they cannot produce the actual traveling speed. The calculations can show the minimum speed the vehicle had to travel to leave the skid marks. Speed alone may not be a factor and other factors contributing to the accident must be identified. Some conditional factors that can change speed or kinetic energy include—

- Coefficients of friction.
- Grade, slope, and superelevation of the roadway.
- Vehicle braking efficiency.

K-2. Collision investigators must identify and account for these conditions. In some cases, the conditions present during the time of the accident may have changed before the arrival of the investigator. Investigators may be required to recreate some of the conditions.

K-3. Kinetic energy or motion energy is created and stored in an object due to two factors: mass and motion. Every object that has mass (weight) and is in motion has kinetic energy. As an object's speed increases, so does its kinetic energy. During a sudden deceleration, the kinetic energy built up in an object must be dissipated; when a vehicle reaches its final resting point (stops moving), it has a kinetic energy of zero. This transfer of energy is evident in a collision through the damage that results from impact (in the form of roadway evidence). Another important means through which a moving vehicle transfers kinetic energy is through friction and heat. The friction between tires and the road surface can create skid marks. The more kinetic energy that is transferred through heat energy via tire and road friction, the longer the skid marks. Skid marks can correlate to the speed of the vehicle. When speed increases, the length of skid marks will also increase. If enough kinetic energy cannot be transferred through heat energy (skid marks) to stop the vehicle, then the remainder of the built-up energy will transfer through other means resulting in damage to vehicles and the occupants within them.

Note. Unless specified otherwise, all numbers and calculations are recorded to the second decimal place. Do not round up or down.

COEFFICIENT OF FRICTION

K-4. It is necessary to determine the coefficient of friction to establish how much drag or resistance the road surface has on a vehicle. The coefficient of friction is the number representing the resistance to sliding between two surfaces. This will vary from roadway to roadway based on specific design, construction material, age, and condition. Slippery pavement offers less drag so the stopping distance is greater. Rough pavement creates more drag and the stopping distance is less. There are two tests commonly used to determine the coefficient of friction: drag sleds and test skids.

Drag Sleds

K-5. A drag sled is used to determine the coefficient of friction of a surface without a test vehicle. The drag sled test requires a sled of known weight and an accurate scale. A drag sled may be purchased through many open source suppliers. The sled has runners made of tire sections; a scale is attached to the sled to measure the force required to move the sled across the road surface. The sled must be pulled in a direction parallel to the road surface. Any upward lift, no matter how slight, will cause the results to be inaccurate. The drag sled should not be used on wet roads or off-road on grass or other like surfaces; these surface conditions will not produce accurate results. Using the drag sled, the coefficient of friction is represented in a formula by the symbol "μ." The value associated with "μ" is found by using the formula: $\mu = F \div W$, where—

- F = force to pull the sled, this number is read off the scale.
- W = weight of sled.
- μ = coefficient of friction.

K-6. The sled should be pulled at least 10 feet at a constant speed; the pull must be smooth with no jerks, bumps, or other variations. Ten separate pulls should be conducted with the measurements recorded; the results of the ten pulls are averaged to determine the average force required and divided by the weight of the sled to find the coefficient of friction for the surface. For example, if a 100-pound sled is pulled across a road surface and it takes 50 pounds of pull, then the coefficient of friction may be determined by using the formula:

- $\mu = F \div W$
- $\mu = 50 \div 100$
- $\mu = 0.50$
- The coefficient of friction is 0.5.

Note. The coefficient of friction is a factor used in calculating distance and speed, and does not have a unit of measure.

Test Skids

K-7. Test skids are the most accurate method used to determine the coefficient of friction of a specific surface. When conducting test skids, the environmental and surface conditions present during the collision should be identical to include the—

- Direction of travel of the collision vehicles.
- Vehicle load.
- Vehicle type.
- Road surface to include the types of road, temperature, and surface conditions such as sand, gravel, ice, wet, or dry.

Speed and Braking

K-8. For safety there should be two people in the test vehicle while conducting test skids; one to drive while the other observes the speedometer. The driver should drive the vehicle in a straight line, at a constant speed about 5 miles per hour faster than the desired test speed, and not exceed 35 miles per hour or the speed limit whichever is less. The driver should then let off the accelerator; when the vehicle slows to the target speed, the driver should—

- Apply hard, constant pressure to the brakes for accurate results. All four wheels of the test vehicle must lock in order to have an accurate test.
- Keep pressure applied to the brakes until the vehicle comes to a stop.
- Avoid hesitation when applying brakes; any hesitation can cause inaccurate results.

K-9. A minimum of two tests must be conducted; use the longest skid measured during the tests. If the two tests cannot be validated using the steps outlined below, additional tests may be required. For safety and accuracy conduct tests at speeds between 15 and 35 miles per hour. Test skids conducted in excess of 35 miles per hour can create an unacceptable level of risk; conduct the tests at 35 miles per hour or the posted speed limit, whichever is less. Tests should not be done at less than 15 miles per hour; tests conducted at less than 15 miles per hour can cause the results to be inaccurate. Slow speeds can cause the coefficient of friction to be higher than actual.

Validating Results

K-10. The validation process ensures that test results are within an acceptable range and do not represent an abnormal result. It is conducted by comparing the longest skid from one test to an established range of the other test. To validate a skid use the following steps:

- **Step 1.** Identify the longest skid of each test.
- **Step 2.** Identify the range associated with the longest skid in test 1. Each skid test should produce four skids, one for each tire (right front, right rear, left front, and left rear). The range is defined as ± 10 percent of the longest skid of the given test. 10 percent of the longest skid can be determined by multiplying the skid distance by 0.10. For example if the longest skid in test 1 is 162 feet, 0.10 x 162 = 16.2 feet. 162 + 16.2 = 178.2 feet and 162 - 16.2 = 145.8 feet; the range is 145.8 feet to 178.2 feet.
- **Step 3.** Conduct comparisons in validation order as follows:
  - *Comparison 1.* Compare the longest skid in test 2 to the range of test 1. If the longest skid in test 2 is within the range of test 1, then the two tests validate. Use the longest skid of the two tests to determine the coefficient of friction (proceed to step 4). If the tests do not validate, a comparison using a third test is required.
  - *Comparison 2.* Compare the longest skid in test 3 with the range of test 1. If the longest skid in test 3 is within the range of test 1, then test 1 and test 3 validate. Use the longest skid of the two tests to determine the coefficient of friction (proceed to step 4). If the tests do not validate, proceed to comparison 3.
  - *Comparison 3.* Compare the longest skid in test 3 with the range of test 2. If the longest skid in test 3 is within the range of test 2, then tests 2 and 3 validate. Use the longest skid of the two tests to determine the coefficient of friction (proceed to step 4). If the tests do not validate, a new series of tests must be conducted and the process repeated.
- **Step 4.** Use the longest skid of the two validated tests to calculate the coefficient of friction.

K-11. Once the skid test has been validated and the longest skid is determined, the coefficient of friction can be calculated. When the skid test is used the formula for calculating coefficient of friction is: $\mu = S^2 \div 30d$ where—

- μ = coefficient of friction.
- 30 = constant for this formula.
- S = speed of the test vehicle.
- d = longest skid distance of the test vehicle taken from a validated test.

K-12. If the test skids were conducted at 35 miles per hour, and the longest validated skid was determined to be 60 feet (using the validation process outlined above), the coefficient of friction is calculated as follows:

- $\mu = S^2 \div 30d$
- $\mu = 35^2 \div [(30)(60)]$
- $\mu = 1{,}225 \div 1{,}800$
- $\mu = 0.68$
- The coefficient of friction is 0.68.

DRAG FACTOR

K-13. The drag factor is an adjusted coefficient of friction. This is to allow for variations in a vehicle's braking efficiency and the roadway in the form of grade, slope, or superelevation. The coefficient of friction must be adjusted when one or both of the following variables exist:

- The braking efficiency of the collision vehicle is less than 100 percent. Braking efficiency less than 100 percent can be the result of erratic braking, failure to apply the brakes (either fully or at all), or mechanical failure.
- Test skids were conducted on a surface with a different grade or slope than that of the collision surface.

BRAKING EFFICIENCY

K-14. The braking efficiency refers to the relative percentage of force applied by each wheel on a vehicle during application of the vehicle brakes. Many factors affect braking efficiency including the type of vehicle, the type of brake system, and the type of drive system. In general, braking efficiency for various vehicles can be assigned the following values under the respective vehicle configurations and conditions:

- **Cars and pickup trucks with rear wheel drive.** For passenger cars and most pickup trucks with rear wheel drive, with or without antilock braking systems, the braking efficiency will be 30 percent for each front tire and 20 percent for each of the rear tires. Therefore, the front would have a combined total of 60 percent and the rear would have a total of 40 percent of the braking efficiency.
- **Cars with front wheel drive.** For passenger cars with front wheel drive, with or without antilock braking systems, the braking efficiency will be 35 percent for each front tire and 15 percent for each of the rear tires. Therefore, the front would have a combined total of 70 percent and the rear would have a total of 30 percent of the braking efficiency.
- **Motorcycles.** Breaking efficiency for motorcycles is assigned as follows:
  - Motorcycles 649 cubic centimeters and under will be 60 percent for the front wheel and 40 percent for the rear wheel.
  - Motorcycles 650 cubic centimeters and over will be 70 percent for the front wheel and 30 percent for the rear wheel.
  - Motorcyclists typically use one brake to stop. If the investigator can prove the use of both brakes, use the total 100 percent brake efficiency (front and rear). If the use of both brakes cannot be proven, use 30 percent or 40 percent (rear only) to adjust for drag factor.

GRADE, SLOPE, AND SUPERELEVATION

K-15. Grade, slope, and superelevation must be taken into account in determining drag factor. If test skids are done on a level surface and the collision occurred on a grade, then the grade must be added to the drag factor. If the collision occurred on a slope, then the slope must be subtracted from the drag factor. If the test skids are done on the actual collision surface, then no adjustment to the drag factor is required. If a drag sled is used, it will be used on the collision surface and no adjustment is needed.

Grade and Slope

K-16. Grade or slope refers to the steepness of a hill. It represents a percentage (ratio) of the distance the roadway rises or falls compared to the horizontal distance along the road surface. The terms "grade" and "slope" are for the most part synonymous. When used in the context of traffic management and collision investigation. The grade or slope of a road surface is relative to the direction of travel. If the vehicle is traveling uphill, use the term "grade." If the vehicle is traveling downhill, use the term "slope." An easy way to remember this is to associate the terms with direction—"You want your grades to go up, and you ski down a slope."

Superelevation

K-17. Superelevation can be either positive or negative. The positive or negative value assigned to a superelevation depends on the roadway configuration rather than the direction of travel of a vehicle. Superelevation refers to the elevation change across a roadway at a right angle to the centerline, from the inside to the outside edges of a curve. This is sometimes referred to as the bank of a roadway.

K-18. The grade, slope, or superelevation of a roadway is calculating by dividing the rise (or fall) of the roadway by the run. Variables for the formula are—

- m = the grade (rise) or slope (fall).
- e = superelevation (or banking).
- rise = the vertical distance (if the direction is uphill) of a road surface relative to another point on that same road surface.
- fall = the vertical distance (if the direction is downhill) of a road surface relative to another point on that same road surface.
- run = the known horizontal distance from the two points on the road surface when measuring the steepness of grade, slope, or superelevation.

Line Level Method

K-19. One of the easiest ways to determine the grade, slope, or superelevation of a roadway is by using the line level method. This method requires a carpenter's level and a ruler. The carpenter's level is used to measure the horizontal distance (the run); the ruler is used to measure the vertical distance (rise). Place the carpenter's level in a level position (exactly horizontal) with one end touching the roadway; the length of the carpenter's level will be used as the value for the run; for example a three-foot carpenter's level will be equate to a run of 3 feet. Next, place the ruler at the elevated end of the carpenter's level and measure the vertical distance (rise or fall) from the roadway surface to the bottom edge of the carpenter's level as illustrated in figure K-1, page K-6. Take multiple measurements along the road in line with the collision skid marks; these measurements can be averaged to obtain a good representation of the slope (grade).

K-20. In the example presented in figure K-1, the calculation will be made to determine the grade (the direction of travel is uphill). A three-foot carpenter's level is used, so a run value of 36 inches (3 feet) is applied; all values must use the same unit of measure. The rise is 4 inches from the road surface. The grade is calculated by dividing the value for the rise (4 inches) by the value for the run (36 inches); $4 \div 36 = 0.11$ (to two decimal places). The roadway has an uphill grade of 11 percent. If feet are used as the unit of measure, convert the inches to feet by dividing the number of inches by the number of inches in a foot (12); for example 4 inches divided by 12 inches per foot equals 0.33 feet. This conversion must be done for both the rise and the run measurements. The calculation would be $0.33 \div 3.0 = 0.11$.

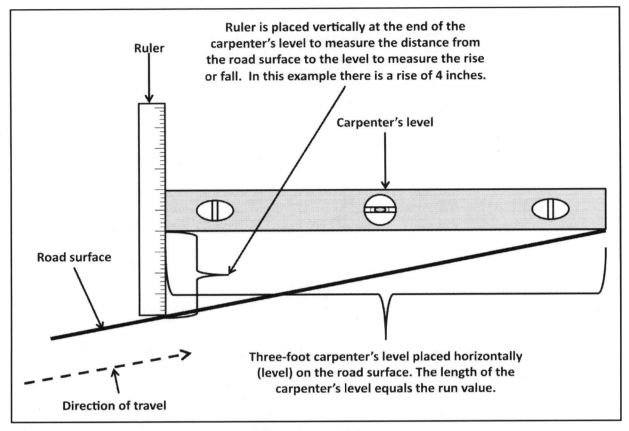

Figure K-1. Determine grade, slope, or superelevation of a roadway using a carpenter's level and ruler

CALCULATING THE ADJUSTED COEFFICIENT OF FRICTION (DRAG FACTOR)

K-21. Once the braking efficiency is determined and values for grade, slope, or superelevation are obtained, the drag factor (or adjusted coefficient of friction) can be determined, if required. The formula for calculating the adjusted coefficient of friction is $f = (\mu \times n) \pm m$ (or e) where—

- f = adjusted coefficient of friction otherwise known as the drag factor.
- μ = 100 percent braking efficiency on a flat, level surface.
- n = braking efficiency.
- m = grade or slope (grade is represented as a positive ratio and slope is represented as a negative ratio).
- e = superelevation.

K-22. For example, if the drag factor for a surface was determined to be 0.65 (μ), the braking efficiency was determined to be 100 percent (n), and the road was determined to have a grade of 0.11 (m), these values can be used to calculate the drag factor (f) using the formula for the adjusted coefficient of friction ($f = (\mu \times n) \pm m$). The calculation to determine the adjusted drag factor is completed as follows:

- $f = (\mu \times n) \pm m$
- $f = (0.65 \times 1.00) + 0.11$
- $f = (0.65) + 0.11$
- $f = 0.76$
- The drag factor or adjusted coefficient of friction is 0.76.

COMPENSATING FOR DIFFERENCES IN GRADE OR SLOPE

K-23. During collisions it may not be possible to conduct a test skid on the collision surface. When test skids are conducted on a surface other than the collision surface and the grade, slope, or superelevation of the test surface is not equal to that of the collision surface, investigators must adjust the coefficient of friction from the resulting test. The method for adjusting the coefficient of friction when test skids are conducted on a different surface is known as the "crow's foot."

K-24. Using the example of a collision occurring on a 3-percent grade and the skid test being conducted on a level surface, investigators will draw the crow's foot; this example is illustrated in figure K-2. The zero line (base leg) of the crow's foot is drawn first; this line is always drawn at zero grade. Next, the investigator draws any required branches. For this example one branch is required to represent the 3-percent grade of the collision surface. The 3-percent grade is represented by the decimal +0.03; the zero-percent grade is represented by the decimal 0.00. The difference between the test surface and the collision surface is determined to find the value for the adjusted grade (m). The rule is to move the test surface to the collision surface (if the direction from the leg representing test skid to the collision surface is up, the value is positive; if it is down, the value is negative). In this example the difference is up indicating a value of +0.03 for the adjusted grade (m).

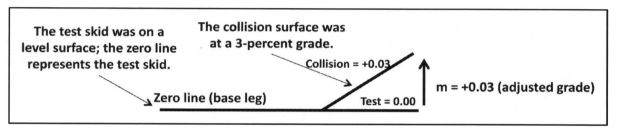

Figure K-2. Example 1 crow's foot

K-25. An example of a case where the collision surface and the test surface are both positive requires a slightly different approach. When using the example of a test surface having a 12-percent grade and the collision surface with a 6-percent grade, the zero line (base leg) of the crow's foot is drawn first. Next, the investigator draws the legs representing the collision grade at 6 percent (+0.06) and a leg representing the test grade at 12 percent (+0.12). The difference between the test surface and the collision surface is determined to find the value for the adjusted grade (m). There is a 6-percent (0.06) difference in grade between the test grade and collision grades. Since the collision grade was less than the test grade, the adjusted grade is negative (if the direction from the leg representing the test skid to the collision surface is up, the value is positive; if it is down, the value is negative). This adjustment shows a negative movement indicating a -0.06 for the adjusted grade (m). This example is illustrated in figure K-3.

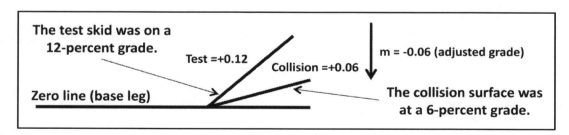

Figure K-3. Example 2 crow's foot

K-26. Using an example of a test surface having a 6-percent grade and the collision surface having a 3-percent slope, the zero line (base leg) of the crow's foot is drawn first. Next, the investigator draws the legs representing the test grade at 6 percent (+0.06) and a leg representing the collision slope at 3 percent (-0.03). Remember slope is down so the decimal representation is negative. The difference between the test surface and the collision surface is determined to find the value for the adjusted grade (m). There is a

9-percent (0.09) difference between the test slope and collision grade. Since the collision grade was less than the test grade, the adjusted grade is negative (if the direction from the leg representing the test skid to the collision surface is up, the value is positive; if it is down, the value is negative). This adjustment shows a negative movement indicating a -0.09 for the adjusted grade (m). This example is shown at figure K-4.

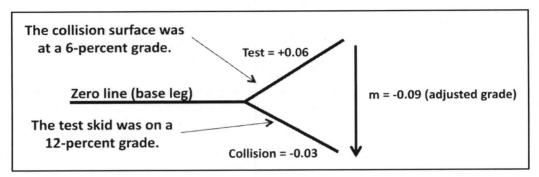

Figure K-4. Example 3 crow's foot

K-27. The formula used to revise the adjusted coefficient of friction to account for differences in grade or slope is $f = (\mu \times n) \pm m$ (or e) where—
- f = revised adjusted coefficient of friction (drag factor).
- μ = the coefficient of friction (obtained from test skids).
- n = braking efficiency.
- m = adjusted grade or slope (taken from the crow's foot).
- e = adjusted superelevation (taken from the crow's foot).

K-28. Using the last example, the adjusted coefficient of friction can be revised to compensate for the differences in the slope or grade of the test surface and the collision surface. Given a drag factor from the test surface of 0.65 (μ), the braking efficiency was determined to be 100 percent (n), a grade on the test surface of 0.06, and a slope on the collision surface of 0.03, the formula is applied as follows:
- $f = (\mu \times n) \pm m$ (or e)
- $f = (0.65)(1.00) - 0.09$
- $f = 0.65 - 0.09$
- $f = 0.56$
- The adjusted coefficient of friction, revised to compensate for the difference in the grade of the test surface and the slope of the collision surface, is 0.56.

BASIC SPEED CALCULATION

K-29. A basic speed calculation may be conducted to determine the minimum speed of a vehicle using the distance of the skid marks of a collision vehicle and the drag factor discussed and calculated previously within this section. The speed from this calculation will be the minimum speed that the vehicle was traveling at the start of the skid; the vehicle could have been traveling faster than the result of the calculation. The skid does not have to be 100 percent straight, slight curves will not affect the accuracy for this formula. For curved skids use a measuring wheel for accuracy. To calculate the minimum speed required to make a specific skid the following factors must be known:
- The coefficient of friction (μ) of the collision surface.
- The grade, slope (m) or superelevation (e) of the collision surface (needed to determine drag factor).
- The braking efficiency (n) of the collision vehicle (needed to determine drag factor).
- The average skid length (ASL) of the collision vehicle's skid marks. The ASL is identified by the variable "d."

Note. This computation cannot be used if the vehicle was towing a trailer.

AVERAGE SKID LENGTH

K-30. The ASL is represented as "ASL" or "d" in formulas. The minimum speed is calculated based upon the physical evidence that exists at the collision scene. If part of the evidence is determined to be a skid mark(s), then it may be used to help determine the minimum speed of the collision vehicle. Before skid marks can be used in any speed equation, the length of the skids must be measured and an ASL calculated. The first thing that must be done is to determine if the skid marks are independent or overlapping.

K-31. Independent skid marks are those left by a single tire making contact with the road surface. Independent skid marks are simply measured from the start to the finish of the skid mark. Overlapping occurs when the vehicle skids in a straight line with multiple wheels locking. Both the front and rear wheels will deposit skid marks, but the rear wheel skid marks will be deposited over the top (overlapping) of the front wheel skid marks. If the vehicle left overlapping skid marks, the vehicle's wheel base must be subtracted from each overlapping skid mark before it is added to the other skid marks. Even though two skid marks were deposited, two overlapping skid marks count as one skid mark. After the type of skid marks have been identified and measured, the lengths are added together and divided by the total number of skid marks to obtain the ASL as depicted in table K-1.

Table K-1. Calculating average skid length

Description of skid marks	Establish the sum of the skid lengths	Determine ASL
Four independent skid marks	Length of RF skid mark + length of RR skid mark + length of LF skid mark + length of LR skid mark = total length	Total length (sum) ÷ 4 = ASL
Three skid marks; two independent and one overlapping (right)	OL of right wheel skid marks – the wheel base length = the overlapping right skid length. Length of LF skid mark + length of LR skid mark + length of overlapping skid = total length.	Total length (sum) ÷ 3 = ASL
Three skid marks; two independent and one overlapping (left)	OL of left wheel skid marks – the wheel base length = the overlapping left skid length. Length of RF skid mark + length of RR skid mark + length of overlapping skid = total length.	Total length (sum) ÷ 3 = ASL
Two overlapping skid marks	OL of left wheel skid marks – the wheel base length = the overlapping left skid length. OL of right wheel skid marks – the wheel base length = the overlapping right skid length. Overlapping left skid length + overlapping right skid length = total length.	Total length (sum) ÷ 2 = ASL

Legend:			
ASL	average skid length	OL	overall length
LF	left front	RF	right front
LR	left rear	RR	right rear

CALCULATING SPEED

K-32. With knowledge of how to calculate the drag factor and determine the ASL, the investigator can conduct a basic speed calculation. The formula for a basic speed calculation is $S = \sqrt{(30df)}$ where—

- S = speed.
- 30 = constant for the formula.
- d = ASL of collision vehicle.
- f = adjusted coefficient of friction (drag factor) of collision surface. Note the following:
  - $f = \mu \times n$, then $\pm m/e$ if not on a level surface.
  - On a level surface, if braking efficiency is 100 percent, then the coefficient of friction and drag factor will be the same.

K-33. Given an ASL of 115 feet and a drag factor of 0.65, the minimum speed of a vehicle at the beginning of the skid can be calculated using the formula $S = \sqrt{(30df)}$. The calculation to determine the minimum speed of the vehicle at the beginning of the skid is completed as follows:

- $S = \sqrt{(30df)}$
- $S = \sqrt{[(30)(115)(0.65)]}$
- $S = \sqrt{2,242.5}$
- $S = 47.35$ miles per hour (to two decimal places).
- The minimum speed of the vehicle at the beginning of the skid is 47.35 miles per hour.

MINIMUM SPEED AND CRITICAL SPEED DETERMINATION

K-34. The formula $S = \sqrt{(15rf)}$ can be used to calculate the minimum speed of a vehicle based on yaw marks left by the vehicle, and in the absence of tire marks, the critical speed of a curve (the maximum speed of the curve before a vehicle starts to lose lateral stability). See paragraph K-38 for a description of the formula variables. The minimum speed calculation is conducted by analyzing the yaw marks left by the vehicle. It determines the minimum speed at which a vehicle must have been going to lose lateral stability on a curve and go off the road. The critical speed is the maximum speed the vehicle can travel and safely negotiate a curve without losing lateral stability. The maximum speed of the vehicle indicates the speed the vehicle must have exceeded to lose lateral stability. The critical speed is calculated when yaw marks are not present. In this case, physical evidence of the vehicle leaving the roadway is not measured; the roadway itself is measured (with no direct evidence indicating the exact track the vehicle took on that roadway).

K-35. While the maximum speed that a vehicle can travel on a curve without losing lateral stability can be calculated, the actual speed of the vehicle cannot be determined based solely on the characteristics of the curve. For this reason, calculating the minimum speed based on yaw marks (positive evidence of what occurred) is preferred.

K-36. A critical speed yaw (scuff mark) occurs when a vehicle is turning in a radius that is too tight for a given speed, causing the vehicle to lose some lateral stability. This causes the rear tires to track outside the path of the front tires. When, this happens the vehicle's tires begin to slide or slip sideways, while still rotating, leaving a characteristic tire "yaw" mark with diagonal striations. In a normal turn (without a yaw), no skid or slip occurs and the rear tires track inside the leading front tires.

Determine Yaw Mark Radius

K-37. The radius of the yaw mark is measured using the chord and middle ordinate method. The chord and middle ordinate method to determine the radius of a yaw mark is illustrated at figure K-5. Select two points on the yaw mark; they will be identified as tangent points. A chord is the straight line distance between two tangent points on a curve. The middle ordinate is the distance from the midpoint of the curve to the midpoint of the long chord. The chord is marked on the yaw mark and is generally not less than 30 feet or more than 100 feet. The chord should start within the first one-third of the yaw mark. Start the chord from the outside edge of the outside yaw mark (usually the darker yaw mark) beginning where the striation marks of the front and rear tires cross over. In the normal controlled negotiation of a curve, the rear tires will trail inside the front tires. As the vehicle begins to skid, the yaw marks of the rear tires will cross over the yaw marks of the front tires passing to the outside. The following values are needed to calculate minimum speed from yaw marks:

- Radius of the yaw mark.
- Half of the collision vehicle's track width.
- Drag factor (adjusted coefficient of friction).

K-38. As the vehicle progresses around the curve, it will generally reduce speed (unless the driver accelerates through the curve). This results in a yaw mark that does not have the same degree of arc on every point. Always start the chord as close as possible to where the striation crossover occurs, and never past the first one-third of the mark. Starting the chord on a segment of the yaw mark any significant distance after the crossover will result in a different (shorter) radius and will result in a lower speed calculation.

K-39. On long sweeping curves, the middle ordinate distance will be relatively small compared to the chord. Measure the middle ordinate in inches and convert to the decimal value in feet. To convert inches to feet divide the inch measurement by 12 (number of inches per foot); for example 6 inches ÷ 12 inches = 0.5 feet, 15 inches ÷ 12 inches = 1.25 feet. The middle ordinate is measured from the outside edge of the yaw mark as shown in figure K-5.

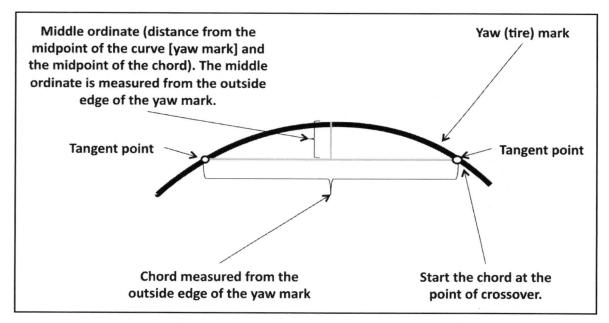

Figure K-5. The chord and middle ordinate method to determine the radius of a yaw mark

K-40. To calculate the radius of the curve, in this case the curve created by the yaw mark, the investigator must use the values obtained for the chord distance and middle ordinate. The formula for determining the radius of a curve is $r = (C^2 \div 8M) + (M \div 2)$, where—

- r = radius.
- C = chord distance.
- M = middle ordinate distance.

K-41. If the chord distance is 38 feet and the middle ordinate distance is 1.25 feet the radius is found by applying the formula $r = (C^2 \div 8M) + (M \div 2)$. The calculation to determine the radius is completed as follows:

- $r = (C^2 \div 8M) + (M \div 2)$
- $r = [38^2 \div (8 \times 1.25)] + (1.25 \div 2)$
- $r = (1,444 \div 10) + (1.25 \div 2)$
- $r = 144.4 + 0.62$ (to two decimal places)

- r = 145.02 feet

K-42. Next determine the vehicles track width. The track width is the distance between the tires of the vehicle; track width is measured from the outside edge of the left front tire to the outside edge of the right front tire, measured in feet. This width is now divided by two to determine half of the collision vehicle's track width. If the distance measured from the outside edge of left front tire to the outside edge of the right front tire is 6 feet, half the track width is 3 (6 feet ÷ 2 = 3 feet). This half track width value is now used to determine the radius traveled by the center of mass of the vehicle. Subtract this value from the yaw mark radius to identify the radius traveled by the center of mass of the vehicle. For example, if the radius of the yaw mark is 145.02 feet (based on the calculation above) and half the vehicle track width is 3 feet, the adjusted radius is 145.02 feet − 3 feet = 142.02 feet. The adjusted radius of 142.02 feet is the radius traveled by the center of mass of the vehicle as it skidded around the curve.

Calculate Minimum Speed

K-43. The minimum speed of the vehicle when it began the skid producing the yaw marks can now be calculated. This calculation is based on physical evidence left on the roadway by the vehicle. The calculation for minimum speed requires the radius determined from measurement and associated calculations of the yaw marks. It also requires the adjusted drag factor discussed earlier in this section. The formula to calculate minimum speed is $S = \sqrt{(15rf)}$ where—

- 15 = a constant for this formula.
- f = adjusted drag factor (adjusted coefficient of friction).
- r = adjusted radius (radius of the yaw curve minus half the vehicle track width).

Note. Braking does not occur when a vehicle produces yaw marks. Yaw marks only occur when the vehicle speed exceeds the coefficient of friction causing the vehicle to slide or slip sideways. The braking efficiency is zero in an adjusted coefficient (f) of friction calculation for a yaw marks. The drag factor formula $f = (\mu \times n) \pm m$ (or e) is simplified to $f = u \pm m$ (or e) and is used to calculate f for a yaw mark.

K-44. Given that the measurements and calculations have been completed to determine radius and drag factor, the adjusted radius (r) has a value of 142.02 feet. The drag factor (f) is 0.62. The calculation to determine the minimum speed of a vehicle that produced the yaw marks is completed as follows:

- $S = \sqrt{(15rf)}$
- $S = \sqrt{[(15)(142.02)(0.62)]}$
- $S = \sqrt{1,320.78}$
- $S = 36.34$ miles per hour
- The minimum speed the vehicle was traveling at the start of the yaw was 36.34 miles per hour.

Calculate Critical Speed

K-45. At times no yaw marks will be visible and the minimum speed of the vehicle cannot be calculated. Instead, determine the critical speed of the curve; this is the maximum speed the vehicle can negotiate that curve without losing lateral stability and being forced off the roadway by centrifugal force. It is not the speed of the vehicle when it left the road surface; it is a calculation based on characteristic of the roadway identifying the maximum speed the roadway can support. The chord and middle ordinate are determined based on the road instead of physical evidence (yaw marks) left on the road. The investigator can conclude through inductive reasoning that the vehicle was traveling faster than the maximum speed, even though the exact vehicle speed cannot be determined. The chord and middle ordinate method to determine radius of a road curve is shown at figure K-6.

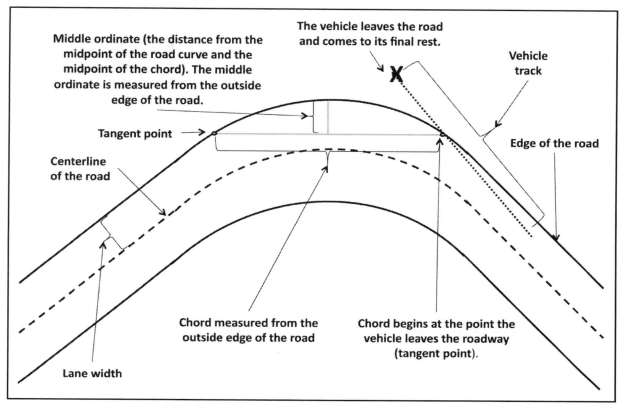

Figure K-6. The chord and middle ordinate method to determine radius of a road curve

K-46. Determine the probable line of travel around the curve. Specifically, take measurements on the premise that the vehicle was traveling in a certain lane, and then use the formula to determine the critical speed of the curve at the center of that lane. Mark two tangent points to establish the chord distance; one at the point the vehicle left the road and one 30 to 50 feet away on the roadway edge. Measure the chord and the middle ordinate in the same manner described for measuring yaw marks, and complete the calculation to determine the radius of the curve. If the chord distance is 75 feet and the middle ordinate distance is 3.0 feet, the calculation to determine the radius is completed as follows:

- $r = (C^2 \div 8M) + (M \div 2)$
- $r = [75^2 \div (8 \times 3.0)] + (3.0 \div 2)$
- $r = (5,625 \div 24) + (3.0 \div 2)$
- $r = 234.37 + 1.5$
- $r = 235.87$ feet (to two decimal places)

K-47. To find the adjusted radius determine the lane width and divide by 2; if the lane width is 10 feet then $10 \div 2 = 5$ feet (half the full lane width). The lane width is used in place of the vehicle track width based on the assumption that a vehicle will travel down the center of the lane. This value is added or subtracted based on whether the radius was calculated from the outside edge or the inside edge of the roadway. Since the radius was calculated based on measurements on the outside of the curve, if the vehicle was in the right-hand lane of a two-lane road, the value determined is subtracted from the radius of the road curve. For this example, the vehicle is traveling in the outside lane so 5 feet is subtracted from the radius of the curve; 235.87 feet – 5 feet = 230.87 feet. The adjusted radius of 230.87 feet is the radius traveled by the center of mass of a vehicle as it travels around the curve. If the vehicle is in the inside lane of a two-lane road, subtract 1.5 x the lane width (1.5 x 10 = 15 feet; 235.87 feet + 15 feet = 250.87 feet). In some cases, the radius may be measured from the inside of the curve due to terrain restrictions or safety concerns. In these cases, measure the chord distance and middle ordinate from the inside of the curve and add the lane width calculation (as presented above) to the radius inside the curve to obtain the adjusted radius.

K-48. The same formula used to calculate the minimum speed of a vehicle at the point of yaw around a curve is used to calculate the maximum speed a vehicle can travel before losing lateral stability and sliding. Along with the adjusted radius (r), the adjusted drag factor (f) is required. Given that the measurements and calculations have been completed to determine radius and drag factor, the adjusted radius (r) has a value of 230.87 feet. The drag factor (f) is 0.62. The calculation to determine the maximum speed that a vehicle can travel around the curve without losing lateral stability is completed as follows:

- $S = \sqrt{(15rf)}$
- $S = \sqrt{[(15)(230.87)(0.62)]}$
- $S = \sqrt{2,147.09}$
- $S = 46.33$ miles per hour
- The maximum speed that a vehicle can travel around the curve without losing lateral stability through the curve is 46.33 miles per hour.

FLIPS AND VAULTS

K-49. Flips and vaults occur when a vehicle strikes an object causing it to become airborne and rotate around in the air. A flip is a sideways rotation of a vehicle or object while in the air. A vault is an end-over-end rotation of a vehicle or object while in the air. The same formula is used to calculate the speed for both flip and vault. The results of the calculations are the minimum speed of the vehicle when it flipped or vaulted. The object that the vehicle impacts (curb, pothole, or other object) must be lower than the center of mass of the vehicle to cause the vehicle to flip or vault.

K-50. The formula can be applied to a collision vehicle (including occupants and cargo in that vehicle), but does not apply to people or items struck by that collision vehicle. It is most accurate when the takeoff and landing are at the same level, and it assumes a 45-degree angle of takeoff; this allows for the greatest distance at the lowest speed. The formula to calculate the minimum speed of a vehicle at the beginning of a flip or vault is $S = 3.87d \div \sqrt{(d \pm H)}$ where—

- S = the minimum speed of a vehicle at the point of impact that causes a flip or vault.
- 3.87 = constant for this formula.
- d = the level distance from the takeoff point to the first landing, measured from the center mass of the vehicle at takeoff to the center mass of the vehicle or object's first landing.
- H = the vertical difference (if any) between the takeoff point and the first landing; in other words, the difference in surface height between the takeoff point and the first landing point. (The vertical distance the vehicle or object travelled in the air is not a consideration.)
- Height may be positive (+), negative (-), or zero (0), depending on where the first landing point is in relation to the takeoff point.

K-51. The formula is different, depending on the vehicle's point of first landing or impact and the vertical height difference between the first landing relative to the takeoff point. The point of first landing following takeoff may be higher, lower, or at the same elevation as the takeoff point. Investigators must choose the correct version of the equation based on the vehicles landing point.

Note. Take all measurements from the center of mass of the vehicles.

K-52. Given a value of 75.0 feet for distance (d) and a value of 8.0 feet for the vertical difference (H), examples are provided below for instances where first landing is above takeoff elevation, below takeoff elevation, or at the same takeoff elevation. When a flip or vault occurs, the minimum speed of the vehicle at the beginning of the flip or vault can be calculated using the examples below when the landing is—

- **Above takeoff.** Use the following formula:
  - $S = 3.87d \div \sqrt{(d - H)}$
  - $S = [(3.87)(75.0)] \div \sqrt{(75.0 - 8.0)}$

- $S = 290.25 \div \sqrt{67.0}$
- $S = 290.25 \div 8.18$
- $S = 35.48$ miles per hour
- The minimum speed of a vehicle at the beginning of the flip or vault is 35.48 miles per hour.
- **Below takeoff.** Use the following formula:
  - $S = 3.87d \div \sqrt{(d + H)}$
  - $S = [(3.87)(75.0)] \div \sqrt{(75.0 + 8.0)}$
  - $S = 290.25 \div \sqrt{83.0}$
  - $S = 290.25 \div 9.11$
  - $S = 31.86$ miles per hour
  - The minimum speed of a vehicle at the beginning of the flip or vault is 31.86 miles per hour.
- **At the same elevation as the takeoff.** Use the following formula:
  - $S = 3.87d \div \sqrt{(d + 0)}$
  - $S = [(3.87)(75.0)] \div \sqrt{(75.0 + 0)}$
  - $S = 290.25 \div \sqrt{75.0}$
  - $S = 290.25 \div 8.66$
  - $S = 33.51$ miles per hour
  - The minimum speed of a vehicle at the beginning of the flip or vault is 33.51 miles per hour.

FALLS

K-53. The fall formula is used to determine a vehicle's minimum speed at takeoff when the vehicle runs off an embankment or level roadway where there is a subsequent drop. Falls are common when a vehicle fails to negotiate a curve or turn. Measurements for this calculation are taken from center of mass at takeoff to center of mass at the first landing. Subsequent rolls or bounces after the first landing point are not considered. This would tend to artificially increase the resultant speed. Grade, slope, and superelevation must be considered in this calculation. To calculate a vehicle's minimum speed at takeoff before a fall, the investigator must determine the—

- Horizontal distance from the takeoff point to the first landing point.
- Vertical distance from the takeoff point to the first landing.
- Percent of slope or grade at takeoff.

K-54. The formula to calculate the minimum speed of a vehicle at takeoff before a fall is slightly different depending on the slope or grade at takeoff. The formula is $S = 2.74d \div \sqrt{(H \pm dm)}$ where—

- S = vehicle's speed at takeoff.
- 2.74 = constant for formula.
- d = horizontal distance from takeoff to first landing.
- H = vertical difference between takeoff and first landing.
- m = Slope or grade at takeoff.
- Use (+) when the takeoff grade is uphill and (-) when the slope is downhill.

K-55. Given a value of 62.0 feet for horizontal distance (d), a value of 11.0 feet for vertical distance (H), and a 0.05 slope, examples are provided below for instances where there is an uphill grade and where there is a downhill grade. Investigators must choose the correct version of the equation based on the slope of the roadway approaching the takeoff point. The minimum speed of the vehicle at takeoff can be calculated per the examples below for falls involving—

- **An uphill grade.** Use the following formula:
  - $S = 2.74d \div \sqrt{(H + dm)}$
  - $S = [(2.74)(62.0)] \div \sqrt{[11.0 + (62.0 \times 0.05)]}$
  - $S = 169.88 \div \sqrt{(11.0 + 3.1)}$
  - $S = 169.88 \div \sqrt{14.1}$

- $S = 169.88 \div 3.75$
- $S = 45.30$ miles per hour
- The minimum speed of the vehicle at takeoff before the fall is 45.30 miles per hour.
- **A downhill grade.** Use the following formula:
  - $S = 2.74d \div \sqrt{(H - dm)}$
  - $S = [(2.74)(62.0)] \div \sqrt{[11.0 - (62.0 \times 0.05)]}$
  - $S = 169.88 \div \sqrt{(11.0 - 3.1)}$
  - $S = 169.88 \div \sqrt{(7.9)}$
  - $S = 169.88 \div 2.81$
  - $S = 60.45$ miles per hour
  - The minimum speed of the vehicle at takeoff before the fall is 60.45 miles per hour.
- **A level takeoff.** Use the following formula:
  - $S = 2.74d \div \sqrt{H}$
  - $S = [(2.74)(62.0) \div \sqrt{11.00}$
  - $S = 169.88 \div 3.31$
  - $S = 51.32$ miles per hour
  - The minimum speed of the vehicle at takeoff before the fall is 51.32 miles per hour.

SPEED AT IMPACT

K-56. Speed at impact is the vehicle's speed at the time of contact with the initial hazard. It is not usually the vehicle's minimum speed; however, the speed at impact could equal minimum speed in some cases. In collisions involving a flip or vault the methods described earlier in paragraphs K-50 and K-51can be used to determine the speed at impact. In cases where a collision does not produce a flip or vault, speed at impact can be determined using the formula $S = \sqrt{(30df)}$ where—S = speed at impact, 30 is a constant for this formula, d = distance from the point of initial impact to the end of the skid, and f = adjusted coefficient of friction. Speed at impact can be determined when the following collision characteristics are present:

- The distance of the collision vehicle's skid marks is measurable.
- There is positive identification of initial point of impact.

K-57. A speed at impact calculation can be conducted using the following scenario: A vehicle traveling on a level surface is following behind a maintenance truck. The load in the maintenance truck shifts causing a large metal box to fall from the truck. The trailing vehicle observes the hazard, applies the brakes, and begins to skid before striking the box and coming to rest. The collision vehicle left skid marks 98.00 feet long before impact with the box, and left an additional 28.00 feet of skid marks after impact to the end of skid; the total distance covered was 126.00 feet. Figure K-7 provides an example for calculating speed at impact.

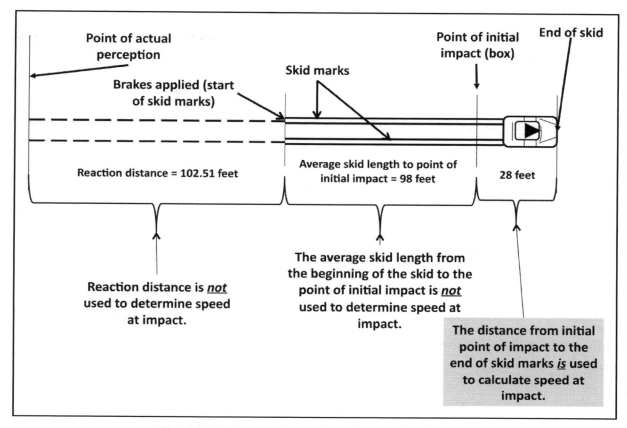

Figure K-7. Scenario to calculate speed at impact

K-58. The speed at impact can be calculated by completing the following steps:

- **Step 1.** Given a coefficient of friction (μ) of 0.65, a braking efficiency (n) of 100% or 1.00, and no slope (level surface) calculate the adjusted coefficient of friction (*f*) using the formula *f* = μ x n (see paragraph K-21) as follows: *f* = 0.65 x 1.00 or 0.65.

- **Step 2.** Given the distances in the previous paragraph, determine minimum speed using the formula S = √(30d*f*) (30 is a constant) (see paragraph K-32) as follows:
  - S = √(30d*f*)
  - S = √(30 x 28.00 x 0.65)
  - S = √546.00
  - S = 23.36 miles per hour
  - The minimum speed at the initial point of impact was 23.36 miles per hour.

COMBINED-SPEED FORMULA

K-59. The combined speed formula can be used to determine the minimum speed of the vehicle at the start of the collision incident when a vehicle travels over multiple surfaces and/or there is a change in braking efficiency, grade, slope or superelevation (conditions that make a single-speed calculation inaccurate). Combined-speed calculations are required when more than one surface is involved, such as when the collision vehicle skids over more than one type of surface. When multiple surfaces are involved, the speeds found for each surface are identified as "on speeds" for that surface. An on speed is the measurement of the loss of kinetic energy over a given surface (in miles per hour). On speeds are then combined in the combined-speed formula to determine a total loss of kinetic energy measured in the unit of miles per hour. The combined-speed formula is Sc = √[$(S_1)^2$ + $(S_2)^2$] where—

- Sc = combined speed, or the minimum speed of the vehicle at the start of the collision incident.

- S_1 = on speed for surface 1 (from start of skid to the next surface).
- S_2 = on speed for surface 2.

Note. Continue adding as many "on speeds" as required for the number of surfaces encountered. The formula is adjusted correspondingly. For example, for three surfaces use $Sc = \sqrt{[(S_1)^2 + (S_2)^2 + (S_2)^3]}$, for four surfaces use $Sc = \sqrt{[(S_1)^2 + (S_2)^2 + (S_2)^3 + (S_2)^4]}$, and so forth.

COMBINED-SPEED CALCULATION (SINGLE FORMULA)

K-60. The appropriate speed formulas discussed earlier are applied to determine the minimum speeds for each surface or speed change caused by a vehicle skidding to a stop. For example, a vehicle skids to a stop and during the deceleration travels over multiple surfaces but does not impact any objects. The speed of the vehicle is found using skids only. Figure K-8 shows the combined speed calculations used for determining speed over multiple surfaces.

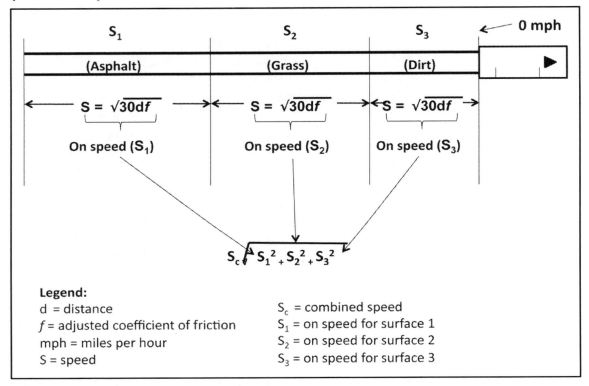

Figure K-8. Combined speed calculation used for multiple surfaces (single formula)

K-61. An example of a combined-speed calculation for a vehicle traveling over two surfaces and stopping without impacting an object is provided in figure K-9 and figure K-10, page K-20. First, determine values for S_1 and S_2 using the basic speed formula; this is discussed at paragraph K-32. The minimum speed for each section of the skids must be calculated separately as shown at figure K-9. Once the values for S_1 and S_2 are calculated, the combined speed formula can be used to calculate minimum combined speed. This is illustrated at figure K-10, page K-20.

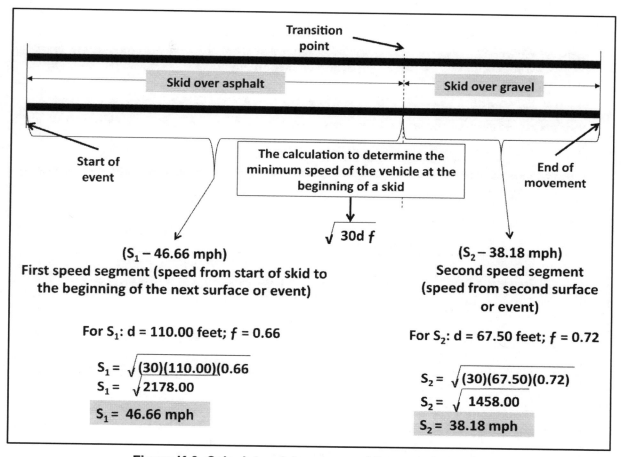

Figure K-9. Calculate minimum speed for each segment

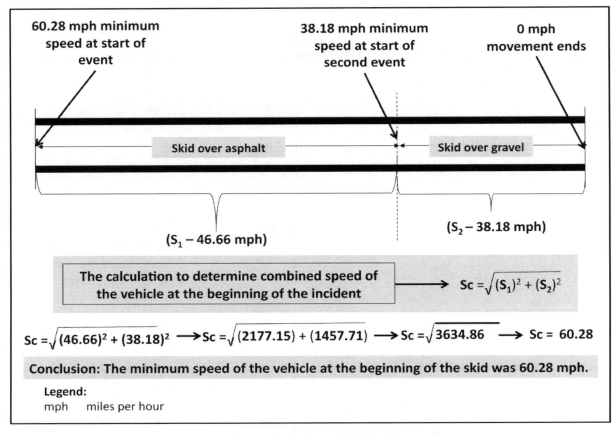

Figure K-10. Calculate combined speed

COMBINED-SPEED CALCULATION (MULTIPLE FORMULAS)

K-62. The combined-speed formula can also be used when more than one type of speed formula is required to compute a combined vehicle speed ; for example, straight skid speed and a vault, fall, or impact. Figure K-11 provides an example for applying the combined speed calculation when multiple formulas are required; in these cases the variables must be known for each of the independent formulas. The appropriate speed formulas discussed earlier are applied to determine the minimum speeds for each surface or speed change caused by collision with an obstacle. For example, a vehicle skids to a stop and during the deceleration the vehicle strikes an object on the roadway. The minimum speed for each section of the skid (before the collision and after the collision) must be calculated separately.

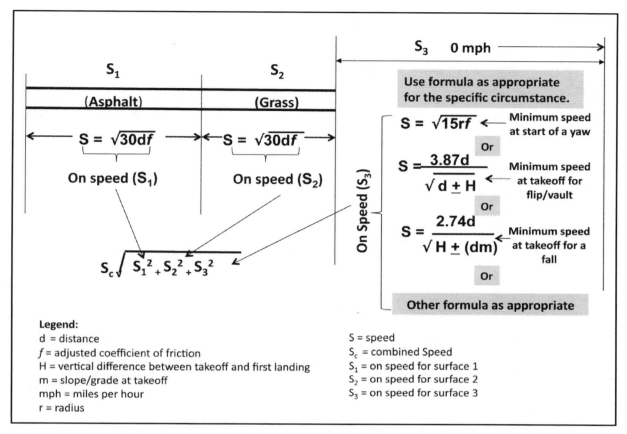

Figure K-11. Combined speed calculation used when multiple formulas are required

K-63. An example of a combined-speed calculation for a vehicle traveling over multiple surfaces and stopping following a flip is provided in figures K-12 and K-13, pages K-22 and K-23. First, determine values for S_1, S_2, and S_3 using the basic speed formula as described in paragraph K-32 and the flip/vault formula as described in paragraph K-50. The minimum speed for each section of the skids must be calculated separately as shown in figure K-12. Once the values for S_1, S_2, and S_3 are calculated, the combined speed formula can be used to calculate minimum combined speed; this step is illustrated in figure K-13.

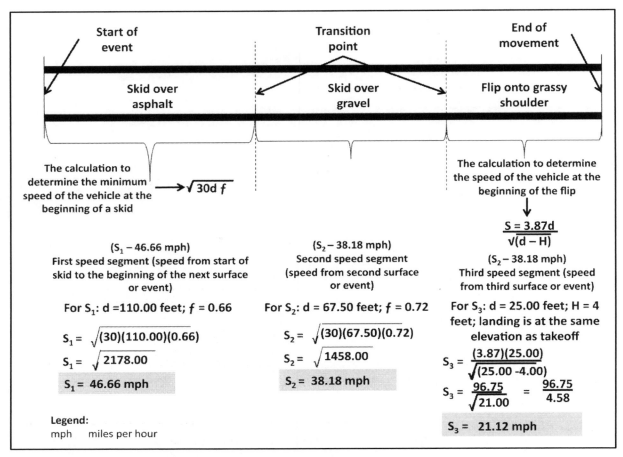

Figure K-12. Calculate minimum speed for each segment using the appropriate formula

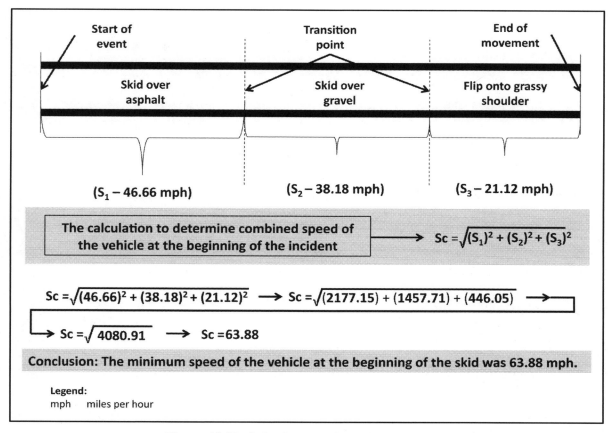

Figure K-13. Calculate total combined speed

TIME AND DISTANCE CALCULATIONS

K-64. Chapter 13 introduced the stages of a collision. These are the sequential events that make up the collision incident; the stages of a collision are depicted in figure 13-1, page 13-7. There are five major events of a collision (occurring sequentially throughout the incident); however, not all events are present in every collision incident. Using points within these stages as reference points, the investigator can calculate some distances and speeds relevant to the collision sequence. Figure K-14, page K-24, shows time and distance measurements.

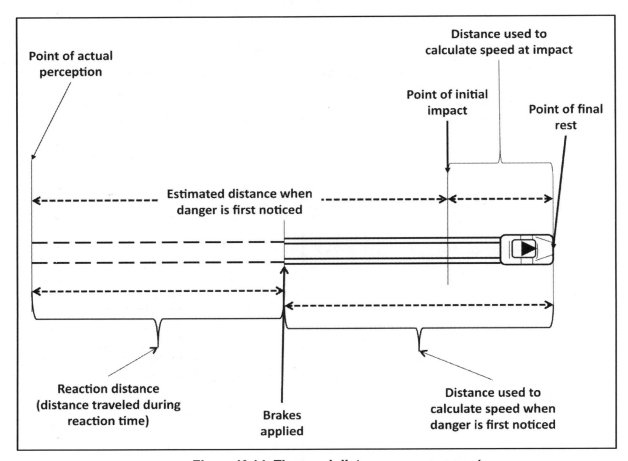

Figure K-14. Time and distance measurements

CALCULATING REACTION DISTANCE

K-65. The following formula can be used to determine unknown distance, velocity, or time when at least two of the variables (d, V, or T) are known: d = V x T where—d = distance (in feet), V = constant velocity (in feet per second), and T = time (in seconds). Velocity is measured in feet per second; speed is measured in miles per hour.

Convert Speed to Velocity

K-66. Using the minimum speed from the formulas above, investigators must convert speed to velocity. To change speed to velocity, use the formula V = S x 1.466 where—S = speed in miles per hour, V = velocity in feet per second, and 1.466 is the constant for the formula. An example for converting speed to velocity is as follows:

- If a given speed is 55 miles per hour—
  - V = S x 1.466
  - V = 55 x 1.466
  - V = 80.63 feet per second

Note. The constant is derived by dividing the number of feet per mile (5,280) by the number of seconds in an hour (3,600). If kilometers per hour are known, convert to miles per hour by the following formula: miles per hour = kilometers per hour x 0.62; for example if a vehicles known speed is 90 kilometers per hour, 90 kilometers per hour x 0.62 = 55.8 miles per hour. 90 kilometers per hour equals 55.8 miles per hour. The formula and constant above can then be used.

Determine Reaction Distance

K-67. The distance traveled between the point of actual perception and the application of the brakes by the driver (reaction time) of a vehicle can be calculated if during a collision sequence before collision (point of initial impact) and application of the brakes—

- The vehicle was traveling at a relatively constant speed.
- The velocity of the vehicle is known (if speed is known, use the formulas presented at paragraph K-66 to convert speed to velocity).
- The standard (constant) reaction time of 1.6 seconds is used.

Note. The stated average reaction time of 1.6 seconds is our industry standard and is applied to drivers who were not expecting any danger at the point a hazard is perceived.

K-68. For example, an investigator determines that a driver was traveling at a speed of 55 miles per hour when a hazard was identified and this subsequently led to a collision. The investigator needs to determine the reaction distance (the distance between the point of actual perception and application of the brakes) by the driver. The speed (55 miles per hour) is known and the reaction time is known (using the standard 1.6 seconds). The distance can be calculated as follows:

- Convert the speed (55 miles per hour) to velocity (feet per second) using the following formula discussed at paragraph K-66:
  - $V = S \times 1.466$
  - $V = 55 \times 1.466$
  - $V = 80.63$ feet per second
- Determine reaction distance using the following formula discussed at paragraph K-65):
  - $d = V \times T$
  - $d = 80.63 \times 1.6$
  - $d = 129.00$ feet
  - The vehicle traveled 129.00 feet during the 1.6 seconds it took the driver to react. This is the distance from where the driver first saw the danger to where the brakes were applied.

CALCULATING ESTIMATED DISTANCE WHEN DANGER FIRST NOTICED

K-69. The estimated distance when danger first noticed (EDDFN) is the estimated distance between the point of actual perception and the point of actual impact. The EDDFN is the combined distance of the ASL before the collision and the reaction distance. Calculating the EDDFN enables investigators to pinpoint the point of actual perception. The EDDFN cannot be determined for every collision. For the EDDFN to be calculated, the driver must have perceived a hazard, some evidence of evasive action must be present (such as skid marks), and the distance associated with evidence of the evasive actions must be measurable. Calculating EDDFN is illustrated in figure K-15, page K-26. You must be able to measure the distance of the collision vehicle's skid marks (ASL) up to the point of initial impact as described in paragraph K-32.

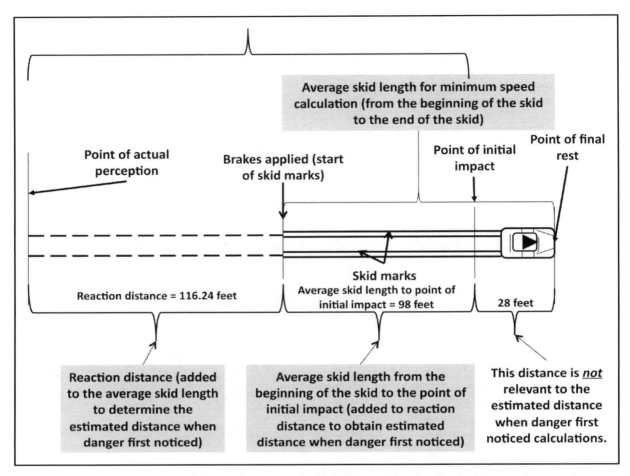

Figure K-15. Estimated distance when danger first noticed calculation requirements

K-70. The EDDFN is calculated using the formula EDDFN = RD + d where—EDDFN = the estimated distance when danger first noticed, RD = the reaction distance (calculated at step 3 below), and d = the ASL (average skid length before collision). The EDDFN can be calculated by completing the following steps:

- **Step 1.** Determine minimum speed using the formula S = √(30d*f*) (see paragraph K-32), given a total ASL (d) of 126.00 feet, a coefficient of friction (μ) of 0.65, a braking efficiency (n) of 100% or 1.00, and no slope (level surface); 30 is a constant as follows:
  - The adjusted coefficient of friction (*f*) must be calculated using the formula *f* = μ x n (see paragraph K-21); *f* = 0.65 x 1.00 or 0.65.
  - S = √(30d*f*)
  - S = √(30 x 126.00 x 0.65)
  - S = √2,457
  - S = 49.56 miles per hour
  - The minimum speed at the beginning of the skid was 49.56 miles per hour.
- **Step 2.** Convert speed to velocity using the result of step 1 and the formula S x 1.466 (see paragraph K-66) as follows:
  - V = S x 1.466
  - V = 49.56 x 1.466
  - V = 72.65 feet per second

- The vehicle traveling at a speed of 49.56 miles per hour has a velocity of 72.65 feet per second.
- **Step 3.** Find reaction distance using the result of step 2 and the formula RD = V x 1.6 as follows:
  - RD = V x 1.6
  - RD = 72.65 x 1.6
  - RD = 116.24 feet
  - The distance traveled between the point where the driver first identified the hazard and the point where the driver applied the brakes is 116.24 feet.
- **Step 4.** Calculate EDDFN using the result of step 3 and the formula EDDFN = RD + d, given the ASL to the point of initial impact is 98.00 feet as follows:
  - EDDFN = RD + d
  - EDDFN = 116.24 + 98
  - EDDFN = 214.24 feet
  - The driver perceived danger 214.24 feet before impact (point of actual perception).

DETERMINING SPEED AS A FACTOR OF COLLISION

K-71. In many cases there is no definitive evidence at the scene of a collision that will reveal the speed the collision vehicle was traveling. Investigators can determine whether speed was a factor in a collision by calculating hypothetical vehicle characteristics using known speeds, drag factors, and other information. The results of these hypothetical calculations can then be used for comparison with actual characteristics associated with a collision to determine whether the collision vehicle was traveling in excess or less than the hypothetical speed. This enables the investigator to determine if speed was a factor in the collision.

CALCULATING SLIDE OR SKID DISTANCES

K-72. The investigator may determine the slide-to-stop distance when a given speed and adjusted coefficient of friction (drag factor) are known using the formula $d = S^2 \div 30f$ where—
- d = distance from slide to stop.
- S = speed (the posted speed limit).
- f = adjusted coefficient of friction.
- 30 = a constant for this formula.

K-73. The slide-to-stop distance is the distance from the start of a skid to the point of initial impact. The results of the distance calculation can enable the investigator to determine if the speed in the collision was a factor contributing to that collision.

K-74. In the example, the distance from slide to stop will be calculated using the formula $d = S^2 \div 30f$ where—
- d = distance from beginning of a skid to stop.
- S = speed (30 miles per hour).
- f = adjusted coefficient of friction (0.59).
- 30 = a constant for this formula.

K-75. The calculation will determine how far a vehicle would skid based on the given speed and a given adjusted coefficient of friction. The distance is determined as follows:
- $d = S^2 \div 30f$
- $d = (30.00)^2 \div (30)(0.59)$
- $d = 900.00 \div 17.70$
- d = 50.84 feet
- A vehicle traveling at 30 miles per hour (S) on a surface with an adjusted coefficient of friction (f) of 0.59 will skid 50.84 feet (d) to a stop.

HYPOTHETICAL ESTIMATED DISTANCE WHEN DANGER FIRST NOTICED

K-76. The hypothetical estimated distance when danger first noticed ([H]EDDFN) is calculated based on a hypothetical vehicle scenario to determine the EDDFN for that hypothetical situation. The resulting (H)EDDFN can be compared to the actual EDDFN to determine if speed was a factor in the collision. The following four steps are required to find the (H)EDDFN:

- **Step 1.** Calculate the slide-to-stop distance (see paragraph K-72) given S = speed (30 miles per hour) (this is normally the posted speed limit), f = adjusted coefficient of friction (0.59), and 30 = a constant for this formula. The calculation will determine how far a vehicle would skid based on the given speed and a given adjusted coefficient of friction. The distance is determined as follows:
  - $d = S^2 \div 30f$
  - $d = (30.00)^2 \div (30)(0.59)$
  - $d = 900.00 \div 17.70$
  - $d = 50.84$ feet
  - A hypothetical vehicle (with 100% braking efficiency) traveling at 30 miles per hour (S) on a surface with a drag factor (f) of 0.59 will skid 50.84 feet to a stop.
- **Step 2.** Convert speed to velocity (see paragraph K-66). Using the formula V = S x 1.466 and the given speed (S) of 30 miles per hour, the velocity (V) can be calculated as follows:
  - V = S x 1.466
  - V = 30.00 x 1.466
  - V = 43.98 feet per second
  - A vehicle traveling at 30 miles per hour has a velocity of 43.98 fps.
- **Step 3.** Find the reaction distance (see paragraph K-65). The variable "RD" is used in place of the variable "d" in the formula. The variable "RD" must be used to designate the reaction distance instead of "d" in the formula d = V x T because in the next calculation the formula (H)EDDFN = RD + d is used; the same variable (d) cannot be used twice in the same formula. Given the industry standard constant 1.6-second reaction time and the velocity (V) from step 2 of 43.98 feet per second, the reaction distance (RD) can be calculated as follows:
  - RD = V x 1.60
  - RD = 43.98 x 1.60
  - RD = 70.36 feet
  - The hypothetical vehicle will travel 70.36 feet in the 1.6 seconds of reaction time (from point of actual perception to application of the brakes).
- **Step 4.** Calculate the (H)EDDFN given the distance (d) of 50.84 feet from step 1 and the reaction distance (RD) of 70.36 feet from step 3 to calculate the (H)EDDFN using the formula (H)EDDFN = RD + d as follows:
  - (H)EDDFN = RD + d
  - (H)EDDFN = 70.36 + 50.84
  - (H)EDDFN = 121.20 feet
  - The estimated distance from danger first noticed to point of impact for the hypothetical vehicle is 121.20 feet. Any vehicle traveling under the same conditions and speed on this road surface should have the same stopping distance.

K-77. After the (H)EDDFN is calculated, compare the (H)EDDFN to the EDDFN of the collision vehicle. For any comparison to be accurate, the distances used must start at the same point. The compared calculations can reveal that—

- Speed *is not* a factor. If the (H)EDDFN equals or exceeds the collision vehicles EDDFN, then speed is not a factor in the collision. Figure K-16 and figure K-17, page K-30, show (H)EDDFN results indicating that speed is not a factor. The calculations show that the collision vehicle was not exceeding the speed limit.

- Speed *is* a factor. If the (H)EDDFN is less than the collision vehicles EDDFN, then speed is a factor in the collision. Figure K-18, page K-31, shows (H)EDDFN results indicating that speed is a factor. The calculations show that the collision vehicle was exceeding the speed limit.

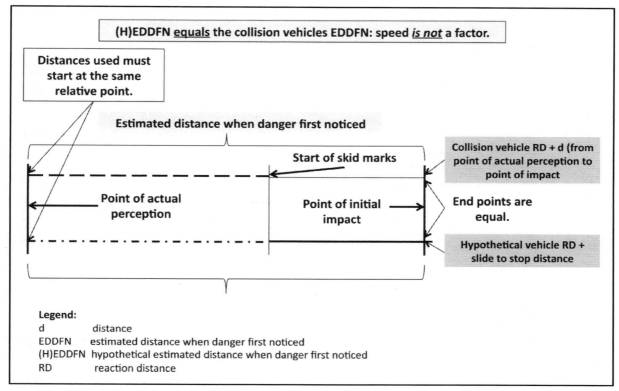

Figure K-16. Hypothetical estimated distance when danger first noticed equals the collision vehicles estimated distance when danger first noticed

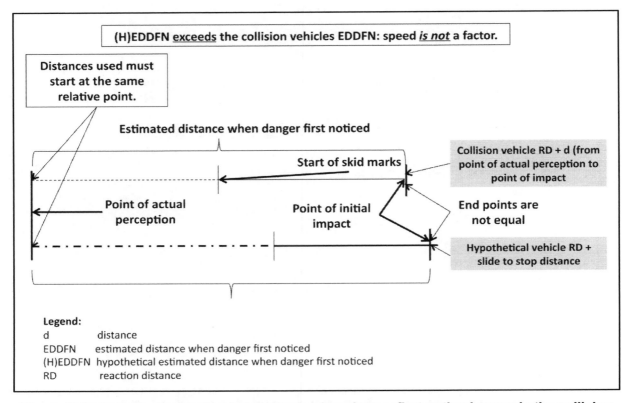

Figure K-17. Hypothetical estimated distance when danger first noticed exceeds the collision vehicles estimated distance when danger first noticed

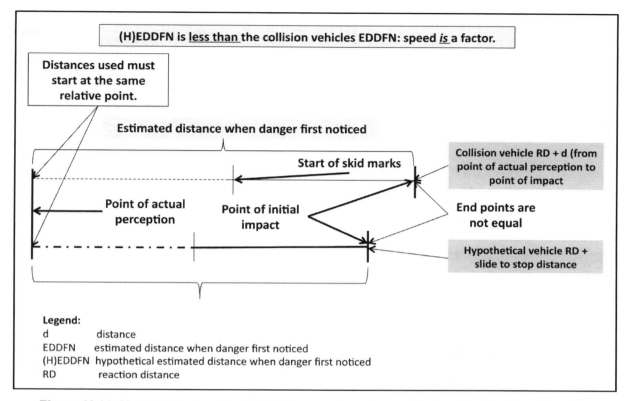

Figure K-18. Hypothetical estimated distance when danger first noticed is less than the collision vehicles estimated distance when danger first noticed

K-78. The (H)EDDFN formula can also be used to determine the total stopping distance required for a vehicle traveling at a specific speed to avoid a potential hazard. Determination of this information can enable appropriate placement of traffic control devices, such as warning signs, cones, or other devices, to afford an appropriate warning distance for vehicle drivers.

K-79. For example, if a road has a warning sign stating "warning, bridge out" and the warning sign is placed 200 feet before the hazard, would a vehicle traveling on that road have time to stop before the hazard? Calculate the (H)EDDFN and compare to the actual distance (200 feet) to determine if there is currently enough stopping distance. Use the following four steps required to find the (H)EDDFN:

- **Step 1.** Calculate the "slide-to-stop" distance (see paragraph K-72) given S = speed (40 miles per hour) (this is normally the posted speed limit), f = adjusted coefficient of friction (0.66), and 30 = a constant for this formula. The calculation will determine how far a vehicle would skid based on the given speed and a given adjusted coefficient of friction. The distance is determined as follows:
  - $d = S^2 \div 30f$
  - $d = (40.00)^2 \div (30)(0.66)$
  - $d = 1,600.00 \div 19.80$
  - $d = 80.80$ feet
  - A hypothetical vehicle (with 100-percent braking efficiency) traveling at 40 miles per hour (S) on a surface with a drag factor (f) of 0.66 will skid 80.80 feet to a stop.
- **Step 2.** Convert speed to velocity (see paragraph K-66). Using the formula V = S x 1.466 and the given speed (S) of 40 miles per hour, the velocity (V) can be calculated as follows:
  - V = S x 1.466
  - V = 40.00 x 1.466

- V = 58.64 feet per second
- A vehicle traveling at 40 miles per hour has a velocity of 58.64 feet per second.
- **Step 3.** Find the reaction distance (see paragraph K-65). Given the industry standard constant 1.6-second reaction time and the velocity (V) from step 2 of 58.64 fps, the reaction distance (RD) can be calculated as follows:
  - RD = V x 1.60
  - RD = 58.64 x 1.60
  - RD = 93.82 feet
  - The hypothetical vehicle will travel 93.82 feet in the 1.6 seconds of reaction time (from point of actual perception to application of the brakes).
- **Step 4.** Calculate the (H)EDDFN given the distance (d) of 80.80 feet from step 1 and the reaction distance (RD) of 93.82 feet from step 3 to calculate the (H)EDDFN using the formula (H)EDDFN = RD + d as follows:
  - (H)EDDFN = RD + d
  - (H)EDDFN = 93.82 + 80.80
  - (H)EDDFN = 174.62 feet
  - The estimated distance from danger first noticed to point of impact for the hypothetical vehicle is 174.62 feet. Any vehicle traveling under the same conditions and speed on this road surface should have the same stopping distance.

K-80. After the (H)EDDFN is calculated, compare the (H)EDDFN to the actual distance of 200 feet. Since (H)EDDFN (the distance required to stop under the stated conditions [174.62 feet]) is less than the actual distance between the warning sign and the hazard (200 feet), a vehicle traveling the posted speed limit will have enough time to stop.

Glossary

Acronym	Definition
ADRP	Army doctrine reference publication
AFMES	Armed Forces Medical Examiner System
ALS	alternate light source
AO	area of operations
AOR	area of responsibility
APO	Army Post Office
AR	Army regulation
ARNG	Army National Guard
ARNGUS	Army National Guard of the United States
ASL	average skid length
ATP	Army techniques publication
ATTP	Army tactics, techniques, and procedures
AUTL	Army Universal Task List
C4	composition 4
CB	composition B
CBRN	chemical, biological, radiological, and nuclear
CCIU	Computer Crimes Investigative Unit
CD	compact disk
CDR	compact disk recordable
CD-ROM	compact disk-read only memory
CFR	Code of Federal Regulations
CID	Criminal Investigation Division
CODIS	Combined Deoxyribonucleic Acid Index System
CPD	controlled prescription drug
CPU	central processing unit
CSA	Controlled Substances Act
CT	computed tomography
DA	Department of the Army
DAIG	Department of the Army Inspector General
DC	defense counsel
DD	Department of Defense
DEA	Drug Enforcement Administration
DFAS	Defense Finance and Accounting Service
DNA	deoxyribonucleic acid

DOD	Department of Defense
DODD	Department of Defense directive
DODI	Department of Defense instruction
DOJ	Department of Justice
DSL	digital subscriber line
DUI	driving under the influence
DVD	digital video disk
DVD-R	digital versatile disk recordable
DWI	driving while intoxicated
EDDFN	estimated distance when danger first noticed
EFL	Expeditionary Forensic Laboratory
EOD	explosive ordnance disposal
EPA	Environmental Protection Agency
FBI	Federal Bureau of Investigation
FFCA	Federal Facilities Compliance Act
FETI	Forensic Experiential Trauma Interview
FIU	Field Investigative Unit
FM	field manual
FPO	Fleet Post Office
FSO	forensic science officer
G-3	operations staff officer
GPS	Global Positioning System
GS	general schedule
GSR	gunshot residue
(H)EDDFN	hypothetical estimated distance when danger first noticed
HIV	human immunodeficiency virus
HN	host nation
IC	incident commander
ID	identification
IED	improvised explosive device
IP	Internet protocol
IR	infrared
ISDN	integrated services digital network
ISO	International Organization of Standardization
JA	judge advocate
L&O	law and order
LAN	local area network
LE	law enforcement
LSD	lysergic acid diethylamide
MCM	Manual for Courts Martial
MCO	major combat operations

MDMA	methylenedioxymethamphetamine
ME	medical examiner
MICR	magnetic ink character recognition
MO	modus operandi
MOU	memorandum of understanding
MPFU	Major Procurement Fraud Unit
MPI	military police investigator
MPR	military police report
MRE	Military Rules of Evidence
MRI	magnetic resonance imagery
MWD	military working dog
N/A	nonapplicable
NAFI	National Association of Fire Investigators
NATO	North Atlantic Treaty Organization
NFPA	National Fire Protection Association
NIC	network interface card
NIJ	National Institute of Justice
NSN	national stock number
OSHA	Occupational Safety and Health Adminisration
PC	personal computer
PCP	phencyclidine
PDA	personal digital assistant
PETN	pentaerythrite tetranitrate
PM	Provost Marshal
POL	petroleum, oils, and lubricants
PPE	personal protective equipment
ROI	Report of Investigation
SA	special agent
SAC	special agent in charge
SAFE	sexual assault forensic evidence
SARA	Superfund Amendments and Reauthorization Act
SARC	sexual assault response coordinator
SF	standard form
SIDS	Sudden Infant Death Syndrome
SJA	staff judge advocate
SLR	single-lens reflex
SME	subject matter expert
SOFA	status-of-forces agreement
SOP	standard operating procedure
SPR	small particle reagent
SUID	Sudden Unexpected Infant Death

SVP	special victims prosecutor
TC	trial counsel
THC	Tetrahydrocannabinol
TMCI	traffic management and collision investigator
TNT	trinitrololuene
TOE	table of organization and equipment
TTL	through the lens
UCMJ	Uniform Code of Military Justice
UN	United Nations
U.S.	United States
USATDS	United States Army Trial Defense Services
USACIDC	United States Army Criminal Investigation Command
USACIL	United States Ary Criminal Investigation Laboratory
USACRC	United States Army Crime Records Center
USAMPS	United States Army Military Police School
USAR	United States Army Reserve
USB	universal series bus
USC	United States Code
UV	ultraviolet
VIN	vehicle identification number
WAN	wide area network

References

Field manuals and selected joint publications are listed by new number followed by old number.

REQUIRED PUBLICATIONS

These documents must be available to intended users of this publication.

ARMY PUBLICATIONS

Most Army doctrinal publications are available online:
< http://www.apd.army.mil/>.

ADP 3-0. *Unified Land Operations.* 10 October 2011.

ADP 5-0. *The Operations Process.* 17 May 2012.

ADRP 3-0. *Unified Land Operations.* 16 May 2012.

ADRP 5-0. *The Operations Process.* 17 May 2012.

AR 27-10. *Military Justice.* 3 October 2011.

AR 70-12. *Fuels and Lubricants Standardization Policy for Equipment Design, Operation, and Logistic Support.* 19 July 2012.

AR 190-5. *Motor Vehicle Traffic Supervision.* 22 May 2006.

AR 190-30. *Military Police Investigations.* 1 November 2005.

AR 190-53. *Interception of Wire and Oral Communications for Law Enforcement Purposes.* 3 November 1986.

AR 195-2. *Criminal Investigations Activities.* 15 May 2009.

AR 195-5. *Evidence Procedures.* 22 February 2013.

AR 195-6. *Department of the Army Polygraph Activities.* 29 September 1995.

AR 200-1. *Environmental Protection and Enhancement.* 13 December 2007.

AR 385-10. *The Army Safety Program.* 23 August 2007.

AR 600-20. *Army Command Policy.* 18 March 2008.

AR 600-85. *The Army Substance Abuse Program.* 28 December 2012.

AR 670-1. *Wear and Appearance of Army Uniforms and Insignia.* 3 February 2005.

AR 735-5. *Property Accountability Policies.* 10 May 2013.

ATP 3-39.35. *Protection Services.* 31 May 2013.

ATTP 3-39.10. *Law and Order Operations.* 20 June 2011.

ATTP 3-39.20. *Police Intelligence Operations.* 29 July 2010.

ATTP 3-39.32. *Physical Security.* 3 August 2010.

ATTP 3-39.34. *Military Working Dogs.* 10 May 2011.

ATTP 3-90.4. *Combined Arms Mobility Operations.* 10 August 2011.

ATTP 3-90.15. *Site Exploitation Operations.* 8 July 2010.

ATTP 4-32. *Explosive Ordnance Disposal Operations.* 19 December 2011.

FM 2-22.3. *Human Intelligence Collector Operations.* 6 September 2006.

FM 3-11.21. *Multiservice Tactics, Techniques, and Procedures for Chemical, Biological, Radiological, and Nuclear Consequence Management Operations.* 1 April 2008.

FM 3-28. *Civil Support Operations.* 20 August 2010.

FM 3-39. *Military Police Operations*. 16 February 2010.

FM 5-19. *Composite Risk Management*. 21 August 2006.

FM 7-15. *The Army Universal Task List*. 27 February 2009.

FM 10-67-1. *Concepts and Equipment of Petroleum Operations*. 2 April 1998.

FM 27-10. *The Law of Land Warfare*. 18 July 1956.

DEPARTMENT OF DEFENSE PUBLICATIONS

DODD 1030.01. *Victim and Witness Assistance*. 13 April 2004.

DODD 3115.09. *DOD Intelligence Interrogations, Detainee Debriefings, and Tactical Questioning*. 9 October 2008.

DODD 5400.11. *DOD Privacy Program*. 8 May 2007.

DODD 5400.11-R. *DOD Privacy Program*. 14 May 2007.

DODD 5500.07-R. *The Joint Ethics Regulation*. 17 November 2011.

DODD 5525.7. *Implementation of the Memorandum of Understanding Between the Department of Justice and the Department of Defense Relating to the Investigation and Prosecution of Certain Crimes*. 22 January 1985.

DODI 1030.2. *Victim and Witness Assistance Procedures*. 4 June 2004.

DODI 5505.8. *Defense Criminal Investigative Organizations and Other DOD Law Enforcement Organizations Investigations of Sexual Misconduct*. 24 January 2005.

DODI 5505.10. *Investigation of Noncombat Deaths of Active Duty Members of the Armed Forces*. 31 January 1996.

DODI 5505.11. *Fingerprint Card and Final Disposition Report Submission Requirements*. 9 July 2010.

DODI 5505.14. *Deoxyribonucleic Acid (DNA) Collection Requirements for Criminal Investigations*. 27 May 2010.

DODI 5525.07. *Justice and the Department of Defense Relating to the Investigation and Prosecution of Certain Crimes*. 18 June 2007.

DODI 6495.02. *Sexual Assault Prevention and Response Program Procedures*. 23 June 2006.

OTHER PUBLICATIONS

Bevel, Tom and Ross Gardner. *Blood Pattern Analysis with an Introduction to Crime Scene Reconstruction*, Third Edition. CRC Press. March 2008.

CID Regulation 195-1. *Criminal Investigation Operational Procedures*. 12 August 1974.

Clean Water Act of 1977.

Fair and Accurate Credit Act of 2003.

Federal Facility Compliance Act of 1992.

Federal Rules of Evidence. As amended to 1 December 2011.

Federal Standard 376B. *Preferred Metric Units for General Use by the Federal Government*. 5 May 1983.

Freedom of Information Act of 1966 with amendments.

Guidelines for the Collection of and Shipment of Specimens for Toxicological Analysis. Published by the Division of Forensic Toxicology, Armed Forces Medical Examiner System. Available at <http://www.bexar.org/bcftl/TOXGUIDE_rev._02-11.pdf>.

Manual for Courts Martial (MCM). 2012.

NFPA 921. *Guide for Fire and Explosion Investigations*. 2011.

Physician's Desk Reference. 2012.

Resource Conservation and Recovery Act of 1976.

Sherman Anti-Trust Act of 1890.

Superfund Amendments and Reauthorization Act (SARA) of 1986.

The Fingerprint Sourcebook. Published by the Scientific Working Group on Friction Ridge Analysis, Study and Technology. Available at the NIJ Web site at <http://www.nij.gov/pubs-sum/225320.htm>.

Title 29 CFR. *Labor.* 2011.

Title 40 CFR. *Protection of the Environment.* 2011.

Title 48 CFR, Part 1. *Federal Acquisition Regulations System. Subpart 1352.2: Text of Provisions and Clauses.* 1 October 2011.

Title 5 USC. *Government Organization and Employees.* Edition 2010.

Title 10 USC. *Armed Forces.* Edition 2010.

Title 18 USC. *Crimes and Criminal Procedure.* Edition 2010.

Title 21 USC. *Controlled Substances Act.* Edition 2010.

Title 32 USC. *National Guard.* Edition 2010.

Traffic Management and Collision Investigations Student Study Guide and Workbook. Available from the Traffic Management and Collision Investigations Course at Lackland Air Force Base.

Uniform Trade Secrets Act of 1979, amended in 1985.

RELATED PUBLICATIONS

These documents contain relevant supplemental information.

A Guide for Explosion and Bombing Scene Investigation. Available from the National Institute of Justice at <www.ojp.usdoj.gov/nij>.

ADP 1-02. *Operational Terms and Graphics.* 31 August 2012.

ADRP 1-02. *Operational Terms and Graphics.* 31 August 2012.

ADP 6-0. *Mission Command.* 17 May 2012.

ADRP 6-0. *Mission Command.* 17 May 2012.

Crime Scene Investigation: A Guide for Law Enforcement. Available from the National Institute of Justice at <www.ojp.usdoj.gov/nij>.

Death Investigation: A Guide for the Scene Investigator. Available from the National Institute of Justice at <www.ojp.usdoj.gov/nij>.

DODD 5205.15E. *DOD Forensic Enterprise (DFE).* April 26, 2011.

DODD 6495.01. *Sexual Assault Prevention and Response (SAPR) Program.* 6 October 2005.

DODI 5505.03. *Initiation of Investigations by Defense Criminal Investigative Organizations.* 24 March 2011.

Electronic Crime Scene Investigation: A Guide for First Responders, Second Edition. Available from the National Institute of Justice at <www.ojp.usdoj.gov/nij>.

Eyewitness Evidence: A Guide for Law Enforcement. Available from the National Institute of Justice at <www.ojp.usdoj.gov/nij>.

Fire and Arson Scene Evidence: A Guide for Public Safety Personnel. Available from the National Institute of Justice at <www.ojp.usdoj.gov/nij>.

FM 1-04. *Legal Support to the Operational Army.* 18 March 2013.

Infant Death Investigation: Guidelines for the Scene Investigator. Published by the Centers for Disease Control and Prevention. January 2007.

Investigations Involving the Internet and Computer Networks. Available from the National Institute of Justice at <www.ojp.usdoj.gov/nij>.

Investigative Uses of Technology: Devices, Tools, and Techniques. Available from the National Institute of Justice at <www.ojp.usdoj.gov/nij>.

Lee, Henry C., Timothy Palmbach, and Marilyn T. Miller. *Henry Lee's Crime Scene Handbook*. Academic Press. July 2001.

Robinson, Edward M. *Crime Scene Photography*, Second Edition. Academic Press. February 2010.

Saferstein, Richard. *Forensic Science: From the Crime Scene to the Crime Lab*. Prentiss Hall. May 2008.

Scientific Working Group on Imaging Technology at <http://www.theiai.org/guidelines/swgit/>.

Wisconsin State Crime Laboratory Physical Evidence Handbook, 8th Edition. Available at <http://www.doj.state.wi.us/dles/crimelabs/physicalevidencehb/>.

REFERENCED FORMS

Unless otherwise indicated, DA forms are available on the Army Publishing Directorate (APD) Web site (http://www.apd.army.mil); DD forms are available on the Office of the Secretary of Defense (OSD) Web site (http://www.dtic.mil/whs/directives/infomgt/forms/formsprogram.htm); Standard Forms (SF) are available on the U.S. General Services Administration (GSA) Web site (http://www.gsa.gov/portal/forms/type/SF). CID Forms on the Law Enforcement Advisory Portal (this is maintained by USACIDC) at https://portal.cims.army.mil/default.aspx#

AFMES Form 1323. *Toxicological Request Form. (available at* http://www.afmes.mil/assets/docs/PM_DNA_Analysis_Request_Form.pdf)

Central Violation Bureau (CVB)Form. *United states District Court Violation Notice (Available at CVB Web site at* http://www.cvb.uscourts.gov)

CID Form 28. *Agent Activity Summary.*

CID Form 36. *Field Test Analysis on Non-Narcotic Substances.*

CID Form 88. *Wanted Poster.*

CID Form 94. *Agent Investigation Report.*

DA Form 2028. *Recommended Changes to Publications and Blank Forms.*

DA Form 2823. *Sworn Statement.*

DA Form 3643. *Daily Issues of Petroleum Products.*

DA Form 3744. *Affidavit Supporting Request for Authorization to Search and Seize or Apprehend.*

DA Form 3745. *Search and Seizure Authorization.*

DA Form 3881. *Rights Warning Procedure/Waiver Certificate.*

DA Form 3946. *Military Police Traffic Accident Report.*

DA Form 3975. *Military Police Report.*

DA Form 4002. *Evidence Property Tag.*

DA Form 4137. *Evidence/Property Custody Document.*

DD Form 518. *Accident – Identification Card.*

DD Form 1408. *Armed Forces Traffic Ticket.*

DD Form 1920. *Alcoholic Influence Report.*

DD Form 2701. *Initial Information for Victims and Witnesses of Crime.*

DD Form 2702. *Court-Martial Information for Victims and Witnesses of Crime.*

DD Form 2703. *Post-Trial Information for Victims and Witnesses of Crime.*

DD Form 2704. *Victim/Witness Certification and Election Concerning Prisoner Status.*

DD Form 2705. *Victim/Witness Notification of Prisoner Status.*

DD Form 2706. *Annual Report on Victim and Witness Assistance.*

DD Form 2922. *Forensic Laboratory Examination Request.*

SF 91. *Operator's Report of Motor Vehicle Accident.*

Index

fixed surveillance, 5-7, *See also* surveillance methods
  observation post, 5-7
  surface undercover role, 5-8
Forensic Experiential Trauma Interview (FETI), 3-9, 9-3, C-1
forensic science officer (FSO), 1-11
framework for law enforcement investigations, 1-1
  collision investigation, 1-2
  criminal investigation, 1-1
fraud and economic crime, 11-1
  against the government, 11-2
  black marketing, 11-8
  check fraud, 11-12
  claims fraud, 11-4
  contracting fraud, 11-6
  credit card fraud, 11-13
  description of fraud, 11-1
  identity theft, 11-11
  petroleum distribution fraud, 11-5
  supply fraud, 11-4
FSO. *See* Forensic Science Officer (FSO)

G

glass. *See* trace evidence
GSR. *See* trace evidence:gunshot residue (GSR)

H

handheld devices (electronics), B-4
  digital camera, B-4
  Global Positioning Systems, B-6
  mobile phones, B-4
  pagers, B-5
  personal digital assistants and electronic organizers, B-5
  tablet computers, B-6

I

impressions and casts, 2-44, 4-21, 10-3, 10-4
  casting a three-dimensional impression, 2-48
  chemical searches, 2-46
  footwear and tire track impressions, 2-30, 2-44, 10-13, 10-15
  impression searches, 2-45

lifting two-dimensional impressions, 2-47
  lighting techniques, 2-46
infanticide, 7-30
initial crime scene response, 4-36
  document actions and observations, 4-40
  ensure safety of personnel, 4-38
  establish and maintain control, 4-39
  observe and assess, 4-37
  transfer control, 4-40
initial crime scene walk-through, 4-43
interrogation approach, 3-17
interrogation environment, 3-15
interrogation phases, 3-14
  body, 3-21
  closing, 3-21
  opening, 3-20
  preparation, 3-14
interrogation preparation phases
  body, 3-14
  closing, 3-14
  opening, 3-14
interrogation themes, 3-16
interrogations, 3-5, 3-9, 3-14, *See also* law enforcement interrogations
interview
  definition, 3-5
interview/interrogation style, 3-9
  advanced/direct, 3-9
  indirect, 3-9
interviews, 3-5, 3-9
  canvass interview, 3-5
  custodial interview, 3-26
  false reports, 3-27
  interpreters, 3-28
  juvenile interview, 3-29
  noncustodial interview, 3-26
  self-incrimination, 3-30
  senior military or civilian interview, 3-30
  suspect interview, 3-5, 3-8
  victim interview, 3-5, 3-6, 3-7, 3-10, *See* also investigating sex offenses
  witness interview, 3-5, 3-7, 3-8, 3-10
investigating arson and explosions, 10-7

investigating burglary, housebreaking, and larceny, 10-3
  evidence, 10-4
  interviews, 10-5
  offender typologies, 10-6
  processing the scene, 10-3
investigating burglary, housekeeping, and larceny crime pattern, 10-6
investigating sex offenses. *See* also sex crimes
  consent determination, 9-5
  crime scene processing, 9-6
  evidence considerations, 9-7
  medical examinations, 9-9
  victim interviews, 9-3
investigator testimony, I-1

L

law and order detachments, 1-12
law enforcement interrogation definition, 3-5
law enforcement interrogations. *See* interrogations
law enforcement investigators, 1-4
  military police investigator, 1-5
  military police Soldier and Department of the Army civilian police, 1-6
  special agent (SA), 1-5
  traffic management and collision investigator, 1-5
levels of collision investigation, 13-8
  cause analysis, 13-10
  initial report and information collection, 13-8
  on-scene investigation, 13-8
  professional reconstruction, 13-9
  technical evaluation, 13-9
lineups, 4-8
  photographic, 4-8
  physical, 4-9

M

Major Procurement Fraud Unit (MPFU), 1-11
mass gravesite investigations, A-5
Military Justice Division, 1-14
  Chief, Military Justice Division, 1-14
  trial counsel, 1-15

By order of the Secretary of the Army:

RAYMOND T. ODIERNO
General, United States Army
Chief of Staff

Official:

GERALD B. O'KEEFE
Administrative Assistant to the
Secretary of the Army
1302401

DISTRIBUTION:

Active Army, Army National Guard, and U.S. Army Reserve: Not to be distributed; electronic media only.

Made in the USA
Lexington, KY
05 October 2016